Culture Shift in
Advanced Industrial
Society

R<small>ONALD</small> I<small>NGLEHART</small>

Culture Shift in Advanced Industrial Society

Princeton University Press, Princeton, New Jersey

Library of Congress Cataloging-in-Publication Data

Inglehart, Ronald,
Culture shift in advanced industrial society / Ronald Inglehart.
p. cm.
Bibliography: p.
Includes index.
ISBN 0-691-07786-X (alk. paper)
ISBN 0-691-02296-8 (pbk.)
1. Social values.   2. Social history—1970–   I. Title.
HM73.I54   1990
303.3'72—dc20   89-34207

This book has been composed in Linotron Times Roman

Princeton University Press books are printed on acid-free paper
and meet the guidelines for permanence and durability of the
Committee on Production Guidelines for Book Longevity of the
Council on Library Resources

Printed in the United States of America

Portions of chapters 1, 2, 3, and 8 of this book appeared in an earlier form in *The American Political Science Review* in December 1988, December 1981, March 1985, and December 1987 respectively. Another portion of chapter 8 appeared in *Government and Opposition* in Autumn 1986.

9   8   7   6   5   4

This book is dedicated to
my wife, Marita, *and my children*,
Elizabeth, Rachel, *and* Ronald

CONTENTS

Figures and Tables

TABLES

PREFACE

THIS book draws on a remarkable series of surveys—the Euro-Barometers—that have been carried out continuously for almost two decades, sponsored by the Commission of the European Communities. Providing regular measures of the attitudes, values, and behavior of the publics of twelve Western nations, this monumental research project was directed by Jacques-René Rabier from 1970 until 1986, and is now being carried out by his successor, Karlheinz Reif. International coordination of these surveys has been undertaken by Helène Riffault, Jean-François Tchernia, Jan Stapel, Norman Webb, and Nicole Jamar.

Another major contribution to this book has been the World Values surveys, carried out in twenty-five countries in 1981–1982 by the European Value Systems Study Group, directed by Ruud de Moor, Jan Kerkhofs, and Jacques-René Rabier, with Gordon Heald playing a leading role in implementing the study on five continents beyond the original West European core area.

Finally, this book draws on a three-nation panel study carried out in 1974–1981 by Samuel Barnes, Barbara Farah, M. Kent Jennings, and me (in the United States); by Dieter Fuchs, Max Kaase, and Hans-Dieter Klingemann (in West Germany); and by Jacques Hagenaars, Felix Heunks, Jacques Thomasson, and Jan Van Deth (in The Netherlands).

It has been a pleasure to work with the people in all three of these groups. This book owes much to their ideas, suggestions, and criticism. I have also benefited from intellectual stimulation and criticism from Paul Abramson, Klaus Allerbeck, David Appel, Wilhelm Buerklin, Marita Carballo de Cilley, Russell Dalton, Harry Eckstein, Sylvia Maria Evers, Juan Diez Nicolas, Juan Diez Medrano, Scott Flanagan, David Handley, Elemer Hankis, Stephen Harding, Martin Heisler, Richard Hofferbert, Marita Rosch Inglehart, Robert Jackman, Wolfgang Jagodzinski, Shinsaku Kohei, Oddbjorn Knutsen, William Lafferty, Franz Lehner, Seymour Martin Lipset, Robert Manchin, Renato Mannheimer, Gregory Markus, Alan Marsh, Anna Melich, Warren Miller, Ichiro Miyake, Ferdinand Mueller-Rommel, Tadao Okamura, Robert Putnam, Akos Rona-Tas, Dusan Sidjanski, Renata Siemienska, Burkhard Strumpel, Dirk Van de Kaa, and Joji Watanuki. It was a privilege to exchange ideas with these people and I would like to express my gratitude. This book could not have been written without them.

I am also grateful to the National Science Foundation, which provided a series of grants for cleaning, archiving, and distributing the Euro-Barometer surveys. Finally, my warm thanks go to Georgia Aktan for expert data processing and to Karen Russell for cheerfully and flawlessly preparing numerous versions of this manuscript.

—Ronald Inglehart

Culture Shift in
Advanced Industrial
Society

The Impact of Economic and Sociopolitical Change on Culture and the Impact of Culture on Economics, Society, and Politics in Advanced Industrial Society

THE peoples of different societies are characterized by enduring differences in basic attitudes, values, and skills: In other words, they have different cultures. During the past few decades, economic, technological, and sociopolitical changes have been transforming the cultures of advanced industrial societies in profoundly important ways. The incentives that motivate people to work, the issues that give rise to political conflict, people's religious beliefs, their attitudes concerning divorce, abortion, and homosexuality, the importance they attach to having children and raising families—all these have been changing. One could go so far as to say that throughout advanced industrial society, what people want out of life is changing.

The change is gradual. It reflects changes in the formative experiences that have shaped different generations. Thus, traditional values and norms remain widespread among older generations; but new orientations have penetrated younger groups to an increasing degree. As younger generations gradually replace older ones in the adult population, the prevailing worldview in these societies is being transformed.

Why do cultures change? Each culture represents a people's strategy for adaptation. In the long run, these strategies generally respond to economic, technological, and political changes; those that fail to do so are unlikely to flourish, and unlikely to be imitated by other societies. Though cultures change in response to changes in the socioeconomic, political, and technological environment, they also shape that environment in return. Significant cultural changes facilitated the rise of the Industrial Revolution in the West; the Industrial Revolution brought a cascade of changes that reshaped Western cultures. These cultural changes, in turn, are now redirecting the trajectory of advanced industrial society, leading to the deemphasis of economic growth as the dominant goal of society and the decline of economic criteria as the implicit standard of rational behavior. During early industrialization, economic factors became so central that economic determinist models were a relatively plausible way to interpret society and culture as a whole. With the emergence of advanced industrial society, economic factors reached a point of diminishing returns, and the plausibility of economic determinist models, such as the classic Marxist worldview, is receding.

In his introduction to an important new series of monographs on politics and culture, Barnes (1986) argues that a culture is a set of beliefs and assumptions developed by a given group in its efforts to cope with the problems of external adaptation and internal integration—one that has worked well enough to be considered valid and taught to new members of the group (cf. Schein 1985). Basically, we agree with this definition. But a people's worldview does not depend solely on what their elders teach them; rather, it is shaped by their entire life experience, and sometimes the formative experiences of a younger generation differ profoundly from those of previous generations. During the decades since World War II, advanced industrial societies have attained unprecedented levels of economic development, with real income per capita now four or five times as high as ever before in history in many countries, and as much as twenty times its highest previous level in some countries. For reasons that will be explored below, this—together with the emergence of the welfare state, changes in the international system, and unprecedented scientific and technological developments—has led to gradual changes in prevailing basic values concerning politics, work, religion, the family, and sexual behavior.

Moreover, partly because they have higher educational levels than older generations, the younger groups have higher political skill levels. Consequently, they have the potential to participate in politics in more active and issue-specific ways than has generally been true in the past.

The implications are far-reaching. Cultural change is shaping both the economic growth rates of societies and the *kind* of economic development they are pursuing. It is reshaping the social basis of political conflict, the reasons people support political parties, the kinds of parties they support, and the ways in which they try to attain their political goals. It is also changing population growth rates, family structure, and church attendance rates.

This book will examine the nature of these cultural changes and their causes and consequences. It carries on an investigation that started in 1970 and gave rise to an earlier book, *The Silent Revolution* (Inglehart 1977). Though a dozen years of additional research and a vast amount of new data have gone into the present book, some of the themes it pursues are stated in the earlier study:

The values of Western publics have been shifting from an overwhelming emphasis on material well-being and physical security toward greater emphasis on the quality of life. The causes and implications of this shift are complex, but the basic principle might be stated very simply: people tend to be more concerned with immediate needs or threats than with things that seem remote or nonthreatening. Thus, a desire for beauty may be more or less universal, but hungry people are more likely to seek food than aesthetic satisfaction. Today, an unprecedentedly large portion of Western populations have been raised under conditions of exceptional economic security. Economic and physical security continue to be valued positively, but their relative priority is lower than in the past.

We hypothesize that a significant shift is also taking place in the distribution of political skills. An increasingly large proportion of the public is coming to have sufficient interest and understanding of national and international politics to participate in decision-making at this level. Mass publics have played a role in national politics for a long time, of course, through the ballot and in other ways. Current changes enable them to play an increasingly active role in formulating policy, and to engage in what might be called "elite-challenging" as opposed to "elite-directed" activities. Elite-directed political participation is largely a matter of elites mobilizing mass support through established organizations such as political parties, labor unions, religious institutions, and so on. The newer "elite-challenging" style of politics gives the public an increasingly important role in making specific *decisions*, not just a choice between two more sets of decision-makers. (P. 3)

Figure 0-1 outlines the topics focused upon in *The Silent Revolution*. Though the scope of our investigation has broadened considerably in the intervening years, these topics remain central to the present book. This continuity reflects a choice of research strategy, for cultural change is a topic that can only be grasped in longitudinal perspective. This book utilizes an eighteen-year time series of cross-national survey data, in which given questions have been asked of representative national samples, year after year. Through analysis of hundreds of thousands of interviews, we can now begin to discern a number of clear trends. But cultural changes take place largely through intergenerational population replacement: One must examine them in the perspective of decades, or even centuries. We have only scratched the surface.

Though we have continued to pursue themes that were central to *The Silent Revolution*, this is quite a different book in several ways. First, the theoretical focus has evolved over time. Our initial focus was on the transition from "Materialist" to "Postmaterialist" values. We continue to ex-

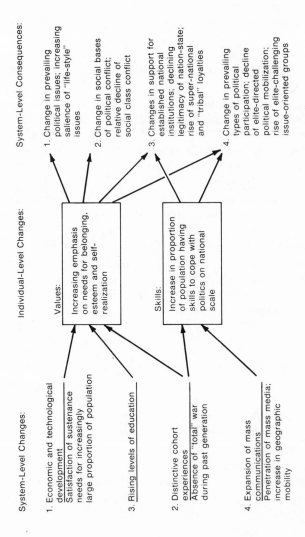

FIGURE 0-1. Overview: The processes of change examined in this book. From Inglehart 1977, 5.

System-Level Changes:

1. Economic and technological development
   Satisfaction of sustenance needs for increasingly large proportion of population

3. Rising levels of education

2. Distinctive cohort experiences
   Absence of "total" war during past generation

4. Expansion of mass communications
   Penetration of mass media; increase in geographic mobility

Individual-Level Changes:

Values:
Increasing emphasis on needs for belonging, esteem and self-realization

Skills:
Increase in proportion of population having skills to cope with politics on national scale

System-Level Consequences:

1. Change in prevailing political issues; increasing salience of "life-style" issues

2. Change in social bases of political conflict; relative decline of social class conflict

3. Changes in support for established national institutions; declining legitimacy of nation-state; rise of super-national and "tribal" loyalties

4. Change in prevailing types of political participation; decline of elite-directed political mobilization; rise of elite-challenging issue-oriented groups

plore this change here; but it has become apparent that it is only one aspect of a much broader syndrome of cultural change, involving the decline of traditional religious orientations and conventional social and sexual norms—along with the emergence of distinctive patterns of economic and political behavior.

The empirical scope of the investigation has grown broader, too. Most of the data in our earlier studies were drawn from the six original member nations of the European Community. The present study utilizes data from more than two dozen societies, including countries in both Eastern and Western Europe, the United States, Canada, Mexico, Argentina, Australia, South Africa, and Japan, with a small but interesting body of data from Hong Kong and the People's Republic of China. This broadened geographic scope has led to a certain amount of theoretical revision, stimulated by the fact that in non-Western societies, cultural change shows patterns that are very different from those it displays throughout the industrialized West.

Finally, the ability to analyze at least some of these topics with a substantial body of time series data puts them in a new perspective. For example, earlier studies hypothesized that as a result of long-term economic security, an intergenerational value change was taking place from Materialist to Postmaterialist priorities (Inglehart 1971, 1977). In the present study, we are able to test this prediction. Through cohort analysis of survey data from 1970 to 1988, we confirm the existence of an intergenerational value change, and calculate the effects of population replacement. We also find empirical confirmation of the predicted linkages with economic security, both in the form of enduring differences linked with security during one's formative years, and in the form of period effects linked with the fluctuations of Western economies. Similarly, in earlier work we predicted the decline of social class conflict and the rise of a new type of political cleavage based on quality of life issues. In the present study, we follow the actual decline of social class–based voting in advanced industrial societies, the erosion of support for the communist parties of Western Europe, and the emergence of new, predominantly Postmaterialist parties on the Left, such as the Environmentalist parties.

These political changes are considerably more complex than prevailing images imply. During the 1980s, the mass media frequently asserted that politics had shifted toward conservatism. The idea is at best half true, and obscures the more complex changes that actually are taking place. Both in the United States and in other advanced industrial societies, the younger and better-educated segments of the population might be described as socially liberal and economically conservative. But even this formulation is oversimplified, for this group is not economically conservative in the traditional sense; rather, the meanings of "liberal" and "conservative" have been transformed. The changing way in which people react to the expanding role of the state provides a striking illustration.

Throughout the first three-quarters of the twentieth century, virtually everyone agreed that support for increasing state intervention was the crucial distinction between Left and Right. From a Marxist perspective, nationalization of industry and state control of the economy constituted the core solution to all other social problems: Abolishing private ownership of the means of production would eradicate exploitation, oppression, alienation, crime, and war.

Though its perspective was less utopian, from the New Deal on, the American Left also viewed increasing state regulation and control as something that was good almost by definition. In the American context, the liberals were those who supported a growing role for the state; the conservatives were those who opposed it. Well into the 1970s, Western political elites continued to define the meanings of "Left" and "Right" in terms of state intervention in the economy and society (see Aberbach, et al. 1981, 115–69 and chapter 9 in this book).

This consensus is dissolving. It no longer seems self-evident that the expansion of state authority constitutes progress—even to those on the Left. One of the key developments of recent years has been a growing skepticism about the desirability and effectiveness of state planning and control, a growing concern for individual autonomy, and a growing respect for market forces. Not surprisingly, this outlook has been endorsed by traditional conservatives, such as Ronald Reagan and Margaret Thatcher. What is new is its growing acceptance by groups traditionally located on the Left. As early as the 1960s, New Left groups emerged that were highly critical of big government, viewed bureaucracy as dehumanizing, and called for the devolution of decision-making power to local communities and to those directly affected by the decisions. East European governments, particularly in Hungary, have been gradually reducing the role of the state for many years. In the 1980s, the pragmatist leadership group that came to power in China after the death of Mao made dramatic changes, experimenting with individual enterprise and an increased role for market forces, and (more hesitantly) increased freedom of expression. In France, a socialist-communist coalition won office in 1981—but after two years of unrewarding experience with nationalization of industry and other traditional policies of the Left, the socialists abandoned this tack and shifted to market-oriented policies. Similar shifts away from reliance on the state, toward market economies, even in states that originally favored socialist models, have been occurring in Asia, Africa, and Latin America. Today, almost no one views nationalization of industry as a panacea; where change is occurring, it is likelier to be the privatization of former state functions. Finally, in the late 1980s even the Soviet Union began allowing a greater role for individual initiative and individual self-expression, under the twin slogans of *perestroika* and *glasnost*. Gorbachev's reforms constitute a major turning point in Soviet history. They have met with fierce resistance from long-entrenched communist party elites, who cling tenaciously to the power, privilege, and perquisites linked with their control of the Soviet economy and society. Moreover, the prospect of change toward a more open but more competitive and less predictable society stirs anxiety among large segments of the Soviet working class; the future of the reform movement is uncertain. At a recent conference on this problem, a leading Soviet scholar predicted that the reforms will endure if Gorbachev can hold on to power for another five years, against "the hard-line conservatives on the Left."

That "the Left" could have become "the conservatives" is virtually a contradiction in terms, but it reflects the current transition in Soviet politics. The Hungarians, however, have been grappling with these problems for much longer—and by the end of the 1980s, it had become normal practice in Hungary to refer to the conservative party bureaucrats as the Right and to the advocates of change toward greater reliance on market forces and individual initiative as the Left.

This change in the nature of political change may seem confusing, but it is coherent in long-term historical perspective. Indeed, this is not the first time that the political polarity of state intervention has shifted. The term "liberal" emerged in nineteenth-century British politics to designate those who advocated *less* government intervention in the economy—at a time when intervention was used primarily on behalf of the landed aristocracy. With the emergence of working-class parties and the rise of the welfare state, the growth of government became almost inseparably linked with the Left (or "liberals" in English-speaking countries). That perception is still widespread, but by no means unanimous.

This change in orientations toward state authority (explored in chapters 8 and 9) can be traced to three main factors. The first is the fact that the welfare state has begun to reach a point of diminishing returns. Paradoxically, this does not reflect the failure of the welfare state, but the fact that it has succeeded in alleviating those problems it can most readily solve—and thereby helped pave the way for new types of problems to become central. The expansion of the welfare state tempered the ruthless exploitation of laissez-faire capitalism, helping it evolve into a stabler and more viable form of society. Today, in contrast with previous history, the masses do not starve, even in times of severe economic downturn; their standard of living has been stabilized at a modest level of economic security. This has reduced social class tensions and helps explain why—in contrast to the widespread political extremism that occurred during the Great Depression of the 1930s—Western nations' politics remained on a fairly even keel during the recessions of the 1970s and early 1980s. But the growth of the welfare state has begun to reach its limits: when government expenditures reach 60 percent of gross national product (as is now the case in a number of Western societies), there is virtually no room for further expansion; taxation becomes massive, and the majority of the public feels the burden.

A second factor that has tipped the scales against state-run economies has been a change in the nature of work. In the early stages of industrial society, most jobs required low levels of skill: the production of relatively simple, standardized, and slow-changing products can be organized according to the traditional assembly line, where a large number of robotlike "hands" perform repetitive tasks, according to routines prescribed from above. A handful of bosses can direct an entire factory, and an entire economy can be run according to one central plan. In advanced industrial society, routine productive and clerical tasks are automated and computerized; innovation becomes the crucial factor. But innovation cannot be prescribed by central authority: it is inherently unpredictable and depends on increasingly specialized expertise that is beyond the grasp of the political authorities. Political elites are incapable of drawing up a plan that can dictate the innovations that are to be made during the next five years in computer programming, superconductivity, genetic engineering, and thousands of other specialties. The evolution of high-tech society requires an organization that allows wide scope for individual judgment and creativity. This is precisely the opposite of the Stalinist model, with its emphasis on centralized planning and authority and political repression.

During the era from the 1930s to the 1970s, capitalist societies adopted various aspects of the welfare state, moving closer to socialist ideals in order to attain a reasonable degree of social and political stability. Today, the functional requisites of high technology favor societies that give relatively wide scope to individual creativity and initiative. Those countries that are least effective in doing so, the socialist group, are under particularly heavy pressure to move away from excessive reliance on central authority. The dismantling of the welfare state is not in the cards, however. Early promises by Ronald Reagan and Margaret Thatcher to cut back on welfare spending ran into a brick wall of political resistance; despite their intense ideological preferences, welfare spending actually continued to rise while these traditional conservatives held power. But it rose at a reduced rate. For the main thrust of social innovation no longer lies in this direction, and support for further *growth* of state authority is reaching a point of diminishing returns. A return to laissez-faire capitalism, however, would bring a predictable renewal of social class conflict. The future lies with those societies that can strike an effective balance between individual autonomy and central authority.

A third factor is important in explaining why, after a century of movement toward increasing central authority, the current shift is toward individual autonomy. It is the process of cultural change that was touched on above and is explored in detail in chapters 2–4. Advanced industrial societies are undergoing a gradual shift from emphasis on economic and physical security above all, toward greater emphasis on belonging, self-expression, and the quality of life. This shift can be traced to the unprecedented levels of economic and physical security that have generally prevailed in these countries since World War II, and to the emergence of the welfare state. Whereas previous generations were relatively willing to make trade-offs that sacrificed individual autonomy for the sake of economic and physical security, the publics of advanced industrial society are increasingly likely to take this kind of security for granted—and to accord a high priority to self-expression both in their work and in political life. Mass demands for a more participatory role are growing in advanced industrial societies, in both East and West. This cultural change reinforces the functional changes described above, further militating against the growth of state authority.

Whether one chooses to label the current shift away from state authority as conservative or liberal (or Right or Left) depends on how deeply one is attached to the concept that the growth of state authority is inherently progressive. Insofar as it is conducive to the emergence of societies with more room for individual self-realization, the new trend seems progressive. What is crucial is the result, not the means by which it is reached.

Some of the political events of the 1980s clearly *were* conservative, however. The emergence of the ''Moral Majority'' in the United States and the rise of the National Front in France are examples. They both represent reactions against change, rather than change in a new direction. Massive and rapid cultural change has been occurring throughout advanced industrial society during the past few decades; chapter 3 traces the shift from Materialist to Postmaterialist values, while chapter 6 explores some of the changes that have taken place in religious orientations, gender roles, and sexual norms. For example, our surveys reveal that younger groups are far more permissive toward divorce than older groups and place much less emphasis on having children than do older groups. These differences square with the fact that during the past twenty-five years, divorce rates rose by as much as 300 percent in Western societies, while during the same period, fertility rates fell to well below the population replacement rate. Similarly, a generation ago, homosexuality was something that was only whispered about. Today, gay and lesbian groups hold official functions, under university sponsorship, demanding legal protection of the right to follow their own sexual preferences. This change is part of a broad intergenerational cultural shift.

In addition to these cultural changes, major immigration flows, especially those from Third World countries, have changed the ethnic makeup of advanced industrial societies. The newcomers speak different languages and have different religions and life-styles from those with which the native population is familiar—further compounding the impression that the culture one grew up in is being swept away. The rise of militant religious fundamentalism in the United States, and of xenophobic movements in Western Europe, represents a reaction against rapid cultural changes that seems to be eroding some of the most basic values and customs of the more traditional and less secure groups in these countries. These are alarming and important phenomena—but they do not represent the wave of the future. On the contrary, they are a reaction against broader trends that are moving faster than these societies can assimilate them.

Some of the findings in this book seem counterintuitive. Everyone has heard that today's youth have turned conservative, and that they are mainly interested in preparing for lucrative careers so that they can become Yuppies and devote their lives to conspicuous consumption. In fact, the empirical evidence provides very little support for this stereotype. It is true that the youth of the 1980s were much likelier to study business than were their counterparts of the 1960s, who were likelier to prepare for academic careers. But this difference in behavior largely reflects a rational response to a changed environment—specifically, an awareness that very few academic jobs were available in the 1970s and 1980s. One's behavior is, of course, constrained by one's environment. But if we probe beneath situational differences, the overwhelming bulk of the evidence indicates that the basic values of contemporary youth are not more materialistic than those of their counterparts a decade or two earlier. Nor are they politically conservative in any basic sense. The problem is that the political program that the Left has employed for the past half-century no longer appeals to them: They see it as unresponsive to the problems of contemporary society. They are, however, potentially far more responsive than their elders to the appeal of a new Left when it addresses the types of problems that are now becoming increasingly crucial (as we will see in chapter 8).

Because populations tend to increase until they meet the available food supply, most cultures have historically been forced to deal with problems of scarcity. For human beings, cooperative behavior is generally a more effective response to this problem than a war of all against all—and virtually all societies tend to temper ruthless economic competition by inculcating norms of sharing, mutual obligation, and cooperation. Similarly, a society in which violence was unrestrained would tear itself apart. Virtually all societies limit the use of violence to narrowly prescribed channels. These limits might, in theory, depend solely on enforcement by superior violence but this would be costly and extremely insecure for the rulers. In practice, all societies attempt to instill norms among their people that bring about voluntary compliance even when no soldier, policeman, judge, or priest is present. Thus, political power is always based on some blend of culture and external sanctions—or legitimate violence, as Weber put it. In so far as the population has internalized the norms "Thou shalt not steal" and "Thou shalt not kill," the society as a whole is far more secure than when order depends solely on the weapons of the local warlord.

To be effective, such basic norms as these must be sufficiently tenacious and inflexible to dominate the urge to kill, even when the urge is strong and external constraints are absent. To be this deeply instilled, these norms generally must be instilled during the prerational phase of early childhood, as part of one's basic character structure. By the same token, this means that basic cultural norms are difficult to change—and that when they do change, the experience is likely to be disorienting and deeply disturbing to those raised under the previous value system. The conscience of the older generation cries out—whether it be the "Moral Majority" in the United States or the hard-line communists in the Soviet Union. Cultural change does occur when changes of sufficient magnitude take place in the economic, technological, or sociopolitical environment. But such changes take place slowly, generally through the socialization of new generations; and the transition tends to be painful. There is a built-in tendency for cultural change to lag behind the environmental changes that give rise to it.

This book analyzes culture change from multiple perspectives. Because it deals with the impact of economic and sociopolitical change on culture, and the impact of culture on economics, society, and politics, it moves from the system level to the individual level and back again to the system level, as indicated in Figure 0-1. But because we now have data from a much larger number of nations than we did in 1977, we now can utilize the nation as a unit in quantitative analysis, and not merely in impressionistic comparisons. Thus, this investigation analyzes cultural change using both the individual and the nation as the unit of analysis; and we gain further insight into the linkages between the two levels by utilizing surveys of elite values and attitudes, as well as surveys of the general public. Our analysis is still limited by an inadequate data base: Our time series is too short at the mass level, and we have too few cases at the national level, to be able conclusively to test the hypotheses suggested by our theoretical framework. But we are able to see the shape of cultural change a good deal more clearly than before.

The phenomenon of cultural change is intimately connected with social, political, and economic change, as the subtitle of this book suggests. To ask, "Which factor *really* explains what is happening?" is meaningless. To illustrate this point, one might ask, "Why did Carl Lewis win the 100-meter run in the 1984 Olympic games—was it because he had strong legs, or because he had strong lungs?" Obviously, he could not have won the race unless he had strong leg muscles *and* a powerful pulmonary system—*and* an excellent circulatory system and strong bones as well. All of them were essential, and to ask, "Which one was really decisive?" is to pose a false alternative. One could push the matter farther, and point out that all of the racers probably had excellent bones, muscles, hearts, and lungs, but what was really decisive was the motivation that drove Lewis to push himself to the limit. Or, moving to a completely different level of analysis, one could even argue that Lewis's victory was determined by political factors: He won because in 1984 the United States did not boycott the games, as it had in 1980. Turning to Lewis's repeat victory in 1988 introduces yet another causal level—he won because his strongest competitor was caught using drugs. Each of these arguments is true in a limited sense; but each factor is part of an interdependent system of causes.

In this book, we do not argue on behalf of cultural determinism—nor do we endorse economic or technological or social or political determinism. Each of these factors is closely related to the others, and while it is interesting and revealing to examine their linkages, it seems pointless to assert that any one of them is the ultimate causal factor that drives the others. We *do* make a more limited claim, however: that culture is an essential causal element that helps shape society—and a factor that today tends to be underestimated. Its importance is underrated, in part, because it is difficult to measure. We have relatively abundant data on economic factors, and contemporary social science is largely data driven; we tend to explain in terms of what we can readily measure.

Cultural factors have rarely been measured quantitatively, and remain poorly explored. Nevertheless, they constitute an essential component of any social system. As the evidence presented in this book indicates, massive but largely unnoticed changes are taking place in the cultural basis of advanced industrial society. Until we measure and understand these events, we will remain in the dark concerning crucial elements of social, political, and economic change.

CHAPTER 1

Culture, Stable Democracy, and Economic Development

INTRODUCTION: THE ROLE OF POLITICAL CULTURE

It is time to redress the balance in social analysis. Since the late 1960s, rational choice models based on economic variables have become the dominant mode of analysis, while cultural factors have been deemphasized to an unrealistic degree. This approach has made major contributions to our understanding of how politics and economics work; nevertheless, it tends to underestimate the significance of cultural factors, if only because economic indicators are readily available and cultural data are not. Thus, rational choice models have fruitfully analyzed the relationships between economics and politics, but left unexplored the linkages that culture has with both politics and economics.

The incompleteness of models that ignore cultural factors is becoming increasingly evident. In Catholic societies from Latin America to Poland, the church plays a major role, despite the demise often predicted by economic determinists. In the Islamic world, Muslim fundamentalism has become a political factor that neither East nor West can ignore. The Confucian-influenced zone of East Asia, by economic criteria one of the *least* favored regions on earth, manifests an economic dynamism that outstrips any other region of the world; it is virtually impossible to explain its performance without reference to cultural factors. Even in advanced industrial societies, religion not only outweighs social class as an influence on electoral behavior (Lijphart 1979), but actually seems to be widening its lead: While social class voting has declined markedly in recent decades, religious cleavages remain astonishingly durable.

There is no question that economic factors are politically important— but they are only part of the story. This chapter argues that different societies are characterized to very different degrees by a specific syndrome of political cultural attitudes; that these cultural differences are relatively enduring, but not immutable; and that they can have major political consequences, one being that they are closely linked to the viability of democratic institutions. Our argument is supported by survey evidence from twenty-five nations, with a substantial time series from eight of them. The findings indicate that examination of political culture is an essential supplement to the rational choice approach, and that the two sometimes focus on different aspects of the same phenomenon. For example, the political economy school has demonstrated that short-term economic success builds support for the government in office. This finding is complemented by analyses of economic and political culture data suggesting that long-term economic success builds mass support for a given type of regime. Given an adequate data base, not only short-term attributes, such as popularity, but also long-term attributes, such as legitimacy, are amenable to empirical analysis.

The emergence of rational choice models was a major advance. But, so far, these models have focused on economics and politics, ignoring cultural variables. Goodhart and Bhansali (1970) and Kramer (1971) were forerunners in analyzing the impact of economic conditions on government popularity and voting behavior. Nordhaus (1975), Hibbs (1977), MacRae (1977), Cameron (1978), and Schmidt (1982) analyzed the impact of politics on economic conditions and economic policy, while Frey and Schneider (1978a, 1978b) analyzed the two-way interdependence between economy and polity. Kinder and Kiewiet (1979) found that the linkage between economics and politics is not simply a narrow pursuit of one's personal economic interests, but instead is in large part "sociotropic"—one votes for a government that is perceived to have served the *nation* well, regardless of whether it has affected one's own pocketbook. This finding, disputed by Kramer (1983) but confirmed by Lewis-Beck (1986) and Markus (1988), raises the possibility that cultural variables, such as a sociotropic orientation, may be important in the interaction between economy and polity—an idea explored more explicitly in this chapter.

Thus far, the focus has been on relationships between short-term fluctuations in economics and politics, such as the impact of current economic conditions on government popularity or of the electoral cycle on business conditions. But this approach can also be applied to the analysis of long-term changes. Easton (1966), for example, argues that favorable government outputs produce feedback in the form of mass support for the authorities in office; but if they are maintained over the long term, such outputs can lead to "diffuse support" for a given type of regime. Lipset (1960) and Rose and Urwin (1969) contend that governmental effectiveness and legitimacy are prerequisites for democracy. We agree, and further suggest that in industrial societies with utilitarian values, the two are closely related. Effectiveness over a long period of time may be the surest way to produce legitimacy, insofar as it leads to the emergence of a public that has absorbed enduring positive orientations toward the regime during its early socialization.

In analyzing such long-term relationships between politics and economics, political culture is a crucial intervening variable. Stable democracy is not a necessary consequence of economic development: It may encourage but does not guarantee the emergence of democratic institutions and a political culture in which they can flourish. In large part, cultural changes reflect the socialization of enduring habits and attitudes. Once established, these orientations have a momentum of their own, and may act as autonomous influences on politics and economics long after the events that gave rise to them. Thus the long-term relationship between economics and politics is complex. Nevertheless, there seems to be a clear empirical linkage between economic development and the emergence of mass democracy, in which rational choice and political culture are not incompatible but complementary modes of explanation.

After flourishing in the 1960s, the concept of political culture came under attack. In 1963, the fountainhead of political culture research, Almond and Verba's *The Civic Culture*, represented a tremendous advance. Previous works that attempted to deal with the impact of culture on politics relied on impressionistic evidence. Cultural influences on the distinctive political behavior of a given people were interpreted in terms of vague but presumably indelible characteristics, such as "national character." One might invoke the *furor Germanicus* described by ancient Roman historians, in order to explain contemporary German militarism—ignoring intervening centuries, when most Germans were seen as beer-drinking music lovers, doomed by nature to be the prey of their more militaristic neighbors, such as the Swedes or the French. By providing, for the first time, a well-developed theory of political culture based on cross-national empirical data, Almond and Verba moved from the realm of literary impressions to that of testable propositions.

In subsequent years, it was often charged that political culture was a static concept and that Almond and Verba had ethnocentrically asserted the (presumably permanent) superiority of Anglo-Saxon culture over that of other nations. Though their theoretical interests concerned possible changes in political culture, their analysis was based on data from a single time point and therefore was necessarily static. The British and Americans were, as hypothesized, found to rank higher on interpersonal trust, pride in their political institutions and feelings of political competence than the publics of Germany, Italy, or Mexico. But since these variables were, in fact, constants for each county, it was impossible to analyze their relationships with other macrophenomena or to trace changes over time. As far as the empirical evidence was concerned, the British and American political cultures might as well have been inherently and indelibly more democratic than those of Germany, Italy, and Mexico.

The concept of political culture came under attack not only for empirical reasons but for ideological ones as well. Traditionally, partisans of the Left tend to view social problems as caused by defects in the social structure; accordingly, they seek the solution in government programs. Conversely, conservatives tend to place the responsibility for social problems on the individual, rather than society. The more rigid ideologues on each side tend to view the causes of any given social phenomenon as either *entirely* due to social structure, with control and responsibility completely outside the individual, or *entirely* a matter of individual responsibility, at the opposite extreme. In fact, most phenomena seem to reflect the interaction of both individual-level and structural-level factors, and the relative importance of these factors can vary a great deal. On one hand, one can conceive of situations so totally and rigidly structured that virtually nothing the individual can do affects his or her fate. The situation of a prisoner in a concentration camp may be very near this extreme. On the other hand, one can also conceive of situations in which what happens mainly reflects the individual's behavior; a libertarian society with lavish and well-distributed resources might approach this ideal. In the real world, one is almost never at either extreme; outcomes reflect both internal orientations and external constraints. Cultural, economic, and political factors all are likely to play a role—and their relative importance in a given situation can more accurately be determined empirically rather than ideologically.

We are now at a stage where it is possible to begin to carry out longitudinal analyses of political culture. Though the data base is still barely adequate, consistent and frequent measures of at least a few key indicators are now available from a number of countries, covering a decade or two. This chapter will focus on one dimension of political culture—a cluster of attitudes that seems linked with the persistence of stable democracy. We will utilize data from the European Community Euro-Barometer surveys carried out from 1970 through 1988, together with the World Values surveys (with fieldwork in 1981 and another wave scheduled for 1990; see Stoetzel [1983] for details). As Kaase (1983) has argued, both the cross-national scope and the relatively extensive time series are crucial to this enterprise, for this book seeks to demonstrate that political culture exists as an autonomous and measurable set of variables with significant political consequences.

Culture is a system of attitudes, values, and knowledge that is widely shared within a society and transmitted from generation to generation. While human nature is biologically innate and universal, culture is learned and may vary from one society to another. The more central and early-learned aspects of culture are resistant to change, both because it requires a massive effort to change central elements of an adult's cognitive organization, and because one's most central values become ends in themselves, the abandonment of which would produce deep uncertainty and anxiety. In the face of major and enduring shifts in societal conditions, even central parts of a culture may be transformed, but they are much more apt to change through intergenerational population replacement than by the conversion of already-socialized adults. Kuhn's (1972) account of paradigm change in scientific revolutions provides an analogy.

The political culture approach today constitutes the leading alternative to rational choice theory as a general explanatory framework for political behavior. The political culture approach is distinctive in arguing that (1) people's responses to their situations are shaped by subjective orientations, which vary cross-culturally and within subcultures; *and* (2) these variations in subjective orientations reflect differences in one's socialization experience, with early learning conditioning later learning, making the former more difficult to undo. Consequently, action can *not* be interpreted as simply the result of external situations: Enduring differences in cultural learning also play an essential part in shaping what people think and do.

As Eckstein sums it up, " 'Cultural' men process experience into action through general cognitive, affective, and evaluative predispositions; the patterns of such predispositions vary from society to society, from social segment to social segment; they do not vary because objective social situations or structures vary but because of culturally determined learning; early learning conditions later learning and learning involves a process of seeking coherence in dispositions" (Eckstein 1988, 792).

These key postulates of the political culture approach have crucial implications for social change. Cultural theory implies that a culture cannot be changed overnight. One may change the rulers and the laws, but changing basic aspects of the underlying culture will take many years. Even then, the long-run effects of revolutionary transformation are likely to diverge widely from revolutionary visions and to retain important elements of the old pattern of society. Furthermore, when basic cultural change does occur, it will take place more readily among younger groups (where it does not need to overcome the resistance of inconsistent early learning) than among older ones, resulting in intergenerational differences. Thus, "in the process of cultural transformation considerable age-related differences should occur. In fact, age, in cases of pronounced discontinuity, might even be expected to be a major basis for subcultural differentiation. If indeed this were found to be so, the cultural perspective upon theory would be enormously strengthened over alternatives. Empirical work pertinent to this expectation, however, is oddly lacking . . ." (Eckstein 1988, 798).

This lack that Eckstein points to has a cause. Strategic though it is, evidence of generational change is very difficult to obtain. Most orientations do not show strong age-related differences—such differences will be found only in domains that are undergoing major change. To detect generational differences, one must have some theoretical guidance that points to those components of culture that one believes *are* changing, and then proceed to measure them regularly and frequently, over a period of many years. Furthermore, one should simultaneously monitor relevant changes in the socioeconomic environment. Only by doing so, does it become possible to distinguish between true generational change and aging effects linked with position in the human life cycle and to distinguish both of these from the impact of short-term effects.

The implications of political culture theory suggest a number of empirical tests, which should indicate whether it or rational choice theory provides the more adequate explanation of political phenomena. Four such tests seem crucial, the first two of which involve historical research:

Test 1. Almond (1983) suggests that the communist experience provides a key test of political culture theory, since it can be viewed as a major attempt to falsify it: Communist elites have consciously attempted to remake the political culture of their societies, according high priority to the task. The evidence indicates that they were only partly successful. Despite massive efforts, these cultures showed considerable resistance to change; moreover, these changes took considerable time, largely occurring as intergenerational population replacement took place (Almond 1983; see also Brown and Gray 1977). Almond sums up the evidence as follows:

> Even in the Soviet Union, where the regime has been in substantial control of the population for two full generations and where the revolution was led by an endogenous elite, the extent of success in remodeling man has been relatively modest. . . . Much of the legitimacy of the Soviet regime . . . results from the fact that the structure of the Soviet system is very much like the preexisting Tsarist one in the sense of centralization, the extensive scope of the government, and its arbitrariness. . . .
>
> The revolutionary aims of creating a "socialist man" have been practically given up in the Soviet Union and Cuba, and were never seriously pursued in Yugoslavia. . . . Were the Soviet threat to be neutralized, there is little doubt that liberal regimes, even ones initiated by communist parties (as was the case in Czechoslovakia in 1967–68) would be established. Communist efforts at resocialization may have been counterproductive in the sense of having created strong liberal propensities in countries such as Poland and Hungary where those orientations were relatively weak in the prerevolutionary era. In Poland after 30 years of revolutionary experience, something like a legitimate pluralist regime emerged in 1981, which allowed the new Solidarity union, the Catholic church and the army to engage in bargaining relations with the communist party. (Almond 1983, 133, 136)

Test 2. The transformation of political culture in West Germany constitutes another crucial historical test. Rogowski (1976) relies mainly on this case as evidence of his contention that cultural reorientation can occur rapidly, in keeping with a rational choice interpretation. It is true that the ruling elites and the laws were changed almost overnight, after Germany's defeat in 1945, and that the public generally accepted these changes. When one's nation has been defeated and devastated, the previous system utterly discredited, the previous ruling elite annihilated or imprisoned and the country occupied by foreign armies, drastic changes like this are possible. Nevertheless, even under these conditions, early learning is resistant to change. The political structure changed suddenly, but, as Baker, Dalton, and Hildebrandt (1981) demonstrate convincingly through a longitudinal analysis of West German survey data, the underlying political culture changed gradually, over a period of many years—and manifested precisely the type of intergenerational differences that cultural theory would predict: The young were reshaped far more readily than the old (cf. Boynton and Loewenberg 1973, 1974; and Conradt 1974). Much the same can be said of the postwar transformation of political culture in Japan (Richardson 1974).

This book will provide additional evidence on each of these two points; but it will address itself primarily to two other tests of political culture theory:

Test 3. Do enduring cross-cultural differences exist, in the basic orientations of the peoples of different societies? Demonstrating that they do— and that they have a significant impact on the attitudes and behavior of these peoples—will be a major task of this chapter.

Test 4. When cultural change takes place, do we observe generational differences? As Eckstein (1988) suggests, this is a crucial test of cultural versus rational choice interpretations, since different generations within a given society are in precisely the same situation: The only factor that differs, apart from age, is the impact of their early socialization. Consequently, if different generations in the same society manifest significantly different responses to the same stimuli, it strongly implies the presence of differences in cultural learning. To demonstrate that this is the case, requires that we distinguish between aging effects and generational effects. Massive evidence of the existence of enduring age-related differences will be presented in chapters 2 and 3, together with cohort analyses, which indicate that they reflect generational differences, linked with differences in the formative experiences of the respective birth cohorts. Before examining this evidence, however, we must deal with the prior question—do enduring cross-cultural differences exist in the basic orientations of different peoples?

This chapter will demonstrate the following theses. (1) There are substantial and enduring cross-cultural differences in certain basic attitudes and habits among the publics of given societies. (2) Though these differences are relatively stable, they are not immutable. We are dealing with variables, not constants. (3) Though changes in these orientations tend to be gradual, they are perceptible and can be traced to specific causes. Among these causes, long-term economic development seems particularly important. (4) Thus, while political economy and political culture deal with two distinct sets of variables, they are closely related. Economic changes help shape cultural change, but they are by no means the only factor involved; moreover, cultural patterns can persist long after the factors that originally gave rise to them have ceased to operate. Thus, they can influence economic life as well as being shaped by it. Finally, (5) one specific cluster of cultural variables is not only linked with economic development but also seems to play a crucial role in facilitating the emergence of modern democracy. Thus, political culture is an intervening variable that helps explain why economic development is conducive to, but does not necessarily lead to, the emergence of modern or mass-based democracy.

The Emergence of a "Civic" Political Culture: Causes and Consequences

The linkage between economic development and modern democracy is complex. Three factors seem particularly crucial: (a) the emergence of a politically powerful commercial-industrial bourgeoisie; (b) the development of preconditions that facilitate mass participation in politics; and (c) the development of mass support for democratic institutions, and feelings of interpersonal trust that extend even to members of opposing parties.

The crucial role played by the commercial-industrial elite in the emergence of democratic institutions has been emphasized by analysts from Marx to Weber, and more recently Lipset (1964). As Moore (1966) succinctly put it in *The Social Origins of Dictatorship and Democracy*, "No bourgeois, no democracy." Similarly, Lindblom (1977) pointed out that, thus far in history, mass democracy has arisen *only* in societies based on market economies. A strong middle class, functioning in a market economy, seems to be a necessary but not sufficient condition for the rise of democracy.

If economic development brings a commercial-industrial elite to power, it facilitates the emergence of elite-level norms that are crucial to democracy. But this broadens the politically relevant universe to only a limited degree. Initially, participation in democratic bargaining tends to be limited to the traditional land-owning elites plus the emerging bourgeoisie. The transition from elite-level democracy to stable mass democracy also requires the development of participatory skills and organizations among the mass public. This phenomenon will be examined in chapter 10; briefly summarized, we argue that industrialization, urbanization, and mass literacy facilitate the organization of labor unions and mass political parties, which lead to the enfranchisement of a growing share of the public; later, as cognitive mobilization takes place, the public develops an increasing potential for more active forms of intervention in political decision making.

The emergence of a strong middle class, and the spread of participatory skills lead to the establishment of democratic political processes among elites and subsequently to a broadening of the politically relevant universe. But the evolution of stable mass-based democracy requires one additional development: the emergence among the general public of norms and attitudes that are supportive of democracy.

One of the most basic of these attitudes is a sense of interpersonal trust. In *The Civic Culture*, Almond and Verba (1963) concluded that interpersonal trust is a prerequisite to the formation of secondary associations, which in turn is essential to effective political participation in any large democracy. A sense of trust is also required for the functioning of the democratic rules of the game. One must view the opposition as a *loyal* opposition, who will not imprison or execute you if you surrender political power to them, but can be relied upon to govern within the laws, and to surrender political power reciprocally if your side wins the next election. Almond and Verba found that their German and Italian respondents ranked relatively low on interpersonal trust. With data from only one time point, it was impossible to determine whether these findings could be attributed to short-term factors—perhaps the harsh conditions of the postwar era—or whether they reflected more enduring differences. Banfield's earlier work (discussed below) suggested that the Italian findings, in particular, might reflect the heritage of historical experiences of many decades.

Banfield (1958) had also found that Italian society was characterized by low interpersonal trust, reaching pathologically low levels in Southern Italy, where the prevailing outlook was "amoral familism": the absence of feelings of trust or moral obligation toward anyone outside the nuclear family. Banfield attributed this phenomenon to a long history of (1) dire poverty and (2) foreign domination. Trusting others is gambling on the expectation that they will reciprocate, rather than abuse your trust. But under conditions of extreme poverty, one has no margin for error: One cannot afford to gamble because if one's trust is abused—if a loan is not repaid for example—one's entire family may starve. Only if a culture has strong and reliably enforced norms of reciprocity is it rational to trust others. The South Italian regional subculture seems to lack such norms; one contributing factor may be an intense distrust of authority resulting from Southern Italy's long history of exploitative foreign domination. Thus, Banfield's explanation is based on an interaction between economic development and other historical experiences.

Not surprisingly, Banfield's interpretation was controversial. One critic, Pizzorno (1966), traced the lack of trust and interpersonal cooperation to the Italian social structure rather than to a specific cultural heritage. Similarly, Lopez Pintor and Wert Ortega (1982) found, in a series of surveys carried out from 1968 to 1980, that the Spanish public consistently displayed low levels of interpersonal trust; they argued that distrust tends to characterize traditional societies in general. While traditional societies can survive even if one trusts only those whom one knows personally, modern society can function only if people do not assume that strangers are enemies. The large-scale enterprises and bureaucracies that make modern economic and political organizations possible depend on predictable and reliable patterns of interaction between people who are total strangers. Since Southern Europe industrialized much more recently than Northern Europe, it still manifests the characteristics of traditional society to a considerable extent.

The relationship between a culture of distrust and the presence or absence of modern social structures has the causal ambiguity of the chicken-or-the-egg question: Does Southern Europe have low levels of trust because it has not yet developed modern organizational structures? Or (in a variation on Weber's Protestant Ethic thesis) did Southern Europe industrialize and develop modern organizational structures later than Northern Europe because its traditional culture was relatively low on interpersonal trust? We cannot answer this question conclusively with the data now available. Banfield's interpretation implies that low levels of trust are a distinctive and persisting feature of given cultures or regional subcultures, which may inhibit economic and political development in those areas. His critics tend to emphasize the impact of economic development on cultural patterns. In our view, a reciprocal causal relationship seems likely.

Important though it is, interpersonal trust alone is not sufficient to support stable mass democracy. A long-term commitment to democratic institutions among the public is also required, in order to sustain democracy when conditions are dire. Even when democracy has no reply to the question "What have you done for me lately?" it may be sustained by diffuse feelings that it is an inherently good thing. These feelings, in turn, may reflect economic and other successes that one experienced long ago—or even learned about secondhand as a part of one's early socialization. Evidence presented below indicates that the publics of certain societies have much more positive feelings toward the world they live in than do those of other societies. One of the best indicators of this orientation is satisfaction with one's life as a whole. This is a very diffuse attitude. It is not tied to the current performance of the economy or the authorities currently in office or to any specific aspect of society. Partly because it is so diffuse, intercultural differences in this orientation are remarkably enduring, and they may help shape attitudes toward more specific objects, such as the political system.

From their 1959 fieldwork, Almond and Verba found that (unlike the British or Americans) few Germans expressed pride in their political institutions; but one of the few aspects of their society in which they did express pride was the way their economic system was working. In the short run, this is an inadequate basis for democratic legitimacy, but in the long run, such feelings may contribute to the evolution of broadly favorable orientations toward the institutions under which one lives. Such feelings may play an important role in sustaining the viability of these institutions, even when favorable economic or political outputs are not forthcoming, for cultural patterns, once established, possess considerable autonomy and can influence subsequent political and economic events. To demonstrate this fact, let us now turn to the analysis of data from cross-national surveys carried out during the past two decades.

CROSS-CULTURAL DIFFERENCES IN OVERALL LIFE SATISFACTION AND THEIR POLITICAL SIGNIFICANCE

The study of political culture is based on the implicit assumption that autonomous and reasonably enduring cross-cultural differences exist and that they can have important political consequences. Intuitively, these assumptions seem plausible. But critics of cultural explanations have questioned these assumptions—and indeed, thus far, very little empirical evidence has been presented to support them. Since they are crucial assumptions underlying a controversial topic, let us examine a substantial body of relevant evidence, in order to see how well these assumptions hold up in longitudinal perspective.

We will start with one of the most basic and central attitudes of all: whether or not one is satisfied with the way things are going in one's life. Figure 1-1 illustrates the cross-national differences in response to the question, ''Generally speaking, how satisfied are you with your life as a whole? Would you say you are very satisfied, fairly satisfied, not very satisfied, or

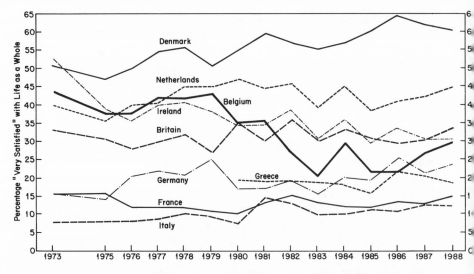

FIGURE 1-1. Cultural differences are relatively enduring, but not immutable. Cross-national differences in levels of satisfaction with one's life as a whole, 1973–1988. Based on Euro-Barometer surveys carried out in each respective year. Data, codebooks, and sampling information for these surveys are available from the ICPSR survey data archive.

not at all satisfied?'' This question has been asked repeatedly in the Euro-Barometer surveys carried out from 1973 to the present. Figure 1-1 sums up the results from the over 200,000 interviews in more than 200 representative national surveys of the publics of nine European Community nations.

We find large and remarkably stable cross-cultural differences. Furthermore, these differences do not reflect objective economic conditions in any direct or simple fashion. Year after year, the Italian public shows the lowest level of satisfaction; from 1973 through 1988, it ranks last in every year but one (when it ranks second lowest); at no time during this fifteen-year period, do more than 15 percent of the Italians describe themselves as ''very satisfied.'' The French manifest only slightly higher levels of life satisfaction than do the Italians, ranking in second-to-last place in all but two years (rising one rank above this level in one year and falling one rank below it in the other year). At no time does more than 17 percent of the French public describe itself as ''very satisfied.''

At the opposite extreme, the Danes manifest the highest level of overall life satisfaction in every year but one (when they rank second); at no time does less than 47 percent of the Danish public describe itself as ''very satisfied.'' On the average, the Danes are six times as likely as the Italians to describe themselves as ''very satisfied.'' The Dutch also rank high consistently, throughout the period from 1973 to 1988; at no time do less than 36 percent describe themselves as "very satisfied" with their lives as a whole.

The other nationalities maintain their relative positions in remarkably stable fashion, with a sole exception: The Belgians, who consistently ranked among the three most satisfied nationalities throughout the 1970s, show a substantial and protracted decline in the 1980s, falling to sixth place by 1986. In the 1970s, 40 to 45 percent of the Belgians consistently described themselves as "very satisfied"; in 1986, the figure had fallen to 25 percent. This drop of 15 to 20 points is not immense when compared with the gap of 50 points that separates the Danes from the Italians; but it does represent a substantial decline in the subjective well-being of the Belgian public—and stands in dramatic contrast to the overall stability of the cross-national differences manifested throughout this period. The cultural differences are reasonably stable, but not eternal. Short-term fluctuations are present, and, as the Belgian case illustrates, significant changes can occur in the relative positions of given nations.

On the whole, the stability shown in Figure 1-1 is truly remarkable, for we must bear in mind that this was a period of sharp economic upheavals. The crises that occurred in the mid-1970s and the early 1980s were the two most severe recessions since the 1930s. Moreover, these crises had a much more severe impact on some societies than others. Our respondents' sense of well-being was affected by these events. The decline of life satisfaction in Belgium can be traced, in part, to the fact that unemployment and inflation in that country soared to extraordinary levels in the 1980s, coupled with the fact that the Belgian government adopted particularly severe emergency austerity measures that cut unemployment benefits and medical benefits and froze pensions and wages. As a result, the Belgian public experienced a 30 percent decline in real income in the early 1980s. From 1973 to 1988, life satisfaction declined significantly in both Belgium and Ireland—two of the three countries most severely afflicted by unemployment and inflation during this period. Conversely, life satisfaction showed a modest but perceptible upward trend in Germany—the country with the lowest inflation rates from 1973 to 1988. Thus we find a fairly good fit between short-term fluctuations in life satisfaction and the economic experiences of the respective societies.

But a far more impressive aspect of Figure 1-1 is the cultural continuity that persisted *in spite of* these short-term fluctuations. Despite dramatic economic upheavals from year to year, and despite large differences between the experiences of the different countries, we find remarkable stability in the relative positions of these publics. Through thick and thin, the Italians and French remain near the bottom and the Danes and Dutch near the top. And despite the fact that the German economy ranks high, both in absolute terms and in relative performance during this period, the life satisfaction levels of the German public consistently rank relatively low (although they show a gradual upward trend). Conversely, both the Irish and the Dutch have much lower per capita incomes than the Germans, and their economies showed considerably higher levels of inflation and unemployment during this era than the German economy did—but nevertheless, both the Irish and the Dutch continued to manifest higher levels of life satisfaction than the Germans. Though cross-cultural differences in life satisfaction respond to economic changes, they do so only with a great deal of inertia.

Our conclusion is very simple but very important: There is a durable cultural component underlying these responses. Virtually any survey response is influenced to some extent by the context in which it is asked, and this question is no exception. Responses reflect both short-term fluctuations (resulting from immediate economic, social, and political events) and a long-term cultural component. Through statistical procedures it is possible to distinguish between the underlying cultural component and the short-term disturbances. In the present case, the long-term cultural differences are so pronounced that one can readily perceive them by mere visual inspection. In more complex cases, statistical analyses may be necessary in order to measure the persisting cross-cultural differences, purged of short-term fluctuations—but the principle remains the same. Though any given survey item is an imperfect indicator of an underlying cultural component, enduring cross-cultural differences do exist and can be measured.

Whether the Danes really are happier than the Italians in some absolute sense is an epistemological question that is inherently difficult to resolve. One way out of this difficulty would be to write off the cross-national differences as a result of poor translation, or to argue that the word for satisfaction has different connotations in different languages: "*satisfait*" and "*zufrieden*" are not equivalent to "satisfied." This explanation may be tempting, but it does not seem tenable.

There are a number of reasons why this seemingly plausible explanation does not stand up under closer inspection. One is illustrated by the case of Switzerland. The Swiss have three different national languages, which coincide with three of the languages used in other nations in these surveys. As data presented in Figure 1-2 demonstrate, the Swiss rank very high on life satisfaction. In fact, the German-speaking Swiss, the French-speaking Swiss, and the Italian-speaking Swiss all express higher levels of satisfaction than do the Germans, French, and Italians with whom they share a language. Indeed, the Swiss rank above all of the other nationalities except the Danes and Swedes, with whom they are essentially on a par. These

Swiss results devastate any attempt to explain the cross-national differences as artifacts of language.

The Swiss case alone is so damaging to the problems-of-translation hypothesis that further evidence seems superfluous, but there is a good deal of it. The Belgian data provide another example. Most Belgians speak either French or a variant of Dutch. But during the period 1973–1979 even the French-speaking Belgians ranked far above the French and roughly on a par with the Dutch in both happiness and satisfaction. Here again, nationality seems to be a much more powerful predictor of subjective well-being than language. In addition, we have the Dutch-German contrast. The two languages are closely related and the Dutch words for both "satisfied" and "happy" are cognates of their German counterparts. But the Dutch consistently rank far above the Germans in both life satisfaction and happiness.

Finally, as we will see in a moment, those nationalities that rank high on life satisfaction also have a strong and consistent tendency to rank high on happiness. In order to attribute the cross-national differences to linguistic artifacts, one would be forced to assume that virtually everyone who has done research on the subject has somehow stumbled onto the same type of noncomparable translation not only for satisfaction, but also for happiness—that, although unable to find equivalent words for the *same* concept, they managed to find words for *another* concept that distorted the results in exactly the same direction and to almost exactly the same degree in country after country. To achieve this by accident would be miraculous.

But exactly what is it that underlies these large and rather stable cross-national differences? Can it be true that the Italians, French, Germans, and Greeks really are a great deal less happy and more dissatisfied with their lives than the Danes, Swiss, Dutch, and Irish? Could fate be so unkind as to doom entire nationalities to unhappiness, simply because they happened to be born in the wrong place? The idea is difficult to accept—not only because it seems unfair, but also because it implies that there are profound differences in how the human organism functions from one nation to another. Could it possibly be true that the Italians experience life as burdensome, while the Swiss, living next door, find it enjoyable? The idea is conceivable, but it seems inconsistent with a large body of social research findings, which indicate that human beings generally function in similar ways. Moreover, it seems incompatible with some of the most striking findings from other research on this very topic (see chapter 7).

We suggest that the cross-national differences have an important cultural component. Though they do not reflect the different languages that were used, they do reflect different cultural norms. Protracted periods of well-being or frustration can raise or lower the norms prevailing in a given society, leading to relatively positive or cynical predispositions that influence responses independently of how well things are going for the individual. The short-term changes do reflect one's immediate experience, but the enduring cross-national differences reflect cognitive cultural norms, rather than individual grief and joy—which does not mean they are superficial. On the contrary, they reflect profound and pervasive differences in outlook. Low levels of life satisfaction are linked with negative orientations toward one's entire society. And, as we will soon see, these orientations have important political consequences. Cross-cultural differences in life satisfaction reflect a deep rooted and empirically reliable phenomenon. Not only is it reliable, with repeated measurements producing similar results year after year, as Figure 1-1 demonstrates; it is also robust, persisting when measured in a variety of different ways. For example, instead of using the four verbal categories described above, the question has been posed using an eleven-point scale ranging from 0, defined as "not at all satisfied," to 10, defined as "very satisfied" with one's life as a whole. The resulting cross-national rankings are virtually identical with those shown in Figure 1-1 (as Figure 1-2 demonstrates).

Moreover, this phenomenon persists even when we ask about it in completely different ways. From 1975 to 1986, in a total of 106 representative national samples, the Euro-Barometer surveys have asked, "Generally speaking, how are things going these days? Would you say you are very happy, fairly happy, or not too happy?" Here, we are not merely asking the question in a different format; we are asking a different question, for happiness and overall life satisfaction are conceptually distinct (Campbell, Converse, and Rodgers 1976; Andrews and Withey 1976). Nevertheless, if happiness and life satisfaction both tap a general sense of well-being, then those publics that rank high on life satisfaction should also rank high on happiness. This expectation is amply supported by empirical evidence: The national-level correlation between happiness and life satisfaction from 1975 to 1986 is .86. Throughout this period, the Italian and French publics consistently manifested the lowest levels of happiness among the nine nationalities that have been members of the European Community since 1973. Conversely, the Dutch and Danish publics consistently manifested the highest levels of happiness, nearly always ranking in first and second place, respectively. Moreover, the Belgian public's declining level of life satisfaction, from 1980 to 1986, is mirrored in a similar decline in reported happiness.

We suggest that the cultural component of these cross-national differences reflects the distinctive historical experience of the respective nationalities. Long periods of disappointed expectations give rise to cynical attitudes. These orientations may be transmitted from generation to generation through preadult socialization. Insofar as early learning tends to be relatively persistent, this contributes to the stability of distinctive cultural patterns. The fact that we can, to some extent, identify the historical causes of given cross-cultural differences does not, of course, make them disappear. They remain important cultural characteristics, which help explain the distinctive behavior of given nationalities.

We suggest that one of the most important sources of cultural variation is a given society's level of economic development: Economic security tends to enhance the prevailing sense of life satisfaction in a society, gradually giving rise to a relatively high cultural norm. Empirical evidence supports this supposition. First, as we have seen, there is a tendency for life satisfaction levels to rise or decline gradually in response to short-term economic fluctuations; for example, despite a predominant pattern of stability, life satisfaction among the Belgian public declined, while that of the German public rose slightly, in response to their respective experiences from 1973 to 1987. But, we suspect, the observed cross-cultural differences reflect long-term historical experiences over generations or even centuries, and not just the past dozen years or so. We cannot test this hypothesis against survey data from the past century or two, but we can use the cross-sectional pattern to provide a surrogate test: If economic security is conducive to relatively high levels of life satisfaction, we would expect the publics of prosperous nations to show higher levels of satisfaction than those of poorer ones. The data shown in Figure 1-2 tend to support this hypothesis.

The overall correlation between gross national product per capita and life satisfaction in Figure 1-2 is .67: Prosperity is linked with relatively high levels of life satisfaction among the twenty-four nations for which we have data from the 1980s. This point has been a matter of controversy in previous studies. Cantril (1965) analyzed data gathered in the 1950s from fourteen countries and found that the publics of richer nations did show relatively high levels of subjective well-being. Easterlin (1974) reanalyzed the Cantril data, and concluded that the correlation was actually rather weak. Emphasizing the fact that some poor nations (such as Egypt) showed higher levels of life satisfaction than did some relatively wealthy ones (such as West Germany), he argued that economic development had little impact on subjective well-being. In a more recent study, based on a broader range of nations, Gallup (1976) found a relatively strong correlation between economic development and life satisfaction; he concluded that the two are linked. The present data also show a relatively strong correlation between economic development and life satisfaction. How we interpret this depends on theoretical expectations. If one approaches the topic with the expectation that subjective well-being is almost entirely a matter

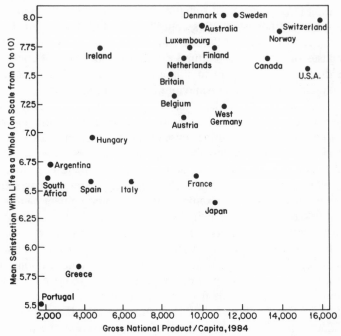

FIGURE 1-2. Mean life satisfaction by level of economic development. $r = .67$.

of economic factors, as Easterlin apparently did, then the crucial finding is that this is not the case. With the data in Figure 1-2, a nation's economic level explains less than half of the variance in life satisfaction. In the data Easterlin analyzed, economic factors explain an even smaller share of the variance. From Easterlin's perspective, economic determinism was clearly discredited.

However, if one approaches the question with the expectation that a nation's level of economic development is only one of a number of historical factors that influence cross-cultural differences in life satisfaction, then the data clearly do support the hypothesis. Here, as in Easterlin's analysis, one can point to some striking deviant cases: Ireland, with a per capita GNP less than half that of West Germany, shows a higher level of life satisfaction. In terms of these data, the Germans and Japanese are underachievers and the Irish are overachievers. The available data suggest that the Mexicans may be even more extreme overachievers than the Irish—but since these data are not based on a representative national sample, we exclude them from these analyses. Nevertheless, the overall pattern is clear: Wealthier nations tend to show higher levels of life satisfaction than poorer ones. It is equally clear, however, that economic development is not the only explanatory variable; other historical factors must also be involved. It may be significant, for example, that the publics of the three Axis powers, Germany, Japan, and Italy, all tend to be under-achievers in life satisfaction. The traumatic discrediting of their social and political systems that accompanied their defeat in World War II may have left a legacy of cynicism that their subsequent social change and economic success has still not entirely erased. We will not attempt to resolve such questions in this analysis. For the moment, our point is simply that, although it is not the only factor involved, economic development does seem to be linked with relatively high levels of life satisfaction.

The Euro-Barometer surveys provide regular readings on political satisfaction levels in each nation. Political satisfaction shows much more short-term fluctuation than does life satisfaction, for it explicitly refers to the political system—and, accordingly, behaves like an indicator of governmental popularity, fluctuating from one month to the next in response to current economic conditions and political events. Figure A-1 (in the Appendix) illustrates this pattern. When a conservative government is in office, those who identify with the Right show higher levels of political satisfaction; when a government of the Left gains power, those who identify with the Left show higher levels. Political satisfaction fluctuates in response to current economic and political events. But it is clear that a significant cultural component *also* is present underneath these fluctuations, since the publics of some countries are consistently more satisfied than others. Moreover, these differences reflect the now-familiar pattern we have found with life satisfaction and happiness. The publics of France and Italy almost always rank lower on political satisfaction than do those of other nations; at the national level, the correlation between life satisfaction and political satisfaction is .41.

Is overall life satisfaction related to stable democracy simply because it is also correlated with political satisfaction? No. If anything, it is the other way around. The length of time democratic institutions have persisted in a given nation is only weakly related to prevailing levels of political satisfaction ($r = .21$); *despite* the fact that political satisfaction has a much more obvious political relevance than does life satisfaction, the latter is far more strongly linked with stable democracy ($r = .73$). Democratic institutions seem to depend on enduring cultural traits, such as life satisfaction and interpersonal trust, more than on relatively fluctuating variables, such as political satisfaction. The latter is a better predictor of the popularity of a given government at a given moment—but precisely because it fluctuates with short-term conditions, it is less effective in maintaining the long-term stability of democratic institutions.

INTERPERSONAL TRUST, ECONOMIC
DEVELOPMENT, AND DEMOCRACY

Following Banfield, Almond and Verba, Wylie, and others, we hypothesized that interpersonal trust is part of an enduring cultural syndrome that
is conducive to the viability of democracy. The first question we must
answer is Do enduring intercultural differences exist in interpersonal trust?
Unless this is true, any argument concerning its long-term political impact
is on shaky ground.

The evidence indicates that given societies are, indeed, characterized by
distinctive levels of interpersonal trust. This even seems to be true of specific regions within given countries. The following question was asked in
Euro-Barometer surveys in 1976, 1980, and 1986: "Now I would like to
ask about how much you would trust people from various countries. For
each country, please say whether, in your opinion, they are generally very
trustworthy, fairly trustworthy, not particularly trustworthy, or not at all
trustworthy."

Figure 1-3 depicts the relative levels of interpersonal trust expressed
during this ten-year period toward people of one's own nationality. As is
immediately evident, trust levels in given countries are extremely stable.
In a pattern that is becoming increasingly familiar, the Italian public ranks
lowest at every point in time (with each of four major regions of Italy
retaining its relative position). The Greeks rank next, followed by the
French. The other nationalities are clustered close together, with relative
rankings consistently remaining within the band between 85 percent and
95 percent. One line in Figure 1-3, labeled "G.B. and Neth.," depicts the
levels of both the British and the Dutch—which are identical at all three
points in time. Remarkably pronounced and durable differences in trust
exist among the various regions of Italy. Precisely as Banfield (1958)
found many years ago, Southern Italy is characterized by lower levels of
interpersonal trust than those of Northern or Central Italy—and lower levels of trust than those of any other Western society for which we have data.

These findings of stable regional differences in Italian political culture
are consistent with earlier findings by Putnam, et al. (1983) based on ecological data covering a much longer period of time. In an imaginative and
elegant analysis, these authors utilize various indicators of social involvement and political mobilization (such as membership in mutual aid societies, union membership, and electoral turnout) to derive a measure of
"civic culture." This variable manifests remarkable stability at the regional level. Their index of civic culture as measured in the 1970s corre-
lates at $r = .91$ with the strength of mass parties in 1919–1921 and at $r = .84$ with the strength of mutual aid societies from 1873 to 1904. Civic

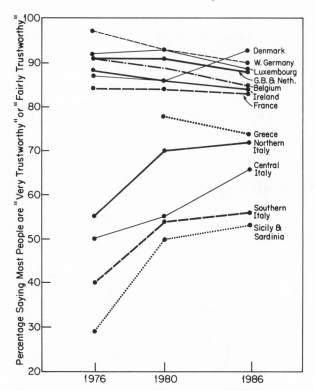

FIGURE 1-3. Interpersonal trust among European publics, 1976–1986. Percentage saying most people of their own nationality are "very trustworthy" or "fairly trustworthy." Based on data from Euro-Barometer surveys 6, 14, and 25.

culture, in turn, proves to be strongly correlated with the relative success of the new regional governments established throughout Italy in 1970. The authors conclude that political success or failure largely reflects the impact of autonomous cultural factors, independent of underlying economic variables:

Contrary to any simple-minded economic determinism, these regional continuities in political culture are strikingly greater than continuities in economic structure or social well-being. For example, the agricultural share of the regional work force in 1970 correlated $r = -.02$ with the same figure in 1870; the equivalent statistic for infant mortality is $r = .01$. Those regions with a relatively agricultural economy in 1970 had not been the more agricultural regions a century earlier, and the regions with good public health in 1970 had not been the healthier ones in 1870. But the regions characterized by political activism and social solidarity in the 1970s were essentially the same regions that had been so a century earlier. In short, we can trace with remarkable fidelity over the last hundred years the historical antecedents of just those aspects of regional political culture—mass participation and civic solidarity—that in turn provide such a powerful explanation for contemporary institutional success. (Putnam et al. 1983, 69–70)

Despite evidence of impressive stability in the propensity to trust others, trust is not a fixed genetic characteristic. It is cultural, being shaped by the historical experiences of given peoples, and therefore is subject to change. Table A-1 (in the Appendix) illustrates this point. As it demonstrates, fieldwork carried out for *The Civic Culture* found that the publics of the two long-established English-speaking democracies had markedly higher levels of interpersonal trust than those of Mexico, West Germany, or Italy. The Italian public, in particular, manifested trust levels that were phenomenally low in 1959. But, as our theoretical framework implies, the economic miracles that took place in both West Germany and Italy during the 1950s and 1960s eventually had an impact on the political culture of these countries. Though the Italian public still remained relatively low on trust in 1981 and 1986, absolute levels of trust had more than tripled by 1981 and almost quadrupled by 1986—a phenomenon that parallels the rise shown by Euro-Barometer survey data for Italy in Figure 1-3. The growth of interpersonal trust among the West German public was proportionately smaller, because they started from a higher level; but in 1981 the Germans had risen to a level much nearer the British, and by 1986 the Germans had actually surpassed the British in interpersonal trust. The other side of the coin is the fact that interpersonal trust was undergoing a long-term decline in the two English-speaking democracies.

Like life satisfaction and happiness, high interpersonal trust goes with relatively high levels of economic development, as Figure 1-4 illustrates. The cross-sectional correlation is .53. The available data do not enable us to determine whether this is because interpersonal trust is conducive to economic development or because economic development leads to an enhanced sense of security that is conducive to trust, or whether (as we suspect) the two processes are mutually supportive. It is interesting that in the two countries from which we have evidence of a dramatic rise in interpersonal trust (West Germany and Italy), this phenomenon took place after a period of dramatic economic recovery. But it is clear that economic factors alone are not decisive, for the publics of both Britain and the United States

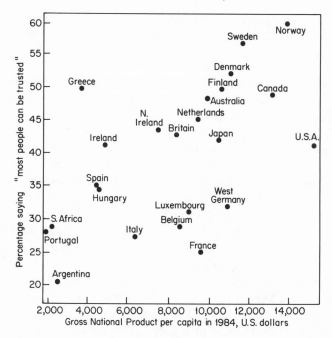

FIGURE 1-4. Economic development and interpersonal trust. Trust levels based on data from World Values survey 1981–1984, and from Euro-Barometer survey 25 (April 1986) for Greece, Portugal, and Luxembourg. $r = .53$.

were wealthier in the 1980s than they were in 1959–1960 but both experienced an erosion of interpersonal trust from 1960 to 1981.

As we will see shortly, high levels of interpersonal trust are also linked with stable democracy. Before analyzing this relationship, let us consider the implications of a recurrent finding in the data we have examined. With remarkable consistency, the publics of France and Italy rank lowest on the syndrome of attitudes that might loosely be called the civic culture. Among those countries for which we have time series data from 1973 to the present, the French and Italian publics nearly always rank lowest on life satisfaction, happiness, political satisfaction, and trust. These are precisely the countries that have been characterized by the largest anti-system parties. In France, since the end of World War I, the communists have normally polled a fifth or more of the total vote in national elections; more recently, a party of the extreme Right, the National Front, won about 10 percent of the vote in nationwide elections in 1984 and again in 1986 and 1988, recalling the sudden mushrooming of support for another extreme Right party, the Poujadists, that took place in the 1950s. Similarly, in Italy, the communists have generally won about a third of the vote since 1945, while the neo-Fascist MSI has won as much as 10 percent of the vote in national elections.

Data from Greece are available only since 1980, but they fit the pattern just described. To be sure, the Greek public has shown relatively high levels of satisfaction with the way democracy has been functioning since democratic institutions were restored in the 1970s, and this variable rose to a new peak in 1981, when the first government of the Left since World War II took office. But, as we have already noted, this variable fluctuates with short-term events. On most of our long-term civic culture indicators, such as life satisfaction, happiness, and support for the existing social order, the Greek public ranks relatively low. In keeping with this pattern, support for anti-system parties has been relatively high in Greece. The communist vote has been higher than in any of the other countries for which we have time series data, apart from France and Italy, and there has also been significant support for parties of the extreme Right.

We believe that relatively low levels of diffuse satisfaction and trust make one more likely to reject the existing political system and support parties of the extreme Right or Left. Again, we have the chicken-or-the-egg question: Does a culture of dissatisfaction and distrust give rise to an extremist vote, or do extremist parties produce distrust and dissatisfaction? The available data do not allow us to give a conclusive answer, but there are reasonably strong grounds for thinking that, while it may work both ways, the former of the two processes is more important. First, knowing the relatively modest place of politics on most people's intellectual horizons, it seems far more plausible to believe that people vote communist or neofascist because they are dissatisfied and distrustful than to believe that they are dissatisfied and distrustful because they vote communist (or, as a Right-wing fantasy might have it, that communism brings unhappiness and distrust). Secondly, low trust, low satisfaction, and low happiness are broad cultural characteristics of the French, Greek, and Italian publics, only marginally more prevalent among the electorates of the communists and extreme Right than elsewhere—if the communists sow unhappiness, they sow it broadly, and not just among their own supporters. Finally, there are indications that gradual cultural change *precedes* changes in the vote. Table 1-1 shows the cross-national pattern of responses to the following question:

> (SHOW CARD) On this card are three basic kinds of attitudes concerning the kind of society we live in. Please choose the one which best describes your own opinion:

1. The entire way our society is organized must be radically changed by revolutionary action.
2. Our society must be gradually improved by reforms.
3. Our present society must be valiantly defended against all subversive forces.

As Table 1-1 demonstrates, there is wide cross-national variation in response to this question. In the early 1980s, support for the revolutionary option ranged from a low of 1 or 2 percent in Northern Ireland and Norway to highs of 12 to 25 percent in Mexico, Portugal, Argentina, and South Africa. Conversely, support for defense of the status quo ranged from highs of 49 and 38 percent, respectively, in Norway and West Germany to lows of 10 to 12 percent in Mexico, Spain, and Portugal. The revolutionary option was most likely to be endorsed in countries with a relatively low

TABLE 1-1. SUPPORT FOR RADICAL CHANGE, GRADUAL REFORM, OR DEFENSE OF PRESENT SOCIETY IN TWENTY-TWO SOCIETIES, 1981 - 1982

Nation	Radical change: "The entire way our society is organized must be changed by revolutionary action" (% agreeing)[a]	Gradual Reform: "Our society must be gradually improved by reforms" (% agreeing)	Defend present society: "Our present society must be valiantly defended against all subversive forces" (% agreeing)	N
N. Ireland	1%	74%	25%	(287)
Norway	2	50	49	(1,146)
W. Germany	3	59	38	(1,149)
Denmark	3	69	28	(1,026)
Japan	3	71	26	(707)
Netherlands	3	70	26	(1,063)
Australia	4	73	23	(1,153)
Sweden	4	80	16	(797)
Ireland	4	76	20	(1,084)
Luxembourg	5	69	25	(760)
Canada	5	74	21	(1,135)
Britain	5	73	23	(1,136)
U.S.	5	73	22	(2,101)
Belgium	7	73	21	(897)
Italy	8	73	19	(1,270)
Spain	8	82	10	(2,091)
Greece	9	63	28	(1,815)
France	9	73	19	(1,123)
Mexico	12	77	11	(1,610)
Portugal	14	74	12	(813)
Argentina	13	77	10	(1,005)
S. Africa	25	54	21	(1,182)

Sources: World Values survey, 1981 - 1982, with Argentine survey in 1984, except that data for Greece and Luxembourg are from Euro-Barometer surveys 15 and 16 (carried out in April and October 1981) and Portugese data are from Euro-Barometer survey 24 (carried out in November 1985; these are the earliest such data available from Portugal).

[a]Percentages may not total 100 because of rounding.

per capita GNP ($r = -.68$), while the conservative option was most likely to be endorsed in countries with a relatively high per capita GNP ($r = .58$). And, as one might expect, support for the revolutionary option is negatively correlated with life satisfaction ($r = -.52$), while support for the conservative option shows a positive correlation with life satisfaction ($r = .31$). In only four countries does support for revolutionary change outweigh support for the present society: Mexico, Portugal, Argentina, and South Africa—all of them countries in which democratic institutions are not fully operative or have had an unstable recent history. In all of the stable democracies, the revolutionary option is heavily outweighed by support for the present society.

Responses to this question among the nine European Community nations from which we have data from 1976 through 1988 are quite stable, but they show a gradual decline in support for the revolutionary option. In 1976, it was supported by almost 10 percent of the public in the European Community as a whole but in 1987 it was supported by only 5 percent. This decline was gradual, never falling by more than one percentage point per year; and it was pervasive, with most nations showing declining support for revolution. But the phenomenon was especially concentrated among the publics of France and Italy, where prorevolutionaries constituted 14 percent of the public in both countries in 1976, but only 7 and 8 percent, respectively, in 1987. This deradicalization of the electorates of France and Italy largely *preceded* the electoral decline experienced by the communist parties of both countries in 1984–1988. Moreover, it may be a harbinger of favorable prospects for the persistence of democratic institutions in these countries, for our data show a correlation of $-.73$ between support for the revolutionary option and the number of continuous years that democratic institutions have functioned in a given nation.

Dramatic and enduring cross-cultural differences also exist in the propensity to discuss politics. This fact will be explored in considerable detail in chapter 10, so we will not discuss it further here. But if the reader wishes to glance ahead at Figure 10-4, it will show striking evidence of the magnitude and durability of the cross-national differences in how often various nationalities discuss politics.

THE CONSEQUENCES OF POLITICAL CULTURE: SOME SPECULATIONS WITH DATA

Let us sum up what we have learned so far. We find a broad syndrome of related attitudes that show substantial and consistent cross-cultural variation, with certain societies being characterized by satisfied and trusting attitudes to a much greater degree than are others. The cross-national differences show impressive stability over time; though they vary gradually (and the variations are of great substantive interest), these tend to be relatively enduring cultural characteristics. Finally, this syndrome is linked with the persistence of democratic institutions.

Life satisfaction, political satisfaction, interpersonal trust, high rates of political discussion, and support for the existing social order all tend to go together: They constitute a syndrome of positive attitudes toward the world in which one lives. What makes this all the more interesting is the fact that this syndrome seems linked with the viability of democratic institutions.

Such causal linkages are difficult to demonstrate conclusively. To do so would require longitudinal political culture data from a large number of nations, some of which became democracies during the course of a long time series, while others did not. Our interpretation suggests that those nations characterized by high levels of life satisfaction, interpersonal trust, tolerance, etc., would be likelier to adopt and maintain democratic institutions than those whose publics lacked such attitudes. Conversely, democratic institutions would be more likely to flounder in nations with low levels of life satisfaction, trust, and so on. Such data are not now available and will be difficult to obtain, both because it will require a long-term data-gathering process in many countries during many decades and because the governments of nondemocratic countries usually make it difficult or impossible to carry out survey research. In principle, however, it is possible to acquire such data, and this is a goal worth striving for; we probably will not attain the optimum, but we can certainly improve on what we have now. In the meantime, let us examine the cross-national pattern. Do democratic institutions seem to have emerged earlier and persisted longer in nations with high levels of overall life satisfaction than in those characterized by relatively low levels?

As Figure 1-5 demonstrates, the answer is yes. There is a remarkably consistent tendency for high levels of life satisfaction to go together with the persistence of democratic institutions over relatively long periods of time. Among the twenty-four nations depicted in Figure 1-5, the overall correlation between life satisfaction and the number of continuous years a given nation has functioned as a democracy is .85. Needless to say, our causal inference would be on firmer ground if we had survey data on life satisfaction levels from some much earlier point in time, such as 1900— but such data is not available. We use ex post facto data from 1981 as an indicator of the relative rankings earlier in history. The evidence indicates that these rankings are pretty stable, but this procedure undoubtedly introduces some error in measurement (which will tend to work *against* our hypothesis). Since our focus is on the effects of domestic political culture, we code democracy as having failed to survive only when it collapsed

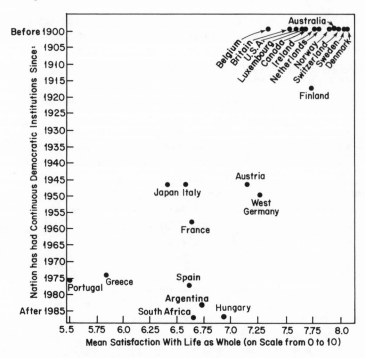

FIGURE 1-5. Mean life satisfaction and stable democracy. Based on data from World Values survey 1981–1984 and Euro-Barometer survey 25. $r = .85$.

through internal causes and not when it did so as a consequence of foreign conquest. By this definition, all of the thirteen nations that have maintained democratic institutions continuously since 1920 or earlier, show relatively high life satisfaction levels (above 7.25 on a scale from 0 to 10). Among the eleven nations in which democratic institutions have emerged only since 1945, or which are not yet fully democratic, every one shows mean life satisfaction levels below 7.25, often far below it.

Our coding of France might be questioned. She is coded as having had continuous democratic institutions only since 1958, since the military uprising that brought the Fourth Republic to an end and brought DeGaulle to power was not of foreign origin but was carried out by the French army. It is true that the last president of the Fourth Republic invited DeGaulle to form a government, but it is also clear that he did so only because of pressure from the French army, which had seized power in Algeria, landed paratroops in Corsica, and seemed on the verge of striking Paris next. Free elections were held shortly afterward, so the suspension of democracy was very brief, but, as the subsequent military uprisings of 1960 and 1962 testify, democracy in France was, for a time, on shaky ground. France is our most ambiguous case. But even if we were to redefine her as having been a stable democracy continuously since 1871, the overall pattern would still show a strong correlation between the presence of high life satisfaction and stable democracy.

It is conceivable that we have the causal arrow reversed. Perhaps many decades of living under democratic institutions produces greater life satisfaction. We don't rule this factor out—indeed, we think it *does* contribute to overall life satisfaction somewhat. But theoretical considerations suggest that it mainly works the other way around. It seems more likely that a global sense of well-being would also shape one's attitudes toward politics than that what is experienced in one relatively narrow aspect of life would determine one's overall sense of satisfaction. In keeping with this reasoning, Andrews and Withey (1976) have found that political satisfaction has only a relatively modest impact on most people's overall life satisfaction; satisfaction with one's job, home, family life, and leisure time all make larger contributions.

Overall life satisfaction is part of a broad syndrome of attitudes reflecting whether one has relatively positive or negative attitudes toward the world in which one lives. Life satisfaction, happiness, interpersonal trust, and whether one supports radical social change or defends one's existing society all tend to go together in a cultural cluster that is closely related to whether or not democratic institutions have persisted for a long time in a given society. These attitudes seem to be a deep-seated aspect of given cultures, constituting a long-term component underlying absolute levels of satisfaction with governmental performance at any given time: Though political satisfaction shows sharp fluctuations from one month to the next, the publics of some societies consistently manifest higher levels of satisfaction than do the publics of others.

This syndrome is also linked with a nation's economic level. The more developed nations tend to rank relatively high on life satisfaction, trust, and the other components of the syndrome. Are both this syndrome and liberal democracy simply joint consequences of economic development— or does political culture make an autonomous contribution to the viability of democratic institutions, as Almond and Verba have argued? Let us emphasize that we do not yet possess a data base that would enable us to answer such questions conclusively. We have established rather clearly the presence of an enduring and cross-nationally distinctive syndrome of basic cultural attitudes and demonstrated that this syndrome is much stronger in those nations that have been stable democracies since 1900 than in those that have been nondemocratic or intermittently democratic. But we do not yet have sufficient data to sort out the causal linkages among political cul-

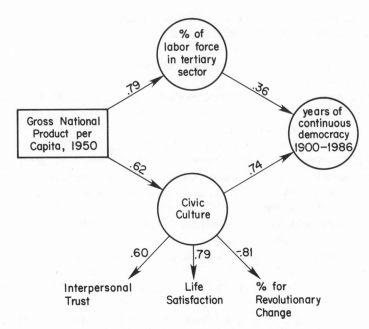

FIGURE 1-6. Economic and cultural prerequisites of stable democracy. LISREL analysis based on data from the societies shown in Figure 1-5. Adjusted goodness of fit index = .88.

ture, economic development, and democracy in a conclusive fashion. To do so would require regular measures of the relevant cultural variables throughout the past century. At present, these data are simply not available. Nevertheless, the patterns shown in Figures 1-2, 1-4, and 1-5 are so striking and their implications are so important that they virtually cry out for further exploration. With the reader's indulgence, the remainder of this chapter will be devoted to some analyses that cannot be conclusive but suggest that cultural factors play an extremely significant role in both political and economic development. Hopefully, they may stimulate further historical analysis, and the development of the longitudinal data base that will be necessary to any definitive analysis of the role of culture.

Figure 1-6 shows the results of a LISREL analysis in which the dependent variable is the number of consecutive years since 1900 that democracy has functioned in a given nation. The results indicate that economic development per se does not necessarily lead to democracy. Only insofar as it brings appropriate changes in social structure and political culture does it enhance the viability of democratic institutions. To take an extreme illustration, such nations as Saudi Arabia, Kuwait, and Libya are quite wealthy, but neither their social structures nor their political cultures seem favorable to democracy.

Clearly, we would prefer to have data gathered at earlier time points for some of our variables, especially the cultural indicators. We use gross national product per capita in 1950 as our indicator of a given nation's level of economic development, 1950 being the earliest time for which we have reliable data from all twenty-two nations. Theoretically, an even earlier time point might better tap the impact of economic development on the growth of the tertiary sector. On the other hand, the 1950 data were measured about thirty years before our political culture indicators (based on 1981 surveys), providing a time lag of about one generation between economic and cultural indicators, which is appropriate for present purposes.

The results suggest that political culture may be a crucial link between economic development and democracy. Although GNP per capita has a strong zero-order correlation with stable democracy, its effects are almost entirely due to its linkages with social structure and political culture, with the latter being the more important of the two. Earlier versions of our LIS-REL model allowed for a direct linkage between economic development and democracy, but its empirical importance was so insignificant ($r = .08$) that the final model shown in Figure 1-6 omits it. A given nation's level of economic development is closely linked with a set of characteristics, which we have labeled the "civic culture" (though it is only roughly equivalent to Almond and Verba's construct). This political culture syndrome is tapped by three indicators: (1) interpersonal trust, (2) life satisfaction, and (3) support for revolutionary change (which is negatively correlated with the civic culture). All three variables are good indicators of this underlying cultural dimension, with the second and third indicators showing almost identical correlations, despite the fact that in face content, overall life satisfaction has no obvious relationship to politics while support for revolutionary change clearly does. Earlier versions of the model also included a fourth indicator of the civic culture, satisfaction with the way democracy is functioning in one's country. Though in face content this variable has the most obvious reference to democratic institutions, it manifests a relatively large amount of short-term fluctuation. This variable seems to reflect governmental popularity at a given time, rather than long-term support for democracy. Consequently, although it has a significant correlation with the civic culture dimension ($r = .54$), it taps it less accurately than the other three indicators do. This is also true of a variable we will discuss in chapter 10, a given public's rate of political discussion: It, too, constitutes part of the political culture syndrome. But for technical reasons we need to avoid using too many indicators. Because of the small number of cases at our disposal, we obtain a better fitting model by omitting these variables.

The underlying civic culture tapped by these three indicators shows a strong linkage with the number of years that democratic institutions have functioned in the given nation. The regression coefficient is .74, controlling for the effects of social structure. This suggests that over half of the variance in the persistence of democratic institutions can be attributed to the effects of political culture alone.

The size of the tertiary sector also has a significant linkage with the persistence of democracy. A measure of the relative size of the middle class, as opposed to those with blue collar or agricultural occupations, it is also an indirect indicator of the strength of commercial elites. The importance of this variable provides empirical support for the arguments of theorists since Marx, who have emphasized the significance of the development of a commercial-industrial middle class. In part, this variable reflects purely economic factors. A less polarized distribution of income and the presence of a middle majority tend to make political conflict less ruthless and less desperate. But, historically, democratic institutions emerged long *before* the redistributive welfare state and the middle majority: Democracy emerged when power passed into the hands of the bourgeoisie. Moore (1966) takes it as axiomatic that there is an inherent affinity between democracy and the bourgeoisie. But if one presses farther and inquires why this is so, one is likely to arrive at a cultural explanation as a crucial intervening variable. Preindustrial agrarian societies are usually dominated by landed aristocracies exercising a military function or by priestly elites, both of which are accustomed to social relations based on a hierarchical chain of command structure. Commercial elites, by contrast, necessarily become accustomed to bargaining: In market relationships the buyer and seller may have diametrically opposed interests—the seller seeking the highest possible price and the buyer the lowest—but unless they can reach a compromise that is acceptable to both sides, neither can do business. Thus, commercial elites accept bargaining among equals, rather than hierarchical authority, as a normal way of dealing with people; these habits and skills are carried over into the emphasis on bargaining, rather than command, that characterizes parliamentary democracy.

It seems clear that viable democracy does not depend on economic factors alone. Specific cultural conditions are crucial—and they in turn are related to economic and macropolitical developments. Long-term economic success can help provide legitimacy for any type of regime in industrial society; thus, it can help maintain the viability of democratic institutions once they are established. But unless economic development is accompanied by certain changes in social structure and political culture, liberal democracy is unlikely to result.

Moreover, external constraints can prevent the emergence of democracy even when internal factors are favorable. Huntington (1984) argues that Czechoslovakia, and probably Poland and Hungary, have social and cultural conditions that would favor increasing democratization in the absence of direct or indirect Soviet intervention. To what degree various East European societies are now characterized by political cultures that would support democratic institutions if the Soviet Union permitted them to emerge, is a fascinating but unanswered question. There are numerous indications of underlying pressures toward political pluralism in East European countries, manifesting themselves in such developments as the emergence of an independent labor movement in Poland, relatively autonomous environmentalist movements in Poland and Hungary, increasingly independent church-related groups throughout the region, and the increasing prevalence of samizdat and the widening margins allowed for public criticism of society in recent years. But at the same time there are indications that the omnipresent threat of Soviet intervention during the past forty-five years has left an imprint on the cultures of certain East European societies.

Table A-2 (in the Appendix) shows some relevant evidence. Representative national samples of the Hungarian and American publics ranked eighteen basic personal values at two time points, in recent years. The results make two important points manifest: (1) Once again, we find pronounced and stable cross-cultural differences; and (2) these differences can be traced, at least in part, to long-term differences in the environments of the respective societies.

The most striking finding that emerges from Table A-2 is the remarkable stability of value priorities within each society. Among the American public, the top eight items occupy exactly the same ranks in 1981 as they did in 1974. The remaining twelve items show slightly more volatility, but none varies by more than two ranks, from 1974 to 1981. Across the eighteen items, the mean change from 1974 to 1981 is about one-half rank (one-twelfth as much movement as would occur by random processes). As we will see in chapter 3, the priorities of the American public show comparable stability over even *longer* periods of time.

The values of the Hungarian public are equally stable: the top six values occupy identical ranks in 1980 and 1983; the same is true of the six lowest ranking values. None of the remaining items varies by more than two places from the early survey to the later one; and the mean change from 1980 to 1983 is less than half of a rank, out of eighteen possible rankings.

When we compare the Hungarians' priorities with those of the United States public, however, we find sizable differences. Both societies rank "a world at peace" and "family security" in the top two places; these values reflect basic human needs for physical and economic security. But other priorities vary strikingly. The mean difference in the rankings of given items between the United States and Hungary is 3.66 places: there is seven times as much cross-national variation as there is change over time within a given society. The Hungarians give "national security" and "social recognition" much higher priorities than do the Americans; the American public gives higher priority to "freedom," "wisdom," and "salvation."

It would be a complex task to identify the reasons underlying these cross-cultural differences. But one of the most interesting contrasts between the Hungarian and American value systems lies in the relative priority given to "national security." For the Hungarians, this is the third most highly valued goal, at both time points. For the Americans, it ranks about twelfth out of eighteen goals. And, while both publics give "world peace" a high priority, the Hungarians rank it first by a very wide margin (with a mean ranking of 1.75 in 1983), while the Americans rank it second (with a mean ranking of 3.42 in 1981). It seems likely that the experience of occupation by the Germans in 1944, Soviet occupation in 1945, revolt and Soviet reoccupation in 1956, reluctant participation in the Soviet invasion of Czechoslovakia in 1968, and witnessing Soviet pressures on Poland in the 1980s have left the Hungarians with a relatively high anxiety concerning foreign intervention.

It would be as gross an oversimplification to believe in sheer cultural determinism as to believe in economic determinism. Stable democracy reflects the interaction of economic, political, and cultural factors. The preceding analyses point to a crucial set of linkages between economic development, political culture and viable democracy. But these are not the only factors involved. The international environment also helps shape the outcome. Democracy has generally arisen in countries that enjoyed a geographically secure position. Thus, economic development does not automatically bring about democracy, but it does seem to be linked with sociocultural changes that enhance democracy's chances.

CULTURAL CHANGE AND ECONOMIC DEVELOPMENT

We have established that certain societies are characterized by relatively high degrees of a durable set of orientations, which roughly correspond to the civic culture discussed by Almond and Verba; and that this cultural pattern shows a strong empirical linkage with stable democracy, even when we control for related aspects of social structure and economic development. In other words, a body of evidence that is not only much larger than that available to Almond and Verba, but also one that extends over a number of years, tends to confirm the basic thesis of *The Civic Culture*.

But the civic culture itself is only one aspect of a still broader cultural syndrome, which seems to reflect a long-term process of social and economic change. To fully understand this process, we must see it in the context of historical developments that have taken place over the past few centuries. Though we do not have survey data that would enable us directly to trace the long-term cultural changes linked with this process, some indicators are available that enable us at least to suggest the broad outlines of what has been happening.

Max Weber (1905) argued many years ago that the rise of capitalism and the subsequent rapid economic development of the West were made possible by a set of cultural changes related to the emergence of Calvinist Protestantism. His Protestant Ethic thesis gave rise to a controversy that endured for decades. Some of the criticisms seem well founded; and the thesis that economic achievement was linked with Protestantism seems unconvincing today, when predominantly Catholic countries have higher economic growth rates than Protestant ones. Nevertheless, though we would not defend Weber's thesis in its entirety, we believe that important aspects of it were correct, provided his work is viewed as an analysis of a specific historical phenomenon (as was clearly Weber's intention), and not as asserting an immutable relationship between economic achievement and Protestantism. Particularly crucial is Weber's insight that culture is not simply an epiphenomenon determined by economics, but an autonomous set of factors that sometimes shape economic events as well as being shaped by them.

In the empirical analyses that follow, we utilize the dominant religious tradition of a given society as an indicator of its preindustrial cultural heritage. This is, of course, an oversimplified indicator, though not as oversimplified as it may seem from today's perspective. Contemporary social scientists tend to underestimate the historical importance of religion, both because they are social scientists, habituated to viewing the world from a secular and scientific viewpoint, and because they are contemporary, living in societies in which the functions of religion have diminished drastically. It may be worthwhile to remind ourselves that in most agrarian societies, religion is an overwhelmingly important force, filling the functions that educational and scientific institutions, the mass media, art museums, and philanthropic foundations, as well as religious institutions, now fill in advanced industrial societies. The total volume of information flows was far smaller than it is today, but what existed was largely integrated and propagated through religious channels. In preindustrial society, to a large extent, culture *is* religion. In modern societies, religion is a far less adequate indicator of the culture as a whole, which becomes more differentiated, and subject to more rapid change. But our interest here is on the impact of the preindustrial cultural heritage of given societies. Clearly, religion is an imperfect indicator of this heritage; we use it as such, simply because we do not possess more refined measures of the value systems prevailing at given times and places in the past.

It may seem implausible that religious traditions that originated centuries ago could still have a major impact on contemporary behavior, for the connection is long-term, indirect, and nonobvious. Clearly, it is not a matter of Calvinist theologians directly indoctrinating people today with attitudes toward economic achievement. Nevertheless, indirect influences may be transmitted through attitudes and habits acquired informally during one's preadult socialization. To illustrate this point, let us examine another piece of evidence concerning the relatively enduring nature of political culture. One of the standard questions included in the Euro-Barometer surveys since 1973 has asked: "When you get together with your friends, would you say you discuss political matters frequently, occasionally, or never?"

While there may be some ambiguity about the distinction between "frequently" and "occasionally," the meaning of "never" is absolutely clear. We use this as the cutting point, to divide respondents into two categories: those who sometimes discuss politics (whether frequently or occasionally), and those who never do. As one would expect, the degree to which people discuss politics fluctuates from year to year; people talk about politics more frequently when national elections take place than when nothing much is happening (see chapter 10 for further details). But underlying such fluctuations, we find large and enduring cross-cultural differences. In the Euro-Barometer surveys carried out from 1973 to 1987, the German public ranks at the top in political discussion rates in every year except one (when it ranks second). The Danes and the Dutch also rank high in virtually every year for which we have data. Conversely, the Belgians, Italians, French, and Irish generally rank low, though elections or crises bring some fluctuations. Overall there is an almost perfect correlation between having a predominantly Protestant historical tradition, and relatively high rates of political discussion. Within given nations, religious differences are usually small; over the centuries, Catholics and Protestants in given societies have become rather similar. But when we combine results from large numbers of surveys, a consistent pattern emerges. In almost every country, Protestants show slightly higher rates of political discussion than do Catholics.

This finding seems significant. For high rates of political discussion are strongly correlated with the syndrome that links the civic culture with stable democracy. In a sense, Protestantism is *also* part of this syndrome—and even though the individual-level differences have dwindled, the impact of historical events still manifests itself in political cultural differences between Catholic and Protestant societies. This linkage between Protes-

TABLE 1-2. POLITICIZATION OF WOMEN IN TWENTY-ONE SOCIETIES
BY PREDOMINANT RELIGION
(Percentage who discuss politics)

Nation	% of Women Who Discuss Politics	Predominant Religion
Finland	77%	Protestant
Switzerland	75	Protestant
U.S.	72	Protestant
Netherlands	70	Protestant
Austria	69	Catholic
W. Germany	67	Protestant
Luxembourg	64	Catholic
Denmark	63	Protestant
Canada	62	Protestant
Britain	60	Protestant
Australia	60	Protestant
N. Ireland	59	Protestant
Greece	58	Orthodox
Hungary	58	Catholic
France	57	Catholic
Ireland	49	Catholic
Italy	47	Catholic
Spain	40	Catholic
Portugal	40	Catholic
Belgium	38	Catholic
Japan	35	Buddhist

Sources: World Values survey, 1981 - 1982, for all countries except
Switzerland and Austria, which are based on Political Action survey,
1974, and Luxembourg, Greece, and Portugal, which are based on cumulated
Euro-Barometer survey data, 1981 - 1986.

tantism and stable democracy is rooted in history, rather than in contemporary influences. Thus, we define predominantly Protestant countries in terms of the dominant historical tradition, rather than the present population mix. While the Netherlands, West Germany, Switzerland, and the United States all have large Catholic and nonreligious populations today, historically their dominant tradition has been Protestant. In a multiple regression analysis of data from ninety-nine nations, Bollen (1979) found that the percentage of Protestants in given countries had a significant effect on political democracy, controlling for economic development but that Protestantism showed no effects on *changes* in the degree of democracy from 1960 to 1965.

Furthermore, the linkage between political discussion rates and Protestantism is gender-specific. When we examine men only, we find a correlation of .50 between Protestant tradition and political discussion, across twenty-one nations. Among women, this correlation rises to .68. Table 1-2 illustrates the latter relationship. All ten of the Protestant nations from which we have data rank among the top twelve nations in frequency of political discussion among women. All nine of the lowest-ranking nations are non-Protestant.

Women are more integrated into political life in historically Protestant

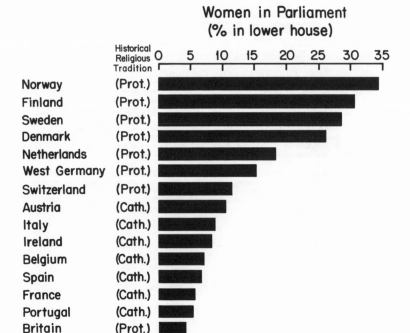

FIGURE 1-7. Political integration of women at elite level by historically dominant religious tradition: percentage of women in lower house of parliament. Adapted from *The Economist*, 29 Feb. 1987, 48.

societies than they are in Catholic ones. This holds true at the elite level as well as among the general public. Figure 1-7 shows the percentage of women in the lower house of parliament in sixteen Western societies, in the late 1980s. All seven of the countries having the highest percentages of women in parliament are societies in which the Protestant tradition was historically predominant. Eight of the nine countries ranking lowest were shaped by the Roman Catholic or Greek Orthodox traditions.

The sole deviant case (Britain) can be explained on institutional grounds. Britain (like the United States) elects her representatives by simple majorities in single-member districts. All of the other countries have some variant of proportional representation, with party lists on which the party leaders can give certain candidates a high ranking, thus ensuring their election (with women allocated a share of these places). Hence, these results reflect differences in the elite political cultures of the respective countries, and it is clear that the political integration of women is more strongly emphasized in historically Protestant than in non-Protestant societies.

These findings converge with those based on mass-level differences in political discussion rates.

Gender differences in political participation have persisted more strongly in Roman Catholic, Greek Orthodox, and Buddhist societies than in Protestant ones. This, in turn, is probably linked with the fact that most Protestant societies adopted women's suffrage at an earlier point in history than did Catholic (and other non-Protestant) countries, which in turn seems linked with the fact that women were integrated into educational systems and the labor force earlier in Protestant countries than in others, which in turn reflects the fact that Protestant countries developed economically at an earlier date, which leads us back, via a causal chain several centuries long, to the Protestant Ethic thesis.

Figure 1-8 diagrams a long-term process of economic and cultural change that helped give rise to the emergence of democracy in the West. As this figure suggests, the relationship between economic and cultural change is one of complex reciprocal causality, with cultural factors not only being influenced by economic change, but also influencing it. Weber argued that Calvinist Protestantism gradually evolved into a value system that viewed the accumulation of wealth for its own sake (and not as a means to survive or acquire luxuries) as a sign of divine grace and that encouraged an ascetic self-control conducive to the accumulation of wealth. This led to an entrepreneurial spirit and an accumulation of capital that facilitated the Industrial Revolution in the eighteenth and nineteenth centuries, which in turn had immense consequences for global economic development in the twentieth century.

We suggest that the Protestant Reformation was only one case of a more general phenomenon: the breakdown of traditional cultural barriers to economic modernization. As the top half of Figure 1-8 suggests, one feature common to traditional value systems is that they emerge in, and are adapted to, economies characterized by very little technological change and economic growth. In this situation, social mobility is a zero-sum game, heavily laden with conflict and threatening to the social system. In a society undergoing rapid industrialization and expansion, by contrast, social mobility may be widespread. But in traditional agrarian societies, social status is hereditary, except when an individual or group forcibly seizes the lands and social status of another. To preserve social peace, virtually all traditional cultures discourage upward social mobility and the accumulation of wealth. These cultures perform an integrating function by, on one hand, providing a rationale that legitimates the established social order and, on the other hand, inculcating norms of sharing, charity, and other obligations that help to mitigate the harshness of a subsistence economy.

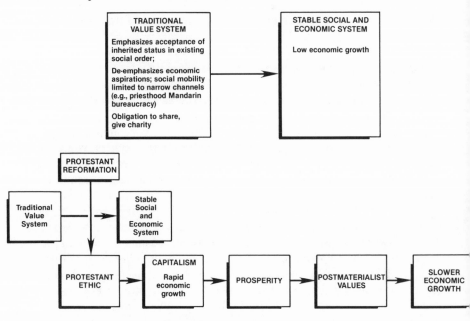

FIGURE 1-8. Long-term economic consequencs of rise of Protestant Ethic. In non-Western countries the impact of the industrialized West serves as a functional equivalent to the Protestant Reformation, although the value system that emerges is shaped by the traditional value system that precedes it.

By their very nature, the traditional value systems of agrarian society are adapted to maintaining a stable balance in unchanging societies; accordingly, they tend to discourage social change in general and the accumulative entrepreneurial spirit in particular. One of the important functions of the Protestant Reformation was to break the grip of the medieval Christian worldview on a significant portion of Europe. It did not accomplish this alone. The emergence of scientific inquiry had already begun to undermine the anthropocentric cosmos of the medieval Christian tradition. But it is difficult to avoid the conclusion that Weber's emphasis on the role of Protestantism captures an important part of reality. Prior to the Protestant Reformation, Southern Europe was economically more advanced than Northern Europe. During the three centuries after the Reformation, capitalism emerged, mainly among the Protestant regions of Europe and among the Protestant minorities of Catholic countries. Protestant Europe manifested a subsequent economic dynamism that was extraordinary, moving it far ahead of Catholic Europe. Shifting trade patterns, declining food production in Southern Europe, and other variables played a role in this shift, but the evidence suggests that cultural factors were also important.

As capitalism led to industrialization and eventually to historically unprecedented levels of prosperity, emulation became more and more attractive and increasing amounts of cross-cultural diffusion took place; but, to a truly remarkable degree, throughout the early stages the Protestant cultural zone was markedly more receptive to industrialization and economic development than any other part of the world. The Industrial Revolution began in England, spreading rapidly to predominantly Protestant Scotland and Wales—but leaving Catholic Ireland largely untouched except for the Protestant region around Belfast. Industrialization spread from England to nearby France, but lagged there in comparison with its rapid implantation in more distant but more receptive areas, such as the United States and Germany, both of which soon became far more industrialized than France. At the start of the twentieth century, the correlation between Protestantism and economic development was still remarkably strong. In Europe, the economically most dynamic nations were Great Britain, Germany, Sweden, Denmark, Norway, the Netherlands, and Switzerland—all of which were predominantly Protestant at that time. The only non-Protestant countries that had attained even roughly comparable levels of economic development were Belgium and France, both of which were geographically near the original core area from which the Industrial Revolution spread and had Protestant minorities who played a disproportionately important role in the process of economic development. In the New World, the United States and Canada had also emerged as developed industrial societies—while virtually all of Latin America remained almost totally unaffected by the Industrial Revolution. Even within Canada, the predominantly Catholic region developed much less rapidly than the rest of the country. Economic development seemed wedded to Protestantism.

But culture is not a constant. It is a system through which a society adapts to its environment: Given a changing environment, in the long run it is likely to change. One major change that took place was the secularization of Catholic (and other non-Protestant) cultures. In much of the world, the role of merchant and profit-making entrepreneur became less stigmatized; in some settings, the entrepreneur even became the cultural hero, as was the captain of industry in the United States of the late nineteenth century.

A contrasting process of cultural change began to take place in the more advanced industrial societies during the second half of the twentieth century. The lower half of Figure 1-8 diagrams this process. Precisely in those regions that had earlier been most strongly influenced by the Protestant Ethic, the long-term consequences of economic development began to be felt, as generations emerged that had been raised in unprecedented prosperity and economic security and were characterized, increasingly, by the presence of Postmaterialist values. The theoretical reasons underlying this process of value change, and a large body of supporting evidence, will be discussed in detail in chapters 2 through 5 of this book.

The Materialist/Postmaterialist thesis is based on two key hypotheses: (1) a *scarcity hypothesis* that one's priorities reflect one's socioeconomic environment so that one places greatest subjective value on those things that are in relatively short supply; and (2) a *socialization hypothesis* that, to a large extent, one's basic values reflect the conditions that prevailed during one's preadult years. Taken together, these two hypotheses imply that, as a result of the historically unprecedented prosperity and the absence of war that has prevailed in Western countries since 1945, younger birth cohorts place less emphasis on economic and physical security than do older groups, who have experienced a much greater degree of economic insecurity, and that, conversely, the younger birth cohorts tend to give a higher priority to nonmaterial needs, such as a sense of community and the quality of life. Cohort analysis based on data from 1970 through 1988 in six Western countries confirms the presence of substantial differences in the basic societal priorities of younger and older generations. Moreover, this analysis, presented in chapter 2, demonstrates that as intergenerational population replacement has occurred, there has been a gradual but pervasive shift in the values of these publics, from predominantly Materialist priorities toward Postmaterialist goals. One consequence of this shift has been a diminishing emphasis on economic growth in these societies, together with increasing emphasis on environmental protection and preserving the quality of life—if necessary, even at the expense of economic growth. Postmaterialists place markedly less emphasis on economic growth than do those with Materialist or mixed values; and they place less emphasis on a high salary and job security than on working with people they like or doing interesting work, as we will see in chapter 5. Moreover, Postmaterialists are economic underachievers, that is, controlling for the fact that they come from more prosperous families and receive better educations, we find that Postmaterialists earn significantly lower incomes than those with Materialist values. Finally, Postmaterialists place more emphasis on protecting the environment and are far more likely to be active members of environmental organizations than are Materialists, as chapter 11 demonstrates. All this suggests that, as societies become increasingly influenced by the growing Postmaterialist minority, they will tend to give economic growth a lower priority. The cross-national data shown in Figures 1-9 and 1-10 support this prediction at the societal level.

Evidence from a cross-national perspective converges with evidence from the individual level, pointing to a long-term cultural process of negative feedback linked with economic growth. On one hand, as Figure 1-9 demonstrates, the publics of relatively rich societies are least likely to emphasize Materialist values, and most likely to emphasize Postmaterialist ones. Since one's values tend to reflect the conditions prevailing during one's preadult years, we allow a lag of about thirty years between the independent variable (level of development in 1950) and the dependent variable (mass value priorities in 1981–1986). Since the median age in our adult sample is about 45, our economic indicator taps conditions when the median individual was about 15 years of age. We find a correlation of − .59 between a nation's per capita GNP in 1950, and the proportion of Materialists among that nation's public in the 1980s. Not only does this result have the predicted polarity and significant strength, but it is stronger than the correlation obtained when we use GNP per capita in 1980 as our independent variable: The time lag that we assumed to exist between economic cause and cultural effect seems to reflect reality.

Figure 1-10 is a mirror-image of Figure 1-9. The wealthier societies are least likely to produce Materialist publics, but Materialist publics seem to produce high economic growth rates. Or, reversing labels, though wealthier societies are most likely to produce Postmaterialists, after an appropriate time lag, the more Postmaterialist societies have the lowest growth rates. The long-term result is that high growth rates eventually lead to lower growth rates. Prosperity engenders a cultural shift toward Postmaterialist values, which eventually leads to a less intense emphasis on economic growth.

Data from roughly two dozen nations reveal a consistent cultural-economic syndrome. The wealthier countries and those with highly developed tertiary sectors are most likely to be long-established democracies, and the publics of these nations tend to show relatively high rates of political discussion, have less Materialist value priorities, and tend to be Protestant in religion (cf. Huntington 1984). These nations, furthermore, tend to have publics that are characterized by high levels of life satisfaction and interpersonal trust, low levels of support for revolutionary social change, high levels of satisfaction with the way democracy is working, and high rates of political discussion. Conversely, the less wealthy, less democratic, and less Protestant nations tend to be characterized by political cultures that show low levels of trust and satisfaction, high levels of support for revolutionary change, and low rates of political discussion. The syndrome is remarkably broad and coherent, combining a distinctive political culture

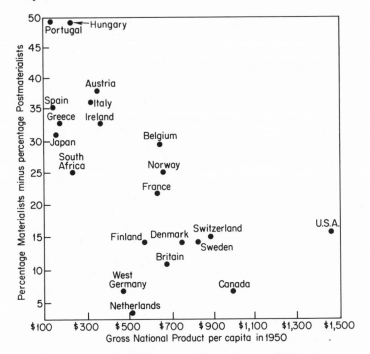

FIGURE 1-9. Economic development and the decline of Materialist values. $r = .63$. Value priorities data from World Values survey, 1981; Euro-Barometer surveys 19–25 (1982–1986); and Political Action, 1974. Gross National Product per capita calculated from *U.N. Statistical Yearbook, 1958* (New York: 1959).

with long-term differences in economic development, which in turn is linked with the Protestant Ethic.

But the Protestant Ethic seems to be unraveling, for the linkage between Protestantism and economic achievement is a thing of the past. While the Protestant Ethic syndrome was strongly correlated with high levels of economic growth in 1870–1913 (the earliest period for which we have data), this correlation weakens and then becomes strongly negative as we move into more recent periods.

Among those countries for which we have long-term historical data, those that had relatively high growth rates a century ago tend to have relatively low growth rates today. Table 1-3 illustrates this phenomenon. In 1870–1913, nearly all Protestant countries had growth rates that were higher than those of almost all Catholic countries. Our table actually understates the extent to which this was true, because the few Catholic countries from which we have reliable historical data are precisely the ones that were *most* developed in the nineteenth century. Spain, Portugal, and Latin

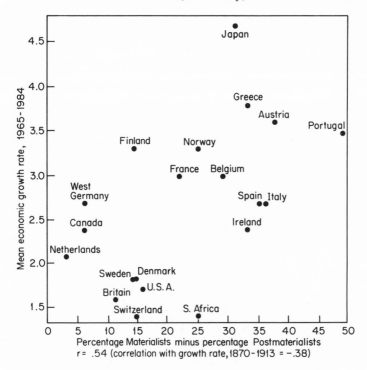

FIGURE 1-10. Materialist values and economic growth, 1965–
1984. $r = .51$. Correlation between 1870–1913 growth rates and
1981–1985 values $= -.38$, i.e., the countries that are most Post-
materialist today had relatively *high* growth rates in 1870–1913.
Growth rates 1965–1984 from *World Development Report, 1986*
(Washington: World Bank, 1986). Growth rates 1870–1913 from
Angus Maddison, *Economic Growth in Japan and the U.S.S.R.*
(London: Allen and Unwin, 1969).

America lagged far behind. Protestant countries still had more dynamic
economies than did most Catholic ones in the interwar years. But in the
past few decades, this situation has reversed itself. During 1965–1984, the
Catholic countries in our sample had higher growth rates than most of the
Protestant ones. Similarly, within the United States, as recently as 1958,
Catholics and Protestants manifested different values concerning various
aspects of economic and family life (Lenski 1963), but these differences
have been dwindling (Alwin 1986).

In part, the recent decline in the relative performance of Protestant countries reflects the fact that it is easier for a poor country to attain a high
growth rate than it is for a rich one: By importing technology that has
already been proven in more developed countries, one can catch up rap-

TABLE 1-3. ECONOMIC GROWTH RATES IN PROTESTANT COUNTRIES,
AS COMPARED WITH CATHOLIC COUNTRIES AND JAPAN, 1870 - 1984

Rank	1870 - 1913	1913 - 1938	1949 - 1965	1965 - 1984
1.	U.S. (P)	Japan (B)	Japan (B)	Japan (B)
2.	Canada (P)	Norway (P)	W.Germany (P)	Norway (P)
3.	Denmark (P)	Neth. (P)	Italy (C)	France (C)
4.	Sweden (P)	U.S. (P)	France (C)	Belgium (C)
5.	Germany (P)	Switz. (P)	Switz. (P)	Italy (C)
6.	Belgium (C)	Denmark (P)	Neth. (P)	W.Germany (P)
7.	Switzerland (P)	Sweden (P)	Canada (P)	Canada (P)
8.	Japan (B)	Italy (C)	Denmark (P)	Neth. (P)
9.	Norway (P)	Canada (P)	Norway (P)	Denmark (P)
10.	Gt.Britain (P)	Germany (P)	Sweden (P)	Sweden (P)
11.	Netherlands (P)	Gt.Britain (P)	U.S. (P)	U.S. (P)
12.	France (C)	France (C)	Belgium (C)	Gt.Britain (P)
13.	Italy (C)	Belgium (C)	Gt.Britain (P)	Switzerland (P)

Mean economic growth rate in
Protestant countries, as a percentage
of mean economic growth rate
in Catholic countries:

152%	120%	98%	72%

Sources: 1870 - 1965 rankings calculated from data in A. Maddison, Economic Growth in Japan and the U.S.S.R. (London: Allen and Unwin, 1969), 148 - 149; 1965 - 1984 rankings calculated from data in World Development Report, 1986 (Washington, D.C.: World Bank, 1986).
    Note: (P) indicates countries in which a majority of the population was Protestant in 1900; (C) indicates countries having a Roman Catholic majority in 1900; (B) indicates countries having a Buddhist majority in 1900.

idly. But in global perspective, it is clear that this is only part of the story, for historically the Protestant countries showed the world's highest growth rates even when they were the richest countries in the world. Moreover, in the contemporary world, plenty of poor nations are *not* showing rapid economic growth, while other poor nations (particularly those of East Asia) have been growing at an extraordinary pace. Conversely, some rich nations (such as Japan) continue to develop relatively rapidly, even when they can no longer rely on imported technology but are increasingly developing their own, while other rich countries have become relatively stagnant. Clearly, some societies are culturally more receptive to economic development than others.

High economic growth was once an almost uniquely Protestant phenomenon; today it has become global in scope and is *less* likely to be found in the Protestant nations than elsewhere. This does not mean that the civic culture that emerged in these nations will disappear; on the contrary, these countries are still becoming richer, and, on the whole, their life satisfaction, political satisfaction, and trust have been gradually rising in recent years. The emergence of democracy is far too complex to allow easy predictions, but the evidence allows us cautious optimism. The syndrome that linked Protestantism with wealth and democracy seems to be becoming less distinctively Protestant because it is permeating other regions of the world.

But, even as it does so, its spread will probably be shaped by cultural influences analogous to those the Protestant Ethic had in an earlier era. Culture is variable, not constant. Hence, it would be misleading to speak of the characteristics of any given cultural zone, such as Protestant Europe or the Confucian cultural area, unless one makes it clear that one is speaking of its attributes at a specific point in history. Keeping this restriction in mind, it does seem clear that given cultural traditions have a coherent and distinctive character that can have important social and economic consequences. Virtually all traditional value systems discourage aspirations toward upward social mobility, while emphasizing social cohesion and stability. In the medieval Roman Catholic world, upward social mobility (other than by force of arms) was possible through only one narrowly institutionalized path—the priesthood, which (normatively at least) required chastity and poverty. Moreover, the productive use of capital was stigmatized as usury and forbidden. The Protestant Reformation secularized the bearers of culture, allowing the priesthood to marry and take on worldly obligations; broadened literacy by making the sacred literature available in the vernacular languages; and eventually removed the stigma from economic accumulation.

The Confucian system was virtually unique among traditional cultures in that it institutionalized a socially accepted and even honored channel for upward social mobility, based on nonviolent individual achievement, rather than ascription. By passing a series of difficult academic examinations that were, in principle, open to any promising young male, one could attain power, status, and wealth as a government official. Consequently, in the sixteenth century, a social scientist from Mars might have ranked East Asia, with its Confucian tradition, as the region of the world that was culturally most conducive to economic development. Though narrowly circumscribed, social mobility through individual achievement was accepted to a degree virtually unknown elsewhere; education, rather than armed force, was the principal means to rise in society; and a secular orientation was relatively conducive to technology and worldly achievement. Indeed, at this point in time, China was economically, technologically, and politically more advanced than any other region of the world.

The Protestant Reformation brought profound cultural changes and eventually led to an explosion of economic and technological development in Protestant Europe, which not only moved it far ahead of Catholic Europe, but gave it a commanding lead over East Asia as well. By the nineteenth century, industrializing states of Europe and North America had attained a degree of technological and military superiority that enabled them to penetrate the Chinese and Japanese empires at will; their traditional political and cultural systems began to crumble.

Though Japan remained isolated from Western contact far longer than did China, the rapidity of Japan's response to Western incursion, once it occurred, was phenomenal. In part, this may reflect the fact that the Japanese society had a long tradition of importing knowledge from abroad; it was relatively easy to substitute a Western model for the Chinese one. The Chinese, by contrast, had for centuries viewed their society as the center of the world, to be emulated by the lesser cultures surrounding it, but with little to learn from the outer barbarians. Moreover, the Japanese bureaucratic elite, though heavily influenced by the Confucian model, were recruited from a former warrior class, which still retained elements of its military ethos. This fact seems significant.

For while cultural superiority is difficult to demonstrate, military superiority can be proven decisively in a single battle. The fact that Commodore Perry possessed unassailable military superiority was sufficient to convince a segment of the Japanese samurai that in order to preserve their most crucial value—military honor—it was essential to adopt Western military and industrial technology. The Chinese scholar elite, on the other hand, preferred to yield rather than descend to the level of the barbarians. Japan's initial confrontation with Western military superiority occurred in 1854. Political power was seized by a modernizing elite in 1868. The speed with which modernization was pursued was staggering. As early as 1870–1913, Japan ranked eighth in economic growth rates among the thirteen nations shown in Table 1-3. In all three of the subsequent time periods, Japan ranked first. By 1894, Japan had attained military superiority over China, defeating her in a brief war. In 1904–1905, she defeated Russia in the Russo-Japanese war, and moved onto the world stage as a major power.

Japan was not geographically near the core areas of industrialization (a factor usually conducive to the diffusion of innovation). And she was not favored with an unusual abundance of natural resources; they were almost totally lacking. Nevertheless, Japanese society was remarkably receptive to economic modernization. We suspect that the Confucian cultural tradition—once its traditional rigidity had been shattered by the impact of the West—was an important element in this. The role of Confucianism is far more complex than can be conveyed in this brief synopsis. Bellah (1957), for example, differentiates between specific Confucian sects that facilitated economic development and others which impeded it (paralleling Weber's emphasis on the role of a specific type of Protestantism in the rise of capitalism). Bellah concludes, however, that during the Tokugawa period (1600–1868), the Japanese traditional culture had already developed a functional equivalent to the Protestant ethic, which combined elements of Confucianism, Buddhism, and Shinto, producing an outlook conducive to economic modernization. Though the advantages of industrialization were recognized earliest by Japanese elites, the entire Confucian cultural zone seems relatively receptive to economic modernization. Table A-3 (in the Appendix) illustrates this point, providing data on recent growth rates for a much larger number of nations than those shown in Table 1-3 above.

By 1950–1965, among seventy-six nations for which we have data, not only Japan but also Taiwan and South Korea (all three shaped by the Confucian tradition) ranked among the top ten in economic growth. Only two Protestant nations ranked among the top ten by then, as compared with four Catholic countries. China, the largest of the Confucian-Buddhist nations, still ranked relatively low, just emerging from civil war at the start of this period, and still recovering from the chaos of the Great Leap Forward at the end of it. Data for Hong Kong and Singapore (both populated predominantly by Chinese) are not available.

During the period from 1965 to 1984, the three fastest growing economies in the world were in countries shaped by the Confucian and Buddhist traditions: Singapore, South Korea, and Hong Kong. Taiwan and Japan also ranked among the top ten and China ranked thirteenth. Moreover, three more of the top twenty countries had significant Chinese minorities that, in each case, played disproportionately important economic roles: Malaysia, Thailand, and Indonesia. Finally, immigrants of East Asian origin have shown disproportionately high rates of economic achievement throughout Southeast Asia and in the United States, Canada, and Western Europe. It is difficult to avoid the conclusion that the Confucian cultural tradition is conducive to economic achievement today.

It would be unrealistic to view these traits as indelible, however. Our broader thesis suggests that the intense emphasis on economic achievement that is now found among peoples shaped by the Confucian tradition, could emerge only when the static orientation of traditional society was broken; it flourishes best in a free market economy, as the contrast between North and South Korea illustrates; and it is likely to gradually erode when future generations have been raised in high levels of economic security. For the present, however, it is a key factor in the world economy.

High levels of economic development do not automatically bring low economic growth. Among the 147 nations for which Taylor and Jodice (1982) provide data, the correlation between absolute level of GNP per capita and economic growth in 1960–1975 is positive, not negative. The very rich nations do show below average growth rates, but this seems to reflect cultural changes rather than economic ones. Among the twenty-two nations for which we have both economic and cultural indicators, relatively high levels of economic development are negatively correlated with economic growth rates during 1965–1984 ($r = -.22$); but the relationship between economic growth and Postmaterialist value priorities among these publics is far stronger ($r = -.54$). In a multiple regression analysis, the partial correlation between growth rate and GNP per capita drops to $-.13$ (which is not statistically significant), while the partial correlation between growth rates and Postmaterialist values remains at $-.52$ (significant at the .02 level). Economic development plays a major role in the emergence of Postmaterialist values; thus, indirectly, economic factors are important. But their *direct* impact on economic growth seems modest; economic development leads to slower economic growth only insofar as it brings cultural change.

CONCLUSION

Both social analysis and social policy would be much simpler if people from different cultures were interchangeable robots, responding uniformly to given situations. But a large body of evidence indicates that they are not. The peoples of given societies tend to be characterized by reasonably durable cultural attributes, which can have major political and economic consequences. If this is true, then effective social policy will be better served by learning about these differences and how they vary cross-culturally and over time than by pretending that they do not exist.

Rational choice models constitute one of the most promising tools now available for political analysis. As currently applied, they are effective in analyzing short-term fluctuations within a given system, taking cultural and institutional factors as constant. But these factors are not constant, either cross-nationally or over time; and current models cannot deal with long-term changes in the basic goals and nature of a system. One of the central debates in the field of political economy seems to reflect this fact. When it was found that political support responds to fluctuations in the economy, it was taken for granted that this reflected the workings of economic self-interest among the electorate. Subsequent research has made this interpretation increasingly doubtful: the linkage between economics and politics seems largely shaped by sociotropic concerns. The classic model of economically determined behavior has a strong grip on the minds of social analysts—probably because, throughout most of the history of industrial society, it provided a fairly accurate description of human behavior. In recent decades, the rising role of Postmaterialist concerns may have helped make sociotropic concerns increasingly important, particularly among the politically more aware segments of the electorate.

Political economy research has demonstrated convincingly that short-term economic changes have significant political consequences. But the long-term consequences of economic change have barely begun to be analyzed in comparable fashion—though they may be at least equally significant. Evidence presented here indicates that the emergence and viability of mass-based democracy is closely related to economic development—*and* that the outcome is contingent on specific cultural changes. Though mass democracy is almost impossible without a certain amount of economic development, economic development by itself does not produce democracy: Unless specific changes occur in culture and social structure, the result may be not democracy but any of a variety of alternatives, examples of which range from Libya to the Soviet Union.

A large body of cross-national survey evidence indicates that enduring cultural differences exist. Though these differences may be related to the economic level of a given nation, they are relatively independent of short-term economic changes. These cultural factors have an important bearing on the durability of democracy, which seems to result from a complex interplay of economic, cultural, and institutional factors. To neglect any of these components may compromise its survival.

Finally, it appears that economic development itself is influenced by cultural variables. In our brief analysis of this, we have utilized an indicator of Materialist/Postmaterialist values that is available from only the past two decades; and another indicator—the dominant religious or philosophic tradition of a given society—that goes back over centuries but is a greatly oversimplified indicator of prevailing worldviews at a given time and place. Clearly, more research will be required before we reach definitive conclusions. But the available evidence supports Weber's insight that culture is not just a consequence of economics; it can shape the basic nature of economic and political life.

CHAPTER 2

The Rise of Postmaterialist Values

INTRODUCTION

A process of intergenerational value change is gradually transforming the politics and cultural norms of advanced industrial societies. A shift from Materialist to Postmaterialist value priorities has brought new political issues to the center of the stage and provided much of the impetus for new political movements. It has split existing political parties and given rise to new ones and it is changing the criteria by which people evaluate their subjective sense of well-being. Moreover, the rise of Postmaterialism itself seems to be only one aspect of a still broader process of cultural change that is reshaping the religious orientations, gender roles, sexual mores, and cultural norms of Western society.

In this chapter, we will present evidence of these trends. We will start by reviewing data concerning the shift from Materialist to Postmaterialist values from 1970 to 1988. In subsequent chapters, we will present evidence that this value shift is itself part of a broader syndrome of intergenerational culture change, in which a growing emphasis on the quality of life and self-expression is accompanied by a declining emphasis on traditional political, religious, moral, and social norms.

In 1970, we hypothesized that the basic value priorities of Western publics had been shifting from a Materialist emphasis toward a Postmaterialist one—from giving top priority to physical sustenance and safety toward heavier emphasis on belonging, self-expression, and the quality of life. This shift was traced to the unprecedented levels of economic and physical security that prevailed during the postwar era (Inglehart 1971). Since this first exploration, the Materialist/Postmaterialist value change hypothesis has been subjected to further analysis by dozens of investigators using fieldwork carried out in the United States, Canada, Australia, Japan, Mexico, Argentina, South Africa, Hungary, Poland, and seventeen West European nations. Measurements at multiple time points are now available for a number of these countries; more than 200 representative national surveys have measured the prevalence of Materialist/Postmaterialist value priorities among the publics of advanced industrial societies. Much of this research has taken place in Germany and Japan—two countries that have experienced rapid economic growth in recent decades, and relatively rapid value change. Less evidence has been gathered in the relatively stagnant

United States, despite the dominant position this country held until recently in empirical social research.

Our data now span almost two decades. Implications for political change that were suggested by the original cross-sectional analysis can be tested in diachronic perspective. We can begin to distinguish between (1) intergenerational value change, based on cohort effects; (2) life cycle, or aging, effects; and (3) period effects. We can examine the impact of the economic uncertainty of recent years on the proportions of Materialist and Postmaterialists among given publics. As we will see, there has been a gradual overall rise in the ratio of Postmaterialists to Materialists among Western publics. Much of the literature on Postmaterialism deals with whether it is a deep-rooted phenomenon having a long-term impact on political behavior or simply a transient epiphenomenon. We will reexamine this issue in the light of recent evidence. If a society's basic values change mainly through intergenerational population replacement, we would expect them to change at a gradual pace. But though short-term changes may be small, close examination of their societal location can provide valuable insight into their long-term implications. Contrary to what some observers assumed (Kesselman 1979), Postmaterialism did not dwindle away in the face of diminished economic and physical security. In most countries, its numbers grew, and in many ways its political influence seems greater now than it was a decade or two ago; but its character and tactics have changed significantly.

One of the most important changes derives from the simple fact that today Postmaterialists are older than they were when they first emerged as a major political factor in the 1960s. Initially manifested mainly through student protest movements, their key impact is now made through the activities of young elites, for the students have grown older, and Postmaterialism has penetrated deeply into the ranks of young professionals, civil servants, managers, and politicians, as we will see in chapter 9. It seems to be a major factor in the rise of a "new class" in Western society—a stratum of highly educated and well-paid young technocrats, who take an adversary stance toward their society (Ladd 1978; Gouldner 1979; Lipset 1979; Steinfels 1979). The debate between those giving top priority to reindustrialization and rearmament versus those who emphasize environmentalism and the quality of life reflects persisting value cleavages.

REEXAMINING THE THEORY OF VALUE CHANGE

Before turning to time series evidence, let us reexamine our theoretical framework in the light of recent findings. It is based on two key hypotheses:

1. *A scarcity hypothesis*. An individual's priorities reflect the socioeconomic environment: One places the greatest subjective value on those things that are in relatively short supply.
2. *A socialization hypothesis*. The relationship between socioeconomic environment and value priorities is not one of immediate adjustment: A substantial time lag is involved because, to a large extent, one's basic values reflect the conditions that prevailed during one's pre-adult years.

The scarcity hypothesis is similar to the principle of diminishing marginal utility in economic theory. The complementary concept of a need hierarchy helped shape the survey items we used to measure value priorities. In its simplest form, the idea of a need hierarchy would probably command almost universal assent. The fact that unmet physiological needs take priority over social, intellectual, or aesthetic needs has been demonstrated all too often in human history—starving people will go to almost any length to obtain food. The rank ordering of human needs becomes less clear as we move beyond those needs directly related to survival. But it does seem clear that there is a basic distinction between the "material" needs for physiological sustenance and safety and nonphysiological needs, such as those for esteem, self-expression, and aesthetic satisfaction.

The recent economic history of advanced industrial societies has significant implications in the light of the scarcity hypothesis. These societies are a remarkable exception to the prevailing historical pattern: The bulk of their population does *not* live under conditions of hunger and economic insecurity. This fact seems to have led to a gradual shift in which needs for belonging, esteem, and intellectual and aesthetic satisfaction became more prominent. As a rule, we would expect prolonged periods of high prosperity to encourage the spread of Postmaterialist values; economic decline would have the opposite effect.

But it is not quite that simple. There is no one-to-one relationship between economic level and the prevalence of Postmaterialist values, for these values reflect one's subjective sense of security, not one's economic level per se. While rich individuals and nationalities, no doubt, tend to feel more secure than poor ones, these feelings are also influenced by the cultural setting and social welfare institutions in which one is raised. Thus, the scarcity hypothesis alone does not generate adequate predictions about the process of value change. It must be interpreted in connection with the socialization hypothesis.

One of the most pervasive concepts in social science is the notion of a basic human personality structure that tends to crystallize by the time an individual reaches adulthood, with relatively little change thereafter. This concept permeates the literature from Plato through Freud and extends to the findings of contemporary survey research. Early socialization seems to carry greater weight than later socialization.

This, of course, does not imply that no change occurs during adult years. In some individual cases, dramatic behavioral shifts are known to occur, and the process of human development never comes to a complete stop (Levinson, et al. 1979; Brim and Kagan 1980). Nevertheless, human development seems to be far more rapid during preadult years than it is afterward, and the great bulk of the evidence points to the conclusion that the statistical likelihood of basic personality change declines sharply after one reaches adulthood (Block 1981; Costa and McCrae 1980; Jennings and Niemi 1981; Jennings and Markus 1984).

Taken together, these two hypotheses generate a coherent set of predictions concerning value change. First, while the scarcity hypothesis implies that prosperity is conducive to the spread of Postmaterialist values, the socialization hypothesis implies that neither an individual's values nor those of a society as a whole are likely to change overnight. Instead, fundamental value change takes place gradually, almost invisibly; in large part, it occurs as a younger generation replaces an older one in the adult population of a society.

Consequently, after a period of sharply rising economic and physical security, one would expect to find substantial differences between the value priorities of older and younger groups: they would have been shaped by different experiences in their formative years. But there would be a sizable time lag between economic changes and their political effects. Ten or fifteen years after an era of prosperity began, the age cohorts that had spent their formative years in prosperity would begin to enter the electorate. Ten more years might pass before these groups began to occupy positions of power and influence in their society; perhaps another decade would pass before they reached the level of top decision makers.

The socialization hypothesis complements the scarcity hypothesis, resolving objections derived from an oversimplified view of how scarcity affects behavior. It helps account for apparently deviant behavior: on one hand, the miser who experienced poverty in early years and relentlessly continues piling up wealth long after attaining material security and, on the other hand, the saintly ascetic who remains true to the higher-order goals instilled by his or her culture, even in the face of severe deprivation. In both instances, an explanation for the seemingly deviant behavior of such individuals lies in their early socialization.

The socialization hypothesis also explains why experimental tests of the need hierarchy have found no positive correlation between satisfaction of a given need at one time and increased emphasis on the next higher need at later time (Alderfer 1972; Kmieciak 1976), for these experiments are based on the implicit assumption that one would find almost immediate changes in an individual's priorities. But if, as hypothesized, an individual's basic priorities are largely fixed by the time he or she reaches adulthood, one would not expect to find much short-term change of the kind that was tested for.

This does not mean that an adult's value priorities are totally immutable—merely that they are relatively difficult to change. Normally, the rewards and deprivations employed in experimental psychology are modest, and the treatment is continued for a fairly brief time. Only in unusual experiments has the treatment been extreme enough to produce evidence of changed priorities among adults. In one such experiment, for example, a conscientious objector was kept on a semistarvation diet for a prolonged period under medical supervision. After several weeks, he lost interest in his social ideals and began to talk about, think about, and even dream about food (Davies 1963). Similar patterns of behavior have been observed among inmates of concentration camps (Elkins 1959; Bettelheim 1979).

From the outset of this research, *The Authoritarian Personality* (Adorno, et al. 1950) seemed to have intriguing implications. A standardized set of authoritarianism items was used in an earlier cross-national exploration of nationalism and internationalism. The results were disappointing: Dimensional analysis showed that the authoritarianism items did not cluster together as they theoretically should (Inglehart 1970b).

Subsequent pilot tests gave similar results. Authoritarianism items showed relatively weak relationships with one another. Some of them seemed closely related to the Materialist/Postmaterialist dimension, but others seemed to tap entirely different dimensions. Authoritarianism, at least as it has been operationalized thus far, has a poor empirical fit with Materialism/Postmaterialism.

The theoretical basis of authoritarianism is not necessarily incompatible with that of the Materialist/Postmaterialist dimension, but there are important differences in focus. The initial concept of authoritarianism emphasizes the psychodynamics of early child-rearing practices rather than influences from the broader economic and political environment. On the other hand, Hyman and Sheatsley (1954), in their critique of the original study, advance a cognitive explanation, arguing that certain respondents, especially those from a lower socioeconomic level, may show an "authoritarian"-type response because this is a more or less accurate reflection of conditions governing their adult lives. Our own interpretation of the genesis of Materialist/Postmaterialist values contains elements of both positions. It emphasizes the importance of relatively early experiences, but links them with environmental factors other than parental discipline.

The original authoritarianism hypothesis fails to predict either the age-group differences or the social class differences that are strikingly evident in the data, as we will see shortly. On the contrary, studies of authoritarianism have found that children tend to be *more* authoritarian than adults. It would not be impossible to reinterpret the authoritarian personality hypothesis in such a way as to explain the age and class differences. One could argue that child-rearing practices vary according to social class, and have changed over time. But in that case, one would need to seek an explanation of why they vary and why they have changed. Quite probably, one would eventually trace this explanation to the economic and political changes on which we rest our own interpretation.

TIME SERIES EVIDENCE FROM THE POSTWAR ERA

Our hypotheses imply that the unprecedented prosperity prevailing from the late 1940s until the early 1970s, has led to substantial growth in the proportion of Postmaterialists among the publics of advanced industrial societies. We believe that this proportion was already rising during the years preceding our first survey of this topic in 1970. We would need a time machine in order to go back and test this proposition, using the battery specifically developed to measure Materialist/Postmaterialist values. Though this is impossible, some available data do seem to tap the relevant dimension.

Data on the priorities of the German public, for example, cover more than twenty years, from 1949 to 1970. In these surveys, representative national samples were asked, "Which of the four freedoms do you personally consider most important—freedom of speech, freedom of worship, freedom from fear, or freedom from want?" In 1949, postwar reconstruction had just begun, and "freedom from want" was the leading choice by a wide margin. But in the following years, Germany rose from poverty to prosperity with almost incredible speed. In 1954, "freedom from want" was still narrowly ahead of any other choice, but by 1958 "freedom of speech" was chosen by more people than all other choices combined (EMNID 1963, 1970).

These changes in the German population's value priorities seem to reflect concurrent changes in their economic environment. Moreover, there is clear evidence of an age-related lag between economic change and value change. In 1962, 59 percent of the Germans from 16 to 25 years old chose "freedom of speech"; the figure declines steadily as we move to older groups; among Germans aged 65 and older, only 35 percent chose "freedom of speech." The fact that the young are much likelier to give "freedom of speech'' priority over ''freedom from want'' fits theoretical expectations neatly. The original data have been lost, and it is not possible to perform a cohort analysis in order to determine how much of this age difference is due to generational change. But the magnitude of the overall shift is so great that each age group must have deemphasized ''freedom from want'' as it aged during this period. The age differences definitely cannot be attributed to life cycle effects. Further persuasive evidence of an intergenerational shift toward Postmaterialist priorities among the German public is found in the massive and definitive analysis of German survey data from 1953 through 1976 by Baker, Dalton and Hildebrandt (1981).

One of the most dramatic examples of economic change in modern history is Japan—a nation that rose from harsh poverty to astonishing prosperity in a single generation. Indicators of the Japanese public's values are available in the Japanese national character studies carried out at five-year intervals, from 1953 through 1983. Analysis of these surveys indicates that Japanese culture changed along several different dimensions during this period, with the perceived sacredness of the emperor declining and emphasis on individuation and political participation rising (Ike 1973; Hayashi 1974; Nisihira 1974; Richardson 1974; Research Committee on the Study of the Japanese National Character 1979; Flanagan 1980a; Inglehart 1982). One of the changes, it seems clear, was a shift from Materialist to Postmaterialist priorities. Among the available survey questions, the most unambiguous indicator of Materialist versus Postmaterialist priorities is the following: ''In bringing up children of primary school age, some think that one should teach them that money is the most important thing. Do you agree or disagree?'' In 1953, a strong majority (65 percent) of the Japanese public agreed that financial security was the most important thing. This figure declined steadily in subsequent surveys; by 1983, only 43 percent of the Japanese public still took this view. As was true of Germany, the trend is in the predicted direction—but in this case, the original data have been preserved, and we can carry out a cohort analysis. Table 2-1 shows the results.

In any given year, the young are a good deal less likely to emphasize the importance of money than are the old. Does this simply reflect an inherent idealism of youth that will disappear as they grow older? Apparently not—for when we follow given age cohorts as they age during this twenty-five-year period, we find no indication whatever of increasing materialism. On the contrary, we find a tendency for a given cohort as it grows older to place *less* emphasis on money. The four cohorts for which we have data throughout the thirty-year period show an average shift of 7 points *away* from giving top priority to money. Almost certainly this was a period effect, with the sharply rising prosperity of the postwar era producing a di-

TABLE 2-1. COHORT ANALYSIS: ANNUAL PERCENTAGES OF JAPANESE COHORTS
AGREEING THAT FINANCIAL SECURITY IS MOST IMPORTANT

Age Group	1953	1958	1963	1968	1973	1978	1983	Change within Given Cohort 1953 - 1983
20 - 24	60	–	43	34	22	18	20	
25 - 29	66		55	49	36	26	24	
30 - 34	63		58	58	42	37	28	
35 - 39	62		56	59	43	43	39	
40 - 44	65		63	59	46	49	42	
45 - 49	66	–	62	62	46	56	48	
50 - 54	72	–	68	65	49	51	54	⟶ - 6
55 - 59	72	–	72	67	60	56	52	⟶ -14
60 - 64	77	–	76	66	59	62	64	⟶ + 1
65 - 69	78	–	72	73	59	62	59	⟶ - 3

Mean: -7

Source: Japanese National Character Surveys carried out by the
Institute of Statistical Mathematics, Tokyo.

minishing emphasis on money within each age cohort, quite independently
of generational change or aging effects. As closer examination of Table 2-
1 indicates, this period effect operated rather strongly from 1953 to 1973
and then reversed direction, so that from 1973 to 1978 each age cohort
came to place slightly more emphasis on the importance of money. This
pattern reflects changes in the economic environment rather faithfully. The
extraordinary rise in prosperity that took place in Japan from 1953 to 1973
was mirrored in a gradual deemphasis on money within each age cohort,
and the economic uncertainty that followed the oil shock of 1973 was accompanied by a temporary reversal of this trend. By 1983, however, the
long-term trend away from Materialism had resumed.

But these period effects are dwarfed by the intergenerational differences. While period effects seem to account for a mean net shift of 7 percentage points away from emphasizing the importance of financial security, we find a difference of 39 points between the youngest and oldest
groups in 1983. Since these data show no evidence whatever that aging
leads to increasing emphasis on money, there is a strong prima facie case
for attributing this 39-point difference entirely to intergenerational change.
It is conceivable that a life cycle tendency toward increasing Materialism
with increasing age also exists, but is totally concealed by stronger period
effects working in the opposite direction. The complexities of distinguish-
ing among aging effects, cohort effects, and period effects are such that
we cannot totally exclude this possibility (Glenn 1976; Knoke and Hout
1976). But belief in such an aging effect must depend on faith alone; it is
totally unsupported by empirical evidence. Jagodzinski (1983) argues that
life cycle effects are present in these data, and tries to measure them with
a regression model. His model is fatally flawed, however, because it sim-

ply assumes that the age differences present at the start of the series in 1953 reflect life cycle differences. This implicit assumption that Japan had a steady-state economy prior to 1953, in which the only difference between generations was based on life cycle effects, is totally untenable. As we saw in chapter 1, Japan was already experiencing one of the world's highest economic growth rates during the period from 1913 to 1938. These data show no evidence of life cycle effects.

Indications of intergenerational change, on the other hand, seem incontrovertible. In 1953, even the youngest group showed overwhelmingly Materialistic priorities—because at that time, all adult age cohorts had spent their formative years during World War II or earlier. These cohorts show only modest changes as they age during the ensuing quarter-century. It is only from 1963 on—when the cohorts shaped by the postwar economic miracle begin to enter the adult population—that we find a clear rejection of financial security as a value having top priority among the younger cohorts. The shift of the Japanese public from a heavy majority giving money top priority, to a minority doing so, seems to reflect intergenerational population replacement above all, with only a minor component due to period effects. In 1953, age differences were relatively small, but since 1963 there has been a tremendous increase in the difference between the priorities of younger and older Japanese. As the leading example of economic growth in the postwar era, Japan constitutes a crucial case for testing our hypotheses. The time series data are unambiguous, clearly indicating that from 1953 to 1983, there was an intergenerational shift away from Materialism among the Japanese public.

MATERIALIST AND POSTMATERIALIST VALUES FROM 1970 TO 1988

Our data from Western countries cover a shorter period than the Japanese data do, but they were specifically designed to measure Materialist/ Postmaterialist value priorities. It is difficult to measure values directly. But their presence can be inferred from a consistent pattern of emphasis on given types of goals. Accordingly, we asked representative samples of citizens from Western nations what they personally considered the most important goals among the following:

A. Maintain order in the nation
B. Give people more say in the decisions of the government
C. Fight rising prices
D. Protect freedom of speech
E. Maintain a high rate of economic growth

F. Make sure that this country has strong defense forces

G. Give people more say in how things are decided at work and in their community

H. Try to make our cities and countryside more beautiful

I. Maintain a stable economy

J. Fight against crime

K. Move toward a friendlier, less impersonal society

L. Move toward a society where ideas count more than money

Our earliest survey (in 1970) used only the first four items, in six countries. The full twelve-item battery was first used in 1973 in the nine-nation European Community and the United States (Inglehart 1977). Both batteries were administered in subsequent surveys, though the simpler four-item battery has been used much more frequently. Items A, C, E, F, I, and J above were designed to tap emphasis on Materialist goals; theoretically, these values should be given high priority by those who experienced economic or physical insecurity during their formative years. The remaining items were designed to tap Postmaterialist goals; they should be emphasized by those raised under relatively secure conditions. If so, certain respondents would favor Materialist items consistently, while others would consistently emphasize the Postmaterialist ones.

Survey results support these theoretical expectations. Those who give top priority to one Materialist goal tend to give high priority to other Materialist goals as well. Conversely, the Postmaterialist items tend to be chosen together. Hence, we can classify our respondents as pure Materialists (those whose top priorities are given to Materialist goals exclusively); pure Postmaterialists (those whose top priorities are given to Postmaterialist items exclusively); or mixed types, based on any combination of the two kinds of items. Though for simplicity of presentation we will sometimes compare the two polar types, we are dealing with a continuum having numerous intermediate categories.

The predicted relationships with social background are confirmed empirically. Within any given age group, those raised in relatively prosperous families are most likely to emphasize Postmaterialist items, and the predicted skew by age group is manifest. Figure 2-1 depicts this age skew in the pooled sample of six West European publics interviewed in our initial survey. Significant cross-national differences exist, but the basic pattern is similar from nation to nation: Among the older groups, Materialists outnumber Postmaterialists enormously; as we move toward younger groups, the proportion of Materialists declines and that of Postmaterialists increases. Thus, among the oldest cohort, Materialists outnumber Postmaterialists by a ratio of more than 12 to 1. Among the youngest cohort, the

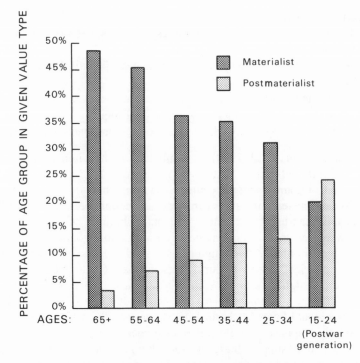

FIGURE 2-1. Value type by age group, among the combined publics of Britain, France, West Germany, Italy, Belgium, and the Netherlands in 1970.

balance has shifted dramatically: Postmaterialists are about as numerous as Materialists.

The Materialist and Postmaterialist types have strikingly different opinions on a wide variety of issues, ranging from women's rights to attitudes toward poverty, ideas of what is important in a job, and positions on foreign policy. Within each age group, about half the sample falls into the Mixed value types. On virtually every issue, their position is about halfway between the Materialists and Postmaterialists; they seem to be a cross-pressured group that could swing either way.

By 1970, Postmaterialists had attained numerical parity with Materialists only among the postwar generation. Furthermore, they were concentrated among the more affluent strata of this age group; among university students, they heavily outnumbered the Materialists. In this light, perceptions of a generation gap in the late 1960s and early 1970s are understandable. Even among the postwar generation, Materialists were about as numerous as Postmaterialists. But in this age group's most articulate and most visible segment—the students—there was an overwhelming preponderance of Postmaterialists. The students lived in a distinct milieu; they had highly developed communications networks with other students but were largely isolated from their nonstudent peers. The priorities prevailing in this milieu were fundamentally different from those shaping the society as a whole.

The existence of such a milieu can play an important part in the evolution and propagation of a given set of values. Indeed, Habermas (1979) argues that the rise of Postmaterialism is not due to the different formative experiences of different generation units, but to exposure to the specific world views inculcated by distinct communications networks (cf. Jaeggi 1979). But this explanation seems to complement, not substitute for, the one proposed here. It helps account for the spread of values in a given milieu, but provides no explanation of why given generation units were disposed to accept given values in the first place, while others rejected them. It seems clear that in virtually all Western nations, the student milieu of the late 1960s did constitute a distinct communications network, propagating a distinctive viewpoint. Given these circumstances, it is not surprising that the student elite saw themselves as part of a counterculture that was engaged in an irreconcilable clash with the culture of an older generation: From their viewpoint, the dictum "Don't trust anyone over thirty" seemed plausible. Our hypotheses imply that as time went by, the Postmaterialists would become older and more evenly distributed across the population. Hence, the plausibility of a monolithic generation gap would fade away. But in 1970, conditions were optimal to sustain belief in a generation gap, with youth all on one side and older people all on the other.

Clearly, there are large empirical differences between the priorities of younger and older groups in Western Europe (and, as subsequent research revealed, the entire industrialized world). But one can advance various interpretations concerning the *implications* of this finding. Though our own hypotheses point to intergenerational change based on cohort effects, we must consider the fact that any given pattern of age differences could, theoretically, result from (1) aging effects, (2) cohort effects, (3) period effects, or some combination of all three.

Aging effects versus cohort effects. Perhaps the most obvious alternative interpretation is one based on aging effects. It would argue that, for biological or other reasons, the young are inherently less materialistic than the old. As they age, however, this model asserts, they inevitably become just as materialistic as their elders, and after fifty years, the youngest group will show the same overwhelming preponderance of Materialists that the oldest group now displays. The aging interpretation, then, holds that the pattern found in 1970 is a permanent characteristic of the human life cycle and will not change over time. The cohort interpretation, on the other hand, implies that the Postmaterialists will gradually permeate the older strata, eventually neutralizing the relationship between values and age.

Period effects. Both the German data and the Japanese data reviewed earlier show period effects: The economic environment of the period up to 1973 apparently induced all age groups to become less materialistic as time went by, quite apart from any processes of aging or generational change. These surveys were carried out during a period of dramatic improvement in living standards, particularly in Germany and Japan; even in the United States (where economic growth was much slower) the real income of the American public approximately doubled from 1947 to 1973.

From 1973 on, however, economic conditions changed dramatically. Energy prices quadrupled almost overnight; the industrialized world entered the most severe recession since the 1930s. Economic growth stagnated and Western nations experienced extraordinarily high levels of inflation and unemployment. By 1980, the real income of the typical American family was actually lower than in 1970.

Western publics were, of course, acutely aware of changed economic circumstances, and responded to them. The most amply documented case is that of the American public, whose economic outlook is surveyed each month. In mid-1972, The University of Michigan Survey Research Center's Index ("SRC Index") of Consumer Sentiment stood at 95, only slightly below its all-time high. By the spring of 1975, the SRC Index had plummeted to 58—the lowest level recorded since these surveys were initiated in the 1950s. With the subsequent economic recovery, consumer confidence revived—only to collapse again in the wake of the second OPEC price shock in late 1979; in April 1980 consumer confidence had reached a new all-time low, with the SRC Index at 53. But with the economic recovery of the mid-1980s, consumer confidence again reached its former high levels. Similar patterns of declining confidence in the economic outlook, followed by recovery, were recorded among West European publics. Clearly (as the scarcity hypothesis implies), the conditions felt during the mid-1970s and early 1980s should work against the development of a Postmaterialist outlook.

Models of cohort, period, and life cycle effects. Which of the three processes—period effects, aging effects, or generational change—was most important? Given the severity of the economic decline and the disappearance of student protest and other dramatic manifestations of a counterculture, one might assume that Postmaterialism was swept away completely by the new, harsher environment. Or—as the socialization hypothesis suggests—are these priorities sufficiently deep-rooted among the adult population to weather such fluctuations in the socioeconomic environment?

The scarcity hypothesis implies short-term changes, or period effects: Periods of prosperity lead to increased Postmaterialism, and periods of scarcity lead to Materialism. The socialization hypothesis implies that long-term cohort effects also exist: the values of a given generation tend to reflect the conditions prevailing during its preadult years. The theory implies nothing about aging or life cycle effects.

Taken together, the two basic hypotheses imply that the process of value change will be characterized by period effects (reflecting short-term fluctuations in the socioeconomic environment) superimposed on long-term cohort effects (reflecting the conditions prevailing during a given age group's formative years).

An empirical test of this theory requires that one distinguish between period effects, cohort effects, and life cycle effects. This is not an easy task. In order to distinguish among the three effects, one must have theoretical grounds for ruling out or controlling for at least one of the three.

The original four-item Materialist/Postmaterialist values battery has now been administered repeatedly to representative national samples of the populations of Britain, France, West Germany, Italy, Belgium, and the Netherlands from 1970 to 1988 in surveys sponsored by the Commission of the European Communities. This massive data base is now reaching the point where it provides measurements at enough time points to trace the rise and fall of period effects and to correlate them with their underlying causes. In order to maximize reliability, this cohort analysis is based on the pooled samples from all six nations. These pooled results, providing an average of approximately 2,000 cases per age cohort in each year, make it possible to follow the value priorities of West European publics across an eighteen-year period that began with high prosperity, was later characterized by two recessions and runaway inflation, and ended with renewed prosperity, mitigated by abnormally high rates of unemployment.

Before we examine the cohort analysis, let us ask: exactly what kind of pattern does each of the three types of effects imply? Figures 2-2, 2-3, and 2-4 depict three possible patterns. Figure 2-2 depicts the pattern of value differences one would find if early socialization were the *only* influence on adult values, so that cohort effects, and only cohort effects, were present.

In this ideal-type model, the younger birth cohorts are less Materialist than all of the older cohorts at all points in time. Because no period effects are present, each cohort's values remain absolutely unchanged, regardless of any changes in the socioeconomic environment. But because of population replacement, the values prevailing in a given society do change over time. During the seventeen-year period depicted here, most of the 1896–

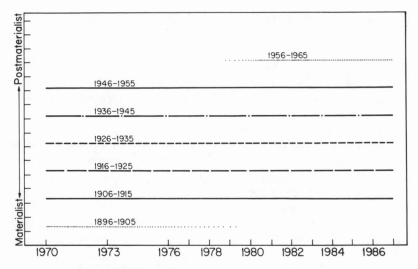

FIGURE 2-2. Cohort effects only.

1905 birth cohort died off and were replaced in the adult population by the cohort born from 1956 to 1965, a group too young to be included in our samples in 1970, but which constituted a major part of the adult public by 1987. The fact that this youngest and much more Postmaterialist cohort replaced the oldest, most Materialist one would tend to produce a net shift toward Postmaterialism.

But since our theory is based on a scarcity hypothesis as well as a socialization hypothesis, one can expect period effects as well as cohort effects. Figure 2-3 depicts a pattern of period effects superimposed on stable cohort differences. Although one can observe substantial fluctuations in response to short-term forces in this figure, the cohort effects are fully as strong as those in Figure 2-2. Consequently, in both cases, the process of intergenerational population replacement tends to produce a gradual shift toward Postmaterialist values.

Figure 2-4 depicts a model in which age-group differences exist, but result entirely from life cycle effects. As a given birth cohort ages, it comes to resemble the next older cohort, so that after ten years have elapsed, a given cohort has shifted to the position held by the cohort that is ten years older. Although each cohort *does* change over time, the values of the society as a whole do not change, because population replacement is offset by life cycle effects. Empirically, life cycle effects can be distinguished from cohort effects because (aside from short-term fluctuations) with life cycle effects, each cohort shows a continuous downward trend, whereas with birth cohort effects, each cohort remains horizontal when

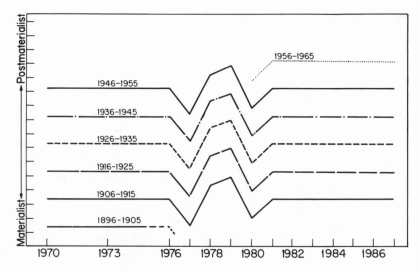

FIGURE 2-3. Cohort effects plus period effects.

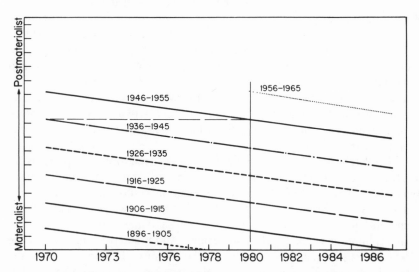

FIGURE 2-4. Life cycle effects only.

plotted as in Figures 2-2, 2-3, and 2-4. The Materialist/Postmaterialist theoretical framework neither predicts nor excludes the possibility of life cycle effects; however, it does predict that there will be substantial and durable cohort effects.

Lehner (1979) argued that values must be either stable or unstable; thus one can have either stable intergenerational differences, or short-term fluctuations, but not both. Fogt (1982), Van Deth (1983a), and Boeltken and Jagodzinski (1985) have all advanced various versions of the same argument; and since they all found short-term fluctuations and anomalies in the values of given groups, they concluded that the hypothesis of intergenerational value change had been falsified.

Superficially, the idea that values must either be stable or unstable sounds plausible. But when translated from nonquantitative labels into the terminology of cohort analysis, it means that one can have either cohort effects or period effects, but not both. A glance at Figure 2-3 will convince the reader that this is not the case. Period effects are perfectly compatible with stable birth cohort differences—indeed, in cohort analysis, one rarely finds intergenerational differences without some period effects as well. The intergenerational differences in Figure 2-3 are exactly as stable as those in Figure 2-2, where period effects are absent; and the two models' implications for the consequences of intergenerational population replacement are identical. Nevertheless, the assumption that short-term period effects are incompatible with a theory of intergenerational value change lies at the heart of these and other recent critiques of the Materialist/Postmaterialist theory.

This assumption is clearly incorrect. The Materialist/Postmaterialist thesis is based on two key hypotheses. The scarcity hypothesis implies period effects. Not only are they not ruled out; they are explicitly predicted, and their polarity is specified: Periods of prosperity lead to increased Postmaterialism, and periods of scarcity lead to Materialism. The socialization hypothesis implies that long-term cohort effects will also exist: The values of a given generation tend to reflect the conditions prevailing during its preadult years.

One might postulate an extreme form of the socialization hypothesis, in which cohort effects were assumed to be so strong that they totally eliminated any period effects. Such an interpretation would require us to assume that once one reaches maturity, no adult learning whatever takes place, and one shows absolutely no further response to one's environment. Such an assumption seems highly implausible. And it clearly is not part of the Materialist/Postmaterialist theory. On the contrary, the implications of the scarcity hypothesis concerning period effects have been discussed explicitly and at some length (Inglehart 1977, 102–06; Inglehart 1981, 887–90).

Taken together, then, the two basic hypotheses underlying the Materialist/Postmaterialist thesis imply that the process of value change is characterized by period effects (reflecting short-term fluctuations in the socioeconomic environment) superimposed on long-term cohort effects (reflecting the conditions prevailing during a given age group's formative years). Thus, an empirical test of this theory requires that one distinguish between period effects, cohort effects, and life cycle effects. This is a difficult task.

A COHORT ANALYSIS OF THE VALUE PRIORITIES OF WEST EUROPEAN PUBLICS, 1970–1988

This task can best be accomplished through cohort analysis, and fortunately we now have a large enough data base to begin to determine what is happening. The original four-item Materialist/Postmaterialist values battery has now been administered to representative national samples of the population of several West European countries at numerous time points from 1970 to 1988 in a series of surveys sponsored by the Commission of the European Communities.

This massive data base is now reaching the point where it provides measurements at enough time points to trace the rise and fall of period effects (if any) and to correlate them with their underlying causes. And (if properly handled) it provides enough cases to obtain reliable measures of the dependent variable, enabling us to follow given age cohorts across time, through successive cross-sectional samples. To do so requires a sample size of at least 1,000 cases for each age cohort, at each point in time and, preferably, an N close to 2,000. The reasons for this are simple:

(1) If a random probability sample shows that 50 percent of those interviewed are Materialists, then with a sample size of 1,000 there is a 95 percent probability that the actual figure for the population surveyed falls within the range from 46.8 percent to 53.2 percent—a confidence interval of 6.4 percentage points. However, we are not dealing with random probability samples, but with quota samples. Here, the margin for sampling error is larger than with random probability samples, but it cannot be calculated precisely. A general rule of thumb is to treat one's effective sample size as half the actual number of interviews when calculating confidence intervals. Thus, with a random sample of 500, there is a 95 percent probability that the true percentage of Materialists falls within the range from 45.5 percent to 54.5 percent—a confidence interval of 9 percentage points. As sample size decreases, the margin one must allow for sampling error increases.

(2) The differences between the values of adjacent cohorts are usually less than 10 percentage points, and sometimes as little as 5 percentage points—thus, with as few as 1,000 cases per cohort, the observed values of two adjacent cohorts could readily overlap each other purely through sampling error, with an older cohort appearing to be less Materialist than the younger one, even if the true values confirmed theoretical expecta-

tions. Or one might observe large fluctuations in the values of a given cohort from one survey to the next, not as a result of period effects but simply because of sampling error.

In short, if our sample size falls below about 1,000 cases per cohort, noise tends to drown out the signal in a cohort analysis, because our margin of error exceeds the actual variation between cohorts, or across time. This is exactly what happens in Van Deth's 1983 analysis. His sample of Dutch respondents is broken down into age cohorts containing as few as seventy-five cases; in order to obtain reliable estimates of their values for cohort comparisons, he would need ten to fifteen times as many cases as he possesses. Not surprisingly, he obtains an erratic pattern in which younger groups are sometimes more Materialistic than older ones. Another analysis based on German data, by Boeltken and Jagodzinski (1985), also obtains anomalous results, for precisely the same reasons. Finding such anomalies does not refute the theory of value change—it merely confirms some basic tenets of sampling theory. When we utilize larger and more reliable samples (of both the Dutch and the German publics) we obtain the theoretically predicted pattern, as Table 2-3 demonstrates.

A simple cross-tabulation of values by age can provide a rough idea of the relationship between the two variables even if the sample contains only a few hundred cases per cohort; but this does not provide the degree of accuracy needed for a quantitative analysis that depends on precise comparisons between a given cohort at one point in time, and the corresponding cohort from another sample at another point in time. For this reason, previous analyses that followed the values of given age groups across time (Inglehart 1977, 1981) have been based on the pooled results of simultaneous samples from six Western nations. The publics of these six nations (Britain, France, Germany, Italy, Belgium, and the Netherlands) were first surveyed in 1970, again in 1973, and subsequently at least once a year from 1976 to the present. These pooled results, providing an average of approximately 2,000 cases per age cohort in each year, enable us to follow the value priorities of West European publics across an eighteen-year period, which began with high prosperity, but later was characterized by two recessions and runaway inflation, first in the mid-1970s and later in the early 1980s.

Figure 2-5 traces the balance between Materialists and Postmaterialists within given age cohorts, born in the years indicated, across this period. This analysis is based on the pooled data from all six nations surveyed from 1970 to 1988. Furthermore, when two surveys were carried out in the same year, the data are combined so that the cohort positions at given time points are generally based on Ns of close to 2,000 cases.

Each cohort's position at a given time is calculated by subtracting the

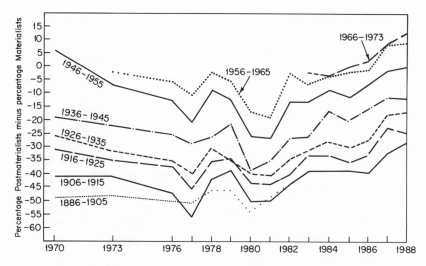

FIGURE 2-5. Value priorities of eight age cohorts across six West European publics, 1970–1988. Based on data from representative national samples of publics of France, Great Britain, West Germany, Italy, Belgium, and the Netherlands, interviewed in European Community surveys of 1970 and 1973 and Euro-Barometer surveys 6 through 29 (total N = 190,129). Principal investigators were Jacques-René Rabier, Karlheinz Reif, and Ronald Inglehart. Data available from ICPSR survey data archive.

percentage of Materialists in that cohort from the percentage of Postmaterialists. Thus, the zero point on the vertical axis reflects a situation in which the two groups are equally numerous (which is about where the cohort born in 1946–1955 was located in 1970). An index of −45 would result if 50 percent of a given cohort were Materialists and only 5 percent were Postmaterialists (with the rest being Mixed types): the oldest cohort was located slightly below this point in 1970. Figure 2-5 summarizes the results from more than 190,000 interviews. It indicates that the age group differences observed in 1970 reflect long-term intergenerational differences, rather than life cycle effects.

Each cohort retains its relative position with striking consistency throughout the eighteen-year period. The 1946–1955 cohort is less Materialistic and more Postmaterialistic than any of the older cohorts at every point in time. The only cohorts that are even less Materialistic are the two other postwar cohorts, the first of which was born from 1956 to 1965 and was too young to be interviewed in 1970; this cohort becomes an increasingly important part of our sample from 1976 on. An even younger cohort, born from 1966 to 1973, begins to enter the sample in the 1980s. Since these samples are limited to the population 15 years and older, this cohort will not have fully entered the sample until 1990, but it was present in substantial numbers by the mid-1980s. This cohort is more Postmaterialist than all of the older groups, though only a trifle more so than the 1956–1965 cohort. Explosive increases in prosperity during the postwar era helped make the 1946–1955 cohort much less Materialist than its predecessors, but the slower growth rates of recent years seem to be reflected in slower rates of value change. The gap between the 1966–1973 cohort and its predecessor is rarely more than a few percentage points and twice falls to zero. This does not mean that the process of value change is coming to a halt, however. It will not do so for decades. What is currently happening is that the 1966–1973 cohort is replacing the 1906–1915 cohort in the adult population—and the difference between these two cohorts is huge, so population replacement continues to produce a substantial shift in values. As Figure 2-5 demonstrates, each of the older cohorts proves to be more Materialist than all of the younger ones at every time point, with only a few minor anomalies. The intercohort value differences are extremely stable, closely resembling the pattern of Figure 2-3.

Moreover, there is no indication at all that each cohort becomes more Materialist as it ages, as would be the case if these differences reflected life cycle effects as Boeltken and Jagodzinski (1985) suggested. At the end of the eighteen-year period, virtually all of the cohorts were fully as Postmaterialistic as they were in 1970. Indeed, there is something of an upward tendency, with most cohorts less Materialist in 1988 than they were in 1970. There are also significant short-term fluctuations, with each cohort showing a brief downward swing in 1977 and again in 1980–1981. These fluctuations reflect period effects, which result largely from the impact of inflation, as will be demonstrated below. But by 1986, inflation had subsided to approximately the 1970 level. With period effects held constant, there is no sign at all of the gradual conversion to Materialism that would be present if a life cycle interpretation were applicable.

The fact that we find a much narrower gap between the 1966–1975 cohort and its predecessors than between the two other postwar cohorts and their predecessors is yet another indication that these value differences reflect historical change rather than some permanent life cycle tendency for the young to be less Materialist than the old. The narrowing of this gap corresponds to the economic conditions of the past fifteen years—but to explain it in terms of life cycle effects, one would need to invent some reason why the human life cycle had made a sudden drastic change in the 1980s. This finding confirms a good deal of other evidence, cited in chapters 1, 3, and 5, which indicates that these values tend to crystallize relatively early in life. The cohort born in 1956–1965 experienced the recessions of the mid-1970s and early 1980s while they were, on the average, about 20 years of age, but this did not prevent this cohort from developing values that are considerably more Postmaterialist than those of the next older cohort. The trend toward rising levels of Postmaterialism among each younger cohort is arrested only when we reach the cohort born in 1966–1975—which lived through these two recessions when they were 1 to 16 years of age. The evidence is compelling. Overall, we find large and enduring intercohort differences, which cannot be attributed to life cycle effects. The pattern reflects intergenerational value change.

These stable intergenerational value differences imply that, other things being equal, we will witness a long-term trend toward Postmaterialist values as one generation replaces another. As we will see below, this is precisely what we do find. Contrary to predictions that Postmaterialism would disappear as a result of the economic crisis, the underlying process of intergenerational change continued to function throughout the period, even though its effect was sometimes masked by negative period effects. When short-term forces returned to normal, the results were manifest. A substantial net shift toward Postmaterialism had taken place—most of it the result of intergenerational population replacement.

The most striking feature of Figure 2-5 is the persistence of stable differences between the value priorities of the respective cohorts across a period of eighteen years. In all years for which data are available, the 1956–1965 and 1966–1973 cohorts are more Postmaterialist than any of the older cohorts. In all fifteen of the years for which data are available, those born in 1956–1965 are more Postmaterialist than any older cohort. At all fifteen time points, the 1946–1955 cohort ranks next, above all of the older cohorts. At all fifteen time points, the 1936–1945 cohort ranks after them; at fourteen of the fifteen time points, the 1926–1935 cohort ranks next; at fourteen of the fifteen time points, the 1916–1925 cohort ranks second to last; and the 1886–1905 cohort ranks last or second to last in all years for which we have reliable numbers. Of 105 data points depicted in Figure 2-5, there are only five anomalies, and all of these are minor ones that involve an overlap between two immediately adjacent cohorts and could be caused by samples that deviate by only a few percentage points from the actual values. The pattern is about as close to perfection as one could hope for: The relative positions of the respective cohorts are extremely stable.

The data show a virtually perfect fit with theoretical expectations. As predicted, there are substantial differences between the values of different cohorts; and, as predicted, the younger cohorts are consistently less Materialist than the older ones. Moreover, as predicted, these differences seem to reflect cohort effects. There is no indication of the long-term downward trend that would be present if we were dealing with life cycle effects. A given cohort does not become more Materialist as it ages. The overall tendency from 1970 to 1988 is horizontal. The respective cohorts are generally at least as Postmaterialist in 1988 as they were in 1970, and whatever net trend exists is upward, toward increasing Postmaterialism.

Some critics have suggested that a cohort analysis based on the mean value scores for each cohort might be more reliable than one based on the percentage difference index used in Figure 2-5. Figure A-2 (in the Appendix) shows the results of such an analysis. For each cohort, the Materialists receive a score of 0, the Mixed types a score of 1, and the Postmaterialists a score of 2. The results are identical with those in Figure 2-5. As hypothesized, we find period effects superimposed on stable cohort differences. There is no overall downward tendency that could support a life cycle interpretation. If we had stopped taking measurements in 1977 or even in 1980 (as Boeltken and Jagodzinski did), the results might have been reconciled with a life cycle interpretation. But with the full time series through 1988, this is implausible. A life cycle model implies that in a ten-year period, each cohort will move downward to the level that the cohort ten years older occupied at the start of the period. The data show no such overall downward tendency.

Instead of following given birth cohorts across time, Figure A-3 (in the Appendix) follows various age groups from 1970 to 1986 using the same values index as in Figure 2-6. If the data fit a life cycle model, we would find horizontal lines here for each age group. What we find, instead, is a clear upward trend. Those who were 65-year-olds in 1986 are markedly more Postmaterialist than those who were that age in 1970; the same is true when we compare the 55- to 64-year-old group in 1987 with the same age group in 1970. Indeed, all six age groups were more Postmaterialist in 1987 than in 1970, in most cases by a substantial margin.

Economic changes furnish a ready explanation for the short-term fluctuations observed in the mid 1970s and early 1980s. But in order to explain this long-term upward trend within each age group, one must either accept the presence of intergenerational value change—or postulate the existence of some mysterious long-term force that no one has yet identified.

The data show no sign whatever of the continuous downward cohort movement that would be associated with the ''continuous aging'' version of a life cycle model. But it is still conceivable that lesser life cycle effects might be present, linked with specific transitions at given points in the life cycle. Thus one might argue that people become more Materialist when they enter the labor force, or that getting married or having children makes them give a higher priority to economic and physical security than they did when they were single and had no children to support. Is it possible that different values of old and young have nothing to do with historical change

TABLE 2-2. IMPACT OF LIFE CYCLE EFFECTS AND COHORT EFFECTS ON VALUES:
MULTIPLE CLASSIFICATION ANALYSIS

	Eta	Beta
Respondent's age cohort	.203	.175
Was respondent ever married?	.144	.071
Family income (quartiles)	.103	.065
Is respondent in labor force?	.082	.061
Does respondent have children?	.021	.043

Multiple R = .234   Multiple R^2 = .055   (N = 221,375)

but simply reflect the fact that the old are likelier to be married and have careers and children than are the young?

Let us test this hypothesis by comparing the values of old and young, this time controlling for whether one has married or not, has children or not, and has a full-time job or not. Table 2-2 shows the results of a multiple classification analysis in which the dependent variable is the index of Materialist/Postmaterialist values used in Figure 2-6. This analysis uses data from all Euro-Barometer surveys that included the relevant questions from 1970 through 1986. The predictors are the respondent's age cohort; the respondent's income (by quartiles within each nation); and dummy variables indicating whether or not the respondent was ever married; has children; and has a full-time job. The results suggest that each of these life cycle transitions may have some impact but that cohort effects are far more important than life cycle effects. In Table 2-2, the respondent's birth cohort has a beta coefficient of .175, which is far higher than that of any of the life cycle indicators. The effects of employment are mixed. On one hand, being in the labor force goes with being slightly more Materialist; on the other hand, having a high income makes one *less* so. The net effect is surprisingly weak. By itself, birth cohort explains more than twice as much of the variance in value priorities as do *all* of the life cycle indicators combined.

Even this may overestimate the impact of life cycle factors, however, for, as we will see in chapter 6, Postmaterialists place much less emphasis on getting married and having children than Materialists do. The life cycle interpretation assumes that people are Postmaterialists because they are not yet married or do not yet have children. But a good deal of evidence suggests that it also works the other way around: People are less likely to get married *because* they are Postmaterialists, and less apt to have children *because* they have distinctive Postmaterialist priorities. Insofar as this is true, we would expect to find a diminishing emphasis on marriage, and declining birth rates in advanced industrial societies—which is exactly what has been taking place ever since Postmaterialists began to enter the adult population in the 1960s. Thus, the linkages between values and marriage and child-bearing shown in Table 2-2 do not necessarily prove that life cycle effects have any impact at all; they merely suggest that this could be the case, and provide an estimate of the upper limits of such effects. Even taking these upper limits at face value, the data indicate that the cohort effects are considerably stronger than the life cycle effects—if the latter exist at all.

In any given sample from a given country, one may find anomalies in which younger groups are more Materialist than older ones (Lafferty 1975; Van Deth 1983a; Boeltken and Jagodzinski 1985). Is the remarkable regularity and theoretical coherence of the cohort differences shown in Figures 2-5 just a fluke that results from pooling cross-national data? No. We obtain results that are equally free from anomalies when we pool the various surveys carried out *within* a given country. Table 2-3 shows the intercohort differences in value priorities within each of the member nations of the European Community, based on the combined data from all surveys carried out from 1970 through 1986. Combining these surveys produces eight large samples of over 20,000 cases each, so that each of the seven cohorts averages nearly 3,000 cases, and three medium-sized samples of from 6,000 to 12,000 cases, with an average of more than 1,000 cases per cohort. The three medium-sized samples are from Greece, which has only been included in the European Community since 1981, and from Luxembourg and Northern Ireland, in which relatively small samples of about 300 cases are interviewed in each Euro-Barometer survey. Finally, we also have two smaller samples, of about 2,700 cases each, from Spain and Portugal, respectively (both of which have been in the Community only since 1986). Each sample now displays a pattern almost completely free from anomalies. As we move from younger to older cohorts, the percentage of Materialists rises regularly and monotonically, whereas the percentage of Postmaterialists declines in similar fashion. Among the eleven large or medium-sized samples, we find only one anomaly, in which an older cohort is less Materialist than a younger one; this occurs in Belgium, where, as we have seen, recent influences have had particularly dire effects. But even here the anomaly is very mild, with the youngest cohort only 1 percentage point more Materialist than the second-youngest one. There are no anomalies at all among the rest of the 154 cells in the large and medium samples. The only large anomaly occurs in one of the two small samples, where we find that the second-oldest Spanish cohort is 5 percentage points more Materialist than the oldest cohort. With a larger data base from Spain, we suspect that this deviation from the general pattern would disappear—and, indeed, this is precisely what happens in later Spanish surveys (see Table 2-4). Deviations from the theoretical pattern are largely a

TABLE 2-3. DISTRIBUTION OF MATERIALIST AND POSTMATERIALIST VALUE TYPES
           BY AGE COHORT IN THIRTEEN SOCIETIES, 1970 - 1986

Birth Years of Age Cohort	Nether- lands Mat PM	West Germany Mat PM	Great Britain Mat PM	Denmark Mat PM	Belgium Mat PM
1956 - 1965	20% 27%	22% 26%	22% 15%	24% 20%	30% 16%
1946 - 1955	23 23	26 19	27 14	25 19	29 16
1936 - 1945	26 19	34 12	29 10	32 12	34 12
1926 - 1935	33 13	41 9	31 9	35 9	37 10
1916 - 1925	35 12	42 9	35 7	38 6	42 7
1906 - 1915	42 8	49 6	40 6	46 4	46 5
1880 - 1905	43 6	53 5	45 4	49 2	51 4
N	(24,197)	(24,401)	(24,336)	(21,142)	(22,569)

Birth Years of Age Cohort	France Mat PM	Italy Mat PM	Repub. of Ireland Mat PM	Luxem- bourg Mat PM
1956 - 1965	26% 20%	30% 14%	31% 11%	22% 22%
1946 - 1955	28 18	34 13	37 8	28 14
1936 - 1945	35 14	48 8	44 5	34 9
1926 - 1935	42 9	51 6	45 5	40 9
1916 - 1925	46 8	55 4	51 3	42 6
1906 - 1915	54 4	57 3	53 3	45 5
1880 - 1905	54 3	58 3	53 3	49 6
N	(26,192)	(26,797)	(20,947)	(6,412)

Birth Years of Age Cohort	Northern Ireland Mat PM	Greece Mat PM	Spain Mat PM	Portugal Mat PM
1956 - 1965	28% 10%	31% 15%	27% 20%	41% 8%
1946 - 1955	42 5	40 13	40 15	47 4
1936 - 1945	47 5	49 7	53 6	55 5
1926 - 1935	48 6	51 6	60 3	60 3
1916 - 1925	50 5	55 6	62 3	70 2
1906 - 1915	55 4	60 3	72 2	72 1
1880 - 1905	56 4	62 4	67 2	74 0
N	(6,019)	(12,216)	(2,690)	(2,728)

Source: Combined results from European Community surveys, 1970 - 1986.

Note: Percentages do not add up to 100% because mixed types are omitted.

function of sample size. As sample size increases, one gets an increasingly accurate picture of reality; and the reality is that younger birth cohorts are less Materialist than older ones.

How does the American public compare with West European publics in this respect? In the early 1970s, among the older cohorts (those born before 1924), the American public showed a higher proportion of Postmaterialists

than did any European public except the Dutch; but among the youngest
cohort, several West European countries showed a higher proportion of
Postmaterialists than did the United States. The overall pattern was similar—in every country, the young were likelier to be Postmaterialists and
less likely to be Materialists. As we noted at the time,

> Again and again, in country after country, we find this same indication
> of change. But the *rate* of change varies from country to country in a
> striking yet consistent and predictable fashion. The American sample
> shows less value change than any other country except Britain. The *old-
> est* American cohort has a higher proportion of Postmaterialists than
> their peers in any European nation—reflecting the greatly privileged po-
> sition this country once had—but the *youngest* American cohort has not
> moved toward Postmaterialism as rapidly as many of their European
> peers. (Inglehart 1977, 36–37)

During the past fifteen years, West European publics have continued to
shift toward Postmaterialist values at a more rapid pace than have the
Americans, and this basic contrast between Western Europe and the United
States still holds true. As Table 2-4 demonstrates, in 1986–1987, *older*
Americans were still more Postmaterialist than most of their European
counterparts—but younger Americans lagged behind, being less Postmaterialist than their counterparts in Western Europe as a whole, and far less
so than their counterparts in the most advanced European countries, the
Netherlands, West Germany, and Denmark.

This contrast between Western Europe and the United States apparently
reflects the facts that (1) throughout the first two-thirds of the twentieth
century, the United States had the highest per capita income in the world;
and (2) compared with the devastation it wrought in Western Europe,
World War II had a relatively mild impact on the United States. Thus, the
older American cohorts were brought up under conditions of greater economic and physical security than those prevailing in Western Europe. But
during the past four decades, the American economy has been relatively
stagnant. West European countries have attained high levels of prosperity,
and their relatively advanced social security systems have contributed to
an atmosphere in which their younger cohorts have grown up with a sense
of security as great or greater than that prevailing in the United States.

The result is that while as recently as the 1960s, the United States was
at the cutting edge of cultural change in advanced industrial society, that
no longer seems to be the case. As evidence presented here and in the
following chapters indicates, the United States is experiencing processes
of cultural change that are basically similar to those of other industrial
societies, but she seems to be encountering them more slowly than are the

TABLE 2-4. DISTRIBUTION OF MATERIALIST AND POSTMATERIALIST VALUE TYPES
BY AGE COHORT IN TWELVE WESTERN NATIONS, 1986 - 1987

Age Range in 1987	Neth. Mat PM	West Germany Mat PM	Denmark Mat PM	Great Britain Mat PM
15 - 24	10% 34%	9% 35%	15% 22%	13% 20%
25 - 34	12 31	14 30	17 27	22 15
35 - 44	14 26	20 26	17 23	20 17
45 - 54	20 21	21 18	20 11	19 14
55 - 64	26 16	20 16	27 11	26 10
65 - 74	22 11	28 13	30 8	30 13
Total	17 25	17 24	21 18	22 15

Age Range in 1987	France Mat PM	Belgium Mat PM	Italy Mat PM	Ireland Mat PM
15 - 24	26% 16%	31% 19%	25% 17%	24% 14%
25 - 34	32 16	30 18	25 14	34 8
35 - 44	32 20	34 15	32 12	36 8
45 - 54	40 7	41 14	42 7	41 7
55 - 64	37 10	45 13	44 7	45 5
65 - 74	48 5	49 8	48 3	52 4
Total	33 14	38 15	35 11	37 9

Age Range in 1987	Spain Mat PM	Greece Mat PM	Portugal Mat PM	European Community Mat PM	United States Mat PM
15 - 24	22% 22%	29% 15%	38% 10%	20% 22%	25% 21%
25 - 34	28 20	37 12	47 7	25 21	18 15
35 - 44	42 12	47 6	50 6	30 16	22 14
45 - 54	55 5	53 5	54 6	34 19	33 19
55 - 64	60 3	56 2	63 4	39 9	24 15
65 - 74	61 3	62 4	70 3	41 7	29 11
Total	42 12	46 8	52 6	30 15	23 16

Sources: Combined results from Euro-Barometer surveys 25, 26, and
27 (carried out in Spring 1986, Fall 1986, and Spring 1987,
respectively); United States data from survey sponsored by the European
Community and carried out by the Gallup organization, in November 1987.
Note: Figures for European Community are weighted according to
population of each country. Ns for each country are: Netherlands,
2,919; West Germany, 2,820; Denmark, 2,848; Britain, 2,930; France,
2,850; Belgium, 2,828; Italy, 3,116; Ireland, 2,921; Spain, 2,702;
Greece, 2,726; Portugal, 2,768; United States, 1,300. Percentages do
not add up to 100% because mixed types are omitted.

economically developed countries of Northern Europe; only Southern Europe still lags behind, and this region is changing rapidly.

The cohort differences are unmistakable in Figures 2-5 and 2-6, but there is clear evidence of significant period effects as well, and our interpretation of the cohort analysis will not be complete until we have accounted for them. It is not difficult to do so. When I formulated the battery

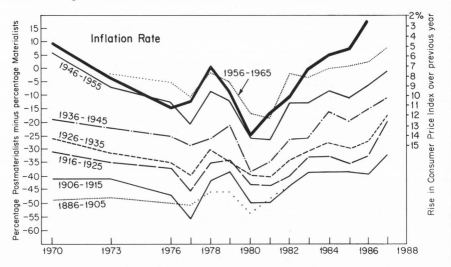

FIGURE 2-6. Value priorities of seven age cohorts and mean inflation rate across six West European countries, 1970–1987. Both the inflation rates and values indices from which these graphs were derived are weighted according to population of each nation.

of items first used to measure Materialist/Postmaterialist value priorities in 1970, I hypothesized that one's sensitivity to inflation would be a good indicator of Materialist priorities. Consequently, one of the two Materialist options in the four-item battery used here is "fighting rising prices." My expectation was that different age cohorts, whose socialization had been shaped by different historical experiences, would respond differently to this item, with the older cohorts more apt to give it a high priority.

When formulating these items in 1969, I did not anticipate the explosive worldwide inflation that would later take place, following the OPEC oil price shocks of late 1973 and late 1979, respectively. But the implications are clear: One would expect such inflation to enhance the chances that a high priority would be given to "fighting rising prices." The theoretically obvious interpretation of the period effects found in Figure 2-5, then, is that they reflect the two waves of inflation that impinged on Western Europe so dramatically in the mid-1970s and again at the start of the 1980s. Is this interpretation confirmed empirically?

Figure 2-6, which shows the answer, is identical to Figure 2-5 except that it also shows the mean inflation rate for the six nations from 1970 through 1987. The inflation rate is indicated by the rise in the Consumer Price Index during the year of the survey; high inflation rates are plotted as a downward movement of the inflation line so that there is the same

TABLE 2-5. VALUE PRIORITIES AND INFLATION RATES AMONG SIX WESTERN
PUBLICS, 1970 - 1987

		% Mats.	% Postmats.	Percentage Difference	Inflation Rate
Netherlands:	1970 - 71	34%	13%	-21	4.2%
	1986 - 87	17	25	+ 8	.3
Britain:	1970 - 71	36	7	-29	6.4
	1986 - 87	22	15	- 7	3.4
Germany:	1970 - 71	44	10	-34	3.0
	1986 - 87	17	24	+ 7	0
France:	1970 - 71	41	11	-30	5.3
	1986- 87	33	14	-19	2.7
Belgium:	1970 - 71	32	14	-18	4.1
	1986 - 87	38	15	-23	1.3
Italy:	1970 - 71	35	10	-25	5.3
	1986 - 87	35	11	-24	5.8
Six nations, weighted	1970-71	39	10	-29	4.9
mean:[a]	1986-87	27	17	-10	2.7

Source: Inflation rates from European Community Eurostatistics
reports.
[a]Weighted according to population of each nation.

polarity for the two sets of variables. In those years for which no survey
data are available, the inflation rate is not plotted either.

Again, the fit between data and theory is remarkably good, so good that
it is immediately apparent even from simply scanning Figure 2-6. Each of
the two dips toward increased Materialism reflects a rise in inflation, and
the upward movements of 1978–1979 and 1982–1987 reflect the abate-
ment of inflation, with roughly a one-year lag. One's impression that the
period effects result largely from changes in the inflation rate is confirmed
by multiple regression analysis of the data in Figure 2-6.

Table A-4 (in the Appendix) shows the inflation rates that prevailed
from 1970 to 1986 in each of the six nations surveyed from 1970 on. Table
2-5 sums up the values shifts from 1970 to 1987, in relation to the inflation
each nation experienced. In five of these nations, by 1986 inflation had
subsided to a level at or below where it was in 1970. In four of these
nations (the Netherlands, Britain, West Germany, and France), we find
impressive shifts toward Postmaterialism. In 1970–1971, Materialists
were three or four times as numerous as Postmaterialists; by 1986–1987,
the two groups were close to parity, with Postmaterialists actually moving
ahead in the Netherlands and West Germany. Part of this shift can be at-

tributed to period effects favorable to Postmaterialism, but an even larger portion can be traced to population replacement, as we will see below.

In Italy, we observe a small net shift toward Postmaterialism in spite of the fact that in 1986 the inflation rate was still higher than in 1970. Here, intergenerational population replacement more than offset negative period effects. Only in Belgium do we observe a net shift toward Materialism. The Belgian deviant case has already been noted in chapter 1, and will be touched upon again in succeeding chapters. This phenomenon seems to be linked with a pervasive malaise in Belgian society during the 1980s. For the six nations as a whole, however, there was a pronounced net shift toward Postmaterialism. The economic turmoil of the 1970s and early 1980s inhibited, but did not stop, the shift toward Postmaterialism linked with intergenerational population replacement.

Not only overall, but on a nation by nation basis, there is an extremely close fit between inflation rates and short-term changes in our dependent variable. This is not a surprising finding, but it is important because it furnishes a substantive explanation of the period effects that baffled earlier investigators—and helps to sort out the impact of period effects, cohort effects, and life cycle effects.

In the mid-1970s and at the start of the 1980s, the world experienced drastic inflation, producing exceptionally strong period effects. By the mid-1980s, inflation rates in most of Western Europe had subsided to their 1970 levels; accordingly, the period effects have now subsided or even reversed their direction. Given the large intergenerational differences in value priorities that our analysis demonstrates, the effects of intergenerational population replacement should be manifest in the value priorities of the public. A great deal of population replacement has taken place since 1970—perhaps more than one realizes. In 1970, those born before 1906 and those born after 1945 were about equally numerous within our sampling universe (which includes all citizens 15 years of age and older). The pre-1906 cohort constituted 17 percent of the public, and the postwar cohort constituted 20 percent. By 1986, major shifts had occurred. The pre-1906 cohort had fallen to less than 5 percent of the public, whereas the postwar cohorts now constituted nearly 50 percent of the public. Are these demographic shifts reflected in the distribution of Materialists and Postmaterialists in Western Europe?

Very much so. In 1970–1971, within the six nations as a whole, Materialists outnumbered Postmaterialists by a ratio of almost 4 to 1. By 1988, this ratio had fallen to 4 to 3. The Postmaterialists were much closer to an even balance with the Materialists. Even in the United States, the change has been substantial. In 1972, Materialists outnumbered Postmaterialists by 3.5 to 1. In 1987, this ratio had fallen to only 1.5 to 1. Part of this shift should be discounted because inflation was lower in 1988 than it had been in 1970–1971. Consequently, period effects are now working to reinforce cohort effects, conveying a somewhat exaggerated impression of how much intergenerational value change has taken place.

A twelve-item battery of questions designed to measure Materialist/ Postmaterialist items was included in the Euro-Barometer surveys in 1973, 1978, and 1988 (for detailed information on the formulation of these questions, see chapter 3). This twelve-item values battery is much less sensitive to the effects of inflation than is the four-item battery. This reflects the fact that in the four-item battery, "fighting rising prices" is one of only two Materialist items, while in the twelve-item battery, it is one of six. Consequently, during periods when inflation is not a major problem, those with Materialist values can shift to one of the five other Materialist items in choosing their top priorities.

This is precisely what happened during the period from 1973 to 1988 (the earliest and most recent years in which the twelve-item battery has been administered in the European Community countries). As Table 2-6 indicates, in 1973 the goal of "fighting rising prices" was chosen by European Community publics as one of their top priorities more frequently than was any other goal. The next most frequently chosen goals were four other Materialist items: "economic growth," "the fight against crime," "maintaining a stable economy," and "maintaining order in the nation." In 1988, inflation had become a minor problem, and "fighting rising prices" fell from first to sixth rank. It was not replaced by a Postmaterialist goal, however. Instead, the various other Materialist goals took up much of the slack, so that the relative positions of Materialist versus Postmaterialist goals were almost unchanged from 1973 to 1988. At both the start and finish of this period, Materialist items held five of the top six positions, and (apart from the sharp drop of "rising prices") they even maintained roughly the same rank order, with "economic growth" moving up from second to first place, "the fight against crime" moving up from third to second place, and so on, down to "strong defense forces," which ranked last in both 1973 and 1988.

Apparently, one Materialist goal can substitute for another, as our theory implies. Nevertheless, the twelve-item battery also reveals a substantial shift from Materialist to Postmaterialist priorities—a shift that parallels the one shown by the four-item index but is of more moderate size. In 1973, Materialist choices outweighed Postmaterialist choices by almost 2 to 1. In 1988, they outweighed Postmaterialist choices by less than 1.5 to 1. The shift in polar types was even more pronounced. If we construct pure Materialist and Postmaterialist types, reflecting those whose top two priorities among these twelve items were exclusively Materialist or exclu-

TABLE 2-6. PRIORITIES OF WESTERN PUBLICS: 1973 VERSUS 1988
(Percentage choosing given goal as first or second most important out of
twelve, among publics of nine nations belonging to European Community in
1973 and 1988)

	1973			1988	
Goal	Polarity	% Choosing	Goal	Polarity	% Choosing
Fight rising prices	(M)	39%	Economic growth	(M)	28%
Economic growth	(M)	24	Fight crime	(M)	27
Fight crime	(M)	22	Stable economy	(M)	21
Stable economy	(M)	22	Maintain order	(M)	20
Maintain order	(M)	19	Fight rising prices	(M)	17
More say on job	(P)	17	Less impersonal society	(P)	18

Less impersonal
  society
	(P)	16	More say in
			  government
				(P)	16

More say in
  government
	(P)	12	Protect free
			  speech
				(P)	16

Protect free speech	(P)	11	More say on job	(P)	13
More beautiful cities	(P)	7	Ideas count	(P)	10
Ideas count	(P)	7	More beautiful cities	(P)	7

Strong defense
  forces
	(M)	4	Strong defense
			  forces
				(M)	6

Materialist total		130			119
Postmat. total		70			80

Source: Based on representative national samples of publics of
France, West Germany, Britain, Italy, Netherlands, Belgium, Luxembourg,
Ireland, and Denmark interviewed in European Community surveys of
September 1973 and April 1988 (Euro-Barometer survey 29).
Note: Percentages are weighted according to population of each
country.

sively Postmaterialist, respectively, we find that in 1973 the pure Materialists outnumber the Postmaterialists by well over 3 to 1; in 1988 this ratio had fallen to barely 2 to 1.

There are various other ways in which we can control for period effects. For example, we can statistically control for inflation in multiple regression analysis. But regardless of whether we control for inflation or estimate the impact of cohort effects (as we do below), it is clear that intergenerational population replacement has brought about a major shift from Materialist to Postmaterialist values.

Needless to say, we cannot guarantee that inflation rates will remain at their present levels. Extraneous factors could set off a third wave of massive inflation that would have a predictable impact on these indicators. Nevertheless, it seems clear that, period effects being equal, the cohort effects demonstrated here create a powerful long-term tendency for the publics of these societies to shift from Materialist to Postmaterialist priorities. Let us try to estimate the impact of these cohort effects more precisely.

THE EFFECTS OF GENERATIONAL REPLACEMENT UPON VALUE CHANGE

Analyses carried out by Abramson and Inglehart (1986, 1987) complement the foregoing findings. Unlike the cohort analyses above (which help distinguish among aging effects, birth cohort effects, and period effects), these analyses estimate the effect of population replacement on value change. Since births and deaths are well documented, they enable one to make precise estimates of how much value change would occur as a result of these demographic changes alone. To do so, one first creates (algebraically) a population in which *no* replacement occurs (see Abramson 1983, 56–61); this serves as a baseline for comparison with the actual population, in which demographic replacement *has* occurred. The first step in creating this baseline is to remove new cohorts from the calculations. Next, one must algebraically immortalize the older cohorts. To do this, we use the distribution of respondents in each cohort in our earliest surveys as our base, multiply the value scores found for each cohort in subsequent surveys by the number of respondents originally in that cohort, sum these products, and divide the sum of these products by the number of cases. This provides a population in which the effects of population replacement have been removed. It can then be compared with the actual value scores among the population. Differences between the actual result and the result with the effects of replacement removed are due to replacement. In the 1970 surveys, respondents with middle-class occupations were overrepresented, which tends to exaggerate the proportion of Postmaterialists; subsequent surveys are more representative. To partially offset this problem, the combined results of the 1970 and 1971 surveys are used as our baseline.

The results of this analysis demonstrate that population replacement affects value change quite markedly, though the actual changes that occurred differ widely from country to country. For the combined European sample, the data shown in Figure 2-7 indicate that replacement is the main force leading to the growth of Postmaterialist values. Figure 2-7 shows Abramson and Inglehart's (1986) estimates. The solid line shows the actual scores on our value index, calculated in the same way as in Figure 2-5. The broken line shows what those scores would have been if there had been no generational replacement. In 1980 and 1981, scores on this value index declined somewhat, largely as a result of the very high inflation prevailing

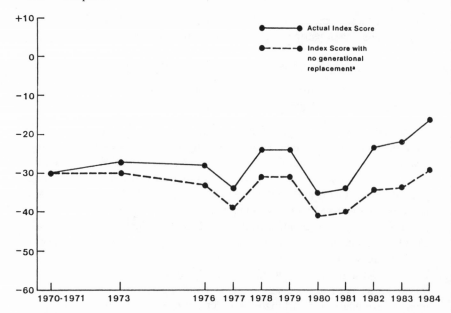

FIGURE 2-7. Percentage of Postmaterialists minus percentage of Materialists in combined sample of six West European publics, 1970–1971 through 1984.

Source: European Community Surveys. For the distribution of respondents by years of birth in all eleven survey years, see Abramson and Inglehart 1986.

ᵃ Assuming that no cohorts born after 1955 entered the adult population and that older cohorts did not diminish through death.

then—but they would have declined even more if there had been no population replacement. In more recent years, however, this decline is more than offset. By 1982, the value index was 7 points above the 1970–1971 starting point; in 1983 it was 8 points higher; and by 1984 it was 13 points above the 1970–1971 baseline. Without replacement, the 1982 score would have been 4 points lower than in the 1970–1971 survey; in 1983 it would have been 3 points lower; and in 1984 it would have been 2 points lower. Postmaterialism rose substantially, but virtually all of this change was due to intergenerational population replacement. In 1984, inflation rates were still higher than in 1970–1971, and without population replacement, there would have been no rise in Postmaterialism.

There will be considerable population replacement in coming years, but the process will slow down, mainly because of low birth rates since the mid-1960s. Between the end of 1970 and the end of 1985, 29 percent of the adult population was replaced. But during the years from 1985 to 2000, only 22 percent of the adult population will be replaced. Both future replacement and the slowdown of that replacement have clear implications for future trends in value priorities.

Abramson and Inglehart (1987) projected the future impact of replacement on West European values from 1985 to 2000. All those who will make up the adult public in 2000 have now been born, so we can calculate demographic shifts with confidence. The only important uncertainty is in estimating the future values of those cohorts that are still too young to have been interviewed. In all past surveys, the youngest cohort entering the adult population has been more Postmaterialist than the next older cohort. Nonetheless, a conservative first projection assumes that all cohorts born after 1965 will enter the adult population with a value score no more Postmaterialist than that of the 1956–1965 cohort. A second projection assumes that, as in all previous surveys, the cohorts entering the adult population will be slightly more Postmaterialist than the adjacent older cohort. Figure 2-8 shows these projections.

Both basic projections assume that cohorts maintain their 1985 levels of Postmaterialism. There will be fluctuations from year to year, of course. But, as our empirical evidence shows, three of the four cohorts that can be tracked over the fifteen years studied here registered virtually identical values scores in 1985 and 1970–1971. This projection of value shifts assumes that the net impact of short-term economic fluctuations from 1985 to 2000 will be similar to their impact from 1970 to 1985. This is a very conservative assumption, because the period effects from 1970 to 1985 were relatively negative, including the two worst recessions since the 1930s. The future could conceivably be even worse, of course. Economic collapse or uncontrollable inflation would affect the outcome—but it would do so in a predictable direction and even to a degree that is at least roughly predictable. The projection presented here simply assumes that economic conditions for the fifteen years from 1985 to 2000 will be roughly similar to those that prevailed during the far from rosy period from 1970 to 1985. The broken line in Figure 2-8 shows our projection based on this assumption. The value index rises slightly by 1990, somewhat more by 1995, and again by 2000. By the year 2000, the overall value index shows a rise of 6 points above the 1985 level purely as a result of generational replacement. This finding that there would be a gain in Postmaterialism is robust, and would obtain as long as young Europeans were no more Materialist than their elders—a finding observed in all survey years thus far.

Let us assume that the two new (and not yet surveyed or only partially surveyed) cohorts will be slightly less Materialist than the adjacent older cohorts. The dotted line in Figure 2-8 shows the overall value scores given these cohort values. While our results for 1990 scarcely differ from our first projection, by 1995 the overall value score will be somewhat higher.

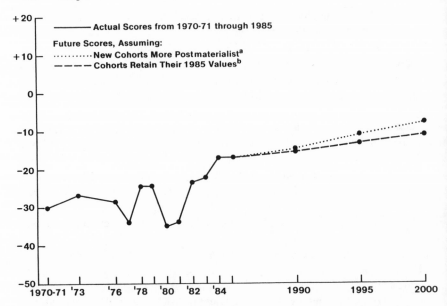

FIGURE 2-8. Projected percentage of Postmaterialists minus percentage of Materialists for six West European publics in 1990, 1995, and 2000.

Source: European Community surveys are used to measure the actual results from 1970–1971 through 1985. We used combined national samples of Germany, Britain, the Netherlands, France, Belgium, and Italy. Projections for 1990, 1995, and 2000 are based on national census projections.

[a] Assumes cohorts will retain their 1985 values, but that cohorts who enter the adult population will be more Postmaterialist than the adjacent older cohort.

[b] Assumes cohorts will retain their 1985 values, but that cohorts who enter the adult population will have the same values as do the 1956–1965 cohort.

By 2000, the overall score shows a 9-point gain over the 1985 value score, with Postmaterialists now being almost as numerous as Materialists.

Slowing rates of generational replacement lead to slower rates of value change. During the fifteen years from 1970 to 1985, there was a 13-point gain in the value index, solely as a result of generational replacement. The population replacement process is slowing down somewhat, but on the basis of our second assumption, we can expect the index to rise an additional 9 points between 1985 and the end of the century. If it rises by more (as now seems likely), the gains will be due to period effects conducive to Postmaterialism.

Even though it is slowing, replacement remains a long-term force pushing Postmaterialism upward. Extremely adverse economic conditions could cause Materialism to rise again, but even under these conditions, generational replacement would slow down any movement toward Materialism.

CONCLUSIONS

The unprecedented economic and physical security of the postwar era has led to an intergenerational shift from Materialist to Postmaterialist values. The young emphasize Postmaterialist goals to a far greater extent than do the old, and cohort analysis indicates that this reflects generational change far more than it does aging effects.

Both Americans and West Europeans became substantially more Postmaterialist from 1970 to 1988, and will probably continue to become more so, but the change created by replacement is relatively slow, for population replacement is gradual in advanced industrial societies, which have relatively low birth rates and death rates, and the decline in birth rates since the mid-1960s will further slow down replacement. Nevertheless, we estimate that almost exactly half the West European adult population (49.8 percent) will have been replaced during the twenty-nine years between the end of 1970 and the beginning of 2000.

Given the gradual impact of replacement, it seems likely that even by the year 2000 Materialists will still be about as numerous as Postmaterialists. The overall proportion of Postmaterialists would then be about twice as great as it was in 1970–1971, when only 1 West European in 10 was a Postmaterialist. Moreover, the key comparison is the ratio of Materialists to Postmaterialists. At the time of our first surveys, in 1970–1971, Materialists held an overwhelming numerical preponderance over Postmaterialists, outnumbering them by nearly 4 to 1. By 1988, the balance had already shifted dramatically, to a point where Materialists outnumbered Postmaterialists by only 4 to 3. This overstates the real long-term change somewhat, since it reflects a combination of intergenerational change *plus* period effects, which had become favorable by 1988. But, even when we discount these period effects, conservative projections based on population replacement alone indicate that by the year 2000 Materialists will outnumber Postmaterialists only narrowly. This may be a sort of tipping point in the balance between the two value types: As we will see in chapters 10 and 11, Postmaterialists are more highly educated, more articulate, and politically more active than Materialists. Consequently, their political impact will probably outweigh that of the Materialists on many issues. The effects of intergenerational population replacement are likely to have a profound effect on the values that prevail among Western publics. Subsequent chapters provide evidence of just how far-reaching these consequences are likely to be.

CHAPTER 3

Stability and Change in Mass Belief Systems

INTRODUCTION

One of the most basic questions in the social sciences concerns the stability of human characteristics. Until a few decades ago, it was taken for granted that enduring orientations and personality traits do exist; more recently, their significance and even their existence have been called into question. Personality researchers, such as Mischel (1968, 1976), rejected the idea of stable traits. Emphasizing cognitive social learning, they saw behavior as shaped more by encoding strategies, personal constructs, and expectations, than by stable personality traits. The rising tide of cognitive psychology shifted attention to explaining behavior in terms of information processing alone without reference to enduring personality characteristics. From another perspective, some economists and some Marxists attempt to interpret human behavior as simply the pursuit of economic interests, with the role of long-term religious, cultural, or personality factors greatly deemphasized. In political science, a large body of literature has questioned whether it makes sense to speak of long-term political party identification. Moreover, the concept of political culture has been attacked so often during the past twenty years that even some of its earliest and most prominent proponents have adopted a guarded, almost defensive tone.

One factor that has facilitated the onslaught on theories that argue the existence and behavioral significance of long-term individual predispositions is that fact that they have an inherently difficult strategic position, for virtually no orientation is so rigidly held that it admits of no exceptions. Even the most committed political partisans sometimes vote against their party, and even someone intensely opposed to taking human life would probably accept it if it were the only way to stop a lunatic from murdering a hundred children. Behavior is almost never determined by long-term predispositions *alone*. They may have an important impact on behavior, but it is a matter of probabilities rather than immutable laws. And long-term stability is inherently much more difficult to demonstrate than short-term variation. With an imaginative research design, one can readily demonstrate dramatic changes in the behavior of a given individual under different circumstances within the space of a few days or even a few minutes.

The inference is then drawn that if behavior can vary so markedly over a short time, it must vary even more over long periods of time and thus it is meaningless to speak of long-term behavioral predispositions. Short-term fluctuations can be demonstrated quickly, but long-term personality or attitudinal traits can be demonstrated only through long-term longitudinal research—of which there is very little. Under pressure to publish or perish, few scholars can devote their time to a research project that will show results only at the end of ten or twenty years—and even fewer funding agencies are willing to support such projects.

The difficulties of demonstrating long-term continuities at the individual level are compounded by the fact that any error in measurement tends to work against the hypothesis. If variation is observed, it tends to undermine evidence of long-term predispositions, regardless of whether this variation is attributable to genuine change or occurred simply because the attitude was measured inaccurately at one time point or another, or because of errors in recording, data processing, etc., at any time during the life of the project. As anyone who is familiar with survey research knows, measurement error is a pervasive and serious problem; what is less obvious is the fact that this systematically weakens the evidence of long-term attitudinal continuities.

Demonstrating the existence of long-term behavioral predispositions is an uphill effort, in short. But it is crucial to understanding many key aspects of human behavior. We believe that attitudinal continuities play an important role at both the individual and the cultural level. Indeed, it is impossible to explain the behavior of given nationalities or individuals without reference to these continuities. As we will demonstrate, some individuals and some nationalities are consistently more interested and more active in politics than others; the intensity fluctuates with short-term factors, but long-term differences persist over the years. Similarly, long-term political party loyalties exist in many countries—and, even though in given elections some people deviate from their usual party loyalties, one's expectations concerning long-term behavior will be very inaccurate if one overlooks the existence of enduring party loyalties.

This chapter utilizes data from the political action panel surveys carried out from 1974 to 1980–1981 to examine evidence of the existence and behavioral impact of long-term orientations (see Barnes, Kaase et al. 1979 for a more detailed description of this study). The fact that this study was carried out in three nations—West Germany, the Netherlands, and the United States—enables us to make cross-cultural comparisons of relative levels on key dependent variables. The fact that it was carried out over six years in West Germany and the Netherlands and seven years in the United

States enables us to examine the stability of attitudes and their impact on political behavior across exceptionally long time periods.

In the cohort analyses presented in chapter 2, we found large differences between the values of different birth cohorts. These differences not only persisted throughout 1970–1988, but seem to reflect distinctive formative experiences that occurred as much as fifty years ago. At first glance, this seems difficult to reconcile with Converse's (1964, 1970) panel-based findings of low constraint and stability among mass attitudes or with similar findings by Van Deth (1983a) and Jagodzinski (1984, 1986). These findings reveal only one aspect of the story, however. Mass attitudes often manifest much more coherent and stable patterns at the aggregate level than would seem possible if one took the results of panel survey analysis at face value. As we will see in this chapter, items designed by Rokeach (1968) and Inglehart (1977) to tap basic value priorities, show modest individual level stability together with remarkably high aggregate stability. Moreover, this aggregate stability is structured in ways that could not occur if random answering were the prevailing pattern. Moreover, as we have already seen, Materialist/Postmaterialist values show large differences between birth cohorts, which not only persisted throughout 1970–1988 but seem to reflect distinctive formative experiences that occurred as much as fifty years ago. These aggregate results are much too skewed to result from equiprobable random answering and cannot be attributed to methods effects; consequently, they must reflect underlying attitudinal predispositions in the respondents themselves. Thus, while random response to given items does play an important role, it is much less widespread than Converse's Black and White model implies, and does not generally reflect an absence of relevant preferences. This chapter will present a structural equation analysis of multiple-item value indicators in panel surveys extending over periods as long as seven years. The results reveal much stabler, broader orientations underlying the response to given items, which account for the high aggregate level stability observed here. Because it usually measures such orientations imperfectly, individual level survey data tend systematically to underestimate constraint and stability in mass attitudes.

THE APPARENT FLUIDITY OF MASS BELIEF SYSTEMS

The development of behavioral research in the postwar era brought forth disturbing evidence about the coherence and stability of mass political orientations, which has haunted us ever since. A central role was played by Converse (1964, 1970), who found that the political ideas of the American public generally display surprisingly little structure and seem to fluctuate capriciously over time. His analysis of panel survey data from 1956, 1958, and 1960 showed that on the average, less than two-thirds of the American public took the same side on important political issues at both points in a two-year period. Since about 50 percent would do so by chance alone, public attitudes seemed dismayingly unstable.

The implications of these findings were disturbing. To many people, they seemed to imply that representative democracy was an unattainable myth. Under democratic norms, public officials are supposed to implement policies that reflect the preferences of the majority of citizens. But if most citizens don't really *have* any coherent or stable preferences about major political issues, why should political decision makers take them into account? Indeed, how could they?

In some quarters, Converse—the bearer of unwelcome news—was even depicted as an advocate of elitism. Though the charge is clearly unwarranted, the implications of his findings are troubling indeed. They have given rise to a wide-ranging, often heated debate (Pierce and Rose 1974; Achen 1975; Erikson 1978; Judd and Milburn 1980; Judd, Krosnick, and Milburn 1981; Converse 1974, 1980; Martin 1981; Jackson 1983; Kinder 1983).

The debate persists. Converse's seminal articles on this topic continue to be cited each year in scores of publications, some agreeing and others disagreeing. There are several reasons why this controversy has been so enduring. The first reason is that it has powerful normative implications, raising the question whether representative democracy is meaningful or even possible, if nonattitudes are as widespread as Converse's analysis implies. Second, it raises the basic epistemological question of survey research: Can we trust the evidence of our measuring instruments? The findings suggest that survey evidence is mostly noise. Converse concluded that more than three-quarters of the public were giving random answers to the question used to illustrate his Black and White model. He never claimed that this held true of all political attitudes, of course; but the impact of his analysis stems from its implications concerning the nature of belief systems in mass publics, not the stability of one particular item. One commonly finds continuity correlations as low as or lower than that found with the item used in the Black and White model—and when one does, the model implies that the overwhelming majority have no real preference and are giving random answers. If this is true, it is important and alarming news for anyone involved in survey research.

There is a third reason why the debate has been so enduring: Both sides were partly right. As we will argue in this chapter, Converse was right: There is a major component of random answering in most survey data.

Moreover, it can be traced to the respondents themselves—it is not simply an artifact of poor questionnaire construction (though vague or confusing questions would increase it). Random answering exists—but it is not nearly as widespread as Converse's analysis indicates; and it is not located where he placed it (concentrated entirely in one of two radically different types of respondents). Instead, the evidence presented here indicates that most respondents *have* preferences that are relevant to most important social issues, but it is difficult to measure them accurately, given the constraints of time and motivation that normally characterize survey research. As a result, survey data tends systematically to underestimate both stability and constraint in mass attitudes.

In short, Converse contributed an immensely important insight—survey data are not nearly as hard as they would seem if one took all marginal distributions at face value. But this insight must be supplemented by another one, growing out of a cumulative body of research—survey data are not nearly as soft as they would seem if one took the turnover displayed in a typical panel survey at face value. Instead, there are underlying elements of stability that can be discerned when one applies more refined measurement techniques and that manifest themselves directly when one examines certain types of survey data at the aggregate level, as we will do here.

To illustrate our argument, let us turn to Figure 3-1, which depicts three different models of attitudinal stability. The first is a Markov Chain model, of the type that Converse (1970) starts with in his analysis of attitudes and nonattitudes. Using this model, let us assume that we find a correlation of .40 between the public's issue preferences at time 1, and the same individuals' preferences on the same issue at time 2, two years later; similarly, we find a .40 correlation between preferences at time 2 and preferences at time 3, four years later than time 1. The broken arrow indicates the correlation that would exist as a result of these two causal linkages. Assuming that no other factors are involved, this model implies that we should find a correlation of .16 between preferences at time 1 and preferences at time 3 (.4 × .4 = .16); one would expect a pronounced decline in the correlation as the time interval gets longer.

But the findings Converse actually observed in his 1956–1958–1960 panel survey deviated drastically from this pattern. The correlations from time 1 to time 2, and from time 2 to time 3, were both approximately .39; but the correlation from time 1 to time 3 was *also* about .39. The correlations over two years were not very high, but they showed no decline when extended over longer periods of time.

These findings were astonishing, since they seemed to violate well-established causal principles. In order to resolve this paradox, Converse developed the Black and White model depicted in Figure 3-1. The observed

1. Markov Chain model:

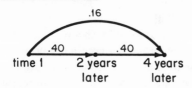

2. Black and White model:

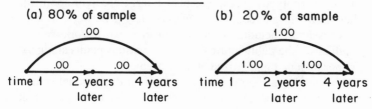

3. Latent Attitude model:

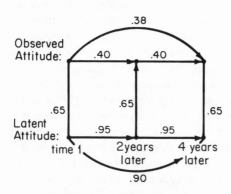

FIGURE 3-1. Three models of continuity and change in mass attitudes.

phenomena could be explained if one assumed that a large share of the sample (80 percent in this case) had no real preferences or "nonattitudes" and were responding at random. Since their responses were random, they would show no correlation whatever from one time to the next, regardless of whether the time intervals were long or short. The remaining respondents' behavior was totally different (hence, the "Black and White" label for this model). This second group not only had real preferences, but their preferences were totally stable; regardless of how much time elapsed, the correlation remained a perfect 1.00. For completely different reasons, the attitudinal stability of both groups shows no change over time. Thus, when the two groups were mixed together in a representative sample of the public, one would observe an overall continuity correlation of only .39 from one survey to the next—but the correlation would not decay over time.

This model fit the data neatly, explaining some findings that otherwise seemed inexplicable. But the Black and White model is problematic. Apart from its alarming normative and epistemological implications, it is inherently implausible. It postulates that the public is dichotomized into two radically different types of respondents—a large group of apoliticals, and a smaller group of rigid ideologues, with nothing in between. A large body of survey research, including some of Converse's own work, suggests that this is unlikely—the public normally falls at various points along a continuum, rather than being polarized at the extremes.

The third model in Figure 3-1, the Latent Attitude model, provides an alternative explanation. This model is based on the assumption that practically everybody has relatively stable underlying preferences that shape their responses to important political questions, but that any given survey question measures those preferences imperfectly. If, as in the example shown here, the latent attitude has a stability correlation of .95 over each two-year period, but there is a correlation of .65 between the observed attitude and the latent attitude at any given time, then one would find a continuity correlation of about .40 between the observed attitude at time 1 and at time 2. And one would find a correlation of .38 over four years, reflecting the product of the three indirect paths ($.65 \times .90 \times .65 = .38$), a figure only slightly lower than the two-year correlation of .40. In empirical research, a difference of this magnitude might not be detected, leaving the impression that there was no decay over time. Over long periods of time, the decline in correlations would become more pronounced, of course. Over an eight-year period, stability in the latent attitude would fall to $r = .81$, resulting in an observed attitudinal correlation of .34, which would be less likely to pass unnoticed. But over a period of four years, the observed results from the Latent Attitude model would closely approximate those from the Black and White model in Figure 3-1.

In other respects, however, the two models have profoundly different implications, which can be tested empirically. Given a two-year continuity correlation of .39, the Black and White model implies that the overwhelming majority of respondents have no real preferences and are giving random answers. The Latent Attitude model postulates that most respondents have real preferences. At any given time, some may be giving random answers (this is one possible interpretation of why there is an imperfect correlation between latent and observed attitudes), but, if so, it holds true of only a minority of the sample. The Black and White model postulates that the public consists of two radically different types of respondents: the "Blacks," characterized by total flux, and the "Whites," characterized by total stability, while the Latent Attitude model implies that the public is characterized by various shades of gray. Finally, the Latent Attitude model implies that one may find certain patterns of aggregate stability in the attitudes of mass publics that could not exist if the Black and White model applied. The next section presents extensive evidence of such stability.

The Black and White model is more parsimonious than the Latent Attitude model in one respect: It deals only with directly observed attitudes, while the Latent Attitude model postulates the existence of a second level of attitudes that is not observed directly. On the other hand, the Black and White model is less parsimonious in that it postulates the existence of two radically different types of respondents, while the Latent Attitude model requires only one. Thus far, no one has been able to identify who are the Blacks and who are the Whites in any sample of the public, and I strongly suspect that the task cannot be accomplished. However, the Latent Attitude model raises the question *"Why* is there an imperfect correlation between underlying preferences and observed responses?"

One possible answer is "Because the questions are too vague or confusingly worded," implying that better-written questions would produce a 1.00 correlation between the respondents' real preferences and the observed responses, resulting in much higher levels of stability over time and much greater ideological coherence. This possibility was emphasized in some of the early criticism of the Black and White model. But, while it undoubtedly has merit in special cases, its general applicability has become almost impossible to maintain. During the past few decades, hundreds of investigators in dozens of countries have attempted to develop and administer clear and meaningful political questions in public opinion surveys. The results have been dismayingly uniform. Political party identification often shows high stability; but apart from methodological artifacts, one almost never finds high levels of constraint or stability in response to questions about policy preferences among the general public. On the other hand, one does find relatively stable and coherent policy attitudes among political elites—even in response to the same questions that produced low stability and constraint among the general public (Putnam, et al. 1979; Converse and Pierce 1986; and see chapter 9). The problem does not seem to lie primarily in the questions themselves.

The problem is largely one of motivation and time. Even if people have preferences that are relevant to a specific sociopolitical question, it may take time and effort to articulate them. In the typical survey situation, a stranger appears at the respondent's door and asks him or her to respond to as many as 300 or 400 questions, with a promise that the interview will be over within a reasonably short time. Most members of the public are cooperative under these circumstances. They give answers, and sometimes very thoughtful ones. But the process of working out the cognitive implications of one's basic preferences involves a lot of work. And when faced with a large number of questions on which he or she has not previously articulated a position, the respondent may be under considerable time pressure. One is most likely to obtain stable responses that reflect basic preferences in connection with those topics that the respondents have frequently discussed and about which they have already made the necessary inferences *before* the interview.

It is probably for this reason that one obtains substantially higher stability coefficients for political party identification than for virtually any other political variable: Throughout one's life, one is repeatedly called on to express overt support for one party rather than another, through explicit actions such as voting, and in political discussions and other forms of political action. One's religious affiliation is one of the few variables that shows a comparable degree of stability, probably for similar reasons. A majority of the American public report that they attend church at least once a month. With both political and religious orientations, the likelihood is relatively high that the respondent has already worked out the necessary cognitive connections before the survey interview takes place.

The key point is that it may take a good deal of effort to put one's gut feelings into words. Zajonc (1980) argues that affective and cognitive orientations are distinct systems that influence each other but have a large degree of autonomy. Furthermore, reversing the tendency to view one's basic preferences as the logical consequence of all one's relevant cognition, he presents evidence that affect may precede cognition (Zajonc 1980; Zajonc, et al. 1982). In other words, one does not necessarily start with articulate, rational considerations, and then derive general preferences from them; rather, it is an interactive process, in which feelings sometimes come first. Reasoning along similar lines, we suggest that even the apparently "random" respondents in panel surveys usually have underlying affective orientations that are only loosely linked with their cognitions about specific public policies but are logically relevant to them. For while affective orientations seem to arise quickly and effortlessly, the process of working out their logical implications for each of the innumerable policy questions that face a society would require a great deal of time and effort. Unless they are involved in daily discussion of policy questions, most people have not made all of the relevant inferences. When asked their opinions in a public opinion survey situation, they do not always stop and take the time required to derive the policy implications of their underlying preferences. Instead, they may give superficial answers that are not necessarily consistent with their basic value preferences. Consequently, random answering is most likely to occur when the respondent does not start the interview with a prefabricated cognitive-affective linkage relating to the given topic.

Thus, while rejecting the Black and White model, we are in partial agreement with Converse: Random answering does play an important role in survey research. But our interpretations differ in several respects. Ours implies the following: (1) Random answering is much less widespread than the Black and White model suggests; evidence presented below indicates that it is limited to 20 to 30 percent of the sample at most. (2) Random answering is not concentrated among a distinct group of respondents who have no relevant preferences and therefore always give random answers on a given topic, but is scattered throughout the sample. (3) Random answering is largely a question of time and motivation. Consequently, under favorable circumstances, the percentage of the public giving constrained and stable answers can become relatively large; conversely, with low incentive and high time pressure, random answering increases. (4) If relevant preferences exist, and the problem is mainly one of measurement error, then multi-item indicators should enable us to tap these underlying preferences much more accurately and with greater stability and constraint than can be done with any of the individual indicators.

During the past decade, the development of increasingly refined techniques has led to cumulative advances in measuring latent variables and estimating the impact of measurement error (Pierce and Rose 1974; Achen 1975; Erikson 1978; Judd and Milburn 1980; Jackson 1983). The results provide increasingly strong support for a latent attitude interpretation. In one of the most advanced of these investigations, Jackson (1983) reanalyzed the data examined by Converse, using the LISREL structural equation approach. He found (1) a substantial amount of measurement error, though he did not determine whether this was attributable to nonattitudes among respondents or to poor questionnaire design; (2) a good deal of constraint, in the form of a common policy orientation underlying the issue questions included in the panel; and (3) a relatively high level of stability, with the common policy orientation showing a continuity correlation of .66 across the four-year period from 1956 to 1960.

Jackson's analysis explains the observed phenomena in an elegant and persuasive fashion. Nevertheless, there is still some room for doubt about this type of explanation, for to some extent the results you get depend on how you construct your model. Though they point in the same general direction, the results obtained by Jackson are significantly different from those obtained by Achen (1975), Erikson (1978), or Judd and Milburn (1980). The raw data are straightforward—and they show low stability. Evidence of underlying stability emerges only after the data have been subjected to some relatively complex processing. As Converse put it, in his response to Judd's and Milburn's LISREL analysis:

> To my eye, the authors obliterate these signs of confusion analytically and then, turn around to proclaim proudly that no such confusion exists, at least not "really," for example in the estimates from the structural model. I am not unaware of what this kind of 'real' means. At the same time, I cannot forget how the data looked before the authors began to process them, and I am convinced that those raw data say something about the reality out there, too. (Converse 1980, 646)

Is the stability that Jackson and others detect produced by statistical sleight-of-hand, or does it reflect stability in the real world, of a kind that sometimes manifests itself directly? In the following section, we will examine a massive body of empirical evidence that strongly supports the latter interpretation. It indicates that the belief systems of mass publics are underpinned by remarkably stable components, which seem to persist not merely over periods of two to four years, but over decades.

This evidence is of two complementary types. The first kind is panel surveys carried out over various intervals, ranging from two months to seven years. In each of these surveys, the respondents gave high or low priority to various societal goals; the results show continuity correlations that are rather modest over short periods, but decay very slowly over long periods of time, in keeping with the Latent Attitude model. The second kind of evidence comes from cohort analysis of these same goals, as ranked by successive cross-sections of Western publics at numerous time points across the period from 1970 through 1988. This evidence has been presented in the preceding chapter. As we saw, the results display a remarkably stable component in the form of substantial differences between birth cohorts that have persisted throughout the tumultuous economic ups and downs that characterized this era. And—of crucial significance here— this stability is structured in a way that is incompatible with a Black and White model. It can be explained only by a Latent Attitude model because the respective birth cohorts manifest very different positions throughout the eighteen-year period. Among the oldest cohort, there is a huge preponderance of Materialist responses over Postmaterialist ones; among the youngest cohort, the two types are about equally numerous. These distinctive skews could not result if more than a small minority were answering at random; and they can not be attributed to methods effects, since both young and old were asked the same questions in the same format. Such a pattern could result only from relatively stable long-term attitudinal pre-dispositions *within* all or most of the respondents themselves.

Examining the panel survey response to these items might lead one to grossly underestimate this underlying stability, however, for the turnover is as high as that found with the items used to illustrate the Black and White model. We have no alternative but to turn to a Latent Attitude model. When we do so, LISREL analysis yields results similar to those Jackson and others have obtained with data from the 1956–1960 panel. Though there is substantial measurement error at any given time, most respondents have underlying preferences that remain stable throughout the seven-year period of our longest panel.

The problem is not nonattitudes so much as measurement error. Accordingly, using better measurement techniques, we find much greater stability. This point can be made more directly, even without going into the complexities of LISREL. In addition to the simple and widely used four-item battery designed to measure Materialist/Postmaterialist value priorities, a broader-based, twelve-item battery was also developed in 1973 and has been used in several surveys since that time. As one would expect, twelve items enable us to tap the underlying attitudinal dimension more accurately than is possible with four items. Consequently the twelve-item index consistently shows greater stability over time and greater constraint with other attitudes than does the four-item index. Similarly, when we move from the public opinion survey situation to a classroom setting, in which the context tends to stimulate higher levels of interest in the task of articulating one's values, and provides a more leisurely setting in which to do so, we find substantially higher levels of stability—even among respondents with relatively modest educational levels.

Let us now examine the empirical evidence on each of these points, starting with a brief review of the implications of the cohort analysis presented in the preceding chapter. We will compare these results with findings from two wave panel surveys carried out in the United States, West Germany, and the Netherlands in 1974 and 1980–1981 and (more briefly) with results from other panel surveys.

EVIDENCE OF UNDERLYING STABILITY IN MASS BELIEF SYSTEMS

The theoretical framework underlying the cohort analysis presented in chapter 2 implies that there has been a gradual intergenerational change in the relative emphasis placed on certain basic goals—a shift from Materialist toward Postmaterialist values. If intergenerational change can be demonstrated, it reflects the persisting effects of distinctive cohort experiences that may have taken place as much as four or five decades ago, and constitutes strong evidence that mass publics have enduring sociopolitical preferences.

In spite of short-term fluctuations, throughout the eighteen-year period from 1970 to 1988, the older birth cohorts consistently manifest value priorities that are much more Materialistic than those of the younger cohorts. These findings are incompatible with the implications of the Black and White model. Although (as we will see shortly) the stability correlations of our values index are no higher than that of the item used in Converse's classic study, the empirical pattern observed here could not possibly result from a situation in which a majority of the respondents were giving random answers. Literally random answering would result in equiprobable response distributions, producing a 50-50 split when there are two alternatives. If as much as 80 percent of the public were giving random answers, they would show a 40-40 split; and even if all of the remaining 20 percent chose the same option (which is highly unlikely), the most extreme skew possible would be a 60-40 split. In the present case, pure random answering would produce equal numbers of Materialists and Postmaterialists— and, indeed, among our youngest cohorts, Postmaterialists are almost as numerous as Materialists. But among the cohort born before 1906, the situation is drastically different. In many countries, well over 50 percent of the sample fall into the pure Materialist category, while only about 4 percent give Postmaterialist responses—though by purely random processes, 16.7 percent would fall into the latter category. The results indicate that no more than 25 percent of the cohort could be giving random answers, even if we assume that *none* of the observed Postmaterialist responses among this oldest cohort reflects genuine preferences within the respondent.

In itself, this point is not entirely new. Years ago, Converse (1974) and Pierce and Rose (1974) had agreed that some observed response patterns could not be attributed to *equiprobable* random answering (such as would result from rolling unloaded dice); the distributions sometimes displayed skews that could only result from random answering that was *not* equiprobable (such as would result from rolling loaded dice).

But a crucial question could not be resolved in this debate, and remained to be answered: What makes the dice loaded?

Pierce and Rose attributed the observed deviations from equiprobable random answering to unmeasured attitudinal predispositions, arguing that the low stability correlations did not result from nonattitudes, but from imperfect measurement of them. Converse, on the other hand, attributed the skew to methods effects and pointed out that if the deviations from equiprobable distributions were due to response set or other artifacts of questionnaire design, rather than to underlying preferences within the respondent, then his thesis that a majority of the public had no real attitude (or "nonattitudes") could still apply.

On this point, our cohort analysis provides decisive evidence. Our older cohorts display skews that deviate enormously from an equiprobable distribution; and it is impossible to attribute these deviations from pure randomness to any sort of methods effect, for both young and old cohorts were asked precisely the same questions, in the same format, at the same time— and they show drastically different distributions. The differences in responses reflect differences in the respondents, not something in the measuring instrument.

Our evidence is incompatible with Converse's interpretation. The results *must* be due to unmeasured attitudinal predispositions. Moreover, the differences in the underlying attitudes of old and young are remarkably enduring. Already, we have direct measurements indicating that they have persisted throughout a period of eighteen years. These findings are derived from a theoretical framework implying that the generational differences can be traced to the persisting impact of formative experiences that took place as much as fifty years ago. In short, the evidence indicates that underlying the relative fluidity of given attitudinal indicators, the sociopolitical orientations of Western publics have components of remarkably great stability.

This stability is by no means limited to the Materialist/Postmaterialist dimension. One of the most influential and widely recognized efforts to analyze human values by means of survey methodology has been the work of Rokeach (1968, 1973, 1974). The Rokeach terminal values survey (Rokeach 1974) was included in both waves of our American panel survey, enabling us to compare these findings with results from a battery designed to measure the entire spectrum of human values.

Though our items refer to sociopolitical priorities, while Rokeach's items generally have personal referents, the stability of the respective Rokeach items varies in the same fashion as does that of the Inglehart items. Stability coefficients for the eighteen items in the Rokeach battery, together with the Materialist/Postmaterialist index, are shown in Table 3-1.

As Table 3-1 demonstrates, Materialist/Postmaterialist values show a substantially lower stability than does the priority respondents give to "salvation." Fully 25 percent of the American panel ranked "salvation" first among the eighteen terminal values in 1974; and of those who did so, 69 percent ranked it first of the eighteen items in 1981 as well. Conversely, a relatively large share of the sample (almost 15 percent) ranked "salvation" last in 1974; and 54 percent of those who did so, ranked it last again in 1981. If one believes in religious salvation, it is the most important thing in the world—one is apt to think about it often, pray, attend church regularly, and consistently give it a very high priority. If one does *not* believe,

TABLE 3-1. STABILITY OF VALUES FROM 1974 TO 1981 AMONG AMERICAN PUBLIC

Value	r^a
Salvation (saved, eternal life)	.68
A comfortable life (a prosperous life)	.44
Mature love (sexual and spiritual intimacy)	.41
National security (protection from attack)	.41
Materialist/Postmaterialist values	.39
A world of beauty (beauty of nature and the arts)	.39
Inner harmony (freedom from inner conflict)	.38
Self-respect (self-esteem)	.36
Equality (brotherhood, equal opportunity for all)	.36
Family security (taking care of loved ones)	.35
An exciting life (a stimulating, active life)	.34
Pleasure (an enjoyable, leisurely life)	.34
Social recognition (respect, admiration)	.32
Happiness (contentment)	.30
Freedom (independence, free choice)	.29
True friendship (close companionship)	.29
A world at peace (free of war and conflict)	.28
Wisdom (a mature understanding of life)	.26
A sense of accomplishment (lasting accomplishment)	.26

Source: Two-wave panel survey of American public carried out in Summer 1974 and Summer 1981 by Survey Research Center, University of Michigan.
Note: Panel N = 933. Fieldwork and sampling are described in *Political Action* codebook.
[a]Product-moment correlations between 1974 and 1981 rankings.

it seems altogether useless. Thus, this basic component of one's religious outlook is by far the most stable of Rokeach's eighteen terminal values.

But the other Rokeach values items all have stability coefficients in the same ballpark as our Materialist/Postmaterialist values index. Indeed, the latter ranks higher than fourteen of the eighteen terminal values. This does not mean that the Inglehart battery is "better" than most items in the Rokeach battery. On the contrary, it is clear that our own values index shows greater stability over time than do most of the Rokeach terminal values simply because it is based on multiple indicators and therefore measures the underlying dimension more accurately than any single item does. The stability across time of our individual *items* is no greater than that found for most of Rokeach's items (and, of course, much lower than that of "salvation"). The problem is not that stable values do not exist, but that it is difficult to measure them. As our measurement techniques improve, stability rises.

Deciding what one's basic priorities in life are is a demanding task for which the only reward is the intrinsic interest of the task itself. Among those who are not interested (at least not at the time of the given survey), some respondents apparently avoid a difficult and unfamiliar job by giving hasty and more or less "random" answers. This process seems to apply to the Rokeach battery as well as to the Inglehart battery. But despite the relatively modest *individual level* stability found with most of the Rokeach

TABLE 3-2.   RANKING OF PERSONAL VALUES AMONG AMERICAN PUBLIC,
1968 - 1981

	Rank			
Value	*1968*	*1971*	*1974*	*1981*
A world at peace (free of war and conflict)	1	1	2	2
Family security (taking care of loved ones)	2	2	1	1
Freedom (independence, free choice)	3	3	3	3
Happiness (contentedness)	4	6	5	5
Self-respect (self-esteem)	5	5	4	4
Wisdom (a mature understanding of life)	6	7	6	6
Equality (brotherhood, equal opportunity for all)	7	4	12	12
Salvation (saved, eternal life)	8	9	10	9
A comfortable life (a prosperous life)	9	13	8	8
A sense of accomplishment (lasting contribution)	10	11	7	7
True friendship (close companionship)	11	10	9	10
National security (protection from attack)	12	8	13	11
Inner harmony (freedom from inner conflict)	13	12	11	13
Mature love (sexual and spiritual intimacy)	14	14	14	14
A world of beauty (beauty of nature and the arts)	15	15	15	16
Social recognition (respect, admiration)	16	17	18	18
Pleasure (an enjoyable, leisurely life)	17	16	16	17
An exciting life (a stimulating, active life)	18	18	17	15

Sources: Representative national samples interviewed by the National
Opinion Research Center, University of Chicago, in 1968 and 1971 (see
Rokeach 1974); and by the Survey Research Center, University of
Michigan, in 1974 and 1981.

items, we believe that they, too, tap basic and deep-rooted values among
the American public. If so, we should find considerable aggregate stability
in the aggregate rankings of these variables.

We can test this expectation against time series data extending over a
thirteen-year period, for the Rokeach terminal values survey has been administered to representative national samples of the American public in
1968, 1971, 1974, and 1981. The overall rankings obtained in each year
are shown in Table 3-2.

The stability we observe is absolutely phenomenal. The six items that
were ranked highest in 1981 are *identical* with the six items ranked highest
in 1968; and—amazing as it may seem in view of the social upheavals that
took place in this era—not one of the six items varies by more than one
rank from its 1981 position in any of the three previous surveys extending
across thirteen years. The stability of the six lowest-ranking items is almost
equally impressive. The six lowest items in 1981 are identical with the six
lowest items in 1968, and most of them do not vary by more than one rank
from their 1981 positions in any of the three previous surveys. The public's
evaluation of an "exciting life" is relatively volatile, rising from eighteenth place in 1968 to fifteenth place in 1981. By most standards, this
would be considered an extremely small change. In the present context, it
is an exceptionally *large* one. Though the middle six items show greater
volatility than the top six or bottom six items, they remain within the mid-

dle zone almost without exception. The overall stability of the Rokeach rankings is extremely impressive. To attribute this stability to sheer chance would strain credulity beyond the breaking point. Despite their modest reliability coefficients, the conclusion is inescapable that the Rokeach items tap orientations that are very stably anchored among the public.

Here again, as with the Materialist/Postmaterialist values items, the distributions are incompatible with the assumption that most of the public is giving random answers. By random processes, each of the eighteen goals would be given top priority (or lowest priority) by about 5.5 percent of the sample. But in fact, both "a world at peace" and "family security" consistently get chosen for top priority by about four times as many people as would do so at random. At the other end of the scale, the deviations from a random model are even more extreme: These two items *combined* are ranked last by less than 1 percent. There is no way in which this could occur if a majority of the sample were answering at random. Even if only 10 percent of the sample were answering randomly, these goals would be ranked last by larger numbers than those we actually observe. Again, it would be extremely difficult to attribute these deviations from equiprobability to methods effects. The respondents chose each value from a pool of items printed on adhesive labels, and gave it a unique ranking. The usual forms of response set—the tendency to agree, or to disagree, or to give the same answer as one gave to the last question—do not apply here (as is also true with the Materialist/Postmaterialist battery). Despite the modest stability correlations, the data manifest a degree of skewed stability that is incompatible with the assumption that nonattitudes are present among more than a small fraction of the sample.

Much of the observed individual level instability in values apparently reflects error in measurement, rather than the absence of preferences. Since our results are generally contaminated by random answering, the responses to any one item provide an imperfect indicator of the respondent's underlying predispositions. Consequently, our multi-item values index shows greater stability over time than any of its constituent items, because it provides a more accurate measure of the underlying concept. And it follows that a still more accurate measure of the Materialist/Postmaterialist dimension should show still higher stability.

Let us try to obtain a more accurate measurement of this dimension. The values index used in our analysis thus far simply consists of the unweighted sum of all Postmaterialist items given top priority. This procedure has the virtue of simplicity: It is intuitively clear what a given score means.

A better measurement can be obtained by using LISREL analysis—a structural equation technique that not only weights indicators but also estimates the amount of measurement error present in given indicators and

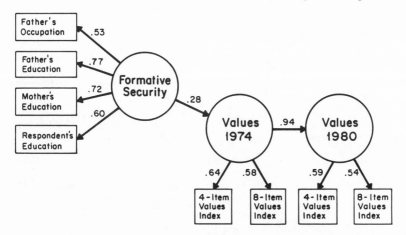

FIGURE 3-2. Value stability in three-nation sample: LISREL model.
$N = 1,850$; T-value for values, 1980 on values, 1974 = 6.29, $P < .0001$.
Adjusted goodness of fit index = .91. Based on data from the Political Action panel surveys. Data, codebooks, and sampling information for these surveys are available from the ICPSR survey data archive. For further information, see Barnes, Kaase, et al. 1979; and Jennings and Van Deth 1989.

controls for correlated error terms. A cross-national panel survey of mass political action has been carried out in the Netherlands, the United States, and West Germany, with a first wave in 1974 (see Barnes, Kaase et al. 1974) and a second wave in 1980–1981 (see Jennings and Van Deth n.d.). A LISREL analysis of the combined data from these surveys produces the results shown in Figure 3-2 (country by country analyses appear below). In this model, rankings of the various items in the original four-item Materialist/Postmaterialist battery are used to construct an additive index, with scores ranging from a minimum for the pure Materialist type to a maximum for the pure Postmaterialist type. The eight newer items were asked as a separate battery in these panel surveys so that we could construct a second, independent Materialist/Postmaterialist index from these responses. Each of these two indices is treated as an indicator of the latent variable "Materialist/Postmaterialist values" for the given year in which the items were administered. This procedure avoids potential problems arising from the fact that, *within* each of these two batteries, the respondent's choice of any one goal is not independent of the choice of another goal. In each of the three countries for which we have panel data, the two values indicators show substantial correlations with the underlying value dimension at each of the two time points where measurements were carried out; these correlations are generally around the .5 level. Respondents' values in 1974 are treated as an independent variable that accounts for their values in 1981.

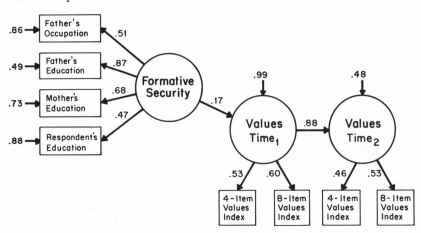

FIGURE 3-3. Value stability in the United States: LISREL model. $N = 660$; T-value for values, 1981 on values, 1974 $= 6.36, p < .0001$. Adjusted goodness of fit index $= .94$.

The underlying values dimension has a remarkably high degree of stability across time. In this three-nation sample, our panel respondents' latent value priorities in 1974 show a .94 coefficient with their values in 1981. This indicates that fully 88 percent of the variance in our respondents' values in 1981 can be attributed to the values these same individuals held in 1974. The social background of our respondents is also taken into account, as an influence on their values (in keeping with the formative security hypotheses discussed below). The occupational level and educational level of one's father together with the educational level of one's mother and one's own education are used as indicators of "formative security." One's parents' educational level tends to be the strongest predictor of this latent variable—and formative security does, indeed, have a significant effect on one's value priorities, with the offspring of better-educated parents generally being more Postmaterialist than the progeny of less educated (and less prosperous) parents. The impact of formative security on one's values in the 1980s, however, seems to work almost entirely through its impact on the values one had in the 1970s. It is not one's current socioeconomic status, so much as one's *early* socioeconomic status (which, in turn, reflects that of one's parents) that seems to influence whether one has Materialist or Postmaterialist priorities.

Figure 3-3 shows the results from a separate analysis of the American panel data, for which the first wave of interviews was carried out in 1974 and the second in 1981. The American results closely resemble those for the other two countries, except that the impact of formative security is less important for the American respondents than for the Dutch and West Ger-

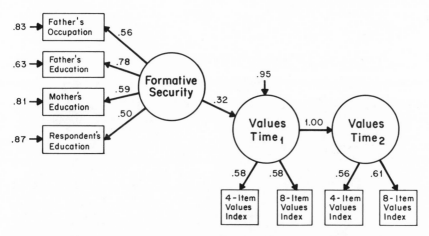

FIGURE 3-4. Value stability in the Netherlands: LISREL model. $N = 500$; T-value for values, 1980 on values, 1974 $= 7.53$, $p < .0001$. Adjusted goodness of fit index $= .94$.

man respondents (shown in Figures 3-4 and 3-5, respectively). This probably reflects the fact that there is greater variability on this dimension in Western Europe than in the United States. Among the European cohorts who lived through World War II, those who experienced low levels of security during their formative years may have been living at the borderline of physical survival. The range of variation has been less extreme on the American scene in modern times.

The Dutch data (see Figure 3-4) show a remarkably high continuity coefficient between values in 1974 and values in 1980; if we were to take it at face value, it would mean that *all* of the variation in values in 1980 can be attributed to variation in 1974. Human beings are not that consistent, and we assume that this reflects imperfect estimation to some degree—but it certainly indicates a high degree of stability in the latent variable. The West German data (see Figure 3-5) show a coefficient of .72, which is still impressive stability, especially when we consider the fact that this is measured over a period of six years. This finding replicates results obtained by Dalton (1981) in analyzing a two-wave German panel survey. Using methods basically similar to ours, Dalton found a .70 correlation between Materialist/Postmaterialist values among German youth in 1976 and in 1979. The fact that we obtain an even *higher* correlation in a panel survey extending over a much longer period (six years, rather than three) may reflect the fact that we used a somewhat different values battery and a different population than did Dalton. But it is also an indication of how surprisingly little these correlations decline over time.

Jagodzinski (1984) asserts that the high stability of the underlying values

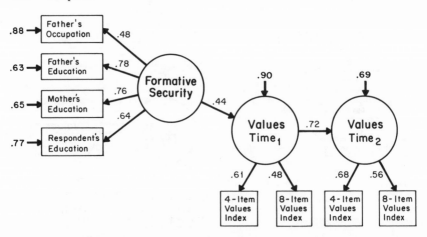

FIGURE 3-5. Value stability in West Germany: LISREL model. $N = 690$; T-value for values, 1980 on values, 1974 $= 6.08, p < .0001$. Adjusted goodness of fit index $= .94$.

found by Dalton (1981) should be discounted because the LISREL technique is unreliable. As evidence, Jagodzinski demonstrates that with LISREL it is possible to obtain high stability coefficients from random data. This, of course, is possible—any technique can be misused. Similarly, one can obtain large but statistically meaningless percentage differences with small samples of survey data. But, in both cases, statistical significance tests enable one to estimate the finding's reliability. Significance tests are a standard feature of the LISREL output, and they provide an immediate indication of whether the results are significant or meaningless. Jagodzinski does not report the standard errors of the stability coefficients from his random data, but they can be calculated and they are not statistically significant at even a modest level. Significance tests for the stability coefficients in our LISREL analyses are reported in Figures 3-3, 3-4, 3-5, and 3-6. In each case, our findings of high value stability over a period of several years are statistically significant at an extremely high level. Similarly, after extensive experimentation with a number of different LISREL models, DeGraaf, Hagenaars, and Luijkx (1987) conclude that Materialist/Postmaterialist values manifest a high degree of stability, as measured by virtually any reasonable model. Finally, Van Deth (n.d.) has analyzed the results of a three-wave panel carried out in the Netherlands in 1974, 1980, and 1985. Though skeptical of the stability of Materialist/Postmaterialist values in earlier work (see Van Deth 1983a), the results of LISREL analysis in this subsequent investigation lead him to conclude that the underlying values are extremely stable.

The panels we have been analyzing span as much as seven years, an

Expected correlations for four-item index
(assuming constant rate of decay in stability of latent variable)

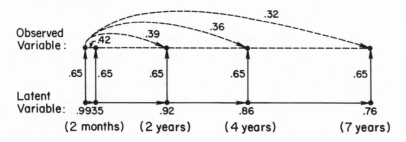

Observed Correlations:

4-item index	.53	.35	.28	.32
12-item index	.82	–	–	.39

FIGURE 3-6. Latent Attitudes model's expected stability of Materialist/ Postmaterialist values over various time intervals and obseved stability over the same intervals. Sources for 2 months—University of Michigan student panel, 1984; 2 years—Dearborn panel, Stockton & Wayman, 1974–1976; 4 years—National Election Study panel, 1972–1976; 7 years—Political Action panel, 1974–1981.

exceptionally long period. The questions used to measure Materialist/Post-materialist priorities have also been asked in a number of other American panels, over shorter periods of time. Let us compare the results.

Figure 3-6 shows the expected and empirically observed correlations between value priorities measured in panels ranging from two months to seven years. The expected values are derived by working backward from the values obtained in the seven-year panel, which shows a continuity correlation in the observed variable of .32 (as measured by the four-item index) and a continuity correlation in the latent variable of .76 (as estimated by LISREL). Given these parameters, a Latent Attitude model implies that we should find a modest but perceptible decline in the continuity correlations over various periods of time, as indicated in Figure 3-1. A Markov Chain model, of course, implies a much more rapid decline in the correlations for the observed variable: If the observed correlation over two months were .42, it would have declined to little more than 0 within less than a year. A Black and White model, on the other hand, implies no decline at all: If the correlation over seven years were .32, it would have been .32 over two months or two decades.

The empirically observed correlations fit a Latent Attitude model much better than they fit either of the other two models. Although they are based on different samples instead of one continuous panel, the figures are in the right ballpark. What we find is a pattern of gradual decay in the continuity correlations.

Surprisingly, however, the four-item index shows a weaker correlation over four years than over seven years. This is a result that none of the models would have predicted. When we examine the details more closely, it seems that this deviation from logical expectations may reflect the problems of time and motivation mentioned above. The four-year panel examined here was carried out in 1972 and 1976. In 1972, these questions appeared fairly early in the interview; but in 1976, they were asked at the very end of a very long interview, coming up after the respondent had already answered more than 400 questions, in an interview that by then had lasted, on the average, about an hour and fifteen minutes. By this point, respondent fatigue may have become an important factor, making some respondents eager to get the interview finished. If so, it would tend to increase the rate of random answering. In the seven-year panel, on the other hand, these questions were asked about seven or eight minutes into the interview, in both 1974 and 1981. Here, respondent fatigue would be much less important, resulting in less measurement error, and thus the phenomenon we observe: a higher stability coefficient over seven years than that observed over four years. Unintentionally, this natural experiment illustrates how heavily measurement error can influence the apparent stability of values and attitudes.

Conversely, the stability coefficient observed in the two-month panel is somewhat above the expected value. This might reflect the fact that here we are dealing with a student sample, instead of a cross-section of the population, as in the other panels. Those with higher educational levels are more likely to discuss politics than those with less education, and consequently are likelier to come to the interview with an answer already articulated that reflects their underlying preferences. But it might also reflect the fact that the two-month panel was carried out in a classroom situation, rather than under typical survey fieldwork conditions. In the classroom situation, the respondents carry out their rankings in a context that reinforces the idea that the task is important, and worth doing carefully. Moreover, the task is performed in a relatively leisurely setting; unlike most other survey respondents, the students are not stealing the time from other activities. Thus, a test-retest experiment carried out in a classroom situation may provide a stronger motivation to answer thoughtfully, with more leisure and fewer distractions present than is true in the usual field interview situation. These factors may at least partially account for the markedly higher stability of results obtained in the classroom situation.

The difference does *not* seem to solely result from the fact that one is dealing with a more highly educated population—for Rokeach (1973) reports test-retest coefficients from samples of seventh- and eighth-grade students that are almost as high as those found among college students. The median test-retest reliabilities reported for the eighteen Rokeach terminal values items, administered to samples of seventh- and eighth-grade students, were about .63 over a three-week period. For college students, they were .78 over three weeks, and (again) .78 over two months (Rokeach, 1973, 58). Thus far, little research has compared the stability and constraint of the responses elicited in experimental situations with the stability and constraint obtained in survey situations. The available evidence suggests that one can obtain significantly higher levels of stability and constraint under experimental conditions, even when the questions and type of respondents are held constant.

If the apparent instability of survey orientations results, in part, from lack of motivation and previous practice in making the relevant linkages between underlying preferences and articulated opinions, we would expect to find higher stability of values among the more educated, and those most interested in societal problems. We do. In the American seven-year panel, our values index shows stability coefficients of .33 for those who say they are not interested in politics, and .40 for those who are very interested. Stability is also greater among the more educated: Among those with an elementary school education the coefficient is .19; for those who attended college it is .46. Van Deth (1983a) reports similar findings from a Dutch panel study of these values.

Our panel surveys provide yet another indication that the apparent instability of mass orientations is due to measurement problems, rather than to nonattitudes. In two of these surveys, the twelve-item Materialist/Postmaterialist values battery was included, as well as the four-item battery (which is one of its components). The broader-based index shows significantly greater stability over both short and long periods of time, presumably because it measures the underlying orientation with greater accuracy. These findings are consistent with previous results, which demonstrated that the twelve-item index also manifests greater constraint with other attitudes than does the four-item index (Inglehart 1977); both stability and constraint rise as one obtains greater accuracy of measurement.

CONCLUSION

Converse's basic insight still stands. There is a significant random component, which must be recognized and dealt with, in survey research. But the Black and White model, with its implications of widespread nonattitudes, is no longer tenable, for the orientations of Western publics show impressive durability, based on latent attitudes that prove to be much more stable than given survey indicators might seem to suggest. These latent attitudes can now be estimated relatively accurately through statistical techniques, such as LISREL, and the results undermine the credibility of a Black and White model. Interestingly, in a recent analysis of the persistence of political party identification, Converse himself applies a Latent Attitude model (Converse and Markus 1979).

Moreover, the stability of these latent attitudes does not exist only in the estimates of structural equation models. Its effects are visible to the naked eye, when we examine certain kinds of aggregate survey results. Throughout Western society, younger birth cohorts are a great deal more likely than older cohorts to emphasize Postmaterialist values. Direct evidence demonstrates that these differences persisted throughout the period from 1970 to 1988. And cohort analysis indicates that they reflect not life cycle effects but *intergenerational* differences. This fact, combined with evidence presented in chapter 5, strongly suggests that they reflect the persisting impact of distinctive formative experiences that (in the case of the oldest cohort) took place as much as fifty years ago. Similarly, responses to the Rokeach terminal values battery show modest individual level stability, together with an almost incredibly high aggregate stability, skewed in ways incompatible with assumptions that random answers are being given by anything more than a small fraction of the respondents.

The conclusion seems inescapable: Mass publics have highly stable sociopolitical orientations, which survey indicators measure imperfectly. We seem to be dealing with two levels of orientations, in which the responses articulated to given questions do not have a one-to-one relationship with the relevant underlying affective orientations. If they have not sorted out these linkages prior to the survey, some respondents may give random answers to given questions, especially if they are answering a large volume of questions in a limited time.

If the correlation between observed survey response and underlying attitude is .7 (roughly the level that applies to the data examined here), then the *observed* correlation between responses to two such items will be less than half as strong as the correlation between the underlying attitudes. This fact helps explain the pervasive finding that with survey data, relatively "strong" correlations between attitudes generally range from about .3 to .45. With aggregate statistical data, the "strong" correlations range from about .6 to .9, with the result that models based on economic indicators tend to explain about four times as much variance as those based on survey data. But when one aggregates survey data to the level of the cohort, as was done above (cf. Dalton 1977; Inglehart 1979a) or to the level of a given party's electorate (see chapter 9), one explains as large a percentage of the variance as one does with economic indicators; at the aggregate level, the random noise in survey data cancels itself out.

Thus, in some respects, the aggregate results convey a more accurate view of the orientations of individuals than individual level survey data do. Only by combining insights from the two perspectives can one obtain the full picture, for—especially when dealing with topics on which the respondent has not articulated a position before the interview takes place—survey research systematically tends to underestimate both stability and constraint in mass attitudes.

CHAPTER 4

Structure in Mass Value Systems:
The Materialist/Postmaterialist
Dimension

INTRODUCTION

Any effort to measure the value priorities of mass publics by means of survey research must be approached with modest expectations. One's basic values are a relatively central, deep-rooted, and early-instilled part of one's outlook on life. Ideally, one would wish to explore them through a series of depth interviews extending over several months, rather than by a brief survey interview, which necessarily tends to elicit responses off the top of one's head.

When the interviewer knocks at the door, many people may not have sorted out what is most important to them in life—and even if they have, they may have difficulty in articulating their basic values quickly, to a person they have never met before. Thus, we are unlikely to observe a well-articulated ideological structure among mass publics. As we saw in the previous chapter, low correlations between items and low stability over time seem inherent in survey research—not necessarily because people do not have real attitudes, but partly because survey research must contend with a relatively high component of error in measurement. Lane (1962) has demonstrated that ordinary citizens *do* seem capable of articulating a coherent political outlook in a series of leisurely depth interviews. Unfortunately, the cost of this approach is prohibitive for present purposes.

The public opinion survey is not the ideal instrument with which to study basic attitudes and values, but it has certain advantages. It can provide a vastly larger number of cases than one could obtain with depth interviews, and this is essential if we hope to make reliable intergenerational comparisons or control for social background factors. Furthermore, the mass survey can provide representative national samples—something extremely useful if one wishes to know what is happening to a society as a whole or to analyze phenomena in cross-national perspective. Finally, the public opinion survey has proven to be quite accurate for many purposes. There may be a dismaying amount of fluctuation at the individual level, but the overall distribution of responses is often remarkably reliable. Surveys of voting intentions do provide accurate predictions of the actual election results; data on consumer attitudes do help predict how the economy is going to behave. The random error inherent in survey research tends to cancel itself out in large samples, especially if one uses multi-item indicators rather than relying on responses to a single question. Survey research is not a perfect instrument, but used skillfully it can be one of the most powerful tools available to social science.

The four-item index of Materialist/Postmaterialist values discussed in the preceding chapters provides a measure of something pervasive and enduring in one's outlook. But we must not overlook this index's shortcomings. The most serious one is the simple fact that it is based on only four items. This means that it may be excessively sensitive to short-term forces. For example, one item in the index concerns rising prices. Western countries have experienced extraordinary fluctuations in inflation in recent years. Our theory implies that the proportion of respondents giving high priority to ''fighting rising prices'' would increase in times of high inflation—not as the result of fundamental value change, but simply because this was a serious current problem. This type of instability probably would be much greater if we simply asked the respondents to rate the importance of rising prices by itself; but in our index, one's choice of this item is constrained by the fact that it must be ranked against other desired goals. Almost everyone was aware that rising prices were a more important problem in 1976 or 1981 than in 1970; but by no means all of those who ranked ''freedom of speech'' above ''rising prices'' in 1970 would be willing to change this ranking simply because inflation got worse. The four items provide a better measure than one, but a more broadly based index would spread the risk over a still larger number of items, making it less likely that an individual's score would be unduly distorted by any particular recent event. Furthermore, a broader-based index would help reduce the amount of error in measurement. In reply to survey questions, many respondents give superficial answers, more or less ''off the top of their heads.'' With a single item, it is impossible to distinguish between those whose answers reflect a genuine attitude and those whose responses are essentially meaningless. But a set of consistent responses to a large series of related questions usually *does* reflect a genuine underlying preference.

DIMENSIONAL ANALYSIS OF
MATERIALIST/POSTMATERIALIST VALUES

In our 1973 surveys, we developed a broader indicator of an individual's value priorities. Analysis of the results should give us a more reliable measure of whether value change is taking place. It also provides a more detailed picture of the respective worldviews of the Materialist and Postmaterialist types. In this chapter, we will analyze the structure of responses to this larger battery of items among the publics of both Western and non-Western societies. A careful examination of the response patterns in given societies can provide a much clearer sense of the underlying worldviews of our respondents. As we will see, there are particularly significant differences between the ways that Western and non-Western publics respond to the same battery of questions.

This larger battery included the four items from the original value priorities index, but they were supplemented with eight additional goals. The following questions were asked:

There is a lot of talk these days about what the aims of this country should be for the next ten years. (HAND RESPONDENT CARD A.) On this card are listed some of the goals which different people would give top priority. Would you please say which one of these you, yourself, consider most important?

CARD A
A. Maintaining a high rate of economic growth.
B. Making sure that this country has strong defense forces.
C. Seeing that the people have more say in how things get decided at work and in their communities.
D. Trying to make our cities and countryside more beautiful.

And which would be the next most important?

(HAND RESPONDENT CARD B.) If you had to choose, which one of the things on this card would you say is most desirable?

CARD B
E. Maintaining order in the nation.
F. Giving the people more say in important government decisions.
G. Fighting rising prices.
H. Protecting freedom of speech.

And what would be your second choice?

Here is another list. (HAND RESPONDENT CARD C.) In your opinion, which one of these is most important?

CARD C
I. Maintain a stable economy.
J. Progress toward a less impersonal, more humane society.
K. The fight against crime.
L. Progress toward a society where ideas are more important than money.

What comes next?

Now would you look again at all of the goals listed on these three cards together and tell me which one you consider the most desirable of all? Just read off the one you choose.
And which is the next most desirable?
And which one of all the aims on these cards is least important from your point of view?

This series of questions enabled us to obtain relative rankings for twelve important goals. The introductory sentences placed the questions in a long-term time framework, and the choices deal with broad societal goals rather than the immediate needs of the respondent; we wanted to tap long-term preoccupations, not one's response to the immediate situation. These twelve options were designed to explore Maslow's (1954) hierarchy of needs. Figure 4-1 indicates the basic need that each item was intended to elicit. Six items were intended to emphasize the physiological needs, "rising prices," "economic growth," and "stable economy" being designed to tap emphasis on economic security and "maintain order," "fight crime," and "strong defense forces" designed to tap emphasis on physical security. While these two types of needs are not identical, both are Materialist in that they are directly related to physiological survival. We hypothesized that they would tend to go together, with only those who feel secure about the satisfaction of both types of needs being likely to give top priority to belonging, self-expression, and intellectual and esthetic satisfaction—needs the remaining items were designed to tap. The remaining six items were designed to tap various Postmaterialist needs. We view the latter needs as potentially universal: Every human being has a need for esteem and aesthetic satisfaction, and an inherent intellectual curiosity. Thus one finds art and music and other products of the search for beauty in all societies, and one finds magic, religion, myths, or philosophy, reflecting the desire to understand and interpret the meaning of life in even the poorest societies. Hungry people may not give top priority to esthetic and intellectual concerns, but given some respite from the struggle for survival, people will act on these needs unless circumstances force them to stifle them. Put another way, "Man does not live by bread alone," particularly when he has plenty of bread. Our expectation, therefore, is that emphasis on the six Materialist items will tend to form one cluster, with the Postmaterialist items in another distinct cluster.

Any culture is multidimensional. Change can occur in sexual norms, tastes in food, or music, political party preferences, trust in government, religious outlook, and numerous other aspects of life. The question is not whether the Materialist/Postmaterialist dimension is the only dimension along which change can occur, but whether such a dimension exists, and,

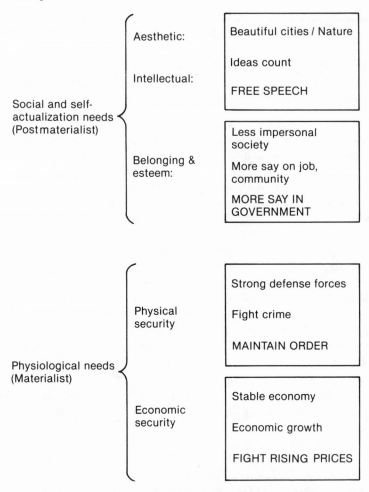

FIGURE 4-1. Items used in the twelve-item battery and needs they were intended to tap. Capital letters indicate items from the original four-item index. Adapted from Inglehart 1977, 42.

if so, whether significant change has been taking place in the predicted direction.

Our theoretical framework implies that emphasis on economic security and on physical security will tend to go together—and that those who feel insecure about these physiological needs have a fundamentally different outlook and political behavior from those who feel secure about them. The latter are likely to give top priority to nonmaterial goals, such as self-expression, belonging, and intellectual or esthetic satisfaction.

The reasons why economic and physical security were expected to go together, very briefly, are as follows: (1) From a macrosocietal perspective, war tends to produce both economic and physical insecurity—both hunger and loss of life. Hence, those generations that have experienced war are likely to feel less secure about both. (2) From a microsocietal perspective, poor individuals tend to be exposed to both economic and physical insecurity—both poverty and relatively high crime rates. The more affluent strata have resources that shield them, to some extent, from both.

Satisfaction of the physiological needs, I argue, leads to growing emphasis on nonphysiological, or Postmaterialist, goals. A large share of the public in Western societies have been socialized in an environment that provides an unprecedentedly secure prospect that the physiological needs will be met. Consequently, Western publics' responses should tend to polarize along a Materialist/Postmaterialist dimension, with some individuals consistently emphasizing Materialist goals, while others tend to give priority to Postmaterialist goals.

In order to test this hypothesis, we performed principal components analyses of the rankings of these goals in each of the ten countries surveyed in 1973. For this analysis, each item was recoded as a separate variable with codes ranging from 1 to 6. If the given item was chosen as the "most desirable" among the entire set of twelve items, it was coded as 1; if it ranked second overall, it was coded as 2; if it ranked last overall, it was coded as 6. If chosen first among its set of four items (but not first or second overall) it was coded as 3; if ranked second in its set of four, it was coded 4. Items not singled out for either high or low rankings were coded as 5. Our variables are based on relative rankings, not absolute scores. This is crucial to operationalizing our hypothesis, but it means that the items are not independent, which would make factor analysis inapplicable with a small pool of items. With only two items, for example, the rank of the first item determines the rank of the second, automatically generating a -1.0 correlation between them. With three items, one would expect negative correlations of about .5. With a pool of four items, random answering would generate negative correlations of about .3 among all four items, so that only two of them could load on the first factor. With a pool of twelve items, the degree to which one item's rank determines that of another, becomes minor. There is still some tendency for all of the items to be negatively correlated, which tends to spread the items over several dimensions. But, as our empirical results show, this effect is dominated by a stronger tendency for Materialist items to be chosen together, on one hand, and Postmaterialist items to be chosen together, on the other. The loadings on the first factor in each country are shown in Table 4-1.

The results show a cross-national consistency that is almost breathtak-

TABLE 4-1. THE MATERIALIST/POSTMATERIALIST FACTOR IN TEN COUNTRIES, 1973
(Loadings of value priorities items on first factor)

	Loading				
Goal	France	West Germany	United States	Bel- gium	Luxem- bourg
More say on job	.636	.562	.451	.472	.659
Less impersonal society	.592	.675	.627	.532	.558
Ideas count	.499	.498	.508	.562	.476
More say in government	.400	.483	.423	.478	.434
Freedom of speech	.486	.575	.409	.564	.527
More beautiful cities	.087	.092	.278	.040	-.089
Fight rising prices	-.305	-.440	-.334	-.511	-.342
Strong defense forces	-.498	-.359	-.464	-.324	-.322
Economic growth	-.412	-.398	-.397	-.297	-.497
Fight crime	-.457	-.418	-.484	-.417	-.347
Stable economy	-.441	-.451	-.435	-.407	-.345
Maintain order	-.558	-.376	-.491	-.497	-.488
Percent of total variance explained by first factor	23%	22%	20%	20%	20%

	Loading				
Goal	Den- mark	Italy	Nether- lands	Britain	Ireland
More say on job	.604	.599	.568	.611	.636
Less impersonal society	.566	.553	.451	.498	.393
Ideas count	.577	.577	.539	.482	.453
More say in government	.464	.566	.514	.506	.572
Freedom of speech	.330	.499	.338	.210	.401
More beautiful cities	.181	-.100	.141	.197	-.073
Fight rising prices	-.154	-.386	-.306	-.238	-.395
Strong defense forces	-.366	-.326	-.414	-.295	-.375
Economic growth	-.517	-.245	-.442	-.536	-.152
Fight crime	-.387	-.490	-.405	-.233	-.465
Stable economy	-.523	-.322	-.410	-.574	-.202
Maintain order	-.440	-.462	-.549	-.346	-.459
Percent of total variance explained by first factor	20%	20%	19%	18%	17%

Source: Inglehart 1977, 44.

ing. In each case, five items—the same five items in every country—cluster near the positive end of the continuum. Six items—again, the same six in every country—are grouped near the negative pole. The remaining item falls near the midpoint.

The items that cluster toward the negative pole are the six Materialist items. And five of the six Postmaterialist items fall into the opposite group. A single item—the one concerning "more beautiful cities" (or "protect nature from pollution," in the American data)—does not fall into either cluster. This item clearly does not behave according to our expectations, a fact that we must explore in more detail. But the other eleven items live up to expectations to an almost uncanny degree. The consistency of responses to these items cannot be attributed to such common sources of spurious correlation as response set, such as often occurs when respondents simply rate a series of items as either "good" or "bad" (or "very important" or "less important"). What frequently happens is that some respondents give similar ratings to a whole series of items. In the present case, this is impossible since respondents had to rank each goal as being more important or less important than the others, in a format that gave no clues to the "right" answer.

Given respondents tend to be preoccupied with a consistent set of needs located toward either the Materialist or Postmaterialist side of the continuum. Eleven of the twelve items fall into two separate clusters, reflecting Materialist and Postmaterialist priorities, respectively (as we see when we compare these results with Figure 4-1). The item designed to tap aesthetic needs fits into neither cluster; with the same consistency by which the eleven other items did fit into their expected places, this one fails to show a loading above the .300 level in any of the ten countries. Why?

The answer, apparently, is that this item does not simply evoke aesthetic needs, as it was intended to do. Instead, it also seems to tap an Industrial/anti-Industrial dimension on which collective economic development is seen as conflicting with one's personal security. Moreover, this item shows a surprisingly strong relationship with the safety needs (see Inglehart 1977, 45–50). For many people, the term "cities" tends to evoke fears of crime.

The relationship between aesthetic concerns and Postmaterialist values is clarified by another analysis utilizing the Rokeach terminal values survey (see Rokeach 1973) together with the Materialist/Postmaterialist battery, both of which were included in the American component of the Political Action study (Barnes, Kaase, et al. 1979).

Factor analysis of the twelve-item Materialist/Postmaterialist battery plus the eighteen-item Rokeach battery reveals a complex and interesting structure. As we would expect, a number of dimensions are needed to capture the configuration of responses. But the Materialist/Postmaterialist dimension remains clearly recognizable, and several of Rokeach's items show substantial loadings on it. Table 4-2 gives results from a second factor analysis, based on the eleven items showing significant loading in Table 4-1, plus the related Rokeach items. In the Materialist cluster, we find Rokeach's items "a comfortable life" and "family security"—two values having an obvious linkage with economic security. Also located in this cluster is an item that is directly relevant to the safety needs, "national

TABLE 4-2. THE MATERIALIST/POSTMATERIALIST FACTOR IN THE UNITED STATES, 1974
(Loadings of eighteen items on first principal component)

Goal	Loading
Ideas count	.58
Less impersonal society	.51
Freedom of speech	.46
WORLD OF BEAUTY[a]	.32
WISDOM	.32
EQUALITY	.30
More say on job	.30
More say in government	.27
INNER HARMONY	.27
Maintain order	-.28
Stable economy	-.30
FAMILY SECURITY	-.37
Economic growth	-.42
Fight rising prices	-.42
NATIONAL SECURITY	-.43
Fight crime	-.45
COMFORTABLE LIFE	-.46
Strong defense forces	-.50

Source: _Political_ _Action_ survey carried out by ISR, University of Michigan, July, 1974.

[a]Rokeach items appear in all capital letters.

security.'' In the Postmaterialist cluster, we find ''equality'' and ''inner harmony,'' plus a pair of items relating to the intellectual and esthetic needs—''wisdom'' and ''a world of beauty.'' Ironically, the item we designed to tap the esthetic needs fails to show the expected empirical relationships, but the item developed by Rokeach does show it. Analysis of the responses to our own item concerning ''more beautiful cities'' revealed an unexpected tendency for this item to be linked with emphasis on ''the fight against crime.'' Inclusion of the word ''cities'' in this context seems to evoke a concern with safety among some respondents; for them, the cities are unbeautiful not only because they are dirty but because they are dangerous. Rokeach's item makes no reference to cities and apparently evokes aesthetic concerns in unmixed form—and consequently falls into the Postmaterialist cluster, as the hierarchy of needs hypothesis would suggest. In short, the anomalous results obtained with this item seem to reflect imperfect formulation of our ''aesthetic'' alternative, rather than an indication that aesthetic concerns are not part of the Postmaterialist syndrome. When unambiguously formulated, they are.

The Materialist/Postmaterialist dimension proves to be exceedingly robust over time. Factor analyses of survey data collected in the nine European Community countries in late 1978 reveal the same pattern as in 1973, and again, it is remarkably uniform across the nine nations. As Table 4-3 demonstrates, in nation after nation, all five Postmaterialist items show

TABLE 4-3. THE MATERIALIST/POSTMATERIALIST FACTOR IN NINE NATIONS, 1978
(Loadings of given items on first principal component)

| | Loading | | | | |
Goal	France	Bel-gium	Nether-lands	West Germany	Italy
More say on job	.57	.55	.65	.63	.53
Less impersonal society	.61	.55	.56	.64	.55
More say in government	.53	.42	.58	.46	.64
Ideas count	.45	.43	.52	.56	.51
Freedom of speech	.46	.47	.31	.49	.50
More beautiful cities	.12	.16	.15	.30	.01
Strong defense forces	-.41	-.21	-.44	-.42	-.43
Fight rising prices	-.35	-.44	-.26	-.24	-.39
Stable economy	-.47	-.49	-.49	-.43	-.33
Fight against crime	-.55	-.31	-.46	-.38	-.52
Economic growth	-.46	-.56	-.57	-.51	-.30
Maintain order	-.58	-.34	-.57	-.46	-.54

| | Loading | | | |
Goal	Luxem-bourg	Denmark	Ireland	Britain
More say on the job	.58	.62	.61	.62
Less impersonal society	.65	.60	.56	.57
More say in government	.45	.57	.56	.48
Ideas count	.46	.57	.57	.52
Freedom of speech	.47	.41	.36	.36
More beautiful cities	.28	.28	-.15	.15
Strong defense forces	.05	-.43	-.24	-.39
Fight rising prices	-.46	-.26	-.26	-.23
Stable economy	-.33	-.53	-.42	-.38
Fight against crime	-.55	-.45	-.45	-.45
Economic growth	-.51	-.50	-.29	-.34
Maintain order	-.53	-.62	-.38	-.48

Source: Data from Euro-Barometer #10 surveys.

positive polarity; and all six Materialist items show negative polarity in every country but Luxembourg, where we find one anomalous loading. With almost incredible consistency in nation after nation, emphasis on the six items designed to tap economic and physical security goes together, forming a coherent Materialist cluster; in every case, emphasis on the five items designed to tap belonging, self-expression, and intellectual satisfaction also goes together, forming a clearly defined Postmaterialist cluster.

This degree of cross-national consistency is remarkable and unusual. An attempted cross-national replication of an authoritarian personality battery, for example, showed different response structures in each of the four Western societies studied (Inglehart 1970b). Figure 4-2 facilitates comparison of the 1973 results with the 1978 results, summing up the overall pattern

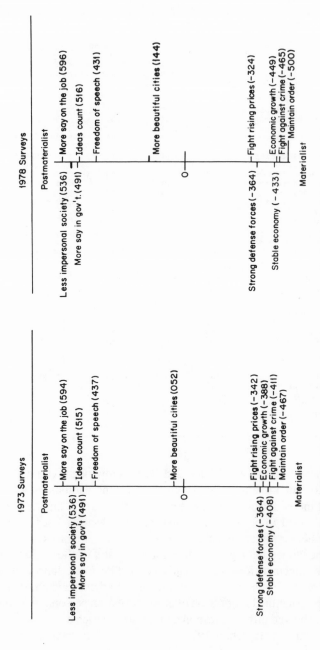

FIGURE 4-2. The Materialist/Postmaterialist values dimension in 1973 and 1978. Mean factor loadings from each of the nine European Community countries surveyed in September 1973 and October/November, 1978. Based on principal components analyses of rankings of the twelve goals.

TABLE 4-4.   THE VALUE PRIORITIES OF CANDIDATES TO THE EUROPEAN
PARLIAMENT:
THE "MATERIALIST/POSTMATERIALIST" AND "CITIES AND CRIME" DIMENSIONS
(Principal components factor analysis)

I. Materialist/Postmaterialist[a]		II. Cities and Crime[b]	
More say on job	.660	Fight against crime	-.717
Less impersonal society	.478	Maintain order	-.611
More say in government	.472	More beautiful cities	-.571
Society where ideas count	.408	Society where ideas count	-.428
More beautiful cities	.315	More say in government	-.309
Freedom of expression	.254		
Controlling inflation	-.436		
Fight against crime	-.442		
Stable economy	-.450		
Economic growth	-.566		
Maintain order	-.588		
Adequate defense forces	-.660		

Source: Survey of candidates to European Parliament; see Inglehart et
al., 1980.

[a]Total variance explained by first factor: 24%.

[b]Total variance explained by first factor: 14%.

by giving the mean factor loading for each item across nine nations in each
year. As a detailed examination of this figure reveals, the response pattern
underlying the 1973 surveys is almost identical with that from the 1978
surveys. Virtually the only significant change is the fact that in 1978 the
"beautiful cities" item has moved a little closer toward the Postmaterialist
cluster it was originally intended to tap.

Analysis of the priorities of candidates for the European Parliament,
based on interviews conducted in 1979, also reveals the same basic pattern
(see Table 4-4). European politicians also tend to respond to the Materialist
items in one way and to the Postmaterialist items in the opposite way. The
similarity between elites and mass publics even extends to the structure of
the second dimension, which reflects the "cities and crime" theme here,
as it does among mass publics. Since we are dealing with an elite sample,
the constraint found here is higher than among the general public. Elites
respond to the item concerning "more beautiful cities" in the way we
originally expected. Here, it *does* cluster with the Postmaterialist items
(apparently because fear of urban crime is a less important part of the outlook of elites). On the other hand, "freedom of expression" shows the
expected polarity, but its correlations are relatively weak. Among candidates for the European Parliament, emphasis on freedom of expression is
almost universal—hence it does not discriminate between Materialists and
Postmaterialists as effectively as at the mass level. On the whole, however,
the structure of elite responses is strikingly similar to that of the general

public. Cross-nationally, across time, and at both mass and elite levels, response to these items shows the same structure. Consistently, the Materialist/Postmaterialist dimension is the main underlying theme.

Does this mean that the data cannot be sliced in any other way? Of course not. In the foregoing, we use principal component analyses to test the hypothesis that these twelve items tap a common underlying Materialist/Postmaterialist dimension. Milkis and Baldino (1978) subjected the 1973 data to varimax rotation—a technique that breaks down the first dimension into four subclusters corresponding, roughly, to the groups of items designed to tap (1) economic security, (2) physical security, (3) belonging, and (4) self-expression.

Taking a similar approach but using a different methodology, Herz (1979) applies multidimensional scaling to the 1973 data and obtains the two-dimensional solution depicted on the left side of Figure 4-3. Like Milkis and Baldino, Herz obtains four clusters of items; the boundaries he draws around these clusters are shown in Figure 4-3. Herz discusses each of these four clusters in detail, and concludes that the Materialist/Postmaterialist dimension has no empirical basis.

He fails to see the forest for the trees. When we project his twelve points onto the main axis of his two-dimensional solution (as shown on the right side of Figure 4-3), the result is an almost perfect replication of the Materialist/Postmaterialist dimension depicted in Figure 4-2. Underlying Herz's four subclusters, we find an overall pattern in which the six Materialist items are situated toward the bottom of the figure and the five Postmaterialist items are grouped toward the top, with one item (once again, "more beautiful cities") located near the center, exactly as in Figure 4-2.

Similarly, in analyses of Japanese data, Flanagan (1982a, 1987) obtains two dimensions and argues that the Materialist/Postmaterialist dimension should be broken down into two components. Flanagan's data are based on ratings rather than rankings and he not only argues that ratings are a better method than rankings—he even maintains that the responses from Western countries also would have shown a structure similar to the one he obtains from Japan if only they had been based on ratings instead of rankings. Rankings, he argues, somehow force all the items onto a single Materialist/Postmaterialist factor. It is difficult to see how rankings could do this, but we need not wonder—Flanagan's hypothesis has already been tested in two Western countries—and the results contradict his expectations. Dalton's (1980, 1981) study indicates that the deviant pattern obtained by Flanagan reflects a difference between Japanese and Western respondents, rather than a difference in methodology, for Dalton has analyzed the responses to the same battery of items used by Flanagan, using the same methodology (ratings). The difference is that Dalton's data come

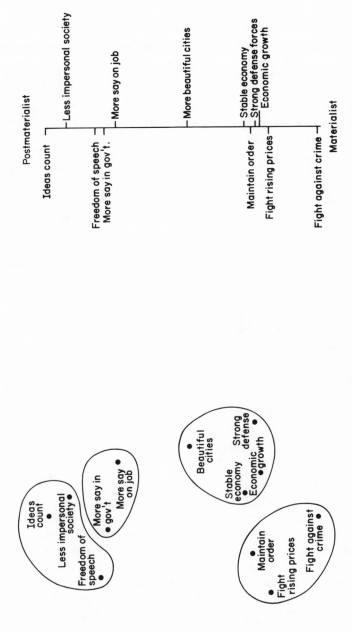

FIGURE 4-3. Structure of value priorities of nine Western publics, 1973. Left: Two-dimensional multidimensional scaling solution, from Herz 1979, 292. Right: The previous multidimensional scaling plot, projected onto its main axis. Note: Compare with Figure 4-2.

from West Germany; and Dalton finds a clear Materialist/Postmaterialist dimension, utilizing both factor analysis and LISREL techniques (Dalton 1980, 1981).

This is not all. Van Deth (1983b) has replicated my twelve-item Materialist/Postmaterialist values battery in a Dutch survey, having his respondents use *both* rankings and ratings. Though previously skeptical of the Materialist/Postmaterialist thesis (Van Deth 1983a), he concludes that the underlying dimension is quite robust, for he obtains a clear Materialist/Postmaterialist dimension from both rankings and ratings and regardless of whether he uses factor analysis, smallest space analysis, or multidimensional scaling.

In various ways, Herz (1979), Milkis and Baldino (1978), Thome (1985), and Flanagan (1982a, 1987) all fall into an analytic fallacy that might be described as the *reductio ad varimax*. On a purely empirical basis, it is perfectly possible to break down the Materialist/Postmaterialist dimension into the two components Flanagan proposes, or the four subclusters Herz proposes; going farther still, one could subject the items in any given subcluster to varimax rotation and discover that there are "really" two or more dimensions underlying it, until one comes up against the limit that, since there are only twelve items, one can obtain no more than twelve dimensions. For certain purposes, such reductionism is perfectly appropriate. If one's hypotheses dealt with attitudes toward physical security, for example, one might focus on that particular cluster; or if one were studying mass attitudes toward crime, one might analyze the responses to that specific item without reference to the other items. But none of the authors discussed here is investigating attitudes toward crime. They are addressing the question whether these twelve items tap an underlying Materialist/Postmaterialist dimension. The answer is an unequivocal yes.

MATERIALISM AND POSTMATERIALISM IN JAPAN

Flanagan (1982a, 1987) seems mistaken in arguing that the Materialist/Postmaterialist dimension does not apply to Western society, and mistaken in arguing that emphasis on economic and physical security do not go together among the Japanese public. But he is correct in perceiving value change as multidimensional. Moreover, when we focus specifically on Japan, the Materialist/Postmaterialist concept must be modified in one important respect, for the Japanese case constitutes a striking contrast to the twenty Western societies we have studied. Japanese data indicate that two cross-cutting processes of value change have been taking place in Japan, though they are not those described by Flanagan (Inglehart 1982). Instead, one seems linked with the decline of the traditional sense of group obligation, rooted in preindustrial Japanese culture; and the other reflects a shift from Materialist to Postmaterialist values that is roughly—but not precisely—similar to what has been taking place in the West. The former has been described as a process of "individuation" (Maruyama 1965; Ike 1973). As Ike (1973, 1203) puts it, "In Western culture, which has long stressed individualism, youth may seek a sense of belonging, whereas in Japanese culture, which has emphasized the group, youth may yearn for individuation and privatization."

Individuation in Japan reflects the gradual decline of an extreme subordination of the individual to the collectivity that may be traced in part to the samurai tradition of feudal obligation and in part to the imperatives of a system of rice culture that depended on communal cooperation to maintain irrigation systems and share water resources, to a degree unknown in modern Western agriculture (Beardsley, et al. 1959). In both cases, strong group ties were closely linked with physical survival. While a similar subordination of the individual to the community may have existed in medieval Europe, the rise of individualism took place relatively long ago in the West—long before the formative years of anyone now living and available to be interviewed in a representative survey. The modernization of Japan is much more recent; it remained a predominantly rural society as recently as 1950. A large share of the Japanese public spent their formative years in a rural setting.

One major consequence is that while a shift from Materialist to Postmaterialist values can be found in modern Japan, it does not encompass a heightened emphasis on "belonging"—the need that Maslow (1954) identified as taking next priority after the needs for economic and physical security had been met. On the contrary, for the Japanese, "belonging" is an aspect of a traditional value system that has been inculcated so heavily that it sometimes interferes with the self-realization sought by Postmaterialists. While contemporary Japanese continue to cherish warm interpersonal relations, there has been a growing resistance to the traditional subordination of the individual to the group. Thus, the rank ordering of the social needs that Maslow viewed as universal actually seems to reflect a Western perspective. For Western Postmaterialists, who have grown up in societies where the individual has long been free from the grip of communal ties, the need for roots is a major preoccupation. For Japanese Postmaterialists, self-realization demands a wider margin of individual freedom from group constraints than the traditional society allowed.

Thus, while my original four-item value priorities index shows the same relationships with age and education in Japan as in the West (Watanuki 1977), one of the newer items, designed to tap emphasis on belonging, shows a strikingly different pattern. This item, dealing with "a less impersonal, more human society," was included in a 1976 Japanese survey. A literal back-translation from the Japanese version reads "a society with harmonious human relations." Throughout Western society, the various versions of this item are substantially more apt to be chosen by the young, the affluent, and the well-educated than by their opposite numbers. In Japan, this item is just as likely to be given relatively high priority by the old, the less educated, and those in rural settings (Miyake 1978).

While emphasis on having "more say in government decisions" is a relatively new component of Japanese culture, "harmonious human relations" connotes the traditional pattern of avoiding conflict by repressing individual differences. As Nakane (1973, 13) puts it, "In the ideal traditional household in Japan . . . opinions of the members of the household should always be held unanimously regardless of the issue, and this normally meant that all members accepted the opinion of the household head." But, on the other hand, "In practice, any decision should be made on the basis of a consensus which includes those located lower in the hierarchy. Such a consensus—reached by what might be termed maximum consultation—might seem a by-product of the post-war 'democratic' age; yet it is not at all new to the Japanese, representing as it does a very basic style of the traditional group operation" (Nakane 1973, 149). Thus, the phrase "harmonious social relations" also has quite positive connotations: it ranks among the most frequently chosen items in Japan, second only to emphasis on "economic stability" (though it ranks fifth among the same eight items, in the West). It attains widespread approval in Japan because it appeals to traditionalists as well as modernists—indeed, it is slightly more popular among the former group. To highly educated Japanese, this item evokes connotations of conformism and authoritarianism that would probably never cross a Westerner's mind. For example, Watanuki (1977, 10) perceives this item as reflecting preindustrial Japanese values and comments that "emperor worship and unconditional obedience to the superior cannot be restored any more." In keeping with Watanuki's interpretation—but in striking contrast to the pattern observed throughout Western society—emphasis on this indicator of "belonging" tends to be linked with emphasis on *Materialist* goals.

In short, Japan constitutes a remarkably distinctive case. Industrialization, urbanization, the attainment of prosperity, and other aspects of modernization have taken place so recently and so rapidly that even while Japan is taking a leading role among advanced industrial nations, some segments of the population are still undergoing the retreat from preindustrial values. The transition from preindustrial to industrial values has been

TABLE 4-5. EMPHASIS ON MONEY AS "MOST IMPORTANT THING TO TEACH A CHILD" AMONG JAPANESE AND AMERICAN PUBLICS

Question: "In bringing up children of primary school age, some think that one should teach them that money is the most important thing. Do you agree or disagree?"

I. Percentage agreeing among Japanese public, 1953 - 1983

1953	1958[a]	1963	1968	1973	1978	1983
65%	-	60%	57%	44%	45%	43%

II. Japan versus United States, 1978

	U.S.	Japan
Agree	5%	45%
Disagree	93	40
Undecided, don't know	2	15

Source: For sampling details and a full report of findings, see Research Committee on the Study of the Japanese National Character 1979. The 1978 survey was carried out in both Japan and the United States.

[a]This item not asked in 1958.

superimposed on the shift from Materialism to Postmaterialist priorities. When they are lumped together, the former process can conceal the latter.

Nevertheless, a shift away from Materialist priorities is taking place in Japan, as in the West. Table 4-5 shows responses of the Japanese public from 1953 to 1983 to the question, "In bringing up children of primary school age some think that one should teach them that money is the most important thing. Do you agree or disagree?"

It would be difficult to design a simpler or more straightforward indicator of a Materialistic outlook. And, it appears, Materialism does exist among the Japanese—and has declined substantially during the past thirty years. Emphasis on money, as the highest priority, has declined from a position endorsed by a 65 percent majority of the Japanese to one endorsed by only 43 percent.

Moreover, the decline of Materialism seems to be based on intergenerational population replacement, as the cohort analysis of this item presented in chapter 2 shows. The priorities of the Japanese public have been shifting away from Materialism.

How Materialistic are the Japanese? By one standard, we would expect them to be more Materialistic than any of the Western publics we have studied, since they emerged only very recently from a grinding Asiatic poverty unknown in the modern West. As recently as 1950, the average annual per capita income in Japan was $200. Though Japan today ranks among the world's wealthiest nations, a large share of its population grew up during times of severe deprivation. Thus, it is not surprising to find that, in some respects, the Japanese public seems relatively Materialistic. Japan manifests a smaller proportion of Postmaterialists than that of any Western society, as measured by my original four-item values index. Similarly, in 1978, 45 percent of the Japanese public still felt children should be taught that "money is the most important thing"—as compared with only 5 percent of the American public surveyed in that year.

On the other hand, we have argued that certain preindustrial values have survived in Japan to a far greater extent than in the West. It has been suggested that the historical growth of Materialism tends to be curvilinear, initially repressed by cultural norms necessary to the functioning of pre-industrial society, but gaining widespread acceptance during the phase of capital accumulation and rapid industrialization, and then declining with the emergence of advanced industrial society (Inglehart 1977, 242–243). Insofar as traditional antimaterialistic norms are still present, we would expect the Japanese to be less Materialistic than Westerners.

Table 4-6 provides some relevant comparisons of societal goals endorsed by the Japanese and by eight Western publics. In one respect, we find similarity, rather than contrast: The top-ranking goal both in Japan and in most Western countries was "a stable economy." By this standard, the Japanese are among the most Materialistic of all publics, with only the Germans emphasizing economic stability more heavily than the Japanese do.

But when we examine the second-ranking goal, we find evidence of another phenomenon. For the Japanese, the second most frequent choice is "a society with harmonious human relations." The Western version, "a friendlier, less impersonal society," is ranked fifth among these eight items (taking the average of the eight Western publics). From the viewpoint of Western society, this is unambiguously a Postmaterialist item, emphasized mainly by the younger, more affluent strata. As we have seen, it has an ambivalent status in Japan. Clearly, it does not represent a Materialistic orientation; but its widespread popularity seems to reflect the persistence of *pre*-Materialist values, rather than the inroads of Postmaterialism.

Interestingly enough, the goal of having "more say in how things are decided at work and in your community" receives less emphasis in Japan than in any Western country. The key phrase probably is "more say." The Japanese already carry out an enormous amount of consultation and consensus-building; few seem to want still more.

The goal that ranks second among Western publics—"the fight against crime"—unquestionably does reflect a Materialist concern. And it re-

TABLE 4-6. SOCIETAL PRIORITIES AMONG WESTERN PUBLICS AND JAPANESE
PUBLIC

	% According High Priority to Goal[a]				
Goal	Britain	West Germany	Nether- lands	Austria	U.S.
Maintain a stable economy	48%	74%	31%	55%	52%
The fight against crime	38	47	48	37	42
More say on the job	29	17	34	20	21
Economic growth	25	22	14	33	15
Friendlier, less impersonal society	11	13	29	9	11
Society where ideas count	16	11	26	10	21
Strong defense forces	20	8	5	9	32
Beautiful cities and countryside	12	8	13	27	6
TOTAL	199	200	200	200	200

	% According High Priority to Goal				
Goal	Italy	Switz- erland	Finland	Western Mean	Japan
Maintain a stable economy	32%	56%	51%	50%	59%
The fight against crime	59	29	35	42	20
More say on the job	25	24	16	23	12
Economic growth	37	7	29	23	9
Friendlier, less impersonal society	18	23	40	19	37
Society where ideas count	16	19	10	16	22
Strong defense forces	6	17	11	14	5
Beautiful cities and countryside	8	24	8	13	36
TOTAL	201	200	200	200	200

Sources: Data from Western nations from Political Action surveys,
1974 - 1976; Japanese data from election survey sponsored by NSF and
NHK.

[a]Based on two top priorities among these eight items except in Japan,
where a maximum of three choices were coded but the mean number of
responses was 2.56. These Japanese data have been standardized to a
base of 200 percent to permit comparison with Western countries.

ceives substantially less emphasis in Japan than in any Western country.
Here again, we have an indication that the Japanese are less Materialistic
than Westerners. But let us go on to inquire why. On one level, the Japanese lack of concern for crime is readily understandable. It reflects the fact
that Japan has a significantly lower crime rate than that of virtually any
Western society (about one-tenth of the prevailing rate for major crimes in

the United States). But if we push the explanation a step further and ask why Japan has such a low crime rate, we would probably trace it to the persistence of a much stronger sense of group affiliation—and consequently more effective social control—in Japan than in the West. Once again, we reach the conclusion that Japan is less Materialistic than the West—but that this may be more attributable to the persistence of preindustrial values than to the rise of Postmaterialism.

Table 4-6 reveals another striking contrast between Japan and the West. "More beautiful cities and countryside," which was the least emphasized item in the West as a whole, is the third-ranking item in Japan. Again, the finding itself is not particularly surprising. In Japan, the second-largest industrial power in the world is packed into an area about the size of Montana; a concern for its environmental impact is understandable (and the Japanese version of this item translates as "make efforts to preserve the environment of this community"). Among the Japanese public, emphasis on this item is positively linked with a concern to preserve "economic stability" but negatively related to emphasis on "economic growth." The corresponding item, "more beautiful cities," had ambivalent polarity throughout the West. Their relatively high emphasis on this goal, therefore, does little to clarify whether we should view the Japanese as more Materialistic or more Postmaterialistic than Westerners.

Table 4-7 provides some additional comparisons between the goals emphasized by the Japanese and by ten Western publics. Despite the fact that the Japanese stress "a stable economy" heavily, few of them consider their salaries the most important feature of their jobs. This may be related to the career pattern typical of a large Japanese corporation, where one starts off with a modest salary, but works in a warm, paternalistic setting, with a strong likelihood of continuous job tenure until retirement. In any case, the Japanese emphasize economic security more than they do their absolute level of pay—but are primarily concerned with such nonmaterial aspects as "working with people you like" and "a feeling of accomplishment." By this standard, the Japanese are among the least Materialistic publics. But of the last two goals, "working with people you like" has an obvious relationship to the stress on "harmonious human relations" discussed above, and a "feeling of accomplishment" may also involve this consideration to some extent. Insofar as this is true, the non-Materialistic outlook of the Japanese might, once again, be traced to the persistence of preindustrial values, rather than to the inroads of Postmaterialism. This interpretation is consistent with the hypothesis that a certain curvilinearity exists in the long-term processes of value change, for emphasis on "working with people you like" and "a feeling of accomplishment" are, very

TABLE 4-7. JOB VALUES IN JAPAN, THE UNITED STATES, AND WESTERN EUROPE

Question: "Here are some of the things people usually take into
account in relation to their work. Which one would you personally
place first?
--A good salary so that you do not have any worries about money.
--A safe job with no risk of closing down or unemployment.
--Working with people you like.
--Doing an important job which gives you a feeling of
accomplishment."

(Percentage "placing first")

A Good Salary		A Safe Job		People You Like		Feeling of Accomplishment	
W.Germany	38%	Ireland	30%	Denmark	34%	U. S.	50%
Britain	37	Italy	29	Japan	30	Japan	38
France	36	W.Germany	28	Netherlands	26	Netherlands	29
Belgium	34	Japan	23	Belgium	20	Luxembourg	29
Italy	33	Belgium	23	Britain	16	Denmark	27
Ireland	30	Luxembourg	22	Ireland	16	France	26
Luxembourg	25	France	21	Italy	14	Britain	25
Netherlands	23	Britain	20	France	14	Ireland	24
Denmark	21	U. S.	19	U. S.	14	Italy	23
U. S.	16	Netherlands	18	Luxembourg	13	Belgium	22
Japan	7	Denmark	16	W.Germany	11	W.Germany	22

Sources: European Community 1973 survey; 1978 Japanese National
Character Survey.

strikingly, characteristic of Postmaterialists in Western countries, as we
will see in chapter 5.

Clearly, the Japan-Western comparison is complex. Items that have one
consistent meaning throughout the West sometimes have a quite different
significance in Japan. On the whole, we would conclude that the Japanese
tend to be less Materialistic than most Westerners, but that this reflects the
persistence of preindustrial values more than it does the rise of Postmaterialism.

The fact that the decline of traditional Prematerialist values is superimposed on the rise of Postmaterialist values in the Japanese case alters the
structure of the Materialist/Postmaterialist dimension in that country.
While emphasis on economic and physical security go together in Japan,
as elsewhere, emphasis on belonging does not constitute part of a Postmaterialist cluster in the way it does throughout the West. While younger
and better-educated Japanese do show a clear-cut preference for having
''more say in important government decisions'' and ''protecting freedom
of speech'' (Watanuki 1977, 34), they may see emphasis on such goals as
''harmonious human relations'' as implying a paternalistic constraint on
individual self-expression. Thus, the twelve-item Materialist/Postmateri-
alist values battery cannot be used in unmodified form in Japan since cer-

tain items that show Postmaterialist polarity with remarkable consistency throughout the West have neutral or even reversed polarity in the context of Japanese society.

This is an important finding. It implies that the nonphysiological part of Maslow's hierarchy of needs is not a universal human pattern, but is contingent on culture. Maslow provides a provocative hypothesis, which helped guide the formulation of our twelve-item battery. But his thesis is only partly tenable. The physiological needs do seem to take precedence over higher-order needs. But, as we concluded some time ago, "There does not seem to be any clear hierarchy within the last set of needs, which Maslow called 'self-actualization needs' " (Inglehart 1977, 22). The Japanese evidence demonstrates this point even more clearly.

Other tests of Maslow's hierarchy reach similar conclusions. Thus, in a review of studies on this topic, Lawler (1973, 34) concludes:

> There is strong evidence to support the view that unless existence needs are satisfied, people will not be concerned with higher-order needs. There is, however, very little evidence to support the view that a hierarchy exists above the security level. Thus, it probably is not safe to assume more than a two-step hierarchy with existence and security needs at the lowest level and all the higher-order needs at the next level.

Our own findings support this conclusion. Consequently, the Materialist/Postmaterialist indices used throughout this book are based on the assumption that people tend to give priority to the safety and sustenance needs, on one hand, or to the higher-order needs, on the other hand—without assuming that there is any specific ordering within the latter group. The pure Materialist and pure Postmaterialist types are located at opposite poles of a continuum, with the various mixed types falling at various points along the spectrum. In Japan, as elsewhere, the physiological needs seem to take first priority. But those who have satisfied them do not automatically turn to the belonging needs as the next item on the agenda. The assumption that they would do so may seem plausible from the perspective of Western society, in which the rise of individualism began centuries ago, and has developed to such an extent that a sense of atomization and anonymity has become a problem. This assumption is less applicable to a society in which traditional modes of survival depended on a relatively extreme subordination of the individual to the group, and where this tradition is still very much alive. In such a setting, those who have satisfied the needs for economic and physical security may feel that self-expression and self-realization require *less* emphasis on certain aspects of group ties.

The basic distinction between physiological and nonphysiological (or Materialist and Postmaterialist) goals seems to be valid in every society for which we have data. But the specific ordering among the nonphysiological goals hypothesized by Maslow does not seem tenable; rather, the ordering varies cross-culturally. Peace and prosperity, in the long run, encourage both Japanese and Western publics to give heightened emphasis to non-material goals. They do not necessarily turn to the *same* nonmaterial goals.

Our theoretical framework implies that the emergence of the Materialist/Postmaterialist dimension reflects the recent historical experience of Western societies; during the past few decades, the publics of these societies have come to polarize along this dimension to an increasing degree, with the emergence of birth cohorts who were socialized under a historically unprecedented degree of economic security, and an unusually prolonged period during which their homelands were secure from invasion. Though Japan has shared in this peace and prosperity, her people have emerged from preindustrial poverty and a quasi-feudal cultural pattern much more recently than have the publics of Western societies. Consequently, as we have seen, the structure of Japanese values differs significantly from that of Western publics.

VALUE CHANGE IN CHINA AND HONG KONG

To what extent do the value systems of peoples in other non-Western societies manifest a structure that diverges from the pattern that has been found to be so pervasive and consistent in Western countries? Some intriguing evidence on this score is available from a recent study carried out in Hong Kong and the People's Republic of China (Ho 1985).

While all the other surveys analyzed in this book are based on oral interviews with representative national samples, Ho's data are based on written questionnaires administered to quota samples of 475 adult residents of Hong Kong and 94 adult residents of China living in the region adjacent to Hong Kong. Clearly, these results cannot be viewed as representative or conclusive; but they hint at the presence of cross-cultural differences that are so interesting and so striking that it seems worthwhile to discuss them. Our analysis suggests an early stage of the Materialist/Postmaterialist dimension in tandem with a preindustrial/industrial one.

The twelve-item Materialist/Postmaterialist values battery, translated into Chinese, was used in the Hong Kong survey (with an item concerning "cultural growth" substituted for the one concerning "more beautiful cities and countryside"). The results of a principal components analysis of these items, performed with the same technique used for the Western surveys, appear in Table 4-8.

The first factor that emerges is basically similar to the Materialist/Postmaterialist dimension found throughout the West. All six of the items in-

TABLE 4-8. TWO DIMENSIONS OF VALUES IN HONG KONG, 1984
(Principal components analysis)

	Materialist/ Postmaterialist Factor	Economic Versus Cultural Goals
More say in government	.60	.16
More say on job	.51	-.07
Ideas count	.42	-.36
Freedom of speech	.35	.14
Less impersonal society	.12	-.40
Cultural growth	.07	-.32
Stable economy	-.10	.74
Economic growth	-.15	.73
Maintain order	-.37	.03
Fight against crime	-.50	-.05
Fight rising prices	-.55	-.24
Strong defense forces	-.64	-.22

Source: Based on quota sample of 475 adult residents of Hong Kong interviewed in Cantonese in Summer 1984; see Ho 1985.

tended to tap Materialist goals have negative polarity on this dimension (though only four of them have loadings above the .3 level); and all six items intended to tap Postmaterialist goals have positive polarity (but again, only four of them have strong loadings). The item dealing with "cultural growth" does no better than did the item it replaced. Interestingly enough, the item dealing with "a less impersonal society" has an ambivalent status in Hong Kong, as in Japan. This may reflect the fact that Chinese society also tends to be far more group-oriented than modern Western society.

The items dealing with "economic growth" and "a stable economy" have the usual Materialist polarity, but weaker loadings than in the West. The explanation may lie in the fact that these items were enormously popular in Hong Kong—so popular that there is not much polarization over them. Fully 70 percent of those interviewed in Hong Kong gave "a stable economy" one of their top two priorities, and 34 percent chose "economic growth" for one of their top two priorities among the eight items shown in Table 4-6 above. The combined total of 104 percentage points for these two items is a higher figure than was found in any Western country or Japan.

Thus, the first factor emerging from the Hong Kong data provides an attenuated but recognizable version of the Materialist/Postmaterialist dimension. It has not yet crystallized as clearly as in Western societies, but the basic configuration is identical, with all twelve items showing the same polarity as in Western societies. This may reflect the fact that Hong Kong has been heavily influenced by Western values for a long time. Under Brit-

TABLE 4-9. TWO DIMENSIONS OF VALUES IN PEOPLE'S REPUBLIC OF CHINA, 1984
(Principal components analysis)

Social Duty Versus Personal Gratification		*Materialist/Prematerialist*	
Feeling of accomplishment	.68	Less impersonal society	.56
Give yourself to society	.66	Give yourself to society	.30
Stable economy	.47	More say on job	.27
Economic growth	.33	Feeling of accomplishment	.23
Work hard and get rich	-.38	A good salary	-.43
Less impersonal society	-.40	Stable economy	-.47
A good salary	-.43	Economic growth	-.55
More say on job	-.58	Work hard and get rich	-.63

Source: Based on quota sample of 94 adult residents of China living in region adjacent to Hong Kong, interviewed in Cantonese in Fall 1984; see Ho 1985.

ish control since early in the nineteenth century, Hong Kong began to develop a powerful merchant class at an early date. By 1910, the British were knighting successful Chinese merchants in Hong Kong. A Materialist orientation has prevailed for some time in Hong Kong—but among the younger, better educated segments of the public, a Postmaterialist outlook is emerging. It is not yet very widespread or full blown, but the demographic correlates of Postmaterialism are similar to those in the West.

The second dimension in this analysis reflects the polarization between traditional personalistic cultural goals and an emphasis on economic growth and stability: a preindustrial versus industrial values tension.

Ho's results from the People's Republic of China provide a striking contrast to those from Hong Kong. Though the data were gathered from a nearby region, using the same language, a quite different configuration of responses emerges. In part, this reflects the fact that some of the items used in Hong Kong were inappropriate for the People's Republic. For example, the topic of "more say in government decisions" was considered too sensitive to use; and the item "fight rising prices" was deemed inappropriate in a society in which prices are set by government decision. Nevertheless, the items that were included convey a sense of the structure of responses, and it seems to reflect a very different worldview from that in nearby Hong Kong, as Table 4-9 demonstrates.

At first glance, the *second* factor that emerges from the Chinese data seems similar to the Materialist/Postmaterialist dimension we have seen elsewhere. This apparent similarity is misleading, as we will see, but let us first examine this second-ranking factor (in terms of variance explained) from the Chinese data. It consists of two fairly distinct clusters; one cluster reflects emphasis on "a less impersonal society," "give yourself to society," "more say on the job," and "a job that gives a feeling of accomplishment"—all of which seem to reflect Postmaterialist priorities. The opposite cluster reflects emphasis on "a good salary," "a stable economy," "economic growth," and "work hard and get rich"—all of which seem straightforward Materialist goals. We would appear to have a clear and unambiguous Materialist/Postmaterialist dimension. True, it is a secondary factor rather than the dominant theme, but its face content seems perfectly coherent, and we would be tempted to view it as a functional equivalent of the Materialist/Postmaterialist dimension found throughout the West and (in somewhat weaker form) in Japan and Hong Kong.

This interpretation collapses when we examine the demographic correlates of these attitudes. In striking contrast to what we find throughout the West, Japan, and Hong Kong, in China the *young* are more apt than the old to emphasize Materialist goals. In this society, the idea of working hard and getting rich is a newly emerging perspective that runs counter to an outlook that was dominant for generations, both in traditional Chinese society and under Mao. Presumably, at an earlier stage of history Western societies also went through a transition in which preindustrial values gradually gave way to Materialist goals—and during this transition, acceptance of these goals must have been more widespread among the young than among the old. If this was the case, it took place long ago in Western societies (and in Hong Kong). These data suggest that a transition to Materialism is occurring now in the People's Republic of China. Accordingly, we have labeled the second factor a "Materialist/pre-Materialist" dimension.

This is a secondary theme, however. The dominant dimension in China, as reflected in the first factor, reflects the polarization between "social duty" and "personal gratification." This dimension does not bear any resemblance to the Materialist/Postmaterialist dimension. It groups together (on one hand) emphasis on "a job that gives a feeling of accomplishment" and "give yourself to society" with two clearly Materialist goals: "a stable economy" and "economic growth." At the opposite pole, we find emphasis on "work hard and get rich" and "a good salary" (both Materialist aspirations) together with "a less impersonal society" and "more say on the job." In the contemporary Chinese setting, this axis of polarization is eminently comprehensible. It reflects the polarization between individual aspirations and the official policy of subordinating all else to the task of building a socialist economy—a goal that has been heavily emphasized by the regime since it came to power in 1949, and that has only recently been relaxed in limited, tentative ways. Our data suggest that the tension between social duty and personal gratification gives rise to a major axis of polarization in Chinese society. And it is the younger, better-educated respondents who tend to emphasize the goals of personal gratification—and the older ones who cling to the emphasis on social duty so heavily inculcated under Mao. It would be naive to view our small Chinese sample as representative of the People's Republic as a whole. These interviews were gathered in a district having atypically close contact with Hong Kong and the West. But this very fact suggests that data from China as a whole would probably show an even greater contrast with our findings from Hong Kong.

The publics of China and Hong Kong seem to hold profoundly different worldviews in some respects. Though both have been shaped by Chinese culture in general and by the Confucian tradition in particular, modern history has propelled them in different directions. The evidence gathered by Ho (1985) suggests that the population of Hong Kong has become imbued with a predominately Materialist orientation but may now be entering the early phase of the emergence of Postmaterialism, while the people of mainland China are still preoccupied with tensions between duty to the collectivity versus personal gratification—in a society in which Materialist orientations are only now beginning to permeate the young. Though Hong Kong will become part of China in 1997, the two societies are so sharply out of phase that it is understandable that the growing impact of economic and cultural influences from Hong Kong has caused shock waves within the People's Republic and been viewed as "spiritual pollution."

We interpret the striking differences between the worldviews found in Hong Kong and the People's Republic of China as reflecting the relatively strong Westernization of Hong Kong, on one hand, and, on the other, the peculiar history of China under Mao, together with the changes that began to emerge when the pragmatists gained power in 1976. Would all communist societies manifest patterns of value polarization similar to that found in China? Probably not—although some contrasts with the way values are structured in Western societies do seem implicit in the nature of communist society.

THE MATERIALIST/POSTMATERIALIST DIMENSION IN POLAND

Data from a representative national survey carried out in Poland shed some light on this question. Gathered on behalf of the Sociological Institute of the University of Warsaw in 1980, a few months before the independent workers' movement Solidarity emerged to prominence, these data include a slightly modified version of the twelve-item Materialist/Postmaterialist values battery (see Inglehart and Siemienska 1988). The results of a principal components analysis appear in Table 4-10.

TABLE 4-10. THE MATERIALIST/POSTMATERIALIST DIMENSION IN POLAND, 1980
(First factor in principal components analysis)

More say on job	.60
More say in government	.55
Freedom of speech	.53
Reorganize the economy	.23
Society where ideas count	.12
Better human relations	-.02
Rapid economic development	-.04
More beautiful cities	-.31
Strong defense forces	-.37
Fight against crime	-.41
Fight against prices	-.41
Maintain order	-.67

Source: Survey of Polish public carried out by OBOP, Warsaw; see Inglehart and Siemienska, 1988.

The pattern indicates that, in contrast to China, a fairly clear Materialist/Postmaterialist dimension *does* exist in Poland (and is the first factor). But the Polish results do not resemble the Western pattern as closely as do our results from Hong Kong.

Postmaterialism is not the same phenomenon in Poland as in the West. In Western countries, those with Materialist values are characterized by the fact that they give top priority to economic and physical security, while Postmaterialists emphasize other goals. But given the fundamentally different relationship that exists between the state and the economy in Poland, as compared with Western nations, the implications of giving top priority to "economic growth," for example, are inherently different from what they would be in the West. Attaining a high rate of economic growth is state policy in Poland, to be attained by sacrificing the production of consumer goods if necessary. It does not have the same connotations of a higher personal standard of living that it does in the West.

In view of these differences in their situation, it is not surprising that the Polish public responds somewhat differently to these items from the way Western publics respond to them. Though most of the items designed to tap Materialist priorities do indeed cluster together in the expected configuration, two of them do not; these items are "rapid economic development" and "reorganize the economy." These deviations from the Western pattern apparently reflect the distinctive role of the economy in Polish society. In the Polish survey, "reorganize the economy" was substituted for the item "maintain a stable economy," because in the Poland of 1980, the latter phrase could be taken to mean maintaining a stagnant economy. In retrospect, however, it seems that our revised translation had an ambiguity of its own. Since the Polish economy could be "reorganized" in a number of different ways, many of which would be more compatible with Post-materialist values than the present economy, selecting this goal could reflect a desire to reform or even reject the existing system, and the fact that it tends to cluster with "more say on the job," "freedom of speech," and "more say in the government" suggests that some of our respondents had such goals in mind when they chose it.

Our revised twelve-item battery does not tap precisely the same dimension as the corresponding battery does in the West. This was more or less inevitable since the social reality that the items refer to is fundamentally different in the two types of societies.

Nevertheless, the broad outlines of the Materialist/Postmaterialist configuration can be discerned in our Polish data. The four items that have the strongest negative loadings were designed to tap Materialist priorities; and the three items that have strong positive loadings were designed to tap Postmaterialist priorities. Though some of our items do not load on it, this first factor is clearly a Materialist/Postmaterialist dimension. Moreover, fortunately enough, all four items from the original four-item battery designed to tap Materialist/Postmaterialist values have substantial loadings on this dimension (these items deal with "order" and "prices" at the Materialist pole and with "free speech" and "more say in the government" at the Postmaterialist pole). This is also true of our results from Hong Kong and Japan. Consequently, we can construct the original four-item index with some confidence that it taps the appropriate dimension in all of the societies studied thus far except China.

When we examine the correlates of Postmaterialism in Poland, our index shows characteristics similar to those found in Western countries. In Poland, as throughout Western Europe and North America, Postmaterialists tend to have higher levels of income and education than do Materialists. And in both Hungary and Poland, as in the West, Postmaterialists tend to be younger than Materialists, perhaps reflecting a similar generational change (see Table A-5 in the Appendix). If so, the implications are important, for in 1980 political discontent in Poland was concentrated among Postmaterialists (Inglehart and Siemienska 1988). Generational change may pose problems for socialist societies that are at least as serious as those in the West.

CONCLUSION

The wide variety of patterns in which responses to these items are structured in non-Western countries makes the uniform structure of the Materialist/Postmaterialist dimension throughout the West all the more remarkable. Since each of the twelve items could show either positive, negative, or neutral polarity in our analyses, there are literally scores of possible combinations. But, in fact, all of the analyses based on data from Western countries manifest the same pattern, with only minor deviations. This pattern, moreover, is one in which eleven of the twelve items conform to theoretical expectations derived from the hypothesis that, at this stage in history, the publics of advanced industrial society tend to polarize between those who give top priority to the traditional goals of economic and physical security and another group who give top priority to such nonmaterial goals as a less impersonal, more participatory society, in which ideas, self-expression, and aesthetic concerns weigh more heavily.

The cross-cultural differences that emerge when we compare the results from Western and non-Western countries make it evident that this pattern of polarization reflects a specific historical situation, and is not inherent in human nature. The cohort analyses presented in chapter 2 also support this interpretation, for they show that Postmaterialist values were originally concentrated among the young but have been permeating the adult population increasingly as time goes by.

Are Postmaterialist values a relatively deep-rooted and central feature of the worldview of given birth cohorts? This question has been debated from a number of different perspectives. One group of investigators raised the question whether these items tapped anything basic, or merely reflected superficial support of currently fashionable causes. Thus, in research carried out in Great Britain, Marsh (1975) found that, despite their comparatively high incomes, Postmaterialists are relatively dissatisfied with their lives in general (including their income) and, above all, with the kind of society and political institutions under which they live. He interpreted this dissatisfaction as evidence that the Postmaterialists are actually more acquisitive than the Materialists: The fact that they support social change and vote for the parties of the Left reflects mere lip service to fashionable causes, he argued, and does not reflect their true personal values.

To test this hypothesis, Marsh developed an index of "personal postmaterialism" in subsequent research. He finds positive product moment correlations of .22 and .21 between it and my two respective indices of societal Postmaterialism (Marsh 1977, 180). In survey research, one rarely obtains attitudinal correlations much above the .3 range unless the relationship is inflated by response set or obvious similarity of face content. In this case, Marsh obtains positive correlations of .21 and .22 between two types of indices based on items that not only have no obvious similarity of face content but were designed with the expectation that they would show *negative* correlations. Marsh's findings provide further validation of the Materialist/Postmaterialist hypothesis. After reviewing the evidence, he concludes that "strong support exists for Inglehart's basic thesis" (Marsh 1977, 192).

Lafferty and Knutsen (1985) go beyond Marsh's work with an even more exhaustive investigation of the relationship between Materialist/Postmaterialist priorities, and the individual's personal values, character values, and democratic values. They find a pervasive and coherent pattern of linkages; they conclude that the Materialist/Postmaterialist value syndrome represents a highly constrained ideological dimension. As the theory implies, it occupies a central position in the worldview of the Norwegian public.

This confirmation of the theory is in a sense all the more significant because it comes from researchers who clearly were not prejudiced in favor of the theory. Both Lafferty (1975) and Marsh (1975) had initially published articles expressing skepticism that Postmaterialist responses tapped anything deep-rooted in the individual's character structure. Each of these scholars subsequently carried out investigations designed to test whether this skepticism was well founded. The fact that they eventually reached conclusions they did not anticipate reflects an impressive scientific objectiveness and intellectual integrity. Their findings gain further support from research carried out in Germany by Schneider (1981), who also finds pervasive linkages between Postmaterialism and personality variables.

Rooted in the distinct experiences produced by major historical changes, the Materialist/Postmaterialist dimension is a central axis of polarization among Western publics, reflecting the contrast between two fundamentally different worldviews. In varying patterns that reflect their own distinctive historical experiences, related dimensions are prominent features of the outlook of the publics of Japan, Hong Kong, and Poland. In the People's Republic of China, this dimension has not yet emerged as an important axis of polarization—instead, we find evidence of a precursor dimension, based on the opposition between Materialist and pre-Materialist values.

CHAPTER 5

Values, Social Class, and Economic Achievement

INTRODUCTION

The relationship between Materialist/Postmaterialist values and socio-economic status (SES) is complex and seemingly paradoxical. On one hand, our theory postulates that Postmaterialist values result from the presence of economic and physical security during one's formative years. This implies that Postmaterialists will be concentrated among the upper socio-economic strata. As we will see shortly, this expectation is amply confirmed: Postmaterialists have better jobs, more education, and higher incomes than Materialists and mixed types.

But Postmaterialist values deemphasize economic achievement. For society as a whole, Postmaterialists give a lower priority to economic growth than to the quality of life; and in their personal lives, Postmaterialists give less emphasis to safe jobs and a high income than to interesting, meaningful work and working with congenial people. Since they are far better educated than Materialists, Postmaterialists tend to earn more. But Postmaterialists seek to maximize status rather than income. When we control for the fact that they are better educated and have better family connections, the Postmaterialists' income advantage narrows or even reverses itself. Indeed, most Postmaterialists actually earn less than Materialists from comparable family backgrounds.

In other words, Postmaterialist values tend to make one an economic underachiever: A larger proportion of one's energies are directed to maximizing goods other than income, such as status and the quality of life. The implications for both social stratification and for economic growth are important. Let us look at the evidence.

VALUES AND FORMATIVE SECURITY

If Postmaterialist values reflect "formative security" (our shorthand term for economic and physical security during one's formative years), we would expect to find a higher proportion of Postmaterialists among relatively prosperous respondents. Granted, virtually all members of the younger generation have been spared some of the harrowing events expe-

TABLE 5-1. OCCUPATIONAL PRESTIGE LEVEL BY VALUE TYPE
(Percentage having an occupation with prestige rating in top quartile for
their nation)

Value Type	U.S.	West Germany	Britain	Neth.	Austria
Materialists	30%	13%	17%	16%	11%
Mixed (Materialists)	27	18	14	22	19
Mixed (Postmat.)	30	26	20	36	30
Postmaterialists	46	44	29	51	41

Value Type	Italy	Switz.	Finland	Total	N
Materialists	9%	16%	14%	16%	(5,221)
Mixed (Materialists)	14	21	16	19	(3,701)
Mixed (Postmat.)	22	29	21	27	(1,854)
Postmaterialists	40	50	30	43	(867)

Source: Political Action surveys.

rienced by virtually all members of the older age groups, such as World
War II and the Great Depression; nevertheless, the impact of these events
was probably milder on the wealthier than on the poorer respondents.
Those who rank in the upper economic strata today did not necessarily rank
there during their formative years, but since there is a fairly strong correlation between one's economic level now and in the past, we would expect
some tendency for upper-status respondents to be less Materialistic.

An analysis of respondents' occupational prestige by value type confirms this expectation very clearly, as Table 5-1 demonstrates. This table
utilizes data from the *Political Action* study (see Barnes, Kaase, et al.
1979), which provides relatively detailed evidence concerning family
background. Here, the respondents' occupations are ranked according to
occupational prestige, using Treiman scores (Treiman 1977). Their value
types are coded on the basis of the twelve-item battery. Those who chose
Materialist goals for at least four of their top five choices are categorized
as Materialists; those who chose Materialist goals for three of their top five
choices are Mixed (Materialist); those who chose two Materialist goals are
classed as Mixed (Postmaterialist); and those who gave one or none of their
top rankings to Materialist goals are classed as Postmaterialists. The percentage of each group with occupations ranking in the top quartile is shown
in Table 5-1. In every country, Postmaterialists are much likelier to have
high-status occupations than are the Materialists; in the eight nations as a
whole, Postmaterialists are more than two and one-half times as likely to
rank in the top quartile as Materialists.

Table 5-2 provides more detailed information about the proportions of
Materialists and Postmaterialists in specific occupations, this time using

TABLE 5-2. RESPONDENT'S VALUE TYPE BY OCCUPATION IN FIFTEEN NATIONS

Occupation	Britain MAT PM		France MAT PM		Belgium MAT PM		Netherlands MAT PM	
Farmer	25%	7%	42%	6%	49%	4%	40%	6%
Manual worker	25	13	43	9	40	8	27	16
Professional	23	20	18	22	24	23	18	28
Executive	24	20	17	31	28	20	15	31

Occupation	W. Germany MAT PM		Italy MAT PM		Luxembourg MAT PM		Denmark MAT PM	
Farmer	38%	11%	59%	3%	44%	6%	37%	5%
Manual worker	31	13	48	5	33	12	32	11
Professional	19	21	30	15	31	16	25	12
Executive	25	19	36	13	27	22	21	15

Occupation	Ireland MAT PM		Greece MAT PM		Spain MAT PM		Portugal MAT PM	
Farmer	45%	5%	51%	5%	44%	0%	65%	0%
Manual worker	38	7	39	9	41	13	43	6
Professional	31	13	30	19	19	28	20	20
Executive	42	6	32	10	31	14	20	40

Occupation	Canada MAT PM		Mexico MAT PM		Japan MAT PM		Total MAT PM	
Farmer	22%	11%	36%	6%	47%	6%	46%	6%
Manual worker	21	17	33	9	38	6	35	11
Professional	14	28	20	15	33	9	24	20
Executive	23	22	18	13	25	14	22	23

Sources: Pooled data for all Euro-Barometer surveys carried out during 1980 - 1986 for all European nations; Canadian, Mexican, and Japanese data from World Values survey, 1981.
Note: Total N = 151,694. Percentages do not add up to 100% because mixed types are omitted.

data from the Euro-Barometer surveys and the World Values surveys. To save space, we do not show the mixed types in this table, and we focus on four occupational groups, located at opposite ends of the Materialist/Post-materialist continuum. Farmers are by far the most Materialist occupational group, with Materialists outnumbering Postmaterialists by almost 8 to 1 in the fifteen nations as a whole. Among manual workers, there is also an overwhelming predominance (about 3 to 1) of Materialists over Post-materialists. On the other hand, Postmaterialists are virtually as numerous

TABLE 5-3. EDUCATIONAL LEVEL BY VALUE TYPE
(Percentage having an educational level in the top quartile for their nation)

Value Type	U.S.	W. Germany	Britain	Nether-lands
Materialists	25%	17%	30%	32%
Mixed (Materialist)	22	24	25	33
Mixed (Postmat.)	26	26	33	54
Postmaterialists	42	51	49	77

Value Type	Austria	Switzer-land	Combined Total	N
Materialists	8%	23%	21%	(4,894)
Mixed (Materialist)	15	26	25	(3,337)
Mixed (Postmat.)	24	34	33	(1,670)
Postmaterialists	29	38	50	(764)

Source: Political Action surveys carried out 1974 - 1976; see Barnes, Kaase, et al. 1979 for details.

as Materialists among professionals and executives. Since farm families tend to have the lowest level of income and economic security, and executives and professionals the highest, these findings are all in the expected direction.

One's education is another indicator of economic status and security, and analysis of values by education shows a similar pattern. As Table 5-3 (based on the *Political Action* data) shows us, the more highly educated are more apt to be Postmaterialists. The relationship of value type with education is even stronger than the relationship with occupation. There are several possible explanations for this fact. One would be that the process of education itself tends to encourage Postmaterialist values—either because they are emphasized in the school curriculum, or because those who receive higher education are exposed to a milieu containing a higher proportion of Postmaterialists. But there is another possible interpretation. Education may be a stronger predictor of value type because it gets closer to the key causal factor, which is formative security. The respondent's occupation is a reasonably good indicator of one's current economic level. But one's education is an indicator of how prosperous one's *parents* were. It is correlated with current income as well, of course, but particularly in Europe, whether or not one went to secondary school is strongly influenced by the socioeconomic status of one's parents. Thus, we have two related but confounding influences mingled here. Let us try to separate them.

The *Political Action* data contain a number of indicators of formative security, the most useful of which are the respondent's answers to the following questions: "During your early youth—let's say when you were

TABLE 5-4. VALUE TYPE BY SOCIOECONOMIC STATUS OF RESPONDENT AND RESPONDENT'S
FATHER
(Percentage predominantly Postmaterialist: i.e., scoring 6 to 10 on values
index)

| Socioeconomic Status | Netherlands | | United States | |
	Status of Respondent	Status of Respondent's Father	Status of Respondent	Status of Respondent's Father
Lower	45%	47%	25%	25%
Medium	47	53	30	30
Upper	65	60	31	38
Gamma	.19	.16	.03	.16

| Socioeconomic Status | W. Germany | | Austria | |
	Status of Respondent	Status of Respondent's Father	Status of Respondent	Status of Respondent's Father
Lower	12%	13%	18%	20%
Medium	18	22	25	28
Upper	45	36	34	42
Gamma	.28	.30	.20	.24

Source: Adapted from Barnes, Kaase, et al., 1979, 328.

between ten and eighteen years old—what was your father's main occupation? What sort of work did he do?'' and ''What was the highest grade of school your father completed?''

Only four of the countries included in the *Political Action* study provide measures of both the father's educational level and the father's occupation during the respondent's early youth. Let us combine these two variables to produce an index of the father's socioeconomic status. If the father had a manual occupation and no more than a primary school education, he is coded as having a ''lower'' socioeconomic status. If the father had a non-manual occupation and a secondary or higher education, he is coded as having ''higher'' socioeconomic status. Those with other occupational and educational combinations are coded as having ''intermediate'' socioeconomic status. The respondent's own socioeconomic status was also coded by the same procedure but utilizing the occupation of the head of the respondent's present household and the respondent's own education.

Now let us compare the two respective indices of socioeconomic status as predictors of the respondent's value type. Table 5-4 shows the results. They provide dramatic evidence of the importance of formative security.

In the Dutch sample, 45 percent of the respondents ranking "low" in socioeconomic status selected predominantly Postmaterialist goals—as compared with 65 percent of the Dutch respondents with "high" socioeconomic status. The full cross-tabulation of values by respondent's status yields a gamma coefficient of .19. When we tabulate value type by the respondent's father's status, we obtain 47 percent Postmaterialists among the "lower"-status Dutch respondents and 60 percent Postmaterialists among the "upper"-status Dutch respondents, with a gamma coefficient of .16. Thus, in the Dutch case, the respondent's own socioeconomic status is a slightly stronger predictor of the respondent's values than is the respondent's father's socioeconomic status. This is far from surprising. Normally, one would certainly expect an individual's own current characteristics to give a far stronger explanation of his or her current attitudes than the status of some other person, particularly since our measure of father's SES is based on recall data reporting the characteristics of another individual at a time that may lie several decades in the past. It follows that our indicator of the father's SES is almost certainly contaminated by a good deal more error in measurement than our indicator of the respondent's own current SES. It is therefore rather surprising to find that in the Dutch case, one's father's SES is almost as good a predictor of one's values as is the individual's own SES.

What is even more surprising, however, is the fact that in each of the other three countries for which we have data, the father's SES is a *stronger* predictor of the respondent's values than is the respondent's own SES. This is an unusual and remarkable finding—but it confirms previous results based on 1971 European Community data (Inglehart 1977, ch. 3). It supports the conclusion that one's values reflect the conditions experienced during one's formative years—perhaps several decades ago—even more than they reflect one's recent experiences.

We find significant linkages between indicators of formative economic security and value types—and a crucial part of these linkages seems to reflect events that took place in the fairly distant past. As we hypothesized, changes in the degree of security experienced during one's formative years may account for the rising proportion of Postmaterialists among the younger age groups.

Taking another approach, Dalton (1977) also attempts to sort out the relative impact of formative experiences, versus current income and education, in shaping one's value priorities. Using the age cohort as the unit of analysis, he undertakes to explain the variance in value priorities across eleven age cohorts in each of eight nations. As an indicator of a given cohort's formative experiences, he uses gross domestic product per capita when a given age cohort in a given nation was 8 to 12 years old. In multiple regression analysis, this indicator proves to be the most powerful predictor of each group's values in adult life: the partial correlation with values is .47. Dalton tested several possible formative periods, using economic conditions when a given cohort was in the age spans from 8 to 12 years; from 13 to 17; and from 18 to 22. The earliest of these formative periods gives the most powerful explanation of values. The generation unit's mean educational level is a decidedly weaker explanatory variable (partial r = .35); life cycle effects rank next (partial r = .25); and current income explains little additional variance. Similar results are obtained by Herz (1979; cf. Inglehart 1980).

In keeping with our hypotheses, we find two types of individual level variation in the West: (1) The postwar age cohorts are more apt to have Postmaterialist priorities because they were raised as a group under conditions of greater economic and physical security than those for the older cohorts; and (2) within given age groups, those raised in relatively prosperous families are more likely to have Postmaterialist values than those raised in less secure circumstances.

In Japan, the former pattern is pronounced, but our data in Table 5-2 suggest that the latter is relatively weak. Japanese professionals and executives are clearly more Postmaterialist than Japanese with farm or manual occupations, but the contrast is not as great as that found in Western countries. Why? One reason may be the fact that Japan is an exceptionally homogeneous society, with less inequality of income distribution than in most Western societies. Consequently, in response to standard public opinion survey questions about subjective social class, fully 90 percent of the Japanese regularly identify themselves as middle class—a finding that seems almost incredible from a Western perspective. In part, this may be one more indication of the strength of group solidarity in Japan, which spans the gap between workers and management in a given enterprise; but it may also reflect an important reality of postwar Japanese society. A large share of the Japanese work force still consists of people working on the production line, doing jobs that require limited skills and pay relatively modest wages; by objective standards they might be categorized as working class. But the annual per capita income in Japan has risen from about $200 in 1950 to about $8,000 in 1980. Even controlled for inflation, the increase is enormous. Compared with the standard of living their parents knew, or the standard of living they experienced when they were young, the overwhelming majority of the Japanese *do* have a middle-class standard of living. Their diet, clothing, housing, transportation, and leisure pursuits all tend to be on a level that was attainable only by the upper middle class a generation ago.

VALUES AND ECONOMIC ACHIEVEMENT

Whether one has Materialist or Postmaterialist values has a significant influence on whether one emphasizes economic or noneconomic forms of achievement. The items we used to measure these values refer to broad societal goals, since we wished to tap long-term preferences in the widest possible perspective. But our theory implies that these choices also tend to reflect personal goals. Do they?

In order to test this assumption, our respondents were asked:

Here are some of the things people usually take into account in relation to their work. Which one would you personally place first? . . . and which next?

— A good salary so that you do not have any worries about money
— A safe job with no risk of closing down or unemployment
— Working with people you like
— Doing an important job which gives you a feeling of accomplishment.

This question refers to much more immediate and personal concerns than the societal goals dealt with above. The first and second alternatives were intended to tap Materialist personal goals: income and security. The third and fourth alternatives were designed to tap "higher order" needs. As we anticipated, the respective pairs tend to be chosen together.

Are our respondents merely giving lip service to goals that are fashionable in their milieu and age group, but unrelated to their personal preferences? Apparently not. We cross-tabulated respondents' job goals by our twelve-item index of Materialist/Postmaterialist value priorities. Table A-6 (in the Appendix) summarizes the results for the nine countries surveyed in 1973. The overall results are summed up in Figure 5-1. In each country, Materialist respondents are relatively likely to choose "a good salary" and "a safe job," while the Postmaterialists tend to choose "working with people you like" and "a feeling of accomplishment." In the nine nations as a whole, the Postmaterialists are more than twice as likely as the Materialists to choose the two latter items. And, with few exceptions, there is a monotonic increase in emphasis on needs for belonging and self-expression as we move from the pure Materialist type, across the four intermediate types, to the pure Postmaterialist type. Figure 5-1 depicts this shift in emphasis on each of the four job goals as we move from Materialist to Postmaterialist; between types "2" and "3," there is a transition point at which a sense of accomplishment begins to outweigh emphasis on salary and congenial co-workers begin to outweigh emphasis on job security. The

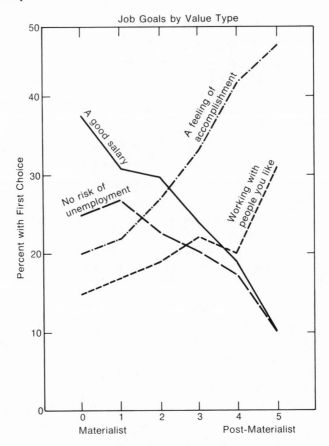

FIGURE 5-1. Job goals by value type. First choice among
"things which are most important in a job." Based on
combined nine-nation European Community sample, 1973
(N = 13,484). Source: Inglehart 1977, 56.

first three types might be described as predominantly Materialist and the
last three as predominantly Postmaterialist.

One's choice of long-term societal goals tends to be integrated with
one's immediate personal goals. This suggests that if Postmaterialist types
are becoming increasingly widespread, changing demands will be made
on employers. There are various indications that this is already occurring
to a certain extent. A high salary alone is no longer enough to motivate the
younger and more skilled segments of the labor force; they are increasingly
concerned with obtaining interesting, meaningful, and congenial work.
Our findings suggest that the current problems encountered in motivating
Western workers are not attributable to the fact that they have become

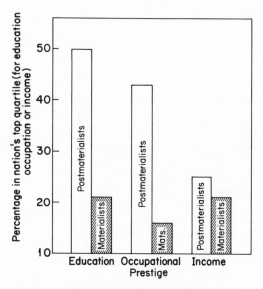

FIGURE 5-2. Value-based differences in respondents' education, occupational prestige,
and income. Based on pooled data from Political Action surveys carried out in 1974–1976
in United States, Britain, West Germany,
Netherlands, Austria, Italy, Switzerland, and
Finland.

lazy—rather, they are motivated by different kinds of goals than those that
proved effective in motivating the labor force in the past.

Value change in Western societies has a number of other implications as
well. In the very nature of things, Postmaterialists tend to be those who
start life with all the advantages; to a considerable extent, that is *why* they
are Postmaterialists. As we have seen, they are two or three times as likely
as Materialists to rank in the best-educated quartile of their society, and
they are correspondingly likely to have high-prestige jobs. But, despite
these advantages, the salaries they earn are only a little higher than those
earned by Materialists. As Table A-7 (in the Appendix) shows, among
those interviewed in the American segment of the *Political Action* study,
the Postmaterialists actually earned less than the Materialists. In West Germany, the differences were negligible, and in most other countries for
which we have data they were not very large. Overall, Postmaterialists are
only 4 percentage points likelier than Materialists to rank in the top quartile
by income in Table A-7. Figure 5-2 depicts this contrast graphically; Postmaterialists are a great deal likelier than Materialists to rank high on edu-

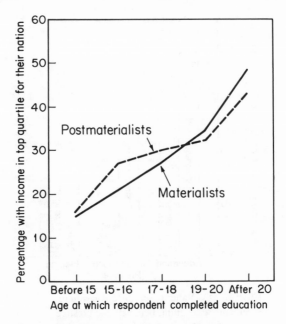

FIGURE 5-3. Economic achievement by value priorities and education among those born since 1945. Based on combined data from European Community surveys carried out in 1970–1986 ($N = 65,752$).

cation and occupational prestige—but they rank only slightly higher on income. They seem to be underachievers in terms of income.

The extent to which this is true varies with age and social background. As Table A-8 (in the Appendix) shows, among the prewar cohorts, Postmaterialists have higher household incomes than those of Materialists at all levels of education. But in the postwar generation, among those whose education continued beyond the age of 18, Postmaterialists earn *less* than Materialists. Figure 5-3 depicts this interaction. The younger, better-educated Postmaterialists are prototypical of their value type, and they seem to embody their values more intensely than do older and less-educated ones, in this and in other respects. Postmaterialists born since 1945 have lived their entire lives under conditions of relative security; to some extent, Postmaterialist values may also have spread among the older cohorts, converting some who have not had a Postmaterialist outlook throughout their entire lives. Such persons are relatively likely to take on Postmaterialist priorities because they have had high household incomes as adults.

Among the younger, better-educated respondents, however, Postmate-

TABLE 5-5. POSTMATERIALISTS AS ECONOMIC UNDERACHIEVERS:
HIGH INCOMES AMONG THOSE BORN SINCE 1945 AND WHOSE EDUCATION
CONTINUED PAST AGE 20
(Percentage with family incomes in top quartile for their nation)

Value Type	France	Belgium	Nether-lands	W. Germany	Italy
Materialist	53%	48%	31%	37%	48%
Mixed	46	46	40	38	42
Postmaterialist	45	46	42	30	41

Value Type	Denmark	Ireland	Britain	Greece
Materialist	54%	76%	49%	54%
Mixed	48	67	48	49
Postmaterialist	45	59	45	48

Source: Combined results of 1970 - 1986 European Community surveys.

rialists consistently tend to have lower household incomes than Materialists. As Table 5-5 shows, this holds true in eight of the nine European Community countries from which we have large numbers of interviews. The Netherlands is the sole exception; in France, Belgium, West Germany, Italy, Denmark, Ireland, Great Britain, and Greece, the younger, better-educated Postmaterialists have lower incomes than Materialists of comparable background—in some countries, by quite sizable margins.

In the preceding paragraph, we spoke of "Materialists of comparable background," because our theory implies that family background is a crucial factor influencing the degree of formative security that shaped one's values. But in fact, the Euro-Barometer surveys do not inquire about the socioeconomic status of one's parents, so we were forced to rely on the respondent's own educational level as a surrogate indicator of formative security, although evidence examined earlier in this chapter indicates that parental background provides a more accurate measure.

The *Political Action* study, however, does provide measures of parental background. Moreover, it also provides information about the respondent's own individual income rather than that of the entire household (as is obtained in the Euro-Barometer surveys). Here, too, we have access to a more accurate measure of what we are interested in: Clearly, one's own income should reflect one's value priorities more faithfully than the income of one's household (a majority of which might be brought in by other persons not necessarily having the same values). The *Political Action* data also provide more accurate measurement of still another variable, for this study utilizes the twelve-item battery (rather than the four-item battery) to

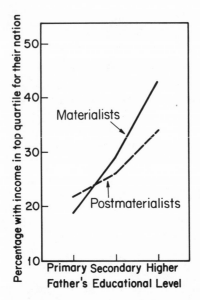

FIGURE 5-4. Economic achievement by value priorities and respondent's father's educational level. Based on pooled data from Political Action surveys in United States, West Germany, Netherlands, and Austria (all age groups) (N = 4,499). "Postmaterialists" consist of pure Postmaterialists plus mixed (Postmaterialist) groups.

measure the respondent's value priorities; and empirical tests indicate that this broader-based battery provides a significantly more accurate measurement of the underlying dimension (Inglehart 1976). Let us therefore replicate this analysis using the *Political Action* data. Table A-9 (in the Appendix) shows the results.

The tendency for Postmaterialists to be economic underachievers becomes considerably more pronounced. It is not limited to the postwar cohorts; it is clearly visible among the better-educated strata of both young and old. As Table A-9 (in the Appendix) indicates, among all respondents whose father's education went beyond primary school, Postmaterialists earn less than Materialists. Figure 5-4 depicts the crossover that occurs. A separate analysis of the postwar generation only (not shown here) reveals that among this group, Postmaterialist values are negatively correlated with income among *all three* levels of parental education.

With more accurate measurement of the respondent's values, his or her own income, and family background, economic underachievement by the Postmaterialists comes into sharper focus. It is still most pronounced among the younger and better-educated groups, but it is found among a majority of all Postmaterialists in this analysis.

Controlling for parental education is clearly more satisfactory than controlling for the respondent's own educational level. While the latter is a reasonably good indicator, parental background is a more direct and less ambiguous measure of formative security. Controlling for the respondent's own education has a certain ambiguity since income and education are closely correlated. When we control for education, we are left wondering whether the Postmaterialists' income advantage narrows or disappears because we are controlling for their higher socioeconomic family background—or simply because in controlling for education, we are also controlling for income to some extent. Controlling for the father's education largely resolves this causal ambiguity. Parental education when one was 10 to 18 years old clearly does have temporal precedence over one's current income; and controlling for this clearly *is* controlling for early social background—and only indirectly (and via an unambiguous causal route) for current income.

Moreover, controlling for an individual's own educational background does not fully control for differences in social background. Postmaterialists of a given educational level tend to come from families with a higher socioeconomic background than was enjoyed by Materialists at the same educational level. The Postmaterialists are more likely to have gone to elite schools than Materialists with the same number of years of schooling; and they may have better family connections, which gives them an edge over Materialists of similar educational level. Controlling for parental background controls for these differences more adequately—and the result is dramatic: A majority of Postmaterialists earn *less* than their Materialist counterparts. They are economic underachievers.

A related analysis by de Graaf and Ultee (1987) reaches similar conclusions. Controlling for education, these authors find that Postmaterialists tend to earn less than Materialists but that they tend to have jobs with *higher* prestige than Materialists. It is not that Postmaterialists are lazy—but that, since they emphasize other values, they quite logically tend to pursue (and attain) other goals.

Using a quite different approach, the aggregate analysis examined in chapter 1 found that nations with relatively high proportions of Postmaterialists show significantly lower rates of economic growth than those of nations with high proportions of Materialists. The evidence examined here suggests that this reflects individual level differences in prevailing motivations, rooted in early-instilled values. It is no coincidence that nations with high proportions of Postmaterialists show relatively low economic growth rates, for Postmaterialists emphasize economic achievement less than Materialists do, and they emphasize other kinds of achievement more. This is not simply a matter of lip service. The evidence examined here indicates that, in their careers, Postmaterialists act to maximize prestige, interesting experiences, and the quality of life in general, rather than sheer income.

CHAPTER 6

Changing Religious Orientations, Gender Roles, and Sexual Norms

INTRODUCTION

Far-reaching though it is, the rise of Postmaterialism is only one aspect of a still broader process of cultural change that is reshaping the political outlook, religious orientations, gender roles, and sexual mores of advanced industrial society. These changes are related to a common concern: the need for a sense of security, which religion and absolute cultural norms have traditionally provided. In the decades since World War II, the emergence of unprecedentedly high levels of prosperity, together with the relatively high levels of social security provided by the welfare state, have contributed to a decline in the prevailing sense of vulnerability. For the general public, one's fate is no longer so heavily influenced by unpredictable forces as it was in agrarian and early industrial society. We believe that this fact has been conducive to the spread of secular and Postmaterialist orientations that place less emphasis on traditional religious and cultural norms—especially insofar as these norms conflict with individual self-expression.

Nevertheless, we do not entirely accept the thesis that modern material values are replacing the traditional spiritual outlook on life (Lenski 1966; Luckmann 1967; Berger 1969; Wilson 1982). Though there seems to be little doubt that Materialist values became increasingly widespread with the rise of industrial society, we suspect that, in the long run, the transition to postindustrial society will entail a renewed emphasis on spiritual values.

There are three basic reasons for the decline of traditional religious social and sexual norms in advanced industrial societies. The first is that an increasing sense of security diminishes need for absolute norms. Individuals under high stress have a need for rigid, predictable rules. They need to be sure of what is going to happen because they are in danger—their margin for error is slender and they need maximum predictability. Postmaterialists reflect the converse phenomenon: Under conditions of relative security, one can tolerate more diversity; thus, one doesn't need the security of the absolute, rigid rules that religious sanctions can provide. The psychological costs of deviating from whatever norms one grew up with are harder to bear if you are under stress than if you feel secure. Taking one's world apart and putting it together again is psychologically stressful in any case. But people with relatively high levels of security, such as the Postmaterialists, can more readily accept deviation from familiar patterns than can people who feel anxiety concerning their basic existential needs. Consequently, we would expect Postmaterialists to accept cultural change more readily than others.

The second reason is that societal and religious norms usually have some functional basis—at least originally. Such basic norms as "Thou shalt not kill" serve an obvious societal function. Restricting violence to narrow, predictable channels is crucial to a society's viability. Without such norms, a society would tend to tear itself apart. Many religious norms, such as "Thou shalt not commit adultery" or "Honor thy father and mother," are linked with maintaining the family unit. This particular function has become less crucial than it once was, which may open the way to gradual erosion of related norms. Although the family was once the key economic unit, in advanced industrial society people's working life is now overwhelmingly outside the home. Similarly, most education now takes place outside the family. Furthermore, the welfare state has taken over responsibility for sheer survival. Formerly, whether children lived or died largely depended on whether their parents provided for them; the relationship reversed when one reached old age. Though the role of the family is still important, the life or death nature of this relationship has been softened by the rise of the welfare state. Today, the new generation can survive if the family breaks up—or even if neither parent is around. One-parent families and childless old people are far more viable under contemporary conditions than they once were. As long as the sheer survival of the children is threatened by it, society is apt to view divorce as utterly wrong, intolerable. It threatens the long-term viability of society.

The functional basis of this norm and other norms reinforcing the two-parent family has eroded. Does this mean that society changes its values? No—not immediately. Cultural norms tend to be internalized very firmly at an early age, and backed up with prerational sanctions. People's opposition to divorce does not simply reflect a rational calculation that "the family is an important economic unit, so people should stay married"; instead, divorce tends to become a question of good and evil. The norms that constrain people's behavior even when they want to do something else are the norms that are taught as absolute rules, and inculcated so that people's consciences torture them if those norms are violated. Such societal norms have a lot of momentum. The mere fact that the function of a given cultural pattern has weakened or even disappeared does not mean that the norm itself disappears. But if the original reason behind a given norm vanishes, it does open the way for that norm to weaken gradually.

Norms linked to the maintenance of the two-parent heterosexual family clearly are weakening, for a variety of reasons, ranging from the rise of the welfare state to the drastic decline of infant mortality rates—meaning that a couple no longer needs to produce four or five children in order to maintain the existing population size. In these realms, one would expect experimentation to take place; gradually, behavior that deviated from traditional norms might become increasingly acceptable—and the groups most likely to accept these new forms of behavior would be the young more than the old, and the relatively secure, more than the insecure.

Conversely, one might interpret such phenomenan as the rise of the "Moral Majority" in the United States as a reaction to recent cultural change by groups who are less educated, have fewer resources, are less secure, and therefore are more threatened by change. This phenomenon is not unique to Western countries. In a curious way, the functional equivalent of the "Moral Majority" in the United States is the hardline communists in the Soviet Union today, who are faced with *perestroika*, and other major changes from the norms under which they were brought up. Even though these norms are quite different from those of the Judaeo-Christian tradition, departure from them strains the conscience and produces anxiety. Accordingly, in the Soviet Union, the intellectuals are more enthusiastic about perestroika than the lower strata of the working class. Thus, reform in the Soviet Union not only faces opposition from elite groups that have a vested interest in keeping the system the way it is but, in addition, gives rise to a conflict between old and new values.

The third reason for the decline of the traditional worldview is a question of cognitive consistency. People struggle for internal consistency. Hence, their worldviews tend to be consistent with their daily experience—and the daily life experience of people today is basically different from the kind of life experience that shaped the Judaeo-Christian tradition. The Old Testament emerged in a pastoral society. Its symbols (the Good Shepherd, feed My sheep, etc.) reflect a pastoral worldview. By the time the New Testament was written, the Jewish people had largely become farmers rather than shepherds—and the New Testament reflects an agrarian society, with rather different norms and a different worldview. But today we live in an advanced industrial society, in which computers are far likelier than sheep to be a part of one's daily experience. Consequently, there is a cognitive mismatch between the traditional normative system and the world most people know from firsthand experience. Not only the social norms, but also the symbols and worldview of the established religions, are not as persuasive or compelling as they were in their original setting.

In agrarian societies, humanity was very much at the mercy of inscrutable and uncontrollable natural forces. Because their causes were dimly understood, people tended to attribute whatever happened to anthropomorphic spirits or gods. Most of the population made their living from agriculture, and were largely dependent on things that came from heaven, like the sun and rain. One prayed for good weather, for relief from disease, or from plagues of insects.

In industrial society, production increasingly moved indoors into an environment built by humans. One did not wait for the sun to rise and the seasons to change—one turned on the lights and heating. One did not pray for good crops—production depended on machines designed and maintained by human ingenuity. With the discovery of germs and antibiotics, even disease ceased to be seen as a divine visitation; increasingly it became a problem within human control.

It was only natural that such profound changes in people's daily experience of how the world worked would lead to changes in the prevailing cosmology. In industrial society, where the factory was the center of productive effort, a mechanistic view of the universe seemed natural. Initially, this gave currency to the concept of God as a great watchmaker who had constructed the universe and then left it to run largely on its own. But as human control of the environment increased, the role ascribed to God dwindled. Materialistic ideologies arose, which proposed secular interpretations of history, and secular utopias to be attained solely by human engineering.

The emergence of postindustrial society seems likely to stimulate further evolution of prevailing views of the cosmos, but not in precisely the same direction as in the early phases of industrialization. In the United States, Canada, and Western Europe, the majority of the labor force no longer works in factories. Instead of living in a mechanistic environment, most people now spend their productive hours dealing with people and symbols. Increasingly, human efforts are no longer focused on producing material objects, but on communicating and processing information—and the crucial product is innovation and knowledge.

We would expect these developments to be conducive to the emergence of a less mechanical and instrumental worldview, one that places more emphasis on understanding the meaning and purpose of human life. The Holocaust and Hiroshima have made it clear that technology is not an unmixed blessing, and environmental problems have given rise to a revived respect for nature. Postindustrial society will not be a return to agrarian society, and a simple reprise of traditional religion does not seem likely, but a renewed concern for spiritual values does. If this is occurring, it is still in its early stages, however. In recent decades, the main trend has been a decline of traditional religious values.

Nevertheless, spiritual concerns are an inherent concern of human beings. In *A Brief History of Time*, theoretical physicist Stephen Hawking relates his efforts to integrate general relativity theory with quantum mechanics, in order to understand how the universe functions. The book, reflecting one of the most modern minds of the twentieth century, working at the frontiers of human knowledge, concludes:

> However, if we do discover a complete theory, it should in time be understandable in broad principle by everyone, not just a few scientists. Then we shall all, philosophers, scientists, and just ordinary people, be able to take part in the discussion of the question of why it is that we and the universe exist. If we find the answer to that, it would be the ultimate triumph of human reason—for then we would know the mind of God. (Hawking 1988, 175)

The concern for the meaning of life, and the meaning of the universe, is not outdated. And Hawking's reference to God is not ironic or incidental—the idea that contemporary science is a spiritual quest pervades his entire book. Hawking's image of God is, of course, a very different concept from the pastoral imagery of the Bible. But a concern for the meaning of life is inherent in humanity. The traditional models that are offered to us are out of date in some profound ways: Their concepts and images are incongruent with much of what most people absorb in both their formal education and their daily life experience. But the basic questions underlying the great religious traditions, concerning the meaning and purpose of life, remain.

TRADITIONAL VERSUS SECULAR VALUES

In preceding chapters, we have seen evidence of major changes in the political and economic priorities of the publics of advanced industrial societies. The rise of Postmaterialism is also linked with a pervasive process of cultural change that goes well beyond these realms, though it has important political and economic implications. Let us examine another dimension of cultural change. In 1981, the European Values Systems Study Group carried out an extensive investigation of the value systems of representative national samples of the publics of ten West European publics (Stoetzel 1983; Abrams, Gerard, and Timms 1985; Halman, et al. 1987; Harding, Phillips, and Fogarty 1986; Fogarty, Ryan, and Lee 1984; Rezsohazy and Kerkhofs 1984); subsequent replications have been carried out in fifteen other countries. This World Values Survey explored beliefs, values, and attitudes of these publics toward religion, family life, work, leisure, and contemporary social issues.

Among the findings emerging from this rich and fascinating study is the fact that the religious and cultural values of these publics show a remarkably high degree of structure and coherence. Compared with the relatively weak correlations generally found between attitudes toward public policy issues, attitudes concerning religion and family show high levels of constraint. As Converse (1964, 1970) has demonstrated, political ideologues are rare among the general public. Nevertheless, a substantial portion of the public manifests a consistent structure of orientations toward a wide range of religious and cultural values. Quite consistently, individuals either adhere to or reject traditional Judaeo-Christian norms, ranging from belief in God, to acceptance of divorce, abortion, or homosexuality.

The fact that we find a more coherent structure among religious than among political attitudes is not entirely surprising. For most people, political activity of any kind is sporadic and infrequent; but for a large share of the population, religious socialization starts early in life and is continued on at least a weekly basis. Table 6-1 demonstrates one aspect of this phenomenon, summing up results from the various publics included in this survey (with similar patterns emerging within each society when analyzed separately).

A principal components analysis reveals that mass orientations toward a diverse range of cultural values can be interpreted in terms of a single underlying dimension that reflects the degree to which one accepts or rejects traditional Judaeo-Christian cultural norms. More than forty attitudes show significant loadings on this dimension, many of them showing correlations that are unusually strong for survey data, especially considering the fact that these questions were asked in a variety of formats and in various sections of the questionnaire, indicating that this relatively high constraint is not simply a methodological artifact.

The attitudes involved here can be grouped into three categories: (1) monotheism; (2) inviolability of family; and (3) the civil order. The first category shows the strongest loadings, and the third, the weakest. The seven highest-loading items (with an average loading of .712) deal with the idea that God exists, that there is only one God, and that He is to be viewed with reverence. Since monotheism is the core belief of the Judaeo-Christian value system, it seems appropriate that the First, Second, and Third Commandments constitute three of the five highest-loading items on this dimension. The highest-loading item, however, is a question that asks: ''And how important is God in your life? Please use this card to indicate— 10 means very important and 1 means not at all important.''

Another group of items deals with the inviolability of the family and child rearing. The specific content is diverse, concerning attitudes toward abortion, divorce, extramarital affairs, adultery, prostitution, and homosexuality. Two questions, based on the Sixth and Ninth Commandments, respectively, fall into this group. The factor loadings for this group range from .538 to .626, and some additional items concerning monotheism also fall into this range—a reflection of the fact that, despite their diverse content, one's responses to these items are closely related to whether or not one believes in God.

A third category of items deals with the civil order—specifically, with stolen property, lying, and violence against other people. Questions based

TABLE 6-1. ACCEPTANCE/REJECTION OF TRADITIONAL JUDAEO-CHRISTIAN VALUES
(Principal components factor analysis)

Value	First Principal Component Loading
God is important in respondent's life (high score on 1 - 10 scale)	.771
"Thou shalt have no other gods before me" applies today	.749
Respondent gets strength and comfort from religion	.736
"Keep the Sabbath holy" applies today	.707
"Thou shalt not take the name of the Lord in vain" applies today	.696
Respondent believes in heaven	.693
Respondent believes in God	.635
Abortion is unjustifiable (low score on 1 - 10 scale)	.626
Respondent believes there is a personal God	.621
Respondent considers self religious	.614
Divorce is unjustifiable (low score on 1 - 10 scale)	.617
Extramarital affairs are unjustifiable (1 - 10 scale)	.606
Respondent believes in a soul	.594
"Thou shalt not commit adultery" applies today	.590
Respondent believes in Hell	.579
Respondent believes in life after death	.579
"Thou shalt not covet thy neighbor's wife" applies today	.577
Respondent believes in the Devil	.560
Prostitution is unjustifiable (1 - 10 scale)	.552
The church gives adequate answers to man's spiritual needs	.551
The church gives adequate answers to moral problems	.544
The church gives adequate answers to the problems of family life	.542
Euthanasia is unjustifiable (1 - 10 scale)	.545
Homosexuality is unjustifiable (1 - 10 scale)	.541
Sex under legal age of consent is unjustifiable (1 - 10 scale)	.538
"Thou shalt not covet thy neighbor's goods" applies today	.531
RESPONDENT ATTENDS CHURCH REGULARLY	.515
Fighting with the police is unjustifiable (1 - 10 scale)	.496
Using marijuana is unjustifiable (1 - 10 scale)	.482
Lying is unjustifiable (1 - 10 scale)	.459
"Thou shalt not bear false witness" applies today	.459

Table 6-1. (Concluded)

Value	First Principal Component Loading
"Honor thy father and mother" applies today	.457
Children should be encouraged to learn religious faith	.456
"Thou shalt not steal" applies today	.450
Buying stolen goods is unjustifiable	.435
Keeping found money is unjustifiable	.438
Not paying fare on public transport is unjustifiable	.415
Cheating on income taxes is unjustifiable	.387
Killing in self-defense is unjustifiable	.338
"Thou shalt not kill" applies today	.330
Political assassination is unjustifiable	.329

Source: Based on combined data from World Values survey, with fieldwork in Spring-Summer 1981 for all countries except the United States, South Africa, and Hungary, where fieldwork took place in Spring-Summer 1982. Fieldwork for respective countries was carried out by the following organizations, with number of interviews in parentheses: Belgium, Dimarso (1,145); Denmark, Observa (1,182); Spain, DATA (2,303); France, Faits et Opinions (1,199); Britain, Gallup Poll (1,231); Northern Ireland and Republic of Ireland, Irish Marketing surveys (1,217 and 312); Italy, DOXA (1,348); Netherlands, NIPO (1,221); West Germany, Institut fur Demoskopie (1,305); United States, Gallup Poll (2,314); Canada (1,250); Japan, Nippon Research Center (1,184); Mexico, IMOP (Mexican Gallup) (1,831); Republic of South Africa, Markinor (1,581); Hungary, Institute of Sociology, Hungarian Academy of Sciences (1,464).

on the Fourth, Fifth, Seventh, Eighth, and Tenth Commandments fall into this group, which shows loadings ranging from .329 to .531.

In the context of survey research, this is a remarkably wide-ranging but cohesive dimension, showing unusually powerful correlations between a diverse set of attitudes. The unifying element holding this value system together seems to be the Ten Commandments of the Old Testament, coupled with the belief that these Commandments reflect the will of an omnipotent deity. If one accepts that belief, it is mandatory that one adhere to the entire system.

As one would expect, those who attend church regularly tend to accept this value system—but it is important to bear in mind that church attendance is only a rough indicator of these associated beliefs. Church attendance is by no means our most sensitive indicator of this dimension; indeed, it does not even rank among the top twenty indicators. Religious practice is shaped by family ties, habits, and social milieu, as well as by personal beliefs; it does not necessarily reflect the individual's personal outlook. Our most sensitive indicator, the question about how important

God is in one's life, explains twice as much of the variance in acceptance or rejection of traditional Judaeo-Christian norms as does church attendance. If we were to base our conclusions on church attendance rates alone, unsupplemented by the more detailed information available from survey research, we would obtain a crude and somewhat misleading picture of mass orientations toward religion. Church attendance statistics are better than nothing, as a rough indicator of trends in religious belief—but they clearly are no substitute for direct measures of these beliefs.

ARE RELIGIOUS VALUES IN DECLINE?

By contrast with the weak structure usually found underlying their political orientations, mass publics seem to have relatively consistent and well-crystallized orientations toward a wide range of religious and moral norms. More interesting still, in every country studied, Materialists are substantially more likely than Postmaterialists to adhere to traditional Judaeo-Christian norms. This holds true even though there is no similarity in either face content or format between the questions used to measure the respondents' religious, moral, and sexual norms and those used to tap Materialist/Postmaterialist values. Indeed, this finding is somewhat paradoxical. The theology of the Judaeo-Christian religions deemphasize the importance of material security in this world and attempt to orient their followers toward nonmaterial goals. Yet, empirically, we find a clear and pervasive tendency for traditional Judaeo-Christian values to be most firmly espoused by the Materialist value type.

This is only an apparent paradox, however. For, as Weber pointed out more than eighty years ago, the actual impact of a given religion can evolve into something very different from its original theology. With the rise of industrial society, a Materialistic outlook became widespread, providing a belief system that was consistent with, and supportive of, the economy and technology underlying that society. By now, the Materialistic emphasis on economic and physical security have become traditional. And it is precisely those who experience the least economic and physical security in their lives who have the greatest need for the guidance and reassurance that familiar cultural norms and absolute religious beliefs provide. The Postmaterialists, on the other hand, have experienced relatively high levels of economic and physical security throughout their formative years. They feel relatively little need for the security and predictability provided by absolute and inflexible rules—on the contrary, they may perceive such rules as an intolerable restriction on individual self-expression.

We find rather strong linkages between Postmaterialism and an agnostic orientation toward traditional Judaeo-Christian norms (by and large, the

TABLE 6-2. PERCEIVED IMPORTANCE OF GOD BY VALUE TYPE AND COUNTRY
(Percentage giving low rating: 4 or below, on a scale from 1 to 10)

Value Type	Denmark	France	Nether- lands	Japan	W. Germany
Materialist	41%	37%	44%	38%	33%
Mixed	55	54	46	45	38
Postmat.	68	64	56	51	61
Total	56	50	48	43	42

Value Type	Britain	Italy	Hungary	Belgium	Spain
Materialist	31%	26%	23%	26%	14%
Mixed	41	33	30	28	32
Postmat.	49	42	46	34	48
Total	40	31	30	28	25

Value Type	Canada	Northern Ireland	Repub. of Ireland	South Africa	Mexico	All Nations[a]
Materialist	8%	15%	3%	5%	2%	23%
Mixed	17	19	14	5	2	29
Postmat.	24	30	23	10	7	44
Total	16	18	10	6	3	29

Source: World Values survey, 1981 - 1982.
Note: U.S. data on Materialist/Postmaterialist values not available in this survey.
[a]Values for "all nations" are based on pooled results, weighted according to population.

correlations are in the .30 range). Table 6-2 gives one example, showing the relationship between Materialist values and the importance of God in one's life, a particularly sensitive indicator of the religious/secular dimension underlying these data. After four decades under communism, the Hungarian public still attaches as much importance to religion as do the Italians. Moreover, the linkage with Materialist/Postmaterialist values that we find in Hungary is very similar to what we find in Western countries. Across the various societies included in this survey, Postmaterialists are about twice as likely as Materialists to indicate that God has little importance in their lives.

From evidence presented in earlier chapters, it seems clear that an intergenerational shift is taking place from Materialist toward Postmaterialist values. Is a similar shift occurring, away from traditional Judaeo-Christian religious and social values?

This last question cannot be answered conclusively because we do not yet have time series data on these religious and cultural values that are comparable to those available on Materialist/Postmaterialist values. But the data that are available suggest that a major intergenerational shift in religious orientations is occurring. It would be a serious oversimplification to describe this process as the decline of religion. In some respects, the emerging generation seems to have a *heightened* sensitivity to spiritual concerns, by comparison with older groups. But the worldview espoused by most of the established religious denominations seems increasingly out of touch with the perceptions and priorities of the younger generation. Thus, we simultaneously find indications of a heightened reverence for nature and an increased concern for the meaning and purpose of life among Postmaterialists together with much weaker support for traditional religious norms. Is the trend toward Postmaterialism mirrored in changing religious orientations?

If an intergenerational value shift were taking place, away from traditional religious and cultural norms, we would expect to find more secular attitudes among the young than among the old. This is precisely what we do find in each of the countries from which we have data. As one illustration of a pervasive pattern, Table 6-3 demonstrates the relationship between age and the importance of God in one's life. As we saw in Table 6-1, this question is our most sensitive indicator of acceptance or rejection of traditional Judaeo-Christian values. In each of these countries, there is an increase in the percentage saying that God is not important in their lives as we move from old to young. The youngest group is about two and a half times as likely to give a secular response as the oldest.

The degree to which the young accord less importance to God than do the old varies greatly from one society to another. This phenomenon seems to characterize Western Europe and Japan to a far greater extent than it does North America and South Africa. If these data reflect an ongoing secularization of mass publics, then the process has had little impact thus far in the United States, South Africa, or Mexico. In each of these countries, the young are likelier than the old to rate God as unimportant in their lives, but most of the population—in each case, over 90 percent—give Him a relatively high ranking. In these countries, even the great majority of the young indicate that God plays an important part in their lives, and the percentage differences between young and old are small. Our results from the Republic of South Africa, incidentally, are weighted according to population so that they primarily reflect the orientations of the Black majority; but a strong emphasis on religion characterizes the white and "colored" populations of South Africa as well as the Black population.

Practically everyone, young or old, attaches importance to God in the

TABLE 6-3. PERCEIVED IMPORTANCE OF GOD BY AGE GROUP

Question: "How important is God in your life? Please use this card to indicate - 10 means very important and 1 means not at all important."

(Percentage giving <u>low</u> rating: 4 or below, on a scale from 1 to 10)

Age Group	Denmark	France	Nether- lands	W. Germany	Japan	Britain
18 - 24	77%	63%	57%	60%	51%	56%
25 - 34	60	63	52	54	44	48
35 - 44	54	49	47	36	45	35
45 - 54	50	30	37	34	37	32
55 - 64	26	35	33	28	28	19
65+	21	33	36	16	32	20
Total	56	50	48	42	42	40

Age Group	Italy	Hungary	Belgium	Spain	Northern Ireland	Canada
18 - 24	34%	33%	43%	37%	36%	20%
25 - 34	42	32	35	37	30	20
35 - 44	24	26	22	18	13	18
45 - 54	21	22	20	19	4	14
55 - 64	31	19	22	18	8	6
65+	27	17	14	12	4	8
Total	31	30	28	25	18	16

Age Group	Repub. of Ireland	U.S.	South Africa	Mexico	Mean[a]
18 - 24	16%	10%	8%	2%	41%
25 - 34	15	10	6	3	37
35 - 44	11	7	4	3	27
45 - 54	4	6	2	2	22
55 - 64	6	5	8	1	20
65+	3	6	2	-	17
Total	10	8	5	3	30

Source: World Values survey, 1981 - 1982.

[a]Mexican sample does not contain sufficient number of persons over 64 years of age for reliable estimates. Consequently, the "mean" is based on all nations except Mexico in order to have the same base for each age group, in this and succeeding tabulations by age.

United States, South Africa, and Mexico. But all thirteen of the other societies show marked differences between young and old. This may be an indication of a precipitous decline in the importance of God in these societies. We emphasize, once again, the impossibility of drawing firm conclusions until a solid time series data base is available. But the available evidence strongly suggests that we are witnessing an intergenerational decline in the subjective importance of God in the lives of these publics. This decline seems gradual in some countries, but in Western Europe and Japan it seems pronounced. Interestingly, the decline of religion as we move from old to young is less pronounced in Hungary than in many Western nations. As chapter 1 suggested, the communist experience seems to have reshaped Hungarian culture only to a limited extent. A gradual process of secularization seems to be taking place, but it is occurring no more rapidly in Hungary than in Western Europe; if anything, communist efforts to instill atheism may have been counterproductive, actually retarding the decline of religious traditions in Hungary and (even more so) in Poland. In some countries—West Germany, for example—the apparent decline is cataclysmic. Among the oldest segment of the German public, only a small minority (16 percent) accord God an unimportant role in their lives. This is roughly comparable to the proportion of the total population who express this attitude today in the United States or Canada. But among the youngest German cohort, a heavy majority (60 percent) feel that God plays a relatively unimportant role in their lives. The West German case is by no means unique. Britain and France indicate almost equally great declines in religious orientation, and Denmark manifests an even sharper age group decline in the importance attached to God. It seems significant that Denmark has for many years been one of the world's most advanced social welfare states; the personal insecurities that (we have suggested) enhance the need for religious certainty are relatively weak in Denmark.

Theoretically, the age group differences observed here might reflect either a historic intergenerational change or life cycle effects. In support of the latter interpretation, one might argue that among the young it is natural for God to be a minor concern, but as the end of one's life approaches, one accords more importance to God, religion, and the afterlife.

But the tremendous cross-national variations we observe in age group differences strongly suggest that there is no inherent linkage between being old and being religious: In some countries, such as Mexico and the United States, most of the young attach great importance to God; in others, such as France or Japan, even among the old, large numbers do not. Danes aged 65 and older are less religious than Americans in their 20s. The age group differences seem to reflect the specific historical circumstances of given societies, rather than anything inherent in the human life cycle.

The fact that a secular orientation is linked with Postmaterialist values suggests that both of these orientations may be part of a broad syndrome of cultural change. The evidence shown in Table 6-4 strengthens this impression. It is based on responses to the question, "Which, if any, of the following do you believe in?" . . . God?"

A majority of the population in every society say they believe in God. The size of this majority ranges from over 60 percent in Japan, Denmark,

TABLE 6-4. BELIEF IN GOD BY AGE GROUP AND COUNTRY
(Percentage saying they believe in God)

Age Group	Japan	Denmark	France	Nether-lands	W. Germany	Britain
15 - 24	57%	37%	56%	60%	66%	67%
25 - 34	64	50	49	62	70	77
35 - 44	56	68	73	73	82	88
45 - 54	57	76	77	80	89	86
55 - 64	77	90	78	86	89	91
65+	72	87	80	83	91	92
Total	62	63	65	71	80	81

Age Group	Hungary	Belgium	Italy	Spain	Canada	Northern Ireland
15 - 24	81%	78%	83%	87%	92%	95%
25 - 34	81	83	84	85	92	90
35 - 44	85	88	91	93	93	98
45 - 54	88	92	94	95	93	100
55 - 64	90	89	90	96	97	100
65+	91	93	92	96	97	98
Total	85	86	88	92	93	97

Age Group	Repub. of Ireland	U.S.	Mexico	South Africa	Mean[a]
15 - 24	95%	97%	99%	98%	76%
25 - 34	95	97	97	99	78
35 - 44	98	98	99	99	86
45 - 54	99	98	98	97	88
55 - 64	99	98	98	98	91
65+	99	99	-	100	91
Total	97	98	98	99	84

Source: World Values survey, 1981 - 1982.
[a]See note to Table 6-3.

and France to near-unanimity in the United States, Mexico, South Africa, and both Northern and southern Ireland (here, as in a number of other respects, the prevailing cultural outlook in Northern Ireland is much closer to that of the Republic of Ireland than to that of Great Britain, which is one reason why we analyze Northern Ireland separately from the rest of the United Kingdom). In this last group of countries, where 97 to 99 percent of the population professes to believe in God, there are, of course, no substantial age group differences. But in each of the other countries, the young are less likely than the old to say they believe in God. Does this reflect a decline of faith? Cross-sectional data cannot give a conclusive answer, but it seems significant that the age differences are largest in those countries where the apparent decline of faith has gone farthest—as if the

TABLE 6-5. RELIGIOSITY BY AGE GROUP AND COUNTRY
(Percentage describing self as "a religious person")

Age Group	Japan	France	Britain	Northern Ireland	Spain	W. Germany
15 - 24	31%	42%	34%	32%	48%	44%
25 - 34	24	40	47	44	52	53
35 - 44	22	56	64	62	67	72
45 - 54	21	62	64	75	72	77
55 - 64	29	64	72	87	76	77
65+	49	70	77	83	80	84
Total	28	53	55	61	64	65

Age Group	Repub. of Ireland	Hungary	Denmark	Netherlands	South Africa	Canada
15 - 24	56%	59%	42%	59%	61%	67%
25 - 34	66	61	56	61	68	74
35 - 44	60	67	76	72	75	76
45 - 54	70	72	84	74	77	77
55 - 64	69	76	89	85	79	90
65+	86	80	90	84	89	86
Total	66	67	69	69	71	76

Age Group	Mexico	Belgium	U.S.	Italy	Mean[a]
15 - 24	77%	73%	75%	78%	53%
25 - 34	76	80	79	77	59
35 - 44	82	80	85	86	68
45 - 54	86	90	89	91	73
55 - 64	90	84	92	89	77
65+	–	88	92	90	82
Total	79	81	83	84	66

Source: World Values survey, 1981 - 1982.
[a]See note to Table 6-3.

older groups tended to hold onto the beliefs in which they were raised, while the young were relatively ready to depart from the traditional faith.

Belief in God is only one aspect of religion. One obtains a rather different perspective from responses to the question, "Independently of whether you go to church or not, would you say you are: a religious person, not a religious person, a convinced atheist?"

Table 6-5 shows the percentage that describes themselves as "a religious person." In almost every country, a considerably smaller proportion of the population considers themselves religious than believes in God (Denmark is an interesting exception). Thus, little more than a quarter of the Japanese public consider themselves religious, and only about half of the French and British publics do so. On the other hand, the Italians, who

TABLE 6-6. RELIGIOUS ATTITUDES BY VALUE TYPE

Value Type	% Saying They Believe in God	% Saying They Believe in a Life after Death	% Describing Self as "a Religious Person"
Materialist	89%	63%	67%
Mixed	83	56	61
Postmat.	69	50	50

Source: World Values survey, 1981 - 1982.
Note: Based on pooled results from sixteen nations, weighted according to population.

ranked only moderately high on belief in God, have the largest percentage who consider themselves religious of any nationality.

In the United States, Mexico, and South Africa, although there is virtually no variation in belief in God, there is variation in the "religious person" indicator of religiosity—and we find the same tendency for the young to be less religious in these three countries that we find elsewhere. In every country, without exception, the young consider themselves less religious than the old.

Each of these attitudes is linked with Materialist/Postmaterialist values: In virtually every country for which we have data, Postmaterialists are significantly less likely to say they believe in God, and less likely to describe themselves as religious, than those with Materialist or mixed values. Table 6-6 sums up the overall pattern in the combined World Values survey.

There is genuine irony in the fact that Postmaterialists seem relatively unattracted to organized religion in Western societies. Since they are less likely than Materialists to be preoccupied by the struggle for survival, theoretically they should have more intellectual and emotional energy to devote to the fulfillment of higher-order needs. And we find evidence that this is in fact the case. Our respondents in each nation were asked, "How often, if at all, do you think about the meaning and purpose of life?" Table 6-7 shows the proportion who said they did so "often," among each value type.

Despite their relative alienation from traditional religion, in each of these societies the Postmaterialists are *more* apt than the Materialists to spend time thinking about the meaning and purpose of life. This holds true despite the fact that older people are more likely to say they do so than younger ones (and the Postmaterialists are, of course, much likelier to be young). In this respect, Postmaterialists have *more* potential interest in religion than Materialists. But, it would seem, most organized religions

TABLE 6-7. FREQUENCY OF THINKING ABOUT THE MEANING OF LIFE
BY VALUE TYPE AND COUNTRY

Question: "How often, if at all, do you think about the meaning and
purpose of life? Often, sometimes, rarely or never?"

(Percentage saying "often")

Value Type	Japan	Belgium	Nether- lands	Spain	Repub. of Ireland	Northern Ireland
Materialist	18%	21%	21%	20%	22%	23%
Mixed	23	22	21	25	28	31
Postmat.	37	28	31	43	42	36
Total	22	23	23	24	27	27

Value Type	W. Germany	Denmark	Hungary	Mexico	Britain	France
Materialist	24%	20%	28%	33%	32%	29%
Mixed	27	30	31	30	30	35
Postmat.	34	32	39	36	43	50
Total	28	29	31	31	33	36

Value Type	Canada	Italy	South Africa	All Nations[a]
Materialist	30%	35%	37%	27%
Mixed	38	37	40	30
Postmat.	44	52	40	41
Total	37	38	39	31

Source: World Values survey, 1981 - 1982.

[a]Values for "all nations" are based on pooled data for all countries
shown in table, weighted according to population of each nation.

today have little to say about the meaning and purpose of life—at least in
terms that are meaningful to the Postmaterialists.

With remarkable consistency, we find that the young and those with
Postmaterialist values place less emphasis on religion than their opposite
numbers. Once again, the most remarkable fact about the Hungarian data
is that the pattern is very similar to that which prevails throughout the
West. The forces underlying cultural change seem to transcend the contrasting political and economic institutions that divide East and West. In
earlier chapters, we saw massive evidence of a gradual intergenerational
shift from Materialist toward Postmaterialist priorities; the present findings
suggest that this shift is linked with a decline of traditional religious values
that is itself part of a still broader syndrome of cultural change.

TABLE 6-8. REJECTION OF HOMOSEXUALITY BY AGE GROUP
(Percentage saying homosexuality can <u>never</u> be justified - a rating of 1
on a scale from 1 to 10)

Age Group	Nether- lands	Denmark	W. Germany	Britain	France	Belgium
18 - 24	11%	18%	26%	31%	28%	42%
25 - 34	13	28	31	30	29	43
35 - 44	19	32	40	38	53	47
45 - 54	23	45	43	40	62	53
55 - 64	39	47	58	67	67	62
65+	52	54	70	72	76	66
Total	22	34	42	43	47	51

Age Group	Canada	Japan	Spain	Hungary	Repub. of Ireland	Italy
18 - 24	42%	35%	38%	44%	41%	50%
25 - 34	41	42	41	47	48	51
35 - 44	46	66	57	56	54	65
45 - 54	52	60	67	63	76	72
55 - 64	72	60	67	69	79	81
65+	82	72	80	76	87	81
Total	51	52	56	56	59	63

Age Group	South Africa	Northern Ireland	U.S.	Mexico	Mean[b]	
18 - 24	66%	60%	55%	70%	39%	
25 - 34	59	53	57	73	40	
35 - 44	65	56	64	74	50	
45 - 54	69	66	77	75	58	
55 - 64	60	75	78	76	65	
65+	64	86	78	-[a]	73	
Total	64	65	65	73		

Source: World Values survey, 1981 - 1982.

[a]The Mexican sample contains too few persons over age 65 for analysis $(N = 6)$.

[b]See note to Table 6-3.

This syndrome involves change in a wide variety of basic social norms. Table 6-8 illustrates another aspect of this syndrome, showing the proportion saying that homosexuality can never be justified, by age group, in sixteen societies. Here, the relative rankings of given nations vary somewhat from those we have seen above, with the Dutch being most permissive toward homosexuality (followed by the Danes and Germans) and the Mexicans least so (followed by the Americans, Irish, South Africans, and Italians). The Mexican and American publics are not only more religious than those of most West European countries, but also less tolerant of homosexuality.

But in almost every society, the young are markedly more tolerant of homosexuality than the old. In the sixteen nations as a whole, the oldest group is almost twice as likely as the youngest group to say that homosexuality can never be justified. Once again, the Hungarian pattern is very similar to that found in the West. Only in Mexico and South Africa is there little evidence of change.

By itself, this does not prove that an intergenerational shift is taking place. The age-related differences are striking but they might reflect life cycle effects rather than historical change based on cohort effects. We will not be able to decide with confidence which is the dominant effect until we have a substantial amount of time series data. In connection with Table 6-8, however, a life cycle interpretation seems highly implausible. Such an interpretation not only implies that the young will be just as intolerant of homosexuality as their elders when they get older; it also implies that in most of these countries, the majority of those who are now over 65 years of age were tolerant of homosexuality forty or fifty years ago. This seems extremely unlikely, in the light of social history. Time series data from both the United States and West Germany indicate that attitudes toward homosexuality have gradually become more permissive (Noelle-Neumann and Piel 1984; NORC 1987).

Permissive attitudes toward homosexuality tend to be linked with Postmaterialist values, as Table 6-9 demonstrates. In every country except Mexico, Postmaterialists are significantly less likely to say that homosexuality can never be justified than other value types. In Mexico, the land of *machismo*, practically nobody accepts homosexuality; fully 73 percent of the total population give it the lowest possible ranking on a ten-point scale. Across these various societies, a 63 percent majority of Materialists hold that homosexuality is never justifiable; among Postmaterialists, only 36 percent take this view.

This is part of a pervasive pattern. As Table 6-10 indicates, Postmaterialists are far more permissive than Materialists in their attitudes toward abortion, divorce, extramarital affairs, prostitution, and euthanasia. As a broad generalization, Materialists are much more likely than Postmaterialists to adhere to traditional societal norms; the dimension in Table 6-1 shows a .36 correlation with our index of Materialist/Postmaterialist values. Although Materialist values are not a core element of traditional religious value systems, in the contemporary historical context they show strong empirical linkages with traditional norms.

Each of the norms dealt with in Table 6-10 also shows striking differences across age groups. Table 6-11 illustrates this point in connection with attitudes toward divorce. In every country but South Africa, the young are far less likely to feel that divorce can never be justified than the

TABLE 6-9. REJECTION OF HOMOSEXUALITY BY VALUE TYPE
(Percentage saying homosexuality can <u>never</u> be justified - a rating of 1
on a scale from 1 to 10)

Value Type	Nether-lands	Denmark	W. Germany	Britain	France	Canada
Materialist	33%	60%	61%	53%	59%	53%
Mixed	29	37	42	43	47	51
Postmat.	17	14	17	30	26	43
Total	28	34	42	43	47	50

Value Type	Belgium	Japan	Hungary	Spain	Repub. of Ireland	Italy
Materialist	52%	58%	66%	69%	70%	72%
Mixed	50	48	53	48	54	60
Postmat.	42	42	31	20	35	40
Total	50	52	55	56	59	63

Value Type	South Africa	Northern Ireland	Mexico	All Nations[a]
Materialist	67%	62%	73%	63%
Mixed	61	70	73	53
Postmat.	77	50	73	36
Total	64	65	73	49

Source: World Values survey, 1981 - 1982.
[a]Values for "all nations" are based on pooled data for all countries
shown in Table, weighted according to population.

TABLE 6-10. MORAL AND SOCIAL ATTITUDES BY VALUE TYPE

Attitude	% Agreeing		
	Mat.	Mixed	Postmat.
Abortion is <u>never</u> justifiable	45%	37%	24%
Divorce is <u>never</u> justifiable	30	23	14
Extramarital affairs are <u>never</u> justifiable	56	49	32
Prostitution is <u>never</u> justifiable	66	54	38
Homosexuality is <u>never</u> justifiable	63	53	36
Euthanasia is <u>never</u> justifiable	42	34	27

Source: Results from combined sixteen nation sample, World Values
survey, 1981 - 1982.

TABLE 6-11. PERCENTAGE SAYING "DIVORCE CAN <u>NEVER</u> BE JUSTIFIED"
BY AGE GROUP AND COUNTRY
(Percentage choosing lowest point on 10-point scale)

Age Group	Denmark	France	W. Germany	Britain	Canada	Nether-lands
15 - 24	7%	7%	4%	8%	15%	7%
25 - 34	6	8	11	13	13	10
35 - 44	11	13	11	9	15	19
45 - 54	14	15	13	13	23	24
55 - 64	12	22	24	22	27	35
65+	24	27	28	29	32	47
Total	11	13	13	14	19	19

Age Group	Japan	Italy	U.S.	Hungary	Spain	Belgium
15 - 24	13%	13%	18%	18%	12%	21%
25 - 34	15	17	15	19	14	18
35 - 44	23	18	23	24	25	26
45 - 54	24	24	31	29	35	32
55 - 64	29	30	23	32	38	35
65+	37	41	35	38	54	43
Total	21	21	22	25	28	28

Age Group	Northern Ireland	South Africa	Repub. of Ireland	Mexico	Mean[a]
15 - 24	12%	42%	26%	43%	15%
25 - 34	12	35	36	45	16
35 - 44	31	33	42	54	21
45 - 54	34	42	58	64	27
55 - 64	45	42	70	62	32
65+	53	42	76	-	41
Total	29	38	45	48	20

Source: World Values survey, 1981 - 1982.
[a]See note to Table 6-3.

old. On the average, the members of our oldest cohort are more than two and one-half times likelier than our youngest group to reject divorce. A similar pattern applies to attitudes toward extramarital affairs. Table A-10 (in the Appendix) demonstrates this point. In all sixteen countries, without exception, the young are more tolerant of extramarital affairs than the old; overall, the old are almost twice as apt as the young to see them as never justifiable.

In most of these attitudes, the publics of Western Europe and Japan are more permissive than those of North America, South Africa, and Ireland—which behaves as if it were an island halfway across the Atlantic. The former group of countries also shows the largest age group differences: if cultural change is occurring, it is doing so at a more rapid pace in Western

TABLE 6-12. PERCENTAGE SAYING "A WOMAN NEEDS CHILDREN IN ORDER TO BE
FULFILLED" BY AGE GROUP AND COUNTRY

Age Group	Nether- lands	U.S.	Britain	Repub. of Ireland	Canada	W. Germany
15 - 24	5%	15%	20%	18%	21%	25%
25 - 34	5	13	18	21	22	30
35 - 44	6	17	20	27	28	31
45 - 54	11	22	22	30	26	44
55 - 64	27	19	21	31	38	42
65+	29	26	33	39	30	55
Total	11	18	22	25	26	36

Age Group	Northern Ireland	Hungary	Belgium	Spain	South Africa	Italy
15 - 24	27%	37%	38%	36%	50%	45%
25 - 34	32	40	39	59	50	48
35 - 44	45	47	50	53	52	51
45 - 54	42	49	50	50	58	55
55 - 64	62	53	56	54	45	67
65+	48	56	51	64	67	61
Total	41	45	47	48	52	53

Age Group	Mexico	Japan	Denmark	France	Mean[a]
15 - 24	51%	67%	61%	66%	35%
25 - 34	53	61	63	63	37
35 - 44	58	68	68	76	42
45 - 54	58	72	74	73	45
55 - 64	63	71	82	78	50
65+	-	76	86	80	53
Total	54	68	70	71	40

[a]See note to Table 6-3.

Europe and Japan than in the former colonies of Western Europe (among which Ireland could be numbered).

Let us turn now to yet another major subject of human concern—the role of child rearing in a woman's life. Traditionally, this has been viewed as a central goal of any normal woman, one of her most important functions in life, and one of her greatest sources of satisfaction. In recent years, this assumption has been increasingly called into question, as growing numbers of women have postponed having children or foregone them completely in order to devote themselves to careers outside the home. This pattern of behavior seems to reflect gradual changes in the outlook of different generations. As Table 6-12 shows, in each of the countries for which we have data, younger respondents are less likely than older ones to feel that "a woman needs children in order to be fulfilled." The correlation

TABLE 6-13. ATTITUDES TOWARD CHILDBEARING BY VALUE TYPE

Value Type	% Saying "A Woman Needs Children in Order to be Fulfilled"	% Approving of Single Woman Having a Child
Materialist	57%	29%
Mixed	48	36
Postmaterialist	33	54

Source: World Values survey, 1981 - 1982 combined data from sixteen countries.

with age is weaker in Mexico and South Africa than elsewhere, but the pattern is pervasive. Here again, the results from an East European country (Hungary) are almost exactly similar to those in Western countries. Interestingly, the American public is one of the *least* conservative on this issue, which coincides with the fact that American women were historically at the vanguard in entering the labor force.

Though the young are less likely to believe that a woman needs to have children, they are also less likely to feel that, if she wants them, she must be married in order to have them. As Table A-11 (in the Appendix) indicates, this, too, is a pervasive pattern, found in all sixteen of the societies for which we have data. Overall, our youngest group is more than twice as likely to approve of single parenthood as our oldest group.

As is true of so many other attitudes, the age group differences are paralleled by value-related differences of roughly equal strength. As Table 6-13 shows, Postmaterialists are far likelier than those with other values to reject the idea that a woman needs children—but to accept single parenthood *if* a woman wishes children. These value differences are not simply a function of the tendency for the young also to be Postmaterialist; multiple regression demonstrates that each of these factors exerts an independent effect, though they tend to reinforce each other. Postmaterialists place more emphasis on self-fulfillment through careers, rather than through ensuring the survival of the species; but they are also more permissive toward single parenthood, perhaps because they are likelier to take the economic viability of the single mother for granted.

Let us now turn to behavioral indicators. Table 6-14 shows the relationship between church attendance and age. There is a marked tendency for the young to manifest less religious behavior than do the old. As we have noted, church attendance is not one of our most sensitive indicators of acceptance or rejection of Judaeo-Christian values. But it has one significant advantage over the attitudinal variables examined in the preceding tables: For many countries, data on church attendance rates are available over a period of several decades. The picture these data give is consistent

TABLE 6-14. CHURCH ATTENDANCE IN SIXTEEN SOCIETIES BY AGE GROUP
(Percentage who attend religious services at least once a month)

Age Group	Denmark	Japan	France	Britain	W. Germany	Belgium
18 - 24	4%	8%	11%	15%	23%	31%
25 - 34	3	6	10	23	23	29
35 - 44	10	7	21	25	33	40
45 - 54	16	16	19	22	40	50
55 - 64	19	24	22	34	46	41
65+	24	29	26	30	59	50
Total	11	12	17	23	35	38

Age Group	Nether-lands	Hungary	Canada	Italy	Spain	U.S.
18 - 24	37%	41%	36%	40%	36%	52%
25 - 34	31	37	41	33	34	57
35 - 44	37	43	46	54	53	59
45 - 54	46	49	48	60	62	68
55 - 64	56	51	58	54	69	70
65+	49	54	59	68	73	70
Total	40	44	45	48	53	60

Age Group	South Africa	Northern Ireland	Mexico	Repub. of Ireland	Mean[a]
18 - 24	59%	50%	74%	83%	35%
25 - 34	55	61	69	82	35
35 - 44	61	66	79	88	43
45 - 54	64	77	83	96	49
55 - 64	62	72	82	96	52
65+	80	84	-	95	57
Total	61	67	75	88	43

Source: World Values survey, organized by European Value Systems Study Group.
[a]See note to Table 6-3.

with an interpretation of Table 6-14 based on intergenerational change. Church attendance rates in most of these countries have been declining gradually, as would be expected from population replacement effects linked with intergenerational differences of the type shown in Table 6-14 (see Schmidtchen 1972; Barnes 1974). Here, too, Hungary resembles the average Western country.

Additional behavioral indications of underlying cultural change are strikingly evident in the demographic statistics of advanced industrial societies from 1960 to 1985. Little more than a decade ago, it was widely believed that unless stringent measures were taken to prevent it, human population would inexorably increase until it reached catastrophic limits (Meadows, et al. 1972; Ehrlich 1978). Instead, starting in the late 1960s, birth rates began to decline throughout the industrialized world. By the 1980s, fertility rates had fallen well below the population replacement level in the United States and most other advanced industrial societies, and a new wave of studies began to explore the possibly devastating consequences of "the birth dearth" (Wattenberg 1987).

Conventional economic interpretations of demographic change are inadequate to explain this phenomenon; for, while previous decline in birth rates had been linked with major economic downturns, this second demographic transition (Van de Kaa 1987) began during an era of unprecedented prosperity and has taken place in advanced industrial societies far more than in Third World countries. It seems to reflect underlying cultural changes, rather than economic factors per se.

Declining birth rates are only one of a number of demographic indications of cultural change. Divorce rates have been rising in advanced industrial societies over the past twenty-five years; so have the rates of abortions and illegitimate births.

Table 6-15 provides aggregate statistical evidence of three trends observed from 1960 to 1985, showing birth rates, illegitimacy rates, and divorce rates among the twelve nations that are now members of the European Community. Birth rates fell in all twelve countries; for the European Community as a whole, the decline was from 19 births per 1,000 people in 1960 to fewer than 12 per 1,000 in 1985. By 1985, fertility rates had dropped below the population replacement level in eleven of the twelve European Community countries—the sole exception being Ireland. Such demographic phenomena are complex, involving economic, political, and other factors, but it seems clear that cultural change was one component of this shift (see Lesthaeghe and Meekers 1986).

Though birth rates fell, the proportion of births that took place outside of marriage rose in all twelve countries, increasing by 250 percent from 1960 to 1985 in the European Community as a whole. This phenomenon shows tremendous cross-cultural variation, remaining below 2 percent of all births in Greece, on one hand, but rising from less than 8 percent to nearly 50 percent of all births in Denmark, on the other hand. Here, too, it appears that cultural factors play a major role.

Finally, divorce rates rose in every country but one—the exception being the Republic of Ireland, where divorce was, and is, illegal. In Italy and Spain, it only recently became legal. For the European Community as a whole, however, divorce increased by 400 percent from 1960 to 1985. And the phenomenon seems symptomatic of underlying changes in the values of these publics. The available aggregate statistical data support the interpretation that norms linked with religion and the inviolability of the family have been growing weaker.

Here, as with almost any major social change, the causes must be examined on more than one level. One could argue, for example, that the dramatic decline in birth rates is due to advances in contraceptive technology. There is no question that developments in contraceptive technology played an important instrumental role—but birth control techniques have existed for many decades. Nevertheless, in the 1950s, birth rates rose to levels far above those of the previous decades; and the decline that is now

TABLE 6-15. EXTERNAL SYMPTOMS OF CULTURAL CHANGE: BIRTH RATES,
ILLEGITIMATE BIRTH RATES, AND DIVORCE RATES, 1960 - 1985

1. Birth Rates (per 1,000 pop.)

Year	W. Germany	France	Italy	Nether- lands	Belgium
1960	17.4	17.9	18.1	20.8	17.0
1970	13.4	16.8	16.8	18.3	14.8
1980	10.1	14.9	11.3	12.8	12.6
1985	9.6	13.9	10.1	12.3	11.6

Year	Luxem- bourg	United Kingdom	Ireland	Denmark
1960	15.9	17.5	21.5	16.6
1970	13.0	16.3	21.8	14.4
1980	11.4	13.4	21.8	11.2
1985	11.2	13.3	17.6	10.5

Year	Greece	Portugal	Spain	European Community
1960	18.9	23.9	21.7	19
1970	16.5	20.0	19.6	16
1980	15.4	16.2	15.2	13
1985	11.8	12.8	–	12(est.)

2. Illegitimate Births (per 1,000 births)

Year	W. Germany	France	Italy	Nether- lands	Belgium
1960	63	61	24	14	21
1970	55	68	22	21	28
1980	76	114	43	41	41
1985	94	196	53	83	–

Year	Luxem- bourg	United Kingdom	Ireland	Denmark
1960	32	52	16	78
1970	40	80	27	110
1980	60	115	50	332
1985	87	189	85	430

Table 6-15. (Concluded)

Illegitimate Births (cont.)

Year	Greece	Portugal	Spain	European Community
1960	12	95	23	45
1970	11	73	14	48
1980	15	92	28	74
1985	17	123	-	113(est.)

3. Divorce Rates

Year	W. Germany	France	Italy	Nether- lands	Belgium
1960	.9	.6	0	.5	.5
1970	1.3	.8	0	.8	.7
1980	1.6	1.5	.2	1.8	1.5
1985	2.1	1.9	.3	2.3	1.9

Year	Luxem- bourg	United Kingdom	Ireland	Denmark
1960	.5	.5	0	1.5
1970	.6	1.1	0	1.9
1980	1.6	2.8	0	2.7
1985	1.8	3.1	0	2.8

Year	Greece	Portugal	Spain	European Community
1960	.3	.1	0	.4
1970	.4	.1	0	.7
1980	.7	.6	0	1.3
1985	.9	.8	-	1.6(est.)

Sources: Eurostat, Demographic Statistics 1987 (Luxembourg: Statistical Office of the European Communities, 1987), 64 – 65; and Eurostat, Basic Statistics of the Community (Luxembourg: 1985), 108.

so dramatically apparent set in only after 1965. The birth dearth reflects a combination of two things:

(1) the availability of effective birth control technology; and
(2) the fact that people choose to use it.

The fact that people have increasingly chosen to have children later in life, or not at all, in recent decades seems to reflect a gradual change in underlying norms. Both components are essential, and to ask which one was the real cause is to pose a false alternative.

Similarly, one might argue that the recent surge in divorces in Italy and Spain is the result of the fact that divorce used to be illegal, but no longer is. This interpretation is perfectly correct as far as it goes—but if one probes somewhat deeper, one is likely to ask, *"Why* did divorce become legal in these countries?" Divorce had been illegal for centuries because it violated deeply held religious norms in those cultures. This still holds true in the Republic of Ireland, where a majority of the public voted against legalizing divorce in a national referendum in 1987. But, as our data suggest, these norms have gradually been weakening over time. Public support for the legalization of divorce became increasingly widespread and articulate in Italy and Spain, until the laws themselves were changed. One consequence was a sudden surge of divorces immediately after the laws were changed. Though this *behavioral* change was sudden and lumpy, it reflected a long process of incremental value change.

Some writers have interpreted this lumpiness of the behavioral symptoms of cultural change as meaning that no long-term decline in traditional norms is taking place. For example, Greeley (1972) and Hout and Greeley (1987) point out that in the United States, church attendance among Protestants has not declined in recent decades, and, while it fell rapidly among Catholics from 1968 to 1975, it has not declined subsequently. The lack of a steady downward trend contradicts the secularization thesis, they conclude.

This argument is not entirely convincing. As we have seen, church attendance rates provide only a very rough indicator of underlying cultural changes. Moreover, this argument assumes that there must be a one-to-one relationship between underlying attitudinal changes and their behavioral consequences. Since they operate on different levels, with behavioral patterns often being more subject to institutional and situational constraints, this is unlikely to hold true. The sudden decline in Catholic church attendance, for example, may have been precipitated by vocal and vigorous opposition to artificial birth control by Pope Paul VI in 1968. But this negative reaction to papal authority reflected, in part, the fact that a majority of American Catholics had come to disagree with the church's position on birth control by that point in time, a development that took place gradually, over a long period of time.

The rise of the West German Greens provides another illustration of disparity between the incremental pace of cultural change, and the sudden emergence of its behavioral symptoms. In 1983, the Greens suddenly achieved worldwide prominence when they won enough votes to enter the West German parliament for the first time, bringing about fundamental changes in the equilibrium of West German politics. But this sudden breakthrough reflected the gradual rise of mass support for environmentalist policies, as we will see in chapter 8. Institutional barriers, such as the fact that a party must win at least 5 percent of the vote to gain seats in the Bundestag, made the party's breakthrough to prominence sudden and dramatic. But its rise reflected long-term processes of incremental change.

In the United States, recent political life has been characterized by a renewed emphasis on religious issues—in particular by a heated antiabortion movement and by a campaign to allow prayer in public schools. This has been interpreted as a manifestation of a swing to the Right on cultural issues.

This interpretation is mistaken. All the evidence we have seen points to a pervasive tendency toward secularization. Clearly, the proprayer and antiabortion movements do have devoted partisans. But their revival of religious issues reflects a reaction among a dwindling traditionalist sector, rather than a general shift toward cultural conservatism among the population at large. Glenn (1987) has examined long-term trends in American survey data on this subject. He finds only a moderate overall decline in church membership, but a substantial decline in endorsement of traditional Christian beliefs. For example, the share of the American public who considered religion very important in their lives declined from 75 percent in the 1950s to 56 percent in the 1980s. Our data suggest that for the past several decades, adherence to traditional cultural norms has been in retreat; the consequences have become manifest in rising rates of divorce and abortion—and in institutional changes that have made them easier to obtain. The intensity with which religious issues have been raised in recent years reflects their adherents' conviction that some of their most basic values are being rapidly eroded, and not the growth of mass support for traditional values. Throughout advanced industrial society, there is evidence of a long-term shift away from traditional religious and cultural norms.

The apparent decline of traditional religious and social norms tends to be linked with the shift from Materialist toward Postmaterialist values, and both processes seem to be components of a broad cultural change characterizing the transition from industrial to postindustrial society. The shift to Postmaterialism and the decline of traditional forms of religion tend to go together because they share a common cause: the unprecedented levels of personal security of contemporary advanced industrial society, which in turn can be traced to the postwar economic miracle and the rise of the welfare state. Postmaterialism and secularization are two distinct phenomena, however, influenced by somewhat different causal factors. For example, unless the spread of AIDS is halted within the near future, we would expect to find a gradual reversal of the growing tolerance toward both homosexuality and extramarital affairs that seems to have emerged in recent decades. This factor would have less impact on other social norms, such as the emphasis on careers over child rearing, and still less impact on the tendency to emphasize the quality of one's working life rather than salary alone.

During the past few decades, however, the publics of advanced industrial societies have become markedly more permissive toward homosexuality. This change seems to be linked with the rise of Postmaterialist values. A relatively secure segment of the population, Postmaterialists tend to take physical survival for granted and are relatively tolerant of behavior that deviates from traditional social norms. As we have seen, Postmaterialists have become increasingly numerous in recent decades, through a process of intergenerational value change. And, as we have also seen, in all advanced industrial societies for which we have data, Postmaterialists are far more tolerant of homosexuality than Materialists. This suggests— but does not prove—that those societies in which Postmaterialists have become most numerous should be relatively tolerant of homosexuality. Are they?

As Figure 6-1 demonstrates, the answer is, emphatically, yes. The vertical axis of this figure reflects the percentage of the public in each society who view homosexuality as never permissible. As we move to the right on the horizontal axis, we find societies with increasingly high proportions of Postmaterialists. As a glance at this figure reveals, the more Postmaterialist societies are far more tolerant of homosexuality than the more Materialist ones. In our most heavily Postmaterialist society, The Netherlands, only 28 percent of the public view homosexuality as "never" permissible. In heavily Materialist ones, such as Italy and Ireland, 60 percent or more of the public hold this view. Mexico would stand out as a deviant case, but is not included in these cross-national comparisons; though it is interesting to examine patterns *within* the Mexican sample, this sample is not representative of the Mexican population as a whole, making it unsuitable for quantitative cross-national analysis. The overall correlation between attitudes toward homosexuality and the proportion of Postmaterialists in a society is strong: $r = .69$ (significant at above the .01 level).

The evidence in Figure 6-1 suggests that the shift toward Postmaterialist values has important societal consequences. And the evidence becomes even more compelling when we examine the relationship between the prevailing values and the divorce rates of given societies, as shown in Figure 6-2. As we already know, within given societies, Postmaterialists are far more permissive toward divorce than Materialists. Interesting and nonobvious though it is, this is only an intracranial correlation, reflecting the linkage between one's values and a given attitude. Do these values have societal consequences? Figure 6-2 indicates that they do, for those societies with relatively high proportions of Postmaterialists are characterized

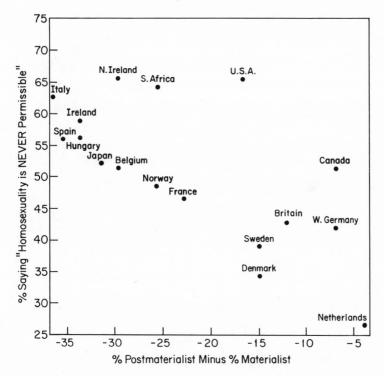

FIGURE 6-1. Attitudes toward homosexuality by value priorities of
given publics. Data from World Values survey, 1981–1982.
$r = -.69$, significant at .003 level.

by much higher divorce rates than those of societies in which the public
has a more Materialist outlook. For example, our most Materialist society
(Portugal) has a divorce rate only one-third as high as that of our most
Postmaterialist society (The Netherlands). The United States is a striking
deviant case, having a divorce rate that is about twice as high as the values
indicator alone would predict. Clearly, values are not the only factor involved. But most societies fall very close to the regression line. The overall correlation is .60, significant at well above the .01 level.

This is a remarkable finding, especially in view of the fact that the values
indicator used here is the simple four-item battery, which provides a considerably less accurate measure of the underlying values dimension than
does the broader-based twelve-item battery (and is much more vulnerable
to distortions linked with short-term fluctuations). Moreover, Postmaterialist values themselves are not inherently linked with predispositions toward divorce; they only facilitate the emergence of other (unmeasured)
attitudes that are directly linked with divorce. *Despite* these problems of

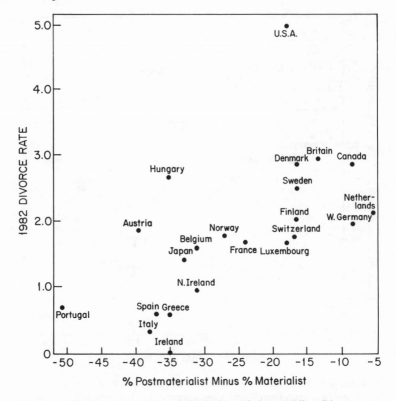

FIGURE 6-2. Divorce rates by value priorities of given publics. Divorce statistics from United Nations, *Statistical Yearbook, 1988* (New York: 1988). Data not available for South Africa. $r = .60$, significant at .003 level.

measurement error, we find a remarkably robust correlation between individual level values and the actual divorce rates of given societies. The presence of a deep-rooted sense of economic and physical security seems to make people readier to accept the financial and emotional costs of divorce. And the heightened emphasis on self-realization that characterizes Postmaterialists probably makes them less willing to remain within marriages that seem stultifying.

This emphasis on self-realization is linked with the fact that Postmaterialists emphasize careers, rather than child rearing, as central to a fulfilling life for women. As Table 6-15 indicates, though most Materialists believe that a woman needs children in order to be fulfilled, two-thirds of the Postmaterialists in our samples reject this view. This is not just a matter of lip service. For, as Figure 6-3 demonstrates, those societies with relatively high proportions of Postmaterialists tend to have much lower birth rates

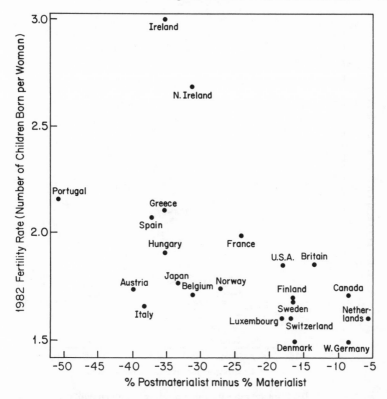

FIGURE 6-3. Fertility rates by value priorities of given publics.
$r = -.50$, significant at .02 level.

than do other societies. The global correlation between values and fertility rates is .50 (significant at almost the .01 level). Ireland stands out as a deviant case here, with a birth rate well above the level one would expect from value priorities alone. In part, this may be traced to institutional factors: The sale of contraceptive drugs and devices is illegal in the Republic of Ireland. Yet this phenomenon also seems to reflect something distinctively Irish—for Northern Ireland (where contraceptive devices are legal) *also* shows an anomalously high fertility rate. Of the twenty-two societies in Figure 6-3, only three had fertility rates above the replacement level (2.1 children per woman), in 1982. By 1985, only two were left (Portugal having fallen below this level). A variety of factors are involved in this phenomenon, with value change apparently playing a significant part. Postmaterialists tend to take personal survival for granted. This may be a reasonable assumption. But their societies are not reproducing themselves.

Another demographic change that seems to reflect cultural change is the

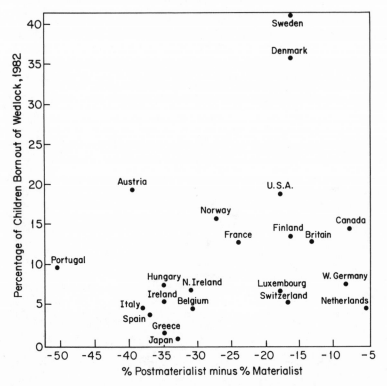

FIGURE 6-4. Illegitimacy rates by value priorities of given publics.
$r = .30$ (n.s.).

dramatic increase in births out of wedlock observed during the past twenty-five years. At the individual level, though Postmaterialists attach less importance to having children as a source of fulfillment, they are relatively likely to feel that *if* one wishes to have children, one need not be married in order to do so. Do societies with relatively high proportions of Postmaterialists have high illegitimacy rates? As Figure 6-4 demonstrates, the answer is yes—but the pattern is complex. Some advanced industrial societies with relatively large numbers of Postmaterialists do have very high proportions of births out of wedlock: Sweden and Denmark are examples. But other relatively Postmaterialist societies do not: The Netherlands and West Germany are examples. Conversely, some much poorer countries with few Postmaterialists, such as Portugal, have rather high illegitimacy rates. Long-established cultural traditions that are specific to given countries enter into the picture. Swedish and Danish society have traditionally been relatively permissive toward birth out of wedlock. To a less striking degree, this has also been true of some Latin American countries and Portugal. Such traditional patterns interact with the more recent trend toward rising illegitimacy rates, which is pervasive throughout advanced industrial society, complicating the picture. Two distinct types of factors influence illegitimacy rates—one of which is rooted in specific preindustrial cultural patterns, and the other of which is linked with the rise of Postmaterialist values. The resulting pattern is complex, and the global correlation between Postmaterialism and illegitimacy rates is in the predicted direction but not statistically significant. Though we are unable to sort out the impact of Postmaterialist value change from the impact of traditional cultural factors in these cross-sectional data, we suspect that time series data would reveal that those societies with rising proportions of Postmaterialists would show disproportionate increases in illegitimate births. The answer must await further research.

On the whole, we find impressive linkages between individual level values and actual behavior of the peoples of given societies—especially considering the fact that the relationships we observe are almost certainly weakened by error in our measurement of value priorities. The actual impact of cultural change is probably underestimated in these analyses, but even the crude measurements available here indicate that changing values have an important impact on the behavior of the peoples of advanced industrial societies, helping to shape the climate of attitudes toward homosexuality and leading to higher divorce rates and lower fertility rates.

But the linkage between the rise of Postmaterialism and the decline of religious orientations more generally is conditional, not inherent. As we have noted, despite their detachment from traditional religion, Postmaterialists are significantly more likely than Materialists to spend time thinking about the meaning and purpose of life. In this respect, Postmaterialists may have *more* potential interest in religion than Materialists do. A religious message based on economic and physical insecurity finds little resonance among Postmaterialists—but one that conveyed a sense of meaning and purpose in contemporary society might fill a need that is becoming increasingly widespread. If a decline of religion is taking place, it is not necessarily built into the conditions of advanced industrial society. The established religions may be losing a growing and potentially mobilizable constituency, by default.

CHAPTER 7

Subjective Well-Being and Value Change: Aspirations Adapt to Situations

INTRODUCTION

Values and subjective well-being have a close but complex relationship. Humans are goal-seeking organisms, and they experience a sense of dissatisfaction until they obtain what they are seeking. Thus, what is valued is related to what is scarce—and one is motivated to seek it by a sense of dissatisfaction.

Conversely, when people get the valued object, they experience feelings of happiness and satisfaction. But this sense of subjective well-being is transient, by its very nature. In the short run, getting what you want may produce euphoria; but in the long run it does not—for if it did, goal-seeking activities would cease. After a while, people take what they have for granted, and either want more or, when they reach a saturation point, turn to the pursuit of other goals. If given goals have been satisfied long enough, people grow up, attaching relatively little value to those goals and value other things more highly. As one generation replaces another, the priorities of an entire society may change. Thus, the process of cultural change is related to the long-term consequences of the pursuit and attainment of subjective well-being.

The crucial point is that, subjectively, the short-term consequences of attaining a given goal are not the same as the long-term consequences. This fact has some seemingly paradoxical implications. The most familiar one (familiar because many people eventually experience it) is the fact that getting what you want doesn't produce lasting happiness. Initially, this is surprising because in the short-term it does. But in the long run, neither an ice cream cone nor a new car nor becoming rich and famous produces the same feelings of delight that it initially did, for subjective well-being reflects a balance between one's aspirations and one's situation—and with long-term prosperity, one's aspirations tend to rise, adjusting to the situation. Thus, happiness is not the result of being rich, but a temporary consequence of having recently become richer.

In this chapter, we will explore two other paradoxes of subjective well being. Though neither of them is a matter of daily experience, both are now well-documented—and both reflect the fact that the long-term consequences of goal attainment differ from the short-term consequences.

The first might be called the paradox of minimum intergroup variation. Everybody knows that some groups are objectively much better off than others, and common sense suggests that the former must be happier and more satisfied with their lives than the latter. But empirical evidence indicates that the actual differences are astonishingly small. In colloquial terms, this paradox might be stated: "Why doesn't money buy happiness?"—or, more precisely, "Why does it cause such small differences between the happiness of rich and poor?"

The second might be called the paradox of large cross-national variation. Happiness and overall life satisfaction vary surprisingly little across stable groups *within* a given country—but, as we saw in chapter 1, they vary a good deal *between* different countries. In concrete terms, we might ask, "Why are the Dutch so much happier than the Germans?"

We will deal with each of these problems in turn, starting with the former.

ASPIRATIONS ADAPT TO SITUATIONS, OR HAPPINESS IS OVER THE NEXT HILL

The paradox of small intergroup variation has been noted by a number of investigators. In an analysis of American data, Andrews and Withey (1976) find that the combined effects of age, sex, race, income, education, and occupation account for only 8 percent of the variance in a carefully validated index of overall life satisfaction. Campbell, Converse, and Rodgers (1976) also find surprisingly weak relationships between social background variables and life satisfaction. In an analysis of data from four Nordic countries, Allardt (1978) reports, "A striking fact is revealed when satisfaction measures are related to common background variables such as . . . occupation, education, sex, age, etc. It appears that within each country the overall satisfaction level tends to be surprisingly constant across categories." Barnes, et al. (1979) report similar findings from the United States and four West European countries. As one would expect, the rich are more satisfied with their incomes than the poor, and the highly educated are more satisfied with their education than the less educated. But the differences are smaller than one might expect; and when we analyze satisfaction with one's life as a whole, the explained variance is very modest indeed.

Just how modest is "modest indeed"? Utilizing data from the United States and eight West European countries, Inglehart (1977) analyzed five different dependent variables, using the following social background variables as predictors: age, sex, income, occupation, education, religious denomination, church attendance, political party identification, labor union membership, region, size of community, and race (in the United States). When a question concerning satisfaction with one's life as a whole is used as the dependent variable, these social background variables explain an average of only 6 percent of the total variance, across the nine nations. But the same set of predictors explain 23 percent of the variance in the respondents' value type; 26 percent of the variance in voting intention; 30 percent of the variance in political party identification; and 33 percent of the variance in self-placement on a Left-Right political scale. In short, the same set of demographic variables explains four to six times as much of the variance in other attitudes as in overall life satisfaction. Why is this true?

One possible explanation lies in the fact that, as Andrews and Withey (1976) have demonstrated, satisfaction with one's life as a whole reflects the sum of one's satisfaction in various domains, such as one's income, housing, occupation, leisure activities, family life, and so forth. Low intergroup variation might result if satisfaction with any one domain were uncorrelated with satisfaction in the others: averaging out across various domains would reduce the variation between groups. But this explanation has limited power, for advantages tend to be cumulative: Those who have higher incomes are also likely to have higher education, hold better jobs, live in more pleasant surroundings, and enjoy better health. While their marriages and family life may be no better than those of people with fewer advantages, at least they are no worse. An averaging out of objective circumstances would still produce a heavy skew in favor of the upper socioeconomic strata. But we find surprisingly little socioeconomic variation in subjective well-being. Some kind of subjective adaptation process must be at work.

Campbell, Converse, and Rodgers (1976) propose such a model. They argue that one's subjective satisfaction with any given aspect of life reflects the gap between one's *aspiration level* and one's *perceived situation* but one's aspiration levels gradually adjust to one's circumstances.

If some such process of adjustment is part of human nature, then one would not normally find large differences between the subjective well-being of different social groups provided that those groups had reasonably stable membership, for in the long run, the aspiration levels of stable groups would have time to adapt to their respective external circumstances. Relatively high or low levels of subjective well-being would be observed only when recent changes had raised or lowered the relative position of a given group.

We would expect this pattern of low intergroup variance to apply most fully to groups that are defined by genetic or ascriptive characteristics, such as sex or religion, since these are stable attributes of given individuals. It would be least true of groups that have a fluctuating membership—especially those for which a change in category coincides with a change in satisfaction level. One's income level, for example, can change a good deal, even over short periods of time—and when it does, the individual concerned may move simultaneously from one income level to another *and* from one satisfaction level to another. When one's income rises into the top quartile, one is almost certain to be pleased about it; and conversely, when one becomes unemployed, one may suddenly experience a sharp decline in both income *and* subjective well-being. Thus we would expect to find a much stronger correlation between income and subjective well-being than between gender and subjective well-being. This is not because economic differences are more important than gender in any absolute sense—but simply because gender is a much more stable characteristic than income.

To illustrate this point, let us consider the difference between income and education. Educational level is generally regarded as being an even more important determinant of socioeconomic status than income; and by and large, education is a stronger predictor of most attitudes than income. But educational level tends to be a more stable attribute of given individuals than income. This generalization is even more applicable to Western Europe than to the United States. Most West Europeans complete their education by the age of 16. Even for the minority that go further, the process is generally completed by their early 20s; from then on, educational level is virtually a fixed characteristic; It rarely rises and never falls. Consequently, if the aspiration-adaptation model is correct, we would expect to find larger differences in subjective well-being linked with income than with education—contrary to our experience with most other attitudes.

Reasoning along similar lines, we would expect to find larger differences in subjective well-being linked with marital status than with gender—not because marital status is a more important determinant of objective circumstances than gender, but simply because people change relatively quickly and frequently from being single to married, or from being married to being divorced, widowed, or separated; thus, being in one of these conditions may reflect a recent change—whereas one's gender is an extremely stable characteristic. And in the long run, aspirations adapt to situations: One adapts to one's stable characteristics.

These expectations may seem counterintuitive at first. Everyone knows that when you get something you wanted, you are more satisfied than you were before you got it; it would seem obvious that subjective satisfaction must respond to external circumstances. Indeed, it does—in the short term. A person who has been lost in a desert undoubtedly is delighted when he or she finally reaches an oasis. But would we expect an ample water supply to still produce delight after weeks or months have passed? Hardly. One begins to take it for granted and starts to worry about other things. And for those who have always lived in an environment where water is plentiful, it may seem virtually valueless, so that the quantity available is completely unrelated to one's subjective well-being.

Thus, intergroup differences in subjective satisfaction reflect the impact of changes over time more than they reflect the absolute levels of external conditions. Within any large sample, one finds a wide range of satisfaction levels, reflecting the fact that some people's recent experiences have exceeded their expectations, while others' have fallen short. When a need is suddenly fulfilled, one feels a heightened sense of satisfaction. But after a time, one begins to take one's situation for granted; aspirations and objective circumstances come into balance. This type of adaptation process is necessary in order for humans to function and survive; otherwise, fulfillment of a given set of goals would lead to a state of contented but satiated immobility.

The process of adjustment is complex, for the balance between needs or aspirations, on one hand, and fulfillment, on the other, is continually being upset and readjusted. Satisfaction of a given need can provide intense pleasure; but eventually one aspires to more or to different things.

But which will it be: more of the same or a shift to different goals? The distinction seems crucial, for the two types of adaptation have quite different implications, and different time frames. On one hand, we are dealing with a quantitative adjustment of aspirations. It does not take place immediately; Campbell, Converse, and Rodgers (1976) conclude that aspiration levels adjust themselves rather slowly. Nevertheless, the evidence indicates that given individuals can and do adjust their aspirations to their situation, shifting them upward with prosperity and (somewhat more slowly) downward with adversity. This process of incremental quantitative changes may take time, but the other process—a qualitative shift from one type of goal to another—seems to work even more slowly. Once adulthood has been reached, most individuals' aspirations seem firmly linked to certain types of goals. It is easier to raise one's sights to more income or a larger house than to shift them to different *kinds* of goals or different ways of life. Major changes in value priorities can take place in a society, but they seem to occur largely as a matter of intergenerational population replacement. In particular, as we have seen, those who have experienced high levels of economic and physical security throughout their formative years tend to take material security for granted, and give Postmaterialist goals top priority. For those with Postmaterialist values, relatively high levels of income do *not* produce high levels of subjective well-being (Inglehart 1977, 1981).

Thus, changes in the economic and social environment can have three different types of impact, each with its own time frame:

1. In the short term, changes in one's objective circumstances can produce an immediate sense of satisfaction or dissatisfaction.
2. Circumstances that persist for some time—probably at least a few years—may gradually raise or lower an individual's aspiration levels *within* a given domain.
3. Circumstances that persist for the very long term can lead to intergenerational value changes, with the result that *different* domains come to be given top priority by the population of a given society.

ASPIRATIONS ADAPT TO SITUATIONS: EVIDENCE FROM SIXTEEN NATIONS

In the following section we will test the hypotheses just outlined. Thus far, most of the empirical research published on subjective well-being has been based on surveys of the American public. Though the results from other societies tend to be similar to the American findings, it is not entirely clear to what extent we are dealing with specifically American phenomena, or with more general human processes of adaptation. The European Community surveys have gathered data on subjective well-being from twelve West European nations, providing an exceptionally large longitudinal data base. Questions about subjective well-being were first administered in 1973 to representative national samples of the publics of Great Britain, Italy, France, West Germany, the Netherlands, Belgium, Luxembourg, Denmark, and Ireland. The same items have been used repeatedly in surveys carried out in each of these nine nations from 1975 to the present; in Greece from 1981 to the present; and in Spain and Portugal from 1985 to the present. Thus by 1986 we had samples of well over 10,000 cases per country from each of the first ten countries. For present purposes, these exceptionally large *N*s are extremely useful. Our hypotheses imply that we will usually find little variation between groups with stable membership, and most of the evidence examined so far points in that direction. To measure very small differences, we will need extremely reliable samples. But in a representative national survey, one must allow for sampling error. With a sample of 1,500 to 2,000 cases, results generally fall within 3 to 5 percentage points of the actual distribution; and as one breaks the sample down into smaller subsamples, the range of sampling error rises. As a consequence, one might observe substantial variation between groups, purely as a result of normal sampling error. As the number of interviews increases, one can be increasingly sure that any variation that is observed, reflects variation in the real world.

Moreover, the fact that subjective well-being has been monitored repeatedly during the past decade enables us to examine variation over time. The European Community surveys already provide a relatively broad range of cultures, but these data are supplemented in this chapter with results from the United States, Canada, Hungary, and Japan, drawn from the World Values survey carried out in 1981–1984. Though these samples are relatively small, they broaden our scope beyond Western Europe. Each of the attributes of our data—variation across time, variation across cultures, and the exceptionally large sample size—will be utilized in the analyses that follow. First, however, let us take an overview of the results.

In September 1973 and subsequently in Euro-Barometer surveys 3 through 11, 13, 15, and 17 through 27, the following question was asked of representative national samples of the European Community publics: "On the whole, are you very satisfied, fairly satisfied, not very satisfied, or not at all satisfied with the life you lead?"

Adapted from previous American research, this question had proven to be an effective indicator of overall life satisfaction. Another item, also adopted from American research, had been found effective in measuring feelings of happiness. First asked in the Euro-Barometer survey 3, carried out in Spring 1975, it had been repeated in a dozen subsequent Euro-Barometer surveys by 1986. This question asked: "Taking all things together, how would you say things are these days—would you say you're very happy, fairly happy or not too happy these days?"

It has been demonstrated that satisfaction with one's life as a whole and happiness are not the same thing, the former being a more cognitive assessment, and the latter a more emotional state (Campbell, Converse, and Rodgers 1976; Andrews and Withey 1976). However, both of these items tap one's overall sense of subjective well-being, rather than assessments of specific aspects of one's life, and it is the former that seems to fit the aspiration-adjustment model most closely. Moreover, responses to these two questions are closely related, with the observed correlations consistently falling in the .5 to .7 range across the societies analyzed here. Recognizing that they tap related but distinct aspects of subjective well-being, we will present results for each variable separately in the tables that follow. Their relationships with social background variables prove to be remarkably similar.

How do West European publics respond to these questions? Figure 7-1 shows the global pattern across ten West European nations, cumulating over 100,000 interviews. Overall, 21 percent of these publics said they

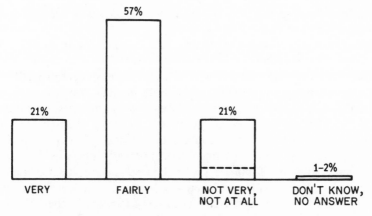

FIGURE 7-1. The distribution of overall life satisfaction and happiness among West European publics, 1973–1983. Based on European Community surveys, weighted according to the population of each nation.

were "very satisfied" with their lives as a whole, 57 percent were "fairly satisfied," 16 percent were "not very satisfied," and 5 percent were "not at all satisfied." When we combine the two latter categories, the result is an almost perfect normal distribution, with "fairly satisfied" being the modal response. Moreover, responses to the question about happiness show almost exactly the same three-category pattern: 20 percent of the West Europeans described themselves as "very happy," 58 percent as "fairly happy," and 20 percent as "not too happy." Again, we have something very close to a normal distribution.

"Don't know" and nonresponse rates to both items are extraordinarily low: Only 1 percent failed to answer the question about life satisfaction, and only 2 percent failed to answer the question about happiness. This is remarkable—in response to questions about major political and social issues, West European publics usually produce nonresponse rates ranging from a minimum of about 4 percent to highs of 20 percent or more, with 10 percent being fairly typical. With these two questions, nonresponse is almost nonexistent. Apparently, they seem clear and meaningful to nearly everyone. A substantial share of the public may not know or care whether more money should be spent on defense, or whether industry should be nationalized; but practically everyone can say whether the shoe pinches them or not.

This finding tends to rule out one potential explanation for low intergroup variation: the possibility that the questions seem meaningless, causing an unusually large share of the public to give random answers. One of the clearest indicators of meaningless or confusing questions is an abnormally high nonresponse rate. But here, nonresponse is about as low as it can get.

Let us turn now to an empirical test of the thesis of minimum intergroup variation. We hypothesized that because gender is an extremely stable characteristic, we should find very little variation in subjective well-being between the sexes. This finding is far from obvious, for it is clear that women face numerous objective disadvantages by comparison with men. If objective circumstances were the main determinant of subjective well-being, one would expect to find substantial differences between men and women; if the aspiration-adjustment model prevails, one would expect to find very small ones. Table 7-1 shows the responses to the question concerning life satisfaction from all Euro-Barometer surveys carried out from 1980 through 1986 in twelve West European countries, plus the 1981–1982 World Values survey results from the United States, Canada, Hungary, and Japan. Table 7-2 shows comparable data in response to the question concerning happiness. We are dealing with an immense body of data; to simplify presentation, in these and the following tables we show just one figure for each group: the percentage that is "high" on well-being. The distributions shown in Figure 7-1 can be dichotomized in two ways, cutting either above the mode or below it. The two procedures produce similar patterns (except that the skew is reversed), and we have dichotomized *below* the mode with life satisfaction, and *above* it with happiness, in order to examine both the high and low ends of the continuum.

Do men and women differ substantially in subjective well-being? Evidence from sixteen industrialized nations indicates that they do not. The results vary slightly from country to country and from one year to the next, but there is no consistent difference. The Hungarians rank among the four least satisfied and least happy publics (which is roughly in line with their economic position) but resemble the other countries in showing an almost complete absence of gender differences in subjective well-being. Here—as throughout the evidence we will examine on subjective well-being (and as was true of the evidence examined in chapter 6)—the most striking feature of the Hungarian data is the fact that they look very similar to those from West European countries. The division between Eastern and Western Europe is a major political barrier, but it does not necessarily reflect a profound cultural contrast.

Overall, the sixteen-nation mean results for both life satisfaction and happiness indicate that women are, if anything, a little *higher* on subjective well-being than men, but the differences amount to only 1 or 2 percentage points. On both life satisfaction and happiness, Ireland and Japan show relatively large gender-related differences, with women being more satisfied than men by margins of 5 and 4 points, respectively, and women being

TABLE 7-1. LIFE SATISFACTION BY GENDER IN SIXTEEN ADVANCED INDUSTRIAL
SOCIETIES, 1980 - 1986
(Percentage "satisfied" or "very satisfied" with life as a whole)

Gender	Nether-lands	Denmark	Canada	Ireland	U.S.	Luxem-bourg
Male	92%	96%	89%	81%	85%	92%
Female	94	96	90	86	84	92

Gender	Britain	Belgium	W. Germany	Spain	Japan	France
Male	86%	82%	85%	74%	73%	74%
Female	87	82	83	72	77	73

Gender	Hungary	Italy	Greece	Portugal	16-Nation Mean
Male	72%	68%	64%	62%	80%
Female	71	66	63	62	80

Sources: Pooled data from Euro-Barometer surveys 13-26 (April 1980 through November 1986) for Western European nations and Ireland; World Values survey, 1981 - 1982 for Canada, United States, Hungary, and Japan.

Note: In each Euro-Barometer survey, representative national samples of about 1,000 were interviewed in each country, except that Greece has been surveyed only since November 1980, and Spain and Portugal only since November 1985. Total N = 163,538. For details of fieldwork and sampling, see the respective Euro-Barometer codebooks, which are available from the Data Archive of the Inter-university Consortium for Political and Social Research. Data from Canada, United States, Hungary, and Japan are from World Values survey, 1981 - 1982; Ns for the four respective countries are 1,245; 2,325; 1,464; and 1,204. A 10-point scale was used to measure life satisfaction in the World Values survey, and we have treated the upper half of this scale (scores of 6-10) as reflecting "satisfied" responses; the marginals obtained in this fashion correspond to the "satisfied" and "very satisfied" proportions in other surveys of these publics. In this table, countries are ranked according to combined scores on both life satisfaction and happiness, giving equal weight to each variable; thus, overall, the Dutch ranked highest from 1980 through 1986, and the Portugese showed the lowest level of subjective well-being.

happier than men by margins of 9 and 4 points, respectively. Normally, differences of this size would pass almost unnoticed. The fact that they are relatively large in the present context reflects just how small the gender-related differences are. Despite very substantial objective differences in career opportunities, personal income, and opportunities for self-expression, throughout industrial society, women are not less satisfied with their lives or less happy than men.

With rare exceptions, one plays the same sex role from birth to death; consequently, the process of aspiration adjustment seems to completely dominate the impact of external differences. Thus, women are no less happy than men. Indeed, when we statistically adjust for the fact that

TABLE 7-2. HAPPINESS BY GENDER IN ADVANCED INDUSTRIAL
SOCIETIES, 1980 - 1986

(Percentage "very happy")

Gender	Nether-lands	Denmark	Canada	Ireland	U.S.	Luxem-bourg
Male	40%	32%	35%	28%	30%	23%
Female	45	37	37	37	32	26

Gender	Britain	Belgium	W. Germany	Spain	Japan	France
Male	25%	25%	15%	20%	14%	13%
Female	28	26	13	22	18	15

Gender	Hungary	Italy	Greece	Portugal	16-Nation Mean
Male	11%	10%	11%	7%	21%
Female	11	9	12	8	24

Source: See note to Table 7-1.

women have lower incomes, lower-status occupations, etc., than men do, the minute differences observed in Tables 7-1 and 7-2 become a trifle larger: Women rank about 3 points higher on life satisfaction and 4 points higher on happiness. The fact that women currently tend to be slightly happier than men may reflect the fact that, as a consequence of the women's movement, their relative position has improved somewhat in recent years.

The evidence from Japan, in particular, points in this direction, for Japan is a society in which women have traditionally been disadvantaged to a far greater degree than in the West. Even today, the opportunities available to women in Japan are much more limited than in most Western societies. Nevertheless, there has been a large *relative* improvement in the position of Japanese women within recent years—one that is far more dramatic than that which has taken place in the West, because it started from a much lower baseline.

A 1973 survey of the Japanese public also found a relatively large difference between the overall life satisfaction levels of men and women—with 73 percent of the men "satisfied" or "reasonably satisfied," as compared with 81 percent of the women (Iwao 1976). Ordinarily, a difference of 8 percentage points would not be considered impressive. But this is not an ordinary variable. In scores of surveys we have examined from numerous Western countries, gender differences in life satisfaction have almost always been negligible. Against this context, the Japanese finding is striking. It is decidedly the largest such difference we have observed. Japanese women were significantly more satisfied with their lives than were men. This would seem almost incredible from a commonsense viewpoint. But it is in perfect accord with the aspiration-adjustment model. For centuries, Japanese women have had a position of extreme subordination—to their fathers in childhood, to their husbands during marriage, and to their sons in later life. Their aspiration levels reflected this fact. And the phenomenon of recent improvement—even though it still falls far short of equality— seems to have produced relatively high satisfaction levels.

The Republic of Ireland resembles Japan to some degree in this respect. Culturally, Ireland is an extremely conservative society, in which both divorce and the sale of contraceptives remain illegal, and where until recently when a woman married she was virtually obliged to give up her career. Since Ireland's entry into the European Community in 1973, both legislation and social norms concerning women have been changing at a relatively rapid rate (and in a favorable direction). This may account for the fact that Irish women currently show significantly higher levels of subjective well-being than those of Irish men.

A good deal has been written about the relationship between subjective well-being and age. Campbell, Converse, and Rodgers (1976) report rising levels of satisfaction with one's life in general and with virtually every specific aspect of life (except health) with increasing age; they attribute this pattern to the attainment of a progressively better fit between aspirations and situation as one moves through the human life cycle. Herzog, Rodgers, and Woodworth (1982) also report this finding, from analysis of more recent American data. A related process of psychological adjustment is suggested by Zajonc (1968), who has shown that how much one likes a given object is a function of familiarity, which is linked with how long one has been exposed to it. On the other hand Campbell (1981) has found that in the 1950s, younger Americans showed higher levels of happiness than did older Americans, while by the late 1970s, the young were significantly *less* happy. Campbell attributes this shift to a birth cohort effect, linked with the experiences of the Vietnam era.

Both life cycle effects and birth cohort effects on subjective well-being have been reported, then. One's birth cohort is a permanent attribute: Consequently, the aspiration-adjustment model implies that people have plenty of time to adjust to any advantages or handicaps linked with their cohort. Accordingly, any intercohort differences in subjective well-being are likely to be transient and situation-specific, probably reflecting the impact of recent events (such as the Vietnam conflict, in the 1970s). One's age,

TABLE 7-3. LIFE SATISFACTION BY AGE GROUP IN ADVANCED INDUSTRIAL
SOCIETIES, 1980 - 1986
(Percentage "satisfied" or "very satisfied" with life as a whole)

Age Group	Nether-lands	Denmark	Canada	Ireland	U.S.	Luxem-bourg
15 - 24	95%	96%	87%	83%	82%	90%
25 - 34	94	97	91	82	85	93
35 - 44	93	96	89	82	86	93
45 - 54	90	95	88	83	85	92
55 - 64	90	95	91	85	87	92
65+	92	95	94	89	86	93

Age Group	Britain	Belgium	W. Germany	Spain	Japan	France
15 - 24	87%	86%	83%	76%	71%	78%
25 - 34	88	84	81	73	74	72
35 - 44	87	83	86	74	78	73
45 - 54	84	81	84	68	75	67
55 - 64	84	77	84	69	73	69
65+	86	79	86	76	84	80

Age Group	Hungary	Italy	Greece	Portugal	Mean
15 - 24	80%	72%	66%	71%	82%
25 - 34	75	65	64	65	80
35 - 44	70	68	65	58	80
45 - 54	76	64	63	58	78
55 - 64	71	66	59	58	78
65+	69	65	61	60	81

Source: See note to Table 7-1.

on the other hand, is constantly changing—but it does so very gradually. One's changing position in the life cycle might give rise to differences in subjective well-being that perennially characterize given ages; but the gradual nature of these changes suggests that they would produce differences of only modest size. Thus, we would not expect either cohort or life cycle effects to give rise to any large and enduring differences in subjective well-being. Tables 7-3 and 7-4 show the overall relationship between our two indicators of subjective well-being and age in the 1970s and in 1982–1983.

Here again, a pattern of minimal intergroup variation is strikingly evident. In the mean figures for this massive data set as a whole, none of the six age groups varies by more than 1 or 2 percentage points from the global mean, either on overall life satisfaction or on happiness. And within given countries, subjective well-being shows little variation by age, although this holds truer for those countries from which we have large samples of many thousand interviews cumulated over 1980–1986 than for those countries from which we have 3,000 cases or fewer (the latter countries being Can-

TABLE 7-4. HAPPINESS BY AGE GROUP
(Percentage "very happy")

Age Group	Nether-lands	Denmark	Canada	Ireland	U.S.	Luxem-bourg
15 - 24	47%	39%	39%	32%	30%	24%
25 - 34	45	35	39	31	34	21
35 - 44	39	33	36	30	33	24
45 - 54	38	33	26	29	32	26
55 - 64	40	32	32	33	30	27
65+	45	34	36	39	30	25

Age Group	Britain	Belgium	W. Germany	Spain	Japan	France
15 - 24	23%	29%	11%	25%	18%	19%
25 - 34	27	28	14	20	20	15
35 - 44	27	25	17	19	13	12
45 - 54	26	23	22	19	16	10
55 - 64	26	22	14	19	16	13
65+	31	26	17	22	13	14

Age Group	Hungary	Italy	Greece	Portugal	Mean
15 - 24	15%	12%	12%	8%	24%
25 - 34	11	9	12	6	23
35 - 44	13	9	10	9	22
45 - 54	9	8	10	7	21
55 - 64	15	8	12	6	22
65+	9	10	13	6	23

Source: See note to Table 7-1.

ada, the United States, Japan, Hungary, Spain, and Portugal). The contrasting findings reported earlier by Campbell, Converse, and Rodgers (1976) and by Herzog, Rodgers, and Woodworth (1982) may reflect the fact that they were based on much smaller samples. However, we do find a slight curvilinear tendency with both indicators, such that satisfaction and happiness decline slightly, from the youngest to the middle-aged groups, and then rise again among the oldest group. When we statistically adjust for the fact that the oldest group has lower incomes and education, is more likely to be widowed, etc., compared to the younger groups, the tendency for subjective well-being to be highest among the oldest group becomes more pronounced. As Table 7-5 demonstrates, there is very little variation across the age groups from age 15 to 64: In overall life satisfaction, these five groups range from a minimum of 76 percent to a maximum of 80 percent satisfied; but the oldest group shows a figure of 86 percent satisfied—a finding that accords well with the aspiration adjustment model. This oldest group is relatively satisfied with their lives despite their comparatively low levels of income, occupation, and other variables;

TABLE 7-5. OVERALL LIFE SATISFACTION AND HAPPINESS BY AGE GROUP,
ADJUSTED FOR DIFFERENCES IN INCOME, OCCUPATION, EDUCATION, MARITAL
STATUS, AND NATIONALITY

Age Group	% "Satisfied" or "Very Satisfied" With Life as a Whole	% "Very Happy"
15 - 24	80%	21%
25 - 34	78	21
35 - 44	80	19
45 - 54	76	16
55 - 64	79	21
65+	86	29

Source: Euro-Barometer surveys 18 and 19.
Note: Adjusted with OSIRIS.IV Multiple Classification Analysis
program. Ns are the same as in Table 7-4.

when we adjust for the depressing effect of these factors, the oldest group emerges as significantly more satisfied than the others.

Precisely the same pattern emerges in connection with happiness, our other indicator of global well-being. As Campbell (1981) found to be the case in the United States in the late 1970s (though not at earlier time points), happiness is highest among the oldest age group. Adjusting for the depressing effects of other variables, those aged 65 and over show 29 percent rating themselves as "very happy"—a figure 8 points above any other age group.

These adjusted figures however, indicate how the world might look if the old had incomes, education, marital status, etc. similar to those of younger groups. In the real world, there is scarcely any variation across age groups. What is remarkable about the satisfaction and happiness ratings of those aged 65 and over, is that they are just as high as those of younger groups despite the fact that, by objective criteria, there is every reason to expect that they would be substantially lower. As is true of women, those over 65 seem to have adapted to a relatively unfavorable situation.

Once upon a time, "the bigger the better" seemed more or less self-evident. Within the past fifteen years, bigness has been diagnosed as pathological. Such books as *Small Is Beautiful* (Schumacher 1973) and *Human Scale* (Sale 1980) have argued that big organizations are inefficient—and big cities unlivable.

There seems to be a measure of truth in this allegation, as Tables 7-6 and A-12 demonstrate. To avoid overloading this chapter with statistics,

Table 7-6 (which deals with life satisfaction by size of community) is shown here and Table A-12 (dealing with happiness by size of community) is in the Appendix. We will also do this with most of the remaining tables that focus on happiness; we do so because both life satisfaction and happiness show virtually identical patterns. This is an important point, and the reader can verify it by referring to the Appendix. But because the two variables tell the same story, most readers will find it easier to simply view the results concerning life satisfaction.

Both Tables 7-6 and A-12 (in the Appendix) reveal that the subjective quality of life among people living in big cities tends to be lower than it is in rural areas, villages, and small or medium-sized towns. But the observed differences are much smaller than the advocates of smallness generally imply. Here (as with sex and age differences) there is remarkably little variation across categories. Indeed, if it were not for the extremely large data base (here at least, a virtue), one would write them off as within the range of normal sampling error. But there is a fairly consistent tendency, across our sixteen nations, for happiness and satisfaction to be lowest in big cities. The differences are rarely large, and the polarity is even reversed in a few instances, but the overall tendency is for subjective well-being to be a little higher in smaller towns. Crowding, pollution, noise, and high crime rates characterize most big cities; they affect subjective well-being adversely. Nevertheless, it seems, if one lives in a big city long enough, one gets used to them to a considerable extent.

Religiosity has been linked to subjective well-being in a number of studies of the American public (Gurin, Veroff, and Feld 1960; Hadaway 1978; Spreitzer and Snyder 1974; cf. Stoetzel 1983). Those who attend church regularly or adhere to some religious faith tend to be happier than those who do not.

Our data from sixteen countries demonstrate that this is not a uniquely American finding, but a general pattern that holds true whether the given nation's prevailing faith is Catholic, Protestant, or Greek Orthodox. In fact, as Tables 7-7 and A-13 (in the Appendix) demonstrate, the differences in subjective well-being linked with differences in religiosity are considerably greater than any of those observed so far. Among these nations as a whole, those who attend church once a week average about 8 points more satisfied with their lives, and 9 points happier, than those who never attend. Religion may play a significant role in adapting to adversity. Moreover, as was suggested in chapter 1, most religious traditions encourage one to dampen one's aspiration levels—which would be a sound strategy to maximize subjective well-being, especially in preindustrial societies having steady-state economies and very limited social mobility.

Education is probably the most important single factor shaping one's life

TABLE 7-6. LIFE SATISFACTION BY PERCEIVED SIZE OF COMMUNITY IN ADVANCED
INDUSTRIAL SOCIETIES, 1980 - 1986
(Percentage "satisfied" or "very satisfied" with life as a whole)

Respondent Considers His/Her Community	Nether-lands	Denmark	Canada	Ireland	U.S.	Luxem-bourg
Rural area or village	94%	97%	90%	87%	87%	93%
Small or middle-size town	94	96	88	86	86	91
Big city	89	95	89	80	82	95

Respondent Considers His/Her Community	Britain	Belgium	W. Germany	Spain	Japan	France
Rural area or village	88%	86%	87%	73%	75%	75%
Small or middle-size town	87	84	84	73	74	73
Big city	84	74	81	73	78	73

Respondent Considers His/Her Community	Hungary	Italy	Greece	Portugal	Mean
Rural area or village	72%	69%	60%	67%	81%
Small or middle-size town	70	65	65	61	80
Big city	71	66	66	57	78

Source: See note to Table 7-1.

in advanced industrial society. One's educational level sets the limits to the type of career one enters, how much money one earns, and how much social prestige one possesses and influences the communications networks one is exposed to throughout life.

As was suggested above, one's educational level is determined early in life and rarely changes significantly during adult years. Precisely because

TABLE 7-7. LIFE SATISFACTION BY FREQUENCY OF CHURCH ATTENDANCE IN
ADVANCED INDUSTRIAL SOCIETIES, 1980 - 1986
(Percentage "satisfied" or "very satisfied" with life as a whole)

Respondent Attends Church:	Nether-lands	Denmark	Canada	Ireland	U.S.
More than once/week	98%	99%	96%	88%	91%
Once/week	96	94	93	86	88
A few times/year	95	97	88	72	83
Never	92	96	86	58	76

Respondent Attends Church:	Luxem-bourg	Britain	Belgium	W. Germany	Japan
More than once/week	95%	90%	86%	73%	76%
Once/week	95	92	89	85	88
A few times/year	95	88	89	88	77
Never	84	84	83	82	73

Respondent Attends Church:	France	Hungary	Italy	Greece	Mean
More than once/week	83%	64%	75%	57%	84%
Once/week	80	74	74	67	86
A few times/year	75	73	64	70	82
Never	71	70	57	64	77

Source: See note to Table 7-1.
Note: Data not available for Spain and Portugal. See note to Table
7-1 re nations shown.

it is subject to relatively little short-term change, we would expect to find
relatively modest differences across educational levels, despite this variable's strong and pervasive impact on one's objective circumstances. This
expectation is borne out by our data from fifteen nations, as Tables 7-8 and
A-14 (in the Appendix) illustrate.

Subjective well-being varies somewhat with education, and the differences are in the direction one would expect: The more educated are happier
and more satisfied with their lives than the less educated. But the differ-

TABLE 7-8. LIFE SATISFACTION BY EDUCATIONAL LEVEL IN ADVANCED INDUSTRIAL
SOCIETIES, 1980 - 1986
(Percentage "satisfied" or "very satisfied" with life as a whole)

Age at Which Respondent Completed Education	Nether- lands	Denmark	Canada	Ireland	U.S.
15 years or less	90%	95%	86%	78%	79%
16 - 19 years	93	96	88	86	85
20 years or older	94	98	93	90	86

Age at Which Respondent Completed Education	Luxem- bourg	Britain	Belgium	W. Germany	Spain
15 years or less	91%	84%	79%	82%	71%
16 - 19 years	93	87	81	85	78
20 years or older	93	91	87	87	75

Age at Which Respondent Completed Education	Japan	France	Italy	Greece	Portugal	Mean
15 years or less	74%	68%	64%	59%	60%	78%
16 - 19 years	75	73	70	68	67	81
20 years or older	79	82	67	71	62	84

Source: See note to Table 7-1.

ence in life satisfaction between the most educated and the least educated amounts to only 6 percentage points, and with happiness the difference is only 2 points. Education seems to have more impact on subjective well-being than does sex, age, or size of community, but somewhat less than does religious orientation.

Does this mean that economic factors are unimportant? No. As we will see shortly, they have considerable impact on subjective well-being—but this impact seems more attributable to short-term changes than to stable differences.

One is much likelier to change one's occupation than to change one's

TABLE 7-9. LIFE SATISFACTION BY OCCUPATION IN ADVANCED INDUSTRIAL
SOCIETIES, 1980 - 1986
(Percentage "satisfied" or "very satisfied" with life as a whole)

Occupation	Nether-lands	Denmark	Canada	Ireland	Luxem-bourg
White collar employee	96%	98%	94%	91%	94%
Retired, student, housewife	94	96	88	88	93
Farmer	93	95	100	86	93
Manual worker	94	96	91	83	89
Unemployed	73	86	76	50	57

Occupation	Britain	Belgium	W. Germany	Spain	Japan
White collar employee	92%	84%	87%	76%	72%
Retired, student, housewife	87	83	85	74	82
Farmer	84	87	87	78	82
Manual worker	87	83	83	69	71
Unemployed	57	67	65	63	62

Occupation	France	Hungary	Italy	Greece	Portugal	Mean
White collar employee	78%	70%	71%	69%	66%	83%
Retired, student, housewife	79	69	68	65	62	81
Farmer	61	71	67	54	71	81
Manual worker	65	75	66	57	60	78
Unemployed	54	71	43	48	43	61

educational level during adult life; accordingly, we would expect to find greater variation in subjective well-being associated with occupation. The data in Tables 7-9 and A-15 (in the Appendix) support this expectation: We find a much wider range of subjective well-being here than in any of our previous tables. Unemployment generally reflects a recent change for the worse. Accordingly, the unemployed show drastically lower rates of life satisfaction than those of any other group; on the average, their life satisfaction levels fall 19 points below those of manual workers, and 25 points below those of white-collar employees. Among those who are employed, however, the differences are relatively modest: Manual workers fall only 6 points below white-collar workers on life satisfaction, and only 2 points below them on happiness (with farmers ranking lowest of all employed groups on happiness).

Income, like occupation, is much less permanently fixed than most of the other factors we have examined so far—which implies that we might find relatively large variation in subjective well-being across income groups. Tables 7-10 and A-16 (in the Appendix) show the relationship between income and each of our two dependent variables, with income levels stratified by quartiles within each nation. Across these fifteen nations, the top quartile averages 14 percentage points more satisfied and 7 points happier than the lowest quartile. This is a much wider range than that between sexes, age groups, or residents of big cities versus small towns. It is even larger than the differences among occupations—though not larger than the differences between the employed and the unemployed. With income, the range of variation is relatively large—but only relatively so. With life satisfaction, for example, one standard deviation covers about 40 percentage points, which is about three times the range between the highest and lowest income quartiles; income explains only a small part of the variance in subjective well-being. As previous research has indicated, money buys surprisingly little happiness or satisfaction.

Another factor that might be expected to have a major impact on subjective well-being is marital status. Few things do more to shape one's daily experience than whether or not one is married, single, divorced, or widowed. Here too, recent changes may play a major role. Being single and being married are relatively long-term states; the typical married respondent has been married a number of years at the time of the survey, and the typical single person has been single all his or her life. Widowhood is apt to be a somewhat more recent condition (though, because of differences in life expectancy plus differences in marriage age, widowed women are likely to live a dozen years or more in that state). Being divorced is even more likely to reflect a recent change, since divorced persons are much more likely to remarry than widowed ones. Separation seems the most likely to reflect recent changes of any of these states; in most settings, it tends to be a short-term situation that precedes divorce. The condition of living as married is a sort of mirror-image of separation; it frequently is a relatively short-term arrangement that precedes marriage.

A crucial question is unanswered: Is marriage a happier state than being single? Both are relatively long-term conditions, so the aspiration-adjust-

TABLE 7-10. LIFE SATISFACTION BY FAMILY INCOME IN ADVANCED INDUSTRIAL
SOCIETIES, 1980 - 1986
(Percentage "satisfied" or "very satisfied" with life as a whole)

Family Income	Netherlands	Denmark	Canada	Ireland	U.S.
Lowest quartile for nation	87%	93%	80%	77%	77%
Second quartile	91	95	91	82	82
Third quartile	95	97	91	87	83
Highest quartile for nation	96	98	91	92	90

Family Income	Luxembourg	Britain	Belgium	W. Germany	Spain
Lowest quartile for nation	85%	75%	75%	74%	64%
Second quartile	93	84	77	82	69
Third quartile	96	90	84	87	77
Highest quartile for nation	94	94	90	90	77

Family Income	Japan	France	Italy	Greece	Portugal	Mean
Lowest quartile for nation	69%	62%	55%	52%	53%	72%
Second quartile	72	69	64	61	59	78
Third quartile	76	77	70	67	62	82
Highest quartile for nation	83	85	76	74	66	86

ment model gives little guidance as to which would show the higher level of subjective well-being. The empirical findings, however, are consistent: Married people tend to be happier than single ones. In other respects, the theoretical rank order seems fairly clear: Widowhood, divorce, and separation all reflect changes that generally must be perceived as changes for the worse. Since separation, in general, tends to reflect the most recent change, we would expect separated people to show the lowest level of subjective well-being.

The levels would then rise, through divorce, widowhood, and being sin-

TABLE 7-11. LIFE SATISFACTION BY MARITAL STATUS IN ADVANCED INDUSTRIAL
SOCIETIES, 1980 - 1986
(Percentage "satisfied" or "very satisfied" with life as a whole)

Marital Status	Nether- lands	Denmark	Canada	Ireland	U.S.	Luxem- bourg
Married	94%	97%	92%	85%	88%	94%
Single	93	96	86	82	80	90
Living as married	95	95	83	62	80	83
Widowed	88	94	93	84	78	89
Divorced	78	90	84	-[a]	79	82
Separated	60	92	63	58	82	73

Marital Status	Britain	Belgium	W. Germany	Spain	Japan	France
Married	88%	84%	87%	73%	80%	75%
Single	86	84	82	74	69	76
Living as married	82	78	75	66	65	69
Widowed	81	71	81	69	59	69
Divorced	68	61	67	82	-	61
Separated	73	68	57	68	-	59

Marital Status	Hungary	Italy	Greece	Portugal	Mean
Married	77%	69%	66%	62%	82%
Single	70	67	62	69	79
Living as married	42	66	68	57	73
Widowed	58	59	50	49	73
Divorced	56	48	51	47	68
Separated	64	45	32	27	61

Source: See note to Table 7-1.

[a]Dash indicates too few cases to be significant.

gle, to being married. Living as married (like separation) is apt to reflect a fairly recent change—but in this case, presumably, a change for the better. We would expect it to rank highest.

Tables 7-11 and A-17 (in the Appendix) show the empirical results from fifteen nations. On the whole, the data support the aspiration-adjustment model. There is relatively little difference between those in the two relatively long-term conditions, married and single (which are, by the same token, by far the two largest groups). Consistent with previous American findings, throughout these nations, married people tend to be both happier and more satisfied with life than single ones. But the differences are modest, ranging from 3 to 7 percentage points. The various formerly married groups broaden the range considerably, and do so in the expected order: Separated persons consistently rank lowest, falling 10 to 20 points below married ones.

Among our six categories, the only one that does not appear in the expected rank order is the living as married group. On theoretical grounds we expected it to rank highest. Empirically, this group ranks a close second on happiness, but in life satisfaction, it falls below both the married and single groups. Apparently, we need to revise our concept of this group. Though it does reflect relatively recent pairings, these pairings are not always satisfying. Those that are so are apt to move into the married category; those that are not revert to the single category. If we view living as married as a sort of filter category, it not only fits better into our overall scheme, but helps explain why the married state—despite a rich folklore to the contrary—tends to be slightly but significantly happier than the single state. The living as married category is, in any case, becoming more prevalent: it constituted 1.86 percent of our samples in 1975–1979, and 4.23 percent of our samples in 1986—having more than doubled in about a decade.

Women are far likelier to fall into the three formerly married conditions than men, as is evident when we compare the Ns in Table 7-12. Not only are women more than three times as likely to be widowed as men; they are almost twice as likely to be divorced and not remarried, and half again as likely.to be separated. Other things being equal, this would tend to make women less satisfied with life and less happy than men. But other things are not equal. Paradoxically, but in keeping with what we have found throughout this analysis, within almost every category, women tend to be happier than men (see Table 7-12).

There are two exceptions. Within the widowed category, men tend to be a little happier, but the differences are extremely small. In the separated category, men are happier and more satisfied than women, and here the differences are relatively pronounced. How can one interpret this reversal of positions? Let us recall that female participation in the work force is a relatively recent phenomenon in most of these countries, and that (especially outside the United States) women, particularly older ones, are less likely to have secondary or higher education than men. Career opportunities for these women are relatively limited. Their postmarital situation may be economically dire. It seems plausible, then, that—especially outside the United States—separation and divorce are more likely to be initiated by

TABLE 7-12. OVERALL LIFE SATISFACTION AND HAPPINESS BY MARITAL STATUS
AND SEX

1. *Percentage "Satisfied" or "Very Satisfied" with Life as a Whole:*

Marital Status	Men		Women	
Married	79%	(31,101)	81%	(30,608)
Living as married	73	(776)	75	(833)
Single	74	(10,885)	75	(9,298)
Widowed	72	(1,391)	70	(5,118)
Divorced	65	(425)	66	(841)
Separated	67	(247)	57	(372)

2. *Percentage "very happy":*

Marital Status	Men		Women	
Married	18%	(20,321)	22%	(20,037)
Living as married	21	(575)	19	(627)
Single	13	(7,157)	17	(6,035)
Widowed	13	(1,058)	12	(3,930)
Divorced	10	(335)	9	(641)
Separated	13	(183)	8	(298)

Source: Combined data from Euro-Barometer surveys 3 - 12 (1975 - 1979).
Note: Percentages are weighted in proportion to population; unweighted Ns appear in parentheses.

men than by women. If so, it is not surprising that the negative feelings linked with this change are greater among women than among men—especially during the initial phase of separation. But, given time, adjustment takes place. Among the divorced and widowed categories, subjective well-being levels are almost identical for men and women. And because women tend to be slightly happier and more satisfied than men in the large married and single categories, the global result is a modest but consistent tendency for women to show higher levels of subjective well-being.

All the evidence we have examined thus far tends to support the aspiration-adjustment model, and suggests that the modest intergroup differences that do appear are in large part due to recent changes. We found, for example, that differences in income levels are linked with different levels of subjective well-being, in the intuitively obvious direction—but that the differences between the top and bottom quartiles amount to only 10 or 15 percentage points. What about the effects of recent changes in one's financial situation? Table 7-13 shows the relative happiness and satisfaction levels of different groups responding to the question:

TABLE 7-13. OVERALL LIFE SATISFACTION AND HAPPINESS BY RECENT CHANGES IN
RESPONDENT'S FINANCIAL SITUATION

During Past 12 Months R's Situation Has Become:	% "Satisfied" or "Very Satisfied" with Life as a Whole		% "Very Happy"	
A lot better	85%	(270)	37%	(270)
A little better	81	(1205)	21	(1185)
Remained the same	83	(3944)	19	(3887)
A little worse	74	(2795)	14	(2779)
A lot worse	57	(1119)	12	(1119)

Source: Euro-Barometer survey 18 (November 1982). For details of sampling and fieldwork, see ICPSR codebook for this survey.

How does the financial situation of your household now compare with what it was 12 months ago? Would you say it:

— Got a lot better
— Got a little better
— Stayed the same
— Got a little worse
— Got a lot worse

The variation across groups was much greater than that found in most of our previous analyses; with spreads of 28 percentage points (in satisfaction levels) and 25 points (in happiness levels). Recent financial changes seem to have a major impact on one's subjective well-being.

The data support our hypothesis about the impact of short-term changes. People seem to adjust to circumstances that persist for some time, as hypothesized. But what about long-term changes? We hypothesized that circumstances that persist for the very long term may lead to intergenerational value changes, with the result that new domains come to be given top priority by given segments of the population. As we saw in chapter 5, the Postmaterialist type is more prevalent among the upper socioeconomic strata than among the lower ones. To be specific, Postmaterialists are more than twice as likely as Materialists to have upper-status occupations, such as executive or professional ones, and they are about three times as likely as Materialists to have a university education. On the basis of their income, occupation, and education, one would expect Postmaterialists to rank high on subjective well-being; quite clearly, they are a relatively privileged group.

TABLE 7-14. LIFE SATISFACTION BY VALUE TYPE IN ADVANCED INDUSTRIAL
SOCIETIES, 1980 - 1986
(Percentage "satisfied" or "very satisfied" with their life as a whole)

Value Type	Nether-lands	Denmark	Canada	Ireland	Luxem-bourg
Materialist	92%	96%	90%	86%	94%
Mixed	93	97	89	83	92
Postmat.	93	94	89	82	91

Value Type	Britain	Belgium	W. Germany	Spain	Japan
Materialist	88%	83%	85%	73%	81%
Mixed	86	81	85	76	73
Postmat.	84	82	81	70	75

Value Type	France	Hungary	Italy	Greece	Portugal	Mean
Materialist	73%	71%	66%	64%	64%	80%
Mixed	74	73	68	64	62	80
Postmat.	78	66	66	63	60	78

Our theoretical framework, however, has entirely different implications. Postmaterialists, according to our reasoning, are Postmaterialists precisely because they take economic security for granted. They are a group that has experienced relatively favorable economic conditions in the long term—in the case of the postwar generation, throughout their lives. Consequently, their relatively high levels of income, education, and occupation do *not* produce particularly high levels of subjective satisfaction, and their priorities tend to be directed toward nonmaterial goals. In short, despite their relatively high levels of income, occupation, and education, we would *not* expect Postmaterialists to show similarly high levels of subjective well-being.

Tables 7-14 and A-18 (in the Appendix) show the overall relationship between values and subjective well-being throughout Western Europe in the 1970s and the 1980s. This relationship conforms to the same pattern that characterizes such stable attributes as sex, rather than relatively variable ones, such as income: There is virtually no variation whatever across the three value types, despite huge differences in income, occupation, and education. Overall, Postmaterialists are slightly *less* satisfied with their

TABLE 7-15. THE MEANING OF HAPPINESS, TO DIFFERENT VALUE TYPES

Question: "When you think about happiness, which one of these things
comes to mind as the most important?" . . . "And in second place?" . . .
"And in third place?"

	% Choosing		
Meaning of Happiness	Materialists (N = 3,440)	Mixed (4,807)	Postmaterialists (1,158)
Disproportionately chosen by Postmaterialists:			
Doing interesting things	9%	14%	25%
Getting along well with your friends	9	13	22
Having enough leisure time	5	7	11
To be thought well of by others	7	12	15
To feel that you are useful to others	13	9	26
Subtotal	43%	55%	99%
Disproportionately chosen by Materialists:			
A successful married life	49%	47%	37%
Good health	87	80	65
Getting on well together in the family	49	44	36
Having enough money to have an agreeable life	43	38	31
Having children	24	22	16

Source: Euro-Barometer survey 19 (Spring 1983).
Note: Since each respondent could name up to three choices, the
percentages above total nearly 300 percent.

lives as a whole and slightly *less* happy than the Materialists or mixed
types. For all practical purposes, one might conclude that there simply are
no differences between value types, in either overall life satisfaction or
happiness.

Nevertheless, though there are virtually no differences in happiness levels, there are striking differences in what makes the different value types
happy. Table 7-15 shows responses to a follow-up question that was asked
in April 1983, after the item about how happy one is these days: "When
you think about happiness, which one of these things comes to mind as
most important? . . . And in second place? . . . And in third place?"

Postmaterialists were markedly more likely to mention interesting and
socially useful activities, being esteemed by others, getting along with
friends, and leisure activities. Materialists were much likelier to emphasize
the importance of marriage, family life, children, good health, and having

enough money. Thus, the emergence of Postmaterialism tends to shift the focus of where happiness is sought, not only away from money and health, but out of the family toward broader social and leisure activities. The declining emphasis on marriage that we noted in the previous chapter, as well as the dramatic decline in birth rates that has taken place throughout Western Europe during the past two decades, definitely seem to be linked with the shift toward Postmaterialist values.

Moreover, the emergence of Postmaterialism, as the postwar generation reached maturity, helps explain an interesting phenomenon that was noted by Campbell (1981): the weakening in the relationship between income and happiness that took place from 1957 to 1978. Among the American public in 1957, there was a difference of fully 25 points in the percentage "very happy" between the top quartile in family income and the bottom quartile. By 1978, this difference had declined to only 7 percentage points (Campbell 1981, 241); Campbell also reports similar findings from Canada (Campbell 1981, 226). The fact that Postmaterialists are a relatively high income group that does not experience relatively high levels of subjective well-being tends to weaken the relationship between income and happiness. And the emergence of Postmaterialists in the late 1960s as an increasingly significant segment of the adult population, fits the timing of the change reported by Campbell. Finally, the emergence of Postmaterialism helps explain still another phenomenon reported by Campbell (1981, 175–81): a shift in the relationship between age and happiness. In 1957, the youngest group of Americans was 15 points happier than the oldest one. By 1978, this difference had disappeared. Campbell attributes this shift to a generational effect, linked with the war in Vietnam. We concur with his general diagnosis, and suspect that the emergence of a relatively substantial Postmaterialist cohort, as the postwar generation reached maturity, contributed significantly to *why* this particular generation had such a negative reaction to the war in Indochina; Postmaterialists had a much more negative response to that war than did those with other values. As we will see in chapter 11, the peace movement today draws its support very disproportionately from the Postmaterialist segment of Western publics.

In the light of this evidence, certain findings seem clear:

1. Subjective well-being scarcely varies at all across groups based on such stable characteristics as sex.
2. Subjective well-being does vary between groups based on less permanent characteristics, such as income or marital status, but even here the amount of variation is surprisingly modest.
3. Subjective well-being shows relatively large variations according to recent *changes* in one's income or marital situation.

TABLE 7-16. MULTIPLE CLASSIFICATION ANALYSIS: PREDICTORS OF
OVERALL LIFE SATISFACTION

	Eta	Beta
Nation	.271	.291
Recent changes in financial situation	.194	.193
Family income	.124	.117
Marital status	.102	.090
Occupation, head of household	.093	.088
Age group	.085	.069
Educational level	.089	.056
Religious orientation	.058	.054
Perceived size of town	.042	.049
Sex	.024	.022
Value priorities	.030	.012

$R = .385 \qquad R^2 = 14.9\%$

Source: Combined ten-nation sample from Euro-Barometer survey 18, for which fieldwork was carried out in November 1982.
Note: $N = 9,581$, weighted according to population of each nation.

All of these findings are precisely what we would expect on the basis of an aspiration-adjustment model, according to which one's aspirations gradually adapt to changes in one's objective situation, and do so in a way that tends to maintain an equilibrium between anguish and joy. Moreover, in the very long term (the time it takes to shape a generation), changes in objective conditions seem to produce value shifts that change the focus of *where* one seeks happiness—and may even change the social background variables most likely to be linked with it.

BUT WHY ARE THE DUTCH SO MUCH HAPPIER THAN THE GERMANS?

All the evidence that we have seen so far fits the aspiration-adjustment model very neatly. But now we must turn to a variable that does not seem to fit that model at all. One's nationality is generally an extremely stable attribute—for most people, it remains unchanged from birth to death. But unlike other stable characteristics, nationality does display a great deal of intergroup variation in levels of well-being. Indeed, both happiness and life satisfaction vary so much cross-nationally that it seems to undermine the credibility of the entire aspiration-adjustment model.

Tables 7-16 and 7-17 present the results of multiple classification analyses that illustrate this point. The evidence here supports our theoretical model on every point but one. In these multivariate analyses, the eta coefficients reflect the zero-order relationship between life satisfaction or happiness and the respective predictor variables, while the beta coeffi-

TABLE 7-17. MULTIPLE CLASSIFICATION ANALYSIS: PREDICTORS OF HAPPINESS

	Eta	Beta
Nation	.235	.247
Recent changes in financial situation	.127	.129
Marital status	.086	.109
Religious orientation	.082	.098
Age group	.089	.097
Educational level	.055	.066
Occupation, head of household	.081	.063
Family income	.063	.056
Perceived size of town	.040	.042
Sex	.021	.033
Value priorities	.038	.027

$R = .316$ $\qquad$ $R^2 = 10.0\%$

Source: Combined data from Euro-Barometer survey 18.
Note: $N = 9,476$.

cients indicate how strong these relationships are, holding constant the effects of each of the other variables.

Recent change in the respondent's financial situation is a stronger predictor of both life satisfaction and happiness than any other variable except nationality. Recent change explains more than twice as much variance in life satisfaction as does absolute level of income, and four times as much variance as does marital status or occupation. Controlling for the effects of the other variables, educational level, religious orientation, the size of one's community, sex, and value type all have negligible effects on life satisfaction.

Much the same pattern holds true of happiness, except that marital status and religious orientation have a relatively strong impact on happiness (ranking immediately after recent changes in one's financial situation), while income itself has a surprisingly weak (indeed, virtually negligible) effect on happiness.

But nationality is by far our strongest predictor of both life satisfaction and happiness: It explains at least twice as much variance as does recent change in one's financial situation, and several times as much as does any of the other predictors. As we saw in chapter 1, there are tremendous cross-national differences in subjective well-being. Furthermore, the differences are consistent regardless of which indicator we use: Those nationalities that rank high on life satisfaction also rank high on happiness; those that rank lowest on satisfaction also rank lowest on happiness. Finally, these differences show considerable stability over time.

We suggest that the observed cross-national differences have an important cultural component: Cultures differ in the extent to which it is permissible to express unhappiness and dissatisfaction with one's life. As Figure 7-1 shows, in Western Europe as a whole, life satisfaction ratings show a positive bias: 78 percent of the European Community's population describe themselves as either "very satisfied" or "fairly satisfied"; while only 21 percent describe themselves as "not very satisfied" or "not at all satisfied." A sizable minority do say they are dissatisfied, but the norm is to describe oneself as at least fairly satisfied. It may seem somewhat disagreeable or impolite to complain about one's condition. Moreover, the distinctive historical experiences of given nationalities seem to have shaped the degree to which the world is seen as generally threatening or benign. As we saw in chapter 1, there are enduring cross-national differences in trust, satisfaction, and support for the existing type of society.

Consequently, given societies may have different cultural baselines for the normal response to questions about how well one is doing. The normal response is *not* the midpoint of the scale in any of the cultures studied: The midpoint of the eleven-point satisfaction scale is 5, but all twenty-three publics for which we have data place themselves at least a little above that level; and the midpoint of the four-point happiness scale is 2.5, but all publics for which we have data place themselves at least slightly above that point.

Exactly how far above the midpoint the mean score for a given public falls seems to be a fairly stable cultural characteristic. But when people from a given culture respond, they have approximately the same positive bias in mind, whether it be relatively weak or strong; and they respond accordingly. If they are feeling especially good at the time of the survey, they may give a response that falls well above their cultural mean; if they are feeling especially bad, their response may fall far below this norm. But because most members of a given society have the same baseline in mind, satisfaction and happiness levels vary relatively little between groups within a given society, even though they vary a great deal between societies.

This interpretation strikes us as plausible, and it seems to reconcile some otherwise highly contradictory findings. But it is only part of the answer, for it immediately raises questions concerning the specific reasons why various Western nations—some of them geographically, culturally, and politically rather similar to one another—have such different cultural baselines concerning the appropriate amount of positive bias to show when asked, "How are you feeling?" At this stage, we can only begin to suggest possible answers.

The evidence in chapter 1 indicates that under extreme conditions, cross-national differences in subjective well-being can be eroded. Distinc-

TABLE 7-18. SUICIDE RATES IN WESTERN NATIONS, 1976 - 1978

Nation	Reported Suicides per 100,000 Inhabitants
Hungary	40.3
Finland	25.0
Denmark	23.9
Switzerland	23.8
Austria	22.7
West Germany	21.7
Sweden	19.4
Japan	17.7
Belgium	16.6
France	15.4
Canada	12.8
U.S.	12.5
Norway	11.4
Netherlands	9.2
Portugal	8.5
Great Britain	7.9
Italy	5.8
Ireland	4.7
Northern Ireland	4.6
Spain	3.9
Greece	2.8

Source: U.N. Demographic Yearbook, 1979.

tive cultural baselines may exist, but they are not immune to the impact of changes in the socioeconomic environment.

The modest but consistent link we have observed between subjective well-being and economic development at the national level may reflect a tendency for cultural baselines to shift gradually when a society experiences protracted periods of misery. When a large share of the population express negative feelings, the norm that one should express positive feelings gradually becomes weakened. Nevertheless, it is clear that we find nothing even approaching a one-to-one relationship between prosperity and subjective well-being at the national level.

Cultural differences in reported subjective well-being may be somewhat similar to cultural differences in suicide rates. Over ninety years ago, Durkheim (1897) observed that suicide rates are markedly higher in Protestant or nonpracticing Catholic countries than in predominantly Catholic countries. Despite immense socioeconomic changes and a widespread decline in religiosity (especially in Northern Europe), the national suicide rates shown in Table 7-18 indicate that Durkheim's finding is still valid to a considerable extent. Though suicide rates fluctuate with economic conditions and other events, a substantial difference persists between the suicide rates of countries in which the public consists primarily of practicing Catholics (such as Ireland, Spain, and Italy) and those of Protestant countries and countries where attachment to the church is weak.

Clearly, the situation is more complex than a simple Catholic versus Protestant or nonpracticing dichotomy would suggest, for by this standard, the Greeks are more Catholic than the practicing Roman Catholics, and Northern Ireland, though mainly Protestant, shows a suicide rate almost identical with that of the Catholic Republic of Ireland. Nevertheless, there is evidence of considerable continuity in cultural attitudes toward suicide.

This continuity gives rise to yet another paradox. Suicide rates tend to be higher in those nations that rank *high*—not low—on subjective well-being. Among the nations shown in Table 7-18, the five that rank highest on subjective satisfaction have a mean suicide rate of 20.7; the five nations ranking lowest on satisfaction have a mean suicide rate of 9.7. In other words, low suicide rates, which superficially might seem to be a good indicator of subjective well-being, in fact prove to be *negatively* correlated with it. This seems astonishing at first glance, but the paradox resolves itself when we look a little closer. For this correlation is almost certainly spurious. Those individuals who commit suicide undoubtedly *are* unhappy; but they constitute a tiny minority of the population of any nation— and whether a relatively large or small minority of the unhappy persons in a given society commits suicide seems to be strongly influenced by cultural patterns. Simply because they are readily available, suicide rates have often been used as an indicator of the subjective quality of life in given countries. More broadly based research indicates that this is misleading. The fact that we find huge gender-related difference in suicide rates demonstrates this point conclusively. Suicide rates reflect cultural norms far more than they do overall happiness levels. For example, within the United States (and most other countries), the suicide rate is about three times as high among men as among women, but there is no evidence whatever that men are three times as likely to be unhappy as women. On the contrary, even common sense would suggest that men should be about as happy as women—and the empirical evidence presented above indicates that there is no significant difference between the sexes in subjective well-being. Here too, the difference in behavior seems to reflect different cultural norms. Once again (as with church attendance rates), we find that aggregate national statistics are a very poor indicator of the feelings and attitudes of the respective publics: they are no substitute for direct measures.

Interestingly, those cultures in which suicide is most widespread tend to have the strongest norms of describing oneself as happy. Conceivably, being deeply unhappy in a society where everybody is expected to be happy may be even more unbearable—or produce a greater sense of social isolation—than it would in a society where misery is not so far from the norm. Thus, we have the paradox of high suicide rates in Denmark—a country in which the overall level of subjective well-being consistently ranks high.

CONCLUSION

Human happiness and satisfaction are complex phenomena. They not only reflect a combination of short-term, medium-term, and long-term processes at the individual level, but also an interaction between cultural and individual level influences.

We have found strong empirical support for an aspiration-adjustment model, at the individual level. Cross-sectionally, there is surprisingly little variation between stable social groups in their levels of subjective well-being. Nevertheless, in the short run economic or social changes for the better do produce significant increases in both happiness and life satisfaction. But one's aspiration level adjusts to conditions that persist over the medium term; after some years, one must get *more* of a given thing to attain an above-average level of subjective well-being. Furthermore, if high levels of economic or physical security persist over the long term (throughout a given generation's formative years), not only does a given level of objective well-being no longer produce above-average satisfaction, but qualitatively different goals may be emphasized. The prevailing values of the society change.

Finally, there are astonishingly large differences between the levels of subjective well-being reported in different societies. These differences can be traced to long-term differences in economic levels to only a limited extent. A given society's level of subjective well-being does seem to respond to recent *changes* in the economic environment, but even this explains only a fraction of the observed variation. In addition, there appears to be an important and enduring cultural component to a given nation's reported level of subjective well-being. In all societies, the modal response is that one's feelings are at least mildly positive, but in some societies the positive skew is much stronger than in others. As we saw in chapter 1, the presence of a relatively positive or negative skew in a given society's norms of subjective well-being is of far more than passing interest. It seems to reflect profound differences in that society's perceptions of how benign or malignant the world is, and has considerable bearing on interpersonal trust and the prospects for stable democracy. These cultural norms are part of a syndrome that has extremely important consequences.

Moreover, the sense of well-being actually experienced within an entire society can deteriorate significantly within a period of a few years, as chapter 1 demonstrated. Similarly, a massive decline in political trust took place in the United States, starting in the Vietnam era (Miller 1974;

Abramson 1983); there are indications that it may have been accompanied by a decline in interpersonal trust more broadly, and by a basic reorientation of which groups were happiest among the American public. As with Materialist/Postmaterialist values, we seem to be dealing with period effects, as well as generational change. The subjective quality of life as it is experienced in entire nations can rise or fall markedly over time. Precisely why and how such phenomena occur is still poorly understood; it merits further research.

CHAPTER 8

The Diminishing Marginal Utility of Economic Determinism: The Decline of Marxism

INTRODUCTION: DIMINISHING MARGINAL
UTILITY AT THE SOCIETAL LEVEL

Ideology lags behind reality. Though Karl Marx died in 1883, his analysis of political conflict continued to fascinate, and sometimes mesmerize, social critics and social scientists for much of the following century. His thesis captured an important part of reality for the early phases of industrial society. But with the evolution of advanced industrial society, new conflicts and new worldviews have emerged, making the economic conflicts Marx emphasized less central to political life.

This development reflects a principle that might be called the diminishing marginal utility of economic determinism: Economic factors tend to play a decisive role under conditions of economic scarcity; but as scarcity diminishes, other factors shape society to an increasing degree. In this chapter we will examine evidence of this phenomenon, first from an aggregate cross-national perspective, and then with time series data at the individual level. The two types of evidence converge, pointing to a diminishing degree of economic determinism, and class-based political conflict, as advanced industrial society emerges. Figure 8-1 provides one of many illustrations.

As Figure 8-1 demonstrates, human life expectancy is closely linked to a nation's level of economic development, especially at the low end of the economic continuum; it is virtually impossible for poor nations to attain a high average life span. A large number of countries cluster tightly together at the low end of the spectrum on both income and life expectancy, with such nations as Chad or Bangladesh showing per capita gross national products below $100 and a male life expectancy of 35 years or less in 1975. Just above them is a group of twenty nations having per capita GNPs of less than $300 and life expectancies of less than 45 years.

The curve rises steeply with relatively modest increases in wealth, until it reaches about $2,000 per capita. Thereafter, the curve levels off. Economic factors become less decisive, and life-style factors more so; longevity becomes less and less a question of adequate nutrition and sanitary

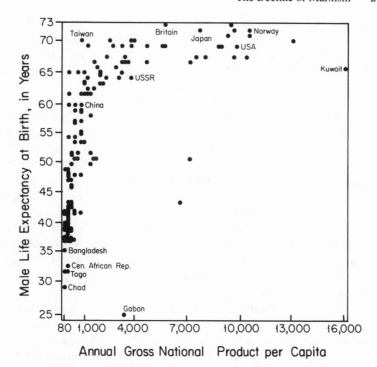

FIGURE 8-1. The diminishing marginal utility of economic determinism: 1975 male life expectancy at birth by gross national product per capita. Based on data from Charles L. Taylor and David A. Jodice, *World Handbook of Political and Social Indicators, III: 1948–1977* (Cologne: Zentralarchiv fuer empirische Sozialforschung, 1982).

facilities, and more and more a question of cholesterol intake, tobacco and alcohol consumption, exercise, levels of stress, and environmental pollution. Some striking recent cultural phenomena could be interpreted as a rational response to this shift. For example, a generation ago, Americans were notorious for their unwillingness to walk anywhere. In recent years, jogging, running, aerobic exercise, and yoga have become pervasive, together with avoidance of cholesterol, smoking and food additives—all of which may reflect a spreading awareness that today, longevity has more to do with life-style than with sheer income.

The leveling off of the curve does not simply reflect ceiling effects. In 1975 only a few nations had male life expectancies above 70 years; but in the ensuing decade, a number of nations raised them by several years. By 1982, female life expectancy in Switzerland had risen to 81 years, and this almost certainly does not represent the ultimate biological ceiling. Most developed nations still have considerable room for improvement—but it no longer is as closely tied to economic development as it once was. Thus, despite rising income, male life expectancy in the Soviet Union has declined in the last decade, apparently because of cultural factors, such as rising alcoholism rates.

As our diminishing returns hypothesis implies, a logarithmic transformation of GNP per capita shows a much better fit with life expectancy than does a linear model: The former explains 61 percent of the variance in life expectancy, and the latter only 37 percent. Figure 8-1 shows untransformed GNP per capita in order to demonstrate directly the diminishing impact of economic gains. Another illustration of this phenomenon is the fact that among the poorer half of these nations, raw GNP per capita explains 44 percent of the variance in life expectancy; while among the richer half it accounts for only 14 percent. Similar patterns of diminishing returns from economic development are found with numerous other indicators of the quality of life. Caloric intake, literacy rates, the number of physicians per capita, and other objective indicators all rise steeply at the low end of the scale, but level off among advanced industrial societies.

Equality of income distribution also increases sharply with economic development, up to a level of about $3,500 per capita; but above that threshold, there is virtually no further rise. Figure 8-2 shows this curve (inverted by comparison with Figure 8-1, since high scores on the vertical axis represent high levels of *in*equality). In 70 percent of the nations with a GNP per capita below $3,500, the top tenth of the population got more than one-third of the total income (in some cases as much as 57 percent). In *none* of the nations with a GNP per capita above $3,500, did the top tenth of the population get more than one-third of the total income; their share ranged from as low as 17 percent, in communist countries, to a high of 33 percent, in Finland.

Does this cross-sectional pattern reflect a longitudinal trend? The point has been debated. The most reliable longitudinal data come from economically advanced countries, which have shown little increase in income equality during the past thirty years. But if we interpret the pattern as reflecting a curve of diminishing returns rather than a linear trend, this finding is exactly what we would expect. It is only in the earlier stages of economic development that we would find large amounts of change. The United States, for example, moved toward substantially greater income equality from 1890 to 1950, but has shown little change since then. Absolute levels of income continued to rise, but relative shares changed only slightly. Conversely, Taiwan, South Korea, Singapore, and Hong Kong all have made dramatic leaps from poverty to prosperity only recently—and all have shown substantial increases in income equality (Chen 1979).

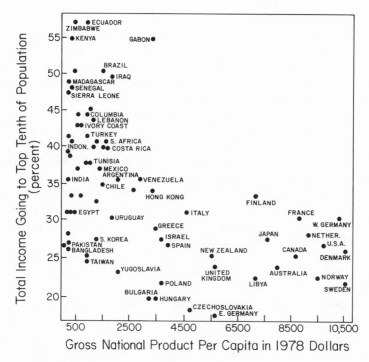

FIGURE 8-2. Economic development and income equality. Based on data from Taylor and Jodice 1982.

Why do we find a curvilinear relationship between economic development and income equality? In the early phase, we believe, it reflects a process of social mobilization, engendered by economic development. Industrialization leads to urbanization and mass literacy, which facilitate the organization of labor unions and mass political parties and the enfranchisement of the working class. Economic development does not *necessarily* bring this about, but it does enhance the *chances* of transforming the masses from isolated and illiterate peasants into organized citizens with the power to bargain for a more equal share of the pie.

But why does the curve level off among mature industrial societies? There are two main reasons. First, as a society approaches perfect equality, it necessarily reaches a point of diminishing returns. At the point where the top tenth had only 10 percent of the income, any further transfer of income would be a move *away* from equality. None of these societies has actually reached this point, but some are getting close; In East Germany, for example, the top tenth get only 17 percent of the total income, according to official sources (these figures may exaggerate the degree of income equality in Eastern Europe—a Czech analysis cited by Connor [1979, 216–

18] estimates that income equality in Eastern Europe is no greater than in some Western countries). In any event, there seems to be a practical limit, for all societies use different rates of pay to motivate their labor forces. China, during the Cultural Revolution, may have emphasized economic equality more heavily than had any other nation in modern times, but even then the country retained some income differences. To motivate the people, the regime relied on a combination of intense moral exhortation and coercion. This system had severe drawbacks; the current Chinese regime has shifted toward less coercion and more reliance on economic incentives. The fact that Norway, Sweden, and Denmark have significantly greater income equality than the United States, West Germany, or France indicates that the latter countries could move further toward equality without winding up with ineffective economies or coercive societies. But the Scandanavian countries seem to be approaching the limit of what is possible in a democratic political system.

Why this is so reflects a second basic principle: Political support for increased income equality reaches a point of diminishing returns at a level well short of perfect equality. Przeworski and Wallerstein (1982) have demonstrated through mathematical modeling that under appropriate conditions workers and capitalists would reach a compromise in rational pursuit of their material interests: Capitalists would consent to democratic institutions through which workers could effectively press claims for material gains. And workers would consent to profits in the expectation that they will be invested productively, improving their future material gains. Thus, given democratic institutions, some inequality of income may be acceptable to the lower-paid groups.

Moreover, as a society moves closer to an equal income distribution, the political base of support for further redistribution becomes narrower. In a poor society where the top 10 percent get 40 to 60 percent of the total income, the vast majority would benefit from redistribution. In a society in which the top tenth get only 20 percent of the total income, far fewer people will benefit from further redistribution, and they will benefit proportionately less; a majority may even stand to lose more than they would gain by additional redistribution. This does not constitute a moral justification for not moving further toward equality; but it does constitute a serious practical problem in democratic societies. Under these conditions, the political base for further development of the welfare state is simply not there—at least not insofar as the citizens are motivated solely by economic self-interest. Ironically, further progress toward equality would come *not* from an emphasis on materialistic class conflict, but through an appeal to the public's sense of justice, social solidarity, and other nonmaterial motivations.

Is there any chance that such appeals would work? We believe that there is. As we have seen above, there seems to be a long-term tendency for the pursuit of economic self-interest itself to reach a point of diminishing returns in advanced industrial societies, and gradually give way to Postmaterialist motivations, including a greater emphasis on social solidarity. Thus, economic development makes a sense of economic deprivation less widespread among mass publics, and consequently a less important cause of political conflict.

This conclusion is not surprising. After the fact, it may even seem self-evident. It is not; it has been hotly debated, and cannot be viewed as conclusively proven even now. A quarter of a century ago, the "end of ideology" (Bell 1960) school concluded that growing prosperity was giving rise to the "politics of consensus in an age of affluence" (Lane 1965); the subsequent explosion of protest in the late 1960s led many to conclude that this school had been completely wrong. In fact, the "end of ideology" school's analysis of what had been happening was partly correct; like Marx, they simply failed to anticipate new developments. While economic cleavages become less intense with rising levels of economic development, they gradually give way to *other* types of conflict.

Thus far we have seen indications that economic development leads to a diminishing impact of economic influences on such objective characteristics as life expectancy and economic equality. But do such changes actually reshape the political preferences of mass publics?

The evidence suggests that at high levels of economic development, public support for the classic economic policies of the Left tends to diminish. Table 8-1 sums up the responses of eleven Western publics to a set of questions dealing with three key issues underlying the classic Left-Right polarization. These questions were asked in Euro-Barometer surveys carried out in 1979, 1981, and 1983 in the ten member nations of the European Community (Greece, not yet a member, was not surveyed in 1979). The questions deal with redistribution of income, government control of the economy, and nationalization of industry—the central elements of the traditional Left's prescription for society. They were worded as follows:

We'd like to hear your views on some important political issues. Could you tell me whether you agree or disagree with each of the following proposals? How strongly do you feel?
(1) Greater effort should be made to reduce income inequality
(2) Government should play a greater role in the management of the economy (in 1983, this item was reversed, to refer to "a smaller role"; its polarity has been recoded accordingly)
(3) Public ownership of industry should be expanded

Though a majority support greater income equality in every country, while further nationalization of industry is rejected by majorities everywhere except in Greece and Ireland, the *relative* levels of support for these three policies among the publics of given nations show impressive consistency—both across items and across time. Taken together, the results add up to a remarkably clear picture of which publics are most favorable to the classic Left economic policies—and the picture does not correspond to conventional stereotypes.

Everyone knows that Denmark is a leading welfare state, with advanced social legislation, progressive taxation, a high level of income equality, and well over half its GNP going to the public sector. Obviously, the Danish public must be relatively favorable to these traditional policies of the Left. Conversely everyone knows that Ireland is a largely rural nation, with a modest public sector and no significant communist or socialist movements. Clearly, Ireland must be a bastion of conservatism on the classic Left-Right issues.

In fact, the conventional stereotypes are dead wrong on both counts. The stereotypes reflect patterns that were true in the past, but precisely *because* Denmark has now attained high levels of social security—and very high levels of taxation—the Danish public has little desire for further extension of these policies. Instead, support for the classic economic policies of the Left tends to reflect a nation's level of economic development (see Table 8-1 and Figure 8-3). As Figure 8-3 demonstrates, Greece is by far the poorest country among the eleven societies surveyed in 1979–1983, and the Greek public has by far the highest level of support for nationalization of industry, more government management of the economy, and reducing income inequality. Ireland is the second-poorest country, and overall Ireland ranks second in support for these policies. At the opposite end of the spectrum, Denmark is the richest country—and has the lowest level of support for these policies. West Germany ranks next to Denmark in economic level—and also in support for the classic Left policies.

The French show more support for these policies than their economic level would suggest—which may be linked with the fact that France also has an incongruously high level of economic inequality. But France constitutes the only significant anomaly. The other ten societies show an almost perfect fit between level of economic development and support for the classic economic policies of the Left.

These findings suggest that the principle of diminishing marginal utility applies at the societal level, as well as the individual level. Greece is an economically underdeveloped country, with many living in extreme poverty and a small, affluent elite. In such a context, the balance between rich and poor can be redressed only by strong government intervention. Den-

TABLE 8-1. SUPPORT FOR THE CLASSIC ECONOMIC POLICIES OF THE LEFT BY
LEVEL OF ECONOMIC DEVELOPMENT, 1979 - 1983

		% in Favor of[a]			
Nation (Ranked by per Capita Gross Domestic Product)	GDP/Capita in European Currency Units, 1982	1. Reducing Income Inequality	2. More Government Management of the Economy	3. More Nation-alization of Industry	Mean for 3 issues
1. Greece	3,958	95%	82%	80%	86%
2. Ireland	5,408	90	72	64	75
3. Italy	6,287	88	68	36	64
4. Northern Ireland	6,852	76	65	57	66
5. Belgium	8,735	87	53	42	61
6. Great Britain	8,755	73	64	46	61
7. Luxembourg	9,407	82	60	31	58
8. Netherlands	9,830	78	64	32	58
9. France	10,237	93	63	44	67
10. W. Germany	10,927	80	52	41	58
11. Denmark	11,194	71	57	19	49

Sources: Attitudinal data are based on combined results from Euro-
Barometer surveys 11, 16, and 19; data on GDP/capita are from Eurostat,
Structural Data (Luxembourg: 1985).

Note: Respective Ns are 8,884 for 1979, 9,909 for 1981, and 9,790
for 1983. See ICPSR codebooks for details concerning fieldwork.

[a]Text of questions: "We'd like to hear your views on some important
political issues. Could you tell me whether you agree or disagree with
each of the following proposals? How strongly do you feel?" (show card):

1. "Greater effort should be made to reduce income inequality."
    (Those who said they "agree" or "agree strongly" are classified as
    favorable to the policy in this table.)

2. "Government should play a greater role in the management of the
    economy."

3. "Public ownership of industry should be expanded."

In the 1983 survey, the polarity of item 2 was reversed; while 70
percent of the ten publics agreed that government should play a greater
role in 1981, only 52 percent rejected the proposal that government
should play a smaller role in 1983. For item 2, values shown in this
table are based on the 1981 and 1983 results only, with equal weight
given to the two formulations. Missing data are excluded from
percentage base.

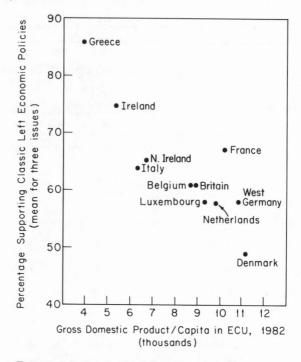

FIGURE 8-3. Support for the classic economic policies of the Left by level of economic development,
1979–1983. Based on responses to three items,
asked in three surveys.

mark, on the other hand, is a rich country that developed and has long had
some of the most advanced social welfare policies in the world—and one
of the world's highest rates of taxation. Almost 60 percent of Denmark's
GNP is spent by the government; the country is approaching the point
where it becomes impossible to move much further in this direction (even
in the Soviet Union, the government's share probably is not over 75 percent despite strong ideological biases against individual enterprise). In
Denmark, further redistribution by the government seems less urgent than
in Greece—and the costs of government intervention impinge on a larger
share of the population. The incentives to press farther with the traditional
economic policies of the Left become relatively weak, and public resistance relatively strong.

In this sense, the policies that dominated the agenda of the Left throughout most of this century are running out of steam. Increased state intervention was desperately needed to alleviate starvation and social upheaval in
the 1930s, was essential to the emergence of the welfare state in the post-

war era, and still makes sense in some areas. But in others, it has passed a point of diminishing returns. The renewed respect for market forces that has emerged throughout most of the industrial world recently reflects this reality.

The neoconservative claim that the classic welfare state policies have failed is false, however. On the contrary, in such countries as Denmark, these policies have largely solved the problems they are capable of solving most readily—and have thereby reduced the demand for more of the same. Insofar as they *succeed*, they reach a point of diminishing returns, and begin to cede top priority to problems that have *not* been solved.

Any attempt to turn back the clock to the savage laissez-faire policies of the early twentieth century would be self-defeating, ultimately leading to a resurgence of class conflict in all its former harshness. But the fundamentalists of the Left are equally self-defeating in their rigid adherence to a traditional program based on class conflict and state ownership and control of the means of production.

This does not mean that economic factors are no longer politically important. On the contrary, some very significant recent research has demonstrated strong linkages between fluctuations in the economies of Western nations and support for the incumbent political party (Kramer 1971; Tufte 1978; Hibbs, Rivers, and Vasilatos 1982). But this research has also produced a surprising finding: While support for the incumbents does reflect the performance of the national economy, it does not seem motivated by individual economic self-interest. The electorates of advanced industrial societies do not seem to be voting their pocketbooks, but instead seem primarily motivated by "sociotropic" concerns; rather than asking "What have you done for me lately?" they ask "What have you done for the *nation* lately?" (Kinder and Kiewiet 1979).

In short, economic factors remain an important influence on electoral behavior—but increasingly, they reflect sociotropic motivations rather than class conflict. The politics of advanced industrial societies no longer polarize primarily on the basis of working class versus middle class; and the old issues, centering on ownership of the means of production, no longer lie at the heart of political polarization.

POLITICAL CHANGE AT THE INDIVIDUAL LEVEL

The argument presented above is implicit in the Materialist/Postmaterialist value change thesis; it is new only in its application to the societal level. In this section we examine political change at the individual level. Here, we have a rare opportunity: the chance to test a set of predictions about social change that were published years before the data by which they are tested came into existence.

At the individual level, our hypothesis concerning the diminishing role of economic factors, is supplemented by a second basic hypothesis: that early-instilled values tend to persist throughout a given individual's life. In the context of the unprecedented economic development of the postwar era, these hypotheses imply a shift from Materialist toward Postmaterialist values. At the individual level, we therefore expected to find sizable and persisting differences between the value priorities of young and old, reflecting their differing formative experiences; but at the societal level, this shift will manifest itself only gradually, as one generation replaces another. Moreover, because this shift involves basic goals, it implies a gradual change in the types of issues that are most central to political conflict, and in the types of political movements and parties people support. Finally, it also implies a decline in social class–based voting and increasing polarization over noneconomic values. These implications for social change were spelled out in earlier publications (Inglehart 1971, 1977).

The intergenerational value differences these hypotheses predict have now been explored extensively. Survey after survey reveals dramatic differences between the goals emphasized by old and young. Moreover, as we saw in chapter 2, cohort analysis demonstrates that there is no tendency for given birth cohorts to become more Materialist as they age; consequently, population replacement has brought a shift toward Postmaterialism.

The predicted intergenerational value shift seems to be confirmed by a massive amount of empirical evidence, but the predicted changes in prevailing types of political cleavages have barely been touched on. Let us examine the relevant evidence.

FROM CLASS-BASED TO VALUE-BASED POLITICAL POLARIZATION

The idea that politics is a struggle between rich and poor can be traced to Plato. But unquestionably the most influential modern version of this idea has been Marx's argument that throughout industrial society, class conflict is the central fact of political life and the key issue underlying the Left-Right polarization is conflict over ownership of the means of production. Marx's influence is reflected not only in a vast literature of social criticism but also in the existence of an entire family of political parties that were inspired by his writings and, in varying degrees, purport to be guided by his analysis. The rise of Postmaterialism makes this analysis less adequate today. Let us consider why.

The Postmaterialist outlook is linked with having spent one's formative years in conditions of economic and physical security. Hence, it is more prevalent among the postwar generation than among older cohorts, and it tends to be concentrated among the more prosperous strata of any given age group.

The political implications are significant and at first seem paradoxical. Postmaterialists give top priority to such goals as a sense of community and the nonmaterial quality of life, but they live in societies that have traditionally emphasized economic gains above all, even at the expense of these values. Hence, they tend to be relatively favorable to social change. Though recruited from the higher-income groups that have traditionally supported the parties of the Right, they tend to shift toward the parties of the Left.

Conversely, when Postmaterialist issues (such as environmentalism, the women's movement, unilateral disarmament, opposition to nuclear power) become central, they may stimulate a reaction in which part of the working class sides with the Right, to reaffirm the traditional Materialist emphasis on economic growth, military security, and domestic order.

The rise of Postmaterialist issues, therefore, tends to neutralize political polarization based on social class. Though long-established party loyalties and institutional ties link the working class to the Left and the middle class to the Right, the social basis of *new* support for the parties and policies of the Left tends to come from middle-class sources. But, at the same time, the Left parties become vulnerable to a potential split between their Postmaterialist Left, which seeks fundamental social change, and their Materialist constituency, which tends to take a traditional stance on the new issues raised by Postmaterialists.

In 1972, this phenomenon temporarily split the Democratic party in the United States, when an insurgent movement won the presidential nomination for George McGovern. Though he won the Postmaterialist vote overwhelmingly, much of the normally Democratic working class electorate voted Republican, and social class–based voting fell almost to zero, as Figure 8-4 demonstrates. This was an extraordinary election, in which nearly half of all Democratic party identifiers voted for the Republican candidate. In subsequent elections, many Democrats returned to their normal political loyalties, partially restoring class voting. Nevertheless, it now hovers at some of the lowest levels to be found anywhere in the Western world.

In 1981, value cleavages contributed to a more enduring division of the British Left, split between a Labour party, which had been captured by a neo-Marxist and neutralist left wing, and a new Social Democratic party, which won over much of the party's mass constituency. Throughout the past decade, the Materialist/Postmaterialist cleavage threatened to split the

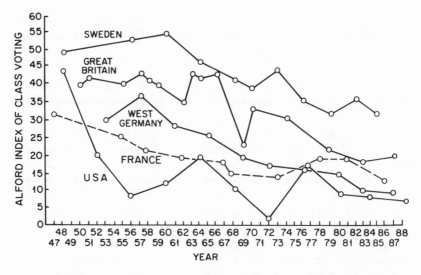

FIGURE 8-4. The trend in social class–based voting in five Western democracies, 1947–1988. Adapted from Lipset 1981, 505; updated by present author with results from recent elections and French elections. Sources: British data— Books and Reynolds 1975; Finer 1980; 1983 and 1987 results calculated from Euro-Barometer survey data. Swedish data—Stephens 1981; Zetterberg 1986. German data—Baker, Dalton, and Hildebrand 1981; Dalton 1984c; and 1987 National Election survey. American data (based on whites only)—Abramson, et al. 1986; and 1988 CBS exit poll. French data—MacRae 1967; later data from surveys conducted by Converse and Dupeux 1962; Converse and Pierce 1986; and Euro-Barometer surveys.

German Social Democratic party, torn between a Postmaterialist "Young Socialist" wing and the labor-oriented main body. Though the Postmaterialist Left was unable to take over the Social Democratic party as long as it still held power in Bonn, it did succeed in launching a Green (ecologist) party, which in 1983 won enough votes to enter the West German national parliament for the first time; in 1987, it received an even larger share of the vote, but began to come under increasing pressure from a Social Democratic party that was also competing for the Postmaterialist electorate.

A long-standing truism of political sociology is that working class voters tend to support the parties of the Left, and middle-class voters those of the Right, throughout Western society. This was an accurate description of reality a generation ago, but the tendency has been getting steadily weaker. As Figure 8-4 illustrates, social class–based voting has declined markedly during the past few decades. If 75 percent of the working class voted for the Left and only 25 percent of the middle class did so, one would obtain an Alford class voting index of 50 (the difference between the two figures). This is about where the Swedish electorate was located in 1948, but by 1985 the index had fallen to 31. Norway, Sweden, and Denmark have traditionally manifested the world's highest levels of social class–based voting, but all have shown declining levels of social class–based voting during the past three decades (Borre 1984, 352). In the United States, Great Britain, France, and West Germany, in the late 1940s and early 1950s, working-class voters were more apt to support the Left than were middle-class voters, by margins ranging from 30 to 45 percentage points. In the most recent national elections in these countries, this spread had shrunken to the range from 8 to 18 points. In the national elections held during the 1980s, class–based voting fell to or below the lowest levels ever recorded to date in Britain, France, Sweden, and West Germany. Though long-established political party loyalties tend to maintain the traditional pattern, it is being eroded both by the fact that new support for the Left increasingly comes from middle-class Postmaterialists and by working-class shifts to the Right in defense of traditional values (Inglehart 1977; Lipset 1981).

It is important to note that the class-conflict model of politics is not a mere straw man: A few decades ago it provided a fairly accurate description of reality. But that reality has changed, gradually but pervasively, to the point where today class voting in most democracies is less than half as strong as it was a generation ago. This change seems linked with intergenerational population replacement, for throughout Western Europe, indices of social class–based voting are about half as large among the postwar birth cohorts as among older groups.

We have argued that Western politics are coming to polarize according to social class less and less, and according to values more and more. We have just seen evidence of the former. Now let us examine evidence of rising polarization according to Materialist/ Postmaterialist values. Figure 8-5 sums up voting intentions by value type from almost 95,000 interviews carried out in Britain, France, Germany, Italy, the Netherlands, and Belgium, from 1970 to 1985. A vast number of nation-specific events took place in these six nations during fifteen turbulent years, which we will not attempt to discuss here. The overall pattern is clear, however. From 1970 to 1985, there was a trend toward increasing polarization on the basis of Materialist/Postmaterialist values.

In 1970, 61 percent of the Materialists intended to vote for parties of the Right and Center, as compared with 40 percent of the Postmaterialists. Materialists were likelier than Postmaterialists to vote for the Right by a ratio of almost exactly 1.5 to 1. This already was a sizable difference—but it has grown steadily larger since 1970. In 1973, the ratio had increased to

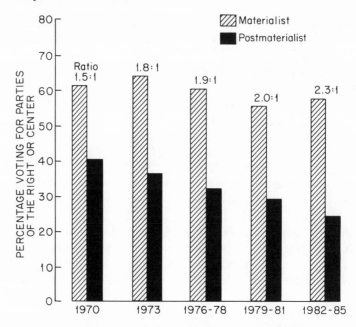

FIGURE 8-5. Percentage voting for political parties of the Right
or Center by value type among combined publics of Britain,
France, Italy, West Germany, Belgium, and the Netherlands,
1970–1985.

1.8 to 1. In 1976–1978, it grew to 1.9 to 1. By 1979–1981 it was slightly
more than 2 to 1. And in 1982–1985, the ratio had risen to 2.3 to 1. This
changing ratio was mainly due to a loss of Postmaterialist votes by the
parties of the Right. In 1970, 40 percent of the Postmaterialists supported
parties of the Right and Center. In 1982–1985, only 25 percent did so; 75
percent were voting for the Left.

But which Left? In order fully to understand the significance of what has
been happening, we must differentiate between various forces *within* a
changing and divided Left. There has been only a modest increase in the
proportion of Postmaterialists voting for the two major long-established
parties of the Left, the Socialist party and the Communist party. In 1970,
they drew 48 percent of the Postmaterialist vote; in 1982–1985, they got
53 percent. Proportionally much larger gains have been made by New Politics parties—above all, ecologist or environmentalist parties, such as the
West German Greens. In 1970 these parties won 13 percent of the Postmaterialist vote. In 1982–1985, they obtained 22 percent. The New Politics gains reflect two countervailing trends: (1) the stagnation or decline of
the Marxist New Left parties of the 1960s and early 1970s; and (2) the

spectacular growth of ecology parties having a distinct, and still evolving, ideology concerning the quality of the physical and social environment. The ecology parties have grown from almost nothing in the mid-1970s to being the largest component of the New Politics parties. Ecology parties recently have won representation in the national parliaments of Belgium, Luxembourg, Austria, Sweden, Switzerland, The Netherlands, Italy, and West Germany—roughly doubling their vote in the 1989 elections, as compared with 1984—and Britain's Social and Liberal Democratic party seems to be moving into the ecology niche.

The rapid growth of the ecology parties and the decline of the New Left parties of the 1960s reflects an important characteristic of both sets of parties: They have not yet developed strong voter loyalties or party organizations. Whether they ever will is an open question. If they do not, in the long run their electorates will probably be absorbed by larger parties that modify their ideological stance sufficiently to present an attractive alternative, just as the Socialist party has absorbed much of the New Left electorate in the Netherlands—partly capturing it, and partly being captured *by* it. We will not attempt to forecast the fate of specific parties in given countries; it is influenced by the parties' leadership, the strategies they adopt, the tactics of their competitors, and nation-specific events, as well as by the values of the electorate. Figure 8-5 makes one thing clear, however: Since 1970 there has been a growing tendency for electoral behavior to polarize on the basis of the Materialist/Postmaterialist value cleavage.

Postmaterialists have become increasingly likely to vote for the Left, but this trend has become increasingly *selective*, with the Postmaterialist vote going to parties that have distinctive programs tailored to Postmaterialist concerns. One striking consequence is that the communist parties have lost their relative appeal to Postmaterialists. In the early and mid-1970s, Postmaterialists were about 2.5 times as likely as Materialists to vote for communist parties. By the mid-1980s, there was little difference between the two groups. This is a remarkable change, which has had a major impact on communist parties throughout the West.

When Postmaterialism first emerged as a significant political force in the 1960s, its proponents tended to express themselves in Marxist slogans, which were then the standard rhetoric of protest in Western Europe. To a large extent the term "Left" *meant* the Marxist parties, and it was natural for the Postmaterialists to think of themselves as Marxists. But in fact there were profound and fundamental disparities between the goals of the Postmaterialists and those of the Marxist Left, as the Postmaterialists gradually discovered. These disparities became apparent in France earlier than in other countries—partly because the crisis of May-June 1968 brought to light the basic contradiction between the bureaucratic and authoritarian materialism of the French Communist party and the Postmaterialist desire for a less hierarchical, more human society, in which the quality of life is more important than economic growth (Inglehart 1977, ch. 10). Even there, ideological reorientation took many years. But today a democratic socialist Left has evolved in France that is increasingly non-Marxist or even anti-Marxist, and increasingly independent of the Soviet Union. The French Communist party, on the other hand, has remained one of the most authoritarian and Moscow-oriented parties in the West—with disastrous electoral consequences. After winning 20 to 25 percent of the vote in most French elections from 1945 to 1978, the Communist party suffered a sharp decline in the 1980s, falling to 16 percent of the vote in 1981 and then to 11 percent in 1984 and dropping below 10 percent in 1986. Though the degree varies from country to country, by the 1980s, communism had lost its disproportionate appeal to the growing Postmaterialist constituency in Western Europe.

ACTUAL ELECTORATES AND POTENTIAL ELECTORATES

The traditional form of Marxism has lost much of the mass electoral appeal it once had, and those parties that remain closest to the hard-line Leninist model are the ones that have lost most heavily. The French Communist party (PCF) illustrates this tendency most clearly. A rigidly authoritarian, Moscow-oriented party, the PCF endorsed the Soviet invasion of Afghanistan and condemned the independent worker's movement in Poland. It continues to call for further nationalization of industry and a state-run economy, despite the unsuccessful experience of the socialist-communist alliance with these policies in 1981–1982. Its decline reached disastrous proportions in the 1986 elections to the National Assembly, when its share of the vote fell below 10 percent—a disaster that was repeated in the 1988 elections. Though this is the most dramatic case of the decline of communism in Western Europe, it is by no means unique. In recent years, the Italian Communist party has also been in decline, and communist parties that had long been represented in the parliaments of Denmark, the Netherlands, and Belgium, have lost their remaining seats.

Election results are one indicator of change, but they do not necessarily tell the entire story. It is conceivable that, despite their diminishing electoral success, the hard-line Marxist parties have a much larger potential electorate than is currently manifest. For example, one of the greatest problems facing the British Liberal party was the perception that it had little chance of winning, so voting for them was wasting one's vote. Conceivably, there is a large constituency that would like to vote for the communists, if they felt they had a better chance of winning (or if they presented candidates in one's constituency, or if other circumstances were more favorable).

Similarly, new parties, such as the West German Greens or the British Social Democrats, have recently emerged in a number of West European countries, but they run up against severe institutional obstacles, for the major established political parties have huge advantages in material assets, national organizations, and voter loyalties. Moreover, the electoral systems of most countries confer additional advantages by setting minimum thresholds, such as the 5 percent requirement in West Germany, and even more stringent requirements in winner-take-all systems, such as those of the United States or Great Britain. Knowing that new parties are unlikely to win seats tends to inhibit voters from voting for them. Consequently, the actual vote for such parties may be far below the size of the electorate they might potentially attract in the absence of such handicaps.

In order to obtain an idea of the size of the *potential* electorate for various types of parties in Western Europe, in Euro-Barometer survey 21 (carried out in Spring 1984), representative national samples of the European Community publics were asked the following question: "I will now mention various political movements. Please tell me, each time, if it is possible or impossible that you would some day vote for a party that corresponds to the description." The respondent was then asked about each of ten types of parties ranging from the far Left to the far Right. This is a simple, straightforward question; but (though one's actual vote or voting intentions have been asked about in thousands of surveys) the *potential* electorates of given parties have rarely been measured, and were never before measured on a cross-national scale such as this. The responses (see Table 8-2) reveal some extremely significant facts about the distribution of underlying preferences that are not shown by the vote itself.

Table 8-2 shows the size of the potential electorates for ten types of political parties in West European countries. Clearly, responses to this type of question differ from those to questions about voting intention. Since the respondent is free to name any party for which he or she would consider voting, the totals for all parties add up to far more than 100 percent. Moreover, liberals tend to be seen as an acceptable second choice by a large share of the public, even though their first loyalty (and actual vote) generally goes elsewhere.

In other respects, the figures in Table 8-2 tend to reflect electoral results. Conservatives show their greatest strength in the British Isles and in Denmark; and socialists are strong almost everywhere, but especially in Greece and France, where they were the ruling party at the time of the

TABLE 8-2. POTENTIAL ELECTORATES FOR VARIOUS TYPES OF PARTIES IN TEN
EUROPEAN COMMUNITY COUNTRIES, 1984

Question: "Please tell me if it is possible or impossible that you would
vote some day for a party that corresponds to the following
description." (show card)

| | % Saying They Might Vote for Party | | | | |
	Communist	Socialist	Liberal	Christian Democrat	Conservative
France	20%	62%	65%	39%	33%
W. Germany	5	55	70	71	46
Italy	38	57	35	57	16
Britain	5	49	77	25	59
N. Ireland	2	33	67	32	68
Netherlands	9	56	41	52	28
Belgium	6	49	40	58	29
Luxembourg	11	69	59	69	21
Denmark	-a	46	42	15	45
Ireland	5	44	60	60	57
Greece	35	74	39	24	30
European Community[b]	16	55	60	49	37

	Extreme Left	Extreme Right	Nationalist	Fascist	Ecologist
France	12%	12%	20%	1%	56%
W. Germany	16	15	13	1	55
Italy	21	15	19	7	52
Britain	10	16	18	1	31
N. Ireland	9	27	25	1	36
Netherlands	14	14	25	2	43
Belgium	16	17	38	1	49
Luxembourg	10	18	24	-	53
Denmark	6	10	5	-	36
Ireland	18	37	60	4	57
Greece	15	15	10	1	27
European Community	15	14	18	2	47

Source: Euro-Barometer survey 21, carried out in April 1984.
Note: N = 9,745. Percentages computed separately for Northern and
southern Ireland.

   [a] Potential electorate for Communists was not ascertained in
Denmark; actual vote in 1984 elections was less than 1 percent.

   [b] Figures for European Community are weighted according to
population of each nation.

survey. Finally, the communists are relatively strong in Italy, France, and
Greece, but weak in the other countries.

These data provide a striking indication of the extent to which Marxism
was a spent electoral force in the 1980s. There is no large hidden reservoir
of potential support for the communists. Overall, only 16 percent of the
West European electorate indicated that they might conceivably vote communist some day. This is not only a far smaller potential electorate than

that of any other major political party; it is also only *one third* as large as the potential electorate for the environmentalist parties.

Perhaps the most striking finding that emerges here, is the remarkably *large* size of the potential electorate for ecology parties. In Germany, France, Ireland, and the three Benelux countries, about half of the electorate said they might vote for such a party. In the European Community as a whole, the figure is 47 percent. This indicates a potential electorate larger than that of the conservatives, almost as large as that of the Christian democrats, and almost *three times* as large as that of the communists.

Until quite recently, it was taken as self-evident that economic growth was inherently good; though there were sharp disagreements on how its benefits should be allocated, the progrowth consensus embraced both labor and management, capitalist and communist. Only in recent years has this assumption been called into question, with the environmental movement holding that economic growth does not always justify the impact it makes on the environment, and with some segments of the movement arguing that economic growth is now becoming either undesirable or even impossible because of the scarcity of natural resources. When environmentalism raises questions of environmental quality versus economic growth, it pits Materialist priorities squarely against Postmaterialist ones. Thus, in 1985, among the Materialists in the European Community publics, 37 percent "strongly approved" of the ecology movement—while 53 percent of the Postmaterialists did so. And while only one-half of one percent of the former claimed to be members of some environmentalist group, 3.3 percent of the Postmaterialists did so.

It is significant that the environmental movement did not collapse during the two major recessions of the mid-1970s and early 1980s. Despite this economic crisis, and a subsequent backlash against environmentalism, environmental protection standards were not abandoned—on the contrary, in a number of respects they became more stringent after 1973, when the energy crisis became manifest. Postmaterialist support for environmentalism remains firm, and the movement continues to win victories. Stricter limitations were enforced on the mining and burning of coal, and on automotive emissions during the height of the energy shortage in the late 1970s. Although the amount of hydroelectric power produced in the United States could be doubled fairly readily, environmentalist opposition has made construction of major new hydroelectric projects virtually impossible. In 1980, a proposed Energy Mobilization Board, designed to facilitate the development of energy resources in the face of environmentalist opposition, died in Congress; and millions of acres of land were added to wilderness areas that are largely closed to exploration for natural resources.

But the most dramatic and emotionally charged confrontation between Materialist and Postmaterialist priorities was the struggle over nuclear power. One can conceive of a world in which Postmaterialists favored the development of nuclear power on the grounds that it disturbs the natural environment less than coal mines, petroleum wells, or hydroelectric dams and that it produces less pollution and has a better safety record than conventional energy sources. This is conceivable—but the reality is quite different.

Nuclear power has come to symbolize everything the Postmaterialists oppose. It carries connotations of the bombing of Hiroshima, reinforced by fears that nuclear power plants might facilitate the spread of nuclear weapons. Based on complex technology, nuclear power was developed by large corporations and the federal government, in the name of economic growth. Postmaterialists are disproportionately active in the antiwar movement, tend to be suspicious of big business and big government—and give low priority to economic growth. They form the core of the opposition to nuclear power. Even during the recent energy crisis, opposition to nuclear power plants did not die away—on the contrary, it brought the development of nuclear power almost to a halt in the United States, West Germany, and several other countries. In 1968, nuclear power produced less than 1 percent of the electricity used in the United States; by 1978 it was providing nearly 13 percent of all electricity consumed. After the Three Mile Island accident this development halted. In 1979, nuclear sources produced only 11 percent of the nation's electricity, and their use is now rising much more slowly than before. Because of the prospect of protracted and unpredictable delays, no new nuclear power plants are currently being ordered and many of those already ordered, have been canceled. In South Korea, where environmental and antinuclear groups have little impact, a nuclear power plant can be built in four years. In the United States, construction time now averages about twelve years. It seems possible that the American power plant industry, which led the world until recently, may shut down completely.

Other nations have chosen to pursue the nuclear option vigorously, and a number of them (including Belgium, Sweden, Switzerland, France, and Great Britain) are already far ahead of the United States in the percentage of electricity they produce from nuclear sources. By 1987 nuclear power plants were supplying over half of Sweden's and Belgium's electricity and fully two-thirds of France's electricity. The contrasting American record reflects technological problems to some extent, but above all it is a question of political and ideological factors.

Like the environmental movement, the struggle over nuclear power reflects a clash of worldviews. For Materialists, the use of nuclear energy is

TABLE 8-3. SUPPORT FOR DEVELOPMENT OF NUCLEAR POWER AMONG NINE WEST
EUROPEAN PUBLICS BY VALUE TYPE, 1979

Question: "Could you tell me whether you agree of disagree with...the
following proposal? ...Nuclear energy should be developed to meet future
energy needs."

| Value Type | % Who "Agree" or "Agree Strongly" | | | | |
	Britain	France	W. Germany	Belgium	Italy
Materialist	79%	77%	69%	56%	57%
Mixed	75	64	58	57	47
Postmaterialist	52	44	46	46	45

| Value Type | % Who "Agree" or "Agree Strongly" | | | |
	Luxem-bourg	Ireland	Nether-lands	Denmark
Materialist	53%	52%	59%	41%
Mixed	59	45	36	40
Postmaterialist	36	35	27	20

Source: European Community survey (Euro-Barometer survey 11) carried
out in April-May 1979. Values index is based on top two priorities
selected from items E-H, cited in Chapter 4.

viewed as desirable insofar as it seems linked with economic growth and
full employment. For them, highly developed science and industry symbolize progress and prosperity. Among Postmaterialists, nuclear power
tends to be rejected not only because of its potential dangers but because it
is linked with big business, big science, and big government—bureaucratic organizations that are evaluated negatively because they are inherently impersonal and hierarchical, minimizing individual self-expression
and human contact. The ideologues of the antinuclear movement argue for
a return to a simpler, more human society in which energy is used spar-
ingly and what is needed comes directly from nature—symbolized by solar
power (Nelkin and Pollak 1981).

Tables 8-3 and 8-4 show the relationship between value type and support
for developing nuclear energy among European Community publics and
among candidates for the European Parliament, respectively. In every
country, Materialists are far more favorable to developing nuclear energy
than Postmaterialists. At the mass level, a majority of the Materialists support the development of nuclear power and a majority of the Postmaterialists oppose it in eight out of nine nations. The differences are even more
pronounced at the elite level. A majority of Materialists support nuclear
power and a majority of Postmaterialists oppose it among the European
Parliament candidates from every one of the nine countries. The percent-

TABLE 8-4. SUPPORT FOR DEVELOPING NUCLEAR POWER AMONG CANDIDATES TO
EUROPEAN PARLIAMENT BY VALUE TYPE, 1979

	% Who "Agree" or "Agree Strongly"[a]				
Value Type	France	W. Germany	Britain	Italy	Belgium
Materialist	95%	98%	77%	55%	100%
Mixed	85	65	54	54	40
Postmaterialist	49	40	24	44	24

	% Who "Agree" or "Agree Strongly"			
Value Type	Ireland	Luxem-bourg	Denmark	Nether-lands
Materialist	54%	71%	86%	64%
Mixed	29	25	14	35
Postmaterialist	0	0	9	5

Source: European Elections Study survey of 742 candidates for the
European Parliament, interviewed in Spring 1979; respondents' value type
is based on top two priorities selected from items A-L cited in Chapter
4.

[a]Figures show percentages who said they "agree" or "agree strongly."
The question about nuclear energy included an "in-between" option (not
proposed to the mass publics) that was selected by from 6 to 26 percent
of given national samples; only in the Netherlands, Denmark, and
Luxembourg were pluralities opposed to developing nuclear energy.

age spread between Materialists and Postmaterialists is at least 46 points
in every country but Italy, where nuclear power was not a major political
issue.

This emerging axis of polarization cuts squarely across traditional left-
right lines. On the antinuclear side one finds intellectuals, some socialists—and much of the upper middle class. On the pronuclear side, one
finds big business—and the AFL-CIO; Gaullists—and the French Communist party. It is not a traditional class struggle, but a polarization based on
Materialist versus Postmaterialist values.

One of the most striking features of the nuclear power controversy is the
extent to which well-informed members of the public and even competent
experts, when exposed to the same body of information, draw totally different conclusions. We believe this reflects a process of cognitive screen-
ing in which given facts are retained and weighted in accord with the individual's basic values. Though support or opposition to nuclear power is
usually justified in terms of objective costs, benefits, and risks, an underlying factor is a clash of worldviews.

Materialists take it for granted that economic growth is crucial, and
weigh the costs and risks of nuclear energy against the costs and risks of
alternative energy sources. Postmaterialists take economic security for

granted and weigh the costs and risks of nuclear power against various no-cost alternatives—among which, reduced material consumption seems not only acceptable but, to some, actually desirable; insofar as it might lead to a more decentralized, less impersonal society that allows freer play for individual self-expression, it has a very positive image (see Schumacher 1973; Lovins 1977; Sale 1980). Thus the debate over nuclear power is based on contrasting visions of the good society, with pronuclear and antinuclear advocates talking past each other because their arguments are implicitly based on different value priorities. To a considerable degree, each side is insensitive to the basic premises of the other.

Postmaterialism has come to manifest itself in new ways under new circumstances; what was a student subculture in the 1960s has evolved into the ideology of ''the new class''. And conflict between those seeking Materialist goals and those seeking Postmaterialist ones has become the basis of a major dimension of political cleavage, supplementing though not supplanting the familiar polarization between labor and management.

There are ironies on both sides. For generations, predominantly Materialist elites took it for granted that nature had infinite resources to withstand consumption and environmental pollution, for the sake of industrial development. But growth did *not* inaugurate the ''politics of consensus in an age of affluence'' (Lane 1965). Instead, after a certain lag, it led to the emergence of new sources of discontent, while a blind emphasis on growth that depended on cheap oil undermined its own future.

More recently, some Postmaterialist elites adopted a mirror image of this view, taking it for granted that industry had infinite resources to support taxation and regulation—sometimes in a needlessly punitive spirit. The irony here was that in the long run Postmaterialism is contingent on material security; the insecurity of the period from 1973 to 1981 arrested its growth and gave impetus to a renewed emphasis on reindustrialization and rearmament.

The rise of Postmaterialism was accompanied by a wave of legislation designed to advance the cause of human equality, raise social welfare standards, and protect the consumer and the environment. There were pervasive changes in national priorities. Prior to 1965, over half of the American federal budget was spent on defense and only about one-quarter on health, education, and welfare. By the end of the 1970s, these proportions had been almost exactly reversed—at which time they began to encounter a vigorous but only marginally successful Materialist counterattack led by such figures as Ronald Reagan and Margaret Thatcher in the 1980s.

It would be gratifying to be able to identify one side as totally right and the other as utterly wrong. But it is not that simple. Both Materialist and Postmaterialist goals are essential elements of a good society, and neither emphasis is automatically appropriate, regardless of circumstances. A healthy economy, and defense forces adequate to deter attack, are essential to the realization of both Materialist and Postmaterialist goals. But they are not the only legitimate political concerns. Beyond a certain point, a military buildup tends to generate countermeasures. The Soviet Union is militarily stronger than ever before, but faces suspicion and opposition from China, Afghanistan, Poland, the West, and much of the Third World. And beyond a certain point, material production produces growing social costs and a diminishing payoff. When there are two cars in every garage, a third adds relatively little; a fourth and a fifth would be positively burdensome. From this perspective, a shift to Postmaterialist priorities, with more time, thought, and resources going into improving the social and natural environment, is simply a rational response to changing conditions.

This should *not* be taken to indicate that the Greens are about to become one of the major political forces in Western Europe overnight. The massive institutional handicaps referred to above make it extremely unlikely; moreover the environmentalist movement has a strong aversion to permanent hierarchical organization, which virtually guarantees problems of factionalism and difficulties in carrying out any well-coordinated long-term strategy. Consequently, the environmentalists will probably never emerge as a new significant political party in countries that have majoritarian electoral systems, such as the United States or Great Britain; their effects in such nations will manifest themselves through the capture or gradual transformation of existing parties. Nevertheless the breadth of this potential electorate is remarkable. If issue preferences alone were what counted, rather than party organizations and loyalties inherited from past decades, the environmentalist parties would outnumber the communist ones today by a wide margin. It is the environmentalists, not the communists, who have a large unrealized potential. They may never convert it into actual votes— but its existence is a key item of information for anyone who is concerned with electoral strategy.

None of the other minor parties listed in Table 8-2 shows a potential electorate of a size that even approaches that of the ecologists. Nationalist parties have significant strength in Belgium and the Republic of Ireland— reflecting the fact that questions of national identity are still not fully solved in these two countries. Potential support for fascist parties is minuscule throughout Western Europe, but highest in Italy where the neofascist MSI is moderately strong.

Fully 14 percent of the West European electorate indicated that they might vote for a party of "the extreme Right." Clearly this term is not seen as synonymous with "fascist" among West European publics. Potential support for the extreme Right is surprisingly widespread. This is alarming information, which should not be ignored, for it gives an indication of potential electoral behavior under favorable conditions. For example, in this survey 12 percent of the French public indicated that they might vote for a party of the extreme Right. Two months later, in the elections to the European Parliament, an extreme Right party, the National Front, actually *did* win about 11 percent of the total French vote—nearly as much as was won by the French Communist party. This result (repeated in 1986 and 1989) has caused considerable concern. Previously an insignificantly small party, the National Front's program stresses law and order, restriction of immigration, opposition to abortion, and anticommunism. Frequently termed fascistic, its leader, Jean-Marie Le Pen, rejected the label, describing the National Front as a party of the national and populist Right.

The emergence of the National Front reflects one aspect of a broader phenomenon that has given rise to Postmaterialist ecologist and New Left parties but can also encourage the emergence of Materialist-backed nationalist and extreme Right parties for the polarization between Postmaterialist and traditional values is incongruent with the axis along which the major established political parties have been aligned for many decades. The tension between these two axes of political polarization tends to destabilize existing political party alignments.

NEW ISSUES AND OLD PARTY LOYALTIES IN POLITICAL POLARIZATION

The political orientations of Western publics today are shaped by two main components: (1) political party loyalties that are largely inherited from the past; and (2) an issue polarization dimension that primarily reflects the new, noneconomic issues. The Left-Right concept is used to subsume *both* of them. This is a serious source of confusion, for the terms "Left" and "Right," like a universal solvent, tend to absorb whatever major conflicts are present in the political system. Accordingly, in the contemporary political vocabulary, the Left-Right concept is used to describe *both* dimensions of political polarization, despite the fact that they are distinct and even, in some respects, contradictory. The degree to which this is true becomes evident when we submit these variables to a principal components analysis. This type of factor analysis is designed to measure the degree to which the variance among a group of variables can be explained by a single underlying dimension. Rather than differentiating between them, it focuses on what they have in common. Table 8-5 presents the results of a principal components analysis of these data. As it demonstrates, most of these variables—whether they tap issue preferences or

TABLE 8-5. PARTISANSHIP, ISSUES, AND IDEOLOGY: LEFT-RIGHT SELF-PLACEMENT AS THE FIRST FACTOR IN A PRINCIPAL COMPONENTS ANALYSIS

		Loading on First Factor in Principal Components Analysis
	R. places self on Left of Left-Right Scale	.73
1. Party Preferences	R. would vote for Communists	.53
	R. would vote for Socialists	.48
	R. would vote for Extreme Left	.45
	R. would vote for Ecologists	.17
	R. would vote for Fascists	.10
	R. would vote for Nationalists	-.18
	R. would vote for Liberals	-.21
	R. would vote for Extreme Right	-.29
	R. would vote for Christian Democrats	-.33
	R. would vote for Conservatives	-.42
2. Issues and Values	Reduce military expenditures	.47
	Liberalize abortion	.47
	Support peace movement	.44
	Postmaterialist value priorities	.40
	Employees deserve more rights in their company	.36
	Reduce income differences	.35
	Homosexuals are people like others	.34
	Labor unions are necessary	.31
	Less government intervention in economy	-.10
	Unemployed don't want to work	-.31
	There are too many immigrant workers	-.34
	Defend the existing social order	-.38
	Religion is important	-.38
	Nuclear power plants essential	-.39
	Scientific research a waste of money	-.41
	Sacrifice self for one's country	-.44
	God exists	-.46

Source: Combined seven-nation data from Euro-Barometer survey 21.

party loyalties—show significant loadings (above the .30 level) on the first factor in this analysis.

By far the highest-loading item in Table 8-5 is the respondent's self-placement on a Left-Right ideological scale. It has been argued that this variable is a resultant that sums up one's preferences on key current issues *and* one's political party loyalties, even if the latter are inherited from the past (Inglehart and Klingemann 1976). The results shown in Table 8-5 strongly support this interpretation. *Both* types of variables show strong loadings. But there is a striking incongruity between which variables among the two subsets show the strongest correlation with the underlying Left-Right dimension. Among the political party type preferences, those corresponding to the large and long-established parties (communists, socialists, Christian democrats, and conservatives) show the highest loadings. Smaller and newer party types, such as ecologist parties, show far weaker loadings. From this evidence, one might conclude that the Left-

Right dimension still reflects essentially the same content that it did forty or fifty years ago.

The issue loadings convey a very different message, however, for economic and social class conflict issues are *not* the strongest indicators of Left and Right. Some, such as support for reducing income differences, have substantial loadings. Others, such as opposition to government intervention in the economy, have surprisingly *weak* loadings. Once an unequivocal indicator of conservative leanings, concern with the growth of government has now become a serious consideration for the New Left as well—and by 1984, this item was only weakly linked with a conservative position. The strongest indicators of whether one is on the Left or the Right are the New Politics issues, such as support for liberalizing abortion and support for the peace movement, at the Left pole, or support for nuclear power plants, belief in God, and patriotism at the other pole. In short, the *issues* that define Left and Right for Western publics today are not class conflict ones so much as reflections of a polarization between the goals emphasized by Postmaterialists, and the traditional social and religious values emphasized by Materialists.

The smallest space analysis shown in Figure 8-6 illustrates the complex reality that underlies the useful but oversimplified concept of the Left-Right dimension of political polarization today. Although a broad Left-Right dimension is visible in Figure 8-6, closer examination reveals how this dimension actually subsumes two distinct components: the traditional Left-Right polarization, and a New Politics dimension.

Those variables with strong positive correlations are close together; those with strong negative correlations are far apart; and those that are essentially unrelated fall in between. For example, those who say they might vote for the communists are *also* very likely to say they might vote for the socialists. Accordingly, the smallest space analysis program places these two parties very near to each other, at the left of Figure 8-6. On the other hand, as one would expect, those who place themselves on the right half of a Left-Right ideological scale are very *unlikely* to say they would vote for either the socialists or the communists. Accordingly, the variable "respondent places self on Right" is located far away from support for the socialist or communist parties, near the righthand edge of Figure 8-6.

As a broad first approximation, a Left-Right dimension is clearly visible in Figure 8-6. The potential electorates of socialists, communists, ecologists, and extreme left are relatively favorable to reducing the defense budget, liberalizing abortion, and social change in general; All of these variables are part of a broad cluster at the lefthand side of Figure 8-6. Conversely, those who support conservatives, Christian democrats, nationalists, or extreme rightists, also tend to believe that God exists, that

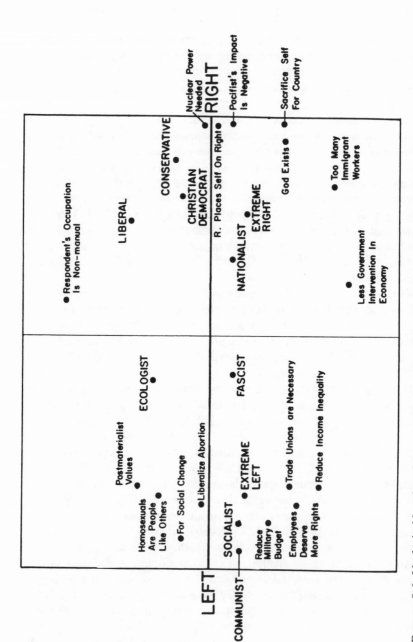

FIGURE 8-6. Ideological location of the potential electorates for major political parties. Smallest space analysis of data from Euro-Barometer survey 21 (April 1984).

the pacifist movements have negative consequences, and that nuclear power plants are needed; all of these variables are part of a broad cluster on the righthand of the smallest space analysis plot.

But this global Left-Right dimension has two distinct components, one linked with established political party loyalties and another based on the new politics. The major established parties polarize along an axis that has one pole in the lower lefthand quadrant of Figure 8-6 and the other in the upper righthand quadrant. Class issues, including attitudes toward labor unions, reducing income inequality, and employee's rights, are linked with the left pole of this axis.

Attitudes toward the ecology parties on one hand, and the nationalist and extreme Right parties on the other hand, are linked with a New Politics axis, which runs from the upper left to the lower right quadrant of Figure 8-6. Postmaterialist values, support for social change, and acceptance of homosexuals and abortion are part of the cluster in the upper left quadrant, while emphasis on patriotism, and religion and opposition to immigrant workers are part of the lower right cluster. Support for reducing the military budget has an anomalous position. It is strongly linked with Postmaterialist values; but it is also strongly linked with support for communist and socialist parties, and appears near them in Figure 8-6.

An indicator of social class—"respondent's occupation is nonmanual"—has an ambivalent position. Not clearly linked with *either* the righthand or the lefthand cluster, it occupies a position above them and toward the center; a nonmanual occupation is linked with support for the more conservative established parties; but it is *also* linked with Postmaterialist values and a liberal stand on the New Politics issues. Its conflicting linkages with these two axes of polarization weakens its relationship with both of them. Thus, despite its central role in social theory, social class today has become an astonishingly weak empirical predictor not only of electoral behavior, but of ideology as well.

The New Politics axis is not congruent with established party alignments. On a number of key issues, such as nuclear power and the peace movement, the established parties of the Left take positions that are unsatisfactory to Postmaterialists—which has led not only to pressures for change within the parties of the Left but also to the emergence of ecologist parties in Western Europe. Conversely, when the established parties of the Right fail to satisfy Materialist concerns in such areas as safety from crime, and problems linked with immigration and cultural change, a Materialist reaction may take place, examples of which range from the rise of George Wallace in the United States of the 1960s, to the recent emergence of the National Front in France.

The rise of Postmaterialism has placed existing party systems under chronic stress. In most countries, these alignments do not correspond to the social bases of support for change, or to polarization over the most heated issues. The major existing political parties were established in an era when economic issues were dominant and the working class was the main base of support for sociopolitical change. Today, the most heated issues tend to be noneconomic, and support for change on these issues comes from Postmaterialists, largely of middle class origin. Insofar as this is true, the social bases of the major parties tends to be inconsistent with their ideological position. The major parties of the Left still tend to have working-class electorates. But, because they are seen as the parties of change, they also tend to attract an increasingly large Postmaterialist electorate and Postmaterialist party activists. The converse applies to the established parties of the Right; they, too, are based on inconsistent combinations of social class and value priorities. The tension between these two factors has contributed to the rise of such new parties as the West German Greens, on one hand, and the French National Front, on the other. Though these newer parties are polar opposites, they have something in common: their social class base is *consistent* with their ideological stance. Hence, they tend to emerge when New Politics issues became heated enough to weaken or split the established parties.

Tables 8-6 and 8-7 show the social class base and prevailing value types of each potential electorate. One of the most striking observations that emerges from these data is an awareness of just how weak the potential for social class–based voting had become among the West European electorate as a whole by 1984. The strongest pattern of social class–based voting, as indicated by both the Alford index and the gamma coefficient, is connected with the Christian Democrats—for whom middle-class support exceeds working-class support by a margin of 12 percentage points. The second-strongest Alford index is that of ecologists—but this index has the wrong polarity, according to conventional notions of Left and Right. Usually viewed as a party of the Left, the ecologists have a predominantly middle-class potential electorate. Accordingly, they have a *negative* index of social class–based voting.

Conventional class–based voting patterns exist for socialists, communists, and extreme leftists, but they can hardly be described as strong. And once again, support for nationalists and extreme rightists violates conventional assumptions. Though almost universally considered parties of the Right, their potential electorate is disproportionately working class.

One way to rescue the class conflict model of politics would be to argue that the problem is simply one of measurement: More complex indicators of social class than the simple but straightforward ones used here would reveal that social class cleavages are the dominant influence after all. In

TABLE 8-6. POTENTIAL ELECTORATES FOR TEN TYPES OF PARTIES
BY SOCIAL CLASS, 1984

Type of Party (Ranked by Degree to Which It Is Disproportionately Working Class)	% Saying They Might Vote for Party			
	Head of Household Has Manual Occupation	Head of Household Has Nonmanual Occupation	Alford-Type Index	Gamma
Extreme Left	19%	13%	+6	.210
Socialist	61	53	+9	.169
Communist	19	15	+4	.144
Extreme Right	17	14	+3	.128
Nationalist	20	17	+3	.089
Fascist	2	2	0	.056
Liberal	58	64	-6	-.117
Conservative	34	42	-8	-.160
Ecologist	44	54	-10	-.203
Christian Democrat	41	53	-12	-.232

Note: Percentages derived from combined data for ten European Community nations, weighted according to population.

fact, empirical analysis provides very little support for this argument. A compound indicator, based on occupational prestige scores, family income, and education improves the explanatory power of social class only marginally, with the traditional parties. Moreover, this index shows the wrong *polarity* with the new types of parties, such as the ecologist ones. Here, upper socioeconomic status goes with voting for the Left. No matter how we slice the data, all three types of parties having a consistent combination of values and social class—that is, the ecologists, on one hand, and the nationalists and extreme rightists on the other—are parties that violate conventional notions of how social class should relate to Left-Right polarization.

Table 8-7 helps explain why this is true. As it demonstrates, the ecologists' potential electorate is, quite disproportionately, postmaterialist. While only 38 percent of the Materialists would consider voting ecologist, 66 percent of the Postmaterialists would do so. The gamma coefficient associated with this is .295—a stronger relationship than any of the social class linkages shown in Table 8-6. Despite their middle-class background, the Postmaterialists' value orientation pulls them toward the ecologists. Conversely, Materialists are about twice as likely as postmaterialists to support nationalists, fascists, or extreme rightists. In each of these cases,

TABLE 8-7. POTENTIAL ELECTORATES FOR TEN TYPES OF PARTIES BY VALUE
TYPE, 1984

Type of Party (Ranked by Degree to Which It Is Disproportionately Materialist)	% Saying They Might Vote for Party			Spread	Gamma
	Materialist	Mixed	Postmaterialist		
Fascist	3%	2%	1%	+2	.271
Nationalist	22	17	13	+9	.177
Christian Democrat	54	48	37	+17	.176
Extreme Right	16	15	8	+8	.139
Conservative	40	42	25	+15	.130
Liberal	56	63	61	−5	−.098
Communist	15	15	24	−9	−.139
Socialist	51	54	72	−21	−.188
Ecologist	38	47	66	−28	−.295
Extreme Left	10	14	26	−16	−.305

the linkage with values is so much stronger than the linkage with social class that the former prevails.

Western politics are coming to polarize according to social class less and less, and according to values more and more. We have already seen evidence of the decline of social class–based voting and the rise in political polarization according to Materialist/Postmaterialist values. Let us examine the latter in more detail. Table 8-8 shows the relationship between actual voting intention and value type from 1970 to 1987 in the six nations for which we have data since 1970.

First, let us examine the trend in the global breakdown between voting for the parties of the Left, versus those of the Right and Center. As Table 8-8 demonstrates, in 1970, 61 percent of the Materialists intended to vote for the Right, as compared with 40 percent of the Postmaterialists. Materialists were likelier than Postmaterialists to vote for the Right by a ratio of almost exactly 1.5 to 1. This is a substantial difference between the two groups—but the difference has grown steadily larger since 1970. By 1982–1987, the ratio had risen to 2.3 to 1. This trend reflects the fact that, despite their middle-class origins, the Postmaterialist electorate was shifting to the Left. But since 1973, socialists have gained very little and communists have actually lost ground among the Postmaterialists. By far the most impressive gains have been made by the environmentalist parties, which have now emerged as the prototypical Postmaterialist parties.

TABLE 8-8. SUPPORT FOR TRADITIONAL LEFT AND NEW POLITICS PARTIES BY VALUE TYPE ACROSS BRITAIN, FRANCE, ITALY, WEST GERMANY, BELGIUM, AND THE NETHERLANDS, 1970 - 1987

	% of Value Type Supporting Party									
	1970		1973		1976-1978		1979-1981		1982-1987	
Party Type	Mat	PM	Mat	PM	Mat	PM	Mat	PM	Mat	PM
Traditional Left parties										
Communists	3%	8%	4%	10%	5%	13%	7%	10%	7%	7%
Socialists and Soc. Dems.	35	40	31	46	33	42	34	42	33	47
New Politics parties										
New Left	1%	11%	1%	7%	1%	8%	2%	10%	1%	6%
Ecologist	-	-	-	-	1	3	2	10	3	14
Ethnic	-	2	1	2	1	2	1	1	1	1
Right and Center	61	40	64	36	60	32	55	27	54	26

Source: Combined six-nation samples from European Community surveys carried out in the years indicated.
Note: Percentages weighted according to population (unweighted N = 109,914).

With this has come the decline of the communists' relative appeal to youth. For decades it had been axiomatic that the young were disproportionately likely to vote Communist: "If a man isn't a communist when he's 25, he has no heart; if he's still a Communist when he's 45, he has no head." This linkage between youth and the Communist party, however, was not a biological constant; it was based on the belief that the goals of a specific younger generation converged with those of the Communist party.

That belief persisted until recently. As Figure 8-7 demonstrates, the two postwar cohorts among the West European publics were markedly more likely to support the Communist party than were their elders in each of the Euro-barometer surveys carried out during the 1970s. But the differences were growing weaker in 1978 and 1979. In the early 1980s, Communist party support among the two postwar cohorts continued to decline, falling to or even below the level of older cohorts. The young and the Postmaterialists had shifted to other parties.

Where did they go? For the most part, *not* to the parties of the right, despite a good deal of recent talk about the growing conservatism of youth.

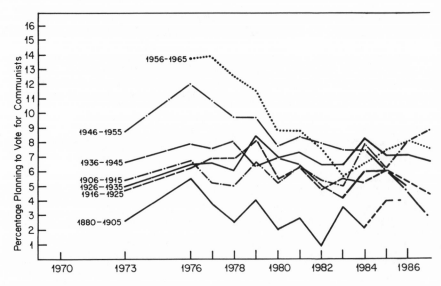

FIGURE 8-7. Percentage planning to vote for Communist party by age cohort, 1973–1987. Based on combined nine-nation sample, weighted according to population of each nation.

The old Left clearly *is* in decline, which presents an opportunity for enterprising and adaptive parties of the Right and Center. But given the option, younger voters gravitate toward New Politics parties, above all the ecologist ones, rather than toward the Right.

As Table 8-9 demonstrates, support for the communists no longer bears much relationship to age. Socialists and social democrats have also lost their special appeal for the young, in most countries. Nevertheless, support for the parties of the Right and Center is substantially *weaker* among the three postwar cohorts than among all of the older groups. There is no overall trend to the Right. Instead, the slack is taken up by a pronounced rise in support for ecologist and other New Politics parties. Consequently, the relative strength of communist parties vis-à-vis New Politics ones has shifted dramatically among the young. Among the cohorts born before World War II, communist support outweighs New Politics support by as much as 2 to 1 or 3 to 1. Among the cohort born in 1946–1955, the New Politics parties are slightly stronger than the communist ones. And among the two youngest cohorts, support for the New Politics parties outweighs support for the communists by margins of 2 to 1 and nearly 4 to 1, respectively.

That the young and the Postmaterialists would eventually move away from dialectical materialism was foreseeable. Commenting on the Post-

TABLE 8-9. SUPPORT FOR TRADITIONAL LEFT AND NEW POLITICS PARTIES BY AGE
COHORT ACROSS BRITAIN, FRANCE, WEST GERMANY, ITALY, DENMARK, IRELAND,
AND BENELUX, DURING 1984 - 1986

		% of Cohort Supporting Party			
Birth Years	Communists	Socialists & Soc. Dems.	Ecologists & Other New Politics Parties	Right & Center	N
1966 - 1970	5%	37%	16%	42%	(2,940)
1956 - 1965	8	38	16	38	(7,437)
1946 - 1955	8	42	9	41	(7,357)
1936 - 1945	6	39	5	50	(6,232)
1926 - 1935	7	38	4	51	(5,846)
1916 - 1925	5	40	3	52	(5,650)
1906 - 1915	5	36	2	57	(3,277)
Before 1906	4	37	1	58	(626)

Source: Combined data from Euro-Barometer surveys 21 - 26 (April
1984 - November 1986).
Note: Percentages weighted according to population of each nation
(total number reporting a voting intention = 39,868). Broken line
indicates threshold between prewar and postwar cohorts.

materialists' attraction to Communism in the 1960s and early 1970s, I
wrote:

> The first and most widespread form of Post-Materialist response has
> been a revival of Marxism itself. It seems ironic that this should occur
> in the West during a period when the younger and more creative ele-
> ments of the Soviet Union and Eastern Europe seem be be abandoning
> Marxism. . . . But Marxism has been a mainstay of social criticism in
> the West, and despite their divergences with the old Left, the New Left
> clings to its rhetoric as to their native language. . . . The danger is that
> their fidelity to traditional categories of thought may put blinders on
> Western protesters in their search for solutions.

Marx provided a brilliant and productive critique of nineteenth-century industrialization, and insofar as the problems we face remain the
same as in his era, his analysis remains relevant. But the problems are
not altogether the same, and many of the most anguishing ones seem to
be inherent to Industrial society, whether Marxist or not. Marx was an
insightful and creative thinker rather than a propounder of orthodoxy. If
he were alive today, he would almost certainly be a Revisionist himself.

A set of new challenges has arisen in the late twentieth century, and they have no pre-fabricated answer. Nationalized factories consume and pollute just as much as privately owned ones. A change in ownership does not seem to make those directing things less rigid or repressive; if anything, Soviet bureaucracy seems more so than Western ones. Nor does it seem to make the routine of the assembly line less tedious or dehumanizing. More experimentation seems to be going on in the West than in the Soviet Union aimed at giving workers a more creative, self-directed role in their work. The military-industrial complex is as powerful in the Soviet Union as in the United States, and the former devotes a much larger share of its Gross National Product to defense than the latter. (Inglehart 1977, 372–73)

In the long run, it was inevitable that the Postmaterialists would become aware of the disparity between their own basic goals and the authoritarian materialism of the established Marxist parties. By the 1980s, they were deserting those parties.

Along with this decline in support for the communists has come a declining belief in one of their key myths: the proletarian revolution that will usher in the last stage of history. Although Postmaterialists have become increasingly likely to vote for the Left in general and ecologist parties in particular, they became *less* favorable to revolutionary change during the period from 1976 to 1987. As Table 8-10 demonstrates, in 1976 Postmaterialists were more than three times as likely as Materialists to favor revolutionary change; by 1987, the difference had diminished considerably. All groups had become much less revolutionary, especially the Postmaterialists (who were still twice as apt to favor radical change as the Materialists).

Neither the young nor the Postmaterialists automatically vote for any party that claims to represent the Left. They are influenced by past loyalties, like other voters. But when they abandon these loyalties, they do so in order to support the parties that seem most likely to attain their goals— which are not necessarily those of the Old Left, and emphatically not those of rigidly authoritarian parties, such as the French Communist party. The Old Left parties are losing ground among the young; they win the support of only 44 percent of the 1945–1965 cohort, and only 36 percent of the 1966–1970 cohort. But the Right need not win them by default. When an option is available that addresses the Postmaterialists' concerns, they tend to take it. The evidence indicates that the Left can win the young *provided* it develops programs that appeal to the Postmaterialists as well as to the Old Left constituency—clearly not an easy task, but not an impossible one.

Though Western communist parties are in severe decline, it is extremely

TABLE 8-10. SUPPORT FOR REVOLUTIONARY SOCIAL CHANGE BY VALUE TYPE
ACROSS NINE NATIONS, 1976 - 1987

	% Favoring Radical Change by Revolutionary Action											
Value Type	1976	1977	1978	1979	1980	1981	1982	1983	1984	1985	1986	1987
Materialists	6%	5%	3%	5%	4%	4%	4%	4%	4%	4%	5%	3%
Mixed	8	8	6	8	8	8	6	6	5	5	5	5
Postmats.	20	17	16	14	14	15	11	7	8	9	7	6
Difference between Materialists and Postmats.	+14	+12	+13	+9	+10	+11	+7	+3	+4	+5	+3	+3

Source: Combined results from Euro-Barometer surveys carried out in Britain, France, West Germany, Italy, Netherlands, Belgium, Luxembourg, Denmark, and Ireland.
Note: Percentages weighted according to population.

unlikely that they will disappear. They still have millions of hard-core loyalists. Moreover, they have made important contributions to politics in their societies: By advocating greater economic equality they stimulated mainstream parties throughout the West to adopt welfare state policies, which were motivated, in part, by the need to meet the challenge from the Left, but which helped their societies adapt to the contemporary world.

Today, Marxism itself needs to readapt—and for the sake of survival, is likely to do so. The Italian Communist party already has reshaped itself extensively. Conservative Marxist parties, such as the French Communist party will eventually be forced to do so, regardless of what the current leadership prefers. The need for change is so clear that it is taking place even in societies ruled by communist parties, with Poland, Yugoslavia, Hungary, and until recently the People's Republic of China moving to relax the grip of central controls and allow greater freedom of expression. As the 1980s drew to a close, the Soviet Union itself was experimenting with ways to liberalize its economy and society. Even Marxist movements must respond to the forces of history.

CONCLUSION

According to the Marxist model, the key political conflict of industrial society is economic, centering on ownership of the means of production and the distribution of income, and support for the Left has a working-class base. With the emergence of advanced industrial society, the impact of economic factors reaches a point of diminishing returns. Noneconomic issues take an increasingly important place on the national agenda, giving rise to a new axis of political polarization; and support for sociopolitical change increasingly comes from a Postmaterialist, largely middle-class base.

Most of the major political parties in Western countries were established in an era dominated by social class conflict, and to a considerable extent the large established political parties are still aligned along a social class–based axis. But support for new political movements and new political parties largely reflects the tension between Materialist and Postmaterialist goals. Accordingly, social class–based voting has been declining, and there has been a growing tendency for Western electorates to polarize according to Materialist versus Postmaterialist values. Unless the established parties of the Left adapt to this new polarization, they risk losing their appeal to the young and Postmaterialist activists; if they move too fast in this direction, they risk losing their traditional working-class constituency.

The rise of a new axis of politics, based on polarization between Postmaterialist values and traditional cultural values, and the decline of class-based polarization, has left Western political systems in a schizophrenic situation. Most of the major political parties have been aligned along the class-based axis of polarization for decades, and established party loyalties and group ties still hold much of the electorate to this alignment. But the most heated issues today tend to be New Politics issues, on which support for change comes mainly from a Postmaterialist, middle-class base. This creates a stress that can be resolved in two ways: by a repositioning of the established parties or by the emergence of new ones. Both have been taking place.

The Marxist interpretation of society seems in decline throughout the industrialized world. Its emphasis on economic factors as the driving force of history provides a good first approximation of reality in the early stages of industrialization, but is of diminishing value as scarcity diminishes and new problems emerge. Similarly, the *policies* that are needed to counter the ruthless exploitation of capitalism in its laissez-faire stage, reach a point of diminishing returns in advanced welfare states. Where government spending is already 40 to 60 percent of GNP, there is less potential to move further in this direction; and the concentration of power in big government itself becomes an increasingly serious problem. The old assumption of the Left that more government was automatically better has lost its credibility. But to elevate government nonintervention into a quasi-theological principle is equally untenable. Some of the emerging problems of advanced industrial society will require more government intervention, not less. Within the next few decades, we will need to shift from petroleum to other energy sources or face dislocations far more severe than the OPEC-triggered recessions of the mid 1970s and early 1980s. Developing solar energy and nuclear fusion to meet this need requires a massive research and development effort, decades ahead of time, that market forces are not making and are not likely to make. Governmental inertia in such areas may be disastrous.

The meaning of "Left" and "Right" has been transformed. The key Marxist issue—nationalization of industry—remains a central preoccupation only to Marxist fundamentalists, such as the embattled hard-liners of the British Labour party. They are out of touch with current reality—and with their electorate. Under their domination, Labour has lost three consecutive elections.

Properly handled, nationalization does little harm; but it is not the panacea it once appeared to be. And insofar as it diverts attention from increasingly pressing problems concerning the nature of modern war and the quality of the physical and social environment, it can be downright counterproductive—for it provides no solution to these problems. Nationalized factories pollute just as much as private ones do. Indeed, insofar as nationalization merges the political regulators and the military-industrial complex into one cozy elite, it may even make things worse. Thus according to a recent UNESCO study, East Germany is the most severely polluted nation in Europe, with air and water pollutant levels two to three times as high as those in West Germany. And it is no coincidence that the only nuclear power plant accident that has cost human lives, occurred in the Soviet Union, where public pressures for safety measures cannot be freely articulated—and where, until recently, nuclear plants were built without containment structures and used a type of graphite reactor that Western countries had stopped building decades ago because it was too hazardous. Though their environmental problems are even more severe, and their arms expenditures at least as high as those in the West, the political systems of the East European countries make the emergence of independent and vigorous environmentalist movements or peace movements vastly more difficult than in the West. It is relatively easy for the ruling elite to simply ignore such issues—officially, the problems underlying them exist only in capitalist countries.

War is as old as human society, but modern technology has given it new implications: Today, it could terminate the human race. This fact has shaped a postwar generation for whom war has a different meaning from what it had in previous history. If one still accepts the Marxist conventional wisdom that war is caused by capitalist greed for profits, then one has a ready solution: Abolish capitalism. But the fact that most of the bloodiest battles of the past decade have been fought *between* nominally communist countries—with Cambodia against Vietnam, Vietnam against

China, China against the Soviet Union, and the Soviet Union against Afghanistan—has led to growing skepticism that the answer is this simple. The problem is rooted in the mentality of a military-industrial complex deeply rooted on *both* sides of an obsolescent ideological boundary. The old ideological paradigm no longer corresponds to reality. Neither the Marxist fundamentalists nor the laissez-faire fundamentalists have adequate answers for the problems of advanced industrial society. The goals of individuals and the challenges facing society are different from those of a generation ago.

CHAPTER 9

The Impact of Values on Ideology and Political Behavior

INTRODUCTION

The preceding chapter demonstrated that the shift from Materialist to Postmaterialist values has had a significant impact on the electoral behavior of Western publics. But voting behavior provides a very conservative indicator of the extent to which politics has been changed, for it is weighted down with an immense inertia: Political institutions, political party organizations, and long-established party loyalties all tend to inhibit change in electoral behavior. Thus, in voting behavior, the old political cleavages of industrial society persist to the greatest extent, with the working class still constituting the bulwark of the Left.

But other, less institutionalized aspects of political behavior are less resistant to change. Thus, in the realm of ideology, political polarization reflects the traditional cleavages to a much weaker degree; though partly shaped by political party loyalties, it is also shaped by new issue cleavages to a considerable extent. It is in the realm of direct political action that the new pattern of politics emerges most vividly. Let us examine these cleavages, starting with the realm of ideology.

TWO FACES OF LEFT AND RIGHT

We hypothesize that a new dimension of political conflict has become increasingly salient, reflecting a polarization between Materialist and Postmaterialist issue preferences. This new dimension is distinct from the traditional Left-Right dimension based on ownership and control of the means of production, and distribution of income. Its existence is working to transform the meaning of Left and Right, and the social bases of these two respective poles. In order to test this hypothesis, let us examine how Western elites and publics polarize in response to a battery of thirteen items included in surveys carried out in all nine nations belonging to the European Community in Spring 1979. Surveys were conducted simultaneously with (1) representative national samples of the publics of each nation (as part of the Euro-Barometer surveys) and (2) a sample of 742 candidates running for seats in the European Parliament. The latter sample gives a reasonably good indication of the issue preferences of West European political elites. It includes politicians belonging to all of the important political parties in all nine nations. In social background, these respondents resemble the members of the respective national parliaments (in which many of them hold seats).

Our battery of questions was designed to measure preferences on a wide range of issues: not only those that have become salient in recent years (such as nuclear power, terrorism, and abortion) but also such classic economic issues as nationalization of industry, redistribution of income, and the government role in the economy.

This battery was worded as follows:

We'd like to hear your views on some important political issues. Could you tell me whether you agree or disagree with each of the following proposals? How strongly do you feel? (Show CARD)

1. Stronger public control should be exercised over the activities of multinational corporations.
2. Nuclear energy should be developed to meet future energy needs.
3. Greater effort should be made to reduce inequality of income.
4. More severe penalties should be introduced for acts of terrorism.
5. Public ownership of private industry should be expanded.
6. Government should play a greater role in the *management* of the economy.
7. Western Europe should make a stronger effort to provide adequate military defense.
8. Women should be free to decide for themselves in matters concerning abortion.
9. Employees should be given equal representation with shareholders on the governing boards of large companies.
10. Economic aid to Third World countries should be increased.
11. Stronger measures should be taken to protect the environment against pollution.
12. Economic aid to the less developed regions of the European Community should be increased.

The respondent was shown a card offering the following categories for response to each item: "agree strongly," "agree," "disagree," and "disagree strongly."

Table 9-1 shows the results of a factor analysis with varimax rotation, based on responses to this battery of items, among candidates for the European Parliament. For reasons of space, only the results from a pooled sample of 742 candidates from all nine nations are shown here; separate

TABLE 9-1. ISSUE POSITIONS OF CANDIDATES TO EUROPEAN PARLIAMENT: FACTOR
ANALYSIS WITH VARIMAX ROTATION

I. Economic Left-Right		II. Non-Economic Left-Right	
More government management of economy	.764[a]	Stronger measures against terrorism	.776[b]
More public ownership of industry	.708	Develop nuclear energy	.733
Reduce income inequality	.642	Stronger defense effort	.727
Public control of multinationals	.633	Women free to choose abortion	-.574
Equal representation for employees	.615	More public ownership of industry	-.451
More aid to Third World	.372		

Source: Survey of candidates for European Parliament conducted in Spring 1979. For sampling details, see Inglehart, et al. 1980.
Note: All loadings above .300 are shown.
[a]Percentage of total variance explained by first factor: 37%.
[b]Percentage of total variance explained by first factor: 14%.

nation by nation analyses show essentially the same patterns, with minor variations.

The expected pattern emerges, with striking clarity. Our first factor is based on six items designed to tap the classic economic concerns; the most sensitive indicators of this dimension are attitude toward government management and ownership of the economy. The second factor shows a quite distinct content; its four highest-loading items are those designed to tap the New Politics. Nuclear energy and abortion are new issues—they did not exist as political issues a generation ago; terrorism has a long history, but its present form is new. Defense, obviously, is not a new issue—on the contrary, it is probably the oldest concern of the state. But domestic opposition to one's own defense establishment took on new overtones during the war in Vietnam. Opposition to the war came to be motivated much less by traditional conservative reasons (above all, opposition to heavy government expenditures and higher taxes) than by a Postmaterialist concern for the impact of the war on the purported *enemy*. Though the defense issue is ancient, both the motivations and social bases that underlie it have changed. A fifth item—concerning public ownership of industry—clearly does not fit our expectations, but it is by far the weakest-loading item. Its presence here signals the fact that this question plays a salient and pivotal role in the ideological structure of professional politicians—something that is not equally true of mass publics. As we will demonstrate shortly (see Table 9-3), the issue preferences of Western publics are structured in an almost identical fashion: Similar analysis also reveals two dimensions, based on almost exactly the same items as those in Table 9-1, except that "public ownership of industry" does not load on the second factor.

We hypothesize that the second dimension reflects a Materialist/Post-materialist polarization, rather than traditional social class conflict. Whether or not this is true remains to be demonstrated. First, let us examine the degree to which we actually have two distinct dimensions.

Varimax rotation can identify two or more independent components of an attitudinal structure even if the variables are only relatively distinct. Among the elites, these two dimensions *are* only relatively distinct. The mean correlation among the three highest-loading items on the first dimension is .50 and the mean correlation among the three highest-loading items on the second dimension is .45 but the mean correlation between the two sets of items is − .33. In other words, at the elite level we find two distinguishable issue clusters, but they are by no means unrelated. In a principal components analysis, all of these items show substantial loadings on an overarching Left-Right ideological dimension, or superissue.

Nevertheless, it is meaningful to distinguish between these two issue clusters. Indeed, unless we do so, we lose sight of a major shift in the meaning and social bases of Left and Right. Moreover, though they tend to be integrated into an overarching Left-Right structure at the elite level, among the general public the two clusters are almost totally unrelated. To be specific, among European publics, the mean correlation among the three items concerning public ownership, public management, and income inequality is .28 and the mean correlation among the items concerning terrorism, nuclear energy, and defense is .23, but the mean correlation between the two sets of items is − .05. At the public level, we are dealing with two completely independent dimensions. In part, this finding reflects a pronounced and pervasive tendency for mass publics to show less attitudinal constraint than do elites (a phenomenon that was discussed in chapter 3). But it is also true, as we will see later, that the two issue clusters are fundamentally different in nature and antecedents.

The fact that the two issue dimensions are distinct and relatively independent does not mean that they are unrelated to a broader Left-Right orientation, even among mass publics. Politics frequently demands a dichotomous choice: A politician must join or oppose a given coalition, or a voter must choose between Chirac and Mitterrand. The effort to build a winning coalition provides a powerful incentive to depict politics in bipolar terms that dichotomize the good guys and the bad guys. The Left-Right image is an oversimplification, but an almost inevitable one, which in the long run tends to assimilate all important issues.

The Left-Right dimension, as a political concept, is a higher-level abstraction used to summarize one's stand on the important political issues of the day. It serves the function of organizing and simplifying a complex political reality, providing an overall orientation toward a potentially limitless number of issues, political parties, and social groups. The pervasive use of the Left-Right concept through the years in Western political discourse testifies to its usefulness. Insofar as political reality can be reduced to one underlying dimension, then one can distinguish readily between friend and foe, and between the "good" and "bad" positions on given issues, in terms of relative distance from one's own position on this dimension.

To be sure, social conflict is rarely, if ever, unidimensional. Thus, to speak in terms of Left and Right is always an oversimplification—but an extremely useful one. In order to describe individually the relationships between a mere dozen issues or parties, one would need to make sixty-six pairwise comparisons; fourteen issues or parties would require ninety-one comparisons. This degree of cognitive complexity is hopelessly unmanageable in practical politics. Ideologues and politicians almost inevitably tend to sum up the alternatives in terms of such all-embracing concepts as Left and Right that provide a relatively simple guideline for forming alliances or appealing for mass support.

The core meaning of the Left-Right dimension, we believe, is whether one supports or opposes social change in an egalitarian direction. Typically, the Left (or, in America, the liberal side) supports change, while the Right opposes it (see Lipset, et al. 1954). It is also important to specify the direction of desired change. While conservative movements may be content to defend the status quo, reactionary ones seek change in the direction of greater *inequality* between classes, nationalities, or other groups.

The utility of the Left-Right concept rests on the fact that through the years, and from one setting to another, the basic political conflicts quite often do reflect a polarization between those seeking social change and those opposing it. The concept is sufficiently general that as new issues arise, they usually can be fitted into the framework. The specific kinds of change may vary, but the question of more or less equality is usually involved, whether it be between social classes, nationalities, races, or sexes. Moreover, there is some continuity in which groups seek change. Generally, those who are least favorably situated in a given social order are most likely to support change. Hence, over the years, certain social groups and political parties have come to be identified with either the Left or the Right.

Representative samples of the publics of the nine European Community nations have repeatedly been asked, ''In political matters people talk of 'the Left' and 'the Right.' How would you place your views on this scale?'' When shown a scale with ten boxes ranging from ''Left'' to ''Right,'' the overwhelming majority of respondents place themselves at some point on the scale with little hesitation. These responses generally bear a coherent relationship to the respondents' other views. For example, in keeping with our concept of the core meaning of Left and Right, those who are most supportive of social change are likely to place themselves toward the Left end of this scale.

A subjective sense of identification with the Left or the Right (or the Center) is widespread in Western Europe—but just what does it mean? It could, conceivably, be something similar to political party identification. In most countries, there is a consensus that given political parties are located at either the Left or the Right (or extreme Left, Center, or extreme Right). Originally, such images may have been based on the party's stand on salient issues, but over time they might become stereotypes that do not necessarily bear much relationship to current issues. How widespread is this phenomenon? The Political Action surveys conducted in Britain, Germany, the Netherlands, Austria, and the United States in 1974 asked the question about Left-Right self-placement cited previously, and then followed it up with this open-ended question: "What does 'Left' mean to you?" . . . "What does 'Right' mean to you?" (For sampling information, see Barnes, Kaase et al. 1979). In the four European countries, from one-fifth to one-half of the respective samples defined "Left" by referring to specific political parties; a slightly larger proportion defined "Right" in the same way. Only about 1 percent of the American public responded with party labels. The terms "Left" and "Right" have come into widespread use only recently in the United States and have not become generally accepted stereotypes for American political parties; but in Western Europe, to a considerable extent, these terms simply reflect the ideological stereotype of whatever party one supports.

One component of the meaning of the Left-Right dimensions, then, seems to be the perception that given political parties are linked with specific points on the continuum. This might reflect an accurate summary of each party's current position on key issues—but it could also be a stereotype that persists long after the events that gave a given party a given image.

It is clear, however, that (for a substantial share of the public, at least) the terms "Left" and "Right" have a meaning that goes beyond outdated stereotypes. In the 1974 surveys, in each country except Britain about half of the sample defined "Left" in terms of some ideology or with reference to more or less government or to social or political change; and about 40 percent defined "Right" in similar broad, abstract terms.

But what is the current meaning of Left and Right in terms of specific issues? In order to answer this, let us examine the correlations between

TABLE 9-2. CORRELATION BETWEEN LEFT-RIGHT SELF-PLACEMENT AND POSITION
ON SPECIFIC ISSUES AMONG WESTERN ELITES AND PUBLICS, 1979
(Pearson product-moment correlations)

Among Candidates for European Parliament		Among Publics of Nine E. C. Nations	
Issue	r^a	Issue	r
More public ownership of industry	.617	Stronger defense effort	-.355
More gov't management of economy	.599	Employees' equal rep. on boards	.277
Stronger defense effort	-.553	Reduce income inequality	.271
More control over multi-nationals	.519	More public ownership of industry	.235
Reduce income inequality	.502	Women should be free to choose abortion	.200
Women should be free to choose abortion	.474	Develop nuclear energy	-.200
More aid to Third World countries	.467	More severe antiterrorist measures	-.198
More severe antiterrorist measures	-.454	More gov't management of economy	.198
Develop nuclear energy	-.454	More control over multi-nationals	.197
Employees' equal rep. on boards	.342	Protect freedom of expression	.191
Stronger antipollution measures	.300	More aid to poorer regions of Europe	.176
Protect freedom of expression	.262	More aid to Third World countries	.174
More aid to poorer regions of Europe	.183	Stronger antipollution measures	.126

[a]Positive polarity indicates that those who support a given issue
tend to place themselves on the Left. Based on pooled data from
candidates from all nine nations and publics from all nine nations,
weighted according to population and (with the candidate data) according
to party strength in the European Parliament.

Left-Right self-placement and the battery of items designed to measure
preferences on both the classic economic issues and some newer issues.
To what extent have the new issues become assimilated to the Left-Right
dimension? To what extent do the new and old issues give rise to separate
axes of polarization?

Table 9-2 provides an answer to the first question. One's stand on the
traditional economic issues shows substantial correlations with Left-Right
self-placement in every case. For example, those who were most supportive of greater efforts to reduce income inequality showed a marked tendency to place themselves on the Left. But by 1979, the new issues were
also integrated with the Left-Right orientation of both elites and mass publics to an impressive degree.

The general pattern is similar among both elites and publics. At both
levels, the items that correlate most strongly with Left-Right self-placement are the top-loading items on the economic Left-Right dimension and

the noneconomic Left-Right dimension, respectively. In other words, our strongest indicators of both dimensions seem to have the greatest impact on whether an individual views himself/herself as located on the Left or on the Right.

But there are significant differences between elites and general publics. For one, these correlations are consistently stronger at the elite level than among the mass public. On the average, one's Left-Right self-placement explains over four times as much variance in issue preferences at the elite level as at the mass level. Constraint is much greater at the elite level, and since virtually identical questions were asked of both elites and general publics, the relatively low level of constraint among mass publics must be due to relatively low levels of political interest or other characteristics of the publics themselves, rather than to some artifact of the survey instrument, such as poor questionnaire construction.

Of more immediate concern, however, is the fact that the economic issues are more closely linked with the elites' sense of Left-Right self-placement than the noneconomic issues. Among the general publics, however, the situation is reversed: The noneconomic issues figure somewhat more prominently. Indeed, the strongest predictor of mass Left-Right self-placement—by a wide margin—is attitude toward national defense.

The classic issues of government ownership and management of industry continue to define the terms "Left and Right" among political elites. These are the textbook examples of Left-Right issues, the stereotypes that figure prominently in the rhetoric and the literature on which the elites were socialized. But the mass public has not read the classic literature. Consequently, the textbook issues do not have the same resonance among mass publics as among elites; for the public, the connotations of "Left" and "Right" are more influenced by current events than they are among elites. Thus, when we perform a factor analysis of issue orientations among the public, the same two dimensions emerge as among elites—but Left-Right self-placement tends to load on the New Politics dimension, far more than on the economic issues factor, as Table 9-3 demonstrates. Among the general public, the issue that showed the strongest correlation with Left-Right self-placement was support or opposition to a stronger military defense effort. The conventional wisdom of the textbooks would certainly not lead one to expect this—but in fact, defense issues are currently a far more intense cause of political polarization among mass publics than the classic economic issues.

At various times in the past the relationship between the Left-Right dimension and support for defense expenditures has fluctuated and even reversed polarity. In the first twenty-two months of World War II, for ex-

TABLE 9-3. ISSUE PREFERENCES AND LEFT-RIGHT SELF-PLACEMENT OF WESTERN
           PUBLICS: FACTOR ANALYSIS WITH VARIMAX ROTATION

Economic Left-Right		Noneconomic Left-Right	
Issue	Loading[a]	Issue	Loading
More economic aid to less developed regions	.615		
Larger government role in managing economy	.583	Stronger military defense effort	.694
Equal representation for employees and owners on boards	.576	More severe penalties for terrorism	.529
Greater effort to reduce income inequality	.559	Nuclear energy should be developed	.516
Stronger effort to protect free expression	.565	Women should be free to decide about abortion	-.346
More economic aid to Third World countries	.553	Equal representation for employees and	
More public ownership of industry	.514	owners on boards	-.300
Stronger antipollution measures	.486	Self-placement on Left-Right scale	.636
Stronger public control over multinationals	.452		
Self-placement on Left-Right scale	-.260		

Source: Pooled data from surveys of nine European Community nations
carried out in April 1979 (Euro-Barometer survey 11) sponsored by
Commission of European Community.
Note: *N* = 8976. For sampling information see ICPSR Codebook for
Euro-Barometer survey 11.
[a]All loadings above .250 are shown.

ample, Western Communist parties opposed taking any part in the war,
which was held to be a struggle among the ruling classes. After the Nazi
invasion of the Soviet Union, partisans of the extreme Left reversed their
position and became some of the most ardent advocates of an all-out effort
against Hitler. In the United States, before Pearl Harbor, Roosevelt and
other liberals struggled desperately to build up the military preparedness
of the United States and the West, against opposition that was particularly
strong in conservative circles. Though the Japanese attack brought virtually unanimous support for the war effort, there was a reprise of the earlier
situation after the war. Conservative Republicans, championed by Robert
Taft, advocated reduced defense expenditures and a withdrawal to Fortress
America, while liberals supported a strong stand in the Cold War. This
pattern seems to have persisted in the United States until at least 1960,
when Kennedy won victory over Nixon with a campaign that promised to
close the "missile gap" between the United States and the Soviet Union.
Accordingly, in his analyses of the issue positions taken by Western political parties from 1957 to 1962, Janda's (1970) expectation was that the

parties of the Left would be relatively favorable to higher allocations to the military. In the West as a whole, he found that support for higher military allocations turned out to be linked with the Right rather than the Left, but the association was very modest. It was probably the war in Vietnam that brought a clear and strong reversal of the earlier relationship. Opposition to the war became a major Postmaterialist cause, linked with humanitarian (rather than economic) concerns, as well as opposition to the hierarchical authority patterns of industrial society. By the end of the 1970s, the military defense issue was—by a clear margin—the strongest correlate of Left-Right self-placement among Western publics. And such new issues as abortion, nuclear power, and measures against terrorism showed correlations with Left-Right self-placement that were as high as, or higher than, those of some classic welfare state issues, such as government management of the economy.

The absorptive power of the Left-Right concept is all the more impressive in view of the fact that attitudes toward nuclear power and terrorism showed quite weak correlations with Left-Right self-placement among older respondents; nevertheless, the relatively strong correlations among the young brought the overall figures up to the levels shown in Table 9-2. To be specific, among West European respondents aged 55 and over, the correlation between Left-Right self-placement and attitudes toward nuclear power and terrorism, respectively, were .118 and .090. Among those aged 15 to 34, the figures were .246 and .265. Buerklin (1982) presents similar evidence: he finds that among older Germans (over 50 years of age), the strongest predictor of Left-Right self-placement is whether or not one is a member of the working class. Among younger Germans (18 to 29 years of age), Left-Right orientations are virtually unrelated to social class—but strongly related to attitudes toward New Politics issues, such as nuclear power and the Green political party. It seems that the linkage between these issues and mass Left-Right orientations is recent, and so far has fully penetrated only the younger groups. For the classic economic issues, on the other hand, age makes no difference. The older groups show correlations between Left-Right self-placement and economic issues that are as strong as, or stronger than, those found among the young.

On the whole, there is a close relationship between the issue positions of the electorate and elites of a given party. Table 9-4 gives the precise correlations. Once again, we find that the most sensitive indicators of the two dimensions shown in Table 9-1 play key roles. The four strongest mass-elite correlations are based on the two highest-loading issues on the economic Left-Right dimension, and the two highest-loading issues on the noneconomic issues dimension.

These issue correlations are handsome indeed. They are all the more

TABLE 9-4. CORRELATIONS BETWEEN ISSUE POSITIONS OF CANDIDATES OF GIVEN
PARTY AND POSITION TAKEN BY ELECTORATE OF THAT PARTY

Issue	r
Develop nuclear power	.645
Stronger measures against terrorists	.607
More government management of economy	.547
More public ownership of industry	.543
Regional aid	.541
Stronger defense	.452
Co-determination	.447
Protection of individual rights	.435
Abortion should be available	.400
Reduce income inequality	.384
Antipollution measures	.384
Aid Third World	.263
Control multinationals	.251

Sources: Electorates — Euro-Barometer survey 11 (April 1979);
candidates — survey carried out in March-May, 1979; for details, see
Inglehart, et al. 1980.
Note: Data set constructed using party as unit of analysis, based on
aggregated responses of the given party's electorate (measured by
reported voting intention) and aggregated responses of the given party's
candidates to the European Parliament.

impressive because they are not intragroup correlations that might conceivably be attributed to some methodological artifact. The correlations are based on two independent data sets, measured at two different levels of the political system. Although they are aggregated to the group level (which tends to reduce the measurement error present in survey data), the correlations found with our best indicators of the two respective dimensions are impressive. The .645 correlation between mass and elite attitudes toward nuclear power, for example, could be interpreted as meaning that almost 42 percent of the variance in the party elite's stand on this issue can be attributed to constituency influences. In fact, we do not believe that the causal linkage is that simple. Part of this agreement may represent the elites' influence on their electorate, for example; or the electorate may support given parties because of the stand they take on key issues, without influencing those positions. Furthermore, the linkages may be based on cues concerning the two broader issue dimensions, rather than the specific indicators.

We will not attempt to determine the specific causal connections that are involved here. For present purposes, our point is simply that strong linkages exist between the positions that the electorates and candidates of given parties take on these issues. It is virtually inconceivable that this pattern could be due to chance alone. It is possible, on one hand, that the politicians of given parties are influencing their electorates; or, on the other hand, it may be that the electorates are influencing the candidates' positions on these issues or, somewhat similarly, that the electorates selectively support given parties and candidates because of their stand on these issues. Each of these factors probably plays a role—and two of the three factors imply that mass issue preferences are an important influence on elite level politics. The net result is a surprisingly close fit between the positions of the electorates and those of politicians of given parties on these issues.

The two most sensitive indicators of the New Politics dimension and the two most sensitive indicators of the economically based Left-Right dimension are the issues that show the strongest elite-mass linkages. But the New Politics issues show even stronger linkages than do the economic issues. Although West European political elites still tend to describe Left-Right political polarization in terms of the classic issues of state ownership and control of the means of production, the evidence suggests that the electorates select their parties more on the basis of the new issues than of the old ones. Issue preferences explain only part of the variance in political party choice, of course. An even larger proportion is probably due to long-term party loyalties. But insofar as issues influence party preferences, the new issues seem to have at least as much impact as the old.

COMPARING CLEAVAGE DIMENSIONS

We hypothesized that the new noneconomic issues dimension reflects a Materialist versus Postmaterialist cleavage, rather than the social class and religious cleavages that gave rise to the conventional Left-Right dimension. Let us now test that hypothesis.

Figure 9-1 shows the strength of the relationship between the issue positions taken by the candidates of given parties and the aggregate characteristics of the electorates of these parties. Table A-19 (in the Appendix) gives the detailed statistics on which Figure 9-1 is based. Again, these are not merely intracranial correlations between various attitudes of the same individuals. They reflect elite-mass linkages, based on independent measurements at each level; and the characteristics examined here tend to be relatively enduring features of given electorates. Thus there are strong grounds for inferring that these mass characteristics have a causal impact on elite attitudes (or lead to selective recruitment of the candidates). In explaining the elite-mass issue correlations shown in Table 9-4, for example, one might plausibly argue that they simply reflect the tendency for the electorates of given parties to follow elite cues when they adopt their issue positions. But it is *not* plausible that the electorates of given parties become predominantly working class, or adopt given religious or value orientations, because of elite cues. It seems far likelier that the elite's issue

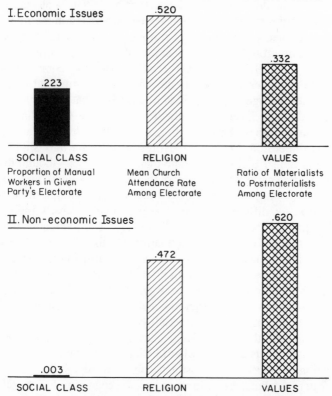

CORRELATES OF ISSUE POSITIONS TAKEN
BY CANDIDATES OF SIXTY-SIX PARTIES
FROM NINE WEST EUROPEAN COUNTRIES

I. Economic Issues

.520

.332

.223

| SOCIAL CLASS | RELIGION | VALUES |
| Proportion of Manual Workers in Given Party's Electorate | Mean Church Attendance Rate Among Electorate | Ratio of Materialists to Postmaterialists Among Electorate |

II. Non-economic Issues

.620

.472

.003

SOCIAL CLASS   RELIGION   VALUES

Source: Issue Battery Included in Survey of 742 Candidates to European
Parliment Interviewed in Spring, 1979 (See Inglehart et al., 1980); and Data
on Electorates From Cumulative results of Euro-Barometer Surveys 3-12.

FIGURE 9-1. Correlates of issue positions taken by candidates
of sixty-six parties from nine West European countries. Sources:
Issue battery included in survey of 742 candidates to European
Parliament interviewed in Spring 1979 (see Inglehart, et al.
1980); and data on electorates from cumulative results of Euro-
Barometer surveys 3–12.

positions are (in one or both of the ways outlined above) influenced by
their constituency's characteristics.

The top half of Figure 9-1 and of Table A-19 (in the Appendix) deal
with three key economic issues. These data demonstrate that of the three
types of characteristics examined here, religiosity has the greatest impact.

Not only has the religious factor been assimilated to the conventional Left-Right dimension—it actually outweighs social class as an influence on attitudes toward economic issues. When Rose and Urwin (1969) and Lijphart (1971) found that religion outweighs social class in its electoral impact in most Western nations, the finding seemed surprising in the light of prevailing social theory. The fact that religion outweighs social class in its impact even on attitudes toward specifically economic issues may seem more surprising still, but our data point to that conclusion. Materialist/ Postmaterialist values also seem to have a significant impact on economic issue attitudes, though their impact is weaker than that of religiosity.

At the individual level, Materialist/Postmaterialist values have an ambivalent relationship to the issues linked with the conventional economic Left-Right dimension. Postmaterialist respondents are only slightly more favorable to redistribution of income than Materialists—though the Postmaterialists are markedly more favorable to increasing economic aid to Third World countries. This suggests that the two groups favor income redistribution for different reasons. Despite their relatively high income levels, Postmaterialists may favor both domestic and foreign income redistribution for the sake of human solidarity. On the other hand, lower-income Materialists may favor domestic income redistribution because they tend to be the ones who benefit from it—but they are not equally favorable to aiding Third World countries, from which they will not benefit. Here, neither group stands to gain material benefits—and the Postmaterialists are much more favorable than the Materialists.

In keeping with their general tendency to support the positions of the Left, Postmaterialists are somewhat likelier than Materialists to favor nationalization of industry. But Postmaterialists are slightly less likely to favor a greater government role in managing the economy. For the Old Left, government ownership, regulation, and control of the economy was inherently good. Almost by definition, a larger government role was viewed as desirable in virtually any situation. For the Postmaterialist Left, big government is inherently dangerous because, like any large, hierarchical, bureaucratic organization, it tends to encroach on individual autonomy and expression.

A question asked in the 1981 World Values survey brings this fact into sharper focus. As we saw in the previous chapter, support for nationalization of industry has become remarkably weak. This does not mean that Western publics have become resigned to traditional laissez-faire capitalism, however—it merely reflects a widely shared perception that nationalization has solved few problems and that government-run industries have generally performed poorly. Nevertheless, there is widespread support for changing the way business and industry is run—with a growing proportion

TABLE 9-5. ATTITUDES TOWARD OWNERSHIP AND MANAGEMENT OF BUSINESS AND
INDUSTRY BY VALUE TYPE

Question: "There is a lot of discussion about how business and industry
should be managed. Which of these four statements comes closest to your
opinion? (show card)
1. The owners should run their business or appoint the managers.
2. The owners and employees should participate in the selection
   of managers.
3. The state should be the owner and appoint the managers.
4. The employees should own the business and elect the managers."

Value Type	% Supporting Ownership/Management by:				
	1. Owners	2. Owners and Employees	3. State	4. Employees	N
Materialists	44%	43%	5%	9%	(3,557)
Mixed	37	48	4	11	(6,397)
Postmaterialists	23	51	4	21	(1,503)
Total	38	47	4	12	(11,457)

Source: Based on pooled results from fourteen nations in World
Values survey, 1981.
Note: Percentages weighted according to population. Percentages may
not total 100 because of rounding.

of Western publics favoring changes that would give employees (not the
government) more say in the selection of managers. Table 9-5 gives the
text of the question and shows how the responses are related to value type.

Here again, there is remarkably little support for statist solutions. Only
4 percent of the publics of fourteen advanced industrial societies supported
the option ''the state should be the owner and appoint the managers.'' But
support for joint employee-owner selection of managers showed impressive strength. Among the four options offered, this alone was selected by
47 percent of the total. Support for the traditional capitalist formula was
significantly less widespread—only 38 percent of these publics favored it.
Moreover, this was a solution favored by those with Materialist values far
more than by those with Postmaterialist priorities; while 44 percent of the
Materialists said they were in favor of retaining untrammeled direction by
owners, only 23 percent of the Postmaterialists did so. In keeping with
their emphasis on self-expression and a meaningful work experience, a
heavy majority of the Postmaterialists favored either co-determination (51
percent) or giving the dominant role to the employees (21 percent).

As Table 9-6 reveals, support for these options is closely correlated with
age cohort. Among those 65 years of age and older, a clear majority favor
the traditional capitalist arrangement. But among those in the 15 to 24 age
group, support for this option falls to only 35 percent of the total; a majority favor giving employees partial or complete control in selection of man-

TABLE 9-6. ATTITUDES TOWARD OWNERSHIP AND MANAGEMENT OF BUSINESS AND
INDUSTRY BY AGE GROUP

Question: "There is a lot of discussion about how business and industry
should be managed. Which of these four statements comes closest to your
opinion? (show card)
  1. The owners should run their business or appoint the managers.
  2. The owners and employees should participate in the selection
      of managers.
  3. The state should be the owneř and appoint the managers.
  4. The employees should own the business and elect the managers."

| | | % Supporting Ownership/Management by: | | | |
Age Group	1. Owners	2. Owners and Employees	3. State	4. Employees	N
15 - 24	35%	49%	4%	12%	(5,194)
25 - 34	41	43	4	12	(3,910)
35 - 44	47	41	3	10	(2,905)
45 - 54	53	37	3	8	(2,249)
55 - 64	53	37	3	7	(1,998)
65+	60	29	4	7	(1,951)

Source: European Values Survey, pooled data from fourteen nations,
weighted according to population.
Note: Percentages may not total 100 because of rounding.

agers. Support for the latter option varies a great deal cross-nationally, as
Table A-20 (in the Appendix) shows, with support weakest in the United
States and Canada and strongest in France, Spain, the Netherlands, and
Belgium. Everywhere, there is an age-linked trend: The young are likelier
to support giving employees a share in selecting managers. But support for
turning industry over to the government is remarkably weak.

This fact poses a dilemma for the Postmaterialist Left. Its adherents tend
to favor social change; and almost any program of social change presup-
poses that the government will be the instrument to bring it about. But the
Postmaterialist Left—far more than the traditional Left—regards the state
as a potential instrument of oppression and exploitation. Though they favor
equality, they are reluctant to use the state to bring it about. One possible
way out of this dilemma might be through decentralizing the state. Hence
Postmaterialists tend to favor regional autonomy. In the November 1981
Euro-Barometer survey, 36 percent of the Materialists were "strongly
for" greater regional autonomy, as compared with 51 percent of the Postmaterialists in the European Community. Big government may be necessary to social change, but the Postmaterialist Left is ambivalent toward it.

On the other hand, the relationship between Materialist/Postmaterialist
values and the noneconomic issues loading on the second dimension is
clear and unequivocal. Materialists are more than twice as likely as Postmaterialists to favor a stronger defense effort, and they are almost twice as

likely to favor developing nuclear power, or taking stronger measures against terrorism. The differences between Materialists and Postmaterialists on these issues are large; and they are consistent, both from issue to issue and from nation to nation.

When we turn to the lower half of Figure 9-1 and of Table A-19 (in the Appendix), we find indications that these preferences have a political impact. Consistently and by a clear margin, the ratio of Materialists to Postmaterialists among the electorate is the strongest predictor of candidate attitudes toward the noneconomic issues. The value preferences of the electorate easily outweigh the impact of both the religious and social class indicators combined, with the latter being negligible: the linkage between the social class composition of a party's electorate and their candidate's stand on noneconomic issues is about as close to zero as it can get. Our religious indicator, on the other hand, does have a significant impact.

The persistence of an apparently flourishing linkage between religious affiliations and political cleavages, coupled with a truly remarkable decline of social class cleavages, may seem paradoxical. But it is very much in keeping with the theoretical framework underlying this analysis. For reasons that we have discussed earlier in some detail (Inglehart 1977, 217–22), the rise of Postmaterialist politics has an inherent tendency to neutralize class-based political cleavages, but it does not have that impact on religious cleavages. On the contrary, it may even give them new life. Postmaterialists tend to be recruited from the more affluent strata that traditionally supported the Right, but they themselves tend to shift their support to the Left; moreover, they may engender a working-class reaction in favor of the Right. Thus, Postmaterialism tends to reverse the polarity of the correlation between social class and the Left-Right dimension. But it does not have this impact on religion. Postmaterialists tend to be recruited from the nonpracticing segment of the religious spectrum, which traditionally has supported the Left, and continues to do so. Furthermore, Postmaterialist support for cultural change may stimulate a conservative reaction on the part of those holding traditional religious values—reinforcing, rather than weakening, their alignment with the Right. The rise of a new kind of value-based politics may give relevance to much older value-based cleavages, rooted in the preindustrial era (Pappi 1977).

THE IMPACT OF SOCIAL CLEAVAGES ON THREE TYPES OF POLITICAL POLARIZATION

We hypothesize that the impact of Postmaterialism would be greatest on those forms of political polarization that are least strongly linked with established political party loyalties. Political party identification is reshaped only gradually by the rise of new values; hence, it helps to preserve old patterns among those variables highly correlated with it. Where voting behavior is closely linked with established political party loyalties, it will polarize according to individual values only slightly. On the other hand, Left-Right ideological self-placement tends to reflect political party ties in part, but it also reflects one's reaction to current issues. Hence, it is more likely to polarize according to one's values. Finally, support for social change is not necessarily tied to political party loyalties at all. Hence, polarization over this basic superissue reflects individual value priorities above all; being only minimally constrained by party ties, it will show a minimum level of social class polarization, under current conditions. Thus we would expect the impact of Postmaterialism to be weakest on voting behavior—a relatively direct expression of party loyalties—and relatively strong on support for social change, a superissue that has no explicit linkage with party ties. Conversely, if it is true that social class conflict was a more important factor a generation ago than it is today, it should be preserved most fully in those forms of polarization that are directly linked with the pattern-preserving influence of long-term party loyalties. The impact of social class on voting should be far stronger than its impact on support for social change. As a hybrid variable reflecting both a partisanship component and an ideological component that sums up one's position on current issues, Left-Right ideological self-placement should occupy an intermediate position between voting and support for social change. As the first step in testing these hypotheses, let us examine the absolute impact of social class, religion, and individual values on each of the three types of political polarization.

Table 9-7 shows how each of the three social cleavages relates to voting patterns, in a pooled sample of the Euro-Barometer surveys carried out in 1980–1986, weighted according to population. This sample's manual-nonmanual breakdown, of course, does not convey the wealth of variation in the respondents' social background characteristics. Nor does it capture the variation from country to country. Table A-24 (in the Appendix) provides a far more detailed picture of social class–based voting, religion-based voting, and value-based voting for each major party in the United States and each of the twelve European Community countries in 1980–1987. Table 9-7 presents a greatly simplified version of this complex reality. It groups parties together into two broad categories—the "Left" (the various communist, socialist, and Social Democratic parties); and the "Right" (the various Christian Democratic, conservative, and some other parties). A minority (about 9 percent of those reporting a party preference) are not classified. The centrist and ethnic nationalist parties are excluded, for example, and the liberal parties are split between some that seem clearly part

TABLE 9-7. ELECTORAL CLEAVAGES BASED ON SOCIAL CLASS, RELIGION AND
PERSONAL VALUES IN WESTERN EUROPE
(Percentage Voting for parties of the Left, 1980 - 1986)

Variable	% Voting for Left	N
1. Social class		
Respondent from family headed by manual worker	59%	(27,583)
Respondent from family with head having non-manual occupation	42	(44,224)
Alford class-voting index	+17	
2. Religiosity		
Respondent attends church at least once a week	31	(5,788)
Respondent attends church at least a few times a year	49	(9,338)
Respondent never attends church	62	(7,908)
3. Value type		
Respondent has Materialist priorities	43	(35,936)
Respondent has Mixed priorities	49	(56,100)
Respondent has Postmaterialist priorities	61	(13,578)

Source: Based on pooled results from Euro-Barometer surveys 13 - 26,
carried out in France, Italy, West Germany, Great Britain, Netherlands,
Belgium, Luxembourg, Denmark, and Ireland.
Note: Percentages weighted according to population of given nation.

of the Right, and others that are considered centrist, and excluded from these tables. Detailed information on how each party is coded appears in the ICPSR code books for the Euro-Barometer surveys.

Though it simplifies a vast number of interesting details, this massive pooled sample does provide an exceptionally reliable data base for analysis of overall patterns of political polarization in Western Europe. As Table 9-7 reveals, class–based voting is still fairly strong in Western Europe. The Alford index of class voting was + 17 for the European Community as a whole. While this is only about half as high as the levels reported for most West European countries in the 1950s, it is still an important political cleavage. It is clear from Table 9-7 that religious cleavages are also very strong. Finally, Table 9-7 indicates that the voting behavior of the various value types is very distinctive. If we simply were to compare the voting intentions of the pure Materialist and pure Postmaterialist types, we would obtain a larger percentage difference than that found with social class. But our values indicator is not dichotomous. Over half of those reporting a preference for parties grouped with the Left or the Right fall into the mixed values type; while the Postmaterialist type shows quite distinctive voting behavior, the sheer percentage differences would convey an exaggerated impression of the impact of values on voting behavior. A multiple classification analysis (see Table A-23 in the Appendix) alleviates this problem, by calculating coefficients that are weighted according to the number of cases in each category of the independent variables.

Table A-21 (in the Appendix) shows the percentage differences associated with self-placement on the Left-Right scale. While the differences linked with church attendance and value type remain quite large, those associated with social class shrink to only 12 percentage points. Traditional party loyalties preserve a relatively large class difference in voting behavior, but it extends less strongly to ideological self-placement.

Finally, Table A-22 (in the Appendix) shows the relationship of social class, church attendance, and value type to support for social change. With all three independent variables, a reformist majority prevails. But even a cursory inspection of this table suggests that values are the dominant factor. There is *no* difference in the degree to which manual and nonmanual respondents support social change. Those with manual occupations are 1 percentage point more likely to favor revolutionary change, but they are also 2 points more likely to favor defense of the present society. Religion, on the other hand, does seem to have an appreciable impact on this orientation. Those who never attend church are about twice as likely to support revolutionary change as those who attend church weekly, and somewhat less likely to favor defense of the established social order. But the differences associated with value type are substantially greater. Postmaterialists are two and one-half times as likely as Materialists to favor revolutionary change, and less than half as likely to favor defending the present society.

Now let us compare the impact of the three social background variables on each of the three types of political polarization. Figure 9-2 shows the results of a multiple classification analysis based on these data. Table A-23 (in the Appendix) shows the more detailed statistics underlying Figure 9-2. In Table A-23, the eta coefficients show the relative strength of each predictor variable, weighted for the number of cases in each category, while the beta coefficients provide a similar statistic, controlling for the effects of each of the other two predictor variables. Figure 9-2 sums up the overall pattern based on the beta coefficients.

As we hypothesized, the impact of social class on voting behavior outweighs that of value type—though our religion indicator shows an even stronger effect than either of them. But when we turn to support for social change, values are the strongest predictor by a wide margin; the impact of

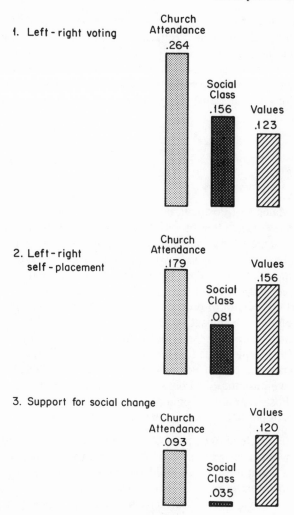

1. Left-right voting

Church Attendance
.264

Social Class
.156

Values
.123

2. Left-right self-placement

Church Attendance
.179

Social Class
.081

Values
.156

3. Support for social change

Church Attendance
.093

Social Class
.035

Values
.120

FIGURE 9-2. The impact of religion, social class, and values on three types of political polarization. Height of each bar is proportional to Beta coefficients in multiple classification analysis of nine-nation sample.

social class is negligible, and while religious practice has a significant effect, it is only about half as strong as that of values. Left-Right self-placement shows an intermediate pattern, consistent with the fact that it is a mixture of partisanship and ideological variables; religion has the strongest impact, followed by values and social class.

The pattern obtained here is by now familiar. As was true with issue polarization, it seems that in relatively recent years, a new axis of political polarization has arisen, which reflects an opposition between Materialist and Postmaterialist goals. Political party loyalties remain tied to the axis based on religion and social class, but they seem to be out of phase with the new cleavage, for support for social change reflects whether one has Materialist or Postmaterialist values far more than it reflects either religion or social class.

THE IMPACT OF VALUES IN 1974 ON POLITICAL ACTION IN THE 1980S: A PANEL ANALYSIS

Though Materialist/Postmaterialist value priorities have less impact on electoral behavior than that of social class or religion, they are a stronger predictor of support for social change than either of these other two long-established bases of political cleavage. Moreover, these values do not just influence one's attitudes: they have enduring and important behavioral consequences. Indeed, as we will see, the values one had in 1974 prove to be a powerful predictor of protest behavior in the 1980s. In order to demonstrate the enduring impact of Materialist/Postmaterialist values, let us turn to the panel data from the Political Action surveys carried out in 1974 and 1980–1981 in the United States, West Germany and the Netherlands.

These data indicate that Postmaterialist values have behavioral consequences as well as attitudinal ones. In formulating our study, we hypothesized that Postmaterialists would be relatively apt to engage in unconventional forms of political action for the following reasons:

(1) Materialists tend to be preoccupied with satisfying immediate physiological needs and their derivatives. Postmaterialists feel relatively secure about these needs and have a greater amount of psychic energy to invest in more remote concerns. This may lead to involvement in a wide variety of activities, among which politics is one possibility.

(2) As a recently emerging minority whose highest priorities tend to be slighted, Postmaterialists are apt to be relatively disaffected with the established social order.

(3) The disruption and property damage that may result from unconventional political action may seem less negative to Postmaterialists since they threaten things to which Postmaterialists give a lower priority than Materialists do (Barnes, Kaase, et al. 1979, 345).

In short, Postmaterialists have a larger amount of psychic energy available for politics; they are less supportive of the established social order;

and subjectively they have less to lose from unconventional political action than do Materialists.

In order to test the hypothesized relationship between values and political behavior, we developed a protest potential scale based on approval of and readiness to engage in, the following activities (ranging from the easiest to the most difficult activities on a Guttman scale):

Signing petitions;
Lawful demonstrations;
Boycotts;
Rent strikes;
Unofficial strikes;
Occupying buildings;
Blocking traffic.

Cross-sectional analysis confirmed our hypothesis: Postmaterialists manifested much higher levels of protest potential in 1974 than did Materialists. Though the data showed a clear relationship, this test had the limitations inherent in cross-sectional analysis. It demonstrated that one's values were correlated with one's level of protest potential at a given point in time. But in a causal relationship, the cause must precede the effect. Could we demonstrate that values measured at one point in time predicted one's behavior at a later time?

Our earlier analysis had an additional problem, which was largely one of presentation. The protest potential scale we used was a hybrid creature, based on a mixture of reported behavior, behavioral intentions, and approval of given actions. The scale was constructed in this way for good theoretical and practical reasons. It was based on Fishbein and Azen's (1967, 1975) reasoning that actual behavior can be predicted accurately from behavioral predispositions, provided one measures respondents' (1) beliefs about the norms governing that specific type of behavior; (2) positive or negative affect toward that behavior; and (3) judgments about the effectiveness of the behavior.

Moreover, only small minorities of the public reported actually having done most of the actions described above. The strategy of basing our protest potential scale on a combination of reported behavior, plus behavioral intentions and approval of given actions, was a means of obtaining a broader base of measurement than would be available if one considered actual behavior only—especially in connection with the more "difficult" forms of behavior, such as occupying buildings and blocking traffic. A drawback of this strategy, however, was that some readers of *Political Action* perceived it as dealing with attitudinal variables alone. This was inaccurate. Actually, a good deal of actual behavior was reported as well, and the analyses that follow will be based entirely on reported *behavior*.

The first point that emerges from these analyses is that the protest potential scale is validated handsomely as a predictor of subsequent actual behavior. The questions about political behavior asked in 1974 were repeated in the 1980–1981 surveys. For the three countries as a whole, among those who ranked low on the protest potential scale (scores of 0–2) in 1974, only 5 percent reported in 1980–1981 that they had actually engaged in two or more of these actions during the past ten years. Among those with an intermediate score on the scale in 1974, 15 percent reported in 1980–1981 that they had engaged in two or more such actions; and among those with high scores (from 4 to 7 on the scale), fully 31 percent reported that they had engaged in two more acts of unconventional political behavior. In short, those with high protest potential scores in 1974 were six times as likely to report having engaged in two or more forms of protest behavior in 1980–1981 as those with low scores in 1974. We anticipated that protest potential, as measured in 1974, would predict protest behavior as measured in 1980 and 1981; this proves to be the case—and it is impressive that the prediction is this strong. This is part of a broad array of evidence demonstrating that, in all three countries, certain individuals have a much stronger predisposition to engage in protest activities than do other individuals—a predisposition that endured throughout the six or seven years that elapsed between the two waves of the panel.

Let us now move a step farther back in the causal chain. We argued that, because of their distinctive formative experiences, Postmaterialists would have a significantly greater propensity to engage in protest activities than do those with Materialist values. Postmaterialists have this propensity despite the fact that they tend to come from the more secure and privileged strata of society, which have the greatest material stake in maintaining the status quo. This hypothesis directly contradicts the class conflict model, which postulates that the economically less privileged groups will be most supportive of social change. Which model generates the more accurate predictions in contemporary society? Table 9-8 gives part of the answer.

As Table 9-8 shows, those who had Postmaterialist values in 1974 were a great deal more likely to report taking part in protest activities in 1980–1981 than were Materialists in each nation. Furthermore, in the three nations as a whole, pure Postmaterialists were more than four times as likely as pure Materialists to have engaged in two or more such activities. The Postmaterialist orientation goes beyond the attitudinal realm. It has pronounced behavioral implications. And its impact seems to extend over long periods of time, since the values one had in 1974 are linked with very sizable differences in one's behavior during the 1980s.

TABLE 9-8. UNCONVENTIONAL POLITICAL BEHAVIOR REPORTED IN 1980 - 1981 BY
VALUE TYPE IN 1974
(Percentage having engaged in two or more types of protest in past ten
years)

Value Type in 1974	W. Germany	Netherlands	U.S.
Materialist	1%	3%	17%
Mixed (Materialist)	2	5	23
Mixed (Postmaterialist)	12	8	25
Postmaterialist	34	23	45
Total	4	9	22
N	(898)	(743)	(910)
Gamma	.39	.37	.16

Table 9-8 illustrates the complex interplay between situational and individual level factors. The general pattern is the same in all three nations: Those who had Postmaterialist values (in 1974) were much likelier to report engaging in two or more types of protest (in 1980–1981) than those with Materialist values. But the strength of this correlation and the absolute level of activities vary substantially between the United States and the two West European countries. On one hand, the average number of activities reported in the United States was much higher than in either West Germany or the Netherlands, with over twice as many Americans as Europeans reporting that they had taken part in petitions, demonstrations, or boycotts. These have now become relatively normal activities for a broad segment of the American public. On the other hand, the correlation between individual values and protest activities was significantly stronger in West Germany and the Netherlands than in the United States. These activities were almost never carried out by Materialists in the two European countries, but were widespread only among Postmaterialists; while in the United States, these activities were much more common among Postmaterialists, but were fairly widespread even among Materialists. In West Germany and the Netherlands, unconventional political behavior remains largely restricted to a Postmaterialist subculture, but has spread beyond it in the United States. This cross-national difference seems to reflect differences in the historical dissemination of new political techniques. The New Politics originated in the United States, in the civil rights struggles of the early 1960s and the Vietnam protests of the late 1960s. The use of unconventional protest techniques was not new even then, but it was developed and disseminated in these struggles and then spread to Western Europe. Probably because of this longer period of contagion, it had attained broader

TABLE 9-9. UNCONVENTIONAL POLITICAL BEHAVIOR REPORTED IN 1980 - 1981 BY
VALUE TYPE IN 1974, CONTROLLING FOR PROTEST BEHAVIOR REPORTED IN 1974

1974 Number of Types of Unconventional Political Behavior Respondent Reported Having Engaged in in Past Ten Years	*1980-1981* *Percentage Who Reported Having Engaged in Two or More Types of Unconventional Political Behavior in Past Ten Years*		
	W. Germany	*Nether-lands*	*U.S.*
None			
Materialists & Mixed (Mat)	1%	2%	8%
Postmaterialists and Mixed (Postmat)	9	8	12
One Type			
Materialists & Mixed (Mat)	1	9	24
Postmaterialists & Mixed (Postmat)	17	14	18
Two or More Types			
Materialists & Mixed (Mat)	8	31	44
Postmaterialists & Mixed (Postmat)	38	39	70

acceptance in the United States by 1981 and is sometimes used even by Materialists in this country—as the opposition to school busing, the anti-abortion movement, and other phenomena of the New Right illustrate.

Causation can never be proven conclusively. Not even the fact that knowing respondents' values in 1974 enables us to predict their behavior six or seven years later proves beyond doubt that the former is shaping the latter. It is always possible that the linkage might be due to some unknown third factor. But we can subject our hypothesis to another, even more stringent test that helps rule out the possibility that some factor other than values is responsible for the linkage.

Let us examine the relationship between respondents' values in 1974 and the protest actions they reported in the 1980s, this time controlling for the number of protest actions they reported in 1974. In doing so, we are controlling for the effects of age, sex, social class, and any other, unknown variables that influenced protest activity in the 1970s. Table 9-9 shows the results for each of the three nations. The respondents in each of the three categories ("none," "one type," and "two or more types") reported the same number of protest actions in 1974. The two subgroups within each of these three categories differ only in their underlying values. Do these values make any difference in their subsequent behavior?

The answer is, emphatically, yes. In the three nations as a whole, among those who had not engaged in any protest actions in 1974, only 3 percent of the Materialists reported engaging in two or more types of such action in 1980–1981. Postmaterialists who had not engaged in any protest in the 1970s were three times more likely to report having engaged in two or more types of protest in 1980–1981. Moving to the next category, among those who reported having engaged in one type of protest activity in 1974, 12 percent of the Materialists had moved into the activist category that engaged in two or more types of protest behavior in the 1980s—as compared with 17 percent of the Postmaterialists. And among the highly active minority who reported having engaged in two or more types of protest in 1974, only 35 percent of the Materialists were still in that category in 1980–1981, as compared with 52 percent of the Postmaterialists. Already in 1974, the Postmaterialists were much more likely to have taken part in protest activities than the Materialists. But even when we control for this difference—and thereby largely control for situational differences and whatever other variables contributed to it—values make a very sizable difference in subsequent behavior.

Situational factors are also important. One does not protest in a vacuum; some objective interest or political issue or moral cause must be at stake, some mode and target of protest must be available, and some organization usually plays a facilitating role. Consequently, some of those who were inactive in the 1970s became active in the 1980s and vice versa. But some individuals, much more than others, have an enduring propensity to protest—and the presence or absence of Postmaterialist values seems to be a major factor underlying this propensity.

The evidence thus far indicates that Materialist/Postmaterialist values have an autonomous impact on protest behavior. Is it possible that these values are simply a surrogate indicator of one's social class or one's religious values, rather than an independent influence on behavior? This possibility is explored in a more extensive analysis of these data in Jennings and Van Deth (1989).

The results show that there is a slight tendency for church attendance to be negatively related to protest behavior, but this tendency is much weaker than the linkage between values and protest. The relationship between the respondent's subjective social class (as reported in 1974) and his or her protest behavior (reported in 1981) is also weaker than that between Postmaterialist values and protest behavior. But what seems even more significant is the fact that the linkage between subjective social class and protest behavior has the opposite polarity from that predicted by the social class conflict model: Protest behavior was most frequent among the upper middle class.

From the viewpoint of anyone whose expectations are shaped by economic determinism, this is a truly surprising finding. According to the traditional class conflict model of politics, social protest is based on the working class, while those with better jobs and higher income normally support the status quo. Could it possibly be true that those who are materially best off, protest most?

Yes. That is precisely what our data show, quite consistently. This phenomenon emerges in each of the countries included in this study, though with interesting cross-national variations. This finding reflects the important role played by "formative security" in instilling a Postmaterialist orientation. Within any given age cohort, those whose parents had relatively high socioeconomic status were most likely to feel a sense of economic and physical security. Thus, those with relatively prosperous parents were most apt to develop Postmaterialist values, which (for the reasons outlined above) are conducive to political protest. But, at the same time, those with prosperous parents were relatively likely to receive a good education and to enjoy other advantages that made them likelier to attain high socioeconomic status themselves when they reached adulthood. Thus, despite the fact that economically they have more to lose through social upheaval, those with higher socioeconomic status are more likely to take part in protest activity than those of lower status.

But the degree to which this is true varies cross-nationally. And it varies according to the degree to which the politics of a given country are class based. Figure 9-3 shows LISREL analyses of the impact of formative security and values on protest potential in the combined samples from the United States, the Netherlands, and West Germany; Figures A-4, A-5, and A-6 (in the Appendix) show separate analyses for each respective country. Formative security, in these analyses, is a latent variable for which the indicators are (1) the occupational prestige level of the respondent's father's occupation; (2) the respondent's father's educational level; (3) the respondent's mother's educational level; and (4) the respondent's own educational level—which tends to reflect the socioeconomic level of one's parents. All of these variables are good indicators of the degree to which the respondent spent his or her formative years in a setting that was relatively shielded from hardship and insecurity. And, in each of our three nations, those who enjoyed a relatively high degree of security during their formative years are most likely to take part in political protest. For the combined three-nation sample, the regression coefficient is .28. This linkage is a good deal stronger in the United States than in either West Germany or the Netherlands, for the United States has never had major class-based political parties. But in both the Netherlands and West Germany, the major party of the Left is a socialist party that has traditionally appealed

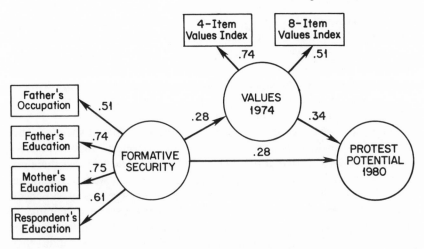

FIGURE 9-3. Impact of formative security and values in 1974 on protest potential in 1980: combined three-nation panel survey (LISREL analysis). Adjusted goodness of fit index = .95.

explicitly to the working class. In both countries, this class-based appeal still exerts a residual influence, mobilizing working-class support for social change and political protest—and partially offsetting the fact that those who experienced the greatest formative security are most apt to engage in protest. The traditional linkage between the working class and support for social change is more than offset by the effects of formative security, even in West Germany and the Netherlands. In the United States, on the other hand, the traditional linkage of working class and support for social change is weaker; and the impact of formative security is stronger accordingly.

Conversely, the linkage between formative security and Postmaterialist values is stronger in both the Netherlands and West Germany than in the United States, probably for the reasons suggested earlier in this chapter. But in all three countries, formative security has a substantial impact on values, with an overall regression coefficient of .28. Moreover, as we saw in chapter 5, these formative experiences have a more important impact on values than do income and occupation at the time of the survey.

Finally, in all three countries, the values respondents had in 1974 have a strong impact on their protest potential as measured in 1980 or 1981. Here, the overall coefficient is .34. Even in the United States, values are a somewhat more powerful influence than social background, but in the Netherlands and West Germany the impact of values dominates that of social background onesidedly, for the traditional and the contemporary influences of social class largely neutralize each other. Thus, the influence of social background on protest potential is complex and partially self-neutralizing, but in advanced industrial society, the haves are more likely to protest than the have-nots—largely because the haves tend to have Postmaterialist values.

The protest movements of the late sixties and early seventies have largely disappeared. Why did this happen, if a relatively high protest potential characterizes the Postmaterialists?

The main answer is that people do not protest in a social vacuum. The Postmaterialists did not protest for the sake of protesting—they responded to specific issues, above all the war in Indochina. The fact that there no longer is a war in Indochina (or, at least, no American war) makes a big difference. Almost nothing can compare with war, in terms of violence, drama, and human tragedy, and nothing on the current scene can command sustained mass attention in the way the Vietnam war did. In the absence of any political cause fully comparable to the war, it is only natural that much of the attention and energies of Postmaterialists have been diverted into other channels.

For some, this means seeking self-actualization through development of the inner self, rather than through social action. The human potential movement is an example. For those who remain politically active, such turning inward seems desertion of the cause; the current crop of youth has been characterized as the Me Generation, practicing a "culture of narcissism" (Lasch 1979). There is a grain of truth but also a lot of misapprehension in this view. At the start of the 1980s, most observers thought that the underlying potential for political protest had vanished. They were taken by surprise. In the early 1980s, the decision to install intermediate-range nuclear missiles in Western Europe gave rise to mass demonstrations (in Europe, though not in the United States) that were even larger than those of the Vietnam era. As we saw in chapter 2, in the late 1980s, the 15- to 24-year-old group was not significantly less Materialistic than the next-older cohort, but their underlying values were far less Materialist than those of older groups, especially the pre-1945 cohorts. If the potential for political protest generally remained only a potential, it was partly because none of the current political causes was as compelling as those of the earlier decade.

POSTMATERIALIST PENETRATION OF ELITE GROUPS

But another major factor has also affected how Postmaterialism manifests itself politically. It springs from the simple fact that the average Postmaterialist is substantially older than he or she was in 1970. Postmaterial-

TABLE 9-10. VALUE TYPE BY OCCUPATION AND AGE GROUP, 1980 - 1986

| | Age Group | | | | | | | | |
| | Under 35 | | | 35 - 49 | | | 50 and over | | |
Occupation	Mat.	PM	N	Mat.	PM	N	Mat.	PM	N
Top management & civil service	19%	27%	(1,150)	23%	25%	(1,415)	24%	15%	(902)
Student	20	24	(11,677)	-	-	-	-	-	-
Professional	20	21	(869)	20	22	(608)	29	15	(505)
Nonmanual employee	25	20	(11,623)	31	14	(7,166)	36	11	(3,871)
Unemployed	28	17	(4,958)	33	11	(1,218)	37	8	(1,565)
Self-employed business	31	12	(2,257)	40	9	(2,797)	41	7	(2,104)
Manual worker	30	13	(10,926)	36	9	(6,904)	41	8	(4,817)
Housewife	36	10	(7,787)	43	8	(7,192)	46	6	(9,824)
Farmer	38	11	(401)	45	8	(706)	46	6	(1,111)
Retired	-	-	-	37	11	(412)	46	6	(19,526)

Source: Based on combined data from Euro-Barometer surveys 13 - 26, carried out from April 1980 through November 1986 in Great Britain, France, West Germany, Italy, Netherlands, Belgium, Luxembourg, Denmark, and Ireland.

ists are no longer concentrated in student ghettos. In many countries, they now are as numerous as the Materialists (or even more numerous) among those in their 30s and well into their 40s. They have moved into positions of influence and authority throughout society. Despite their minority status in society as a whole, they outnumber the Materialists in a number of key sectors.

Table 9-10 shows how the two pure value types are distributed by age and occupation among the publics of the European Community countries. This table pools the data from all of the surveys carried out in 1980–1986 in all nine countries that were members of the Community in 1980. This massive sample provides reliable data for certain small but important elite groups. A national sample survey normally contains only a handful of professionals, for example; but here we have large enough numbers not only to compare this occupational category with others but to break it down by age group.

Overall, the pure Postmaterialist type constitutes only about 9 percent of the manual workers and 7 percent of the farmers; in these occupational groups, pure Materialists outnumber Postmaterialists by ratios of at least 5 to 1. On the other hand, Postmaterialists outnumber Materialists in the student milieu. This is significant but not surprising. What *is* surprising is the fact that among those less than 35 years old with jobs that lead to top management and top civil service posts, Postmaterialists outnumber Materialists decisively; their numerical preponderance here is even greater than among students. This is all the more astonishing since these young technocrats are older, on the average, than the students. This phenomenon reflects the fact that the young managers and officials are a highly select stratum, recruited according to considerably more demanding criteria than those for admission to a university; there are many more students than young technocrats. In social background, the young managers and officials correspond to the students at the most prestigious schools, rather than to the student population as a whole. In general, the more selective our criteria become, the higher the proportion of Postmaterialists—and the young technocrats represent the elite of the recent university graduates. Already occupying influential positions, many of them should reach the top decision-making level within the next decade.

In addition to students and young technocrats, young professionals are the only remaining category in which Postmaterialists outnumber Materialists. Postmaterialists are slightly more numerous than Materialists in the professions—not only in the under-35 age group but in the 35- to 49-year-old category as well. In the 1970s, Materialists still held a narrow preponderance in both these groups (Inglehart 1981). Today, there is an almost even balance between Materialists and Postmaterialists among those aged 35 to 49 in top management and top civil service posts.

The fact that there is a preponderance of Postmaterialists over Materialists among young professionals and managers contradicts a solidly entrenched piece of folk wisdom. For some years now, it has been a widely accepted factoid that yuppies are an overwhelmingly materialistic group, interested only in attaining the highest possible standard of living. But if our data are to be believed—and they represent a massive number of surveys from nine Western nations—today's young professionals are far less materialistic than the population as a whole. Furthermore, this conclusion is supported by exhaustive analyses of two major studies of American data. Both Jennings and Markus (1984) and Delli Carpini (1986) have traced the generation that came of age during the 1960s into the 1980s—and have found that this group as a whole, and its upper-status segment in particular, remain politically and socially more liberal than preceding generations.

How is it, then, that the yuppies have acquired such an image of self-indulgent materialism? We believe that it reflects four characteristics of the yuppies themselves, probably compounded by a certain amount of envy.

The yuppies, or young urban professionals, are characterized by being (1) highly educated; (2) if married or living together, likely to have two careers and thus two incomes; and (3) for reasons discussed in chapter 6, relatively likely to have no children. All this adds up to the fact that they tend to have considerably more disposable income than was true of most young couples in earlier decades. Finally, (4) they grew up with a relatively high sense of economic security, and feel little anxiety to accumulate for the future. In short, they have high disposable income—and are willing to dispose of it. This results in a visibly high (and distinctive) level of consumption, sometimes referred to as the brie and Volvo syndrome.

It would be misleading, however, to conclude from this that their basic motivations are narrowly materialistic. The young urban professional category is not identical with Postmaterialism, and some Yuppies undoubtedly are flagrantly materialistic—but for the young professionals as a whole, the evidence points in the opposite direction. Like Postmaterialists in general, they are relatively open to social change, and potentially receptive to being mobilized by progressive political parties. But the appeal must make sense in terms of their worldview. It must address such problems as peace, ecology, the quality of life, and social solidarity; they cannot be mobilized by continuing to repeat the same political formula that the Left was using in the 1930s. For this constituency, the wave of the future was not captured by Ronald Reagan—but neither was it captured by Walter Mondale or Michael Dukakis. Reagan, at least, was responding to the problems of the 1980s, although often in a negative fashion. For Mondale, these problems simply were not there.

Among those 50 and older, the Materialists hold a clear preponderance in every occupational category. Among self-employed people in business and trades in this age group, Materialists are six times as numerous as Postmaterialists. Even among the self-employed under 35, Materialists predominate by a ratio of nearly 3 to 1: young professionals and young technocrats may be Postmaterialistic, but young self-employed businesspeople definitely are not.

By the mid-1980s, Postmaterialism had become a powerful influence among technocrats and professionals—not only those in their 20s but also those in their 30s and 40s. This does not mean that it will automatically become the dominant influence in Western societies. Postmaterialists remain a numerical minority, better equipped to attain their goals through bureaucratic institutions or the courts than through the electoral process. They may encounter the backlash of resurgent Materialism, as some recent events in the United States and Western Europe suggest. Nevertheless, by the 1980s Postmaterialism had not only made deep inroads among young

TABLE 9-11. VALUE TYPE BY AGE GROUP AMONG CANDIDATES FOR EUROPEAN
PARLIAMENT, 1979

| | % in Age Group | | |
Value Type	25 - 54	55 - 86	Total % in European Parliament
Materialist	31%	43%	35%
Mixed	34	34	34
Postmaterialist	36	23	32
N	(439)	(221)	(660)

Source: Interviews with 742 candidates for seats in the European
Parliament, carried out March-April-May, 1979 as part of the European
Election Study organized by Karlheinz Reif. Principal investigators
were Ian Gordon, Ronald Inglehart, Carsten Lehman Sorensen and Jacques-
René Rabier. This sample includes 62 percent of those actually elected
in June 1979.

Note: Percentages are weighted in proportion to actual number of
seats each party and nationality had in the European Parliament as of
June 1979. Accordingly, candidates from parties that won no seats are
excluded from this table. Unweighted Ns appear at foot of each column.
One column does not add up to 100 because of rounding.

professionals and technocrats; but it had also, to a surprising degree, penetrated the West European political elite.

Table 9-10 may actually understate the degree to which younger Western elites had become Postmaterialist, for these data are based on representative national samples. Even when we break them down into relatively fine categories as in Table 9-10, even the top management and civil service group is heterogeneous, ranging from relatively modest levels to the truly elite stratum. Generally, the higher the stratum, the more Postmaterialist we would expect it to be.

For an indication of the values prevailing among genuine West European political elites, let us now turn to some data from interviews with the candidates running for seats in the European Parliament in 1979. This sample includes candidates from all significant political parties in all nine countries that were then members, drawn in proportion to the number of seats each party held in the European Parliament. In background, these candidates were roughly similar to members of the respective national parliaments (in which many of them held seats). Though somewhat younger than the average member of the national parliaments, they provide a reasonably good sampling of the West European political elite.

Table 9-11 shows the distribution of value types among our sample of the European Parliament, weighted in proportion to how many seats each party and nationality obtained in 1979. In the Parliament as a whole, Materialists narrowly outnumbered Postmaterialists in 1979. But while Post-materialists (as defined here) then constituted little more than one-eighth of the general public of these countries, they made up nearly one-third of the European Parliament. And when we break our sample down by age group, we find a pronounced skew. Among those 55 years of age and over, Materialists are almost twice as numerous as Postmaterialists. But among those under 55, the Postmaterialists outnumber the Materialists.

A comprehensive study of West German elites carried out by Wilden-mann et al. (1982) confirms that Postmaterialists have made massive in-roads among elite groups in that country. Indeed, as Figure 9-4 demon-strates, by 1981 (when the fieldwork was executed), Postmaterialist values were predominant among most of the elite groups in West Germany, in-cluding top-level civil servants, the presidents of universities and large research organizations, the political editors and top journalists of television and print media, labor union leaders, and the politicians of two of the three largest political parties, the Social Democrats (SPD) and Free Democrats (FDP). The Greens had not yet entered the Bundestag when this study was carried out, and consequently were not included as part of the political elite—but if they had been, it is virtually certain that they, too, would have ranked as an overwhelmingly Postmaterialist group. Among the eleven elite groups studied by Wildenmann, et al., only four showed a predomi-nance of Materialists over Postmaterialists: the officers of business and farm associations, the directors of major industrial corporations and banks, top Christian Democratic (CDU/CSU) politicians, and generals and admirals.

Most of these eleven elite groups are decidedly more Postmaterialist than the West German public. As we saw in chapter 3, the mean value scores of Western publics fluctuated significantly with the rise and fall of their economies during the 1970s and 1980s. Consequently, the score shown for the West German public in Figure 9-4 is based on the cumulated results of all Euro-Barometer surveys carried out from 1976 to April 1987. On this basis, the West German public shows approximately the same bal-ance between Materialists and Postmaterialists as do the Christian Demo-cratic politicians, with a percentage difference index (PDI) of − 15. If we were to use the results from 1981 only (the year in which the elite data were collected), the West German public would rank as more Materialist than all of the elite groups. This procedure would probably be somewhat misleading, however, since 1981 happened to be the low point of Post-materialism among the West German public. But even if we were to utilize only the data from the latest surveys, in which the West German public shows the highest level of Postmaterialism ever recorded, it would still fall between the generals and admirals and the top civil servants—ranking as

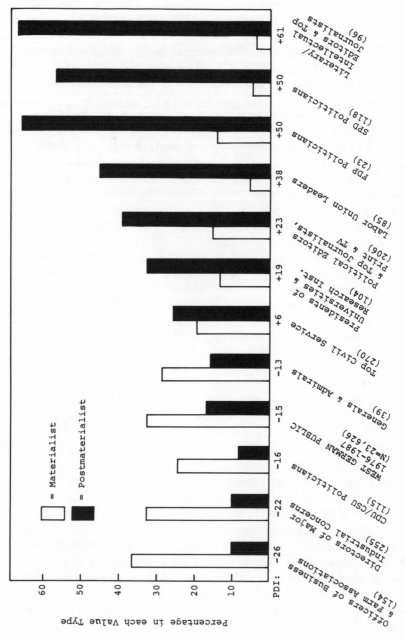

FIGURE 9-4. Balance between Materialist and Postmaterialist value priorities among West German elites and West German public. Figures for elites from Rudolf Wildenmann, et al., *Fuehrungsschicht in der Bundesrepublik Deutschland, 1981: Tabellenband* (Mannheim: University of Mannheim, 1982), 50–60;

more Materialist than seven of the eleven elite groups. Any way you slice it, the evidence is clear that most of these elite groups are more Postmaterialist than the West German public as a whole.

This is not a case of the public's simply following elite cues. At the time of the 1981 surveys, West Germany was governed by a coalition of the Social Democrats and Free Democrats, both of which were far more Postmaterialist than the German public as a whole. But in October 1982 this coalition broke up, and the Christian Democrats became the main governing party, in coalition with a divided Free Democratic Party.

In the ensuing 1983 elections, West German politics realigned along the Materialist/Postmaterialist axis to a considerable extent, with environmentalist issues and the peace movement taking on unprecedented salience. The Free Democratic party split, at both mass and elite levels, with about half of the party's previous electorate abandoning it. The Green party won enough votes to enter the West German parliament for the first time, reflecting the rising strength of Postmaterialism. But, at the same time, the Christian Democratic party won a solid victory, reflecting the fact that, on this newer axis, the average West German voter was closer to the CDU/CSU than to any other party.

This phenomenon provides one more illustration of the tactical dilemma of the Left in contemporary society. Postmaterialist forces have become powerful at the elite level; they demand major policy shifts in key areas, and they are far too influential among the militants and elites of Left parties to be ignored. But Postmaterialists are not equally strong at the mass level—which means that the parties of the Left are in danger of electoral defeat if they swing too far to the Postmaterialist side. The recent experience of both the West German Social Democrats and the British Labour Party seems to reflect this fact.

Recent research in the United States by Rothman and Lichter (1984) suggests that Postmaterialism has become widespread among American elites also, particularly among the media elite. In 1979–1980, Rothman and Lichter interviewed 240 journalists at the country's most influential media outlets, randomly selecting individuals from news department executives, editorial or production staffs, and working reporters. They also interviewed top- and middle-level executives from three Fortune 500 industrial firms and one firm each drawn from Fortune lists of the fifty leading American retail outlets, banks, and public utilities. In addition, they studied top leadership in the television and motion picture industries and 200 top-level administrators in agencies of the federal government. Since Rothman and Lichter developed their own instrument to measure Materialist/Postmaterialist values, their results cannot be compared directly with results from other studies at either the elite or mass levels; but they find intergroup differences that are striking and that parallel those found in West Germany. Rothman and Lichter (1983) also have reported that corporate executives and government bureaucrats gave top ranking to Materialist over Postmaterialist goals by margins of 2 to 1; by contrast, public interest group elites and television and film elites preferred Postmaterialist goals by margins of at least 2 to 1.

The results from Rothman and Lichter's version of the Materialist/Postmaterialist values index cannot be compared directly with those from the American public. But in November-December 1987, the Gallup organization interviewed a national sample of the American public, and simultaneously interviewed 387 opinion leaders drawn from six key decision-making groups in the United States. These groups were (1) business leaders, selected randomly from among top executives in Fortune 500 companies; (2) policymakers, including members of the U.S. Congress serving on committees dealing with foreign affairs and members of the White House staff, the National Security Council, the Agency for International Development, and the Departments of State, Commerce, Defense, and Transportation; (3) media representatives, consisting of news directors and newscasters from the three major television networks and radio and television stations in major cities, plus editors and columnists from major newspapers in nine major cities, editors of fifteen leading newsmagazines and specialized foreign affairs magazines, and foreign news editors from the three primary wire services; (4) agricultural decision-makers, consisting of members of Congress serving on agricultural committees, personnel from the Department of Agriculture, chief executives of international firms that produce or sell agricultural products, chief executives of agricultural organizations, and editors and publishers of farm-oriented media; (5) research institute experts, consisting of leaders of both private foreign policy organizations and university foreign policy institutes; and (6) labor leaders, consisting of top leaders from the national offices of the largest labor unions concerned with international issues. In this survey, the four-item Materialist/Postmaterialist values battery was administered in both the mass and elite interviews. Figure 9-5 shows the results reported for the American public and each of the elite groups.

The Gallup organization's American results are strikingly similar to our data from West Germany. In both countries, the only elite groups that are significantly more Materialist than the general public are the agricultural and business elites. In both countries, the media elites, research elites, and labor elites are far more Postmaterialist in their values than the general public. This also holds true of the governmental policymaking elites in the United States, even though these interviews were conducted during the Reagan administration. The policymakers subsample contains people

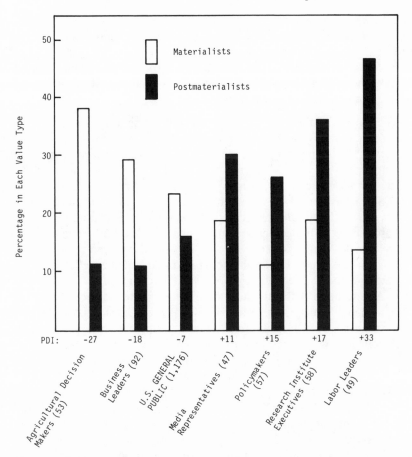

FIGURE 9-5. Balance between Materialist and Postmaterialist value priorities among elites and public in the Untied States, 1987. Based on surveys of American public and U.S. opinion leaders carried out by the Gallup organization in November 1987 (#G08217).

drawn from both major parties and some independents; the group as a whole was predominantly Postmaterialist.

These results reveal a great deal of polarization along the Materialist/ Postmaterialist dimension among American elites. It would be a great oversimplification to view the situation as one in which monolithically Postmaterialist elites are imposing their preferences on a relatively Materialist public, for in both Germany and the United States, business and agricultural elites are even more Materialist than the general public. Armed with very different resources, economic elites are struggling against communications elites to pull the public in opposite directions.

Nevertheless, these results confirm Rothman and Lichter's finding that media elites and intellectuals tend to have a significantly more Postmaterialist outlook than does the public as a whole.

Rothman and Lichter (1984) cite Bell (1976) as arguing that the traditional American emphasis on achievement and instrumental rationality was derived from a Protestant religious heritage:

> The erosion of this inheritance, along with rising affluence, has weakened these motivational patterns and substituted for them the narcissistic pursuit of "stimulating" experiences. The erosion is most pronounced among those groups at one remove from the central economic institutions of the society, i.e., artists, intellectuals, journalists, etc.
>
> Since the turn of the twentieth century, Bell suggests, such groups have leveled a sustained attack upon business and other traditional elites based upon both ideological commitment and lifestyle preferences. In contrast to business men, who are motivated by achievement needs (i.e., the need to live up to an internalized standard of excellence), these elites are power orientated and somewhat narcissistic.
>
> According to Bell and others these cultural elites have contributed to fundamental changes in American life. Perhaps most importantly they have gradually eroded the faith of both traditional elites and ordinary Americans in the values and institutions of their society.
>
> On the other hand, Habermas (1975) has argued that these elites possess a sharper perception of the internal contradictions in capitalist societies than do those most closely involved with the central institutions of capitalism. In contributing to the loss of legitimacy of capitalist societies, they may well be contributing to an evolutionary adaptation which will lead to a higher level of social integration. Habermas's thesis receives some empirical support from the work of Inglehart, whose findings suggest increased support for "post-materialist" values among such elites. (Rothman and Lichter 1984, 29–30)

Though Bell and Habermas both agree that the cultural elites are playing a crucial role in American society, they disagree profoundly about whether this role will have constructive or destructive effects. Rothman and Lichter (1984) attempt to assess this question by measuring the background and personality attributes of the media elite, and comparing them with those of the business elite. Interestingly enough, the media elite tend to come from higher social status backgrounds than do the business elite; the fathers of the media elite are nearly twice as likely to have graduated from college as are those of the business elite. Rothman and Lichter also find that the business elite rank significantly higher than do the media elite on need achievement, while the media elite are significantly higher on narcissism and the need for power. While "achievement" is a more positive-sounding label than "narcissism," by itself this tells us little about the impact of various types of elites: achievement motivations could produce either harmful or beneficial consequences. However, the authors do cite evidence indicating that the media elite have an important impact:

> Michael Robinson (1975) has demonstrated a link between reliance on television news and political alienation. He attributes this finding, in part, to anti-institutional themes in network news. More recently, Miller et al. (1979) uncovered similar patterns among newspaper readers. Based on a national survey, they found that people who read newspapers highly critical of American political institutions tend to distrust such institutions significantly more than those who read more favorable newspapers. The *New York Times* and *Washington Post* were among the most "critical" papers they studied. (Rothman and Lichter 1984, 48)

The authors conclude:

> The pointed views of the national media elite are not mere wishes and opinions of those aspiring to power, but the voice of a new leadership group that has arrived as a major force in American society. Cosmopolitan in their origins, liberal in their outlooks, they are aware and protective of their collective influence. The rise of this elite has hardly gone unnoticed. Some hail them as the public's tribunes against the powerful—indispensable champions of the underdog and the oppressed. Others decry them for allegiance to an adversary culture that is chiseling away at traditional values. (Lichter and Rothman 1981, 60)

The emergence of a new style of politics, linked with the rise to power of Postmaterialist politicians, has been most dramatic in Western Europe, where it has given rise to new political parties. It is taking place in the United States less conspicuously but with equally important consequences. As one would expect, Postmaterialist politicians still tend to be relatively young; and thus far, they have broken through to hold top office only at the local level. Where they have done so, the results are striking. Describing the rise of what they term "the new mayors" in both France and the United States, a cross-national group of sociologists comments:

> In the late 1970s a new type of political leader emerged in the U.S. . . . They are most successful at the local level, and thus have had only moderate media attention. But here their success is considerable—including Mayors Dianne Feinstein in San Francisco, Kathy Whitmire in Houston, William Green in Philadelphia, and many others in smaller cities. The

Democratic Presidential candidate in 1984, Senator Gary Hart from Colorado, stressed similar themes, but was defeated by the more traditional Walter Mondale in the Democratic Primary election.

How are these leaders different? They share five traits which distinguish them from the traditional Left and Right.

They are *fiscal conservatives*, preferring lower taxes. While less fiscally conservative than traditional Republicans like Ronald Reagan, they are distinctly more cautious than the classic New Deal Democrats from Franklin Roosevelt through Lyndon Johnson.

Yet *on social issues they are progressive*. Here they are closer to the more traditional Left in favoring more equal treatment of racial and ethnic minorities, women, and tolerance of diverse life-styles such as gays. They share a youthful acceptance of these life-styles that disturb many older persons.

They appeal in *populist* manner to individual citizens. They thus rely heavily on the media, direct mail campaigns, door-to-door visits, and similar activities which convey their concerns to individual citizens.

They *distrust organized groups*: unions, churches, ethnic group associations, and especially party organizations are far less legitimate. Usually New Fiscal Populists come to power by campaigning against these groups which have supported more traditional (especially Democratic) candidates. Once in office they seek to implement policies that can be responsive to the disadvantaged and maintain services, while also not increasing taxes. This means improving productivity, which often leads to "breaking heads" of some government workers, especially union leaders who resist these changes.

Fifth, they tend to *stress public goods which appeal to all citizens* rather than private or separable goods which are consumed individually. Low taxes and productivity are classic goods stressed by New Fiscal Populists, in contrast to patronage and clientelism—the awarding of contracts to one's friends and allies in more traditional Leftist manner. But they differ from the traditional Right in seeking to maintain services. They thus do not propose simple across-the-board cutbacks or tax reductions like Ronald Reagan and other traditional conservatives. Improving productivity, doing more for less, "new ideas," are the slogans of New Fiscal Populists. Were these only heard on the campaign trail, the normal reaction would be to treat them as vacuous—still the case for many national commentators. But at the local level where New Fiscal Populists (NFPs) have held office, they have actually implemented programs improving productivity in ways that have been documented; they not only mean what they say, they are implementing these approaches across America. (Balme et al. 1986/1987, 264–65)

POSTMATERIALISM AND THE RISE OF THE NEW CLASS

Clearly, Postmaterialism is no longer a student phenomenon. When the postwar generation first became politically relevant in the 1960s, the universities may have been the only major institutions in which they were the dominant influence. Their youth, their minority status in society as a whole, and their relative lack of representation at decision-making levels dictated a protest strategy. Postmaterialists had little access to key decision-making posts; but they were highly motivated and articulate. They could not control decision making, but they could disrupt it—and they made use of unconventional political protest techniques.

The relative youth and powerlessness of the Postmaterialists may have dictated a strategy of student protest in the 1960s. But Postmaterialism has moved out of the student ghetto. By 1980, a Postmaterialist outlook had become more common than a Materialist one among young technocrats, professionals, and politicians in Western countries. As experts, congressional staffers, and members of ministerial cabinets, Postmaterialists had direct access to the command posts of the sociopolitical system. Protest was no longer their most effective tool. The impact of Postmaterialism was no longer symbolized by the student with a protest placard, but by the public interest lawyer, or the technocrat with an environmental impact statement.

In recent years, a growing number of Western intellectuals have focused their attention on the rise of a Western version of "the new class." In contrast with the establishment-oriented "new class" of Eastern Europe described by Djilas (1966), the new class in the West is an elite characterized by its adversary stance toward the existing social order (Podhoretz 1979; Bruce-Briggs 1979); by its "culture of critical discourse" (Gouldner 1979, 28–29); and by a "new liberalism" (Ladd 1978, 48–49). Broder (1980) describes the emergence of a new generation of political elites with many of these characteristics as a "changing of the guard."

There is no clear consensus on the criteria that define the new class. Ehrenreich and Ehrenreich (1977) describe it as those in the census categories of "professional and technical" plus "managers and administrators"—precisely the categories we have found to be most heavily Postmaterialist. But Ladd (1978) extends its limits to include anyone with a college education. There is even less consensus concerning *why* this well-paid and increasingly powerful stratum of society is critical of the existing economic and political order and participates in leftist political movements. There is a tendency to view an adversary culture as something inherent in higher education or in certain occupations, but the reasons are not clear. Highly educated groups have existed for a long time, but in the past they generally were politically conservative. High levels of education and information are certainly the resource that enables the New Class to play an important role—but they do not explain why today an increasing share of the most highly educated and informed strata choose to take an adversary stance toward their society.

I suggest that the rise of Postmaterialism and its subsequent penetration of technocratic and professional elites has been a major factor behind the emergence of the new class, for this group is distinctive not only in its occupational and educational characteristics, but also in its values—and the ideology attributed to the new class reflects Postmaterialist values rather closely (Ladd 1976, 1978). If this is true, it explains why a new class having these specific characteristics has emerged at this particular point in history.

For the distinctive values of the new class reflect an historical change that cannot be attributed simply to a changing educational and occupational structure. Rising levels of education and a shift of manpower into the "knowledge industries" have played a major role in the rise of this new elite, as Bell (1973, 1976), Lipset and Dobson (1972), Lipset (1979), and others have argued. But, as Table 9-10 makes clear, an "adversary culture" is not an inherent concomitant of the education or adult role of professionals and technocrats. Older professionals and technocrats are preponderantly Materialist; it is only among the younger segments of these groups that Postmaterialist priorities outweigh Materialist ones.

Because both the political environment and the social location of Postmaterialists have changed significantly, their tactics have also changed. Though the war in Indochina no longer plays an important role in Western politics, some of the most important movements on the current scene reflect the clash of Materialist and Postmaterialist worldviews—among them, the women's movement, the consumer advocacy movement, the environmental movement, and the antinuclear movement. These movements involve questions of whether one gives top priority to economic growth or to the individual's right to self-realization and the quality of life. These movements are increasingly becoming the major vehicle through which social change is attained in advanced industrial society. We will examine them in more detail in chapter 11.

CONCLUSION

Long-term predispositions play a major role in shaping political orientations and political behavior. There is no question that situational factors and external mobilizing factors also play important roles, and the attention that recent literature has directed toward them is well placed. But the fact remains that, in any given situation, certain individuals have internal predispositions that make them vastly more likely to engage in political action than other individuals. As we have seen, these dispositions are durable characteristics of given persons. Panel survey data demonstrate that given respondents had an enduring tendency to emphasize either Materialist or Postmaterialist values, which lasted over the period from 1974 to 1980–1981 in our three respective nations. Moreover, the values they held in 1974 were a good predictor of their subsequent political preferences and behavior in the early 1980s. Gradual changes in basic values are reshaping the politics of advanced industrial societies.

Building the welfare state and restoring economic growth were, understandably, the dominant political concerns of the 1930s and the postwar era. In the 1960s and 1970s, Postmaterialist forces captured the issue agenda of the West European Left and of American liberals. The effects of this coup have not yet been fully assimilated into either the rhetoric or the party alignments of Western nations.

Protest has become divorced from partisanship, to a remarkable degree. Two main axes of political polarization exist side by side, with the leading parties aligned along the familiar Left-Right axis based on religion and social class, in uneasy coexistence with a largely independent polarization between Materialists and Postmaterialists. The latter continue to dominate the issue arena. For a decade after the OPEC oil shock in 1973, Western economies functioned in an atmosphere of insecurity and diminishing expectations. Although at the start of the decade, practically everyone assumed that the issues of the 1980s would be economic issues, the ones that actually evoked political activism were mainly Postmaterialist ones.

The rise of Postmaterialism has placed existing party alignments under chronic stress, for in most countries these alignments do not correspond to either the social bases of support for change or to polarization over the most heated issues. The resulting stress can be resolved in various ways. One is dealignment, with a gradual decline of party loyalty and party identification, insofar as the most salient issues no longer provide an incentive that attaches new voters to existing parties. Another is realignment, with existing parties splitting or being taken over by reorienting elites.

There is yet another possibility. In the long run, the new axis of polarization based on Materialist/Postmaterialist values may be assimilated into a new synthesis.

A Materialist consensus provided the rationale and the legitimating myth of industrial society. Its Postmaterialist antithesis has not yet led to the emergence of a new synthesis. But it seems likely that the wave of the future is not undiluted acceptance of Postmaterialist goals. The Postmaterialists brought into the political arena a number of issues that had been largely ignored and neglected; in doing so, they help correct a course that tended to sacrifice the quality of life to one-sided economic considerations. But carried to an extreme, Postmaterialism can be equally self-defeating. The antiindustrial outlook of some of the movement's ideologues could lead to neglect of the economic base on which Postmaterialism ultimately depends. In the long run, a new synthesis of Materialist and Postmaterialist orientations will almost certainly emerge, through sheer functional necessity.

CHAPTER 10

From Elite-Directed to Elite-Directing Politics: The Role of Cognitive Mobilization, Changing Gender Roles, and Changing Values

INTRODUCTION: GROWING PARTICIPANT POTENTIAL AMONG MASS PUBLICS?

Economic development should lead to rising levels of mass political participation, for three good theoretical reasons. (1) The publics of advanced industrial societies have developed enhanced abilities to participate; their educational levels have risen dramatically during the past half-century, and political information has become much more readily available. (2) Social norms have become much more permissive toward political participation by the female half of the public. A generation or two ago, women did not even have the right to vote. Today not only are they legally enfranchised in all Western democracies, but there is increasing informal acceptance of their playing an equal role in politics, and female role models have become more widespread. Finally, (3) there is evidence that the value priorities of Western publics have gradually been shifting from Materialist toward Postmaterialist values. If this trend has indeed been occurring, it, too, should tend to raise the political participation rates of mass publics. Being freed from the need to focus their energies primarily on the struggle for economic and physical security should enable them to devote more attention to Postmaterialist concerns—such as politics.

All of these considerations suggest that the political participation rates of Western publics should be gradually rising. To be sure, these are not the only kinds of influences involved; a dramatic political conflict at a given time and place can temporarily mobilize the public, regardless of such underlying factors as educational levels or social norms. But over the long haul, the three processes just outlined should tend to raise the publics' participant potential.

At least in theory. But impressionistic evidence, and some kinds of quantitative indicators, seem to point in precisely the opposite direction. In most Western nations, the public in general and students in particular seem much less politicized than they were in the late 1960s and early

1970s. And the evidence is not merely impressionistic. Voter turnout in American presidential elections has declined in recent decades; in 1988 it hit the lowest level since the 1950s. Voter turnout in Western Europe has not been rising, and in many countries is somewhat below the level it showed two or three decades ago.

Common sense and theory point in opposite directions—or so it seems. When we look at the matter in broader perspective, however, the disparity between theory and reality disappears. This chapter will present evidence that as a result of three long-term processes linked with the evolution of advanced industrial society, mass publics are gradually becoming more involved in politics. We will argue that the potential for political participation of Western publics has been rising gradually over recent decades, as a result of three factors: (1) rising levels of education and political information; (2) changing norms governing political participation by women; and (3) changing value priorities, which tend to place less emphasis on immediate survival needs and give higher priority to self-expression. The immediate consequences of these long-term changes, however, have been partly masked by the fact that, while the individual level preconditions for political participation have been improving, external mobilization has been in decline, as a result of the decay of political party machines, labor unions, and religious institutions. The net result has been a stagnation of electoral turnout and other forms of elite-directed participation, on one hand, together with the growth of elite-directing forms of participation, on the other hand. Elite-directing participation originates among members of the general public having no special role in existing institutions, other than those created ad hoc, in order to cope with the specific problem. Rising rates of political discussion, an increase in unconventional forms of political participation, and the rise of new social movements are all manifestations of the rise of elite-directing participation. We will draw on evidence from many nations spanning a wide spectrum of economic development and will examine data that extend over a number of years. But, first, let us briefly discuss these three processes, and the reasons why they should tend to increase the political activity of mass publics.

COGNITIVE MOBILIZATION: THE SHIFTING BALANCE OF POLITICAL SKILLS

In early face-to-face political communities, such as the tribe or city state, political communication was by word of mouth and dealt with people or things one knew firsthand. Virtually everyone possessed the skills necessary for political participation, so politics could be relatively democratic, with decision making sometimes taking place through councils in which every adult male had a voice.

The emergence of extensive political communities, based on much larger areas and governing millions rather than thousands of people, required special skills, starting with literacy. Word-of-mouth communications were no longer adequate; written messages had to be sent and received across great distances. Human memory was no longer capable of retaining such details as the tax base of thousands of villages or the military manpower they could raise; written records were needed. And personal chains of loyalties were inadequate to hold together large empires; legitimating myths or ideologies based on abstract symbols had to be propagated.

The extensive political community had a greatly enlarged population and resource base, and it eventually drove smaller competitors out of existence. But a heavy price was paid. Elites with specialized skills developed to perform the necessary coordinating functions. A wide gap opened between ordinary people, who did not have the specialized training needed to cope with politics at a distance, and a small elite, which was involved in national politics. The peasant masses became more or less irrelevant to the politics of large agrarian nations.

Industrialization makes it possible to narrow the gap between elites and masses again. Lerner (1958) has analyzed the profound changes that take place as parochial peoples become urbanized and literate and come into contact with mass media—and consequently, able to relate to the national political community rather than to just their village or tribe. Deutsch (1964, 1966) gave further insight into this transformation with his analysis of "social mobilization." This process begins when people are uprooted from physical and intellectual isolation, and from old traditions, occupations, and places of residence. Gradually they became integrated into modern organizations and extensive communications networks—expanding their horizons beyond the scope of word-of-mouth communications and increasingly coming into touch with national politics.

Western countries long ago completed the outwardly visible stages of social mobilization, such as urbanization, basic industrialization, widespread literacy, mass military service, and universal suffrage. Nevertheless, the core of the process continues: the dissemination of skills needed to cope with an extensive political community. The term "cognitive mobilization" refers to this aspect of the social mobilization process (Inglehart 1970a, 1977; Dalton 1984a; Dalton, Flanagan, and Beck 1984). Though formal education is by no means the same thing as cognitive mobilization, it is probably the best readily available indicator.

Almond and Verba (1963) demonstrated that the more educated a person is, the more likely he or she is to have a sense of "subjective political competence"—and to take part in politics. Numerous other studies in various countries have found that people with higher socioeconomic status are most apt to participate in politics (Milbrath and Goel 1977; Verba, Nie, and Kim 1978; Barnes, Kaase et al. 1979). But is this attributable to cognitive mobilization, or to social status itself? In other words, are the better educated more likely to have more say in politics because they have the skills needed to press their demands more effectively—or simply because they have better social connections, and more money with which to induce officials to listen to them?

It would be naive to think that wealth and personal connections are irrelevant. But rising levels of skills and information are important too; and from the standpoint of long-term changes, these cognitive variables are particularly significant. By definition, there will always be an upper third, a middle third and a lower third in socioeconomic status. But pronounced growth has occurred in *absolute* levels of education and information, and this may be shifting the balance of political skills between elites and mass, giving the citizens a better chance to make significant political inputs.

Other observers have emphasized other consequences of economic development. Nie, Powell, and Prewitt (1969) argue that economic development leads to higher rates of political participation, but does so chiefly because of its impact on a society's class structure and organizational infrastructure. Verba, Nie, and Kim (1978) emphasize similar factors, arguing that economic development increases the size of the middle class, which in turn leads to higher rates of membership in formal organizations.

Education undoubtedly is an indicator of social status, but it is also an indicator of communications skills. The distinction is important, for in multivariate analysis, cognitive variables, such as education and political information, prove to be much more powerful predictors of political participation than do such relatively pure social class indicators as income or occupation (Inglehart 1977). Communications skills seem to be even more important than social status per se.

Verba and Nie (1972), Nie, Powell, and Prewitt (1969), and Verba, Nie, and Kim (1978) find that organizational membership is strongly associated with political participation. They conclude that the masses can become participants by joining organizations, even without changes in basic attitudes or skills. This is true. But it leads to very limited *types* of participation. Membership in traditional bureaucratic organizations mainly seems to encourage *elite-directed* rather than *elite-directing* forms of participation. It may not reflect the impact of public preferences on elite decisions, so much as the successful marshaling of the public by elites.

Inglehart (1977) argues that participation springs from two fundamentally different processes, one underlying an older mode of political participation, the other, a newer mode. The institutions that mobilized mass political participation in the late nineteenth and early twentieth centuries—labor union, church, and mass political party—were hierarchical organizations, in which a small number of leaders or political bosses led a mass of disciplined troops. They were effective in bringing large numbers of newly enfranchised citizens to the polls in an era when universal compulsory education had just taken root and the average citizen had a low level of political skills. But while these elite-directed organizations could mobilize large numbers, they usually produced only a relatively low qualitative level of participation, generally the simple act of voting (Converse 1972).

A newer, elite-directing mode of participation expresses the individual's preferences with far greater precision and in much more detail than the old. It is issue-oriented, and based on ad hoc groups rather than on established bureaucratic organizations. It aims at effecting specific policy changes rather than simply supporting the representatives of a given group. This mode of participation requires relatively high skill levels.

Thus, if we take formal education as an indicator of political skills, we find that sheer literacy seems sufficient to produce voting. The bulk of Western citizens reached this threshold generations ago. But while literacy alone may be sufficient to produce a high rate of voting, taking the initiative at the national level seems to require at least a secondary education, and probably a university education. This is particularly true of the more elite-directing types of political behavior: As Barnes, Kaase, et al. (1979) demonstrate, high educational levels are very closely associated with participation in unconventional forms of political action. But their study also goes a step farther and develops measures of political skills. It finds that a high level of political conceptualization is an even stronger predictor of unconventional political behavior than education—and far stronger than social class per se.

It seems likely that the rise of a postindustrial society, or information society (Bell 1973, 1976), also leads to a growing potential for citizen participation in politics. Increasingly, not only formal education but job experience as well develop politically relevant skills. The traditional assembly-line worker produced things, working in a hierarchical system that required (and allowed) very little autonomous judgment. Workers in the service and information sectors deal with people and concepts; operating in an environment where innovation is crucial, they need autonomy for the use of individual judgment. It is inherently impossible to prescribe innovation from above, in hierarchical fashion. Accustomed to working in less hierarchical decision structures in their job life, people in the information and service sectors are relatively likely to have both the skills and the inclination to take part in decision making in the political realm as well.

High skill levels are needed for elite-directing action, because modernization "discourages participation by creating complex organizational networks based on high specialization and division of political labor that requires participants to possess unprecedented expertise" (DiPalma 1970). Today most national officials have a university education. The citizen with only a primary school education is hardly on a footing of equality with them in mastery of bureaucratic techniques, or even in figuring out whom he or she should contact in order to articulate a specific grievance. As a result, he or she is likely to depend on some kind of broker, such as a patron or a political boss who purports to represent one's interests in general.

The newer mode of political participation is far more issue specific and more likely to function at the higher thresholds of participation. It is new in the sense that only recently has a large percentage of the population possessed the skills required for this form of participation. And it is new in that it makes the public less dependent on permanent, oligarchic organizations.

We suggest that at high levels of development, traditional kinds of organizational involvement become progressively less effective. With a wide range of alternative channels of information and redress, people rely less and less on such established organizational networks as labor unions, churches, and old-line urban political machines. Both union membership rates and church attendance have been falling in most Western countries, and traditional political party ties have been weakening. This can have the effect of *depressing* certain types of political participation, such as voting, that are heavily dependent on elite-directed mobilization and may require little or no cognitive response to current issues. But, at the same time, elite-directing types of participation, aimed at influencing specific policy decisions, are becoming more widespread. The iron law of oligarchy is very gradually being repealed.

Political participation remained dependent on permanently established organizations as long as most of the people with bureaucratic skills held positions within these institutions. But today ad hoc organizations can be brought into being more or less at will, because the public has an unprecedentedly large leavening of nonelite members with high levels of political skills. A balance between elites and mass that was upset centuries ago is in the process of being redressed.

Strong organizational networks can help less advantaged groups attain higher participation rates than those of groups with higher skill levels. Situational factors are also important; indeed, during a given period, they may well swamp the effects of more gradual, underlying changes. But from a long-term perspective, changes at the individual level are even more significant. Exciting periods tend to alternate with dull periods of politics. In the short run, the period effects predominate; but in the long run, they are apt to cancel one another out. The long-term effects of individual level change, on the other hand, tend to be cumulative. They set new limits to the rise and fall of activism in response to given events. Thus, it is crucial to analyze participation in longitudinal perspective, as we will attempt to do here. Cognitive mobilization may be gradually raising the baseline of potential political participation, particularly the potential for elite-directing types of political behavior.

The impact of cognitive mobilization is reinforced by two other processes that increase the public's participant potential. One of them is the gradual breakdown of gender-based differences in political roles. As recently as the start of this century, the only significant political role available to women was that of hereditary monarch, and even that became open only when no male heir existed (and even then, only in certain countries). As evidence presented in chapter 1 demonstrated, women are still far less integrated into political life than men—but the degree to which this is true varies markedly, by cultural pattern.

In the United States, Great Britain, Germany, and Scandinavia, women did not win the right to vote until around 1920. In Belgium, France, and Italy, they were not enfranchised until after World War II. In Switzerland, women won the right to vote in national elections only in 1971. Moreover, the sheer fact of being legally enfranchised did not instantly erase gender differences in political participation. Those generations who were socialized when women did not play an active political role have different expectations than do those who take women's political participation for granted; furthermore, the younger birth cohorts have increasingly been exposed to female political role models. Until 1979, none of the democracies of Western Europe or North America had been governed by a woman; as of 1986, women held the chief executive office in four of these countries, (all of them countries that had extended the franchise relatively early). Given these differences in formative experiences, it seems likely that it will take a long-term process of intergenerational population replacement to overcome the female deficit in political participation.

A third process that also implies long-term changes in mass political participation is the intergenerational shift from Materialist toward Postmaterialist value priorities that is gradually transforming the publics of advanced industrial society. Postmaterialists are free to redirect some of the attention and energy that were formerly focused primarily on physical survival and security. Politics is only one possibility among a variety of broader, more abstract concerns—but it is one of the activities that Post-materialists engage in disproportionately. Consequently, the gradual shift toward Postmaterialism should also tend to increase the politicization of Western publics.

We believe that these three social processes are gradually raising mass participation potential, and increasing the likelihood of elite-directing political participation. Yet it is not immediately apparent that mass political participation is increasing. Voting turnout rates have been stagnant in most Western countries for many years, and one hears a good deal of talk about political apathy among Western publics. What is the underlying reality?

To answer this question, we will draw on a large body of survey data concerning rates of political discussion. In surveys carried out repeatedly since 1973, and in nineteen different countries, representative national samples of the public have been asked: "When you get together with your friends, would you say you discuss political matters frequently, occasionally, or never?"

There are a number of reasons why our analysis focuses on responses to this question. First, data are available from a large number of nations over a considerable period of time—which is crucial for any analysis of trends thought to be inherent in advanced industrial society. Fluctuations in political interest in any given country are almost inevitable; the recent trend in the United States seems downward, but the overall trend in the industrial world may be up. Secondly, we believe that responses to this item provide a relatively accurate indicator of the potential for political activity among Western publics. Clearly, it is a better indicator of political activism than voter turnout rates, which can be extremely misleading; in Italy and Belgium, for example, voting is legally required of all citizens, producing extremely high rates of turnout, but, as data presented below illustrate, the Belgian and Italian publics show much lower rates of political involvement than do most Western publics. Voting is an important activity, but it is an elite-directed form of participation, and constitutes a poor indicator of more active forms of participation, which are becoming increasingly significant. The process of cognitive mobilization gives rise to sophisticated electorates who are less closely linked to the political machines that bring people to the polls but show a higher potential for issue-specific forms of participation.

POLITICAL INVOLVEMENT IN CROSS-NATIONAL PERSPECTIVE

Now, let us take a look at actual political discussion rates in twenty societies from which we have data, from Euro-Barometer surveys plus the

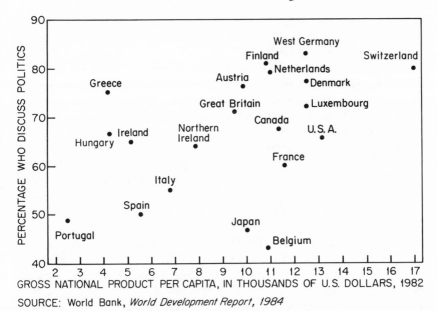

SOURCE: World Bank, *World Development Report, 1984*

FIGURE 10-1. Political discussion rates by level of economic development.
Sources: Economic data from World Bank, *World Development Report, 1984*; discussion rates from Euro-Barometer surveys and World Values survey, 1981.

Political Action surveys and the World Values survey carried out in 1981. Figure 10-1 shows the percentage of the public in each society who "frequently" or "occasionally" discuss politics, with the twenty societies arrayed according to levels of economic development. Our overall hypothesis is that economic development is conducive to rising levels of political activity, since each of the three specific processes we have discussed is linked with economic development. Our analysis here focuses on the distinction between those who "never" discuss politics and those who do so either "frequently" or "occasionally." While there might be some ambiguity about the cutting line between "frequently" and "occasionally," the meaning of "never" is quite clear. And a surprisingly large proportion of the population report that they never discuss politics.

The relationship between economic development and political discussion is clearly positive. The majority of the nations are arrayed along the diagonal from the lower lefthand corner to the upper righthand corner of Figure 10-1. Eight of the nine nations with political discussion rates over 70 percent have per capita gross national products over $9,000 per year; and all eight nations with a gross national product per capita over $11,000 have political discussion rates over 60 percent. Conversely, three of our poorest countries—Portugal, Spain, and Italy—show some of the lowest rates of political discussion, with about half of the population reporting that they never discuss politics.

There are some striking deviant cases, however. The Greeks are over-achievers, showing high rates of political discussion despite the fact that Greece is one of the poorest nations in our sample. This phenomenon may reflect a tradition that dates back to widespread political discussion in the *agora* of the ancient city-state democracies—a tradition that is still a source of pride in contemporary Greece. On the other hand, the Japanese and Belgians are pronounced underachievers: These economically devel-oped nations manifest very low levels of political discussion. For Japan, this is a familiar pattern, for strong cultural norms emphasize conformity to a group consensus, and the avoidance of topics that might make conflict manifest. Politics, of course, is inherently conflict laden. For Belgium, we have no ready explanation, but the phenomenon seems to be an enduring aspect of Belgian society. In all of the Euro-Barometer surveys carried out from 1973 to 1987, the Belgians consistently show low levels of politici-zation. We have three striking deviant cases, then; but the other sixteen nations fall on or near the diagonal from the lower left to upper right, reflecting rising political discussion rates with rising economic develop-ment.

Our thesis deals with change, and one cannot prove a longitudinal theory with cross-sectional data. Nevertheless, Figure 10-1 shows precisely the type of pattern that would result if rising levels of economic development led to rising levels of politicization. This cross-national overview does not prove the thesis, but it does provide prima facie support, with a good fit between theory and the empirical pattern.

Let us examine the evidence more closely. Table 10-1 shows the per-centage who discuss politics, by level of education. Theoretically, one of the main reasons why politicization should be rising is because the educa-tional levels of Western publics have risen dramatically during recent de-cades and the more educated tend to be politically more active. For reasons of space we show only the overall results in Table 10-1, but the pattern applies to each of the twenty countries from which we have data. Overall, among those who left school before reaching 15 years of age, nearly half never discuss politics, while among those who completed their education at the age of 22 or over, only 12 percent never discuss politics. In other words, those who leave school before age 15 are about four times as likely to be apolitical as those who receive a university education. In view of the fact that the former group, though still sizable, is rapidly diminishing, while the university-educated segment is becoming a much larger share of the adult public, should we expect a substantial rise in the politicization of

TABLE 10-1. POLITICAL INVOLVEMENT BY EDUCATIONAL LEVEL IN TEN WESTERN
SOCIETIES, 1973 - 1984
(Percentage who discuss politics "frequently" or "occasionally")

Age at Which Respondent Left School	Percentage Who Discuss Politics	N
Before age 15	54%	(66,666)
15	64	(23,372)
16	66	(23,161)
17	71	(15,591)
18	73	(16,163)
19	79	(6,715)
20	80	(4,769)
21	85	(3,989)
22 and over	88	(13,277)

Sources: Combined results of European Community 1973 Survey and
Euro-Barometer surveys 3 - 21 (1975 - 1984) carried out in Britain,
France, Italy, West Germany, Netherlands, Belgium, Luxembourg, Ireland,
Denmark, and Greece.

Western publics? Or is education a purely positional good, with the more educated citizens being more active politically simply because of their relative position, regardless of absolute levels?

Table 10-2 gives a partial answer to this question, demonstrating that younger birth cohorts in Western societies are substantially more apt to discuss politics than are their elders and that this difference is due, in large part, to the fact that the younger cohorts are more highly educated. When we statistically adjust for differences in education levels, much (though not all) of the age-linked difference disappears. It appears that the effects of education are not merely positional: the political discussion rates of an entire generation can be raised by obtaining more education.

This pattern may mean that as more educated cohorts replace the less educated ones in the adult population, we will witness a rising level of politicization. But before we can draw this conclusion, we need to distinguish between life cycle effects and enduring characteristics of given birth cohorts. It *could* be the case that the younger cohorts are more apt to discuss politics simply because they are young—and will progressively disengage from politics as they grow older. Furthermore, the youngest cohort in Table 10-2 is less apt to discuss politics than the next older group. Does this mean that whatever trend might be reflected in these data has recently reversed itself?

TABLE 10-2. POLITICAL INVOLVEMENT BY BIRTH COHORT IN TEN WESTERN
SOCIETIES, 1973 - 1984

Cohort's Birth Years	% Who Discuss Politics		N
	Actually Observed	Adjusted for Education	
1956 - 1965	66%	59%	(26,295)
1946 - 1955	73	69	(38,081)
1936 - 1945	71	71	(32,476)
1926 - 1935	66	69	(28,773)
1916 - 1925	64	68	(26,129)
1906 - 1915	58	63	(21,133)
Before 1906	49	56	(9,574)

Sources: See Table 10-1.

In order to clarify this question, we performed a cohort analysis, following given birth cohorts across time, to see whether they become less involved in politics as they age, or whether they retain relatively stable positions. Figure 10-2 shows the results, based on over 200,000 interviews carried out in the nine countries from which we have data from 1973 to 1987. This analysis demonstrates two important points:

(1) Given cohorts do not become less politicized as they age. If age-related differences reflected life cycle effects, each of our cohorts (spanning ten years) should drop to the level of the next-older cohort after ten years have elapsed. No such pattern is visible. With one exception, each cohort remains at approximately the same level throughout the entire fourteen-year period, showing only minor fluctuations. The cohort born from 1906 to 1915 declined slightly, but by no means enough to erase the apparent generational difference. If the age differences were entirely due to life cycle effects, this cohort should have fallen below the 50 percent level by 1983. It is nowhere near that point. There is a faint hint of disengagement among the oldest cohort, but by no means enough to account for the overall cohort differences.

(2) The youngest cohort examined here (the group born from 1956 to 1965) starts out as the second least politicized group in 1973 (when its members were all less than 18 years of age); its position rises rapidly as its members reach adulthood, and by 1983 (when its members are 18 to 27 years old) it has become one of the two most politicized cohorts, roughly on a par with the 1946–1955 birth cohort. Here, life cycle effects clearly are present—but they work in the opposite direction from that specified by

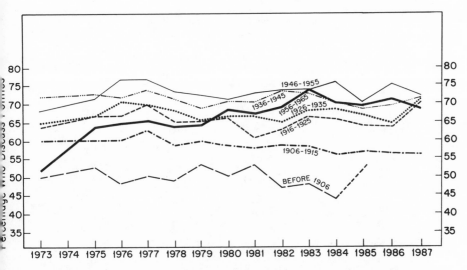

ɪɢᴜʀᴇ 10-2. Percentage who "frequently" or "occasionally" discuss politics by birth co-ort, 1973–1987. Based on combined samples of publics of Great Britain, France, West Ger-ɪany, Italy, the Netherlands, Belgium, Denmark, Ireland, and Luxembourg, interviewed in 973 European Community survey and in Euro-Barometer surveys 3 through 27. Total un-veighted N = 204,322.

the "aging produces disengagement" hypothesis: People are less apt to discuss politics during their preadult years, but upon reaching adulthood, the younger and more educated cohorts show higher rates of political discussion than do the older cohorts. This explains the anomaly in Table 10-2: The youngest age group is, at any given point in time, less politicized than some of the older groups not because of a reversal of trends but because it has not yet reached political maturity.

Our results imply that intergenerational population replacement will lead to a gradual increase in political involvement. This is not attributable to rising education alone. As we saw in Table 10-2, not all of the age-related differences in political discussion rates are due to educational differences: Some differences persist even when we control for education. One reason, we suggest, is the gradual erosion of traditional gender roles that formerly severely inhibited political action by women and still exert lingering effects.

THE FADING OF THE GENDER GAP IN POLITICIZATION

Table 10-3 illustrates one aspect of this phenomenon. In each of the twenty societies for which we have data, women are less likely to discuss politics than men. The size of this gender gap ranges from very small in

TABLE 10-3.   POLITICAL INVOLVEMENT: THE GENDER GAP IN TWENTY SOCIETIES
(Percentage who discuss politics)

1.	ITALY	Men	74%	(11,131)	11. AUSTRIA	Men	84%	(647)
		Women	47	(11,349)		Women	69	(933)
	Gender gap:		-27		Gender gap:		-15	
2.	PORTUGAL	Men	65	(3,426)	12. DENMARK	Men	77	(9,725)
		Women	40	(5,269)		Women	63	(10,631)
	Gender gap:		-25		Gender Gap:		-14	
3.	GREECE	Men	82	(3,861)	13. BRITAIN	Men	73	(10,414)
		Women	58	(4,138)		Women	60	(11,688)
	Gender gap:		-24		Gender Gap:		-13	
4.	JAPAN	Men	58	(565)	14. CANADA	Men	75	(618)
		Women	35	(589)		Women	62	(626)
	Gender gap:		-23		Gender Gap:		-13	
5.	HUNGARY	Men	80	(679)	15. FRANCE	Men	70	(10,781)
		Women	58	(757)		Women	57	(11,776)
	Gender gap:		-21		Gender Gap:		-10	
6.	IRELAND	Men	70	(9,938)	16. SWITZERLAND Men		85	(641)
		Women	49	(10,185)		Women	75	(647)
	Gender gap:		-21		Gender Gap:		-10	
7.	SPAIN	Men	58	(2,572)	17. N. IRELAND	Men	69	(1,244)
		Women	40	(2,962)		Women	59	(1,245)
	Gender gap:		-18		Gender Gap:		-10	
8.	W.GERMANY	Men	85	(10,076)	18. U.S.	Men	82	(1,771)
		Women	67	(11,208)		Women	72	(2,236)
	Gender gap:		-18		Gender Gap:		-10	
9.	BELGIUM	Men	54	(10,045)	19. FINLAND	Men	86	(607)
		Women	38	(10,806)		Women	77	(607)
	Gender gap:		-16		Gender Gap:		-9	
10.	LUXEMBOURG	Men	80	(3,200)	20. NETHERLANDS Men		75	(9,831)
		Women	64	(3,081)		Women	70	(11,250)
	Gender gap:		-16		Gender Gap:		-5	

Sources: Pooled data from European Community surveys carried out from 1973 through 1985. For the United States, Canada, Hungary, and Japan, data are from the World Values survey, with fieldwork in 1981 and 1982; for the United States (additional data), Austria, Finland, and Switzerland, data are from the Political Action survey, 1974 - 1976.

the Netherlands, to massive in Italy, Portugal, Greece, and Japan. To some extent, the low ranking of certain countries in Figure 10-2 is simply a reflection of the fact that the women in these countries are largely apolitical, but this is by no means the whole story. Greece, again, is exceptional: The overall cultural emphasis on discussing politics is so strong that the Greek public ranks relatively high, despite the presence of a large gap between men and women. These data show striking signs of the persistence of long-term cultural influences, as we saw in chapter 1.

The impact of these influences is gradually fading, however. One major factor that tends to erase the gender gap in politicization is formal education. As Table 10—4 shows, the gender gap is largest among the least educated, and shrinks almost to zero among the highly educated. Among

TABLE 10-4. POLITICAL INVOLVEMENT BY EDUCATIONAL LEVEL AND GENDER IN
TEN WESTERN NATIONS, 1973 - 1974
(Percentage who discuss politics "frequently" or "from time to time")

Age at Which Respondent Left School	Men	N	Women	N	Gender Gap (% Men-% Women)
Before age 15	66%	(30,729)	44%	(35,887)	22
15	73	(10,958)	56	(12,401)	17
16	73	(10,593)	60	(12,553)	13
17	76	(6,887)	67	(8,696)	9
18	79	(7,349)	68	(8,797)	11
19	83	(3,355)	74	(3,355)	9
20	84	(2,458)	76	(2,307)	8
21	87	(1,975)	82	(2,014)	5
22 and over	89	(8,617)	86	(4,652)	3

Sources: See Table 10-1.

those who left school before the age of 15, men are far likelier to discuss politics than are women. The traditional apolitical role of women still influences the behavior of the majority of these women. But formal education provides new inputs that erode the traditional heritage—and the 22-point gender gap found among the least educated dwindles to 3 points among those with a higher education.

The data in Table 10-4 have longitudinal implications, for not only have absolute levels of education been rising, but the difference in educational levels of men and women has been narrowing. A generation or two ago, it was exceptional for women to receive higher education. Today women are almost as likely as men to attend a university in most of these countries. Hence, the size of the gender gap should gradually diminish over time.

Figure 10-3 shows the relevant evidence. It demonstrates that the gender gap tends to get smaller as we move from the older to the younger (historically more recent) birth cohorts. Among the cohorts born before 1906 and those born from 1906 to 1915, the gender gap averages about 20 percentage points. Among the cohort born from 1956 to 1965, it is about half that size. Not only are overall educational levels rising, but the female politicization deficit seems to be eroding. Both factors should increase the potential for political participation.

We suggested that another process should also work in this direction: the gradual shift from Materialist to Postmaterialist values. Those who have

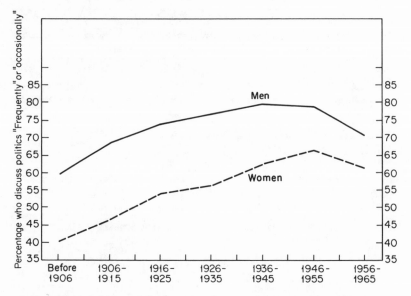

FIGURE 10-3. The shrinking gender gap: political discussion rates among men and women born in the years indicated. Based on eight-nation data, 1973–1984.

grown up under conditions of relatively great economic and physical security are relatively apt to take them for granted, and focus on attaining other goals. Among other things, they are more apt to devote energy and attention to political concerns. Barnes, Kaase et al. (1979) have demonstrated that Postmaterialists are far more likely to engage in mildly disruptive forms of unconventional political participation than those with Materialist or mixed values. As Table 10-5 demonstrates, this also applies to the present indicator: Postmaterialists are a good deal likelier to discuss politics than those with other types of values.

Postmaterialists tend to be recruited from the more affluent segments of society; hence, they tend to have relatively high educational levels. Given the sharp differences in the amount of economic and physical security experienced by those who grew up in Western Europe in the 1920s, 1930s, and 1940s, by comparison with those who grew up in the postwar era, Postmaterialists are much more numerous among the younger cohorts than among the older ones. But even when we control for the fact that they tend to be younger and better educated than the rest of the population, those with Postmaterialist values remain likelier to discuss politics than those with other value priorities.

Table 10-5 illustrates the apparent impact of education, gender, value priorities, birth cohort, and occupation on political discussion rates. Education, gender, and values all seem to have significant effects—and their impact persists when we control for the effects of the other variables, in a multiple classification analysis. For example, men overall are 15 percentage points more likely than women to discuss politics; this difference is reduced (to 12 points) but by no means disappears when we adjust for the effects of the other independent variables in this analysis.

As Table 10-5 demonstrates, significant age group differences also persist when we adjust for the effects of the other variables; indeed, the youngest (preadult) cohorts fall even farther below their elders when we adjust for the fact that they are better educated and more Postmaterialist

TABLE 10-5. POLITICIZATION OF WESTERN PUBLICS BY EDUCATION, SEX, VALUES, BIRTH COHORT, AND OCCUPATION
(Percentage who discuss politics)

Age at Which Respondent Completed Education	Unadjusted	Adjusted for Sex, Values, Birth Cohort and Occupation	N
Before age 15	56%	58%	(60,100)
Age 15 - 16	66	66	(43,528)
Age 17 - 19	73	73	(37,654)
Age 20 - 22	86	78	(22,005)
Still in school	73	75	(14,086)

Sex	Unadjusted	Adjusted for Education, Values, Birth Cohort, and Occupation	N
Male	75%	73%	(86,283)
Female	60	61	(91,433)

Values	Unadjusted	Adjusted for Education, Sex, Birth Cohort, and Occupation	N
Materialist	58%	61%	(65,657)
Mixed	69	69	(92,324)
Postmaterialist	85	80	(19,846)

Birth Year of Respondent's Birth Cohort	Unadjusted	Adjusted for Education, Sex, Values, and Occupation	N
1966 - 1970	55%	46%	(5,022)
1956 - 1965	67	61	(31,405)
1946 - 1955	74	69	(35,842)
1936 - 1945	72	71	(29,804)
1926 - 1935	67	71	(26,804)
1916 - 1925	64	70	(23,867)
1906 - 1915	59	67	(17,820)
Before 1906	51	60	(6,995)

Table 10-5. (Concluded)

Respondent's Occupation	Unadjusted	Adjusted for Education, Sex, Values, and Birth Cohort	N
Executive	88%	73%	(5,124)
Professional	87	74	(3,132)
Clerical, sales	79	73	(30,761)
Student	72	70	(14,776)
Small business	72	68	(10,287)
Farmer	71	71	(5,911)
Manual worker	65	65	(32,375)
Unemployed	62	62	(8,203)
Retired	59	64	(25,594)
Housewife	57	64	(38,321)

Source: pooled data from twelve-nation European Community surveys, 1970-1985.
Note: Total N = 177,827.

than the other cohorts. As indicated above, this seems to reflect life cycle effects.

Finally, as the literature on postindustrial society suggests, there are significant differences in politicization according to occupational type, with those in the service sector considerably more apt to discuss politics than those engaged in manufacturing or agriculture. These differences diminish markedly when we adjust for differences in the other independent variables. For example, Table 10-5 shows an unadjusted difference of 23 points between executives and manual workers; but this gap shrinks to only 8 points when we control for the fact that the executives are better educated, more Postmaterialist, etc. Though it is not the dominant cause, the changing occupational structure also seems to encourage rising politicization.

Table 10-6 summarizes the results of a multiple classification analysis using the above variables plus nationality as predictors of whether or not one discusses politics. The eta coefficient indicates the strength of the zero-order relationship, while the beta coefficient shows how much impact a given variable has after we adjust for the effects of the other predictors. Nationality proves to be the strongest predictor of political discussion, and large cross-national differences persist even when we control for differences in education, values, occupation, and other variables. In chapter 1, we examined some of the historical factors, such as religion and early industrialization, that help shape political culture; a full analysis would go beyond the scope of this chapter. But our findings suggest that historical events that took place long ago, can leave a lasting imprint on a nation's rate of political participation.

Education, alone, explains almost as much of the variation in political

TABLE 10-6. MULTIPLE CLASSIFICATION ANALYSIS: PREDICTORS OF POLITICAL DISCUSSION RATES IN TWELVE NATIONS

	Eta	Beta
Nationality	.183	.172
Education	.211	.166
Gender	.161	.133
Value type	.171	.111
Age cohort	.125	.107
Occupation	.193	.071
$(N = 180,521)$	$R = .354$	$R^2 = .125$

Source: Based on analysis of combined data from Euro-Barometer surveys carried out from 1973 through 1985 in France, Italy, West Germany, United Kingdom, Belgium, Luxembourg, Netherlands, Ireland, Denmark, Greece, Spain, and Portugal.

participation as does nationality, even after we control for the effects of all the other variables included in this analysis, some of which are closely related to education. Gender, value type, and age cohort rank next. The net effects of occupation are relatively modest, though significant. While the zero-order relationship between occupation and political discussion rates is strong, this relationship weakens a great deal when we control for the fact that those in given occupations also tend to have distinctive educational levels, gender, and values and (to some extent) belong to different age cohorts.

These cross-sectional results have longitudinal implications. The better educated, the Postmaterialists, and those employed in the service sector all show relatively high rates of political discussion. Because all three of these categories are becoming more numerous in the adult population, we would expect a gradual rise in mass political participation. Moreover, the female role has traditionally exerted a strong inhibiting effect on political participation, but this effect is markedly weaker among the younger cohorts than among the older ones. This, too, would lead us to expect a gradual rise in political discussion rates as intergenerational population replacement takes place. Is any such phenomenon discernible?

The answer is yes. Figure 10-4 shows political discussion rates measured in each of the eight larger countries from which we have survey data throughout the period from 1973 to 1987 (data from Luxembourg are also available, but the number of respondents interviewed in that country is relatively small, and the results less reliable). The pattern is complex—as one would expect. There is considerable short-term fluctuation, with rates rising and falling in response to current conditions. As Scheuch (1968) has argued, there is some tendency for political discussion rates in a given

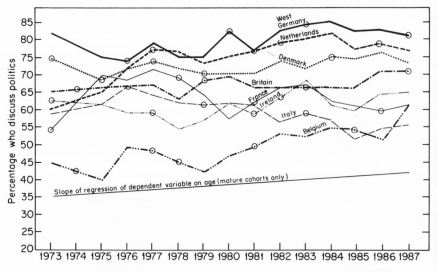

FIGURE 10-4. Percentage who discuss politics in eight nations, 1973–1987. Circle indicates year in which elections took place.

country to be higher in an election year. One nation—Italy—even shows an overall downward trend during this period. But when we examine the results from many countries, across a substantial period of time, we find an overall upward trend—and it rises at just about the rate that would be produced by intergenerational population replacement. Certain nations have a long-term tendency to show relatively high or relatively low rates of political discussion. The Germans always rank relatively high and the Belgians low, but nearly all of them also show an upward tendency. The amount of change is modest: on the average, only a few percentage points per decade. Thus the fluctuations from one year to the next can easily swamp the underlying trend in any given nation—making the trend invisible except in a large cross-national data array such as this. But in the long term, the cumulative effects of this process may be transforming the nature of politics in advanced industrial societies.

Table 10-7 shows the net change over time in each of these countries, grouping the surveys from several years together to minimize the impact of short-term fluctuations. Among the eight nations for which we have data from 1973 through 1987, seven show an increase in political discussion rates, while one shows a decrease. Across these eight nations there is an average increase of 4.5 percentage points. Data from Greece are also available, though only since 1980. The Greek public also shows an upward

TABLE 10-7.   POLITICAL DISCUSSION RATES OVER TIME, 1973 - 1987
(Percentage who discuss politics "frequently" or "occasionally")

	W. Germany	Denmark	Britain	Netherlands	Ireland
1973 - 1975	78%	70%	66%	63%	62%
1976 - 1978	76	72	66	75	57
1979 - 1981	78	70	68	74	59
1982 - 1987	83	74	68	78	64
Net change	+5	+4	+2	+15	+2

	Italy	France	Belgium	Greece	
1973 - 1975	60%	62%	42%	–	
1976 - 1978	64	68	47	–	
1979 - 1981	61	61	46	66%	
1982 - 1987	56	63	53	74	
Net change	-4	+1	+11	+8	

shift, indeed, a rather sharp one, which would raise the overall average if the Greek data were included with those from the other eight countries.

The reasons underlying the downward shift in our one deviant case, Italy, are no doubt complex. One factor however, is probably the increasing secularization of the Italian Communist party, which has evolved from an antisystem party, dramatically different from the mainstream parties, to a close approximation of a normal social democratic party that accepts the democratic rules of the game. This may be a healthy development for the future of democracy in Italy; but it means that Italian politics have become less exciting, less of a conflict between good and evil, and more of a choice between parties that are only incrementally different on key policy questions. If this is indeed contributing to the decline of political discussion among the Italian public, one might expect to witness a similar trend among the French public when the French Communist party ceases to be viewed as a radical alternative and possible threat to democratic institutions. But this decline would probably be a short-term phenomenon: for advanced industrial societies as a whole, the long-term trend is toward an increase in the more active, elite-directing forms of political participation.

RISING POLITICIZATION AND DECLINING PARTISANSHIP

It is important to specify precisely what is happening, however, for we are dealing with two distinct and seemingly contradictory trends. Despite the fact that the younger, better educated birth cohorts in Western Europe

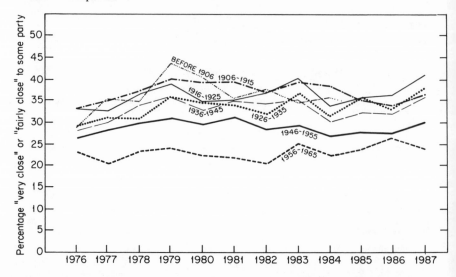

FIGURE 10-5. Strength of partisan loyalties by age cohort, 1976–1987. Based on combined samples from France, Italy, West Germany, the Netherlands, Belgium, Great Britain, Ireland, Luxembourg, and Denmark, weighted according to population of each country.

show consistently higher political discussion rates than do their elders, they have lower levels of political partisan loyalty. In surveys carried out from 1976 to 1987, our respondents were asked: "Do you consider yourself to be close to any particular political party? [if yes] Do you feel yourself to be very close to this party, fairly close, or merely a sympathizer?" Figure 10-5 shows the results of a cohort analysis of the responses. The pattern is virtually an inverted version of Figure 10-2. Throughout the past decade the older birth cohorts reported relatively high rates of political party loyalty, while the postwar cohorts were consistently less likely to feel close to some political party. This finding parallels a pattern of intergenerational decline in party identification that has been found among the American electorate during the past two decades (Nie, Verba, and Petrocik 1979; Pomper 1975; Abramson 1979); and it may help explain the fact that most West European countries have shown higher rates of electoral volatility in recent years than was generally true in the past (Pedersen 1979; Dalton, Flanagan, and Beck 1984). What makes this finding paradoxical, however, is the fact that the better educated and those who are most involved in politics are *most* apt to identify with some political party. The younger cohorts are better educated and, as we have seen, more apt to discuss politics—but in spite of this they are distinctly *less* likely to have a sense of party loyalty.

Have education and political involvement lost their power to encourage a sense of party loyalty among the young? No. Among this group, as among their elders, the highly educated and those who discuss politics are markedly more likely to feel close to some party than the less educated and politically uninvolved. Thus, their education and politicization predispose them to identify with *some* political party. But they have less incentive to identify with any specific political party, among the available choices. For the older cohorts, religion and social class gave powerful cues in establishing one's political party loyalties. The younger cohorts have a weaker tendency to polarize according to social class, and religion plays a less important role in their lives, as we saw in chapters 6 and 8. Moreover, the established political parties came into being in an era dominated by social class conflict and economic issues, and tend to remain polarized on this basis. But in recent years, a new axis of polarization has arisen based on cultural and quality of life issues. Today, the established political party configuration does not adequately reflect the most burning contemporary issues, and those who have grown up in the postwar era have relatively little motivation to identify with one of the established political parties.

Figure 10-5 suggests that the younger birth cohorts are characterized by lower political party loyalty rates than those of the older ones, and that these differences reflect cohort effects rather than aging effects. If this is true, then intergenerational population replacement should produce a gradual overall decline in political party ties. Like the rise in political discussion rates, this type of process would not produce dramatic short-term shifts. In any given country, the change from one year to the next would be scarcely perceptible, and could easily be swamped by nation-specific events. But in the long run, in most advanced industrial societies we should witness a gradual decline in partisan loyalty rates. Is any such phenomenon perceptible? Table 10-8 enables us to examine this question, showing party loyalty rates derived from data from a total of 207 representative national surveys carried out in the nine nations that have been members of the European Community since 1973.

Here, as with political discussion rates, the detailed trend is complex. When we examine it country by country, we find a large amount of short-term fluctuation, with the rates sometimes rising in one country at the same time as they are falling in another. The picture is further complicated by the fact that in Great Britain and Ireland, the surveys carried out prior to 1978 asked, "Do you consider yourself a *supporter* of any particular political party?" rather than "close to any particular political party?" Nevertheless, an overall tendency is reasonably clear, and remains present whether we include the British and Irish data, exclude them, or analyze them separately: Political party loyalty rates tend to fall. This trend is not

TABLE 10-8. POLITICAL PARTY LOYALTY RATES, 1976 - 1987
(Percentage who consider themselves close to some political party)

Year	Loyalty Rate	N
1976	69%	(17,103)
1977	67	(17,605)
1978	67	(17,351)
1979	70	(17,472)
1980	66	(8,835)
1981	71	(16,455)
1982	63	(17,954)
1983	65	(17,508)
1984	64	(17,655)
1985	61	(17,767)
1986	61	(17,650)
1987	61	(8,653)
Net change	-8	

Source: Combined data from Euro-Barometer surveys carried out in given years, in France, Italy, Great Britain, West Germany, Netherlands, Belgium, Luxembourg, Ireland, and Denmark.
Note: Percentages weighted according to population.

monotonic, for we find a high point in 1981, but this peak is anomalous, being inconsistent with the years immediately before and after it. The overall trend is downward, showing a net decline of 8 percentage points from 1976 to 1987.

In contrast to the trend toward rising rates of political discussion, there is no theoretical reason to expect the decline of partisanship to continue indefinitely. A realignment of political party systems that makes party polarization correspond more closely to issue polarization could bring it to a gradual halt. Such a realignment already seems to be taking place in some West European countries. But for the present the overall trend is downward.

The Impact of Cognitive Mobilization

This downward trend in party loyalties, interacting with the rising politicization brought by cognitive mobilization, is transforming the nature of partisanship among Western electorates. In order to measure the impact of cognitive mobilization reliably, we constructed an index of this process, based on two key indicators: (1) political discussion rates, measured as outlined above; and (2) the respondent's educational level, based on the age at which he or she left school. In constructing this index, we trichotomized educational levels, with the school-leaving ages of 16 through 19 constituting the middle category; since the question about political discussion also had three categories, the two variables produce an additive index with scores ranging from 1 to 5. For simplicity of discussion, we will speak of an individual as "low" on cognitive mobilization if he or she has a score below 3 on this index: in other words, if the respondent's education ended before age 16 and he or she discusses politics at most "occasionally" *or* if the respondent's education ended by age 19, and he or she never discusses politics. Those with scores higher than 3 on this index will be described as ranking "high" on cognitive mobilization. When we analyze the cognitive mobilization scores of our respondents, we find pronounced cohort effects. The pattern here is even stronger than that shown in Figure 10-2, because educational levels are less strongly influenced by the life cycle effects that complicate and weaken the relationship between age and political discussion.

Figure 10-6 illustrates these cohort differences for the combined nine nations for which we have data from 1973 to 1987. The intercohort differences in cognitive mobilization levels are large indeed: Cumulating the data from all available years (not shown in figure), we find that among the oldest birth cohort (those born before 1906), only 24 percent rank "high" on our cognitive mobilization index. Among the youngest cohort, fully 60 percent rank "high" on cognitive mobilization. Once again, we have clear indications of stable cohort differences, so once again let us ask the question "Does population replacement seem to be producing an overall shift in the indicated direction?" The answer, again, is yes. Among the nine nations as a whole, we find a shift from 41 percent who ranked "high" on our cognitive mobilization index in 1973 to 49 percent ranking "high" in 1986. The shift is gradual but significant; over a period of several decades, it could transform the modal position of the electorate from one predominantly uninvolved except at elections to one ready to intervene actively in the political process.

COGNITIVE MOBILIZATION AND
ELITE-DIRECTING POLITICAL ACTION

The consequences of cognitive mobilization do not end with an increased propensity to discuss politics. On the contrary, cognitive mobili-

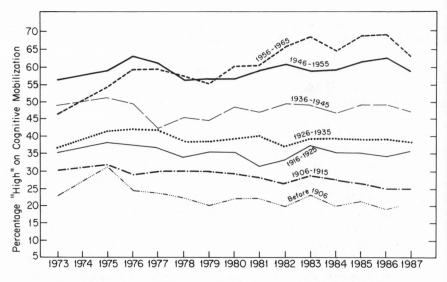

FIGURE 10-6. Percentage "high" on cognitive mobilization by age cohort, 1973–1987. Based on combined data from France, West Germany, Great Britain, Italy, the Netherlands, Belgium, Luxembourg, Ireland, and Denmark, weighted in proportion to population.

zation greatly increases the likelihood that citizens will engage in a broad repertoire of elite-directing political actions, ranging from petitions to demonstrations to boycotts, unofficial strikes, occupying buildings, and blocking traffic, in order to articulate political grievances and put pressure on policymakers to comply with their demands. Table 10-9 illustrates this point with data showing political activism vis-à-vis cognitive mobilization level in each of eight Western democracies.

The dependent variable in Table 10-9 is based on a Guttman scale that measures the respondent's propensity to engage in unconventional political behavior. The protest activities just described are scalar—that is, they can be arrayed in a given order, ranging from "easy" actions, such as taking part in a lawful demonstration, to relatively "difficult" ones, such as occupying buildings or blocking traffic. Those respondents who are willing to take part in any given type of activity, are probably also willing to undertake any of the "easier" types of action (Barnes, Kaase et al. 1979, 57–96). Table 10-9 shows the percentages in each nation who are willing to take part in a boycott or more difficult actions, broken down by cognitive mobilization level.

The relationship between cognitive mobilization and unconventional political action is strong. In each of the eight nations in which the political

TABLE 10-9.   UNCONVENTIONAL POLITICAL PARTICIPATION BY COGNITIVE
MOBILIZATION IN EIGHT NATIONS
(Percentage who have taken part in a boycott or more difficult activity)

R's Level of Cognitive Mobilization	Britain	W. Germany	Netherlands	U.S.
1. Low	12%	15%	28%	7%
2. Medium-low	23	21	33	21
3. Medium	30	28	48	32
4. Medium-high	46	40	53	41
5. High	53	61	52	57

R's Level of Cognitive Mobilization	Austria	Italy	Switzerland	Finland
1. Low	6%	20%	13%	7%
2. Medium-low	15	28	18	15
3. Medium	20	29	29	25
4. Medium-high	37	46	51	40
5. High	39	70	55	33

Source: Eight-nation Political Action survey, 1974 - 1976.

action study was carried out, those with high cognitive mobilization scores are far likelier to report that they have taken part in a boycott, or would be willing to do so, than those with low levels of cognitive mobilization. Across the eight nations as a whole, among those with a cognitive mobilization score of 1 (that is, those who left school by age 15 and who never discuss politics), only 14 percent report that they have participated in a boycott or are willing to do so. Among those with scores of 5 (those whose education continued beyond age 19 and who frequently discuss politics), 53 percent report this level of unconventional political participation. In other words, a high level of cognitive mobilization almost quadruples propensity for elite-directing behavior.

When we combine the effects of cognitive mobilization with those of Materialist/Postmaterialist value change, the impact is even greater. Figure 10-7 illustrates this phenomenon, using the combined results from the eight nations just discussed. As we saw in the preceding chapter, Postmaterialists are more likely to engage in unconventional political protest than Materialists. Moreover, values interact with cognitive mobilization in such a way that at high levels of cognitive mobilization, the differences between value types are magnified considerably. At every level of cognitive mobilization, Postmaterialists show higher levels of protest potential than do Materialists. A group that has emerged recently, in societies that are still dominated by Materialist goals, the Postmaterialists are relatively apt to be

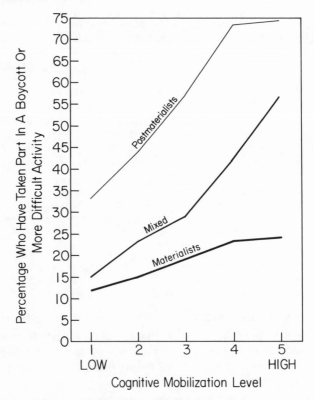

FIGURE 10-7. Unconventional political participation by cognitive mobilization and value type. Combined eight-nation data from Political Action study, 1974–1976.

dissatisfied with the established social order; and the disruption and property damage that may result from unconventional political action weighs less heavily for the Postmaterialists, threatening things they value less than the Materialists do.

But rising levels of cognitive mobilization widen the distance between Postmaterialists and Materialists: Those with high levels of cognitive mobilization become more likely to act on the basis of their underlying values. The combined effects of these two variables are powerful indeed. Among those with Materialist values and low levels of cognitive mobilization, only 12 percent have taken part, or are willing to take part, in a boycott or more difficult activity. Among Postmaterialists with high levels of cognitive mobilization, 74 percent have done so or are ready to do.

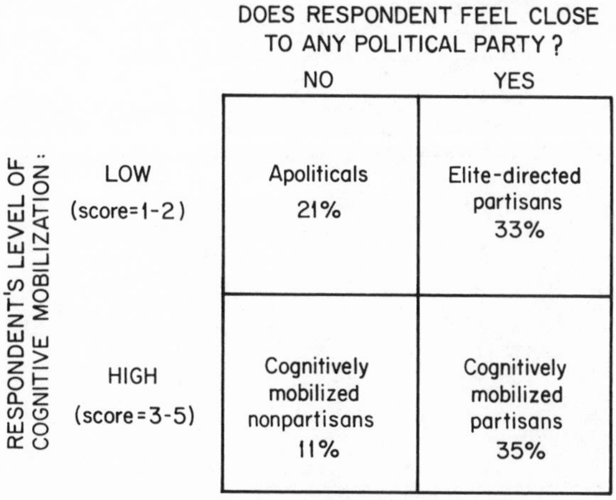

DOES RESPONDENT FEEL CLOSE
TO ANY POLITICAL PARTY ?

		NO	YES
RESPONDENT'S LEVEL OF COGNITIVE MOBILIZATION:	LOW (score=1-2)	Apoliticals 21%	Elite-directed partisans 33%
	HIGH (score=3-5)	Cognitively mobilized nonpartisans 11%	Cognitively mobilized partisans 35%

FIGURE 10-8. Political mobilization typology.
Adapted from Dalton 1984a.

CHANGING PATTERNS OF POLITICAL PARTISANSHIP

The process of cognitive mobilization seems to be increasing the potential for elite-directing political action among Western publics. It also seems to be changing the nature of partisan support (Dalton 1984a) and the types of political parties Western electorates are willing to support.

One component of this change results from the interaction between cognitive mobilization, on one hand, and the decline of partisan loyalties, on the other hand. As Figure 10-8 illustrates, these two factors give rise to four patterns of partisanship: (1) apoliticals—those with low levels of education and political involvement (or cognitive mobilization) who do not feel close to any political party; (2) elite-directed partisans—those with low levels of political skills who nevertheless feel close to some political party (a type of partisanship particularly prevalent in the early stages of industrialization, when a relatively uneducated public is led to the polls by hierarchical, elite-directed organizations); (3) cognitively mobilized partisans—those with high levels of political skills who feel close to some party (the ideal type of the informed and involved party identifier); and (4) cognitively mobilized nonpartisans—those with high political skills who do not feel close to any party. This fourth type is a deviant one—for high levels of education and political involvement usually lead to development of partisan loyalties. This still tends to be the case: Among the cognitively mobilized, partisans are more than three times as numerous as nonpartisans (while among those low on cognitive mobilization, they are only one

TABLE 10-10. INTERGENERATIONAL CONTRASTS IN TYPES OF POLITICAL
MOBILIZATION

Cohort's Birth Years	Apoliticals	Elite-Directed Partisans	Cognitively Mobilized Partisans	Cognitively Mobilized Nonpartisans	N
1956 - 1965	22%	17%	41%	21%	(22,661)
1946 - 1955	17	24	44	15	(26,220)
1936 - 1945	19	33	38	10	(24,340)
1926 - 1935	22	38	31	8	(21,153)
1916 - 1925	23	42	28	7	(19,036)
1906 - 1915	23	47	24	5	(15,732)
Before 1906	28	49	19	4	(5,892)

Source: Combined data from Euro-Barometer surveys carried out from 1973 through 1984.
Note: Percentages for some cohorts do not total 100 because of rounding.

and a half times as numerous). Nevertheless, the cognitively mobilized nonpartisans are a growing group, and play a crucial role, providing the cutting edge for ongoing processes of political realignment.

As we might expect, the cognitively mobilized nonpartisans are far more numerous among the younger birth cohorts than among the older ones. Table 10-10 provides the evidence on this score. Among the two oldest cohorts, this is a tiny deviant group, comprising no more than 4 or 5 percent of the electorate. Among the two postwar cohorts it is far more numerous, constituting 21 percent of the group born from 1956 to 1965. Insofar as the differences registered from oldest to youngest cohort reflect a pattern of historical change, this type seems to be becoming much more widespread; it is five times as prevalent among the youngest cohort as among the oldest.

Cognitively mobilized partisans also become much more numerous as we move from the oldest to the youngest cohort, but the proportional change is not as dramatic. This type becomes roughly twice as widespread as we move from old to young, reflecting the gradual emergence of an increasingly sophisticated electorate.

In absolute magnitude, the largest change of all is the decline in the ranks of the elite-directed partisans—the loyal troops, oriented by group ties more than by concerns for specific political decisions. This type constitutes nearly half of the entire electorate among the two oldest cohorts. Among the youngest cohort, they have dwindled to only 17 percent, and actually are less numerous than the cognitively mobilized nonpartisans (whom they outnumber by 12 to 1 among the oldest cohort). There is little change among the apoliticals, whose rise in cognitive mobilization manifests itself mainly in the decline of elite-directed partisanship.

These cohort differences imply (but, of course, do not prove) that we are experiencing some large and basic changes in the nature of political partisanship in Western democracies. Our findings suggest that the elite-directed partisanship that was the basis of the disciplined, hierarchical political parties that dominated the scene for much of this century, is in severe decline. Elite-directed partisans have shifted from being the mode (and virtually the majority) among the older generation to being an uncharacteristic, almost deviant type of citizen among the youngest generation of voters. The new modal pattern is that of cognitively mobilized partisanship, involving a shift from unquestioning loyalty to a more informed, and more conditional, loyalty. Moreover, along with this, has come the rise of a politically sophisticated group that has not been mobilized by any institution, but has an autonomous concern with politics—and may be available for involvement in new political movements or new political parties, or the takeover of existing ones.

New political movements have arisen in profusion in recent years. In most countries, launching a new political party is far more difficult than launching a movement, since it is severely limited by the electoral laws and political institutions of a given society, but even this has occurred recently in Great Britain, West Germany, and France, where, respectively, the Social Democrats, the Greens, and the National Front have emerged as significant political factors during the past several years.

Is there any evidence that the cohort differences shown in Table 10-10 are being translated into longitudinal changes through the population replacement process? The data in Table 10-10 reflect seven cohorts that span a period of sixty years. The longitudinal data presently available cover a period of only a dozen years. Consequently, the changes over time shown in Table 10-11, are smaller than the cohort differences shown in Table 10-10, and correspondingly more vulnerable to distortion through the impact of short-term fluctuations. Nevertheless the longitudinal changes shown in Table 10-11 tend to confirm the changes implicit in the cohort differences. The two largest changes shown in Table 10-11 are (1) a decline in elite-directed partisanship, which falls from 34 percent of the sample in 1976 to only 27 percent in 1987, corresponding to the massive decline of elite-directed partisanship shown in Table 10-10, and (2) a rise in the proportion of cognitively mobilized nonpartisans, from 10 percent of the sample in 1976 to 16 percent in 1987, making them 60 percent more numerous than they were a decade earlier.

TABLE 10-11. DISTRIBUTION OF POLITICAL MOBILIZATION TYPES, 1976 - 1987

Year	Apoliticals	Elite-Directed Partisans	Cognitively Mobilized Partisans	Cognitively Mobilized Nonpartisans	N
1976	20%	34%	36%	10%	(16,731)
1977	22	32	35	11	(17,389)
1978[a]	22	34	33	10	(17,015)
1979	20	36	34	10	(17,303)
1980	23	34	33	11	(8,685)[b]
1981	18	35	36	11	(1,069)
1982	23	29	34	14	(17,672)
1983	21	30	35	14	(18,019)
1984	22	31	34	13	(17,209)
1985	24	28	33	15	(17,767)
1986	24	27	33	17	(17,920)
1987	23	27	34	16	(8,831)

Source: Combined results of Euro-Barometer surveys 5 - 27, carried out in the nine nations that were members of European Community in 1976.

[a]The question about political party loyalties was modified in Britain and Ireland starting in 1977; however, subsequent British and Irish surveys show a continuation of the same downward trend as in previous surveys. Starting the series in 1978, or excluding the British and Irish data, we still witness a gradual downward trend.

[b]The N for the 1980 surveys is smaller than in other years because in the Fall 1980 survey the question about party loyalty was asked in a noncomparable format; these data have been excluded.

The two other changes shown in Table 10-11 are small, but do not correspond to the cohort differences. Table 10-10 shows a slight decrease in the percentage of apoliticals as we move from old to young, but longitudinally we find an increase. And Table 10-10 shows a sizable increase in cognitively mobilized partisanship, but the longitudinal results shown in Table 10-11 show a slight decrease. We suspect that the latter may reflect short-term fluctuations; the availability of data covering a longer time span will demonstrate whether or not this is the case. In any event, both the decline of elite-directed partisanship and a pronounced growth in the ranks of cognitively mobilized nonpartisans seem to be confirmed; and these are the theoretically crucial shifts.

Each of these trends facilitates change in the type of political parties that Western electorates support. The decline of elite-directed partisanship tends to erode the base of support for established political parties, especially those that persist largely because of traditional ties rather than be-cause of their position on contemporary issues. Conversely, the emergence of growing numbers of cognitively mobilized nonpartisans, creates a po-tential constituency for new parties. Table 10-12 gives the cumulative re-sults for each of the nine countries from which we have a large enough number of cases to yield reasonably reliable results, even for certain small, but interesting new parties. As this table demonstrates, the four respective political mobilization types support very different kinds of political par-ties. Within the Left, for example, the Socialist and Communist parties tend to have disproportionate support from elite-directed partisans. Con-versely, newer parties, such as the West German Greens, the French and

TABLE 10-12. VOTING INTENTION BY POLITICAL MOBILIZATION TYPE,
1976 - 1984

Party	Apoliticals	Elite-Directed Partisans	Cognitive Partisans	Cognitive Nonpartisans	N
1. France					
Left Socialist (PSU)	6%	2%	4%	5%	(858)
Communist	8	12	13	3	(2,439)
Socialist	33	39	39	27	(8,333)
Ecologist	10	3	6	19	(1,581)
Left Radical	3	3	3	4	(610)
Democratic Center	4	4	4	8	(994)
Radical	3	2	1	2	(407)
Giscardian	17	17	14	16	(3,478)
Gaullist	16	18	17	15	(3,839)
2. Belgium					
Communist	2	2	3	4	(501)
Socialist	31	35	22	20	(5,841)
Ecologist	3	2	4	9	(709)
Liberal (3 parties)	11	11	16	20	(2,774)
Flemish People's	6	5	10	7	(1,523)
Francophone	5	4	6	8	(1,106)
Christian Social	42	41	38	32	(8,261)
3. Netherlands					
Communist	2	1	1	1	(275)
Pacifist Socialist	2	1	4	4	(591)
Radical	1	1	3	3	(507)
Socialists	41	42	28	27	(6,948)
Democrats 1966	6	4	9	15	(1,668)
Dem. Soc. 1970	1	-	1	1	(148)
Liberal	11	11	23	18	(3,865)
Christian Democrat	30	35	27	26	(6,220)
Conservative religious parties	6	4	3	5	(676)
4. West Germany					
Communist	1	-	1	-	(85)
Social Democrat	43	46	38	38	(8,855)
Greens	2	1	6	10	(872)
Liberals	5	4	7	10	(1,277)
Christian Democrat	48	49	48	42	(10,153)
Neo-Nazi	-	-	-	1	(43)

TABLE 10-12. (Concluded)

Party	Apoliticals	Elite- Directed Partisans	Cognitive Partisans	Cognitive Nonpartisans	N
5. Italy					
Proletarian Democrat	1%	1%	4%	9%	(495)
Radical	1	1	4	4	(540)
Communist	16	23	27	10	(5,305)
Socialist	20	19	17	17	(4,046)
Social Democrat	5	4	4	7	(899)
Republican	3	3	5	14	(944)
Christian Democrat	48	42	28	29	(8,228)
Liberal	4	2	4	8	(742)
Neo-Fascist	4	5	7	3	(1,304)
6. Britain					
Labour	43	43	33	30	(8,445)
Social Democrat	7	3	6	10	(1,238)
Liberal	13	8	8	14	(2,166)
Ecologist	2	2	2	2	(376)
Conservative	36	43	52	46	(9,860)
7. Ireland					
Labour	17	13	11	15	(2,644)
Workers' Party	1	1	1	1	(141)
Fine Gael	27	27	36	37	(6,298)
Fianna Fail	56	59	52	47	(11,083)
8. Denmark					
Communist	1	2	3	2	(407)
Left Socialist	1	1	6	9	(733)
Socialist People's	5	4	11	14	(1,589)
Social Democrats	45	47	29	25	(7,762)
Democratic Center	4	2	3	5	(591)
Radicals	4	3	5	5	(835)
Single Tax	2	1	2	3	(367)
Conservative	14	13	20	18	(3,280)
Christian People's	3	3	2	2	(469)
Right Liberals	11	17	12	10	(2,832)
Progress	10	7	7	7	(1,487)
9. Greece					
Communist (Moscow)	4	8	18	6	(998)
Communist (Interior)	1	1	4	7	(232)
Socialist	58	58	56	57	(4,545)
Union of Dem. Center	1	1	1	2	(72)
New Democracy	33	29	19	22	(1,893)
Democratic Unity	1	—	1	3	(64)
Liberal	2	1	—	2	(72)

Belgian Ecologists, the Dutch Democrats '66, and the Proletarian Democrats (in Italy), and even the National Front (in France) draw their support
largely from cognitively mobilized nonpartisans. This also holds true,
though to a lesser degree, of Britain's Social Democratic party—a new
party, in a sense, but one that was formed by the breakup of a long-established party and is closely linked with another long-established party.

CONCLUSION

The potential for political action among Western publics is gradually rising. This fact is only intermittently evident, however, for in any given country, the amount of activity that takes place at any given time is conditioned by the issues and the political situation currently prevailing. But when we examine evidence from a score of advanced industrial societies, with a substantial time series from a number of them, we find an overall rise in individual level politicization. This increase can be traced to three factors: (1) rising rates of education and exposure to political information among younger birth cohorts, as compared with older ones; (2) the dwindling of the female deficit in politicization— while the traditional female role was incompatible with most forms of political action, gender differences are modest among those cohorts that reached maturity most recently; and (3) the spread of Postmaterialist values—being raised with a sense of economic and physical security apparently encourages one to devote a larger share of attention to relatively remote and abstract concerns, such as politics.

The impact of all three of these processes is linked with intergenerational population replacement; consequently, it makes itself felt only gradually. Data from eight West European countries, from 1973 through 1987, show a mean increase in political discussion rates of 4.5 percentage points across these eight countries, over the fourteen-year period. This amount of change could easily be overlooked, or swamped by short-term fluctuations, if we were examining data from only one country, or over a shorter period of time. But its cumulative long-term effects may be substantial.

The impact of this process tends to be concealed by the fact that it is occurring jointly with falling rates of political party loyalty (which showed a mean decline of 8 percentage points in the same eight nations from 1976 to 1987). While electorates are becoming more politicized, their behavior is becoming less constrained by established organizations. Thus, the rising individual level potential for political activism is partially offset by a decline in the organizations that have traditionally provided external mobilization. The iron law of oligarchy has been weakened, and the old-line political elites are gradually losing control. This, together with the new issues raised by Postmaterialism, has been conducive to the emergence of new political movements and political parties. The rise of the West German Greens, for example, reflects both the emergence of a Postmaterialist constituency whose outlook is not captured by the existing political parties and the emergence of a growing pool of voters who are politicized but do not feel tied to established parties. From 1976 to 1987, the proportion of cognitively mobilized nonpartisans in Western Europe nearly doubled. This points to a growing potential for elite-directing political behavior, aimed at achieving specific policy changes, rather than simply providing support for one set of elites instead of another. Politics in Western societies is gradually becoming less institutionalized and less predictable, but is being brought under increasingly close public scrutiny.

CHAPTER 11

New Social Movements: Values, Ideology, and Cognitive Mobilization

THE MULTIPLE CAUSES OF NEW SOCIAL MOVEMENTS

Participation in new social movements reflects the interaction of a number of factors and can be analyzed on several different levels. On one level, it reflects the existence of objective problems, such as the degradation of the environment, the exploitation of women, the coldness and impersonality of industrial society, or the danger of war; people rarely engage in political action unless there is some problem to solve. On another level, it is difficult for isolated individuals to engage in effective political action; political participation is facilitated by the existence of social networks or political organizations that coordinate the actions of many individuals. But people do not act unless they want to attain some goal. The existence of problems and organizations would have no effect unless some value system or ideology motivated people to act.

The boundary between an ideology and a value system is not sharply defined; both are belief systems that may lead to a coherent orientation toward a whole range of specific issues. But the term "ideology" is generally understood to refer to an action plan propagated by some specific political party or movement; it is adopted more or less consciously as the result of explicit indoctrination. A "value system," on the other hand, reflects one's socialization as a whole, particularly that of one's early years. An ideology might be adopted or rejected from one day to the next through rational persuasion. Values are less cognitive and more affective and tend to be relatively enduring. They may motivate one to adopt an ideology. Thus, a given ideology, per se, would not necessarily be associated with enduring intergenerational differences, except insofar as they reflected differences in underlying values.

Even when we take account of problems, organizations, values, and ideology, we still have not considered all the major influences on participation in new social movements. Effective political action requires the presence of certain skills among the relevant individuals. Even severe problems or a superb organization may fail to mobilize a population consisting of illiterate and apolitical people. The term "cognitive mobilization'' refers to the development of the political skills that are needed to cope with the politics of a large-scale society; as we saw in the preceding chapter, relatively high or low levels of these skills are an enduring characteristic of given individuals and of given political cultures.

Finally, there is a significant interaction between values and cognitive mobilization. Values, we have argued, have a relatively strong affective component; they may be present even when their cognitive implications have not been worked out. "Preferences need no inferences," as Zajonc (1980) puts it. Considerable thought and effort may be required to develop the logical connection between given values and the appropriate political stance. Consequently, the impact of values on political behavior tends to be greatest among those with relatively high levels of education, political information, political interest, and political skills: in short, among those with high levels of cognitive mobilization. For the remainder of the public, values and issue-specific attitudes (and behavior) may be only weakly correlated. The potential influence of values remains latent until a situation arises that makes their implications salient. Accordingly, we are likely to find more relationship between basic values and active participation in a movement than between values and relatively passive expressions of attitudes. This is because active participation occurs when the given topic has become salient; one has thought about it and worked out the cognitive implications of one's central values. In survey research, we can elicit responses concerning almost any topic; but these responses often reflect superficial reactions produced on the spur of the moment. The fact that given survey responses may be shallow does not mean that relevant values do not exist, as we saw in chapter 3; under appropriate conditions, when the individuals are given the time and incentive to work out the implications of their basic orientations, or when the given topic becomes a salient part of their lives, the observed connection between values and behavior may be very strong.

As this chapter will demonstrate, the Materialist/Postmaterialist dimension has played a crucial role in the rise of the wave of the new social movements that became increasingly prominent in recent years. Clearly, the emergence of new values has not been the sole factor involved. Objective problems, organizations, and ideologies have all been at work. And the emergence of the new social movements owes much to the gradually rising level of political skills among mass publics, as education has become more widespread and political information more pervasive. But the emergence of new value priorities has also been an important factor. The rise of the ecology movement, for example, is not simply due to the fact that the environment is in worse condition than it used to be; it is not even clear that it is. Partly, this development has taken place because the public has become more sensitive to the quality of the environment than it was a generation ago. Similarly, women do not seem to be more disadvantaged today than they were a few decades ago; but it does seem clear that they have come to place greater emphasis on self-fulfillment and on the opportunity to have a career outside the home.

Schmidt (1984), Mueller-Rommel (1984), and Buerklin (1984) all found that support for the West German Green party very disproportionately came from Postmaterialists. We believe that this represents merely one case of a much broader phenomenon. Postmaterialist values underlie many of the new social movements—for the Postmaterialists emphasize fundamentally different value priorities from those that have dominated industrial society for many decades. The established political parties that control electoral politics in most Western societies emerged in an era when social class conflict dominated the political agenda; and existing alignments still largely reflect this orientation. But the old alignments do not adequately reflect such new issues as the women's movement, the environmentalist movement, or the opposition to nuclear power. Because they seek goals that the existing political parties are not well adapted to pursue, Postmaterialists are likely to turn to new social movements. In the takeoff phase of industrial revolution, economic growth was the central problem. Postmaterialists have become increasingly numerous in recent decades, and they place less emphasis on economic growth and more emphasis on the noneconomic quality of life. Their support for environmentalism reflects this concern—in explicit reference to the quality of the physical environment and (less overtly, but at least equally important) in a concern for the quality of the social environment, with Postmaterialists seeking less hierarchical, more intimate and informal relations between people. It is not that the Postmaterialists reject the fruits of prosperity—but simply that their value priorities are less strongly dominated by the imperatives that were central to early industrial society.

Similarly, the rise of the peace movement reflected many factors and can be analyzed on a number of levels. It can be traced to specific political decisions made by specific political leaders, in a specific strategic context. The presence of Postmaterialists would not automatically have generated the movement in the absence of these other factors. But it does seem clear that the emergence of Postmaterialism was one of the key conditions that facilitated the development of the peace movement in Western Europe in the 1980s, and that enabled it to mobilize larger numbers of supporters than any of its various forerunners, from the early days of the Cold War through the Vietnam era.

Why were Postmaterialists so much likelier to be active in the peace movement than those with other values? Was it because they are more afraid of war? The answer to the latter question is no. Postmaterialists are concerned with war, but they are no likelier to feel that World War III is imminent than the rest of the public. Instead, the linkage between Postmaterialism and the peace movement seems to reflect two main elements, one of which is a relative sense of security. Postmaterialist values develop from a sense of economic and physical security, and the latter part of the syndrome includes a sense of national security as well as domestic security. Postmaterialists are likelier than Materialists to take national security for granted. Accordingly, West European Postmaterialists are more apt to feel that the American presence in Europe is unnecessary and that additional arms are superfluous.

The other side of the coin is that Postmaterialism has emerged in a setting in which war seems absurd. Since the end of World War II, it has seemed that the only war likely to take place in Western Europe would be a total war involving both of the superpowers. In the thermonuclear age, the costs of such a war would almost certainly outweigh the gains by a vast margin. Indeed, if the nuclear winter hypothesis is correct, it would wipe out human life in the entire Northern hemisphere, and possibly the Southern one as well. By any cost-benefit analysis, this is not a paying proposition.

This has not always been the case. Throughout most of history, it has been at least conceivable that the material gains of a given war might exceed the material costs. In an economy of scarcity, it was even possible that under extreme conditions, a given tribe or nation's only hope for survival might lie in a successful war to seize a neighbor's land or food or water supply. In advanced industrial society, the cost-benefit ratio has swung far in the opposite direction. On one hand, the costs of war have become very high; and, on the other hand, the benefits are relatively low; with a high level of technology, there are easier and safer ways to get rich than by plundering one's neighbors (as the recent history of Germany and Japan illustrates). From a Postmaterialist perspective, war seems absurd.

The rise of the new social movements is not a result of values alone; to some extent, the emergence of these movements also reflects explicit ideological indoctrination. But to pose the question as one of values *or* ideology is a false choice. It is both. Moreover, the rise of new values constitutes a key element in any explanation of why a new ideological perspective has arisen, for the ideology of the new social movements is not simply the traditional ideology of the Left. Except in the very general sense that the Left (then as now) constitutes the side of the political spectrum that is seeking social change, the traditional and contemporary meanings of "Left" are very different: the Old Left viewed both economic growth and technological progress as fundamentally good and progressive;

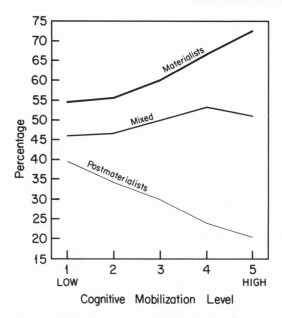

FIGURE 11-1. Percentage voting for parties of
the Right and Center (Christian Democrats, Conservatives, Liberals, etc.) by value type and level
of cognitive mobilization. Combined nine-nation
sample, 1973–1984 (N = 104,934).

the New Left is suspicious of both. The Old Left had a working-class social
base; the New Left has a predominantly middle-class base. To a great extent, the spread of new values and the rise of new issues have already
reshaped the meaning of "Left" and "Right." To mass publics, the core
meaning of "Left" is no longer simply state ownership of the means of
production and related issues focusing on class conflict. Increasingly, it
refers to a cluster of issues concerning the quality of the physical and social
environment, the role of women, nuclear power, and nuclear weapons.
The meaning of "Left" is changing—imperceptibly but steadily.

THE IMPACT OF POSTMATERIALIST VALUES AND
COGNITIVE MOBILIZATION

For the reasons outlined above, Materialist/Postmaterialist values have
their greatest impact on the behavior of those individuals who rank highest
on cognitive mobilization. Figures 11-1, 11-2, and 11-3 illustrate the relationship among cognitive mobilization, Materialist/Postmaterialist values, and voting behavior that holds true throughout Western Europe and is

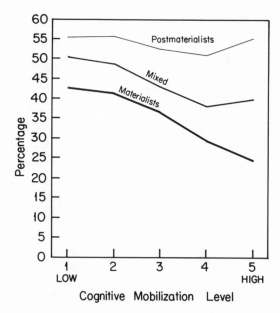

FIGURE 11-2. Percentage voting for traditional
Left parties (Communists, Socialists, and Social
Democrats) by value type and level of cognitive
mobilization. Combined nine-nation sample,
1973–1984 (N = 104,934).

based on scores of thousands of interviews. As Figure 11-1 demonstrates,
those with Materialist values are substantially more likely to vote for the
parties of the Right and Center than are those with Postmaterialist or mixed
values. The basic values of the former group correspond relatively well to
the priorities that have long prevailed in industrial society. Hence, Materialists are relatively likely to support conservative political parties.

But the impact of one's values on how one votes is vastly greater among
the more educated and the politically involved than among those who give
relatively little attention to politics. Among those who rank lowest on our
cognitive mobilization index (that is, those who left school before the age
of 16 and who ''never'' discuss politics with their friends), 55 percent of
the Materialists vote for the parties of the Right or Center, while only 40
percent of the Postmaterialists do so—a difference of 15 percentage points.
Among those who rank highest on our cognitive mobilization index (that
is, those whose schooling continued until they were 20 or older and who
''frequently'' discuss politics with their friends), the respective figures are
72 percent and 20 percent, a gap of more than 50 percentage points. This

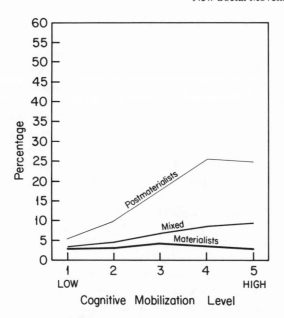

FIGURE 11-3. Percentage voting for New Politics parties (New Left, ecologist, and ethnic parties) by value type and level of cognitive mobilization. Combined nine-nation sample, 1973–1984 (N = 104,934).

is a powerful illustration of the fact that thought and attention are required in order for one's basic values to become articulated with one's behavior.

Among those with Materialist values, the more educated and politically involved one is, the more likely one is to vote for the parties of the Right and Center. Conversely, among the Postmaterialists, those who are most informed about politics and who discuss politics most frequently find a discrepancy between their own goals and the priorities emphasized by the conservative parties. Despite the fact that Postmaterialists tend to come from relatively prosperous middle-class strata that have traditionally supported the parties of the Right, only a small minority of the cognitively mobilized Postmaterialists vote for the Right or Center.

With rising levels of cognitive mobilization, Postmaterialists desert the parties of the Right and Center overwhelming. Yet, as Figure 11-2 shows, cognitive mobilization produces scarcely any increase in Postmaterialist support for the traditional established parties of the Left. Where do the cognitively mobilized Postmaterialists go? They give their backing to New Politics parties, and to ecology parties in particular. The West German

Greens, for example, are above all a party of Postmaterialists with high levels of cognitive mobilization.

Thus, the established parties of the Left are fighting on two fronts. Their core constituency is predominantly Materialist—and under current conditions, rising levels of cognitive mobilization encourage this group to gravitate toward the Right, as a heightened political involvement makes them more aware of the erosion of traditional cultural values. But, at the same time, the established parties of the Left do not necessarily gain the support of those most sympathetic to cultural change, the Postmaterialists. Postmaterialists tend to find the established parties of the Left too conservative on these issues, and with rising cognitive mobilization, they tend to be drawn to new parties that are more responsive to Postmaterialist goals than is the leadership of the established Left parties.

Ecology parties have a much larger potential electorate than their share of the vote in national elections might seem to indicate. As we saw in chapter 8, a far larger share of the West European electorate now say they might vote for an ecology party than would consider voting for a communist party. Because they are new and tend to be poorly organized, faction-ridden, and inadequately financed, these parties are unlikely to outpoll the highly organized and disciplined communist parties in the foreseeable future. But they represent one symptom of a broad underlying process of political change that has given rise to the environmentalist movement and a variety of other new social movements.

Participation in these movements is strongly related to whether one has Postmaterialist or Materialist values, in each of the twelve nations of the European Community, as Table 11-1 demonstrates. This table is based on responses to the following question, included in Euro-Barometer surveys 17, 22, and 25: "There are a number of groups and movements seeking support of the public. For each of the following movements, can you tell me (a) whether you approve (strongly or somewhat) or disapprove (somewhat or strongly); and (b) whether you are a member or would be likely to join, or would certainly not join."

These movements include "the ecology movement," "movements concerned with stopping the construction or use of nuclear power plants," and "anti-war or anti-nuclear weapons movements." These items were originally developed by Nicholas Watts and David Handley, and included in the Euro-Barometer surveys under the sponsorship of the Berlin Science Center. Table 11-1 shows each country's percentages of Materialists, Postmaterialists, and mixed types saying they are members of, or might join, each of these three movements in 1986.

The proportion saying that they are members or would join these movements varies greatly from one nation to another. It is consistently lowest

TABLE 11-1. MEMBERSHIP OR POTENTIAL MEMBERSHIP IN NEW SOCIAL MOVEMENTS
BY MATERIALIST/POSTMATERIALIST VALUES IN TWELVE NATIONS, 1986

1. Respondent Is Member of, or Might Join, ECOLOGY MOVEMENT:

Value Type	Belgium	Denmark	France	Portugal	Britain	Italy
Materialist	4%	8%	8%	8%	10%	15%
Mixed	9	9	11	17	21	31
Postmaterialist	10	26	23	21	45	38
Total	8	11	12	12	22	26

Value Type	Ireland	Lux.	W. Germany	Neth.	Spain	Greece
Materialist	27%	26%	13%	28%	31%	40%
Mixed	32	35	34	35	42	52
Postmaterialist	43	57	64	52	72	78
Total	31	35	37	38	42	50

2. Respondent Is Member of, or Might Join, MOVEMENT AGAINST NUCLEAR
POWER PLANTS:

Value Type	Belgium	France	Portugal	Italy	Lux.	Denmark
Materialist	1%	5%	7%	9%	9%	14%
Mixed	9	6	16	19	17	13
Postmaterialist	3	13	24	21	24	29
Total	5	6	12	15	15	16

Value Type	Neth.	Britain	Spain	W. Germany	Ireland	Greece
Materialist	10%	9%	21%	9%	30%	41%
Mixed	12	17	30	30	40	53
Postmaterialist	31	37	55	59	51	77
Total	17	18	30	34	38	50

3. Respondent Is Member of, or Might Join, ANTIWAR MOVEMENT:

Value Type	Belgium	France	Portugal	Denmark	Britain	Neth.
Materialist	3%	5%	9%	14%	8%	10%
Mixed	9	10	19	15	17	17
Postmaterialist	5	28	32	30	41	40
Total	6	11	15	17	18	22

Value Type	Lux.	Italy	Spain	Ireland	Greece	W. Germany
Materialist	19%	15%	24%	30%	43%	32%
Mixed	22	30	36	40	56	58
Postmaterialist	36	40	62	53	77	82
Total	23	25	35	38	53	59

Source: Euro-Barometer survey 25 (April 1986).

in Belgium, which is characterized by the most apolitical culture in Western Europe, as we saw in chapter 10. Rates of participation in the ecology movement are highest in Greece, and it is significant that metropolitan Athens probably has the most severe pollution problems of any major city in the European Community. Participation in the antiwar movement was highest in West Germany, the country that was scheduled to receive the largest contingent of Pershing and cruise missiles of any NATO member—a fact that probably contributed to the emergence of a particularly strong and widespread antiwar movement in that country. Thus, examination of the data in cross-national perspective suggests that situational factors are very important, and that we must take account of long-term factors (such as the political culture of a given society), intermediate ones (such as the severity of pollution in a given country in a given period), and short-term ones (such as the NATO decision concerning the installation of intermediate-range missiles, and its subsequent implementation). Such factors almost certainly contribute to the wide range of cross-national variation in membership and potential membership in new social movements.

But it is equally clear that, in addition to such situational factors, the presence of Materialist/Postmaterialist values constitutes another major component underlying support for the new social movements. In each of the twelve nations, Postmaterialists are far more likely than Materialists to be members or potential members of these movements. In any given country, Postmaterialists are at least twice as likely as Materialists to be members, and the ratio is often 3 to 1, or even 4 to 1 or 5 to 1.

This relationship persists over time, moreover, as Tables 11-2 and 11-3 demonstrate in regard to the antiwar movement. Though levels of approval (shown for five nations in Table 11-2) and levels of reported and actual membership (shown for five nations in Table 11-3) may rise or fall in response to given events in given countries, those with Postmaterialist values consistently remain far more likely to give their approval—and their active participation—than those with Materialist values. Consistently, year after year, across these five nations as a whole, those with Postmaterialist values are at least five times as likely to be members of the antiwar movement as those with Materialist values. Though the pure Postmaterialist type constitutes only one-eighth of the public, they consistently furnish an absolute majority of the movements' activists.

Values, Ideology, and Cognitive Mobilization

One's ideological predispositions also influence support for the new social movements. In this analysis, we will use the respondent's self-placement on a Left-Right scale as an indicator of his or her ideological affiliation. The following question is a standard part of the Euro-Barometer surveys: "In political matters, people talk of the 'left' and the 'right.' How would you place your views on this scale?" (The respondent is handed a

TABLE 11-2. SUPPORT FOR PEACE MOVEMENTS BY VALUE TYPE

Question: "Can you tell me whether you approve (strongly or somewhat) or disapprove (somewhat or strongly) of the antiwar and antinuclear weapons movements, such as the Campaign for Nuclear Disarmament?"

(Percentage who "approve strongly")

Value Type	France			Netherlands			W. Germany		
	1982	1984	1986	1982	1984	1986	1982	1984	1986
Materialist	31%	28%	26%	35%	27%	21%	20%	10%	10%
Mixed	38	32	31	36	33	27	26	23	21
Postmaterialist	53	44	53	61	59	52	66	57	52

Value Type	Italy			United Kingdom			Western Europe[a]		
	1982	1984	1986	1982	1984	1986	1982	1984	1986
Materialist	72%	39%	52%	25%	14%	26%	43%	26%	28%
Mixed	72	58	62	28	23	28	47	33	35
Postmaterialist	79	70	67	44	40	50	63	52	55

Sources: Euro-Barometer surveys 17 (April 1982), 22 (November 1984), and 25 (April 1986).

[a]Figures for Western Europe are weighted according to population of each country. Data are available at all three time points only for these five countries.

scale consisting of ten boxes with the word "left" at the left end and the word "right" at the right end.)

Responses to this item tap a general sense of identification with the parties and the issue positions of the Left (Inglehart and Klingemann 1976). We will use this item to measure the degree to which given individuals support the new social movements because of previous ideological influences (for example, whether they are environmentalists because they have always been on the Left). Clearly, this procedure exaggerates the influence of ideology on support for the new social movements, since the meaning of "the Left" has already changed, under the impact of new social movements; today, many people consider themselves to be on the Left because they are environmentalists, rather than the other way around. We will nevertheless use this somewhat exaggerated estimate of ideological influence in order to provide a conservative estimate of the impact of Materialist/Postmaterialist value priorities on support for the new social movements.

TABLE 11-3. MEMBERSHIP IN PEACE MOVEMENT BY VALUE TYPE

Question: "Can you tell me whether you are a member, or are likely to join, or would certainly not join...the antiwar and antinuclear weapons movements, such as CND?"

(Percentage saying they "are a member")

Value Type	France			Netherlands			W. Germany		
	1982	1984	1986	1982	1984	1986	1982	1984	1986
Materialist	.0%	.3%	.0%	1.0%	.0%	.0%	.5%	.0%	.9%
Mixed	.4	.2	.0	1.1	1.1	.6	4.1	1.7	1.4
Postmat.	3.3	1.0	.6	5.5	7.4	3.0	10.4	6.8	3.5

Value Type	Italy			United Kingdom			Western Europe[a]		
	1982	1984	1986	1982	1984	1986	1982	1984	1986
Materialist	.8%	.3%	.7%	.6%	1.3%	.5%	.5%	.4%	.5%
Mixed	2.7	1.0	1.2	1.1	1.6	1.4	1.4	1.2	1.0
Postmat.	5.6	10.1	6.7	5.6	5.7	10.8	5.0	5.9	5.3

Sources: See Table 11-2.
[a]See note to Table 11-2.

As we will see, this impact is substantial, even when we control for the effects of one's Left-Right ideological orientation.

What is the relative impact of ideology, cognitive mobilization, and Materialist/Postmaterialist values in building support for the new social movements? The answer depends on whether one is focusing on approval or action. In regard to general approval of the ecology movement, Left-Right self placement is a considerably stronger predictor of attitude than Materialist/Postmaterialist values. Moreover, the respondent's level of cognitive mobilization is totally unrelated to this attitude. But in regard to behavioral intentions and actual behavior, cognitive mobilization is an important predictor and Materialist/Postmaterialist values are the most important predictor of all. As Table 11-4 demonstrates, Postmaterialists are significantly more likely to approve of the ecology movement than Materialists, but the difference is relatively modest (gamma = .077). Self-placement on a Left-Right ideological scale shows a much stronger linkage

TABLE 11-4. ATTITUDES AND BEHAVIOR TOWARD ECOLOGY MOVEMENT BY LEFT-RIGHT IDEOLOGY, COGNITIVE MOBILIZATION, AND MATERIALIST/POSTMATERIALIST VALUES

	% Who Strongly Approve of Ecology Movement	% Who Might Join Ecology Movement	% Who Are Members of Ecology Movement	% Who Will Vote for Greens (W. Ger. only)
Respondent's self-placement on Left-Right ideology scale				
Right,Center-Right (7 - 10)	29% (2,373)	17%	.9% (2,110)	2% (332)
Center (5 - 6)	33 (3,534)	23	.6 (3,197)	4 (377)
Left,Center-Left (1 - 4)	43 (3,072)	36	1.7 (2,673)	13 (267)
gamma	.209	.261		
Respondent's cognitive mobilization score				
Low, Medium-Low (1 - 2)	37% (5,097)	19%	.5% (4,667)	4% (465)
Medium (3)	32 (2,997)	28	.8 (2,637)	8 (398)
High, Medium-High (4 - 5)	41 (1,931)	37	2.8 (1,670)	13 (156)
gamma	.015	.305		
Respondent's value type				
Materialist	37% (2,746)	15%	.6% (2,540)	1% (177)
Mixed	33 (5,300)	25	.7 (4,696)	4 (565)
Postmaterialist	46 (1,484)	45	3.3 (1,269)	23 (187)
gamma	.077	.427		

Source: Combined data from twelve nations surveyed in Euro-Barometer survey 25 (fieldwork completed April 1986).
Note: N = 11,831.

with approval of the ecology movement (gamma = .209)—though, to some extent, this may reflect the tendency for ecology-minded people to place themselves on the Left, rather than a tendency for the traditional constituency of the Left to be particularly ecology-minded.

However, the linkage between ideology and behavior is only slightly stronger than the linkage between ideology and attitudes. Those who place themselves on the Left are almost twice as likely to be members of the environmentalist movement as those who place themselves on the Right (gamma = .261). The linkage between values and behavior, on the other hand, is far stronger than the linkage between values and attitudes: Those with Postmaterialist values are five and a half times as likely to be members of the environmentalist movement as those with Materialist values (gamma = .427).

In moving from the realm of attitudes toward environmentalism to the realm of proenvironmentalist behavior, we are moving from a relatively "soft" indicator that contains a large component of spur of the moment response to a relatively "hard" indicator that refers to specific activities one either has or has not done. Only a small minority (about 1 percent) of the public claim to be members of the ecology movement. But this small active group consists of people who have given the ecology movement a great deal of time and thought. Consequently, the relationship between Materialist/Postmaterialist values and active participation in the movement is very strong. The same is true of electoral behavior concerning the largest and most salient of the ecology parties, the West German Greens, for which the linkage between votes and values is extremely strong (Postmaterialists are twenty-three times as apt to vote for them as are Materialists). A strong linkage between values and party choice does not necessarily hold true of electoral behavior in general, as we saw in chapter 8; with many parties, voting behavior is largely shaped by the inertia of long-established loyalties. But the Greens are a new party. Hardly anyone votes for it except those who see it as acting on behalf of their own basic values.

Moving from attitudes to behavior does not have a comparable effect on the relationship with Left-Right ideology. This variable is not much more strongly linked with behavior than it is with attitudes. This reflects the fact that the Left-Right dimension (unlike the Materialist/Postmaterialist dimension) has been a major fixture of West German and West European politics for many decades. Practically everyone can place themselves on this dimension—but many do so out of traditional loyalties, and others as a reflection of their orientations toward current issues. Traditionally, the Left has been favorable to change-oriented movements, and those who identify with the Left tend to give at least lip service to the new social movements. Yet more active involvement in these movements is not linked with a markedly stronger correlation between behavior and Left-Right ideology, for Materialists remain a major component of the Left—and for them, a closer examination of the relationship between their beliefs and the goals of the new social movements does not have the same unequivocal result that it does among Postmaterialists. From the viewpoint of the Materialist Left, it is not unambiguously clear that the environmentalist and antiwar movements will enhance their top priorities—economic and physical security.

The impact of cognitive mobilization, on the other hand, does show a dramatic increase as we move from attitudes to behavior and behavioral intentions. In their attitudes, those with high levels of political skills are not necessarily more favorable to the ecology movement than those with low levels. But high levels of political skills are virtually a prerequisite for active participation in such a movement, and cognitive mobilization shows a strong linkage with our behavioral indicators.

TABLE 11-5. ATTITUDES AND BEHAVIOR TOWARD THREE NEW SOCIAL MOVEMENTS BY VALUES, COGNITIVE MOBILIZATION, AND LEFT-RIGHT IDEOLOGY
(Cell entry is gamma coefficient)

	Gamma	
	Approval of Movement	Membership or Potential Membership in Movement
Left-Right ideology's linkage with:		
Ecology movement	.209	.261
Anti-nuclear power movement	.233	.339
Antiwar movement	.295	.299
Mean linkage	.246	.300
Cognitive mobilization's linkage with:		
Ecology movement	.015	.305
Anti-nuclear power movement	.066	.279
Antiwar movement	.026	.295
Mean linkage	.036	.293
Materialist/Postmaterialist values' linkage with:		
Ecology movement	.077	.427
Anti-nuclear power movement	.048	.433
Antiwar movement	.116	.465
Mean linkage	.080	.442

Source: See Table 11-4.

These findings apply to the anti–nuclear power movement and the anti-war movement as well as to the ecology movement. Table 11-5 compares the linkages between our three independent variables, on one hand, and attitudes and behavior and behavioral intentions toward each of these three types of movements on the other hand. Figure 11-4 sums up the overall results in graphic form. For each of these three kinds of movements, across the twelve nations of the European Community, Left-Right ideological location is the strongest predictor of attitudinal approval. But cognitive mobilization is an equally strong predictor, and Materialist/Postmaterialist values are a much stronger predictor, of behavioral intentions and actual behavior.

The rise of these new social movements has reshaped the meaning of the old, familiar Left-Right ideological spectrum, as much as it has been shaped by it. One major component of the meaning of "Left" and "Right" today is simply the connotations of specific political parties that have traditionally been considered to be on the Left or on the Right. Originally, these Left-Right locations reflected, above all, the fact that certain

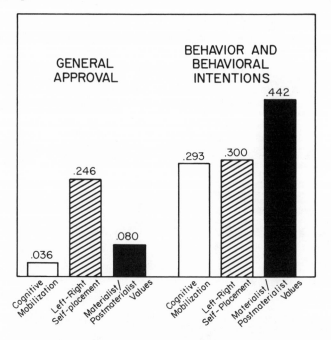

FIGURE 11-4. Linkage of attitudes and behavior toward new social movements with cognitive mobilization, Left-Right ideological self-placement, and Materialist/Postmaterialist values. Mean gamma coefficients of each factor's association with orientations toward three types of movements, among publics of twelve European Community nations, 1986. Based on Euro-Barometer survey 25.

parties represented the workers (on one hand) or the privileged classes (on the other hand). Conventionally, the communists occupied the leftmost position on the spectrum, followed by the socialists and then the liberals and various other more conservative groups. But this conventional component of the Left-Right dimension has an ambiguous relationship to the new social movements. As Table 11-6 demonstrates, the communist electorate is not markedly more supportive of the ecology and the antinuclear movements than the electorate of the extreme right. Instead, one finds a curvilinear relationship, with the socialists being more favorable to these movements than the communists. By far the most dramatic rise in the support for social change comes when we reach the ecology parties—which most observers initially placed somewhere near the middle of the Left-Right spectrum. Today, one might argue that they really should be placed to the left of the communists—which would then create a relatively clear,

TABLE 11-6. MEMBERSHIP AND POTENTIAL MEMBERSHIP IN NEW SOCIAL MOVEMENTS
BY VOTING INTENTION ACROSS TEN WESTERN NATIONS
(Percentage saying they are members or might join given movement)

1. Ecology movement

Communist	23%	(399)
Socialist	28	(1,924)
Ecologist	69	(254)
Liberal/Giscardians	19	(499)
Christian Dem./Conserv./Gaullists	17	(1,845)
Extreme Right (MSI, FN, NPD, etc.)	21	(93)

2. Anti-nuclear power movement

Communist	15	(404)
Socialist	20	(1,941)
Ecologist	53	(242)
Liberal	6	(497)
Christian Dem./Conserv./Gaullists	7	(1,850)
Extreme Right	11	(90)

3. Antiwar movement

Communist	30	(400)
Socialist	33	(1,977)
Ecologist	60	(244)
Liberal	16	(505)
Christian Dem./Conserv./Gaullists	17	(1,847)
Extreme Right	10	(94)

Source: Based on combined ten-nation data from Euro-Barometer
survey 21 (April 1984).
Note: Percentages weighted according to population of each nation.

monotonic relationship between the Left-Right dimension and support for
the new social movements. There is no reason why we could not adopt this
convention—but we should bear in mind that if we did so, it would represent a redefinition of the Left-Right spectrum in the light of new facts,
rather than the shaping of the new movements by the traditional Left
ideology.

The degree to which the Left has been reshaped by such new social
movements, rather than the other way around, is put in clearer perspective
when we compare the deep-rooted Communist parties of France and Italy,
with the Communist parties of the new party systems that have emerged
since democratic institutions were restored in Greece, Spain, and Portugal
in the 1970s. Thus far, the new movements have had only a relatively
modest impact on the long-established and heavily bureaucratized Communist parties of France and Italy; within these countries, the electorates
of various other parties are more supportive of the ecology movement than
are the communists. But in the newer party systems of Greece, Spain, and
Portugal, the Left-Right partisan space coincides more closely with support for the new social movements, with the Communist party being the
most proecologist party in the system. These newer Communist parties

emerged in an era when the environmentalist and antinuclear movements were already major issues, and their positions have been relatively responsive to them.

THE IMPACT OF AGE, INCOME, RELIGION, AND PARTISANSHIP: MULTIVARIATE ANALYSIS

The new social movements reflect a variety of factors, as we have argued. Not all of them can be readily measured by survey research, but let us attempt to estimate the relative importance of those that can. Some of these variables are correlated with others; age, for example, is linked with both Materialist/Postmaterialist values and Left-Right self-placement. Is it possible that both of the latter variables show strong linkages with membership in the new social movements simply because younger people are most likely to join them? Similarly, both cognitive mobilization and Postmaterialist values are linked with relatively high levels of income and education. Are they both simply surrogate indicators of social class?

In order to answer such questions, and gain a clearer understanding of the relative impact of given variables, controlling for the effects of others, we performed a series of multiple classification analyses. Membership and potential membership in given social movements were the dependent variables in these analyses (dichotomizing those who said they were members or might join the given movement and those who said they would not join). As predictor variables, we used Materialist/Postmaterialist values, Left-Right self-placement, cognitive mobilization, age, income, religiosity, and closeness to a political party. A number of additional demographic variables were included in preliminary analyses, but those which had neither theoretical significance nor empirical importance were eliminated from our final version of these analyses, reported in Tables 11-7 through 11-10.

Table 11-7 shows the percentages who say they are members of the ecology movement, or might join it, within the respective categories of each of our seven predictor variables, for the European Community as a whole. Table 11-8 provides the summary statistics from a multiple classification analysis based on these variables. Tables 11-9 and 11-10 provide comparable information concerning membership and potential membership in the antiwar movement. The results from our analysis of the anti–nuclear power movement are so similar to these results that we will not present them here.

Materialist/Postmaterialist value priorities prove to be our strongest predictor of participation in both the ecology movement and the antiwar movement across these twelve nations. This holds true of both the zero-

TABLE 11-7. PREDICTORS OF MEMBERSHIP/POTENTIAL MEMBERSHIP IN ECOLOGY
MOVEMENT ACROSS TWELVE WEST EUROPEAN NATIONS
(Percentage saying they are members or might join)

Variable	%	N
1. Materialist/Postmaterialist values		
Materialist	15	(2,540)
Mixed	26	(4,695)
Postmaterialist	48	(1,268)
2. Self-Placement on Left-Right ideology scale		
Left (1-2)	17	(514)
Center-Left (3-4)	18	(1,595)
Center (5-6)	24	(3,196)
Center-Right (7-8)	37	(1,982)
Right (9-10)	40	(690)
3. Age of respondent		
Ages 15 - 24	37	(1,744)
Ages 25 - 39	31	(2,618)
Ages 40-54	24	(2,002)
Ages 55+	15	(2,598)
4. Cognitive mobilization level		
Low (left school before age 16,		
and "never" discusses politics)	15	(1,781)
Medium-Low	23	(2,616)
Medium	29	(2,420)
Medium-High	39	(1,393)
High (schooling beyond age 19, and		
"often" discusses politics)	43	(397)
5. How religious does respondent consider self?		
1-2 (not at all religious)	33	(1,517)
3-4	33	(1,181)
5-6	24	(2,544)
7-8	24	(2,256)
9-10 (very religious)	20	(1,370)
6. Closeness to a political party		
Very close	28	(725)
Fairly close	31	(1,398)
Merely a sympathizer	26	(2,726)
Not close to any party	23	(3,433)
7. Family income		
Lowest quartile	21	(1,772)
Second quartile	25	(1,493)
Third quartile	27	(1,936)
Highest quartile	32	(2,098)

Source: Euro-Barometer survey 25, combined twelve-nation data.

order relationship (indicated by the eta coefficients in Tables 11-8 and 11-10) and the partial relationship, controlled for the effects of all the other predictors included in these analyses (as indicated by the beta coefficients in Tables 11-8 and 11-10). These results demonstrate that the impact of values is not a spurious one; it cannot be attributed to the fact that Post-materialists are younger, better educated, more inclined to the Left, and so forth. Values are the strongest predictor of activism and potential activism in both of these new social movements, and remain so even when we control for the effects of these other variables.

TABLE 11-8. MEMBERSHIP AND POTENTIAL MEMBERSHIP IN ECOLOGY MOVEMENTS:
MULTIPLE CLASSIFICATION ANALYSIS

	Eta	Beta
Materialist/Postmaterialist values	.228	.153
Left-Right ideology (self-placement)	.184	.129
Age of respondent	.182	.122
Cognitive mobilization level	.184	.092
Religiosity of respondent	.109	.043
Closeness to a political party	.063	.042
Family income (quartiles)	.083	.028
(N = 8,607)		R = .313

Source: Based on twelve-nation data from Euro-Barometer survey 25.

Left-Right self-placement and cognitive mobilization also have substantial impact when we control for the effects of other variables. Their impact is not just an indirect manifestation of social class conflict. Indeed, these results demonstrate rather vividly just how little social class conflict has to do with the rise of the new social movements, for income proves to be a feeble predictor of activism in both of these movements. Moreover—and this is even more important—it shows the wrong polarity: The upper-income groups are more likely to belong to these presumably Left-oriented movements than the lower-income groups. If we view this phenomenon as reflecting these groups' relative levels of cognitive mobilization, it is perfectly in keeping with our expectations. But it is not at all what we would have predicted if we viewed these movements as manifestations of the class struggle.

Age does have a significant impact on activism in these movements. It is the third strongest predictor of membership and potential membership in the ecology movement, and the second-strongest predictor of membership in the antiwar movement. This holds true when we control for the impact of Materialist/Postmaterialist values (which are, of course, closely related). Age plays a significant role even apart from the associated generational differences in value priorities and Left-Right self placement. It seems likely that life cycle effects are involved, though we cannot be sure whether this is true without longitudinal data.

Religiosity has a fairly pronounced zero-order relationship with membership in the new social movements: only 20 percent of those who consider themselves "very religious" are members or potential members of the ecology movement, for example—as compared with 33 percent of those who consider themselves "not at all religious." But this linkage fades into marginal significance when we control for the effects of the other variables (including the fact that the more religious respondents are

TABLE 11-9. PREDICTORS OF MEMBERSHIP/POTENTIAL MEMBERSHIP IN ANTIWAR
MOVEMENT ACROSS TWELVE WEST EUROPEAN NATIONS
(Percentage saying they are members or might join)

Variable	%	N
Materialist/Postmaterialist values		
Materialist	15	(2,592)
Mixed	27	(4,831)
Postmaterialist	51	(1,310)
Self-placement on Left-Right ideology scale		
Left (1-2)	43	(713)
Center-Left (3-4)	39	(2,016)
Center (5-6)	26	(3,279)
Center-Right (7-8)	18	(1,641)
Right (9-10)	16	(520)
Age of respondent		
Ages 15 - 24	40	(1,853)
Ages 25 - 39	33	(2,667)
Ages 40 - 54	22	(2,025)
Ages 55+	17	(2,632)
Cognitive mobilization level		
Low (left school by age 16, never discusses politics)	15	(1,916)
Medium-Low	25	(2,891)
Medium	31	(2,668)
Medium-High	37	(1,361)
High (schooling beyond age 19, often discusses politics)	47	(355)
Self-placement on religiosity scale		
Not at all religious (1-2)	36	(1,576)
Points 3-4	34	(1,242)
Points 5-6	26	(2,606)
Points 7-8	25	(2,252)
Very religious (9-10)	20	(1,413)
Closeness to some political party		
Very close	32	(807)
Fairly close	32	(1,559)
Merely a sympathizer	28	(2,726)
Note close to any party	24	(3,815)
Family Income		
Lowest quartile	24	(1,798)
Second quartile	29	(1,587)
Third quartile	27	(1,863)
Highest quartile	30	(1,940)

Source: Euro-Barometer survey 25 data.

less likely to be Postmaterialists, are less likely to place themselves on the Left, and tend to be older and lower on cognitive mobilization).

Closeness to a political party plays even less of a role in determining membership or potential membership in the new social movements. Those who say they are very close to some political party are somewhat more apt to be active in these movements than those who are not close to any party, but the impact of this variable fades to an insignificant level when we control for the effects of the other variables. This negative finding has consid-

TABLE 11-10. MEMBERSHIP OR POTENTIAL MEMBERSHIP IN ANTIWAR MOVEMENT:
MULTIPLE CLASSIFICATION ANALYSIS

	Eta	Beta
Materialist/Postmaterialist values	.251	.175
Respondent's age	.195	.139
Left-Right ideology	.200	.136
Cognitive mobilization	.183	.087
Religiosity of respondent	.125	.043
Closeness to a political party	.066	.043
Family income (quartiles)	.050	.036
(N = 9,000)		R = .337

Source: Based on twelve-nation data from Euro-Barometer survey 25.

erable theoretical significance. It demonstrates the fact that these new social movements are genuinely new; the established political parties, which for decades have played a crucial role in mobilizing political participation, are only a marginal factor in building support for these new movements. The new social movements represent a different type of political participation, one that is less elite directed than has generally been true of participation in the past, and one that is shaped to a far greater degree by the individual's values, ideology, and political skills. The new social movements are new not only in their goals but also in their political style and in the factors that mobilize their activists.

CHAPTER 12

Cultural Change and the Atlantic Alliance

INTRODUCTION: POSTMATERIALISM AND THE ATLANTIC ALLIANCE

The existence of the Atlantic Alliance has helped Western Europe to remain independent, prosperous, and at peace throughout the past generation. In doing so, the alliance contributed to the sense of economic and physical security that allows Postmaterialists to emphasize values other than national security. But, ironically, the very fact that the alliance has functioned well may have contributed to a process that is gradually eroding the political consensus on which it originally was based.

In the wake of World War II and the Soviet occupation of nine formerly independent East European nations, the presence of American forces in Western Europe was widely viewed as a factor that protected that region from a fate similar to that of Poland, Hungary, East Germany, or Czechoslovakia. The Czech coup and the Berlin blockade in 1948 helped confirm that feeling. Throughout the 1950s, West European publics generally showed predominantly favorable attitudes toward the United States (Merritt and Puchala 1968). By the final year of Kennedy's presidency, these attitudes were overwhelming among the publics of West Germany, Britain, France, and Italy, with those having a favorable opinion of the United States outnumbering those with unfavorable opinions by ratios of about 5 to 1, overall, and by as much as 10 to 1 in West Germany.

That situation no longer holds true, as Table 12-1 demonstrates. In 1954–1955, among the four West European publics shown in Table 12-1, people with favorable opinions of the United States were about four times as numerous as those with unfavorable ones. In terms of the index used in this table, this translates into an average rating of +41 for the United States. No other nation among those rated received ratings that even approached this level. USIA survey data reported by Merritt and Puchala (1968, 235–48) reveal that feelings toward Great Britain were relatively positive at this time, but her ratings by West European publics translate into a mean index of +20—only about half as high as the ratings of the United States. At the same time, the British, French, and Italian publics gave West Germany an average rating of +8, meaning that good opinions

TABLE 12-1. WEST EUROPEAN OPINIONS OF THE UNITED STATES, 1954 - 1987

Question: "Do you have a very good, good, neither good nor bad, bad or
          very bad opinion of the United States?"

(Percentage favorable minus percentage unfavorable opinions)

Nation	1954	1955	1956	1957	1958	1959	1960	1961
West Germany	57	56	55	58	65	65	65	71
Great Britain	40	54	51	41	52	65	49	56
Italy	49	57	65	62	53	68	57	53
France	0	17	6	4	23	31	33	42

Nation	1962	1963	1964	1965	1969	1971	1972	1973
West Germany	68	75	84	73	63	51	46	45
Great Britain	52	44	66	57	41	37	49	–
Italy	61	68	74	62	52	–	60	57
France	36	36	41	28	38	32	38	–

Nation	1976	1978	1981	1982	1984	1985	1987
West Germany	50	81	45	43	37	37	42
Great Britain	24	63	14	20	20	37	40
Italy	25	64	39	39	31	47	48
France	28	49	31	25	18	31	37

    Sources: U.S. Information Agency surveys, 1954 - 1982; and Euro-
Barometer surveys 22, 24, 27, and 28 (the latter two surveys are
combined, for the 1987 results). When more than one survey was carried
out in one year, the results have been averaged.
    Note: From 1954 through 1976, a five-point scale was used that
included a neutral "neither good nor bad" category; in subsequent
surveys, this neutral category was dropped. Thus, the absolute
percentages from before and after 1976 are not comparable, but the
balance between positive and negative opinions does seem to be roughly
comparable across time.

outweighed bad ones by only 8 percentage points. France was rated
slightly below this level in 1954–1955, with a mean rating of + 5. The
mean rating for Italy was − 12: Bad opinions outweighed good ones by 12
percentage points. Finally, feelings toward the Soviet Union and China
were overwhelmingly negative during this period: the two countries received mean ratings of − 37 and − 41, respectively.

    In the 1980s, attitudes toward the United States were generally less fa-
vorable than they had been in the early 1960s, but the picture is quite differentiated when examined in detail, country by country, and year by year.
For example, the relative positions of the French and West German publics
show a dramatic shift over the three decades for which we have data (see
Table 12-1). On one hand, the West Germans (generally the most pro-
American ally during the 1950s and 1960s) had developed markedly less

favorable attitudes by the 1980s; conversely, the French (formerly the least reliable ally and almost evenly divided between positive and negative orientations in the 1950s) showed an upward trend and by the 1980s had attitudes almost as favorable as those of the other three publics. Though the causal relationships are complex, these contrasting trends are almost certainly linked with the decay of the French Communist party, on one hand, and the rise of powerful neutralist currents among both the Green and Social Democratic parties in West Germany. The only question is, to what extent do these attitudes reflect the partisan changes, and to what degree did they help bring them about? Moreover, the impact of current events is evident: Sizable shifts occur from year to year in the attitudes of given publics. Thus, one can see traces of the impact of the defeat of EDC in French attitudes in 1954; and an echo of Kennedy's "Ich bin ein Berliner" in German attitudes in 1963–1964. Nevertheless, despite the complexities of detail and the contrast between trends in France and elsewhere, there is an overall downward trend, with the decay of favorable attitudes toward the United States most pronounced in West Germany and Great Britain—and with only the French as favorable in 1987 as they were in the early 1960s.

Does it matter? Or are these attitudes simply an epiphenomenon, reflecting the impact of recent events and cues given by leaders in given nations? We think it does matter. To be sure, it seems clear that current events have an impact. The Atlantic Alliance is in trouble—and the current strains in the alliance reflect real problems linked with different reactions to global events, questions of who should pay for Western defense, balance of trade difficulties, interest rates, and other problems. But it is not simply a matter of malleable publics responding to external events and elite cues. On the contrary, it is evident that relatively autonomous public preferences also have an impact on elite policy. Thus, the proposal to install American intermediate-range missiles in Western Europe was initiated by the leader of the West German Social Democratic party, Helmut Schmidt, out of concern over the newly installed Soviet SS20 missiles; his party later repudiated this policy under the pressure of widespread and articulate public opinion that not only opposed this specific measure but has increasingly voiced opposition to the American presence in Europe and to the Atlantic Alliance in general.

In other words, though public attitudes in this area clearly do react to short-term forces, there is also a long-term component. This long-term component reflects deep-rooted cultural orientations, which change only rather slowly and which can act as a constraint on policymakers at a given point in time. These long-term factors are complex; in some respects, they are potentially conducive to world peace. But they also tend to erode public support for the Atlantic Alliance.

We have already dealt with one of these factors: the shift toward Postmaterialist values. Postmaterialists tend to be relatively unfavorable to the Atlantic Alliance in general. Moreover, while not predominantly anti-American, Postmaterialists tend to have less favorable attitudes toward the United States than do the rest of their compatriots. The first point reflects something inherent: Postmaterialists are a group that was raised in relative economic and physical security. Hence, they tend to take national security for granted. Accordingly, West European Postmaterialists are apt to feel that the American presence in Western Europe is unnecessary and that additional arms are superfluous. Consequently, the Soviet invasion of Afghanistan and the installation of SS20 missiles targeted on Western Europe did not evoke a rallying around NATO on their part; on the contrary, Postmaterialists tended to perceive the installation of American missiles as needless provocation. This perception, in turn, was facilitated by a second factor—something that is not inherent in Postmaterialism but reflects an historical accident: the fact that the first large cohort of Postmaterialists entered maturity during the Vietnam era. This experience left a lasting residue of suspicion of the United States and a predisposition to see the Americans as the aggressors. For earlier generations, who had experienced the Soviet occupation and repression of Eastern Europe, the bias ran the other way: the Soviets were viewed as profoundly dangerous and the Americans as a much-needed and relatively benevolent ally. But for the postwar generation, the overwhelming focus on Vietnam from the mid-1960s to the mid-1970s has had a lasting impact. It has contributed to an intergenerational shift in some of the basic attitudes that condition West European publics' orientations toward East-West relationships and the Atlantic alliance.

TRUST BETWEEN NATIONS: ENDURING CULTURAL BIASES

As we saw in chapter 1, a sense of interpersonal trust plays a crucial role in political cooperation, facilitating the emergence of democratic institutions. A predisposition to trust or distrust other nationalities seems to be an enduring cultural characteristic—one that can facilitate or hinder international cooperation.

Trust or distrust helps shape expectations under conditions of imperfect information; trust can be a crucial factor when the leaders of one nation interpret the actions of another nation. Trust is the expectation that another's behavior will be predictably friendly; distrust is the expectation that another's behavior will be harmful or unpredictable (Pruitt 1965). Thus, trust or distrust predisposes one to interpret another's actions as friendly or threatening when ambiguity exists. The consequences can be vitally important.

In the early 1980s, for example, it was ambiguous why the Soviet Union developed intermediate-range nuclear missiles and installed them within range of Western Europe. One interpretation is that it was a defensive measure intended merely to offset the nuclear predominance the United States had held since the end of World War II. Another interpretation is that the Soviets neutralized the American nuclear advantage in order to exploit their superiority in conventional weapons and eventually be able to dominate Western Europe.

If Western decision makers perceive Soviet action as threatening, they will feel they must take countermeasures; if the Soviet leaders, in turn, interpret the countermeasures as motivated by hostile intent, it can become a vicious circle of mutual paranoia. Ironically, the United States and the Soviet Union have no trade rivalries, no border conflicts, complementary economies and an immense common interest: a mutual stake in avoiding World War III. If it is true that their ideological differences are fading, the main thing that separates them may be simply a question of trust—but this may turn out to be a matter of life and death.

Distrust tends to become a self-fulfilling prophecy, as history amply illustrates. From 1866 to 1945, each generation of Frenchmen and Germans anticipated the coming war between their two nations—eagerly or with foreboding, but with the conviction that it was inevitable, virtually a law of nature. Dramatic changes have occurred since 1945; such seeming laws of nature can be abolished. But the process is not easy, for trust or distrust between two mutually salient nations tends to be persistent—especially if it is rooted in cultural differences. Since political elites are socialized within a given political culture, their outlook is likely to reflect the stereotypes of trust or distrust prevailing within the culture in which they grew up.

The tendency for given nations' actions to be interpreted differently within different cultural areas is illustrated vividly by the Falkland Islands crisis of 1982. To a remarkable extent, Spanish-speaking regimes, regardless of whether they were located on the Left, Right, or Center, supported an Argentine military dictatorship in the conflict, while Great Britain's partners in the European Community, together with English-speaking nations, such as Canada, Australia, New Zealand, and the United States, supported Great Britain. Even within the European Community, reactions differed according to cultural zones. Italy, for example, condemned Argentine seizure of the islands, but refrained from applying economic sanctions.

Trust between nationalities may be vital—but can anything be done about it? Insofar as it is linked with primordial ties, such as race and ethnic ties, it is relatively intractable. But geographic proximity and race seem to be declining influences on cross-national trust or distrust; and, though language is important, its significance lies more in the fact that it can be a channel of communication or a barrier to communication flows than in its importance as a fixed ethnic characteristic (Inglehart and Rabier 1984b). Though trust or distrust between nationalities shows an impressive tendency to persist over time, it is a variable not a constant, and subject to human intervention.

In a number of Euro-Barometer surveys carried out since 1970, representative national samples of the publics of the European Community countries have been asked a series of questions about how much they trusted or distrusted peoples of various other nationalities. In each of these surveys, the publics were asked: ''Now I would like to ask about how much you would trust people from different countries. For each country please say whether, in your opinion, they are in general very trustworthy, fairly trustworthy, not particularly trustworthy, or not at all trustworthy.''

The questions were asked in the context of surveys dealing with international relations. The key word ''trust'' was translated into German as *Vertrauen*, into French as *confiance*, into Danish as *trovaerdige*, in Italian as *Fiducia*, and into Dutch as *vertrouwen*.

Table 12-2 shows the relative levels of trust toward various other nationalities that were expressed by the publics of the nine countries that were members of the European Community in 1976, and the levels of trust expressed by these same nine publics a decade later in 1986. There was a wide range of variation in the ratings of various nationalities. The indices shown here reflect the fact that in 1976, for example, 71 percent of the combined European publics trusted the Swiss and only 14 percent distrusted them, while, on the other hand, fully 74 percent distrusted the Russians and only 20 percent trusted them. As this table demonstrates, both the absolute and relative levels of trust that West European publics have for other nationalities are extremely stable. Indeed, the rank order of all thirteen nationalities that were asked about in both surveys remain virtually identical across the ten years from 1976 to 1986. The Swiss were the most trusted nationality and the Russians were the least trusted both in 1976 and in 1986. The eleven nationalities in between also maintain virtually identical positions, apart from slight shifts for the Dutch and the Danes, who were ranked second and third, respectively, in 1976 but ranked third and second, respectively, in 1986. The Germans and Luxembourgers show a

TABLE 12-2. TRUST IN OTHER NATIONALITIES AMONG NINE WEST EUROPEAN
PUBLICS, IN 1976 AND 1986
(Rank and mean rating of each nationality by the combined nine publics)

	1976			1986		
Rank	Nationality	Trust Rating	Rank	Nationality	Trust Rating	Shift, 1976 to 1986
1.	Swiss	.68	1.	Swiss	.70	+.02
2.	Dutch	.65	2.	Danes	.66	+.02
3.	Danes	.64	3.	Dutch	.65	.00
4.	Germans	.64	4.	Luxembourgers	.64	+.01
5.	Luxembourgers	.63	5.	Germans	.63	-.01
6.	Belgians	.62	6.	Belgians	.61	-.01
7.	Americans	.59	7.	Americans	.58	-.01
8.	British	.57	8.	British	.58	+.01
9.	French	.55	9.	French	.57	+.02
10.	Irish	.45	10.	Irish	.53	+.08
11.	Italians	.42	11.	Italians	.51	+.09
12.	Chinese	.31	12.	Chinese	.48	+.17
13.	Russians	.30	13.	Russians	.38	+.08
	Mean	.54			.58	+.04

Sources: Pooled data from representative national samples of publics of France, Britain, West Germany, Italy, the Netherlands, Belgium, Luxembourg, Ireland, and Denmark, surveyed in November 1976 (Euro-Barometer survey 6) and in April 1986 (Euro-Barometer survey 25).

Note: Results from each country are weighted according to population. Mean score is based on overall ratings for each nationality, with 0 = "not at all trustworthy," .33 = "not very trustworthy," .67 = "fairly trustworthy," and 1.00 = "very trustworthy." Thus, a mean score of .50 is the neutral point where positive ratings equal negative ratings.

similar slight shift; all other nationalities show *exactly* the same rankings in 1976 and 1986. Table 12-1 presents the results from nine European Community publics as a whole, but the ratings made by given publics within the Community show a similar stability; relatively trustful or distrustful predispositions toward specific nationalities are a stable feature of given political cultures.

This is true not only of trust toward specific nationalities, but of entire configurations of trust toward other peoples, as Figures 12-1 and 12-2 demonstrate. These figures present the results of smallest space analyses based on the correlations between trust ratings of various nationalities. In these diagrams, nationalities whose ratings are closely correlated are located near one another. The results reveal that those who gave relatively high ratings to the Russians, for example, were likely to give similar ratings to the Chinese as well; the fact that both societies were governed by communist systems probably accounts for the tendency for them to receive similar ratings. The Chinese and Russians occupy proximate positions not only in 1976 but in 1986 as well. Since both nationalities were ranked

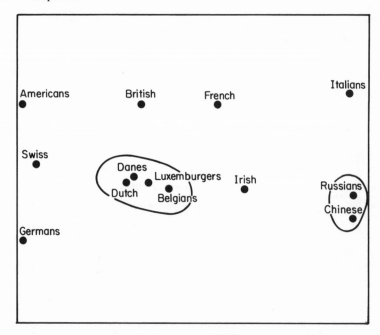

FIGURE 12-1. Trust ratings of thirteen nationalities by the publics of
nine European Community nations, 1976 ($N = 9,210$). Smallest
space analysis based on ratings by representative national samples of
publics of France, Britain, West Germany, Italy, the Netherlands, Belgium, Ireland, Denmark, and Luxembourg in Euro-Barometer survey
6. Kruskal's stress = .09.

relatively low on trustworthiness, they are located at the low trust pole (the
right side of these figures); the Italians also tend to receive low ratings, but
are perceived as culturally different, so they also appear on the right, but at
some distance from the Russians and Chinese. Another group that is perceived as similar consists of the Danes, the Dutch, the Belgians, and the
Luxembourgers: West European publics tend to see them as similar, and
give them similar ratings. The same is true, to a somewhat lesser degree,
of the Germans and Swiss. The entire cognitive map of which nationalities
can be trusted and how the ratings of one nationality go together with ratings of others, shows remarkable stability across the decade: The overall
pattern for 1976 is virtually identical with that for 1986.

Trust and distrust of given nationalities seems to be part of a stable cognitive map in the minds of given publics. But these patterns are not immutable. If we turn again to Table 12-2, we notice a very interesting phenomena: The ratings of most nationalities tend to be slightly higher in 1986
than they were in 1976. Though the rank order remains very stable, nine

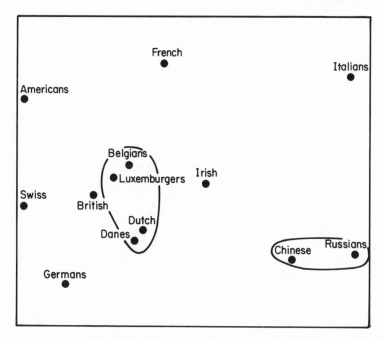

FIGURE 12-2. Trust ratings of thirteen nationalities by the publics of nine European Community nations, 1986 ($N = 8,823$). Smallest space analysis based on ratings by representative national samples of publics of France, Britain, West Germany, Italy, the Netherlands, Belgium, Ireland, Denmark, and Luxembourg in Euro-Barometer survey 25. Kruskal's stress = .12.

of the thirteen nationalities received higher ratings in 1986 than they had in 1976; one remained unchanged and three received slightly lower ratings; the overall mean rating rose by .04 points, and two nationalities that had received predominately negative ratings in 1976 (below .50) rose above this threshold, with both the Irish and the Italians receiving predominately positive ratings in 1986. The Chinese showed an unusually steep rise, moving to near this threshold in 1986; and the Russians also made impressive gains.

The Americans were one of the three nationalities that declined, moving against the overall upward trend. Though the amount of change that took place from 1976 to 1986 was very slight, this decline seems to be part of a long-term trend. Table 12-1 indicates that favorable opinions of the United States declined sharply from 1964 to 1976 (the era of the war in Vietnam) and then showed a recovery, which was offset by another decline in the early 1980s, followed by a partial recovery in 1985–1987. Thus, there is a mild absolute decline since the late 1950s and early 1960s—and a very sharp *relative* decline, for, as noted above, in the 1950s, the United States received much more favorable ratings than did Britain, West Germany, or France and incomparably more favorable ones than Italy, China, and the Soviet Union, all of which received predominantly negative ones.

The trust ratings shown in Table 12-2 are not directly comparable to the overall good or bad opinion ratings traced in Table 12-1, but they seem to follow a common trajectory. By 1976, the level of trust felt toward the Americans was well below that felt for the Germans—almost certainly a sharp reversal of what we would have found if this question had been asked in 1954–1955. The Americans still ranked .02 points above the British and .04 points above the French in 1976; but by 1986, the Americans were exactly tied with the British and only .01 point above the French. Mass opinions of the United States and trust in the American people remain predominantly positive. But their absolute level has declined slightly and the relative position of the United States has declined greatly, which means that her position as natural leader of the Atlantic Alliance has deteriorated. In the 1950s, the alliance was inherently and almost inevitably American centered; in the 1980s, intra-European bonds have become stronger in some cases than the Atlantic tie—and the psychological gulf between East and West has become narrower.

There is no reason to doubt that policy changes could bring significant short-term shifts toward more favorable attitudes toward the United States. But there is also evidence of a long-term structural component leading to the erosion of public support for the Atlantic Alliance. The shift toward Postmaterialism is a contributing factor. Partly, this simply reflects the historical accident that the first large Postmaterialist cohort entered the political stage during the Vietnam era. This did not result in Postmaterialists becoming anti-American; the historical, political, economic, and cultural bonds between the United States and Western Europe were too strong for that. But it did apparently contribute to making the Postmaterialists less favorably predisposed toward the United States and less trusting of the American people than those with other values.

Figure 12-3 illustrates this complex phenomenon. On one hand, Postmaterialists in general tend to be *more* trusting toward other nationalities than Materialists or mixed types. This is precisely what we would expect, since the Postmaterialists as a group were raised under conditions of relatively high economic and physical security and, for reasons suggested in Chapter 1, insecure persons are unlikely to trust strangers. In this respect, economic development tends to be generally conducive to trust between nations. Postmaterialists are relatively trusting of most nationalities—but they make an exception for the United States. Not only do West European Postmaterialists feel substantially less trust for Americans than do their

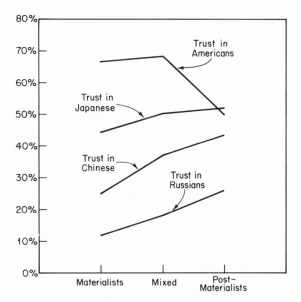

FIGURE 12-3. Trust in various nationalities by value type. Percentage saying that in their opinion the people indicated are "very trustworthy" or "fairly trustworthy," rather than "not particularly trustworthy," "not at all trustworthy," or "don't know." Based on combined data from Euro-Barometer survey 17 (April 1982).

Materialist or mixed-values compatriots; they actually trust Americans less than they trust the Japanese, and only slightly more than they trust the Chinese.

Our interpretation of this anomaly attributes it, in part, to the residual impact of the Vietnam experience, which engaged Postmaterialists to an exceptional degree. We do not have adequate data to test this interpretation. Insofar as it is correct, the tendency for West European Postmaterialists to be relatively anti-American should gradually fade over time. But this tendency was still clearly visible a decade after the war had ended and seems to be fading only gradually (if it is doing so).

The still positive but relatively low levels of trust toward Americans that we find among West European Postmaterialists do not necessarily mean that they are anti-American or opposed to political cooperation with the United States. But anti-Americanism does exist in Western Europe; we know this not merely from indirect inferences, but from the evidence of attitudes openly declared by substantial portions of the public.

In the 1980s, about one-fourth of the public in the four main European

TABLE 12-3. ANTI-AMERICANISM BY VALUE TYPE AMONG FIVE WESTERN PUBLICS IN 1982
AND 1984

Question: "Recently there have been some expressions of anti-American feelings
among West Europeans. How would you describe your own
feelings? Strongly anti-American, somewhat anti-American,
somewhat pro-American or strongly pro-American?"

(Percentage "strongly" or "somewhat" anti-American)

Value Type	France		W. Germany		Italy		Britain		Greece		Weighted Total[a]	
	1982	1984	1982	1984	1982	1984	1982	1984	1982	1984	1982	1984
Materialist	26%	13%	16%	12%	13%	17%	25%	29%	46%	45%	21%	19%
Mixed	29	20	19	18	19	25	37	34	61	57	27	24
Postmat.	44	34	41	38	42	38	43	44	80	78	43	37
Total	31	19	19	20	20	22	36	34	58	51	27	24

Sources: Euro-Barometer survey 17 (April 1982) and Euro-Barometer survey
22 (November 1984). In 1984 this question was asked only in these five
nations.

[a]Weighted according to population of each country.

NATO nations plus Greece described their own feelings as anti-American.
Though the evidence is still inadequate, there are indications that anti-
Americanism may be linked with the long-term shift toward Postmaterialism in those countries. As Table 12-3 demonstrates, Postmaterialists in all
five countries are relatively likely to be anti-American; in the five countries
as a whole, they are twice as apt as Materialists to express anti-American
feelings.

We should be cautious in interpreting this finding. It is not based on
anything like the massive body of data that points to a long-term trend
toward Postmaterialism. The linkage between Postmaterialism and anti-
Americanism suggests that the two variables may be following a common
trajectory, but it will require a good deal of additional research to establish
whether a trend exists. The linkage between anti-Americanism and Postmaterialism could be a transient phenomenon, perhaps resulting from the
campaign against the deployment of American missiles that was active in
the early 1980s. Clearly, anti-Americanism is not an inherent component
of Postmaterialism: There is no theoretical reason why the two would necessarily go together. Indeed, we would expect Postmaterialists to manifest
relatively low levels of xenophobia, because of their comparatively secure
socioeconomic status—and, in general, they do manifest relatively positive attitudes toward other nationalities. The linkage between Postmaterialism and anti-American feelings was durable at least from 1982 to 1984.

TABLE 12-4. ATTITUDES TOWARD ATLANTIC ALLIANCE BY VALUE TYPE

Question: "All things considered, what do you think is better for (respondent's country) national interest? To coordinate our foreign policy closely with the United States; or to conduct our foreign policy without giving special consideration to the interests of the United States?"

(Percentage saying "coordinate closely with the United States")

Value Type	France	W. Germany	Italy	Britain	Greece	Weighted Total[a]
Materialist	35%	66%	47%	51%	16%	44%
Mixed	33	64	41	46	8	41
Postmaterialist	16	36	25	35	5	24

Source: Euro-Barometer survey 17 (April 1982). This question was asked only in these five nations.
[a]Weighted according to population of each country.

Though the prevalence of anti-American feelings fell in some countries and rose in others, with a modest overall decline, the underlying values-based component persisted. In both 1982 and 1984, Postmaterialists were about twice as likely as Materialists to express anti-American feelings. A conclusive interpretation of this finding is not yet possible. But regardless of whether a long-term anti-American trend exists, it seems clear that a pro-American consensus no longer exists.

Moreover, support for the Atlantic Alliance itself seems to have eroded even more than have favorable feelings toward the Americans. As Table 12-4 illustrates, public support for coordinating one's own nation's foreign policy with that of the·United States varies a great deal from nation to nation. But across the four main NATO partners plus Greece, less than 40 percent of the public were in favor of a coordinated Atlantic foreign policy in 1982. Here again, we find a pronounced linkage with Materialist/Post-materialist values. Overall, Postmaterialists are only about half as likely as Materialists to support a coordinated foreign policy. Again, how stably the two attitudes are linked is an open question. But the findings are suggestive.

The Atlantic Alliance, of course, consists of more than the United States. Conceivably, it could even exist without that country. But the United States is the strongest member of the alliance and close cooperation with the United States is now supported by only a minority among the West European publics. In most member countries, strong majorities still favor continued participation in NATO. Data from the November 1984 Euro-Barometer survey indicate that only in Greece does opposition to NATO membership outweigh support for remaining in NATO. But opposition to NATO membership is widespread, with 15 to 35 percent of the public opposing it in the various other member countries. Moreover, this opposition may be growing, for it is more common among the young and the Postmaterialists than among other groups.

Whatever the impact of long-term trends, however, it seems clear that West European publics' evaluations of current American politics have been important too—and in the early 1980s, a large share of these publics saw current American policies as harmful. The NATO decision to deploy new American intermediate-range nuclear missiles in Western Europe, while negotiating with the Soviets to reduce the number of their own new intermediate-range missiles, gave rise to tremendous controversy in Western Europe from 1979 to 1984. Protest groups became active throughout Western Europe and hundreds of thousands of demonstrators marched or surrounded United States military bases in an effort to prevent deployment. Although the decision to install these missiles was originally prompted by West Germany and was made by the various NATO governments, the move was strongly backed by the American government—and was perceived as an American policy by many, perhaps even most, of the protesters. After much debate and various delays, deployment finally began late in 1984. Almost unquestionably, this was what most West Europeans must have had in mind when they were asked, at that time, "On balance, do you think that United States' policies and actions during the past year have done more to promote peace or done more to increase the risk of war?"

As Table 12-5 demonstrates, in all seven countries for which we have data, more people thought United States policies had increased the risk of war than thought they had promoted peace. But these responses depended heavily on the respondent's national perspective. Opinion was about evenly divided in Italy and Ireland, while in Britain, Belgium, and the Netherlands, clear majorities felt that United States policies had increased the risk of war; and among the Greek public—characterized as we have seen, by strongly anti-American predispositions—an overwhelming majority thought United States policies had been conducive to war.

But it was not only national perspective that shaped perceptions of United States policy: these perceptions were also heavily influenced by values and generation. As Table 12-6 demonstrates, the Materialists among West European publics were about evenly divided in their assessment of whether United States policies had done more to promote peace or more to promote war. But those with Postmaterialist values were more than *four times* as likely to perceive American policies as having increased the risk of war as they were to see them as conducive to peace. It was not simply the objective events that gave rise to dissent; the cultural filter through which one viewed them was also immensely important. The young were also significantly more likely to perceive American policies as war-

TABLE 12-5. WEST EUROPEAN EVALUATIONS OF WHETHER U.S. POLICIES AND
ACTIONS DURING 1984 HAVE PROMOTED PEACE

Question: "On balance, do you think that United States policies and
actions during the past year have done more to promote peace or done
more to increase the risk of war?"

Public	Peace	Don't Know	War
Italy	42%	14%	43%
Ireland	36	23	41
Belgium	34	18	48
Netherlands	32	21	47
West Germany	30	31	39
Britain	29	17	54
Greece	13	22	66

Source: Euro-Barometer survey 22 (November 1984). Question not
asked in France, Denmark, or Luxembourg.

TABLE 12-6. EVALUATIONS OF WHETHER U.S. POLICIES DURING 1984 HAVE
PROMOTED PEACE BY VALUE TYPE AND AGE GROUP

	Peace	Don't Know	War
1. By value type			
Materialist	29%	43%	27%
Mixed	27	36	37
Postmaterialist	13	32	55
2. By age group			
15 - 24	20	40	39
25 - 39	21	39	40
40 - 54	30	35	36
55+	30	40	30

Source: See Table 12-5.

like than were the old, but the relationship was a good deal weaker than
that with values; it seems that the young tended to perceive American policy as warlike because many of them were Postmaterialists, rather than that
Postmaterialists saw things that way because they were young.

The specific events that took place from 1982 to 1984 were extremely important, and they probably tended to make all nationalities view American actions as having increased the risk of war. But people of different nationalities, and people with different values, reacted very differently to precisely the same events at the same time and place. The evidence indicates that in addition to the influence of current events, there is also a long-term component at work shaping people's assessments of what has happened, with Postmaterialists far likelier to put a negative interpretation on United States defense policy.

The same point can be made in connection with United States economic policy. In 1984, the American government was maintaining exceptionally high interest rates, in an effort to cope with a huge negative balance of payments; this was causing considerable economic difficulty in some West European countries, especially Great Britain, which experienced a heavy flow of capital to the United States. These problems were widely discussed in Western Europe, and in every one of the seven countries for which we have 1984 data, a strong plurality of the public felt that United States economic policies had been harmful to their country's economy (see Table 12-7). One year later, economic conditions had begun to change, and public attitudes shifted sharply; by 1985, in almost half of the European Community countries, solid pluralities assessed United States economic policy as having been favorable. There seems to be little question that changes in the real world led to dramatic changes in mass perception. But, once again, there is strong evidence that a long-term component also helped shape these perceptions—for in 1984, Postmaterialists were almost twice as likely as Materialists to perceive United States economic policy as having hurt their nation's economy, and in 1985, though the overall distribution of attitudes was much more positive, Postmaterialists were *still* about twice as likely as Materialists to make a negative assessment of United States economic policy (see Table 12-8). The judgments of mass publics reflect an interaction between their response to current events and enduring predispositions.

THE DECLINE OF NATIONALISM AND PATRIOTISM AMONG WEST EUROPEAN PUBLICS

The rise of Postmaterialism seems to be one of two factors that are working to erode mass support for the Atlantic Alliance. Another important process is also occurring: the decline of nationalism and patriotism among West European publics. This trend can be traced to some of the same factors that give rise to Postmaterialism: the emergence of a public that has become accustomed to economic and physical security, and is less likely

TABLE 12-7. WEST EUROPEAN EVALUATIONS OF WHETHER U.S. POLICIES HELPED
OR HARMED THEIR NATION'S ECONOMY, IN 1984 AND 1985

Question: "From what you have heard or read, do you think that the
economic policies and actions of the United States have been more
helpful or more harmful to the economic situation in our country, or
have they had little effect on our country?"

Country	1984		1985	
	Helped	Harmed	Helped	Harmed
Netherlands	27%	37%	40%	25%
Italy	25	41	43	22
West Germany	20	40	34	26
Portugal	-	-	32	12
Ireland	19	27	30	15
Denmark	-	-	23	28
Belgium	15	46	21	30
Spain	-	-	19	31
Greece	10	52	19	49
Britain	7	56	15	38
France	-	-	11	36

Source: Euro-Barometer survey 22 (November 1984) and survey 24
(November 1985).
Note: The percentages saying that American policies "helped" or
"hurt" their country's economy do not add up to 100; the remainder said
they "had little effect" or "don't know." In 1984, this question was
asked only in the seven nations for which results are given.

to feel threatened by neighboring peoples. Indeed, the rise of Postmaterialism contributes to this tendency. But the decline of patriotism and nationalism goes beyond the Postmaterialist syndrome, for it also reflects an
historical change in West European publics' orientations toward war—a
change that seems linked with the experience of World War II, on one
hand, and an awareness that modern technology would make a third world
war vastly more destructive than even the cataclysm of 1939–1945. Finally, the emergence of the European Community institutions has contributed to making the perspective of the nation-state seem outmoded, giving
rise to a faint but growing sense of European citizenship.

This is a very positive development in most respects. But insofar as
NATO bases its appeal on the nationalistic and patriotic sentiments that
characterized European publics during the balance of power era, another
component of its long-term mass support is gradually eroding. Indeed, as
we will demonstrate, in some important respects mass support is already
far eroded.

TABLE 12-8. EVALUATIONS OF WHETHER U.S. POLICIES HELPED OR HARMED ONE'S
NATION'S ECONOMY BY VALUE TYPE AND AGE GROUP, IN 1984 AND 1985

	1984		1985	
	Helped	*Harmed*	*Helped*	*Harmed*
1. By value type				
Materialist	14%	28%	29%	24%
Mixed	15	36	25	31
Postmaterialist	9	51	22	48
2. By age group				
15 - 24	11	34	24	30
25 - 39	12	38	23	33
40 - 54	15	35	29	29
55+	16	33	28	27

Source: See Table 12-7.

Table 12-9 presents evidence concerning one aspect of this process. In all six countries for which we have data from 1970, there are indications of a decline in national pride during the fifteen years from 1970 to 1985. In some cases—that of Belgium in particular—this decline is astonishingly large. In 1970, fully 70 percent of the Belgian public described themselves as "very proud" to be Belgians; in 1985, only 26 percent did so. The Belgian case is exceptional, since, as evidence noted throughout this book has indicated, cataclysmic changes have been occurring in the political culture of that country. The enormous size of this shift (in which the Belgians went from being one of the peoples that ranked highest on national pride to one that ranked lower than everyone but the Germans and Japanese) suggests that the collapse of a spirit of national unity in the 1970s helped account for the distinctive Belgian malaise that we have witnessed. But Belgium was not the only country that experienced declining feelings of national pride. A similar though milder trend is also visible in each of the other five countries that were surveyed in 1970: the publics of Luxembourg, Italy, France, the Netherlands, and West Germany all show declines from 1970 to 1985, ranging from 17 to 24 points in the percentage who were "very proud" of their nationality. No consistent pattern appears in the brief two-year period from 1983 to 1985; if anything, national pride seemed to have risen in that time. But the long-term decline is mirrored in the response patterns of the respective age groups and value types. As Table 12-10 reveals, Postmaterialists are only about half as likely as Ma-

TABLE 12-9. FEELING OF NATIONAL PRIDE IN TWENTY-TWO NATIONS,
1970 - 1985

Question: "Would you say you are very proud, quite proud, not very
proud, or not at all proud to be (nationality)?"

(Percentage saying "very proud")

Nation	1970	1981	1983	1985
Greece	-	-	76%	72%
U.S.	-	76%	-	-
Australia	-	70	-	-
Hungary	-	67	-	-
Mexico	-	65	-	-
Spain	-	51	-	64
Canada	-	62	-	-
Luxembourg	81%	-	51	62
Iceland	-	58	-	-
Britain	-	53	57	54
Ireland	-	67	52	53
Argentina	-	49	-	-
Italy	62	40	40	45
Norway	-	41	-	-
France	66	31	36	42
Denmark	-	30	39	40
Sweden	-	30	-	-
Netherlands	54	20	34	34
Portugal	-	-	-	33
Belgium	70	29	24	26
Japan	-	30	-	-
West Germany	38	21	17	20

Sources: European Community survey carried out in February-March
1970; World Values survey, 1981 - 1982; Euro-Barometer survey 19 (April
1983), and Euro-Barometer survey 24 (October-November 1985).

terialists are to describe themselves as "very proud" of their nationality;
and the youngest age cohort in Table 12-10 is far less likely to be "very
proud" of their nationality than the oldest cohort. Once again, we have
indications of an intergenerational shift, which the available longitudinal
evidence tends to confirm.

At the same time, there is evidence of the gradual emergence of a sense
of European citizenship. In the April 1983 Euro-Barometer survey, and
again in the November 1985 survey, the publics of the European Community countries were asked, "Do you ever think of yourself not only as
a citizen of [your nation] but also as a citizen of Europe?"

Both times, about half the public in the European Community as a whole
responded that they "often" or "sometimes" thought of themselves as
citizens of Europe. Postmaterialists and younger respondents were more
apt to express this feeling than were Materialists and older respondents.
This is still far short of a consensus—half of the public "never" think of
themselves as Europeans—and, given the weakness of the European institutions, this development has limited significance at present. But in the
long run, it could become significant.

TABLE 12-10. NATIONAL PRIDE AMONG WEST EUROPEAN PUBLICS BY VALUE TYPE
AND AGE GROUP, 1983

Question: "Would you say you are very proud, quite proud, not very
proud, or not at all proud to be (nationality)?"

(Percentage saying "very proud")

	%	N
1. By value type		
Materialist	47%	(3,380)
Mixed	40	(4,655)
Postmaterialist	24	(1,127)
2. By age group		
15 - 24	29	(1,834)
25 - 34	35	(1,632)
35 - 44	37	(1,637)
45 - 54	39	(1,433)
55 - 64	52	(1,385)
65+	54	(1,439)

Source: Based on data from Euro-Barometer survey 19 (April 1983).
Note: Percentages weighted according to population of each nation.

The majority of these publics may not yet be citizens of Europe. But it is equally clear that they are no longer the fervent nationalists of yesterday. The feeling that the nation-state incarnated a supreme value, as the haven and the sole defense of a unique way of life, has largely vanished in contemporary Western Europe. One of the most important practical consequences is that today large segments of the public would not be willing to fight for their country.

In the 1981 World Values survey, and again in the November 1985 Euro-Barometer survey, representative samples of the respective publics were asked, "Of course, we all hope that there will not be another war, but if it were to come to that, would you be willing to fight for your country?"

As Table 12-11 demonstrates, there is a wide range of cross-national variation in the responses. One point is clear, however: The European members of the NATO alliance are less ready to fight for their country than are the Americans—who, themselves, manifested severe dissension over this question during the war in Vietnam. The sole exception to this pattern is found among the Greeks–ironically, the one public having a majority in favor of withdrawal from NATO. Quite likely, what many Greeks have in mind is not an all-out East-West war, but a local nonnuclear conflict between Greece and Turkey.

Even within Western Europe, the percentage willing to fight for their

TABLE 12-11. WILLINGNESS TO FIGHT FOR ONE'S COUNTRY IN TWENTY-TWO
SOCIETIES

Question: "Of course, we all hope that there will not be another war,
but if it were to come to that, would you be willing to fight for your
country?"

(Percentage saying "Yes")

Nation	1981	1985
Mexico	89%	–
Sweden	87	–
Hungary	87	–
Australia	75	–
United States	74	–
Iceland	74	–
Greece	–	76%
Spain	66	69
Luxembourg	–	67
Portugal	–	65
Canada	64	–
Denmark	72	63
Britain	68	61
Argentina	59	–
South Africa	59	–
France	48	57
Netherlands	57	52
Ireland	61	45
Italy	36	38
Belgium	34	36
West Germany	47	33
Japan	32	–

Sources: World Values survey, 1981 - 1982; and Euro-Barometer survey
24 (October-November 1985).

country ranges from 60 percent or more in Denmark, Great Britain, and
Spain to as little as one-third of the public in Belgium, West Germany, and
Italy. It seems significant that willingness to fight for one's country is
markedly lower in the three defeated former Axis powers, Germany, Japan, and Italy, than in most of their neighbors. The glories of war were
vastly overrated by the men who led these countries nearly two generations
ago; and the defeat they met in World War II seems to have discredited its
appeal in lasting fashion.

Thus, an unusual confluence of forces works to undermine willingness
to fight for one's country in Western Europe. On one hand, the emergence
of Postmaterialism contributes to this orientation. As Table 12-12 demonstrates, Postmaterialists are significantly less willing to fight for their country than Materialists. But this interacts with life cycle effects and an historical experience that is particularly intense among the older generation,
particularly in the countries that were defeated in World War II. The net
effect is that the correlation with age is relatively weak with this item and
the old are actually less willing to fight for their country than the young.

Changing situations can make people see things from a different per-

TABLE 12-12. WILLINGNESS TO FIGHT FOR ONE'S COUNTRY BY VALUE TYPE AND
AGE GROUP, IN 1981 AND 1985
(Percentage willing to fight)

	1981	1985
1. By value type		
Materialist	65%	54%
Mixed	68	53
Postmaterialist	55	38
2. By age group		
15 - 24	66	52
25 - 34	66	50
35 - 44	73	52
45 - 54	70	49
55 - 64	67	47
65+	56	44

Sources: World Values survey, 1981; and Euro-Barometer survey 24 (1985).

spective. The British students who vowed not to fight for King and Country during the Oxford peace movement of the 1930s fought resolutely when World War II arrived. And the responses of given publics show considerable fluctuations even in the relatively short period from 1981 to 1985. Nevertheless, the evidence in Table 12-11 cannot simply be ignored.

France, West Germany, and Italy are crucial NATO allies—and the publics of all three countries are seriously divided on whether they would be willing to fight for their countries. In France, roughly half the public indicated that they would be willing to do so; in both West Germany and Italy, in both 1981 and 1985, the majority indicated they were *not* willing to fight. Though the absolute level of these responses would undoubtedly vary with actual situations, we cannot assume that in the event of an actual conflict, willingness to fight would automatically move *upward*: West Europeans' willingness to fight is far below the level found in the United States, where unwillingness to fight became so intense during the Vietnam conflict that eventually the military draft was abolished. The future is unpredictable. But it would be unwise to ignore evidence of negative trends underlying mass support for the Atlantic Alliance.

Waning Support for NATO: Implications

There is a tendency for those concerned with the Atlantic Alliance to blame its current difficulties on short-term factors, such as the tactical errors of given politicians or the influence of Soviet-funded pressure groups. Fundamentally, the argument goes, NATO is just as healthy as it ever was and will no doubt play a major role for another generation.

If, as the evidence presented here suggests, declining support for the Atlantic Alliance proves to be part of a long-term trend linked with intergenerational population replacement, this interpretation is unrealistic—and it might be wise to begin openly considering a future without NATO. Already, the alliance has experienced extreme difficulty in implementing basic strategic decisions because of the erosion of public support. The principal West German opposition party, which originally proposed deployment of intermediate-range missiles, later became deeply divided on the subject and officially opposed them. The Dutch government went through a crisis over this question and survived by patching together a compromise that postponed deployment but satisfied neither side. Subsequent Soviet-American negotiations resolved this specific problem, but left the basic dilemma unchanged.

In a sense, the present arrangements obtain the worst of both worlds: A large and apparently growing part of the European public takes it for granted that the United States will defend Western Europe but views the American forces as dangerous and provocative. The presence of American military forces in Western Europe provides a rationale to do nothing and shift the responsibility to the United States. In the long run, this is an untenable position for the United States. Moreover, the credibility of the American nuclear guarantee is genuinely open to doubt. The United States no longer has a monopoly or even a preponderance of strategic nuclear missiles. Given nuclear parity, how realistic is it to assume that an American president will commit national suicide in order to preserve the independence of Western Europe? Rather than wait for an open policy split to occur, which might suddenly leave Western Europe without any credible counterweight to Soviet military pressures, it might be wise to plan phasing out the American military presence in a gradual fashion that would enable the West Europeans to develop an independent defense system if they choose to do so.

Today, in contrast with the postwar era, Western Europe is perfectly capable of defending itself. The Atlantic Alliance was founded at a time when Western Europe lay devastated by World War II and divided by resentment and hatreds, which were especially deep between the peoples of France and Germany. Under these conditions, American military protection may have been the only alternative to a Soviet-dominated Europe. Circumstances have changed profoundly. Today, Western Europe is becoming increasingly unified in a European Community, which by 1992 will abolish the remaining barriers to trade and the movement of people within a twelve-nation economic unit. The Community has a growing sense of political unity, as well. A majority of the French public now consider West Germany their closest ally and the people they trust most (In-

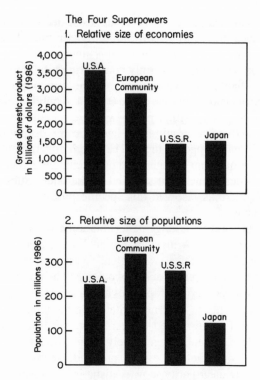

FIGURE 12-4. The four superpowers: relative
size of economic base and population of
United States, European Community, Soviet
Union, and Japan in 1986.

glehart and Rabier 1984). While psychological ties with the United States
have become less paramount, feelings of West European solidarity have
grown stronger.

It remains true that, individually, no single West European nation is
capable of dealing with the Soviet Union on equal terms. But a united
European Community is not only equal to but, in most respects, potentially
stronger than the USSR. As Figure 12-4 demonstrates, the European Community as a whole constitutes one of the world's four economic superpowers, together with the United States, the Soviet Union, and Japan. The
European Community's economic base ranks second only to that of the
United States, and the united European Community ranks first among the
four superpowers in population. China is a potential fifth superpower, with
a population as large as that of the four superpowers combined—but an
economic base that is still less than one-tenth as large as that of the European Community. The combined nations of the European Community

have a larger population, a much larger industrial base, and a higher technological level than the Soviet Union does. Given the will and the time to prepare, there is no question that a united European Community could maintain its independence without an American military presence. It may be time to begin planning for this possibility.

THE EVOLUTION OF SUPPORT FOR EUROPEAN UNIFICATION

Public support for European integration has stabilized at a high level during the past two decades. It is stronger among the publics of the European Community's original six member nations and among the publics of the two new members, Spain and Portugal, than among the publics of the countries that first entered the Community during the economic distress of the mid-1970s and early 1980s; but overall, solid majorities favor membership in the European Community and support further efforts to unify Western Europe.

At the close of World War II, Western Europe was prostrate and divided by deep antagonisms. World War II had been the third round of a seemingly endless conflict between Germany and France. The European movement was launched, in large part, to avoid yet another round of West European civil war.

Public support for European integration has grown gradually since that time, with major advances and setbacks. The best available indicator of these long-term changes is a question that was first asked in a series of U.S. Information Agency (USIA) surveys in the 1950s and 1960s and has been included in the European Community's Euro-Barometer surveys in modified form from 1970 on. The question asks: "Would you say that you are very favorable, rather favorable, indifferent, unfavorable or very unfavorable to the efforts being made to unify Western Europe?"

This question is designed to tap the respondent's general feeling of support or opposition to European unification. It is virtually the only relevant item that has been asked repeatedly over a period of many years. But clearly it cannot be viewed as an absolute measure of support levels. It has a floating referent: the "efforts toward uniting Europe" that the question evoked in 1952 may have been the comparatively modest Coal and Steel Community; in 1957, respondents probably would have thought of the Common Market. In the 1980s, far more ambitious plans were being discussed, including a plan for political integration into a European Union.

Bearing this is mind, let us turn to Figure 12-5, which charts the rise and fall of responses to this question over a thirty-five-year period in Britain, France, Germany, and Italy (the USIA generally carried out European

FIGURE 12-5. Percentage "for" efforts to unify Western Europe, 1952–1987. Missing data are included in percentage base (thus, in 1952, 70 percent of the West German public were "for," 10 percent were "against," and 20 percent were "undecided"). Source: USIA surveys from 1952 to 1964 and European Community surveys from 1970 through 1987.

surveys only in these four countries). The pattern reveals several important points. First, let us note that in the period prior to 1958—the year the Common Market began to function—responses in all four countries fluctuated together, apparently in reaction to current events. We cannot demonstrate the causal linkages, of course, but it seems likely that the Korean War, together with the founding of the Coal and Steel Community in 1952, gave an early impetus to support for European integration: North Korea's invasion of the South gave rise to fears that Western Europe might be next on the Soviet agenda; and the achievement of integration in the steel industry may have encouraged the feeling that further integration was feasible. Conversely, the failure of the European Defense Community in 1954 apparently depressed European morale and led to a withdrawal of support, while renewed fears of war, stimulated by the Soviet invasion of Hungary and the Suez crisis late in 1956, may have rekindled a sense of urgency about European unification.

In any case, we find a series of pronounced upward and downard shifts in the 1950s, in which all four countries move together. But, starting in about 1958, the pattern changes. The British—who had ranked second only to the Germans in support for unification—start to move out of phase with the other three publics. Within the three Common Market countries, fluctuations taper off and support levels gradually converge upward toward the German level; by the mid-1970s, the Italians and the French were virtually indistinguishable from the Germans. Previously, the Germans had consistently been the most pro-European public, but in the 1970s and 1980s, the Germans, French, and Italians all showed strong prointegration consensuses, and in a given year any one of the three might rank highest. The British level, by contrast, fell drastically after creation of the Common Market, dropping below the 50 percent mark at the time of the first veto of British entry to the European Community and far below it after the second veto. Britain finally was admitted in 1973; two years later, British support for integration again rose above the 50 percent line, and continued moving upward for the next few years; nevertheless, a decade later there was still a large gap between the British and the three original European Community publics, although the British were gradually moving toward convergence. This does not mean that the British were less European in 1975 than in 1952; on the contrary, in 1952 they were unwilling to join even the Coal and Steel Community by a decisive margin. What the pattern does indicate is that a large relative gap opened up between the British, on one hand, and the publics of the original six Common Market countries, on the other. Until 1973, the British remained outside the European Community framework, while the publics of the Six shared common experiences, and gradually developed an increasingly European outlook.

Aside from the divergence between the British and the other three publics, Figure 12-5 shows another, almost equally striking phenomenon. The French and Italian publics—who originally were far less European than the Germans—progressively narrowed the gap, to the point where it had virtually disappeared by 1975. By 1987, the French and Italian publics were slightly more European than the Germans. This reflects the development of a pro-European consensus among the French and Italian publics; and the most important element in the process was winning over the large communist electorates in these countries.

Today, the prospect of a European Community that is united not only economically but also politically is no idle dream. To a surprising extent, the publics of the twelve member nations are already ready to accept it. The overwhelming majority are favorable to the general idea of unifying Western Europe; as Table 12-13 shows, across the twelve nations, supporters of unification outnumber opponents by almost 8 to 1. Moreover,

TABLE 12-13. SUPPORT FOR EUROPEAN UNIFICATION IN TWELVE EUROPEAN
COMMUNITY NATIONS, 1987

Question: "In general, are you for or against efforts being made to
unify Western Europe?"

Nation	% For	% Against
Italy	86%	5%
France	85	6
Netherlands	79	12
Belgium	78	7
West Germany	76	15
Spain	74	5
Portugal	70	5
Greece	66	17
Ireland	62	13
Luxembourg	60	11
Britain	70	17
Denmark	43	45
European Community	77	10

Source: Euro-Barometer survey 28 (November 1987).
Note: The difference between the totals shown above and 100%
reflects the percentage giving no opinion. Thus, in Italy, 9% of the
public gave no answer.

support for unification outweighs opposition by an overwhelming margin
in eleven of the twelve countries. The sole exception is Denmark, where a
plurality of the public opposes it.

When we move from the general idea of unification to the specific proposal to form a European government, responsible to the European Parliament, we are dealing with a much more demanding test of commitment to
European integration. But here, too, pro-European sentiment is remarkably widespread, with those favoring the formation of a European government outnumbering its opponents by 2 to 1 (see Table 12-14). Solid majorities favor this proposal in ten of the twelve nations; a plurality oppose
it in Britain, and an overwhelming majority oppose it in Denmark.

CONCLUSION

Evidence presented here suggests that declining support for the Atlantic
Alliance may be part of a long-term trend linked with intergenerational
population replacement. The continued erosion of political support for
NATO is not likely to occur rapidly; but it may be difficult to avoid in the
long run.

If this is true, then it may be time to begin planning for a future without
NATO, rather than to wait for a policy split to occur that might leave Western Europe without any credible counter to possible Soviet military pressures. Given the will to do so and the time to prepare, there is no question
that a united European Community could maintain its independence even

TABLE 12-14. SUPPORT FOR FORMATION OF A EUROPEAN GOVERNMENT, 1987

Question: "Are you for or against the formation of a European
government, responsible to the European Parliament?"

Nation	% For	% Against
Italy	70%	11%
France	60	19
Belgium	55	12
Luxembourg	52	21
Spain	49	10
Netherlands	45	21
Portugal	42	14
West Germany	41	28
Ireland	39	23
Greece	39	21
Britain	31	45
Denmark	13	64
European Community	49	24

Source: Euro-Barometer survey 28 (November 1987).

without an American military presence. And there are signs of the gradual emergence of a sense of European identity.

The parochial nationalism that seemed so pronounced in France under DeGaulle has vanished. Today, the French are among the most solidly pro-European publics in Europe. Only in Denmark is opposition to the construction of a politically united Europe overwhelming. But Denmark, with less than 2 percent of the European Community's population, is not crucial to the enterprise; a United Europe could flourish with or without Denmark. British membership, on the other hand, probably is crucial. For the time being, British opposition constitutes a major obstacle to political unification. But in Britain, unlike Denmark, opinion is fairly evenly divided. Moreover, the British have come a long way, from refusing to join the Common Market at all when it was founded, and being divided about whether to remain in the Community until recently, to a current consensus in favor of membership and a very favorable attitude toward the broad idea of European unification. If British attitudes continue to evolve as they have during the past two decades, European political unity may come about early in the coming century.

CHAPTER 13

The Role of Culture in Social Change: Conclusion

PEOPLE live in the past far more than they realize. We interpret reality in terms of concepts and worldviews based on past experiences. This is inevitable—what we experience consists of millions of sensations, and we cannot focus on all of them. Making them coherent means abstracting a few simplified concepts that seem relevant to important goals.

Few people invent concepts. It is vastly easier to take prefabricated ones from the available stock, based on experiences interpreted earlier by members of one's society. Having built an interpretation of reality around given concepts as one grows up, to reconstruct it anew would be a daunting task. Only the most traumatic experiences ever drive people to it. Thus, one orients one's life by following old road maps. They may be crude and they may be out of date, but even a crude map gives more guidance in reaching one's goals than does striking out on a random walk.

Prevailing worldviews differ from society to society, reflecting the different historical experiences of different peoples. Consequently, we find enduring, but not immutable, differences between the values, attitudes, and habits of different peoples. This means that different individuals and groups of people react differently in similar situations. As we have seen, surveys carried out repeatedly over many years show enduring cross-national differences in levels of overall life satisfaction, happiness, political satisfaction, interpersonal trust, and support for the existing social order. These attributes are part of a coherent syndrome, with given nationalities consistently ranking relatively high (or relatively low) on all of them. High or low scores on this syndrome have important consequences for the political and social behavior of given peoples, shaping the prospects for viable democracy, among other things. As we have seen, large cross-cultural differences in this syndrome of attitudes persisted throughout the period from 1973 through 1988; and fragmentary additional evidence suggests that these differences can be traced back into the 1950s.

These cross-cultural differences show considerable durability, then; but they are not immutable. For example, while the Italian public showed much lower levels of interpersonal trust than did other Western publics from the 1950s through the late 1980s, Italian trust levels have been rising, gradually approaching those of other publics. Moreover, we find similar subcultural differences within Italy, with interpersonal trust levels in the south, Sicily and Sardinia ranking far below those in the north—but with trust levels rising throughout the country and moving toward convergence among the various regions of Italy, as in the West in general. West Germany presents an even more striking example of cultural change. In 1959, the West German public ranked far behind the British and American publics, and only marginally ahead of the Italians, in interpersonal trust and other aspects of the civic culture syndrome. But by the mid-1970s the West Germans had risen to a level almost as high as that of the British on overall life satisfaction, slightly higher on interpersonal trust, and well above the British on political satisfaction and support for the existing social order. Several decades of prosperity, together with a relatively effective and stable political system, contributed to the development of an increasingly strong civic culture among the West German public. Change has occurred—but it did so gradually.

Other dimensions of political culture show comparable stability, with only gradual change. Isolated attitudes can change overnight, but change in a central component of people's worldview seems to take place, in large part, as one generation replaces another. Thus, throughout the period from 1973 to 1988, the Germans, Dutch, and Danes showed a relatively strong propensity to discuss politics, while the Irish, Italians, and Belgians were much less likely to do so. But the younger and better-educated birth cohorts consistently showed higher levels of politicization than did the older groups in their country; and politicization levels have been gradually rising in most countries as younger cohorts replace older ones in the adult populations.

Similarly, throughout advanced industrial society, younger birth cohorts are much likelier to have Postmaterialist values than their elders. A massive body of survey evidence demonstrates that these cohort differences persisted throughout the period from 1970 to 1988; consequently, intergenerational population replacement during this period led to a gradual decline in the proportion of Materialists and an increase in the proportion of Postmaterialists among Western publics.

Materialist/Postmaterialist values seem to be part of a broader syndrome of orientations involving motivation to work, political outlook, attitudes toward the environment and nuclear power, the role of religion in people's lives, the likelihood of getting married or having children, and attitudes toward the role of women, homosexuality, divorce, abortion, and numerous other topics. The facts that all of these are closely related to whether one has Materialist or Postmaterialist values *and* that the outlook of younger birth cohorts differs greatly from that of older cohorts suggest that we may be witnessing a broad cultural shift, with one worldview replacing another. Whether this broad cultural shift is actually occurring has not yet been demonstrated empirically; but it is already clear that an intergenerational shift is taking place in at least one component of this syndrome—the shift from Materialist to Postmaterialist values. Whether one has Materialist or Postmaterialist priorities seems to reflect the impact of one's formative experiences—experiences that may have taken place as much as fifty or sixty years ago.

In short, the worldviews that prevail in given societies can change—but they change gradually, in large part through intergenerational population replacement. This inherent slowness of cultural change can be dangerous, for it means that the values and assumptions upon which both elites and mass publics operate may be based on a bygone reality—and there is considerable evidence that this does indeed happen.

For example, the policy of basing the West's defense planning on a strategy of massive nuclear deterrence may have been rational as long as only the West had a deliverable nuclear capability. Today, it has become a system whereby both the Soviet Union and the United States (together with everyone else in the Northern Hemisphere) live perpetually on the brink of annihilation, with thousands of nuclear weapons targeted on one another and ready to go off at a few minutes' notice. This system no longer provides a really credible deterrent to aggression, but it is enormously dangerous—particularly to those who possess it. A rational observer from another planet would probably view the current defense system as remarkably foolish, dangerous, and irresponsible; but political elites, for the most part, calmly accept it because, in the back of their minds, they see the world as if they still were living in an earlier era

Before the emergence of advanced industrial society, it was taken for granted that all nations were inherent rivals, seeking to conquer one another unless prevented from doing so. Wars of conquest seemed inevitable because they were potentially profitable. Throughout history, tribes and nations have fought to control hunting grounds, water, agricultural land, and other natural resources. Under conditions of extreme scarcity, such wars might be the only means for a given people to survive. Even for nations with a somewhat more advanced level of technology, wars of conquest could bring riches, as Spain and Portugal demonstrated long ago. The costs were relatively low, and successful wars might bring substantial gains.

For high-technology societies, the cost/benefit ratio has changed decisively, but national strategies involving hundreds of billions of dollars and hundreds of millions of lives continue to reflect outmoded assumptions. On one hand, for one high-technology society to attack another would be irrational because the costs would vastly outweigh any conceivable gains: Nuclear weapons, together with equally deadly bacteriological and chemical ones, enable both sides to destroy in minutes far more than they would gain even in the event of total victory and enslavement of the enemy. Even a lightly armed high-technology society, such as Japan, makes a somewhat dubious target. She is well enough equipped to exact considerable costs; and if one conquered her, there is relatively little plunder to carry off since her wealth lies primarily in the skills and knowledge of her people.

On the other hand, wars against preindustrial nations have also become unprofitable, for a different set of reasons. There is now such a disparity between the standard of living of an advanced industrial society and an agrarian one that the costs of imperialism outweigh the potential gains. During the American war in Vietnam, for example, it cost approximately $50,000 per year to maintain one American soldier there—in a country with a per capita income of less than $200 per year. The Vietnamese could field an army of a given size for about 1 percent of what it would cost the Americans. The Americans were motivated by political misperception rather than financial gain, but if they had been a classic imperial power seeking enrichment, victory would have been futile because there was not enough available capital in the entire country to pay the costs of their involvement. Imperialism loses its cost-effectiveness for societies with a high technological level, which may be why the last Western power to give up her colonial empire was Portugal—by far the poorest country in Western Europe, with a per capita income about one-quarter of that of Britain or France.

The declining economics of imperialism seem to be reinforced by an accompanying cultural shift: With economic development and the rise of Postmaterialist values, people not only have less need to plunder their neighbors, but seem to become less willing to do so. At the close of World War II, the United States may have become the first victorious power in history to extend economic aid to her defeated foes instead of plundering them. But subsequently, former colonial powers, such as Britain, France, and the Netherlands, have extended small but significant amounts of economic aid to their former empires. And the Soviet Union has now joined them. Though in the immediate postwar era, capital equipment taken from Eastern Europe was an important source of Soviet reconstruction, for most of the past fifteen years, the Soviet Union has been subsidizing her client states, with the costs of the Soviet empire clearly outweighing the economic gains.

In short, not only does the cost/benefit ratio become unfavorable to imperialism at high levels of technology; even more important, safer and easier ways to get rich become available. With a primitive technology, plundering your neighbors may be the only available means to obtain wealth. But advanced technology offers the potential to amass much greater wealth without leaving your homeland. The amount of territory and natural resources one controls become secondary considerations; increasingly, the key resources are knowledge and innovation. Stripped of her empire, Japan has developed a per capita income forty times as high as the highest level she attained in the prewar era. It is probably no coincidence that both Germany and Japan, defeated in World War II and greatly reduced in territory and natural resources, nevertheless emerged as the two great success stories of the postwar era. This phenomenon has sometimes been attributed to the fact that their industrial plants were largely destroyed in the war, leaving them free to develop new, more modern factories. But if this had been the secret of their success, any other country could have copied them and built from scratch. It may be more important that their total defeat, by banishing any illusions of military conquest, freed them psychologically to concentrate on more productive activities.

Old worldviews are remarkably persistent, shaping human behavior long after the conditions that gave rise to them have faded away. Soviet and American leaders continue to spend hundreds of billions of dollars each year on weapons systems of no utility except as an instrument of psychological warfare. The supposition that the two countries are doomed to fight each other rests almost entirely on subjective factors: It corresponds to no objective motivation. Like the persistent stereotypes of trust or distrust that given nationalities hold for others, enduring over decades, the danger of nuclear war persists—based on little more than mindsets that bear no relationship to the objective situation today. Located on opposite sides of the world, the United States and the Soviet Union have no border rivalries. Moreover, they have complementary economies: Competing against each other in very few domains, they are potentially good customers for each other's products. Ultimately, the only reason for conflict between the superpowers is an outmoded ideology of inevitable conflict—which, insofar as it persists, could become a self-fulfilling prophecy.

Ideological stereotypes tend to depict the East-West comparison as a black and white contrast, when the reality is one of incremental differences—some of which have been getting smaller as time goes by. For example, the stereotype tends to depict ''communist'' states as having totally state-run economies, and ''capitalist'' countries as having economies completely in private hands. Today that is far from reality. On one hand, with increasing government regulation and intervention and the growth of the welfare state, the state's share of the pie has steadily increased throughout the West. Seventy years ago, government expenditures in most Western countries were less than 10 percent of total national product. Today, governmental expenditures range from about one-third of gross national product, in the United States, to over 60 percent in such countries as the Netherlands and Sweden. In this respect, there is only a marginal difference between the latter countries and Eastern Europe or the Soviet Union, where governmental expenditures amount to about 70 percent of gross national product—and where the current trend is moving in the direction of reducing state intervention and control. Throughout the communist world, various regimes are experimenting with ways to diminish the stultifying effects of excessive centralized control and to give greater scope to individual initiative. At the same time, the West seems to be moving away from the classic model of capitalism in another way. Although there no longer is much support in the West for increasing government ownership of industry as we saw in chapter 9, there is widespread and apparently growing support for greater employee participation in selection of management.

There may be a long-term tendency toward East-West convergence in the political realm as well. The emphasis that Mikhail Gorbachev has recently placed on restructuring Soviet society reflects a broader process, which is common to advanced industrial societies: As they develop, it becomes increasingly difficult to govern them in a hierarchical, authoritarian fashion. A determined and cohesive political elite can repress the pressures to permit more autonomy and broader participation in decision making, but it does so at the risk of economic and political stagnation. During the long years of Brezhnev's reign, precisely this was happening, with a resulting decline in productivity and economic growth and a general deterioration of morale. Western societies have felt the impact of repeated waves of demands for increased mass participation in politics. These demands led to the enfranchisement of the working class around the turn of the century, followed by the suffragette movement, the birth of the welfare state, and the wave of activism in the United States in the 1960s that resulted in the extension of civil rights to blacks in the South and extension of the vote to 18-year-olds. The process of cognitive mobilization continues today, with such contemporary phenomena as the environmentalist movement, the women's movement, and other new social movements.

The relative openness of Western democracies meant that they felt these demands relatively early, and responded to them incrementally. The more tightly controlled societies of Eastern Europe were subject to the same forces that gave rise to these movements, but tended to repress them. Thus, limited reforms and liberalization began to emerge under Khrushchev; these events stimulated various writers in the 1960s to develop the thesis that mature industrial states tend to converge toward a common model. But, as subsequent events demonstrated, the process is not automatic: After Khrushchev, there came a phase of reaction and consolidation. Nevertheless, the basic insight may have been well founded. A strategy of repression, such as that followed by Brezhnev, may be effective in the short run, but it gives rise to increasingly serious problems in the long run. Contemporary Soviet elites, led by Gorbachev, clearly are aware of the difficulties engendered by the rigid policies of the Brezhnev era and are making a serious effort to find ways to make Soviet society more open. Their motivation may be primarily a concern to restore the Soviet economy to a competitive position, but doing so will necessarily entail increased freedom of communication and a somewhat less hierarchical, more pluralistic society—for developing the mature technology and economy of advanced industrial society brings many benefits that are highly attractive to the Soviet elite. But it also gives rise to a labor force that is capable of, and likely to seek, more significant input into decision making in both the economic and political domains. There are two fundamental reasons why this is true, the first functional and the second cultural.

The first reason is the fact that a technologically advanced economy requires a highly educated labor force, working in a fashion that requires a good deal of autonomy. The rulers of a primitive agricultural economy can run it with slave labor; and when industrial society first emerged, the early factories were run with unskilled "hands," performing simple repetitive tasks according to a routine prescribed from above. But the crucial tasks of advanced industrial society require increasing amounts of individual judgment and initiative. Routine mechanical and clerical operations are taken over by automated machinery and computers; increasingly, people are employed only where human judgment, empathy, and creativity are needed. Sheer muscle power is no longer in demand; the crucial input is innovation. The Japanese economy has become the pacesetter for industrial society partly because it is well adapted to giving free play to human initiative and judgment in avoiding errors in the production process, but primarily because it is geared to continually introducing new products and improving existing ones.

Innovation is crucial. But innovation cannot be prescribed from above; by definition, it does not consist in following existing routines. It requires individual autonomy, and can flourish only when the individual feels free to express his or her ideas regardless of what the authorities believe. An authoritarian atmosphere stifles creativity. But once an individual becomes accustomed to exercising independent judgment and expressing ideas freely in the workplace, he or she may be increasingly inclined to exercise these skills in politics as well (Nie, Powell, and Prewitt 1969; Verba, Nie, and Kim 1978). This tendency is reinforced by the fact that introducing the technological infrastructure of a knowledge-based society tends to open up communications channels in ways that are difficult for the central authorities to police and control. If a government allows copying machines to become widespread, it opens the door for rapid and widespread *samizdat*. If a nationwide network of personal computers grows up, citizens suddenly have freedom of the press. Not surprisingly, Soviet political elites have resisted such developments—but doing so means falling farther and farther behind world standards in economic productivity and innovation, and in the long run an obsolete economy means an obsolete military establishment. In short, economic modernization does not make political liberalization inevitable, but it does make it increasingly difficult to avoid.

The impact of technological modernization is reinforced by parallel cultural developments that take place in advanced industrial society. As we have seen, economic development and the emergence of social welfare institutions give rise to a sense of economic security, which in turn leads to a gradual shift from Materialist to Postmaterialist values among both elites and the general public. Though the Soviet Union still lags behind the West in absolute levels of income, we would expect her relatively high standards of job security and other forms of social security to give rise to an increasingly Postmaterialist outlook. This seems already to have occurred in Poland (as we saw in chapter 4). Though we do not have relevant survey evidence from the Soviet Union itself, a recent study of Soviet émigrés suggests the presence of large intergenerational differences in the political orientations of the Soviet public (Zimmerman and Yarsike n.d.). Evidence from numerous countries makes it clear that Postmaterialists are far likelier than Materialists to give a high priority to self-expression, not only on the job and in the community, but in national politics as well. We suspect that a similar cultural shift is taking place in the Soviet Union.

By themselves, such cultural preferences are not necessarily decisive. They are only one component of a complex system of causal factors. They constitute an important motivational factor that, in the long run, tends to encourage political liberalization, reinforcing the other factors we have mentioned. We do not expect major changes to take place overnight. On the contrary, there is a great deal of institutional and cultural inertia working against change. But the long-term outlook seems more conducive to convergence than to polarization between Soviet and Western societies. It would be ironic if they destroyed each other over differences that are gradually fading.

The impact of cultural factors varies from one situation to another. But situational factors now seem conducive to culture's becoming an increasingly important factor in the politics of both Western countries and the Soviet Union. In order to see why this is true, let us ask, "Under what conditions is culture a crucial factor?"

Under certain circumstances, an essential variable, whether it be economic or cultural, may have no apparent impact. For an illustration, let us return to the analogy of the racers. It is absolutely necessary to have strong leg muscles, bones, heart, and lungs, in order to win a race, but if all the runners have equally strong legs, muscular strength will be uncorrelated with success. In other words, if there is no variation in a given factor, it will be of no help in predicting or explaining the outcome. Among Olympic runners, there probably is little variation in muscular strength; for in order to compete at that level, one must have strong legs. But among a random group of people, including everyone from toddlers to feeble old people, there will be a great deal of variation in muscular strength—making it an important predictor of their relative success. In both cases, muscular strength is essential, but its statistical impact is suppressed when variance is minimal or nonexistent.

Similarly, Materialist/Postmaterialist values have no explanatory power in a society consisting almost entirely of Materialists (even though the behavior of these people is shaped in crucial ways by the fact that they are Materialists); but with the emergence of substantial numbers of Postmaterialists, this dimension may become a major explanatory variable. Precisely this seems to have happened in advanced industrial societies within the past few decades. Prior to the emergence of Postmaterialism, one could take this aspect of culture largely for granted, basing one's model of society on the assumption that people behaved as Economic Man, motivated primarily by materialistic goals.

There is another situation in which the impact of an essential variable will be masked, even when it has considerable variation: when all parties involved are above a threshold at which they have more than enough to meet the demands of the given situation. Using the analogy of the runners again, strong bones are essential to a runner and some runners may have considerably stronger bones than others. But above a certain point, additional strength does not contribute to greater speed. Bone strength, even if it varies greatly, will not decide the outcome, and the crucial factor will be one that *is* in short supply. In long distance races, the limiting factor tends to be the rate at which oxygen can be supplied to the muscles, which depends primarily on the pulmonary and circulatory systems. These systems may also interact with motivational factors: The race may be won by a runner who persists at high speed, despite the fatigue and pain induced by oxygen starvation. But the critical variable will be one that is in short supply.

Throughout the history of preindustrial society, and continuing well into early industrial society, population tended to increase to meet the available food supply—at which point food became the limiting factor. It determined how most individuals spent most of their time and effort. At the societal level, it determined population size. It might determine foreign policy as well, if the tribe or nation attempted to expand its territory at the expense of its neighbors. As long as getting enough to eat is the crucial problem for most people, economic determinism provides a reasonably good first approximation, in attempting to explain human behavior. Even here, it is only a first approximation, however, since virtually all societies develop ways of limiting the impact of scarcity, through norms of sharing and mutual obligation, and partially effective ways of limiting population growth, through norms governing when one may marry. Such norms are a crucial way in which a society minimizes internal violence, maintains group cohesion, and adapts to an environment of scarcity.

During the early industrialization process in the West, traditional religious norms and restraints were breaking down. This rendered stark economic determinism more plausible than it had been earlier, because the effectiveness of cultural restraints had become weaker and less apparent. Thus, the Marxist model appeared at a point in history when a univariate model of society seemed relatively plausible. The ability to come up with a plausible one-factor model gave Marx an immense advantage, which helps explain the tremendous impact he had, and still has, on the way people throughout the world interpret reality. The fact that Marx himself unquestionably saw reality as more complex than sheer economic determinism, is irrelevant. In his bolder moments, he spoke as if reality were a matter of simple economic determinism, and understandably, this was the version that caught on and has had immense social and political impact— for the simpler the model, the more powerful it seems, and a model that purportedly explained all of history and human destiny on the basis of one key factor had immense appeal. It was simple and dramatic enough to be grasped by millions. Moreover, because it was built on one factor, it avoided the ambiguities inherent in any multivariate explanation. When more than one variable is required to explain reality, the implications become ambiguous: History is changed from a simple conflict of good versus evil to a matter of striking a balance between various competing goods; there is no simple solution, no obvious moral prescription.

In advanced industrial society, economic determinism becomes less and less credible because of two important developments. First, economic growth reaches a point of diminishing returns. An increasingly large share of the population has more than enough to eat. Economics is no longer the limiting factor. Economic goods continue to be sought for reasons of prestige, but this is something that can also be obtained in a variety of other ways. Secondly, in advanced industrial society, population does not increase to meet the food supply. Far from it, in advanced industrial society, population growth has fallen below replacement levels even as economic growth continues. Thus, in these societies, not only has economic supply risen far above the subsistence level, but demand has stopped increasing. Consequently, in advanced industrial society, economics remains important, but it is no longer the critical factor. Motivations of prestige and self-realization become more salient. Since both prestige and self-realization are culturally defined, cultural factors become a more crucial influence on human behavior.

Measuring the impact of culture is difficult, because we do not yet have adequate data. The evidence analyzed in this book provides only a rough estimate of the influence of cultural factors. But the available evidence indicates that the values and cultural norms held by given peoples are a major influence on whether or not democratic institutions are viable. Moreover, as we have seen, societies with relatively large proportions of Postmaterialists have markedly lower rates of economic growth, much higher divorce rates, and much lower birth rates, than do societies that remain predominantly Materialist. Culture not only responds to changes in the environment; it also helps shape the social, economic and political world.

Culture provides maps of the universe. The maps are crude, but we use them because they provide some guidance on how to get where we want to go and a sense of what life means. These maps are necessarily crude; for a human being to attempt to describe the nature of the universe and the meaning of human life, is as ambitious as for an ant who has never been more than a hundred yards from its anthill to give an account of the cosmos.

The maps are crude, but they have gradually evolved. Within the Judaeo-Christian tradition, we can trace the evolution of human conceptions of God, from the God of genocide and human sacrifice in the early books of the Bible, to the God of love in the later books. In Marx's worldview, sacred concerns left the scene and the analysis of secular forces became central; history replaced God, but humanity's pursuit of salvation remained the central theme. Contemporary physics and astronomy have elaborated a view of the universe that is a breathtaking display of how far human ingenuity can reach, probing billions of light years into space and billions of years back in time, to deduce in detail just what happened during the first twenty minutes after the Big Bang that created the universe. But if one asks what caused the Big Bang, the answer, for now, is, "It was just one of those things that happens from time to time." The account is fascinating, and it takes us amazingly far in explaining how we got here. But it does not even attempt to tell us why we got here—and that is a question that remains profoundly meaningful to every human being, including the physicists.

Though secular concerns took the center of the stage in the nineteenth century, religion did not die out, as expected. On the contrary, it manifests remarkable vitality in a variety of guises, from Brazil to Poland to Afghanistan. In advanced industrial society, and particularly in Western Europe, the appeal of the traditional churches seems to be fading among the younger generation—but it is precisely here that a Postmaterialist worldview is emerging that shows a relatively great concern for the meaning of life, and that places renewed emphasis on the sacred—though it tends to see the sacred in nature rather than in churches. Just as the desire for beauty is universal, the desire to know and understand is inherent in human nature. How to make a living may be the first question people ask, but the question of *why* we live will probably always be with us.

Today the maps reach farther than they used to, but what we have is still a rough approximation. However desperately we may want to be certain that our map is right, future generations will probably marvel at how much we missed. We still see the meaning of our existence through a glass darkly.

Perhaps this is inherent in the situation: Humanity builds meaning into the universe, and the job is not finished. The story of humanity may turn out to be a cruel joke, if we use our technological cleverness to exterminate the species. Or we could go on to heights still undreamed of, reaching a nobility a little lower than the angels. The answer is not yet in.

Appendix

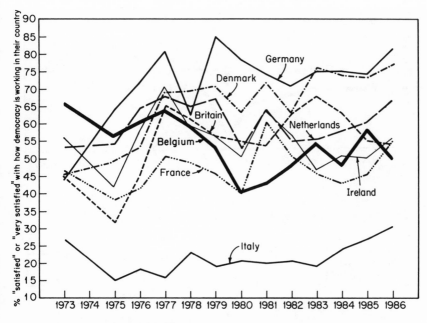

FIGURE A-1. Satisfaction with the way democracy is working in one's own nation in six nations, 1973–1986. Based on Euro-Barometer surveys.

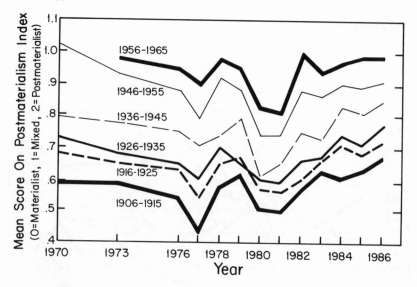

FIGURE A-2. Materialist/Postmaterialist values from 1970 to 1986 among the combined publics of six West European nations: birth cohort analysis.

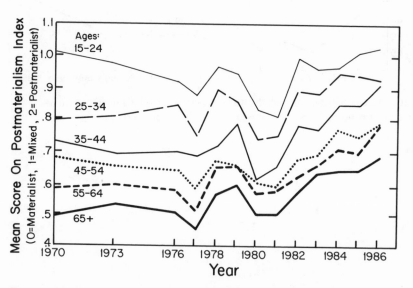

FIGURE A-3. Materialist/Postmaterialist values from 1970 to 1986 among the combined publics of six West European publics: life stage analysis.

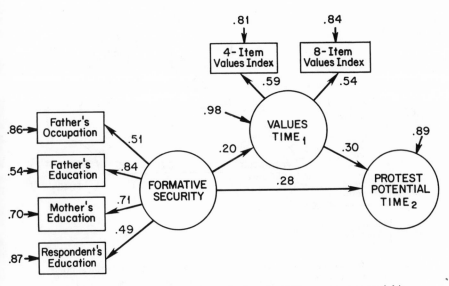

FIGURE A-4. Impact of formative security and values in 1974 on protest potential in 1981: United States panel. Adjusted goodness of fit index = .97.

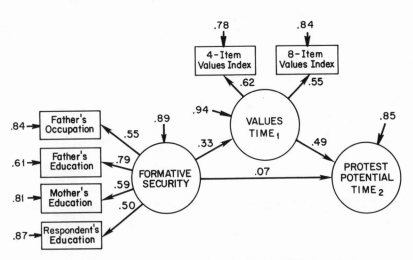

FIGURE A-5. Impact of formative security and values in 1974 on protest potential in 1980: Netherlands panel. Adjusted goodness of fit index = .94.

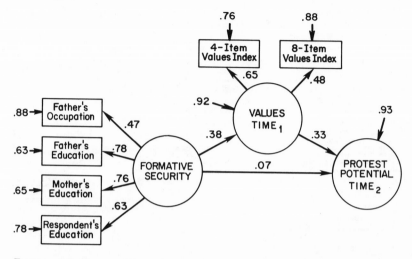

FIGURE A-6. Impact of formative security and values in 1974 on protest potential in 1980: West German panel. Adjusted goodness of fit index = .95.

TABLE A-1. INTERPERSONAL TRUST IN THE LATE 1950S AND THE 1980S IN FIVE
NATIONS
(Percentage saying "most people can be trusted")

	1959	1981	1986
U.S.	58%	41%	–
Britain	56	43	40%
Mexico	31[a]	18	–
West Germany	24	32	43
Italy	8	27	30

Sources: 1959 – Civic Culture study (Almond and Verba 1963); 1981 – World Values survey; 1986 – Euro-Barometer survey 25.

[a]The Civic Culture sample for Mexico was based on the urban population only (those living in cities of at least 10,000 population).

TABLE A-2. VALUE PRIORITIES OF AMERICAN AND HUNGARIAN PUBLICS:
STABLE CROSS-CULTURAL DIFFERENCES

United States		Hungary	
1974	1981	1980	1983
1. Family security	1. Family security	1. World at peace	1. World at peace
2. World at peace	2. World at peace	2. Family security	2. Family security
3. Freedom	3. Freedom	3. National security	3. National security
4. Self-respect	4. Self-respect	4. Happiness	4. Happiness
5. Happiness	5. Happiness	5. Sense of accomplishment	5. Sense of accomplishment
6. Wisdom	6. Wisdom	6. Comfortable life	6. Comfortable life
7. Sense of accomplishment	7. Sense of accomplishment	7. Social recognition	7. Inner harmony
8. Comfortable life	8. Comfortable life	8. Freedom	8. Freedom
9. True friendship	9. Salvation	9. Inner harmony	9. Social recognition
10. Salvation	10. True friendship	10. Self-respect	10. Equality
11. Inner harmony	11. National security	11. True friendship	11. True friendship
12. Equality	12. Equality	12. Equality	12. Self-respect
13. National security	13. Inner harmony	13. Mature love	13. Mature love
14. Mature love	14. Mature love	14. Pleasure	14. Pleasure
15. World of beauty	15. An exciting life	15. An exciting life	15. An exciting life
16. Pleasure	16. World of beauty	16. Wisdom	16. Wisdom
17. An exciting life	17. Pleasure	17. World of beauty	17. World of beauty
18. Social recognition	18. Social recognition	18. Salvation	18. Salvation

Source: Hungarian data from Hankiss and Manchin 1983; U.S. data from Political Action surveys carried out in 1974 and 1981.

TABLE A-3. MEAN ECONOMIC GROWTH 1965 - 1984 BY CULTURAL TRADITION

1.	Singapore	Con-Bud	7.8%	38. W. Germany	Prot	2.7
2.	South Korea	Con-Bud	6.6	39. Spain	Cath	2.7
3.	Hong Kong	Con-Bud	6.2	40. Mauritius	Hindu	2.7
4.	Hungary	Cath	6.2	41. Trinidad-Tobago	Cath	2.6
5.	Oman	Islam	6.1	42. Panama	Cath	2.6
6.	Saudi Arabia	Islam	5.9	43. Philippines	Cath	2.4
7.	Taiwan	Con-Bud	5.7	44. Ireland	Cath	2.4
8.	Indonesia	Islam	4.9	45. Canada	Prot	2.4
9.	Jordan	Islam	4.8	46. Mongolia	Budd	2.3
10.	Japan	Con-Bud	4.7	47. Burma	Budd	2.3
11.	Brazil	Cath	4.6	48. Netherlands	Prot	2.1
12.	Malaysia	Islam	4.5	49. Guatemala	Cath	2.0
13.	China	Con-Bud	4.5	50. Denmark	Prot	1.8
14.	Syria	Islam	4.5	51. Sweden	Prot	1.8
15.	Paraguay	Cath	4.4	52. Uruguay	Cath	1.8
16.	Tunisia	Islam	4.4	53. U.S.A.	Prot	1.7
17.	Yugoslavia	Orth	4.3	54. Australia	Prot	1.7
18.	Egypt	Islam	4.3	55. Costa Rica	Cath	1.6
19.	Thailand	Budd	4.2	56. Great Britain	Prot	1.6
20.	Greece	Orth	3.8	57. India	Hindu	1.6
21.	E. Germany	Prot	3.7	58. Poland	Cath	1.5
22.	Austria	Cath	3.6	59. Switzerland	Prot	1.4
23.	Albania	Islam	3.6	60. New Zealand	Prot	1.4
24.	U.S.S.R.	Orth	3.6	61. Sudan	Islam	1.2
25.	Algeria	Islam	3.6	62. Venezuela	Cath	.9
26.	Portugal	Cath	3.5	63. Bangladesh	Islam	.6
27.	Norway	Prot	3.3	64. Honduras	Cath	.5
28.	Finland	Prot	3.3	65. Argentina	Cath	.3
29.	France	Cath	3.0	66. Mauritania	Islam	.3
30.	Belgium	Cath	3.0	67. Bolivia	Cath	.2
31.	Colombia	Cath	3.0	68. Nepal	Hindu	.2
32.	Turkey	Islam	2.9	69. Peru	Cath	-.1
33.	Mexico	Cath	2.9	70. Jamaica	Prot	-.1
34.	Sri Lanka	Budd	2.9	71. Kuwait	Islam	-.1
35.	Morocco	Islam	2.8	72. Chile	Cath	-.1
36.	Israel	Judaic	2.7	73. El Salvador	Cath	-.6
37.	Italy	Cath	2.7	74. Libya	Islam	-1.1
				75. Nicaragua	Cath	-1.5

Source: Mean annual economic growth rates from World Bank, _Annual Development Report, 1986_ (Washington, D.C.: 1986).
   Cultural traditions coded by author: "Cath" = Roman Catholic; "Prot" = Protestant; "Islam" = Islamic; "Budd" = Buddhist; "Con-Bud" = Confucian + Buddhist.

TABLE A-4.   RISE IN CONSUMER PRICE INDEX OVER PREVIOUS YEAR IN SIX WESTERN
NATIONS, 1970 TO 1986

			CPI Rise				
Year	Netherlands	W. Germany	Britain	Belgium	France	Italy	Weighted Mean[a]
1970	4.2%	3.0%	6.4%	4.1%	5.3%	5.3%	4.9%
1973	8.6	7.2	9.4	6.3	7.1	10.8	8.5
1976	9.0	4.3	16.5	9.2	9.6	16.8	11.4
1977	6.4	3.6	15.9	7.1	9.4	17.0	10.9
1978	3.4	2.8	8.3	5.0	9.1	12.2	7.6
1979	4.3	4.1	13.4	3.9	10.7	14.8	9.9
1980	7.0	5.5	18.0	6.7	13.6	22.7	14.0
1981	7.5	5.9	11.9	7.6	13.4	19.5	12.1
1982	6.0	5.3	8.6	8.7	12.0	16.4	10.2
1983	2.8	2.9	4.3	7.7	9.0	14.7	7.4
1984	3.2	2.4	5.0	6.3	7.3	10.8	6.1
1985	2.2	2.2	6.1	4.9	5.9	9.2	5.6
1986	0.3	0.0	3.4	1.3	2.7	5.8	2.7

Source: Eurostat, Monthly Bulletin of General Statistics (Luxembourg: Statistical Office of the European Communities, 1971 - 1986).

[a]Weighted according to population of each country.

TABLE A-5. VALUE PRIORITIES BY AGE GROUP IN POLAND AND HUNGARY

	Poland			Hungary		
Age	Mat	Postmat	N	Mat	Postmat	N
16 - 19	18%	20%	(102)	41%	5%	(95)
20 - 29	22	18	(481)	48	5	(218)
30 - 39	24	18	(304)	46	3	(270)
40 - 49	25	16	(319)	57	2	(217)
50 - 59	26	14	(407)	50	2	(221)
60+	41	10	(99)	60	1	(334)

Sources: Representative national survey of Polish public, carried out in March 1980 by the Center for Public Opinion Research (OBOP) of Polish Radio and Television, for Institute of Sociology, University of Warsaw; and representative national survey of Hungarian public carried out in 1982 by the Institute of Sociology, Hungarian Academy of Sciences.

[a]Percentages do not total 100 because "mixed" value types are omitted.

TABLE A-6. WHAT PEOPLE LOOK FOR IN A JOB BY VALUE TYPE AND NATIONALITY (Percentage choosing "people you like" or "feeling of accomplishment" as first choice)

Value Type	France	Belgium	Netherlands	W. Germany	Italy
Materialist	34%	33%	51%	26%	29%
Score = 1	38	33	46	31	40
Score = 2	39	44	59	42	46
Score = 3	47	51	63	55	59
Score = 4	56	59	68	70	60
Postmaterialist	70	71	85	89	87

Value Type	Luxembourg	Denmark	Ireland	Britain
Materialist	35%	60%	35%	39%
Score = 1	48	59	41	41
Score = 2	32	61	46	43
Score = 3	63	64	57	56
Score = 4	77	82	55	59
Postmaterialist	79	86	90	77

Source: Inglehart 1977, 55.

TABLE A-7. RESPONDENT'S INCOME LEVEL BY VALUE TYPE
(Percentage having an income in top quartile for their nation)

	U.S.	W. Germany	Netherlands	Austria
Materialists	31%	23%	18%	17%
Mixed (Materialists)	25	20	22	24
Mixed (Postmat.)	23	20	30	22
Postmaterialists	21	24	39	29

	Switzerland	Finland	Total	N
Materialists	17%	20%	21%	(3,327)
Mixed (Materialists)	19	16	21	(2,308)
Mixed (Postmat.)	23	24	23	(1,167)
Postmaterialists	25	23	25	(565)

Source: Political Action surveys.

TABLE A-8. VALUES AND ECONOMIC ACHIEVEMENT BY EDUCATION AMONG THE PREWAR
COHORTS AND THE POSTWAR GENERATION
(Percentage with family income in top quartile for their nation)

Age at Which Respondent Completed Education	Prewar Cohorts (Born before 1945)		Postwar Cohorts (Born since 1945)	
	Materialists	Postmaterialists	Materialists	Postmaterialists
Under 15	10% (30,266)	16% (2,888)	15% (4,060)	16% (762)
15 - 16	21 (10,000)	24 (2,165)	21 (5,511)	27 (2,181)
17 - 18	31 (5,426)	38 (1,705)	27 (3,823)	30 (2,184)
19 - 20	41 (1,713)	52 (601)	34 (1,455)	32 (1,189)
Over 20	52 (2,316)	58 (1,758)	48 (1,323)	43 (2,364)

Source: Combined data from all European Community surveys, 1970 -
1986.

TABLE A-9. RESPONDENT'S INCOME BY VALUE TYPE, CONTROLLING FOR FATHER'S
EDUCATION
(Percentage having income in top quartile for their nation)

	Respondent's Father's Education Level		
	Primary	Secondary	Higher
Materialists	19% (1,553)	29% (571)	43% (81)
Mixed (Materialists)	20 (863)	28 (397)	38 (81)
Mixed (Postmat.)	21 (320)	25 (237)	43 (56)
Postmaterialists	24 (151)	27 (161)	24 (58)
gamma	.05	-.11	-.24

Source: Pooled Political Action data from U.S., West Germany,
Netherlands, and Austria (all countries for which all three variables
are available).

TABLE A-10. PERCENTAGE SAYING "MARRIED MEN/WOMEN HAVING AN AFFAIR CAN
NEVER BE JUSTIFIED" BY AGE AND COUNTRY

(Percentage choosing lowest point on 10-point scale)

Age	France	Japan	W. Germany	South Africa	Nether- lands	Britain
15 - 24	15%	25%	27%	49%	34%	30%
25 - 34	16	35	38	44	45	44
35 - 44	24	50	53	46	49	49
45 - 54	32	53	50	48	56	56
55 - 64	33	55	60	61	69	71
65+	47	75	67	68	74	82
Total	25	44	46	48	50	51

Age	Belgium	Italy	Spain	Hungary	Canada	Denmark
15 - 24	47%	42%	36%	43%	47%	42%
25 - 34	45	43	45	49	55	52
35 - 44	48	58	53	57	49	68
45 - 54	59	66	63	63	61	68
55-64	61	64	65	69	76	77
65+	70	69	75	78	77	87
Total	54	54	55	56	58	62

Age	Mexico	U.S.	North. Ireland	Repub. of Ireland	Mean
15 - 24	56%	50%	58%	59%	40%
25 - 34	61	58	46	71	46
35 - 44	70	60	77	75	54
45 - 54	70	76	80	84	61
55 - 64	70	79	87	91	68
65+	-	83	96	91	76
Total	62	64	72	75	54

Source: World Values survey, 1981 - 1982. Mean is based on surveys
from all nations except Mexico, where we do not have the full range of
ages.

TABLE A-11. PERCENTAGE APPROVING OF A SINGLE WOMAN HAVING A CHILD BY
AGE GROUP AND COUNTRY

Question: "If a woman wants to have a child as a single parent, but she
doesn't want to have a stable relationship with a man, do you approve or
disapprove?"

Age	Japan	Repub. of Ireland	North. Ireland	W. Germany	South Africa	Britain
15 - 24	19%	34%	36%	35%	30%	42%
25 - 34	18	27	24	37	27	49
35 - 44	8	22	31	31	32	30
45 - 54	12	11	22	22	30	30
55 - 64	7	11	11	17	26	22
65+	8	5	9	13	18	10
Total	13	22	23	27	28	33

Age	U.S.	Belgium	Nether- lands	Canada	Hungary	Italy
15 - 24	45%	50%	41%	47%	46%	40%
25 - 34	44	39	42	47	44	52
35 - 44	39	35	38	37	35	39
45 - 54	20	28	27	28	30	35
55 - 64	19	20	24	25	26	27
65+	15	16	18	13	21	24
Total	34	34	35	36	37	38

Age	Spain	Mexico	France	Denmark	Mean
15 - 24	57%	56%	73%	80%	45%
25 - 34	57	57	74	77	44
35 - 44	39	42	63	82	38
45 - 54	31	36	61	70	31
55 - 64	26	32	57	67	26
65+	14	-	45	54	19
Total	39	50	65	74	36

Source: World Values survey, 1981 - 1982. Mean is based on surveys
from all countries except Mexico, where we do not have the full range of
ages.

TABLE A-12. HAPPINESS BY PERCEIVED SIZE OF COMMUNITY
(Percentage "very happy")

Respondent Considers His/Her Community:	Netherlands	Denmark	Canada	Ireland	U.S.	Luxembourg
Rural area or village	47%	31%	35%	31%	35%	27%
Small or middle-size town	42	37	37	32	33	23
Big city	36	34	35	33	28	19

Respondent Considers His/Her Community:	Britain	Belgium	W. Germany	Spain	Japan	France
Rural area or village	31%	28%	15%	21%	17%	13%
Small or middle-size town	27	24	13	20	16	16
Big city	22	24	13	22	17	14

Respondent Considers His/Her Community:	Hungary	Italy	Greece	Portugal	Mean
Rural area or village	10%	10%	12%	8%	23%
Small or middle-size town	11	9	11	6	22
Big city	13	9	11	7	21

Source: See note to Table 7-1.

TABLE A-13. LIFE SATISFACTION AND HAPPINESS BY RELIGIOUS ORIENTATION, 1982

Question: "Independently of whether you go to church or not, would you say you are a religious person, not a religious person, or a convinced atheist?"

	Percentage "Satisfied" or "Very Satisfied" with Life as a Whole	Percentage "Very Happy"
A religious person	78% (6,516)	25% (6,470)
Not a religious person	79 (2,188)	19 (2,178)
A convinced atheist	68 (407)	16 (400)

Source: Euro-Barometer survey 18 (November 1982).

TABLE A-14. HAPPINESS BY EDUCATIONAL LEVEL
(Percentage "very happy")

Age at Which Respondent Completed Education	Nether- lands	Denmark	Canada	Ireland	U.S.
15 years or less	38%	33%	33%	28%	26%
16 - 19 years	47	37	35	34	31
20 years or older	43	32	38	37	33

Age at Which Respondent Completed Education	Luxem- bourg	Britain	Belgium	W. Germany	Spain
15 years or less	25%	26%	24%	15%	20%
16 - 19 years	24	27	25	12	25
20 years or older	25	28	28	18	17

Age at Which Respondent Completed Education	Japan	France	Italy	Greece	Portugal	Mean
15 years or less	17%	11%	9%	12%	8%	22%
16 - 19 years	17	14	8	11	6	24
20 years or older	15	21	8	10	3	24

Source: See note to Table 7-1.

TABLE A-15. HAPPINESS BY RESPONDENT'S OCCUPATION
(Percentage "very happy")

Respondent's Occupation	Nether-lands	Denmark	Canada	Ireland	Luxem-bourg
White collar employee	43%	37%	38%	35%	24%
Retired, student, housewife	45	35	36	38	26
Manual worker	45	34	30	26	23
Farmer	48	18	34	25	22
Unemployed	22	29	30	17	16

Respondent's Occupation	Britain	Belgium	W. Germany	Spain	Japan
White collar employee	30%	25%	15%	20%	11%
Retired, student, housewife	28	27	14	22	22
Manual worker	25	26	13	21	14
Farmer	-	31	13	18	14
Unemployed	12	20	15	19	22

Respondent's Occupation	France	Hungary	Italy	Greece	Portugal	Mean
White collar employee	15%	7%	10%	10%	8%	22%
Retired, student, housewife	16	11	9	13	7	23
Manual worker	10	14	10	10	7	21
Farmer	6	12	12	10	8	19
Unemployed	12	13	7	6	5	16

Source: See note to Table 7-1.

TABLE A-16. HAPPINESS BY FAMILY INCOME
(Percentage "very happy")

Respondent's Family Income	Netherlands	Denmark	Canada	Ireland	U.S.
Lowest quartile for nation	33%	30%	25%	27%	26%
Second quartile	41	32	36	31	25
Third quartile	43	38	41	34	27
Highest quartile	52	37	35	38	36

Respondent's Family Income	Luxembourg	Britain	Belgium	W. Germany	Spain
Lowest quartile for nation	20%	20%	20%	11%	18%
Second quartile	25	26	20	12	19
Third quartile	25	25	27	14	18
Highest quartile	27	32	34	18	23

Respondent's Family Income	Japan	France	Italy	Greece	Portugal	Mean
Lowest quartile for nation	18%	10%	8%	11%	4%	19%
Second quartile	19	13	8	11	8	22
Third quartile	12	15	10	11	7	23
Highest quartile	14	19	11	12	8	26

Source: See note to Table 7-1.

TABLE A-17. HAPPINESS BY MARITAL STATUS
(Percentage "very happy")

Respondent's Marital Status	Nether- lands	Denmark	Canada	Ireland	U.S.	Luxem- bourg
Married	47%	36%	39%	34%	37%	27%
Living as married	47	35	34	38	30	18
Single	40	34	34	30	26	22
Widowed	27	30	19	33	25	17
Divorced	21	24	19	-	19	13
Separated	8	29	13	13	23	11

Respondent's Marital Status	Britain	Belgium	W. Germany	Spain	Japan	France
Married	31%	28%	16%	22%	17%	15%
Living as married	20	17	10	27	19	18
Single	21	27	11	21	14	15
Widowed	18	16	11	15	36	10
Divorced	13	9	8	20	-	6
Separated	16	7	5	4	-	7

Respondent's Marital Status	Hungary	Italy	Greece	Portugal	Mean
Married	14%	10%	12%	7%	25%
Living as married	5	13	20	7	22
Single	7	9	9	8	21
Widowed	4	5	10	5	18
Divorced	2	2	5	3	12
Separated	12	1	16	-	12

Source: See note to Table 7-1.

TABLE A-18. HAPPINESS BY VALUE TYPE
(Percentage "very happy")

Respondent's Value Type	Nether- lands	Denmark	Canada	Ireland	Luxem- bourg
Materialist	44%	34%	37%	33%	26%
Mixed	45	36	35	32	24
Postmat.	37	28	35	29	22

Respondent's Value Type	Britain	Belgium	W. Germany	Spain	Japan
Materialist	28%	25%	11%	19%	15%
Mixed	27	27	16	25	17
Postmat.	24	23	12	20	18

Respondent's Value Type	France	Hungary	Italy	Greece	Portugal	Mean
Materialist	12%	10%	9%	12%	8%	22%
Mixed	14	13	10	12	7	23
Postmat.	21	15	9	10	5	21

Source: See note to Table 7-1.

TABLE A-19. CORRELATION BETWEEN POLICIES SUPPORTED BY CANDIDATES OF A GIVEN
PARTY AND CHARACTERISTICS OF THAT PARTY'S ELECTORATE

1. Economic Issues

Characteristics of Electorate	More Government Management of the Economy	More Public Ownership of Industry	Reduce Income Inequality	Mean Correlation, 3 Issues
Percentage of manual workers among electorate	.325	.224	.120	.223
Church attendance rate among electorate	.460	.621	.480	.520
Ratio of Materialists to Postmaterialists among electorate	-.180	-.510	-.306	-.332

2. Noneconomic Issues

Characteristics of Electorate	Develop Nuclear Power	Stronger Defense Effort	Stronger Measures against Terrorists	Mean Correlation, 3 Issues
Percentage of manual workers among electorate	-.017	-.077	.086	-.003
Church attendance rate among electorate	-.554	-.414	-.448	-.472
Ratio of Materialists to Postmaterialists among electorate	.677	.512	.670	.620

Sources: Data on electorates based on cumulative results of Euro-Barometer surveys 3 - 12; candidates' positions based on interviews with candidates to European Parliament representing sixty-six parties in nine nations.

TABLE A-20. ATTITUDES TOWARD OWNERSHIP AND MANAGEMENT OF BUSINESS AND
INDUSTRY BY AGE GROUP AND COUNTRY

Question: "There is a lot of discussion about how business
and industry should be managed. Which of these four statements comes
closest to your opinion? (show card)
1. The owners should run their business or appoint the managers.
2. The owners and employees should participate in the selection
of managers.
3. The state should be the owner and appoint the managers.
4. The employees should own the business and elect the managers."

(Percentage choosing "owners and employees" or "employees")

Age	North. Ireland	U.S.	Canada	Ireland	Britain
15 - 24	43%	48%	49%	53%	57%
25 - 34	33	45	45	50	56
35 - 44	35	37	39	48	43
45 - 54	44	26	34	46	33
55 - 64	32	34	26	39	46
65+	28	26	38	31	37
Total	37	39	41	46	48

Age	South Africa	W. Germany	Denmark	Japan	Italy
15 - 24	60%	67%	69%	71%	69%
25 - 34	55	58	65	57	63
35 - 44	56	48	58	58	59
45 - 54	36	51	48	44	61
55 - 64	40	34	46	53	56
65+	32	32	31	51	51
Total	49	51	57	58	62

Age	Mexico	Belgium	Nether-lands	Spain	France	Mean
15 - 24	69%	62%	71%	77%	84%	63%
25 - 34	60	58	67	73	80	58
35 - 44	59	55	65	65	79	53
45 - 54	55	50	64	64	77	48
55 - 64	55	41	65	57	70	46
65+	-	46	61	52	55	41
Total	62	64	66	67	76	54

Source: Pooled data from fourteen nations in World Values survey, 1981.

TABLE A-21. LEFT-RIGHT SELF-PLACEMENT BY SOCIAL CLASS, RELIGIOUS PRACTICE, AND
PERSONAL VALUES, 1980 - 1986
(Percentage placing selves on Left half (codes 1-5)
of Left-Right scale)

	% Placing Selves on Left	N
1. By social class		
Manual head of family	65%	(35,359)
Nonmanual head of family	57	(52,652)
2. By religious practice		
Respondent attends church at least once a week	48	(7,279)
Respondent attends church a few times a year	56	(12,157)
Respondent never attends church	69	(10,912)
3. By value priorities		
Materialist	53	(42,895)
Mixed	58	(65,636)
Postmaterialist	78	(15,831)

Source: Pooled results of Euro-Barometer surveys 13 - 26.

TABLE A-22. SUPPORT FOR SOCIAL CHANGE BY SOCIAL CLASS, RELIGIOUS PRACTICE, AND PERSONAL VALUES, 1980 - 1986

	Respondent Favors:			
	Revolutionary Change	Gradual Reform	Defense of Present Society	N
1. By social class				
Manual head of family	7%[a]	63%	30%	(35,720)
Nonmanual head of family	6	67	28	(52,127)
2. By religious practice				
Attends church at least weekly	4	60	36	(6,239)
Attends church a few times a year	4	63	32	(11,399)
Never attends church	9	64	26	(8,953)
3. By value priorities				
Materialist	4	62	34	(44,242)
Mixed	6	64	30	(65,939)
Postmaterialist	10	74	16	(15,258)

Source: Pooled results from Euro-Barometer surveys 13 - 26, carried out in France, Italy, West Germany, Great Britain, The Netherlands, Belgium, Luxembourg, Denmark, and Ireland, weighted according to population of given nation.

[a]Percentages may not total 100 because of rounding.

TABLE A-23.   POLITICAL CLEAVAGES BY SOCIAL CLASS, RELIGION, AND PERSONAL
VALUES: MULTIPLE CLASSIFICATION ANALYSES

	Eta	Beta
1. Left-Right Voting		
Church attendance	.264	.242
Social class	.179	.162
Value priorities	.14	.126
2. Left-Right Self-Placement		
Church attendance	.201	.195
Value priorities	.188	.179
Social class	.095	.084
3. Support for Social Change		
Value priorities	.185	.172
Church attendance	.111	.094
Social class	.032	.020

Source: Pooled data from surveys of European Community carried out 1973 -
1979 (1976 - 1979 with support for social change).

TABLE A-24. ELECTORAL CLEAVAGES IN TWELVE NATIONS, 1980 - 1987
(Percentage voting for given party by value type, social class, and church attendan

Respondent Would Vote for:	Value Type			Social Class		Church Attendance		
	Mat.	Mixed	Postmat.	Manual Occ.	Nonmanual Occ.	Weekly	Monthly or Less	Never
United States (1984)								
Reagan	71%	59%	46%	52%	59%	61%	54%	60%
Mondale	29	40	52	47	40	37	45	39
Other	1	1	2	1	1	2	1	1
(N)	(132)	(419)	(115)	(455)	(778)	(590)	(548)	(158)
West Germany								
Communist	-	-	1	1	-	-	-	1
Greens	2	6	27	7	10	2	4	11
Social Dems.	38	44	47	52	37	22	47	56
Free Democrats	5	5	5	3	6	4	6	6
Christian Dems.	55	45	19	37	45	71	43	25
(N)	(3,436)	(6,404)	(1,985)	(1,940)	(4,606)	(520)	(1,273)	(635)
Great Britain								
Labour	29	35	49	46	24	38	33	44
Soc. Dem.- Liberal	23	25	28	24	26	25	25	24
Scottish/Welsh	1	1	2	2	1	1	1	1
Conservative	48	39	21	28	49	36	41	30
(N)	(4,183)	(9,669)	(2,086)	(4,447)	(3,758)	(202)	(450)	(520)
Denmark								
Communist	1	1	2	1	1	2	1	2
Soc. Peoples, Soc. Left	7	12	47	20	19	8	8	21
Social Dems.	38	35	25	51	26	19	37	41
Radicals, Single Tax	5	6	9	4	7	10	8	7
Democratic Center	3	3	1	2	4	1	2	2
Conservative	25	25	8	10	30	15	22	17
Christian Peoples	2	2	-	2	1	21	2	-
Liberals	15	13	5	6	9	23	17	6
Progress Party	5	4	1	5	3	3	4	5
(N)	(2,866)	(6,129)	(1,612)	(2,424)	(4,164)	(100)	(1,057)	(761)

(continued)

Table A-24. (Continued)

spondent ıld Vote for:	Value Type			Social Class		Church Attendance		
	Mat.	Mixed	Postmat.	Manual Occ.	Nonmanual Occ.	Weekly	Monthly or Less	Never
aly								
Proletarian Dems., Radicals	2%	7%	23%	5%	7%	2%	4%	12%
Communist	18	26	34	37	18	7	25	40
Socialist	18	18	16	18	18	10	19	15
Social Dems.	5	4	2	3	4	4	4	4
Republicans	4	5	6	2	7	5	5	5
Christian Dems.	44	31	16	31	34	64	34	14
Liberals	3	4	2	1	5	3	3	4
Neo-Fascists	6	6	2	4	7	4	6	6
(N)	(4,462)	(4,780)	(829)	(2,315)	(4,658)	(770)	(908)	(392)
eece								
Communist (Moscow)	8	17	28	17	14	4	12	29
Communist (Eurocomm)	1	4	10	3	6	1	3	10
Socialist	52	54	50	57	52	61	60	51
New Democracy	38	23	11	20	25	32	22	10
(N)	(3,122)	(3,800)	(828)	(1,780)	(2,858)	(277)	(685)	(218)
therlands								
Communist	1	1	3	2	1	-	-	3
Pacifist Soc., Radicals	1	4	17	4	7	2	4	7
Socialist	30	31	44	44	25	12	26	50
Democrats '66	7	9	12	9	11	6	14	14
Liberals	19	20	9	8	25	8	22	18
Christian Dems.	37	31	13	26	25	63	31	7
Conserv. Calvinists	5	4	2	5	4	10	2	1
(N)	(3,017)	(6,845)	(2,551)	(2,757)	(3,349)	(660)	(543)	(1,069)
ain								
Communist	5	9	19	8	6	3	1	14
Other Left	1	3	11	3	2	1	1	3
Socialist	58	57	50	66	51	50	69	61
Dem. Reform	2	3	2	2	1	1	1	1
Basque, Catalan	10	12	10	7	11	9	10	11
Popular Alliance	23	14	6	14	26	37	18	10
(N)	(631)	(802)	(202)	(2,465)	(2,625)	(571)	(215)	(456)

Table A-24. (Concluded)

Respondent Would Vote for:	Value Type			Social Class		Church Attendance		
	Mat.	Mixed	Postmat.	Manual Occ.	Nonmanual Occ.	Weekly	Monthly or Less	Never
France								
Unif. Socialist	3%	3%	7%	5%	3%	1%	2%	6%
Ecologist	7	10	18	10	13	7	9	13
Communist	8	9	11	14	7	2	6	15
Socialist	35	34	43	42	35	20	37	39
Republican Left	3	3	3	2	3	2	2	4
Gaullists,UDF	41	39	18	27	39	63	40	22
Nat. Front	3	2	-	3	2	3	1	1
(N)	(3,877)	(5,346)	(1,393)	(5,877)	(6,139)	(276)	(791)	(991)
Belgium								
Communist	1	1	4	2	1	1	1	4
Ecologist	4	10	23	9	12	3	9	10
Socialist	27	31	30	39	21	11	10	15
Liberal	11	11	10	11	21	11	10	15
Ethnic Nat.	8	10	10	8	12	12	12	19
Christian Soc.	42	31	18	30	30	65	36	12
(N)	(2,983)	(3,771)	(914)	(2,200)	(2,540)	(520)	(421)	(528)
Ireland								
Labor; Workers	10	13	22	20	9	12	29	32
Fine Gael	33	33	33	24	39	32	36	35
Fianna Fail	57	54	44	56	51	56	35	31
(N)	(3,920)	(4,892)	(542)	(3,068)	(2,077)	(1,693)	(122)	(42)
Portugal								
Communist	8	16	18	15	9			
Socialist	36	30	30	39	29			
Other Left	7	9	13	8	9		N.A.	
Social Democrat	42	37	35	31	46			
Soc. Dem. Center	6	7	3	5	7			
(N)	(1,709)	(1,438)	(176)	(1,232)	(1,091)			

Source: Based on pooled data from Euro-Barometer surveys, 1980 - 1987.

REFERENCES

Aberbach, Joel D., et al. 1981. *Bureaucrats and politicians in Western democracies.* Cambridge: Harvard University Press.

Abrams, Mark, David Gerard, and Noel Timms. 1985. *Values and social change in Britain.* Houndmills and London: Macmillan.

Abramson, Paul R. 1979. Developing party identification: a further examination of life-cycle, generational and period effects. *American Journal of Political Science* 23:78–96.

———. 1983. *Political attitudes in America: Formation and change.* San Francisco: Freeman.

Abramson, Paul R., and Ronald Inglehart. 1986. Generational replacement and value change in the six West European societies. *American Journal of Political Science* 30:1–25.

———. 1987. The future of Postmaterialist values: Population replacement effects, 1970–1985 and 1985–2000. *Journal of Politics* (February).

Abramson, Paul R., et al. 1986. *Change and continuity in the 1984 elections.* Washington, D.C.: C. Q. Press.

Achen, Christopher H. 1975. Mass political attitudes and the survey response. *American Political Science Review* 69:1218–31.

Adorno, Theodor W., et al. 1950. *The authoritarian personality.* New York: Harper. An excellent recent reexamination appears in Fred I. Greenstein, *Personality and politics* (Chicago: Markham, 1969), 94–119.

Alderfer, Clayton P. 1972. *Existence, relatedness, and growth: Human needs in organizational settings.* New York: Free Press.

Alford, Robert R. 1963. *Party and society: The Anglo-American democracies.* Chicago: Rand McNally.

Allardt, Erik. 1978. Objective and subjective social indicators of well-being. *Comparative Studies in Sociology* 1:142–73.

Almond, Gabriel. 1983. Communism and political culture theory. *Comparative Politics* (January):127–38.

Almond, Gabriel, and Sidney Verba. 1963. *The civic culture: Political attitudes and democracy in five nations.* Princeton: Princeton University Press.

———. *The civic culture revisited.* Boston: Little, Brown.

Alwin, Duane F. 1986. Religion and parental child-rearing orientations: Evidence of a Catholic-Protestant convergence. *American Journal of Sociology* 92:412–40.

Alwin, Duane F., and Jon A. Krosner. 1986. The measurement of values in surveys: A comparison of ratings and rankings. *Public Opinion Quarterly* 49:535–52.

Andrews, Frank, and Stephen Withey. 1976. *Social indicators of well-being in America.* New York: Plenum.

Aron, Raymond. 1955. Fin de l'age ideologique? In *Sociologica*, edited by Theodor W. Adorno and Walter Dires, 219–33. Frankfurt: Europaische Verlaganstalt.

Axelrod, Robert. 1984. *The evolution of cooperation*. New York: Basic Books.

Baker, Kendall L., Russell Dalton, and Kai Hildebrandt. 1981. *Germany transformed*. Cambridge: Harvard University Press.

Balme, Richard, et al. 1986/87. New mayors: France and the United States. *The Tocqueville Review* 8:263–78.

Banfield, Edward. 1958. *The moral basis of a backward society*. Chicago: Free Press.

Barnes, Samuel H. 1974. Religion and class in Italian electoral behavior. In *Electoral behavior: A comparative handbook*, edited by Richard Rose. New York: Free Press.

———. 1986. *Politics and culture*. monograph series prepared for U.S. Department of State. Ann Arbor: Institute for Social Research.

Barnes, Samuel H., Max Kaase, et al. 1979. *Political action: Mass participation in five Western democracies*. Beverly Hills: Sage.

Beardsley, Richard K., et al. 1959. *Village Japan*. Chicago: University of Chicago Press.

Bell, Daniel. 1973. *The coming of postindustrial society*. New York: Basic Books.

———. 1976. *The cultural contradictions of capitalism*. New York: Basic Books.

———. 1960. *The end of ideology*. Glencoe: Free Press.

Bellah, Robert. 1957. *Tokugawa religion*. New York: The Free Press.

Bendor, Jonathan. 1987. In good times and bad: Reciprocity in an uncertain world. *American Journal of Political Science* 31:531–58.

Berger, Peter. 1969. *A rumor of angels*. New York: Doubleday.

Bettelheim, Bruno. 1979. *Surviving*. New York: Knopf.

Block, J. 1981. Some enduring and consequential structures of personality. In *Further explorations in personality*, edited by Albert I. Rabin, et al., 27–43. New York: Wiley-Interscience.

Boeltken, Ferdinand, and Wolfgang Jagodzinski. 1985. Postmaterialism in the European community, 1970—1980: Insecure value orientations in an environment of insecurity. *Comparative Political Studies*, 17:453–84.

Bollen, Kenneth A. 1979. Political democracy and the timing of development. *American Sociological Review* 44:572–87.

Books, John W., and Jo Ann Reynolds. 1975. A note on class voting in Great Britain and the United States. *Comparative Political Studies* 8:360–75.

Borre, Ole. 1984. Critical electoral change in Scandanavia. In *Electoral change in advanced industrial democracies*, edited by Russell J. Dalton, Scott C. Flanagan, and P. A. Beck, 330–64. Princeton: Princeton University Press.

Boynton, Gerald R., and Gerhard Loewenberg. 1973. The development of public support for parliament in Germany, 1951–1959. *British Journal of Political Science* 3:169–89.

———. 1974. The decay of support for the monarchy and the Hitler regime in the Federal Republic of Germany. *British Journal of Political Science* 4:453–88.

Brim, Orville G., Jr., and Jerome Kagan, eds. 1980. *Constancy and change in human development*. Cambridge: Harvard University Press.

Broder, David S. 1980. *Changing of the guard*. New York: Simon and Schuster.

Brown, Archie, and Jack Gray, eds. 1977. *Political culture and political change in communist states*. New York: Holmes and Meier.

Bruce-Briggs, B., ed. 1979. *The new class?* New Brunswick, N.J.: Transaction Books.

Brzezinski, Zbigniew, and Samuel P. Huntington. 1964. *Political Power: USA/USSR*. New York: Viking Press.

Buerklin, Wilhelm. 1981. Die Gruenen und die 'Neue Politik.' *Politische Vierteljahresschrift* 22:359–82.

————. 1982. Konzept und Fakten. *Politische Viertels jahresschrift* 23:339–45.

————. 1985a. "The Gruenen: Ecology and the New Left." In *West German politics in the mid-eighties*, edited by H. Peter Wallach and George Romoser. New York: Praeger.

————. 1984b. Value change and partisan realignment in West Germany, 1970–1983: Recent findings and political interpretations. Paper presented at the meetings of the American Political Science Association, Washington, D.C.

Calista, Donald J. 1984. Postmaterialism and value convergence: Value priorities of Japanese compared with their perceptions of American values. *Comparative Political Studies* 16:525–55.

Cameron, David. 1978. The expansion of the public economy: A comparative analysis. *American Political Science Review* 72:1243–61.

Campbell, Angus. 1981. *The sense of well-being in America*. New York: McGraw-Hill.

Campbell, Angus, Philip E. Converse and W. L. Rodgers. 1976. *The quality of life*. New York: Russell Sage.

Cantril, Hadley. 1965. *The pattern of human concerns*. New Brunswick, N.J.: Rutgers University Press.

Chen, E.Y.K. 1979. *Hyper-growth in Asian economies*. New York: Holmes and Meier.

Christie, Richard. 1954. Authoritarianism revisited. In *Studies in the scope and method of "The Authoritarian Personality,"* edited by Richard Christie and Marie Jahoda. Glencoe: Free Press.

Cofer, C. N., and M. H. Appley. 1964. *Motivation: Theory and research*. New York: Wiley.

Connor, W. D. 1979. *Socialism, politics and equality: Hierarchy and change in Eastern Europe and the U.S.S.R*. New York: Columbia University Press.

Conradt, David. 1974. West Germany: A remade political culture? *Comparative Politics* 7:222–38.

Converse, Philip E. 1964. The nature of belief systems among mass publics. In *Ideology and discontent*, edited by David Apter, 201–61. New York: Free Press.

————. 1970. Attitudes and non-attitudes: continuation of a dialogue. In *The quantitative analysis of social problems*, edited by Edward R. Tufte, 168–90. Reading, Mass.: Addison-Wesley.

————. 1972. Change in the American electorate. In *The human meaning of social change*, edited by A. E. Campbell and Philip E. Converse. New York: Russell Sage.

———. 1974. Comment: The status of nonattitudes. *American Political Science Review* 68:650–60.

———. 1980. Comment: Rejoinder to Judd and Milburn. *American Political Science Review* 45:644–46.

Converse, Philip E., and Georges Dupeux. 1962. Politicization of the electorate in France and the United States. *Public Opinion Quarterly* 26:1–23.

Converse, Philip E., and Gregory Markus. 1979. Plus ca change . . . The new CPS election study panel. *American Political Science Review* 73:32–49.

Converse, Philip E., and Roy Pierce. 1986. *Political representation in France*. Cambridge: Belknap-Harvard University Press.

Costa, Paul T., Jr., and Robert McCrae. 1980. Still stable after all these years: Personality as a key to some issues in adulthood and old age. In Vol. 3 of *Life-span development and behavior*, edited by Paul B. Baltes and Orville G. Brim, 65–102. New York: Academic Press.

Croon, M., and Phillip Stouthard. 1984. Some applications of the singular values decomposition technique on "political action" data. Presented at annual meetings of the European Consortium for Political Research, Salzburg, Austria, April 13–19.

Dalton, Russell J. 1977. Was there a revolution? A note in generational versus life-cycle explanations of value differences. *Comparative Political Studies* 9:459–75.

———. 1980. *Values in change: A panel study of German youth, 1976–1979*. Washington, D.C.: U. S. International Communications Agency.

———. 1981. The persistence of values and life cycle changes. *Politische Vierteljahresschrift: sonderheft* 12:187–207.

———. 1984a. Cognitive mobilization and partisan dealignment in advanced industrial democracies. *Journal of Politics* 46:264–84.

———. 1984b. Environmentalism and value change in Western democracies. Paper presented at the meetings of the American Political Science Association, Washington, D.C..

———. 1984c. The West German party system between two ages. In *Electoral change in advanced industrial democracies: Realignment or dealignment?* edited by Russell J. Dalton, Scott C. Flanagan, and P. A. Beck, 104–33. Princeton: Princeton University Press.

Dalton, Russell J., Scott C. Flanagan, and Paul Beck, eds. 1984. *Electoral change: Realignment and dealignment in advanced industrial democracies*. Princeton: Princeton University Press.

Davies, James C. 1963. *Human nature and politics*. New York: Wiley.

Davis, James A., and Tom W. Smith. 1982. *General social surveys, 1972–1982: Cumulative code book*. Chicago: National Opinion Research Center.

De Graaf, Nan Dirk, and Wout Ultee. 1987. 'Who Does Not Like Getting Ahead?'' Paper presented to ISA Research Committee on Social Stratification, Cambridge, Massachusetts, September 2–4.

De Graaf, Nan Dirk, Jacques Hagenaars, and Ruud Luijkx. 1987. Intragenerational stability of Postmaterialism. Unpublished manuscript, University of Utrecht.

Delli Carpini, Michael X. 1986. *Stability and change in American politics: The coming of age of the generation of the 1960s*. New York: New York University Press.

Deutsch, Karl W. 1964. Social mobilization and political development. *American Political Science Review* 55:493–514.

———. 1966. *Nationalism and social communication*. Cambridge: MIT Press.

Deutsch, Karl W., et al. 1957. *Political community and the North Atlantic area*. Princeton: Princeton University Press.

DiPalma, Giuseppi. 1970. *Apathy and participation: Mass politics in Western societies*. New York: Free Press.

Djilas, Milovan. 1966. *The new class*. London: Unwin.

Durkheim, Emile. [1897] 1958. *Suicide*. Glencoe: Free Press.

Easterlin, Richard A. 1974. Does economic growth improve the human lot? Some empirical evidence. In *Nations and households in economic growth*, edited by Paul A. David and Melvin W. Reder. New York: Academic Press.

Easton, David. 1966. *A systems analysis of political life*. New York: Wiley.

Eckstein, Harry. 1988. A culturalist theory of political change. *American Political Science Review* 82:789–804.

Ehrenreich, Barbara, and John Ehrenreich. 1977. The professional-managerial class. *Radical America* 2:7–31.

Ehrlich, Paul R. 1968. *The population bomb*. New York: Ballantine Books.

Elkins, Stanley. 1959. *Slavery: A problem in American institutional and intellectual life*. Chicago: The University of Chicago Press.

EMNID. 1963. *Pressedienst*. Cited in *Encounter* 22:53.

Erikson, Robert S. 1978. Analyzing one variable-three wave panel data: A comparison of two models. *Political Methodology* 5:151–61.

Finer, Samuel E. 1980. *The changing British party system, 1945–1979*. Washington, D.C.: American Enterprise Institute.

Fishbein, Martin. 1967. Attitudinal prediction of behavior. In *Readings in attitude theory and measurement*, edited by M. Fishbein. New York: John Wiley.

Fishbein, Martin, and Icek Azen. 1975. *Belief, attitude, intention, and behavior*. Reading, Mass.: Addison-Wesley.

Flanagan, Scott C. 1980a. Value change and partisan change in Japan: The silent revolution revisited. *Comparative Politics* 11:253–78.

———. 1980b. Value cleavages, economic cleavages and the Japanese voter. *American Journal of Political Science* 24:178–206.

———. 1982a. Changing values in advanced industrial society. *Comparative Political Studies* 14:403–44.

———. 1982b. Measuring value change in advanced industrial societies: A rejoinder to Inglehart. *Comparative Political Studies* 15:99–128.

———. 1987. Changing values in industrial societies revisited: Towards a resolution of the values debate. *American Political Science Review* 81:1303–19.

Fogarty, Michael, Liam Ryan, and Joseph Lee. 1984. *Irish values and attitudes*. Dublin: Dominican Publishers.

Fogt, Helmut, 1982. *Politische Generationen*. Opladen: Westdeutscher Verlag.

Frey, Bruno S., and F. Schneider. 1978a. An empirical study of politics. Economic interaction in the United States. *Review of Economics and Statistics* 60:174–83.

———. 1978b. A political-economic model of the United Kingdom. *Economics Journal* 80:243–53.

Gallup, George H. 1976. Human needs and satisfactions: A global survey. *Public Opinion Quarterly* 41:459–67.

Gastil, Raymond D., ed. 1982. *Freedom in the world.* Westport, Conn.: Greenwood Press.

Glenn, Norval D. 1976. Cohort analysis' futile quest: Statistical attempts to separate age, period and cohort effects. *American Sociological Review* 41:900–904.

———. 1987. Social trends in the United States: Evidence from sample surveys. *Public Opinion Quarterly* 51:109–26.

Goodhart, C. A. E., and R. J. Bhansali. 1970. Political economy. *Political Studies* 18:43–106.

Gottlieb, Avi, and Ephraim Yuchtman-Yaar. 1983. Materialism, postmaterialism, and public views of socioeconomic policy: The case of Israel. *Comparative Political Studies* 16:307–35.

Gouldner, Alvin. 1979. *The future of the intellectuals and the rise of the new class.* New York: Seabury.

Greeley, Andrew. 1972. *Unsecular man: The persistence of religion.* New York: Shocken Books.

Greiffenhagen, Sylvia, and Martin Greiffenhagen. 1979. *Ein schwieriges Vaterland.* Munich: Liszt.

Gurin, Gerald, Joseph Veroff, and Sheila Feld. 1960. *Americans view their mental health.* New York: Basic Books.

Habermas, Jurgen. 1975. *Legitimation crisis.* Translated by T. McCarthy. Boston, Mass.: Beacon Press.

———. 1979. Einleitung. In *Stichworte zur 'Geistigen Situation der Zeit,'* edited by Jurgen Habermas. Frankfurt: Suhrkamp.

Hadaway, C. K. 1978. Life satisfaction and religion: An analysis. *Social Forces* 57:636–43.

Halman, Loek, Felix Heunks, Ruud de Moor, and Harry Zanders. 1987. *Traditie, secularisatie en Individualisering.* Tilburg: Tilburg University Press.

Hankiss, Elemer, and Robert Manchin. 1983. *Stabilitas es Valtozas a Magyar Ertekrendszerben* (Stability and change in the Hungarian value system). Budapest: Hungarian Academy of Sciences.

Harding, Stephen, and David Phillips, with Michael Fogarty. 1986. *Contrasting values in Western Europe.* London: MacMillan.

Hawking, Stephen W. 1988. *A brief history of time.* New York: Bantam.

Hayashi, Chikio. 1974. Time, age, and ways of thinking—from the Kokuminsei surveys. *Journal of Asian African Studies* 10:75–85.

Herz, Thomas. 1979. Der Wandel von Wertvorstellungen in westlichen Industriegesellschaften. *Koelner Zeitschrift fuer Soziologie und Sozialpsychologie* 2:282–302.

Herzog, A. Regula, Willard L. Rodgers, and J. Woodworth. 1982. *Subjective well-being among different age groups.* Ann Arbor: Institute for Social Research.

Heunks, Feliz J. 1979. *Nederlanders en hun Samenleving.* Amsterdam: Holland University Press.

Hibbs, Douglas A. 1977. Political parties and macroeconomic policy. *American Political Science Review* 71:467–87.

Hibbs, Douglas A., Douglas Rivers, and Nicholas Vasilatos. 1982. The dynamics of political support for American presidents among occupational and partisan groups. *American Journal of Political Science* 26:312–32.

Hildebrandt, Kai, and Russell Dalton. 1977. Die neue Politik: Politischer Wandel oder Schoenwetter Politik? *Politische Vierteljahresschrift* 18:230–56.

Ho, Edric Seng-liang. 1985. Values and economic development: Hong Kong and China. Ph.D. dissertation, University of Michigan.

Hout, Michael, and Andrew M. Greeley. 1987. The Center doesn't hold: Church attendance in the United States, 1940–1984. *American Sociology Review* 52:325–45.

Huntington, Samuel P. 1984. Will more countries become democratic? *Political Science Quarterly* 99:193–218.

Hyman, Herbert H., and Paul B. Sheatsley. 1954. "The Authoritarian Personality": A methodological critique. In *Studies in authoritarian personality,* edited by Richard Christie and Marie Jahoda, 50–122. Glencoe: Free Press.

Iijima, K. 1982. The feelings of satisfaction and happiness of the Japanese and other peoples. *Bull. Nippon Research Ctr.,* May: 112–31.

Ike, Nobutaka. 1973. Economic growth and intergenerational change in Japan. *American Political Science Review* 67:1194–1203.

Inglehart, Ronald. 1970a. Cognitive mobilization and European identity. *Comparative Politics* 3:45–70.

———. 1970b. The new Europeans: Inward or outward looking? *International Organization* 24:129–39.

———. 1971. The silent revolution in Europe: Intergenerational change in post-industrial societies. *American Political Science Review* 65:991–1017.

———. 1976. Changing values and attitudes toward military service among the American public. In *The social psychology of military service,* edited by Nancy Goldman and David R. Segal. Beverly Hills: Sage.

———. 1977. *The silent revolution: Changing values and political styles among Western publics.* Princeton: Princeton University Press.

———. 1979a. Value priorities and socioeconomic change. In *Political action: Mass participation in five Western democracies,* edited by Samuel H. Barnes et al., 305–42. Beverly Hills: Sage.

———. 1979b. Political action: The impact of values, cognitive level and social background. In *Political action: Mass participation in five Western democracies,* edited by Samuel H. Barnes et al., 343–80. Beverly Hills: Sage.

———. 1980. Zusammenhang zwischen soziooekonomischen Bedingungen und individuellen Wertprioritaeten. *Koelner Zeitschrift fuer Soziologie und Sozialpsychologie* 32:144–53.

―――. 1981. Post-Materialism in an environment of insecurity. *The American Political Science Review* 75:880–900.

―――. 1982. Changing values in Japan and the West. *Comparative Political Studies* 14:445–79.

―――. 1983. Changing paradigms in comparative political behavior. In *Political science: The state of the art,* edited by A. Finifter. Washington, D.C.: American Political Science Association.

―――. 1985. New perspectives on value change: Responses to Lafferty and Knutsen, Savage, Boeltken, and Jagodzinski. *Comparative Political Studies* 17:485–532.

―――. 1989. Observations on cultural change and postmodernism. In *Politics and contemporary culture,* edited by John Gibbins. London: Sage.

Inglehart, Ronald, and Avram Hochstein. 1972. Alignment and dealignment of the electorate in France and the United States. *Comparative Political Studies* 4:343–72.

Inglehart, Ronald, and Hans D. Klingemann. 1976. Party identification, ideological preference and the left-right dimension among Western publics. In *Party identification and beyond,* edited by Ian Budge, Ivor Crewe, and Dennis Farlie, 243–73. London and New York: Wiley.

Inglehart, Ronald, and Jacques-Rene Rabier. 1984a. Du bonheur . . . sentiment personnel et norme culturelle. *Futuribles,* (October):3–28.

―――. 1984b. La confiance entre nations. *Revue Francaise de Science Politique.* 34:5–47.

Inglehart, Ronald, Jacques-Rene Rabier, Ian Gordon, and Carsten J. Sorenson. 1980. Broader powers for the European parliament? The attitudes of candidates. *European Journal of Political Research* 8:113–32.

Inglehart, Ronald, and Renata Siemienska. 1988. Political values and dissatisfaction in Poland and the West: A comparative analysis. *Government and Opposition* 23:440–57.

Iwao, S. 1976. A full life for modern Japanese women. In *Changing values in modern Japan,* edited by S. Nishiyama, 95–111. Tokyo: Nihonjin Kenkyukai.

Jackson, D. J., and Duane Alwin. 1980. The factor analysis of ipsative measures. *Sociological Methods and Research* 9:218–38.

Jackson, John E. 1983. The systematic beliefs of the mass public: Estimating policy preferences with survey data. *Journal of Politics* 45:840–65.

Jaeggi, Urs. 1979. Drinnen und draussen. In *Stichworte zur 'Geistigen Situation der Zeit,'* edited by Jurgen Habermas, 443–73. Frankfurt: Suhrkamp.

Jagodzinski, Wolfgang. 1983. Materialism in Japan reconsidered: Toward a synthesis of generational and life-cycle explanations. *American Political Science Review* 77:887–94.

―――. 1984. Wie transformiert man Labile *In* Stabile *REL*ationen? Zur Persistenz postmaterialistischer Wertorientierungen. *Zeitschrift fuer Soziologie* 13:225–42.

―――. 1986. Die zu stille Revolution: Zum Aggregatwandel materialistischer und postmaterialistischer Wertorientierungen in sechs westeuropaeischen Laendern zwischen 1970 and 1981. In *Wertwandel, oekonomische Krise und Politik in der*

Bundersrepublik Deutschland, edited by D. Oberndorfer et al. Berlin: Duncker and Humblot.

Janda, Kenneth. 1970. *A conceptual framework for the analysis of political parties.* Beverly Hills: Sage.

Jennings, M. Kent, Klaus R. Allerbeck, and Leopold Rosenmayr. 1979. Generations and families: General orientations. In *Political action,* edited by Samuel H. Barnes et al. Beverly Hills: Sage.

Jennings, M. Kent, and Gregory Markus. 1984. Partisan orientations over the long haul: Results from the three-wave socialization panel. *American Political Science Review* 78:1000–1018.

Jennings, M. Kent, and Richard G. Niemi. 1981. *Generations and politics.* Princeton: Princeton University Press.

Jennings, M. Kent, and Jan Van Deth, eds. 1989. *Continuities in political action.* New York and Berlin: DeGruyter-Aldine.

Judd, Charles M., J. Krosnick, and M. A. Milburn. 1981. Political involvement and attitude structure in the general public. *American Sociological Review* 46:660–69.

Judd, Charles M., and M. A. Milburn, 1980. The structure of attitude systems in the general public: Comparisons of a structural equation model. *American Sociological Review* 45:627–43.

Kaase, Max. 1983. Sinn oder Unsinn des Konzepts "Politische Kultur." In *Wahlen und politisches System,* edited by Max Kaase and Hans-Dieter Klingemann, 144–71. Opladen: Westdeutscher Verlag.

Kaase, Max, and Hans-Dieter Klingemann. 1979. Sozialstruktur, Wertorientierung und Parteiensysteme. In *Sozialer Wandel in West Europa,* edited by Joachim Mattes. Frankfurt: Campus Verlag.

Kemp, David A. 1979. The Australian electorate. In *The Australian national elections of 1977,* edited by Howard R. Penniman. Washington, D.C.: American Enterprise Institute.

Kerr, Henry, and David Handley. 1974. Conflits des génerations et politique étrangère en Suisse. *Annuaire Suisse de Science Politique,* 15:127–55.

Kesselman, Mark. 1979. Review of *The Silent Revolution,* by Ronald Inglehart. *American Political Science Review* 73:284–86.

Kinder, Donald R. 1983. Diversity and complexity in American public opinion. In *Political science: The state of the discipline,* edited by Ada W. Finifter, 389–428. Washington, D.C.: American Political Science Association.

Kinder, Donald, and D. Roderick Kiewiet. 1979. Sociotropic politics: The American case. *British Journal of Political Science* 11:129–61.

Klingemann, Hans D. 1979. Ideological conceptualization of politics: Indicators and distribution. In *Political action,* edited by Samuel H. Barnes, et al. Beverly Hills: Sage.

Kmieciak, Peter. 1976. *Wertstrukturen und Wertwandel in der Bundesrepublik Deutschland.* Goettingen: Schwartz.

Knoke, David, and Michael Hout. 1976. Reply to Glenn. *American Sociological Review* 41:906–8.

Knutsen, Oddbjorn. 1982. Materialisme og Post-Materialisme i Norge. Oslo: Institutt for samfunnsforskning.

Kramer, Gerald H. 1971. Short-term fluctuations in U.S. voting behavior, 1896–1964. *American Political Science Review* 65:131–43.

———. 1983. The ecological fallacy revisited: Aggregate versus individual-level findings on economics and elections and sociotropic voting. *American Political Science Review* 77:92–111.

Kuhn, Thomas. 1972. *The structure of scientific revolutions.* Chicago: University of Chicago Press.

Ladd, Everett C., Jr. 1976. Liberalism upside down: The inversion of the New Deal order. *Political Science Quarterly* 91:577–600.

———. 1978. The new lines are drawn: Class and ideology in America. *Public Opinion* 1:48–53.

Lafferty, William M. 1975. Basic needs and political values: Some perspectives from Norway's silent revolution. *Acta Sociologica* 19:117–36.

Lafferty, William M., and Oddbjorn Knutsen. 1985. Postmaterialism in a social democratic state: An analysis of the distinctness and congruity of the Inglehart value syndrome in Norway. *Comparative Political Studies* 17:411–31.

Lane, Robert. 1962. *Political ideology.* New York: Free Press.

———. 1965. The politics of consensus in an age of affluence. *American Political Science Review* 59:874–95.

Lasch, Christopher, 1979. *The culture of narcissism: American life in an age of diminishing expectations.* New York: Norton.

Lawler, Edward E. 1973. *Motivation, work, organization.* Monterey: Brooks/Cole.

Lehner, Franz. 1979. Die "Stille Revolution": Zur Theorie und Realitaet des Wertwandels in hochindustrialisierten Gesellschaften. In *Wertwandel und gesellschaftlicher Wandel*, edited by Helmut Klages and Peter Kmieciak, 317–27. Frankfurt: Campus Verlag.

Lenski, Gerhard. 1963. *The religious factor.* New York: Anchor-Doubleday.

———. 1966. *Power and privilege: A theory of social stratification.* New York: McGraw-Hill.

Lerner, Daniel. 1958. *The passing of traditional society.* New York: Free Press.

Lesthaeghe, Ron, and Dominique Meekers. 1986. Value changes and the dimensions of familism in the European Community. *European Journal of Population* 2:225–68.

Levinson, Daniel J., et al. 1979. *The seasons of a man's life.* New York: Alfred A. Knopf.

Lewis-Beck, Michael. 1986. Comparative economic voting: Britain, France, Germany, Italy. *American Journal of Political Science* 30:315–46.

Lichter, Linda S., S. Robert Lichter, and Stanley Rothman. 1983. Hollywood and America: The odd couple. *Public Opinion* (January):54–58.

Lichter, S. Robert, and Stanley Rothman. 1981. Media and business elites. *Public Opinion* (October/November):42–60.

Lijphart, Arend. 1971. *Class voting and religious voting in the European democracies.* Glasgow: University of Strathclyde.

———. 1979. Religious vs. linguistic vs. class voting: The crucial experiment of comparing Belgium, Canada, South Africa and Switzerland. *American Political Science Review* 73:442–61.

———. 1984. *Democracies: Patterns of majoritarian and consensus government in twenty-one countries*. New Haven: Yale University Press.

Lindblom, Charles E. 1977. *Politics and markets: The world's political-economic systems*. New York: Basic Books.

Lipset, Seymour M. 1960. *Political man: The social bases of politics*. Garden City: Doubleday.

———. 1964. The changing class structure and contemporary European politics. *Daedalus* 93:271–303.

———. 1979. The new class and the professoriate. In *The new class?* edited by B. Bruce-Briggs, 67–68. New Brunswick, N.J.: Transaction Books.

———. 1981. *Political man: The social bases of politics*. 2d ed. Baltimore: Johns Hopkins University Press.

Lipset, Seymour M., and Richard B. Dobson. 1972. The intellectual as critic and rebel. *Daedalus* 101:137–98.

Lipset, Seymour M., and Stein Rokkan. 1967. Cleavage structures and voter alignments. In *Party systems and voter alignments*, edited by Seymour M. Lipset and Stein Rokkan. New York: Free Press.

Lipset, Seymour Martin, et al. 1954. The psychology of voting: An analysis of political behavior. In Vol. 2 of *Handbook of social psychology*, edited by Gardner-Lindzey et al. Reading, Mass.: Addison-Wesley.

Lopez Pintor, Rafel, and Jose Ignacio, Wert Ortega. 1982. La otra Espana: Insolidaridad e intolerancia en la tradicion politico-cultural Espanola. *Revista Espanola de Investigaciones Sociologicas* (July-September):292–307

Lovins, Amory. 1977. *Soft energy paths: Toward a durable peace*. New York: Harper.

Luckmann, Thomas. 1967. *The invisible religion*. New York: Macmillan.

Luhmann, Niklas. 1979. *Power and trust*. Chichester and New York: Wiley.

McNeil, William H. 1976. *Plagues and Peoples*. New York: Anchor-Doubleday.

MacRae, Duncan. 1967. *Parliament, parties and society in France, 1946–1958*. New York: St. Martin's Press.

———. 1977. A political model of the business cycle. *Journal of Political Economics* 85:239–63.

Maddison, Angus. 1969. *Economic growth in Japan and the U.S.S.R.* London: Allen and Unwin.

Markus, Gregory B. 1983. Dynamic modeling of cohort change: The case of political partisanship. *American Journal of Political Science* 27:715–39.

———. 1988. The impact of personal and national economic conditions on the presidential vote: A pooled cross-sectional analysis. *American Journal of Political Science* 32:137–54.

Marsh, Alan. 1975. The silent revolution, value priorities, and the quality of life in Britain. *American Political Science Review* 69:1–30.

———. 1977. *Protest and political consciousness*. Beverly Hills and London: Sage.

Martin, Steven S. 1981. New methods lead to familiar results: A comment on Judd and

Milburn, 'The structure of attitude systems.' *American Sociological Review* 46:670–75.

Maruyama, Masao. 1965. Patterns of individuation and the case of Japan: A conceptual scheme. In *Changing Japanese attitudes toward modernization*, edited by M. B. Jansen. Princeton: Princeton University Press.

Maslow, Abraham K. 1954. *Motivation and personality*. New York: Harper and Row.

Meadows, Donella H., et al. 1972. *The limits to growth*. New York: Universe.

Merritt, Richard L., and Donald J. Puchala. 1968. *Western European perspectives on international affairs*. New York: Praeger.

Milbrath, Lester W., and M. Goel. 1977. *Political participation*. 2d ed., 114–28. Chicago: Rand McNally.

Milkis, Sidney, and Thomas Baldino. 1978. The future of the silent revolution: A reexamination of intergenerational change in Western Europe. Paper presented at the annual meeting of the Midwest Political Science Association, Chicago.

Miller, Arthur H. 1974. Political issues and trust in government: 1964–1970. *American Political Science Review* 68:951–72.

Miller, Arthur H., et al. 1979. Type-set journalism: Impact of newspapers on public confidence. *American Political Science Review* 71:67–84.

Miller, Warren E., and Teresa Levitin. 1976. *Leadership and change: New politics and the American electorate*. Cambridge, Mass.: Winthrop.

Mischel, Walter. 1968. *Personality and assessment*. New York: Wiley.

———. 1976. *Introduction to personality*. 2d ed., 499*ff*. New York: Holt Rinehart & Winston.

Miyake, Ichiro. 1978. Yakusha atogaki. In Inglehart, Ronald, *Shizukanaru Kakumei*, 391–99, Tokyo: Toyo Keizai Shinposha.

———. 1982. Trust in government and political cleavages: A cross-national comparison. *Doshisha Law Review*, nos. 171 and 172.

Moehler, Peter. 1986. Mustertreue abbildung: Ein weg zur Losung des stabilitaetsfluktuations problems in Panelumfragen. *ZUMA Bericht* (November):31–44.

Moore, Barrington. 1966. *Social origins of dictatorship and democracy*. Boston: Beacon Press.

Mueller-Rommel, Ferdinand. 1982. Ecology parties in Western Europe. *West European Politics* 2:68–74.

———. 1984. Die Gruenen: Aus der Sicht der Wahl und Elitenforschnung. In *Die Gruenen*, edited by Thomas Klage, 125–41. Frankfurt: Fischer.

Nakane, Chie. 1973. *Japanese society*. New York: Penguin Books.

Nardi, Rafaella. 1980. Sono le condizioni economiche a influenzare I valori? Un controllo dell'ipotesi di Inglehart. *Rivista Italiana Scienza Politiche* 10:293–315.

Nelkin, Dorothy, and Michael Pollak. 1981. *The atom besieged: Extraparliamentary dissent in France and Germany*. Cambridge, Mass.: MIT Press.

Nie, Norman, with Kristi Andersen. 1974. Mass belief systems revisited: Political change and attitude structure. *Journal of Politics* 36:540–91.

Nie, Norman, G. Bingham Powell, and Kenneth Prewitt. 1969. Social structure and political participation: Developmental relationships. Parts I and II. *American Political Science Review* 63:361–78 and 808–32.

Nie, Norman, Sidney Verba, and John Petrocik. 1979. *The changing American voter*. Cambridge, Mass.: Harvard University Press.

Nishihira, Sigeki. 1974. Changed and unchanged characteristics of the Japanese. *Japan Echo* 1:22–32.

Noelle-Neumann, Elisabeth, and Edgar Piel. 1984. *Allensbacher Jahrbuch der Demoskopie*, 1978–1983. Munich: Saur.

N.O.R.C. 1987. *General social surveys, 1972–1987: Cumulative codebook*. Storrs, Conn.: Roper center.

Nordhaus, W. D. 1975. A preliminary survey of the theory and findings on vote and popularity functions. *European Journal of Political Research* 9:181–99.

Nowak, Stefan. 1981. Values and attitudes of the Polish people. *Scientific American* 245:45–54.

Pappi, Franz-Urban. 1977. Sozialstruktur, gesellschaftliche Wertorientierung und Wahlabsicht. *Politische Vierteljahresschrift* 18:195–229.

Pedersen, Mogens N. 1979. The dynamics of European party systems. *European Journal of Political Research* 7:1–26.

Pierce, John C., and D. Rose. 1974. Nonattitudes and American public opinion: Examination of a thesis. *American Political Science Review* 68:626–49.

Pizzorno, Alessandro. 1966. Amoral familism and historical marginality. *International Review of Community Development* 15:55–66.

Podhoretz, Norman. 1979. The adversary culture and the new class. In *The new class?* edited by B. Bruce-Briggs, 19–32. New Brunswick, N.J.: Transaction Books.

Pomper, Gerald M. 1975. *The voter's choice: Varieties of American electoral behavior*. New York: Dodd, Mead.

Pruitt, Dean G. 1965. Definition of the situation as a determinant of international action. In *International behavior: A social-psychological analysis*, edited by Herbert C. Kelman. New York: Holt Rinehart & Winston.

Przeworski, A., and M. Wallerstein. 1982. The structure of class conflict in democratic capitalist societies. *American Political Science Review* 76:215–38.

Putnam, Robert D. 1987. Institutional performance and political culture: Some puzzles about the power of the past. Paper presented at the 1987 annual meeting of the American Political Science Association, Chicago, September 3–6.

Putnam, Robert, Roberto Leonardi, and Rafaella Y. Nanetti. 1979. Attitude stability among Italian elites. *American Journal of Political Science* 23:463–94.

Putnam, Robert D., et al. 1983. Explaining institutional success: The case of Italian regional government. *American Political Science Review* 77:55–74.

Rankin, W.L., and J.W. Grube. 1980. A comparison of the ranking and rating procedures for value system measurement. *European Journal of Social Psychology* 72:666–73.

Research Committee on the Study of the Japanese National Character. 1979. *A study of the Japanese national character: The sixth nation-wide survey*. Tokyo: Institute of Statistical Mathematics.

Rezsohazy, Rudolf, and Jan Kerkhofs. 1984. *L'univers des Belges*. Louvain-la-Neuve: CIACO.

Richardson, Bradley M. 1974. *The political culture of Japan*. Berkeley: University of California Press.

Robinson, Michael. 1975. Public affairs television and the growth of political malaise. *American Political Science Review* 69:409–32.

Rogowski, Ronald. 1976. *A rational theory of legitimacy*. Princeton: Princeton University Press.

Rokeach, Milton. 1968. *Beliefs, attitudes and values*. San Francisco: Jossey-Bass.

————. *The Nature of Human Values*. New York: Free Press.

————. 1974. Change and stability in American value systems, 1968–1971. *Public Opinion Quarterly* 38:222-238.

Rose, Richard, and Derek Urwin. 1969. Social cohesion, political parties and strains in regimes. *Comparative Political Studies* 2:7–67.

Rothman, Stanley, and S. Robert Lichter. 1983. How liberal are bureaucrats? *Regulation* (November–December):16–21.

————. 1984. Personality, ideology, and world view: A comparison of media and business elites. *British Journal of Political Science* 15:29–49.

Sale, Kirk. 1980. *Human scale*. New York: Coward, McCann and Geoghegan.

Schein, Edgar, 1985. *Organizational culture and leadership*. San Francisco: Jossey-Bass.

Scheuch, Erwin. 1968. The cross-cultural use of sample surveys: problems in comparability. In *Comparative research across cultures and nations*, edited by S. Rokkan. Paris and The Hague: Mouton.

Schmidt, Manfred. 1982. *Wohlfahrtsstaatliche Politik unter buergerlichen und sozialdemokratischen Regierungen*. Frankfurt: Campus Verlag.

————. 1984. Konkurrenz, Demokratie, Wohlfahrtsstaat und neue soziale Bewegungen. *Beilage: Das Parlament* 11:3–14.

Schmidtchen, Gerhard. 1972. *Zwischen Kirche und Gesellschaft*. Freiburg: Herder Verlag.

Schneider, Manfred. 1981. Postmaterialistische Wertorientierung und Persoenlichkeit. *Politische Vierteljahresschrift* 22:153–67.

Schumacher, E. F. 1973. *Small is Beautiful: Economics as if people mattered*. New York: Harper and Row.

Siemienska, Renata. 1985. Values, aspirations and expectations in Polish society, and perspectives on need fulfillment. Paper presented at conference on Politics, Economic and Social Mechanisms for Fulfillment of Needs in Polish Society, Grzegorzewice, Poland, June 20–23.

Spreitzer, E., and E. E. Snyder. 1974. Correlates of life satisfaction among the aged. *Journal of Gerontology* 29:454–58.

Statistical Office of the European Communities. 1985. Demographic statistics. Brussels: Statistical Office of the European Communities.

Steinfels, Peter. 1979. *The Neo-Conservatives*. New York: Simon and Schuster.

Stephens, John D. A. 1981. The changing Swedish electorate. *Comparative Political Studies* 14:163–204.

Stockton, Ronald R., and Frank W. Wayman. 1983. *A time of turmoil: Values and voting in the 1970s*. East Lansing: Michigan State University Press.

Stoetzel, Jean. 1983. *Les valeurs du temps present*. Paris: Presses Universitaires de France.

Szabo, Stephen F., ed. 1983. *The successor generation: International perspectives of postwar Europeans*. London: Butterworths.

Taylor, Charles, and David Jodice. 1982. *World handbook of political and social indicators*. 3d ed. New Haven: Yale University Press.

———. 1982. *World handbook of political and social indicators, III: 1948–1977* (codebook). Cologne: zentralarchiv fuer empirische sozialforschung.

Thomassen, Jacques, et al. 1983. *De Verstomde Revolutie*. Alphen aan den Rijn: Samsom Uitgeverij.

Thome, Helmut. 1985. Wandel zu postmaterialistischen Werten? Theoretische und empirische Einwaende gegen Ingleharts Theorie-versuch. *Soziale Welt* 36:27–59.

———. 1985. *Wertewandel in der Politik*. Berlin: Wissenschaftlischer Autorenverlag.

Tufte, Edward R. 1978. *Political control of the economy*. Princeton: Princeton University Press.

United Nations. 1959. *U.N. statistical yearbook*. New York: United Nations.

United Nations. 1979. *Demographic yearbook*. New York: United Nations.

Van de Kaa, Dirk J. 1987. Europe's second demographic transition. *Population Bull.* 42:3–57.

Van Deth, Jan W. 1983a. The persistence of materialist and postmaterialist value orientations. *European Journal of Political Research* 11:63–79.

———. 1983b. Ranking the ratings: The case of materialist and postmaterialist value orientations. *Political Methodology* 9:407–32.

———. 1984. *Politieke Waarden: Een Onderzoek naar politieke waarde-orientaties in Nederland in de periode 1970 tot 1982*. Amsterdam: CT Press.

Verba, Sidney. 1980. On revisiting the civic culture: A personal postscript. In *The civic culture revisited*, edited by Gabriel A. Almond and Sidney Verba. Boston: Little, Brown.

Verba, Sidney, and Norman H. Nie. 1972. *Participation in America: Political democracy and social equality*. New York: Harper & Row.

Verba, Sidney, Norman H. Nie, and Jae-On Kim. 1978. *Participation and political equality*. Cambridge and New York: Cambridge University Press.

Watanuki, Joji. 1977. *Politics in postwar Japanese society*. Tokyo: Tokyo University Press.

———. 1979. *Japanese politics*. Tokyo: Tokyo University Press.

Wattenberg, Ben J. 1987. *The birth dearth*. New York: Pharas Books.

Weber, Max. 1925. *Wirtschaft und Gesellschaft*. 2d ed. Tuebingen: Mohr.

———. [1904–1905] 1958. *The Protestant ethic and the spirit of capitalism*. New York: Scribners.

Wildenmann, Rudolf, et al. 1982. *Fuehrungsschicht in der Bundesrepublik Deutschland, 1981: Tabellenband*. Mannheim: University of Mannheim.

Wilson, Bryan. 1982. *Religion in sociological perspective*. New York: Oxford University Press.

World Bank. 1986. *World development report, 1986*. New York: Oxford University Press.

Zajonc, Robert B. 1968. Attitudinal effects of mere exposure. *Journal of Personality and Social Psychology, Monograph Supplement* 9:1–27.

——. 1980. Feeling and thinking: Preferences need no inferences. *American Psychologist* 35:151–75.

Zajonc, Robert B., Paula Pietromonaco, and John Bargh. 1982. Independence and interaction of affect and cognition. In *Affect and cognition*, edited by Margaret S. Clark and Susan T. Fiske, 221–27. Hillsdale, N.J.: Erlbaum Associates.

Zetterberg, Hans. 1986. Class voting in Sweden, 1979–1986. Personal communication.

Zimmerman, William. 1987. *Politics and culture in Yugoslavia.* Ann Arbor: Institute for Social Research.

Zimmerman, William, and Deborah Yarsike. n.d. Intergenerational change and the future of Soviet foreign policy. Unpublished paper.

INDEX

Aberbach, Joel, 8
abortion, 195–96, 275, 277, 290
Abrams, Mark, 181
Abramson, Paul, 99, 101, 247, 356
absolute norms, 177, 178
Achen, Christopher, 107, 113–14
Adorno, Theodor, 70
adversary culture, 332
aesthetic concerns, 5, 68, 138, 160
affective orientations, 112, 128
age-related differences, 19, 21
aging effects, 20–21, 73, 77–78, 93
agrarian society, 49, 53, 179
AIDS, 205
Alderfer, Clayton, 70
Alford index, 278
Allardt, Erik, 213
Almond, Gabriel, 17, 20, 23, 25, 44–45, 48, 337
Alwin, Duane, 59
Andrews, Frank, 43, 213–14
anti-Americanism, 403–5
anti-system parties, 37
antiabortion movements, 205
antinuclear movement, 269, 332, 385
antiwar movement, 379–80, 385, 391–92
apoliticals, 363
aspiration-adjustment model, 214–15, 217–18, 223, 241, 246
aspirations, adjustment of, 216
assembly line, 339
Atlantic Alliance, 393, 395–96, 402, 405, 415
attitudinal stability, 7, 47, 108, 110, 121–24, 126–29
authoritarianism, 70–71, 139, 146, 263
Axis powers, 33, 413
Azen, Icek, 311

Baker, Kendall, 21, 72
Baldino, Thomas, 142, 144
Balme, Richard, 330
Banfield, Edward, 23–24
Bangladesh, 248
Barnes, Samuel, 4, 105, 121, 137, 163, 200, 213, 310, 338–39, 350, 360
Beardsley, Richard, 145
Beck, Paul, 337, 356
behavior, vs. attitudes, 385
Bell, Daniel, 253, 328, 332, 339
Bellah, Robert, 62

belonging, 11, 134, 145–46, 169
Berger, Peter, 177
Bettelheim, Bruno, 70
Bhansali, R. J., 16
Big Bang, 432
big business, 269
big government, 269, 302, 304
birth cohorts. *See* cohort effects
birth control, 204, 209; technology, 203
birth rates, 89, 201–2, 208; illegitimate, 201–2, 210–11
Black and White model, 106–11, 113, 115–16, 125, 127–28
Block, J., 69
Boeltken, Ferdinand, 82, 84, 88, 90
Bollen, Kenneth, 51
bourgeoisie, 22–23, 46
Boynton, Gerald, 21
Brezhnev, Leonid, 427–28
Brim, Orville, 69
Broder, David, 331
Brown, Archie, 20
Bruce-Briggs, B., 331
Buddhism, 63
Buerklin, Wilhelm, 298, 373
Bundestag, 323
bureaucratic organizations, 8, 263, 269, 302, 340
business leaders, 327

Calvinist Protestantism, 49, 53
Cameron, David, 16
Campbell, Angus, 213–14, 216, 223, 225–26, 240
candidates' policy positions, 299
Cantril, Hadley, 31
capitalist societies, 10, 286
Catholic countries, 15, 55, 58, 245
CDU/CSU politicians, 324
centralized control, 10–11, 427
changes in one's income or marital situation, 240
Chen, E.Y.K., 250
childbearing, 198–99, 206, 208
Christian Democratic party, West German, 274, 278–80, 323
Christian norms, 179, 182–83, 185, 190, 432
church attendance, 184, 199–200, 204, 340
civic culture, 17, 23, 34, 37, 45–46, 48
The Civic Culture, 17, 23, 36, 48
civil service posts, 320